FROM MOREE TO MABO

Pamela Burton lives in Canberra where she studied Law at the Australian National University. Her Master's thesis was a study of the radical High Court Justice, Henry Bournes Higgins. She founded her own law firm in 1976 and later practised as a barrister at the Canberra Bar. Pamela has participated on a range of Federal government tribunals and committees.

FROM MOREE TO MABO

THE MARY GAUDRON STORY

PAMELA BURTON

UWA PUBLISHING

First published in 2010 and reprinted in 2017 by
UWA Publishing
Crawley, Western Australia 6009
www.uwap.uwa.edu.au

UWAP is an imprint of UWA Publishing
a division of The University of Western Australia

This book is copyright. Apart from any fair dealing for the purpose of private study, research, criticism or review, as permitted under the *Copyright Act 1968*, no part may be reproduced by any process without written permission. Enquiries should be made to the publisher.

The moral right of the author has been asserted.

Copyright © Pamela Burton 2010

National Library of Australia
Cataloguing-in-Publication data:
Burton, Pamela.
From Moree to Mabo : the Mary Gaudron story / Pamela Burton.
ISBN: 9781742580982 (pbk.)

Includes bibliographical references and index.
Gaudron, Mary, 1943-
 Lawyers—Australia—Biography.
Judges—Australia—Biography. Women
judges—Australia—Biography.

347.9403534092

Cover: *Mary Gaudron* by Sally Robinson, 2006. Detail.
This painting is from the NSW Bar Association Collection, Sydney.
Typeset by J & M Typesetting
Printed by Lightning Source

In memory of my sister, Dr Clare Burton, a leader in Australia's struggle for gender equity in the workforce. Mary Gaudron and Clare Burton were sisters in the fight for recognition of women's worth.

CONTENTS

Foreword by The Hon. Michael Kirby AC CMG	ix
Acknowledgments	xv
Prologue: The Evatt Connection	1
1 Home Ground	7
2 The Getting of Knowledge—and Religion	27
3 Sydney University Law School	40
4 Facing Challenges	58
5 A Labor 'gal' at the Bar	75
6 The Pat Mackie Case	95
7 Equal Pay—in Principle	112
8 A Seat on the Arbitration Commission	135
9 A Dramatic Departure	158
10 NSW Solicitor General	183
11 Crime and Corruption	206
12 Taps, Leaks and Buckets of Muck	228
13 High Ground	250
14 Getting to Mabo: The Mason Court at Work	275
15 Equal Justice: Gaudron at Work	299
16 Adapting to change—the Court under Chief Justices Brennan and Gleeson	320
17 Law, Gaudron-style	345
18 Moving On: A Time to Speak Out	369
Notes	402
Select Bibliography	464
Index	474

FOREWORD

The Hon. Michael Kirby AC CMG

Mary Gaudron is a bright star of the Australian legal firmament. Because of her role as the first woman Justice of the High Court of Australia she is assured of her place in the nation's history. So with her work in the law, before and after she took her seat on the Court. So with her remarkable personality and character, demonstrated in the decades of her public life.

We have it on the authority of this book that Mary Gaudron has a horror of biographies, believing that some events in life belong in the past and should be left there, undisturbed by prying eyes. Yet hers is a story that demands the telling. Judicial biography in Australia is a neglected genre. In Mary Gaudron's case, Pamela Burton has done well to repair this neglect.

Reading these pages, I learned much about the life and motive forces of Mary Gaudron that I did not previously know. And this is so although I would claim to have been an acquaintance, colleague and ultimately a friend, over virtually our entire lives in the law. The early years demonstrate how life hangs by a thread, depending upon strange events that appear to happen by chance.

In the young Mary's case, inspiration for the public life that was to unfold may have been given an energetic start in her imagination by the fortuitous events of her 'dawdling round town' in Moree, New South Wales, when she came upon the then Labor Party leader, Dr. H. V. Evatt (a past Justice of the High Court). He was addressing her father's friends in the street, urging them to vote 'no' in the 1951 referendum on communism. An interchange with Evatt led to his posting the young girl a copy of the Australian Constitution, whose interpretation was later to become one of her main judicial responsibilities. Decades later she remembered the arrival of the envelope from Evatt, boldly marked 'OHMS', bringing the booklet to her humble parental home.

The inspiration of wonderful and strong women teachers in the convent school in Moree inspired her to make the most of her manifest abilities. Sister Vianney, then one of the influential Mercy nuns, got it right when she explained why Mary was a 'delight to teach'. She was 'enthusiastic, attentive, observant, studious, caring and alert'. Yet would these gifts have come to the fore if she had not applied for, and received, a bursary to pay the school fees that her father, a railway fettler, could never have afforded? Would she have stayed in education to win a Commonwealth scholarship to university, but for the inspiration, and urging, of wonderful teachers?

As the author points out, there is a kind of irony in the fact that the nuns of Mary Gaudron's childhood encouraged the quick-witted pupil in their care to make the best of her abilities; to question everything; and even to challenge (and mostly to reject) the religious doctrines that underpinned their Faith. As a young girl, she boldly wrote an essay to prove that God did not exist. And when, on the other side of town, she had a chance to take on the boys at the De La Salle College, she knew at once that she had a talent in public speaking and advocacy. The path ahead of her began to become clear.

Mary Gaudron and I were fortunate to enter Sydney University in the same decade, when there were many creative students and a number of highly influential law teachers. Mary Gaudron resented the way her teachers addressed the classroom as 'Gentlemen'. It was something I did not even notice. In truth, in those days, there were very few women. Her skills in analysis and her inclination to audacity quickly marked her out. The competing influences for her conceptions of law, provided successively by Julius Stone, Frank Hutley and Bill Morison were to lay the ground for her judicial philosophy, which it is a main purpose of this book to explore and explain.

Mary Gaudron demonstrated to fellow students and teachers alike the special quality of fearlessness that was necessary, especially in those hostile days, for a woman to stand out in the law. Repeatedly, she confronted the chauvinism of the judiciary and legal profession of that time, earning for herself the label of 'Mary the Merciless'. The same spirit often made her relationships turbulent. In a professional group dynamic, which was then even more conformist than it is today, she was remarkable for being unrestrained and unself-conscious when so many others (including myself) were well and truly buttoned-up. She was fun (most of the time), histrionic, often egocentric, given to tantrums (many strategic) and quite a personality. None of this fitted into the then general expectation of how a young woman should behave in the world of Australian law.

Nevertheless, it was these very qualities that quickly got Mary Gaudron noticed in the circles that mattered. What her intellectual brilliance and University Medal in Law had not immediately done, her feistiness, mixed with a warm and humorous personality, began to break the ice of frigid social expectations. By chance events (including terrifying last-minute abandonments by QC leaders), she secured opportunities in appellate advocacy where her intellect could shine and be noticed. And shine it did. Union leader Clyde Cameron, who would later become one of Gough Whitlam's ministers, saw her capacity in protracted litigation involving a union colleague. Later, following her brilliant success as counsel for the Commonwealth in the *Equal Pay Case* of 1975, he sought to persuade the Whitlam Cabinet to appoint Mary Gaudron at thirty-one to the Arbitration Commission. His praise of her talents ultimately led Whitlam to exclaim: 'Next, you will tell me that she was born in a bloody manger'. But appointed she was.

The troubled and difficult years that the young Mary Gaudron experienced first as a deputy president of the Australian

Conciliation and Arbitration Commission and then as Solicitor-General of New South Wales, are not glossed over in this book. In the former, she emerges from her resignation as a judge to be a person of very strong principles. In the latter, she demonstrated, as her departmental head declared, impeccable professionalism and perfect knowledge about the applicable law.

When Lionel Murphy was dying of a cancer probably aggravated by his long ordeal under criminal accusations ultimately rejected by a jury, he exclaimed that what was needed in the Justice of the High Court who would replace him, was 'a keen mind and a good heart'. Following his death, Mary Gaudron and I spoke at Justice Murphy's memorial service in the Sydney Town Hall. Her speech, typically, approached the subject laterally and with great insight into Lionel and the moment. It therefore came as no real surprise that the call to take Murphy's seat went to Gaudron.

Present at her welcome to the High Court was Dame Roma Mitchell, her predecessor in the struggle for women's equality in the Australian legal profession and judiciary. The Moree *Champion* reproduced a circled photograph from the convent school days declaring that the decision that brought the young Mary to the High Court bench was one that had been effectively made 'years ago'.

The largest part of *From Moree to Mabo* is devoted to an analysis of the leading cases in which Mary Gaudron participated whilst a Justice of the High Court. The record demonstrates the confidence which she displayed in her own intellectual abilities and the large reserves of emotional energy upon which she could always call. It is not for me to comment on the many decisions that are analysed here. A large number of them after 1996 were written in cases in which I also participated. Some of them we wrote jointly together.

As has become customary in recent times, the author puzzles over the labels that media and some other commentators are pleased to assign to judges, according to whether they are to be considered 'black letter lawyers' or 'judicial activists'. Not every judge accepts that dichotomy or the particular label attributed to a judge's work. Sometimes the labels represent little more than code language, designed to reflect approval or disapproval of particular judicial conclusions; modes of reasoning; references to past authority; or invocation of policy and principle as well as precedent in fulfilling the judicial task.

The discussion of the constitutional validity of the cross-vesting legislation in the High Court in *Re Wakim* (where Justice Gaudron and I differed) may not, as suggested, show her 'legalism' in contrast to my suggested 'activism'. Rather it may show, in that case as in others, our respective conceptions of where our notions of 'legalism' differentially led us. In our judicial system, judges are obliged to provide reasons for their decisions. Those reasons display for all to see the grounds and arguments that the judge invokes to support the orders to which he or she ultimately comes. Chief Justice Brennan is quoted, correctly in my view, as disclaiming the label of 'activism' when assigned to the High Court during the years when Mary Gaudron, Chief Justice Mason and he sat together. What was different about those years, he explains, was the greater openness of the Mason Court in acknowledging the range of considerations that had led it to its reasons.

These were days in which many important decisions were written that had the effect of re-expressing the law of Australia on many topics. In virtually all of those decisions, Mary Gaudron was a powerful, and usually a concurring, voice. None of the decisions of that time was more important than that written in the second *Mabo Case* in 1992. At that moment, the High Court of Australian re-expressed the common law of Australia to reverse more than a century of earlier judicial holdings that had denied Aboriginal Australians title to their traditional lands. *Mabo* was pronounced with the strong participation of Justice Gaudron, before my arrival on the High Court. I can take therefore neither praise, nor blame, for its conclusions. Critics of its holding still exist in the Australian legal profession. However, I believe that future generations will say that, along with the *Communist Party* decision of 1951, and a few other notable cases, this was an historic blow for equal justice under law in Australia.

Justice Gaudron's lifelong commitment to equality and non-discrimination shine forth in *Mabo* as in other opinions. What democratic parliaments had failed over 150 years to provide, the High Court secured in *Mabo*. If there was particular passion in the language of the joint reasons that Justice Gaudron wrote with Justice Deane, it may, in her case, have derived from her early years in Moree. Witnessing discrimination and inequality close up. Sharing the feelings of injustice and outrage. Writing a new chapter in the nation's legal chronicle. Correcting an unrepaired legal wrong.

Mary Gaudron continues to make contributions to the law and society. In recent times, her activities have been mainly in the field of international law. Yet, through it all, she has remained herself. A fine technical lawyer who never lost faith in the law. A complex personality who achieved professional triumphs whilst enjoying the sometimes more elusive successes as wife, mother and convivial companion to her select circle of friends.

When Mary Gaudron left the High Court of Australia in 2003, things were never quite the same again. It had been a long journey from the railway worker's timber home in Moree to the grand building on the lake in Canberra. Suddenly, for us who were left, the covert cigarettes were gone. The ready bottle of champagne was no more. The convivial laughter was not heard amid the silence. The turbulence and occasional tantrums disappeared. In the icy stillness of a Canberra night, one yearned for Mary's deep voice, her sense of compassion and convivial humour. There were no more Irish songs to astonish dignified guests at lunchtime. The Justices drifted back to holding their functions at gentlemen's clubs which did not admit women members, something they would never have dared to do in Mary Gaudron's time. The respectful isolation of the individual chambers was restored. A walk across the book-lined corridor had never been too difficult for 'Mary the Merciless'.

Great courts need formal, predictable and unerringly polite judges with quiet voices and serene personalities. But to fulfil their true greatness, they also need lateral thinkers, people with unusual backgrounds who can be noisy, with fiery tempers and occasional minds and tongues to match. It will be a while before there is another judge in Australia's apex court quite like Mary Gaudron.

Michael Kirby
August 2010

ACKNOWLEDGMENTS

This biography, a personal initiative, arises from my interest in the High Court of Australia and, as I increasingly came to recognise, the considerable contribution to its activity during the last decade of the twentieth century by Mary Gaudron, a justice of the High Court from 1987 to 2003. I soon found that there was so much more to Gaudron's life. Research took me on her historic journey from life in a New South Wales country town divided by racism in the 1950s, to the big end of town—of which the legal profession formed a part in Sydney in the 1960s, industrial turmoil and inflation in the 1970s, scenes of crime and corruption in the 1980s, then to life on the bench of Australia's highest court.

This biography is not in any sense authorised. The Hon. Mary Gaudron, QC, was not interviewed; she did not assist the project nor allow access to personal papers. She explained her dread of biographies. It became clear that as a justice of the High Court, she held an optimistic view of the future, was motivated to use the law to improve people's lives and was not interested in dwelling on the past.

Blank pages were soon filled with words generated by people

who knew her and agreed that Mary Gaudron's extraordinary story should be told. Cathy Allan and Peter Gaudron helped in my search of the Gaudron family history. Lyall Munro introduced me to members of the Moree community, including Sammy Sabine, Noeline Briggs-Smith, Betty Carter, and classmates of young Mary, among others. All contributed their memories of life in and around Moree in the 1940s and 1950s. Former principals of St Philomena's school, Moree, Kevin Humphries and Patrick Roohan, together with Father Paul McCabe and Tom Campbell gathered information about the local Catholic schools. The Mercy nuns who taught Mary shared their memories. I also acknowledge the assistance given by the Ursuline nuns and others of the Catholic faith, and high school friends of Mary Gaudron who helped my understanding of the influences of a Catholic education on a young girl.

Few people are aware of the role Mary Gaudron played – when she was wife of veteran caver, Ben Nurse – in the work of the Sydney Speleological Society. I thank Society members for their contributions and Ben Nurse, Ross Ellis and Warwick Counsell, in particular, for the time they spent speaking to me.

Many people provided insights into life at the NSW Bar in the late 1960s and early 1970s, and the notable characters with whom Mary Gaudron associated. Janet Coombs, barrister, collected and preserved a boxful of news clippings about the first women at the NSW Bar, which provided a chronology of Gaudron's achievements. Former Justice Jim Staples explained the intricacies of the Pat Mackie defamation case in which he and Gaudron appeared as barristers. Professor Marian Sawer and Kathy MacDermott commented on the equal pay cases. Jim Staples, Pauline Hansen and John Blackley proved rich sources of anecdotes concerning Gaudron's time as a deputy president of the Commonwealth Conciliation and Arbitration Commission.

Of her time as Solicitor General of New South Wales, the Hon. Don Stewart, the Hon. Frank Walker, Justice Terry Sheahan, Judge Greg Woods and Mike Steketee, among others, gave generously of their time and knowledge to enlighten me about this politically volatile time. Former prime minister Bob Hawke, former NSW premier Neville Wran and Associate Justice John McLaughlin each offered their perspectives on Mary Gaudron.

The work of the High Court of Australia is clouded in mystery for many Australians. I thank former chief justices, Sir Anthony Mason and Sir Gerard Brennan, Justice William Gummow and former justices Michael Kirby and Ian Callinan for talking to me about their time on the Court. I am grateful for the cooperation and provision of information by the High Court, and for the help given by Magistrate Margot Stubbs, Christopher Doogan, Dr Hanna Jaireth and Fiona Hamilton.

Over the years I have had many conversations with professional colleagues and friends of Mary Gaudron, most of whom are listed in the bibliography. Others asked not to be named. I thank them all for their help.

I especially thank the Moree Northern Regional Library, the University of Sydney Law School Library, the NSW Bar Association Library, the NSW Parliamentary Library, the State Library of NSW, the National Archives, the NSW Labor Party, the High Court of Australia library, and the National Library of Australia, whose friendly staff members unearthed material required to make this work possible.

Depiction of Mary Gaudron's colourful personality was enhanced by artist Sally Robinson's portraits, and by the official High Court photographs taken by David Coward. Both helped me create a picture in words of the many faces of Mary Gaudron, and kindly gave permission to use their work in the book. I also thank the High Court of Australia, National Archives, AAP, Newspix, Fairfax, *Moree Champion,* the United Nations, Australian Women Lawyers, Jennifer Batrouney SC, Judge Jeanette Morrish, the Sydney Speleological Society, Ben Nurse, Ross Ellis, Betty Carter, Lalie Fletcher, and Alan Ross, for providing and permitting their photos to be used in the book.

This biography has benefited enormously from much advice and many suggestions from Professor Emeritus Leslie Zines and Professor Emeritus Tony Blackshield. Professor Zines, supervisor of my Master's thesis on High Court Justice Henry Bournes Higgins, read the chapters on the High Court with a close critical eye.

Addressing his observations greatly enhanced this central part of the book. Professor Blackshield was an invaluable source of information about the Sydney University Law School and the respective influences of Julius Stone and Frank Hutley. In conversation, he provoked me with questions about Gaudron's contribution to the High Court. He subsequently read an advanced draft, providing many further comments and suggestions.

Collecting information is one matter. It is another to piece it together to form a coherent account of a person's life and work, and to write the story. John Nethercote read the text several times and allowed me to draw on his extensive experience as an editor as well as his considerable knowledge of Australian government and politics. Dr Doug Cocks has been by my side as a writing mentor, a constant source of support and encouragement, a sounding board, and a reader and editor of drafts at various stages. My sister Meredith Edwards, stepmother Betty Nathan, and many friends supported and encouraged me, reading and commenting on the manuscript as it developed. I would like to thank Michael Sexton, SC, and Dr Heather Roberts for reading the full text closely when in draft form and for providing many constructive suggestions. Others who commented on chapters at various stages include Professor Kim Rubenstein, Carmel Meiklejohn, Caroline White and Robin Gibson.

A measure of boldness is required to write a biography of a living person who is not enthusiastic about it being written. John Elliot's interest provided me with the determination to continue. June Sutherland's enthusiasm gave me courage to talk publicly about it. The Independent Scholars Association of Australia and the National Centre for Biography kindly hosted discussion. Support and encouragement came from authors Ann Moyal, Kate Grenville, Christine Wallace and Jacqueline Kent.

No author could have been better supported than I was by my agent, Gaby Naher. She saw the importance of Australians knowing more about Mary Gaudron, and demonstrated faith in me as author of the book. Her search for a publisher of high standing led to Terri-ann White, Director, University of Western Australia Publishing. Terri-ann's efficiency, dedication and 'nothing is impossible' attitude where deadlines were concerned kept the book's production on track. Susan Midalia, as editor, worked tirelessly to turn the manuscript into a book. I thank these three wonderful women for their patience, knowledge, expertise and for making my vision into a readable reality. I also thank Madeleine Davis who prepared the index; Gillian Evans for her thoroughness in checking references; and David Walker for sorting and organising the illustrations.

None of those who assisted in the writing of this biography carries responsibility for the final text; responsibility for errors and inadequacies rests with me alone.

Prologue

THE EVATT CONNECTION

In 1951, as now, few Australians possessed a copy of the Australian Constitution. Fewer still had read it even as they came to vote at a referendum to amend it to outlaw the Communist Party in Australia. Mary Genevieve Gaudron, a child in the outback New South Wales town of Moree, however, obtained one and cherished it. But she was much too young to vote.

Mary Gaudron, the first woman to become a justice of the High Court of Australia, was only eight years old when she met Herbert Vere Evatt, leader of the Australian Labor Party. It was early September 1951. Dust swirled around the dry streets of Moree. Evatt, known as 'the Doc' or 'Bert' Evatt, had been leader of the ALP for the few months since Ben Chifley's death in June of that year. Evatt was campaigning to persuade people to vote 'No' in this referendum. If passed, the Menzies Government intended to ban the Communist Party of Australia and criminalise advocacy of communism.[1] Evatt saw this as an attack on the fundamental right of freedom of speech.

A crowd assembled in Jellicoe Park, Moree, to listen to the Doc. He was speaking from the back of a blue Holden utility. The man can be imagined bellowing into the loudhailer gripped tightly in his right hand, his left hand alternating between gesturing emphatically and pushing back the undisciplined lock of hair that fell over his forehead; he would occasionally remove his round, tortoiseshell-framed glasses to wipe his brow. He had a down-to-earth air that appealed to working men and women. His voice was strong and his message intense.

In the days before, Evatt had addressed crowds in many New South Wales country towns and had visited workplaces and talked to unionists who had set up 'Vote No' committees. In particular, Evatt addressed a meeting of five hundred Eveleigh railway workers in Redfern.[2] From the rousing reception he received there, he measured the support he could draw from railway union members and their families. Moree railway workers were among the crowd at Jellicoe Park.

Young Mary Gaudron was, as she puts it, 'dawdling round town' when she saw a small group of her father's friends gathered around the truck, talking passionately about something called the 'Constitution'.[3] The young girl absorbed the talk and the exchanges that took place between Evatt and his audience. She was curious about the repeated references to the 'Constitution'.

She put her hand up and attracted the attention of the visiting campaigner. The gentleness in his boyish smile no doubt encouraged the question she asked of him: 'Please sir, what's a Constitution?'[4] Mary's youthful freckled face, framed by braided ginger-red hair, could not disguise the adult curiosity shown in her blue eyes. Evatt made time for this spirited child. He explained that it was the law by which Parliament was governed. She put her hand up again and asked, 'Is it like the Ten Commandments?' Evatt responded, 'You could call it the Ten Commandments of government.' With this, she asked where she could get a copy. He replied, 'You can write to me, Dr H.V. Evatt, Parliament House, Canberra, and I will send you one.' She did; he kept his word.[5]

As the locals remember it, Ted Gaudron, Mary's father, a committed unionist and Labor Party man, was at Jellicoe Park. Evatt accepted an invitation to meet some of the unionists at the Gaudron cottage in Morton Street, in the heart of the railway community in

East Moree. Twenty or so railway workers assembled in the small Gaudron cottage to talk with their hero.

Evatt's campaign effort was an overwhelming and unexpected success. On 22 September 1951 the referendum was defeated. It had been thought that in the anti-communist climate of the Cold War, Australians would support the Government's plans despite the more usual tendency to oppose amendments to the Constitution.

Gaudron treasured the document she received in the mail from Evatt. It provided her with a focus. Before she received it, however, she went to school and bragged that she was to receive her own Constitution, somehow implying that it would be some magnificent document or 'two tablets of stone' perhaps. Gaudron recalled years later how, while waiting for the arrival of the document, she was teased by the school bully asking every now and then, 'Where's your Constitution then?'[6] When the small pamphlet arrived in a brown envelope marked 'OHMS', she felt obliged to produce it. Her friends mocked her enthusiasm. 'What are you going to do with that?' they asked. The bully laughed at it being 'just a book', and said, 'It's no use to anyone.' Knowingly, young Mary retorted, 'It's our Constitution. Lawyers know what to do with it.' He said, 'You're not a lawyer.' Humiliated and backed into a corner she declared, 'Well, that's what I'm going to be—a lawyer.' She never doubted she could. 'It made sense…What else was one to do?' she reflected years later: 'I didn't have the talent or educational background for anything else. I was ignorant of lots of other fields. We had never heard of computer science. But I knew there were lawyers and I knew what they did.'[7]

Her encounter with Evatt and her copy of the Constitution were pathfinders to her future. They suggested a direction she might not have later considered. As one newspaper version or another came back to haunt her, Gaudron had some regrets about telling the story of Evatt having inspired her to become a lawyer.[8] Perhaps she believes too much has been made of the childhood encounter. Yet when Gaudron became an advocate to be reckoned with—one with leftist political leanings and a passion for equality and justice—her meeting with Evatt was an obvious event for the press to relate, especially as so little else was known about her. She is a private person and, apart from a few such stories, she has largely succeeded in keeping her private and family life out of public view.

Still, she has often told of her meeting with Evatt and confirmed not only its influence on her but the influence of the man and his thinking as well. The story resurfaced on her appointment as a justice of the High Court of Australia. Evatt, after all, had been a predecessor on the Court, the final arbiter on interpretation of the Australian Constitution, the very document that he had so propitiously placed in her hands so many years earlier. The event was a 'watershed experience' in her life.[9]

Gaudron particularly admired Evatt's contribution to the formation of the United Nations. He was at the San Francisco Conference of 1945 which drew up the United Nations Charter. He led Australia's delegations at the first three sessions of the United Nations in 1946, 1947 and 1948. In 1948 Evatt was elected President of the United Nations General Assembly and presided over the drafting of the landmark Universal Declaration of Human Rights. Gaudron describes this document as being 'the emanation of his pen'[10] and, in an address in 2006 entitled 'Remembering the Universal Declaration and Australia's human rights record', that it was 'arguably the most important document ever reduced to writing, whether on paper, papyrus, vellum or tablets of stone...'[11]

By the time Gaudron embarked on her Arts-Law degree in 1959, Evatt's passionate and unpredictable personality had contributed to the destruction of his political career. In February 1960 he was appointed Chief Justice of the Supreme Court of NSW where he remained for two and a half years before declining health compelled his resignation. Gaudron never met Evatt again after the day he talked to her from the back of the Holden ute in Jellicoe Park, although as a student she attended the Supreme Court to watch him preside at a hearing of the Full Court.[12]

Herbert Vere Evatt died on 2 November 1965. In the same year Mary Gaudron completed her law degree at the University of Sydney. Like Evatt and his niece, Elizabeth Evatt, who would become the first Chief Justice of the Family Court of Australia, Gaudron received the University Medal in Law.[13] Like Evatt, Gaudron became a champion of the rights of society's most vulnerable and disadvantaged, and saw possibilities for the law to be used as a tool to advance social justice.

Throughout her career, further Evatt associations appeared. She mingled with other lawyers in the Evatt family, and like many of them and other 'Labor lawyers' who excelled in the law, she would be recognised by Labor politicians as worthy of judicial appointment. She worked and appeared in the NSW Supreme Court with Evatt's brother, Clive Evatt, QC, Elizabeth's father. She spent some happy times at the historic Evatt home, Leuralla, at Leura in the Blue Mountains, now a toy and railway museum which contains a 'Doc Evatt Memorial Room'. Gaudron followed Elizabeth Evatt to the Conciliation and Arbitration Commission. In 1980, Gaudron delivered a Herbert Vere Evatt Memorial Lecture on the rights and dignities of employees.[14]

Twenty-two years after Evatt's death, Gaudron was appointed to the High Court of Australia. Evatt had been the youngest appointee to the Court. Gaudron, at age forty-four, became its third youngest judge. She was ultimately to deliver many significant judgments on constitutional cases. One of these was *Mabo*,[15] remarkable for its passion and powerful reasoning in support of justice and land rights for Australian Aborigines. Mary Gaudron became a strong advocate against discrimination of all kinds, and of human rights generally. Bold as well as brilliant, Gaudron, against the odds, joined Evatt in taking an important place in Australia's legal and constitutional history.

Palm Sunday family photo of Mary Gaudron's great-grandmother, Elizabeth Hille (centre), great-grandfather Johann 'John' (right middle row), grandfather John 'Jack', (top left) and his siblings. (Courtesy Peter Gaudron.)

Elizabeth Hille. (Courtesy Peter Gaudron.)   Jack Gaudron. (Courtesy Peter Gaudron.)

The Gaudron cottage, Morton Street, Moree, New South Wales.

Chapter One

HOME GROUND

You have to know from whom and where you come from—
to know where you are going.[1]

Rhineland roots

Behind Mary Gaudron's much-loved holiday cottage in the Loire Valley in France is a small and well-kept graveyard. In spring and early summer it is alive with colour from freshly laid flowers. That she might have French connections entered the realm of possibility when she first came across a family of Gaudrons in this walled, well-packed home of the dead so near to her Loire retreat. As she pours her guests red wine from the nearby Vouvray vineyard of Sylvain Gaudron, Mary tells her fanciful dinner table tale that she might be of French descent. The pleasant discovery that the nearby vineyard carries both her name and champagne to her taste further fed speculation about a French heritage.

Gaudron in fact lays no claim to any of the French Gaudrons as an ancestor, though the romantic notion of a French connection cannot be ruled out. At the root of the Australian Gaudron family tree were Mary's father's great grandparents, Jacob and Appoloniae Gaudron, who arrived in Sydney in 1855 as assisted immigrants from Oberheimbach in the sometimes French, and sometimes German, ruled region of the Rhineland. Shipping records confirm family oral history that they regarded themselves as German.[2] Jacob declared when he arrived in Australia, 'I left the country as a German and I arrive here as a German'.[3] Importantly for Mary Gaudron's possible 'French connection', one of Jacob's brothers purportedly settled in France.

At other times Gaudron has declared she is 'bog Irish'. This is easy to accept given her sandy-red hair, freckles, a fiery temper to match, and her strong Catholic background. She claims, however, to be 'only a quarter Irish'.[4] On one occasion, when giving a speech to a bevy of judges and aspiring lawyers, she described herself as 'a lapsed Irish Catholic chain-smoker'.[5]

Being playful about her origins on another occasion, she boasted a prestigious legal connection. She suggested to a colleague at the Bar that she could be a descendant of Sir Frederick Jordan, a former Chief Justice of New South Wales, after whom Frederick Jordan Chambers was named.[6] Well, why not? After all, the family name of her Gaudron grandmother, also Mary, was 'Jordan'.

Mary Gaudron is an engaging storyteller, whether the stories are fanciful or true, and 'holds court' with her lively personality at dinner parties, or anywhere amongst close friends and colleagues. Amongst people she trusts, she is frank about her thoughts, fears and beliefs, but she is a private person when it comes to her personal and family life. Speaking about her childhood is something she rarely does. She enjoys life in the present, looks optimistically to the future, and prefers not to revisit sadness and sensitive issues of the past.

Yet her childhood and family background are important to understanding who Mary Gaudron is, her many faces, her world view, how and why she became the first woman to be a justice of Australia's High Court, and what she brought to the role. Her 'where do I come from?' story is a typical Australian immigration story of hard times and sadness, perseverance, courage and success—all descriptions and attributes which equally apply to

Mary Gaudron's life passage—and establishes her working-class origins.

Jacob and Appoloniae, with their three children, Johann aged nine, Jacob eight, and Susannah three, were passengers on *Cateaux Wattel*'s maiden voyage to Sydney. It was a 941-ton, three-masted wooden sailing ship built in 1854.[7] It was an eventful journey from start to finish; one that took its toll on the children. Before the ship left the dock, a fire broke out in the galley where oil had spilled. The repairs took some three weeks and the passengers had to endure the wait. Once underway the vessel was plagued with an outbreak of dysentery from contaminated water; twenty infants died at sea.[8] Young Susannah and Jacob Gaudron were two of those children, and were buried at sea. Only the oldest child, Johann, survived the journey.[9] He was Mary Gaudron's great-grandfather.

On 9 March 1855 *Cateaux Wattel* arrived in Sydney Cove.[10] The grieving Gaudrons, together with the other passengers, were detained in quarantine for several days because of the death of a little girl just days before the ship docked in Sydney. Jacob and Appoloniae (known by her easier to pronounce second name, Therese) settled in Patrick Plains in the Richmond River area, near Singleton. They had two more children, one of whom died at seventeen. Their oldest son, Johann, known as 'John', married a German, Elizabeth Hillë, and in the early 1880s moved to the Casino area, a bustling sawmilling and trade locality near Lismore, where John became a successful sugar-cane farmer and a pioneer of the dairy cattle industry in the region. They had a daughter and five sons. Their second son John, known as 'Jack', was a first generation Australian. He was Mary Gaudron's grandfather. Following the marriages of all of Johann and Elizabeth's sons, a large clan of Casino Gaudrons contributed to the flourishing Australian branch of the Gaudron family. They became sugar cane farmers in the Richmond River area, and cane and banana growers in the Lismore, Coffs Harbour and Casino areas.

Mary Gaudron's grandfather, Jack, married Mary Ann Jordan in 1906. They settled in the river junction town of Coraki, south-east of Casino. They had thirteen children. The oldest of the eight boys, Edward John Michael Gaudron, was born in 1907. He was Mary Gaudron's father.

Mary Gaudron never knew her paternal grandmother well. In 1940 Grandma Mary was shot by a stray hunting bullet which lodged behind her eye, causing serious problems. She spent some time at home in a wheelchair and died in hospital in 1945 when Mary was two. Grandfather Jack continued to live on the family farm with one of his children. Mary visited with her family for various Sunday lunch reunions.

Mary Gaudron's father, Ted, left school at fourteen to work with NSW railways. He obtained work as a fettler, maintaining and repairing the wooden railway sleepers. Two brothers, John and Alfred, also worked on the railways. The rapidly developing NSW railway network provided young boys with the opportunity of sweeping railway station platforms for pocket money and learning about the work of fettlers and engine drivers. Four of Ted's brothers, Peter, Bernie, Joseph and James, later served in the Second World War. All came home safely. Ted's work on the railways took him to Moree, an inland town 600 kilometres north-west of Sydney.

Moree, New South Wales

Mary Gaudron's childhood in Moree was an unlikely beginning for a High Court justice. She was born into a Catholic working-class family and raised in a black and white community uncomfortable with its differences. But it gave her a rich education from a young age. It exposed her to issues of social and racial inequality and to the political and industrial realities of the times.

Her life as a child was one of contradictions. She lived in a volatile household that fluctuated between love and anger. Her family lived in a complex and struggling railway community of battlers whose standard of living, however, was so much higher than the nearby neglected and significantly poorer indigenous community. Furthermore, while racial prejudice divided the wider community, Mary as a child had the benefit of being immersed in a section of it that was welded together by union solidarity.

This childhood provided much for Gaudron to reflect upon when formulating the beliefs and values she lived by. Having chosen a career in law, she believed that the use of the law was the best means of addressing discriminatory attitudes and injustices generally that troubled her. This belief culminated symbolically in *Mabo*, the 1992 landmark case concerning indigenous land rights in which she participated as a justice of the High Court.[11]

The outback NSW town of Moree was settled in the mid-1800s. Squatters, attracted to the rich black soil and fertile flood plains, established pastoral runs, and the 'butcher, baker, and candlestick maker' effect followed the closer European settlement of the region. The predominant crops were wheat, cotton and olives; the expansion of cotton in recent years adding large stretches of snowy white fields in summer to the brown and green patchwork landscape. Squatters became sheep graziers and, as the wool industry grew, shearers came to the region for work. Moree was gazetted as a township in 1862. Rail came to Moree in 1897, swelling the population with the work and people it attracted.

By the time Mary's father, Ted, arrived in Moree, there was a well-established, relatively poor and mostly white, community of railway workers and their families who lived in cottages or tin huts, or who camped on the land surrounding the railway yards. Socio-economically, the railway community fell between Moree's wealthier pastoralists and business community and the town's poor Aboriginal community, who, dispossessed of their land, fled to Moree and established settlements there from the early 1920s to the late 1960s. Geographically, the wealthier European townsfolk lived mainly in 'West Moree', north of the river; the railway community and an Aboriginal community were situated in East Moree, south of the Mehi River which runs through the middle of the town.

Ted met Grace Mawkes, 'Bonnie' to family and friends, at a dance in Moree where Bonnie was working as a clerk. Born in Inverell, NSW, Bonnie came to Moree as a child. She grew up and went to school there. Bonnie was twenty-four and Ted eleven years older when they married in 1942 in Ted's local church, St

John and St Henry Catholic Church, East Moree. They made Moree their home. Their first child, Mary Genevieve Gaudron, was born into East Moree's railway community on 5 January 1943.

Ted and Bonnie Gaudron raised their family in 90 (now 306) Morton Street, East Moree, an old timber cottage sitting in a line of railway workers' timber and fibro houses across the road from the Moree railway station. They rented the home, purchasing it years later in 1960. This was decent housing, a far cry from the railway camp of tents, sheds and huts that housed the fettlers and other railway workers and their families on the railway land across the road, and from the humpies, tin sheds and makeshift homes of 'Top Camp', one of Moree's larger Aboriginal camps that lay behind Morton Street along the banks of the often flooding Mehi River.[12]

Aboriginal researcher, Noeline Briggs-Smith, known as 'Auntie Noeline', is well placed to describe the living conditions in both communities. Three years older than Mary Gaudron, Noeline Briggs-Smith was born in Top Camp and lived as a child in a dwelling made from flattened Arnott's biscuit tins and kerosene containers that gave off an offensive odour. When she was seven, her family moved into a house in 'Soapie Row', so-called because a soap factory had previously occupied the area.[13] As an adult she lived with her husband in the railway camp. Their accommodation was makeshift, comprising a tent and a tin shed on land owned partly by the council and partly by NSW railways. The railway camp lay uncomfortably between the noisy railway line and the smelly cattle trucks that stood overnight beside the 'wool appraisal' shed where sheep fleece were classed. Noeline Briggs-Smith recalls:

> Living in the tin huts made out of metal from kerosene cans meant living with the smell of kerosene, with the smell of cow dung and trying to sleep with the noise of the trains shunting at night.[14]

Mary Gaudron has claimed or, more accurately, boasted, possibly in typically self-mocking jest, that she was 'born in a tent in the bush where her father was working as a fettler on the railway

Top Camp memorial plaque on the bank of the Mehi River, East Moree, New South Wales.

Old Church of St Henry, later St Francis Xavier's primary school, Moree East, which Mary Gaudron attended. (Courtesy Lalie Fletcher.)

Church interior converted to school classroom. (Courtesy Lalie Fletcher.)

lines.'[15] This would suggest that Ted and Bonnie lived in the railway camp before moving into Morton Street across from the railway station. One of Gaudron's teaching nuns recalls that when the girl, at age eleven, arrived as a boarder at St Ursula's College in Armidale, she said that the dormitory was her first experience of sleeping on a 'real' rather than 'a dirt' bedroom floor.

While many railway families did live in tents and shacks on the railway property, the recall of local residents is that the Gaudrons did not endure this, the family having moved into their home in Morton Street from another rented house in East Moree. Gaudron's mention of 'dirt floors' can be explained, however, whether or not she had spent any part of her early life in a tent. As a child Mary slept in a shack at the back of the Morton Street home. The floor of the front part of the house was timber. The 'add-on' shack at the back, like other houses with 'add-on' living areas at the time, had a dirt floor. The severe floods that caused Morton Street houses to install and raise their floors occurred in 1955 and 1956, shortly after Mary left for Armidale.

The railway community

In the 1940s and 1950s when Mary Gaudron was growing up, there was a spirit in the railway community akin to a sense of family that provided social support networks. The railway community was an entity in itself. Everyone knew each other. It was home to McElhone's pub, the meeting place of the railway workers and a stronghold for unionists and Labor Party supporters, located at the north end of Morton Street.

The railway workers, from all accounts, were supportive of their Aboriginal neighbours. The proximity of Top Camp to the railway community, and the poverty of both communities, meant that Aboriginal relations with non-Aborigines in East Moree were more congenial than with the white townspeople across the river. The railway workers were battlers like the Aborigines and empathised with their plight. Most of the few Aborigines who obtained work in the area were employed in shearing sheds and some as labourers with the railways, and this resulted in some mixing of the black and white communities, with Aboriginal railway workers living in tents and huts alongside white railway workers.

Though the pastoralists and West Moree's townsfolk were predominantly conservative, the influx of shearers during the wool boom in the 1950s and the large railway community and its powerful union turned Moree politically into a 'Labor town'. The Moree branch of the Railway Workers' Union numbered around 300 in the 1950s—close to a hundred percent of the workers. It was led by a strong secretary, Roy Warrener. Mary's father, Ted, was a committed and active unionist.

Non-Aboriginal Sam Sabine, a respected community leader, and Aboriginal elder Lyall Munro both attribute the good treatment provided to the workers, black and white alike, to the Union and the NSW railway bosses. Both men started out as junior porters, or railway 'call boys', tasked with waking up Ted Gaudron and other steam 'loco' engine drivers, and taking notes to them about their day's work before the steam 'locos' disappeared in the late 1950s. Good railway industrial policy did not, however, ensure equal opportunity for Aborigines. The handful of Aborigines fortunate enough to obtain work on the railways were given the 'shit jobs' to do—the work of fettlers, laying and maintaining the timber sleepers on the tracks.[16] Most did not progress. Few became porters, or gangers who oversaw the work of the fettlers. Not until the late 1950s or early 1960s did an Aborigine, William Duke, become an engine driver. Mechanisation soon drove fettlers out of work and reduced opportunities for the few Aborigines employed there. Some obtained work at the 'loco depot'. Employment opportunities in the town for Aboriginal men were even worse outside the railway community.

How did Mary Gaudron picture this? She was born on the 'wrong side' of the railway tracks in a racially divided town in a community that was struggling both socially and economically. Importantly, however, she did not perceive herself as disadvantaged. Mary and her siblings were well-fed, always neatly attired and provided with the best education their parents could afford. According to a close school friend, their childhood in the railway community was happy, safe and carefree.[17] Lalie Schmidt has fond memories of playing with Mary in the Gaudrons' large back yard. It butted on to a vacant strip of land, on which Mary's father developed a garden full of vegetables and flowers. Lalie would sit on the swing under the grape vine behind the house watching the chickens pecking around while waiting for Mary to finish her strictly supervised piano practice.

Lalie and Mary spend many happy hours playing in the local spa baths, after which on hot summer days they would buy ice-creams or cold drinks from Peter Notaris' café, or look out for George Poulis in his white apron pedalling his ice cream cart along Morton Street. Clydesdales clopped slowly along Morton Street pulling carts of milk, and bringing fresh bread to the cottage doors. Ice was delivered to replenish ice chests in the cottages which had not yet acquired kerosene refrigerators and to the railway camp dwellers. Burt Hand's nearby corner store provided groceries and other goods for the community. This was particularly important to the Aboriginal community, who were not permitted to shop in West Moree.

Whatever socio-economic disadvantages Mary suffered paled into insignificance in comparison to the neighbouring community of Aborigines who, she observed, were 'very considerably less than equal'.[18] Discrimination against Aborigines was much more obvious to Gaudron as she grew up than any discrimination against women. She was barely conscious of women's inferior role during her childhood in Moree. In working-class families, she says, women were often the mainstay, handling the finances and organising the children's education. It was only at university that she began to appreciate that there were 'special problems for women'.[19] Speaking out years later she observed that, while forty years ago an Australian woman had fewer rights than a man, 'her legal status was infinitely superior to that of Aboriginal Australians'. She noted that in New South Wales, 'there was no guaranteed freedom of movement for Aboriginal Australians, and no guaranteed freedom for them to communicate with non-Aboriginal Australians'.[20] She summed up its impact on her:

> It was impossible—absolutely impossible—not to be aware that, in the phrase made famous by George Orwell, some people were more equal than others—indeed, significantly so.[21]

Nor did she forget it.

Moree's dark history

In their High Court judgment in *Mabo*, Justices Deane and Gaudron together described the dispossession of Aboriginal people from their land as 'the darkest aspect of the history of this nation'.[22] Gaudron should know. Living on the doorstep of a community of dispossessed indigenous people in Moree, she had witnessed the social impact of the dispossession of Aborigines of their land and the segregation policies that followed—in short, Moree's dark history.

For some time the written history of Moree, like Moree's crest, reflected the culture and values of the European settlers of the land, ignoring those of the original inhabitants.[23] The record was significantly corrected by 1999 when three volumes of pictorial history, by and about the Aboriginal community, were compiled by Briggs-Smith. Her comments reveal what Mary Gaudron learned was the case in other parts of Australia from extensive research she carried out for the purpose of *Mabo*:

> The early explorers did not know about the way the first Australians lived. Their ways of living were so different that they couldn't understand each other. It was the beginning of all the misunderstandings between the European newcomers and the Aboriginal people who had always lived here, and looked at the country and all its land as theirs, because they knew it belonged to them.[24]

Notably, though there is now some acceptance that Moree means 'long waterhole' or 'spring',[25] the rising sun, originally thought to have been the meaning of 'Moree', remains the emblem on Moree's crest.[26]

Mary Gaudron (circled), class photo, 1949. (Courtesy Lalie Fletcher.)

Mary Gaudron, Moree, 1950.
(Courtesy Allan Ross.)

Betty Cutmore, childhood friend of Mary
Gaudron, 1950. (Courtesy Betty Carter.)

The township's non-Aboriginal population in Mary Gaudron's childhood was estimated at somewhere between 5,000 and 6,000.[27] The Kamilaroi people, the second largest indigenous group in eastern Australia, had lived extensively across the Moree Plains.[28] The number of Aborigines who settled in Moree is not known. Neither they, nor the Torres Strait Islander population, were counted in the national census prior to the 1967 amendment to the Constitution. In 1965 it was known that the Moree region had by far the largest Aboriginal stations in NSW, with more than 400 residents, but there were estimated to be more in other Moree locations, including Top Camp.[29]

Throughout her life, Gaudron was troubled about the way Australia treated its Aboriginal peoples. In 1998 she stated frankly that the racism she saw directed towards indigenous Australians while she was growing up shaped her attitude towards all forms of discrimination.[30] As a child, she witnessed the fact that Moree's Aborigines were not allowed to enter the Town Hall or to use public toilets, or other council-controlled buildings.[31] In 2005 she described what she saw:

> Aborigines were not allowed on the bus that travelled from East to West Moree, nor in the Municipal swimming pool. They were allowed into the picture theatre but only in the front rows which were roped off from the rest of the audience. Aboriginal children did not go to school like the rest of us, although some few received a rudimentary schooling on the Mission. And if they were ill, Aboriginal people were treated, if at all, in the isolation ward of the local hospital.[32]

Briggs-Smith confirms this picture of racial discrimination. Aborigines, she writes:

> [w]ere not served in hotels, clubs (Aboriginal ex-servicemen were served on ANZAC day at the RSL), certain cafés and shops. The few clothing shops that did allow them to enter did not allow them to try on clothes. They were not allowed in hairdressers or barber-shops, to rent houses in town or

enter the Bore Baths. Very few worked in town for most of the work was acquired by the men in shearing sheds or doing property work with cattle and wheat. A few women worked in town as domestics in private homes and hotels. The only place young women could look forward to a career was in nursing at the McMaster Ward.[33]

Clear rules about black and white rights had been established by the European community as soon as settlement commenced, and persisted in many country towns of NSW and Queensland well into the 1960s.[34] In 1883 'protection' of indigenous peoples became government policy. It was formalised by the *Aborigines Protection Act 1909* (NSW) which set up a Board with the power to declare reserves and to compel Aboriginal people to live on them.

It was the impact of these policies on Terry Hie Hie,[35] an Aboriginal reserve, fifty kilometres south-east of Moree on the Gwydir's Wee Waa Creek tributary,[36] which contributed to the settlement of 'Top Camp'. The Aborigines Protection Board started to take Aboriginal and part-Aboriginal children away from their parents and place them in institutions.[37] Many children were removed from their families without parental consent to be trained as domestics and labourers in special government institutions set up for the purpose. This continued until 1963.

By 1922 the harshness of the Reserve Manager's rule and the fear of the 'men on horses' coming without warning to seize and remove their children caused many of Terry Hie Hie's Aboriginal residents to flee. Some fled to Queensland; some who came to Moree established 'Top Camp'.

For the whole time Mary Gaudron lived in Moree, until as late as 1955, the Moree Council enforced a policy of excluding all Aborigines from council premises and town baths. An Aboriginal couple was barred from hiring the town hall for a wedding reception. Conflicts became more explicit and intense in the early 1960s. Vic Simms, celebrity musician and Aboriginal elder, was enjoying a swim in the Moree pool with a group of white Australians with whom he was touring. He was asked to leave by the pool manager.

The whole group, including singers Col Joye, Peter Allen and Judy Stone, left the pool in protest.[38] Other similar stories of segregation of black and white people and prejudicial council policy provoked Charles Perkins, Aboriginal activist and University of Sydney graduate, to lead a bus group of university students in protest in 1965. Amongst other things, the 'freedom riders' noisily demanded that Aborigines have access to Moree swimming pool. Their action led to an eruption of racial tensions because it brought a deeper awareness in the Australian community of the lack of rights and privileges suffered by Aboriginal people.[39] The intervention brought some changes in official policy but did not effect great change in social practices. Noeline Briggs-Smith sums up:

> The saddest part of our past is that the colour bar has put Moree, and its district, well behind other Aboriginal communities elsewhere, and in most instances we are still trying to catch up.[40]

The legacy of these times has left Moree with a lingering reputation for continuing racial tension. Briggs-Smith says,

> Sadly, those who live in the Aboriginal community today still suffer as a result of the past, and whatever their motives, those in local government authority at that time created a part of history that is ill-remembered about Moree.[41]

Home life

Religion was a large influence in Mary's upbringing. Ted and Bonnie were practising Catholics, Bonnie having converted to Catholicism on marrying Ted. Ted was active in the church community, befriending the parish priest, Father Lynami O'Reilly. In the longer term the family's strong church connection was all-important in Mary's education. Mary was also influenced by Ted's keen interest in social and political matters. Politics was a constant topic of discussion in the Gaudron household. Ted had experienced life in the Great Depression and he wanted a better deal for workers and for Aborigines. He had visions of an egalitarian Australian society, and he imparted to others his strongly held views with a passion. He thought about them and talked about them, at work, at the pub, and at home. At one point Ted, a long-serving Labor Party member, sought preselection for State Labor, with the support and encouragement of Father O'Reilly.

As a child, Mary had thrust upon her every aspect of social justice and the injustice that her father associated with Australian society's class and racial prejudices. Ted sat around the family kitchen table with his workmates and thumped it passionately while expressing his views. He sometimes talked of 'derailing trains', which scared young Mary.[42] His workmates considered that Ted took his interest in politics too far.[43] On the mention of politics, 'he was up on a box like a shot out of a gun'.[44] Some, on entering the public bar at the railway community's 'local', McElphone Hotel, and seeing Ted talking, would leave and head for the saloon. He would approach people to confront them with his view that the 'Government was ruining the country', and his opinions on industrial and union matters and the country's need for Labor Party rule.[45] Sometimes his passion for politics turned into aggression. 'You didn't want to be with him when he had been drinking,' according to one workmate. 'It took only two or three beers before Ted would express his political views forcefully to those around him. After a few more, he was capable of stirring up trouble.'[46]

Ted Gaudron had progressed from his earlier work as a fettler to shunting steam engines. Eventually he became an engine driver. He spent his entire working life in Moree with the railways. It was demanding work, and the drivers had to shovel and stoke the coal themselves. It was often hot, and always dirty, work. His 'Moree track' took him to Armidale, Inverell, the Lindsay Range and Brisbane. 'Sleepovers' away from home for several days at a time were common.

Ted was out of town when tragedy occurred. Less than two years after Mary's birth, her parents suffered the heartbreak of losing their next child, a son, Robert James. 'Bobbie', as he was affectionately called, was born in March 1944. He died on 12 December from respiratory complications at the Moree district hospital. It took Ted nearly a day to return to his grieving wife in time to bury Bobbie in the Roman Catholic part of the Moree Cemetery. Bobbie's death cast a shadow over Bonnie for the rest of her life, and she was, as a consequence, especially protective of her children. Two girls followed—Margaret and Kathleen. Bonnie rarely let the girls as small children out of the house unaccompanied.[47] In 1955, another boy, Paul, was born.

Mary's home life both confused and toughened her. Her father's political values and union support were a strong influence. But his sometimes violent moods disrupted the household. Like most of his railway colleagues at the time, Ted accepted the notion that children should be given 'a clip on the ear when they misbehaved'.[48] While he would not harm his children, Ted's behaviour was sometimes dangerously violent. He created tension because no one ever knew when he would 'go off'. After a few beers, domestic disruption was expected. He would erupt, take his anger out on Bonnie and throw things around in the house, which frightened the children.[49]

Bonnie learned to anticipate his violence, and keep as much of it as she could hidden from the children. On one or two occasions, Mary was bundled off to sleep the night at Daisy ('Nan') Cutmore's, several doors along the street. Daisy Cutmore was a respected Aboriginal woman who worked as a cook in many of Moree's hotels. She purchased her own house in Morton Street in 1949—the first Aboriginal family to own a house in the railway community. Her daughter, Dorothy, and grand-daughter, Betty, lived with her. Betty and Mary became good friends. They walked to their respective schools together, Mary's Catholic primary school being on the way to the public school Betty attended in the early 1950s.

Gaudron's friendship with Aboriginal Betty Cutmore (now Carter) helped Gaudron to understand the irrationality of discrimination on the basis of skin colour. Betty, living in the same street as the Gaudrons, felt 'free', despite her Aboriginality, to 'knock around' with Mary as a child. She and Mary swam at the local pool, notorious for its colour ban. Betty claims she was never asked to leave, adding, 'other than when I was kicked out in 1960 for wearing a very brief pink bikini'.[50] Her experience, while shared by some other Aboriginal children, was not typical for most Aboriginal children in the community at the time. She had the privilege of living with her well-respected grandmother in a regular house which may have shielded her from some of the prejudice generally experienced by indigenous children. Betty was also lighter in skin colour than many of her Aboriginal friends, and entering the pool with Mary, she did not appear noticeably 'black'. Briggs-Smith reports that she, too, 'could sometimes enter the baths but my sister who was dark skinned could not and she had to wait outside and peer through the fence'.[51]

The strong and loving female figures of Mary Gaudron's mother and grandmother helped to counteract Ted's instability. Bonnie's formidable mother, Violet Grace Mawkes, the 'Nan' whom Mary Gaudron talks about as a role model, describing her as 'a woman of great ingenious resourcefulness',[52] lived for a time with the Gaudron family and helped to raise the children as they came along, freeing Bonnie to go to work. Violet had an imposing presence enhanced by her signature black taffeta dress and her grey hair pulled back in a bun. Incongruously, she covered her dress with a floral apron, and wore slippers—in and outdoors.

Violet had married George Mawkes, a builder two years her junior, in Inverell in 1908. They moved to Moree where Bonnie went to school. George Mawkes was one of eight children. His father, Albert Mawkes, was also an assisted immigrant, having arrived in Australia on the vessel *Sirocco* (2) from Plymouth in 1864 at age seventeen.[53] Violet died in 1957 when Mary was only fourteen.[54]

Bonnie, like her daughter, Mary, was bright in personality and intellect. She excelled at school, having been Dux at the Intermediate level of Moree Public School in 1933.[55] Untrained, but with a talent for figures, Bonnie worked as bookkeeper for a large general store in the township of Moree. A sound and sensible woman, she worked hard to keep the family together throughout their difficulties. Ted, too, was resourceful and intelligent. He was well-built and fine looking in a rugged way. He dressed simply and had a quiet sense of dignity. In addition to his railway work, Father O'Reilly arranged for him to engage in some share farming on a small piece of land just outside Moree. There, with the help of the farmer and a small tractor, he tended to his plot.

Despite the unpredictability of Ted's behaviour he was well-liked and respected by the railway community and his Aboriginal workmates. He participated in community work, including volunteer work for St Vincent de Paul, and he introduced like-minded people to each other, quietly working behind the scenes to encourage better community and race relations.[56] Later, in the 1970s, he helped Lyall Munro establish the Aboriginal Legal Service in Moree. At about this time Ted Gaudron sought help from Alcoholics Anonymous and played a role in helping others with drinking problems.

In contrast to Ted, Bonnie was calm. She was very well-liked; friendly, a chatterbox who enjoyed talking to her neighbours over the front gate as they passed to pick up goods from Mr Poulis' small shop, 'Burroo's', next door. But she kept the family's problems to herself. Church members came to collect flowers cut from the Gaudrons' colourful garden, and their children might enter the kitchen for a glass of water. Otherwise, Bonnie maintained the family's privacy, and children, other than Mary's close school friends, were not encouraged to visit.

The Gaudrons were notable in the community for their cleverness—the parents and children alike. Ted assisted with the running of the Railway Institute Library across the road at the railway station. It housed operations and safety manuals, and reading and reference books. It was the social hub for railway employees, who held union meetings and other activities there.[57] The railway workers' children used the library, and it was a welcome resource for parents like Bonnie and Ted who keenly oversaw their children's homework.

Ted loved his children and was 'immensely proud of his daughter, Mary'.[58] However, Mary Gaudron did not altogether like him and his aggressive behaviour in particular, though she was proud of and influenced by her father's sound social values.[59] Ted was scathing of social distinctions, opposed racial discrimination, and he was a passionate advocate of workers' rights. He exposed her to his political views and gave her an early awareness of the impact of politics on social and industrial issues. He did not seek credit for his community work, wanting only to see things done. He had a strong personality and was proud of being working-class. Mary has a similarly complex makeup that includes a forceful and volatile personality, emotions that often erupt, pride about her social origins, and modesty about her achievements. As a child she was forthright, often surprising her teachers and other adults by her intelligence and outspokenness. She was mature beyond her years, and 'acted like a little lady' and never talked about the problems at home.[60] Here lies the probable origin of her preciously guarded family privacy throughout her later public life.

Chapter Two

THE GETTING OF KNOWLEDGE—AND RELIGION

> Give me a child until he is seven and I will give you the man.
> Francis Xavier[1]

A Catholic education

Mary Gaudron's mother, Bonnie, on becoming Catholic, adopted the faith and agreed to raise the children as Catholics and send them to Catholic schools. Both parents placed great importance on the children's education, though they did not have the wealth to provide their children with any special educational opportunities. Encouraged by their parents' interest, the Gaudron children all did well at school, particularly the bright and enquiring Mary.

The Catholic education system looked after young Mary particularly well. It plucked her out of ordinariness and provided her with the opportunity to make use of her exceptional abilities. Her education instilled sound social values and encouraged independent thinking that, ironically, gave her the tools to free her from unquestioning acceptance of religious dogma, and equip her to become a lawyer of integrity and influence.

Mary's primary education was typical of a convent education in a rural town at the time—caring but basic. From 1948 until 1953, she attended St Francis Xavier, a small Catholic school in East Moree for her infant and primary education. The Sisters of Mercy nuns who taught Mary were not formally trained but were highly dedicated. The paucity of their physical resources was matched by the richness of their beliefs and values. They instilled in their charges an ethos of social justice as well as a conventional Christianity.

The Catholic Church fostered the intellectual potential of its students from a young age through means-tested bursaries for very bright children. Gaudron later benefited from an education by Ursuline nuns, somewhat more sophisticated and liberal-minded than the education likely to be provided by the more prevalent and poorer Irish Catholic high schools.

St Francis Xavier Primary

The Sisters of Mercy arrived in Moree in 1899 and opened a small primary school room in East Moree before establishing a primary and secondary convent school in the main township of West Moree. The development of two distinct school campuses in Moree in Mary Gaudron's childhood translated, by reason of geography, to the children from the lower socio-economic families of the railway community attending the East Moree school, St Francis Xavier's, while the children from wealthier families were more likely to attend St Philomena's on the 'better off' side of town.[2]

The Mercy nuns accepted children of all denominations and social backgrounds. The order was founded by Catherine McAuley in Ireland, in 1831. Its stated mission was 'to serve the needy with courage and compassion, with a special concern for women'. Mother Mary Aloysius and Mother Mary Vincent Mulhall, who founded the Mercy order in the Armidale diocese, had a vision for the diocese to provide an education and moral and religious training to all children. Accepting children from wealthy families allowed the Mercy nuns to provide affordable or free education for the children of the poor, particularly the children of itinerant agricultural workers. Certainly this was the case in Moree.

In 1948, when Mary commenced school, racial segregation was entrenched in the community. Bishop Doody, the fifth Bishop of Armidale, arrived in the same year and was appalled to learn that Aboriginal children were not admitted to the Catholic schools. He took action to desegregate Catholic schools in the diocese, particularly in Armidale and Moree, the two main centres of Aboriginal people, in both of which there was serious racial injustice and tension.[3] Aborigines were still excluded from public schools, and Mary's friend Betty Cutmore had to travel much further to the mission school each day, until she was permitted to attend the public school in her later primary years.

Neatly dressed in school uniform, her reddish hair plaited and tied with a navy ribbon, Mary walked to school, meeting other children at the end of Morton Street. There they crossed the railway line and a vacant paddock to Warialda Street. They arrived in time to play in the school yard before school commenced. She was a chubby child, full of energy and enthusiasm.

The school was small. In 1930, when a new brick Church of St John and St Henry was built in Warialda Street, East Moree, the old weatherboard church attached to it was converted for the school's use until the 1960s when it closed and its students were transferred to St Philomena's. Three teaching nuns, including the principal, took charge of three mixed-age classes. Kindergarten, first and second class were taught in the old church, and the rest of the primary children were schooled in the attached hall, third and fourth classes at one end, fifth and six at the other.

Bernie Frize, later a priest in the Armidale diocese, was an older boy in the same 'classroom' as Mary, though at the other end of the hall. Through his child eyes his perception was that Catholic schools were 'good' and public schools were 'bad'. He was particularly troubled by the public telephone outside St Francis Xavier School and wanted to know why there was not a 'Catholic' phone booth. As with Mary, the school brought out Frize's potential. He received a diocesan bursary to attend St Joseph's in Hunters Hill, Sydney, where he met and became a long-standing friend of Murray Gleeson. In later years, Gaudron sat on the High Court with Chief Justice Murray Gleeson, permitting Frize to boast of schooling with two High Court justices.

Mary is remembered because of her brightness and willingness to speak out. Monica Horan, then Sister Mary Bernardine, taught her in third and fourth class. Sisters Mary Borgia and Mary Vianney (now Mavis Dick) were her teachers in fifth and sixth grades. Mavis Dick never forgot Mary Gaudron because she was 'a delight to teach—enthusiastic, attentive, observant, studious, caring and alert. If she did not understand something, she would ask.' Horan quickly recognised Mary's intelligence and observed that, though very young, the girl thought and acted independently. There was an occasion when Father Edward Meehan visited the school to conduct an inspection. Mary had prepared for this. He reached the third and fourth classes late in the day and when he finished his inspection Horan recalls him saying, 'Sister, I think these boys and girls could go a little bit early. They have been very good while I examined them.' Mary Gaudron's hand went up, before Sister Horan could answer, and she said, 'Father, you haven't looked at our sewing yet.' 'Oh,' he said, 'I must see your sewing and the boys' handwork.' Gaudron had correctly assessed the mood of the class. The children rummaged around and from under the desks came an array of sewing and woodwork items.[4]

It was a different atmosphere when the unpopular Monsignor O'Reilly, 'Monsignor Bulldog' to the children,[5] visited the school, often without warning. His practice was to enter the school hall from the door behind the teacher. On one occasion, Mavis Dick, then Principal of the school, visibly shook when she became aware of his presence. This was not lost on ten-year-old Mary Gaudron who, both observant and caring, saw the effect of the power imbalance. It stayed with her, recalling it with Mavis Dick many years later.[6]

Gaudron was well-liked, popular with other girls in her class, participating in whatever was happening and not putting herself above the other pupils. She also learnt to handle embarrassments and to save face. Her excited re-telling to her school friends of her encounter with 'the Doc', Bert Evatt, and the important document he promised to send her, speaks to this. The copy of the Constitution she received from Evatt's office which, because of its importance, she expected to be if not cast in stone then at least a leather-bound volume, turned out to be an unimpressive slim paperback book, its pages pinned together by a couple of large staples. It mattered. Gaudron's boasting about its importance invited the teasing she had to endure. She was quick to convert her humiliation into pride. She made a dignified assertion that understanding this document would make her into 'someone'—a lawyer, she declared. To adults who enquired, she was more specific. She asserted that she intended to be a barrister.[7]

Words were an important tool for Gaudron from a young age; whether in written form in a barely comprehensible document such as the Australian Constitution, or as a quick-witted put down of anyone who presumed to mock her. Her brilliant verbal gifts helped to disguise a very real modesty and natural shyness.

Mary, at age ten in sixth class, sat the exam for a diocesan bursary. In addition to scholarships that paid the school fees of the poorer students, bursaries were granted by local bishops to girls and boys with intellectual potential, irrespective of their family's income. Mary gained the top aggregate marks in the Armidale Diocesan Primary Qualifying Certificate finals, winning a bursary that allowed her to attend St Ursula's High School in Armidale the following year.[8] The diocesan bursary covered all fees payable to St Ursula's for the first three years.

The Gaudron family would not have been able to afford boarding school fees. At the time her parents had the education of their other two daughters to consider, and another child would soon be on the way. Mary would probably have attended St Philomena's High School on the other side of the river and obtained whatever work she could on leaving school, possibly as early as fifteen years.

Gaudron remained humble about her superior intellect and achievements, probably a product of her father's constant reminder: 'Don't get above yourself.'[9] Her father's attitude possibly accounts for her loathing, even as an adult, of formal acclaim of her achievements.

St Ursula's, Armidale

Gaudron, just eleven years old, arrived as a boarder at St Ursula's College, Armidale. The discipline of a boarding school contrasted with her more relaxed primary school days. Travelling to and from Armidale on her own at the beginning and end of term was an ordeal in itself. The train from Moree went only to Werris Creek. There she had to wait alone, for several hours, for the Sydney train to Armidale. Once at St Ursula's, the girls' routine was regimented, and Armidale was cold. They rose early most mornings to attend morning Mass in the chapel. Rugged up with coats and mittens they braved the cold to attend the chapel. As soon as they returned, according to a school friend, they would back up to the heaters, bend over and raise the skirts of their maroon tunics to warm their bottoms! The Ursuline nuns experimented with less regimented practices. Once, they let the girls choose whether they wanted to attend morning Mass or not. Given the choice of Mass and freezing bottoms or a warm bed, that freedom of choice was soon abandoned because of the drop in attendance at Mass.

There were about twenty-five girls in each dormitory. As in a hospital ward, once the curtain was drawn around a bed, there was not much room to move. Bed making had to be perfected with 'hospital corners'. They were required to wear uniforms in and out of school, and day clothes only to socials, picnics and some other outings. Gaudron, however, did not have money to spend on clothes. She was nevertheless always neat and tidy, and did not rely on being fashionable for her popularity. She was liked because she was kind, clever and had a sense of fun.

One of the teaching nuns recalls that when she came to St Ursula's, Gaudron was a shy little girl. She did not remain so for very long, however, and immediately impressed the nuns as being very bright. Sister Pat Kennedy—'Mother Campion'—describes Gaudron as a brilliant student in a high-spirited and academically bright class. She remembers her as a 'quick-witted girl who was determined to make the best of her abilities'.[10] She arrived with an enquiring mind and an eagerness to learn, and soon felt comfortable enough for her spirited nature and cheeky personality to emerge.

The German Ursulines were well-educated and sophisticated women who promoted academic excellence. St Ursula's was a school with a good academic reputation. It boasted of former pupils in the professional, cultural and educational sectors of Australian society. Australian writer Dymphna Cusack preceded Gaudron as a notable St Ursula's student. The school accepted a diverse range of students. Tania Szabo, born in 1943 in the United Kingdom, daughter of Violette Szabo of the British Special Operations Executive in the Second World War and heroine of the film, *Carve Her Name in Pride*, attended the school with Gaudron. There were also students from Thailand and Indonesia as well as girls from other areas of Australia.

Gaudron's intelligent curiosity served her well with the relatively liberal-minded Ursuline Order. She is remembered by her teachers and fellow students for questioning everything in her eagerness to understand. If she did not agree with the answers she was given, rather than argue she would go away and quietly research the matter for herself, and, if appropriate, raise it again another time. In this way there were discussions about philosophical and moral issues that might have been avoided but for Gaudron's interest and initiative. According to her classmates, this was done without a hint of showing off.

Gaudron was not a swot. One of her teachers testifies that she was not consistently studious. Schoolwork came easily to her, and she could afford to take learning in her stride. A story Gaudron cheekily tells is that one of the Sisters told her she was going to fail one year 'not because the Blessed Mary says so, but because I mark the exam papers and I say you will fail'. The story, if largely apocryphal, nevertheless expresses Gaudron's perception that one Ursuline Sister thought she might fail, and whether or not the Sister's treatment was so designed, it successfully motivated Gaudron to prove her wrong.

Gaudron was particularly fortunate to have university graduate Sister Kennedy as one of her teachers throughout her five years at St Ursula's, including five of her six Leaving Certificate subjects. She was an excellent teacher, interesting and well-prepared for her lessons and one who encouraged independent thinking and challenging questions. Gaudron's friend Margaret Hogan recalls that no pupil failed Kennedy's subjects in the Leaving Certificate in Gaudron's final year in 1958.

Gaudron cockily claims that, had she studied medicine, she would have been as good a doctor as she was a lawyer.[11] No one would doubt it. But, while the school was equipped with a laboratory and Gaudron may have taken science as a subject, the nuns were not trained to teach it. According to another of Gaudron's teachers, Sister Pauline Kneipp, Catholic schools were rather slow to embrace the increasing emphasis on science and technology that occurred in Australian education generally in the 1950s and 1960s.[12] Gaudron's interest in law and the humanities was more likely to have been encouraged.

Great emphasis was still placed on scripture, theology and philosophy, in all of which Gaudron no doubt received a thorough grounding. Scholarly Father Tom Fitzgerald, Dominican priest at the University of New England, visited the school to teach the philosophy of religion. Religion was a compulsory subject and one which Sister Kennedy also taught. Father Fitzgerald also conducted a course in basic logic in Gaudron's fourth year, the influence of which can be seen in her adherence to logical argument throughout her career in law. Father Fitzgerald was exacting. He asked questions of the students, selecting those whose minds he could see had drifted at that moment, or who had not been listening. In similar manner, Gaudron was later impressed and influenced by Sydney University law lecturer, Frank Hutley, who also had a disciplined mind and high expectations of his students.

From all accounts the more progressive of the nuns engaged well with students like Gaudron who had the spirit and courage to question. They encouraged their students to read widely and think for themselves. The economics students, for example, had access to *The Economist* and some radical social welfare papers. Further, they had the education and confidence to handle the difficult scientific and moral questions children tended to ask about the Creation, Darwinism, sex and abortion. These were topics that Gaudron and her friends discussed in the school yard in the context of their Catholic upbringing.

Gaudron and her friends were also politically aware. Gaudron's time at high school between 1954 and 1958 was a time of turmoil in the Australian Labor Party, especially the 'Split' over Communism in 1955–56. Catholics dominated an anti-Communist 'right wing' of the Labor Party which became the Democratic Labor Party (DLP) in Victoria, and later Queensland. Government subsidies for denominational schools had been withdrawn in the last half of the nineteenth century—a hard blow to the Catholic school system. The DLP had the support of the Catholic schools and revived the demand for government aid to non-state schools. Religion and politics were entangled. Both Gaudron's and Hogan's fathers, though strong Catholics, continued to support the Australian Labor Party. Mary Gaudron as an adult identified politically with the Labor Party.

The 'Ursuline spirit' is the phrase coined by the Ursulines to describe their teaching aim of encouraging, within the Catholic tradition, the growth of a faith community in which each person would be helped to develop, in her unique way, 'all her physical, intellectual, moral and religious faculties'. It also conveys the need to take care to appreciate the individual's potential.[13] Gaudron had no difficulty with two of these: the development of her intellectual and moral faculties. Throughout her professional career she received acclaim for her acute intellect and was a strong advocate of social justice.

The nuns, however, failed to persuade her of the existence of God or the worth of Catholic liturgy and ritual. In her second year at St Ursula's, Gaudron told one of the nuns that she could not believe in the existence of God. She wrote an essay on why she thought God did not exist.[14] On later occasions she reaffirmed this, and on one occasion, when she spoke of her 'loss of faith', she tells of being punished by being sent outside or given punishment tasks to occupy her.[15] It did nothing to change Gaudron's thinking.

The nuns were not so successful, either, with Mary's physical education. As an adult, apart from her interest in caving (inspired by Sister Pat Kennedy's ancient history classes),[16] she was not an active or competitive sportswoman. Gaudron was, however, a fiercely competitive debater; adept at outwitting opponents with her quick thinking. Debating was encouraged in the school and Gaudron loved it. St Ursula girls took on the boys at De La Salle College. The De La Salle boys were intimidated by the three very bright St Ursula girls—Gaudron, Marie McCanna and Lyndall Reid—intellectual rivals and close friends. All three were well ahead of the best of the boys of the same year. Paul McCabe, later an Armidale priest, attended De La Salle in the same years that Gaudron attended St Ursula's. He recalls Gaudron's intellect with awe.

Gaudron excelled at public speaking. She was clear, succinct and outspoken. If her accent gave away her working-class origins it would not have mattered to the nuns, confident that they could smooth out the rough edges of this intelligent child with lessons in elocution. By the time she reached adulthood Gaudron pronounced her words in the cultured but not affected voice of the educated Australian. However, her extraordinarily large vocabulary included notoriously colourful words, making it clear to everyone that, as an adult, she was comfortable about her origins. She was not allowed to swear at school. Instead, she let her vocal chords loose in song.

Surrounded by song

Gaudron loved to sing and music is an important part of education in Ursuline schools.[17] The students were surrounded by a strong musical culture. They sang in the Cathedral choir, whether they had ability or not. Some of her friends had outstanding singing voices. Gaudron did not. As an adult, she continued to sing often and loudly, laughing and enjoying her off-key sounds and possibly other people's amusement at functions with friends and colleagues.[18]

St Ursula's music rooms were alive with music for most of each day. The College had a dozen pianos. Gaudron had played the piano at home and her grandmother hoped she would be a concert pianist. Gaudron laughed at the idea: 'I'm tone deaf, clumsy, and that was not on,'[19] although she boasted later in life that she once played the mandolin with a band called Jock Strap and his Elastic Band.[20] There was such a band; established by one of her and her husband's caving friends. But she was not a member of it. Perhaps on caving trips she joined in the singalongs. Other friends of Gaudron's do attest to her strumming a banjo around a camp fire in later years, and that her poor musical ear never deterred her from breaking out in song whenever she felt inclined. At school she acquired the nickname 'Cush', taken from *Macushla*, the Irish folk song she sang—'*Macushla! Macushla! Your sweet voice is calling…*'

She did not enjoy hymn singing as much. The nuns sang hymns composed by Bishop Doody, and Gaudron's grievance was that sometimes she, with other of the girls, was compelled to sing them.[21] Many of the students, if only to escape boarding school for a few hours, also attended local classical concerts, such as the Australian Broadcasting Commission's annual concert. This gave Gaudron an early opportunity to appreciate classical music.

The boys' school, De La Salle College, and St Ursula's held four or five joint functions a year. Dancing was not taught at St Ursula's. The girls played their own music and improvised when dancing at the organised socials. They were expected to behave, however, as well-bred young ladies should. They were often told that 'young ladies do not do that', such as crossing their knees in public. They were groomed to the standards of the upper class so that they could be accepted as respectable women in any stratum of society. There were other functions at which De La Salle boys and St Ursula's girls would mix. Students from both Colleges sang in the choir during religious feasts and special occasions in the church calendar.

Vocational choices

After three years, on completion of her Intermediate year, Gaudron's family expected her to return home and work at a local radio station or join the Postmaster-General's Department as a telephonist, like other young female school leavers in Moree. Moree's magneto manual telephone exchange was a large, busy, hot and difficult place in which to work. This is not what Gaudron had in mind. But her bursary had expired and the family could not afford to keep her at school. She sought the local Bishop's help and secured an extension of the bursary to finish her education at St Ursula's.[22] On the results of the Intermediate Certificate examinations of 1956, both she and Marie McCanna received a means-tested monetary grant to complete their final two years of secondary education.[23]

Her aptitude for debating and public speaking may have been a factor in Gaudron's decision to settle on law as a career. One of the Thai students at St Ursula's predicted to Gaudron that she would be the first female to become a High Court judge. It is significant that Gaudron never forgot the remark, telling her first High Court associate, Margot Stubbs, about it. Predictions of that kind can in themselves influence a person's drive to see the prophecy realised. They sow the seed of possibilities in impressionable young minds. In Gaudron's case it would need to germinate quickly and grow strong enough to withstand the barriers which she would soon find blocking her path. The first discouragement came quickly.

In 1958, her last year at school, she approached local solicitor Dick Webb. At that time Gaudron had no reason to believe that women could not be lawyers, or judges for that matter. She asked him to take her on as an articled clerk so that she could study law through the NSW Solicitors' Admission Board. 'You've set your sights too high,' he told her. 'Girls don't do law.' He suggested that instead she take a job as a typist or secretary. When she became a High Court judge thirty years later, he chuckled over how wrong he had proved to be.[24]

The incident did nothing to dampen Gaudron's ambition and drive to prove that she was as able as any man, and intellectually as good as the best. Her compulsion, even in jest, to talk about being as good as any man is strong evidence that even though she was confident in her own ability, she was all too aware of the constant need to prove that ability to her male peers. A determination to prove people like Webb wrong, and women like her Thai classmate right, became embedded in Gaudron's psyche.

Fifth year students had to undertake the diocesan final examination in Religion. It always took place the day after the feast of Christ the King. The girls did not take it very seriously. Everyone passed Religion. More important were the external

Leaving Certificate examinations. All the Leaving Certificate students from all schools in Armidale had to go to Armidale High School to sit the exams. They commenced on the first Tuesday in November—Melbourne Cup day. This annoyed the girls who wanted to listen to the famous horse race.[25] Gaudron's subjects were English, Latin, French, general maths, modern history and ancient history. She matriculated with straight 'A's in all subjects, in addition to passing an oral examination in French.[26] This secured her a Commonwealth Scholarship, enabling her to attend the University of Sydney.[27]

Gaudron professed that she did not enjoy her time at St Ursula's, despite her academic success and the lasting friendships she made with Sister Kennedy and some of her classmates. Gaudron's discomfort might have been the product of having felt different in status or wealth from many of the other girls, but it is more likely that, coming to St Ursula's as a boarder after living a freer life in Moree, she did not enjoy being told what to do and how to do it when not in the classroom. By way of contrast, her friends Margaret Hogan and Lesley Moore loved their time at St Ursula's, having been boarders as youngsters in less advantaged boarding schools. However, Gaudron eventually acknowledged her good fortune in being given the opportunity to attend St Ursula's. Many years later she gave several graduation talks to Ursula students at the Australian National University in Canberra, where she acknowledged the positive influence of the nuns and the spirit of the school.

Chapter Three

SYDNEY UNIVERSITY LAW SCHOOL

It was not until I got to university that the idea of special problems for women began to percolate through the old grey cells.

Mary Gaudron, 1981[1]

Just sixteen

Gaudron's outstanding school Leaving Certificate results ensured her admission to the University of Sydney. She modestly records the relative ease of gaining admission to its Law School: 'Entry was guaranteed by 4 Bs (one of them in English) in the old Leaving Certificate. A gentleman's pass was 2 As and 4 Bs; anything in excess was in poor taste.'[2]

In 1959, at just sixteen, she was too young to be admitted directly into the Law School.[3] When she did commence law studies in 1961 Gaudron awoke to the obstacles for women and prejudices against them entering a profession. In addition, undertaking a degree part-time posed great difficulties for law students. Those with wealthy parents could dedicate themselves to their studies. Gaudron needed to work to supplement her finances, and her task ahead called for dogged determination, boldness and brilliance. She had those attributes.

Gaudron moved to Sydney where she boarded with a family in Auburn, and embarked on a combined Arts-Law degree, the first two years of her course consisting of Arts subjects alone. A Commonwealth scholarship paid her university fees and gave her a small allowance. She also had a £50 prize from the Moree and Bullaroo Council.

In her second year, she did some nursing at night and weekends and during vacations at a convalescent home in Randwick. The work supplemented her finances, but had its drawbacks. Elderly people tend to die in the early hours of the morning. Gaudron had the unenviable task of laying out the bodies when they died on her shift.

For a young Catholic country girl, entering the gates of the University of Sydney was a daunting experience. Forty years later, giving an Address on the occasion of conferral of an honorary Doctorate of Laws by the University of Sydney, she recalled,

> I arrived then with high hopes and a shiny new briefcase, almost evenly counterbalanced by a shaming weight of ignorance and naiveté.
>
> My first impressions were not of the magnificent sandstone buildings that then predominated, nor of the remote and intimidating academics in their austere black robes, but of the sophistication of my fellow students. They had all the answers. They knew, for example, what was and was not examinable, what had to be read and what could safely be ignored, whose ideas were in and whose were out. All this they imparted to me and a clutch of other awestruck freshettes from the bush with solemn superiority. They also told us that the carved sandstone lions which flanked the steps to the old Fisher Library roared out loud every time a virgin walked past. Thereupon, some of us set about losing our virginal status. I decided it was easier to give the library a miss.
>
> It took a while but it gradually became apparent that it was sometimes wise not to believe those with all the answers.

Rather, it was the question that was all important. Moreover, to find the answer, one could not avoid the library no matter how loud the lions might roar. Perhaps, that is the essence of a University education.[4]

So, at the risk of the student world labelling her the virgin Mary, in pursuit of the correct questions and answers, Mary Gaudron let the lions roar.

Gaudron collected some credits and passes with merit during her two years of study of English, philosophy and psychology, and one year of Latin.[5] This was also a time when there was fun to be had in establishing her place at the university, including some self-exploration, making new friends, taking up social and recreational activities, and in finding and pursuing a male companion. She accomplished all of these in a reasonably short time.

She joined the Ngunnagan Club, a social and recreational club, which met every Sunday evening, to suit the needs of students who were working as well as studying. There she met Ben Nurse. Nurse had founded the Sydney Speleological Society in 1954 as a breakaway club from the University Speleological Society, and has been its president for almost the whole of its existence.[6] Gaudron joined the Sydney cavers and caving became a major part of her off-campus social and recreational life. It is a hobby of the curious—people who want to explore places where no one has been before. More men than women were serious cavers in those days, although it was a recreation that wives and girlfriends could enjoy without necessarily being involved in the strenuous activity that keen speleologists undertook. Gaudron enjoyed the weekend caving trips, the socialising, the outdoor life and camping. She became a proficient caver, exploring underground into her thirties. Her interest was perhaps influenced by her exposure in Armidale to the beauty of New England's landscape and its granite gorges, and certainly by her interest at school in ancient history as told from archaeological diggings.[7] And she was interested in her cave man, Ben Nurse. Gaudron was taken with him. He was strong, attractive, some years her senior, financially secure and a figure of authority with the cavers. He had engineering skills, and was in business. She pursued him. She succeeded. They courted and married.

Times, they are a-changing

Gaudron's time at university coincided with an exuberant period in Australia's social history. The baby boomers hit the universities in the 1960s. Those with left political leanings and those from conservative backgrounds, the religious and the irreligious, the brilliant and those with bare passes, mingled and exchanged views on university campuses. Times were 'a-changing' and adapting to new breeds of unconventional people.

Gaudron was drawn to the unconventional, people whose unrestrained behaviour encouraged her own. She inclined towards more politically radical people whom she perceived to be like-minded. They were much more fun than those of conservative upbringing; people who made love to people they loved when they were moved to do so. A new world opened up before her and she walked into it with seeming ease.

Writer Bob Ellis recalls Gaudron as one of those who flourished from their life at the University of Sydney:

> ...on one university campus in one-half decade, Robert Hughes, Clive James, Les Murray, Michael Kirby, Mary Gaudron, Germaine Greer, John Bell, John Gaden, Bruce Beresford, Geoffrey Robertson, Arthur Dignam, Richard Wherrett, Richard Walsh, Richard Butler, Richard Brennan, Richard Bradshaw, Mungo MacCallum, Laurie Oakes, Henri Szeps, Hall Greenland and me.
>
> The campus was Sydney and the half-decade 1959-64 and if its budget then had been cut in the way it has lately been cut we'd be most of us driving buses now or dead or drunk or teaching English in Yokohama or running a whorehouse in Bolivia, or worse.[8]

'The Push', an intellectual anti-establishment group of men and women within the University of Sydney, emerged during the 1950s.[9] Controversial feminist Germaine Greer, a product of a convent education, moved to Sydney from Melbourne in 1959 and associated herself with the Push. In principle, at least, women were regarded by the group as equal to men; and it attracted other free thinking women like Lillian Roxon and Eva Cox, whose feminist beliefs encouraged women into careers and political activity. Gaudron befriended Lillian Roxon and describes her as 'a really outspoken, uncompromising feminist'.[10] Gaudron's new-found freedom from institutional living, at a place and a time when risqué behaviour was regarded by the intelligentsia as their right, might account for her taking up 'unladylike' behaviour that she could not engage in at St Ursula's. She took to smoking, social drinking and a fairly uninhibited use of language that was then regarded as the preserve of men.

The Push had a rebellious approach to life, challenging authoritarian rules, elitist attitudes and censorship. John Anderson, Challis Professor of Philosophy at the University of Sydney from 1927 to 1958, had a significant impact on Australian philosophy and was a strong influence on Push personalities. He attracted people to him on campus, and for many years he was the president of the University Libertarian Society. The Andersonian influence and the Libertarian Society were an entrenched part of left-wing culture by the time Gaudron entered the University gates. The philosopher Eugene Kamenka, a protégé of Anderson's, succinctly described the new world that opened up before Gaudron:

> He admired neither war memorials nor virginity. He thought religion was a force of evil and that sexual repression engendered stupidity and facilitated political repression. Education should have no aim outside the acquisition of knowledge and critical understanding.[11]

Ironically, Gaudron's Catholic Ursuline education, in so far as it encouraged the expression of ideas, opened the way for her to escape the confines of the Church's teaching. It led her into a university education that permitted and encouraged exploration and radical thought. Gaudron did not stay wedded to Catholic teachings, although they served to reinforce her strong sense of right and wrong. While not rejecting Catholicism for the sake of rejection, she discarded large parts of it that clashed with her ideas of equality, fairness and freedoms. Having already revealed herself at school as an independent thinker, it is likely that the influence of the feminist members of the Push appealed to her, particularly as her eyes were soon opened to discrimination against women, both at university and in the workforce.

The 1960s were times of new freedoms. Conventions were being challenged. Sexually and morally permissive society had arrived. New ideas and ideals confronted the old. The students of the day could assume they were the power brokers of tomorrow. It was all possible. The 'new left' had new confidence. According to Blanche d'Alpuget:

> Values were confused, extremes of behaviour flourished. The nation's youth smoked, ate and some injected themselves with illicit drugs; they wore funny clothes and fornicated in a casual fashion which perhaps lacked the piquancy of guilt, but was fun.[12]

A boys' domain

Gaudron entered the Sydney University Law School in 1961. It was not situated on the Camperdown campus where the lions might roar, but in the city of Sydney near the Phillip Street law courts. It was small and outmoded with limited study facilities[13] and, outside the lecture room, students were segregated. Gaudron describes it as something of a shock when she first arrived at the Law School:

> The first indication that things might be amiss was when I was taken to the Women's Common Room and could not fail to observe that it had in the previous year served as a men's urinal. The next thing that indicated things weren't entirely as they should be was when I attended lectures, all of which commenced with the salutation, 'Gentlemen'. Just that—'Gentlemen'.[14]

Her understanding of the previous use of the Common Room might not be entirely correct, but near enough, given the hurried renovations that took place to cater for the small but growing number of women.[15] The Law School consisted then of the 'old building' in Phillip Street and at the back, awkwardly attached to it, was a newer but no prettier building facing Elizabeth Street. The men's Common Room was on the eighth floor in the newer building. The women's Common Room, meanly furnished with four chairs and a lounge, was on the second floor of the old building. Adjoining it was a men's toilet just outside the Department of International Law and Jurisprudence. This was converted into a women's washroom, where, as Gaudron noted, 'a two stand urinal stood as testimony to their equality before the law'.[16] There was a lingering 'aroma' in the washroom, not as savoury perhaps as the 'fine tang of faintly scented urine' of James Joyce's mutton kidneys.[17]

Gaudron and other female law students before her were fortunate in having Ada Evans, a pioneering suffragette of the 1920s, to open the gates of the university Law School for them. Evans was alone in her battle against deeply entrenched sexism in the Law School. The then Dean, Professor Pitt Cobbett, had tried to persuade her to leave the Law School, suggesting that 'she lacked the physique and should do medicine instead'.[18] She persevered and graduated from the Law School in 1902. It was a pyrrhic victory. She was refused registration as a student-at-law on the ground that there was no precedent for a woman doing this. Gaudron explains:

> Instead, there was a line of judicial authority, testimony to the creative genius of the common law as administered by men, that women were not 'persons' and could not avail themselves of rights or privileges not specifically conferred on women.

Evans spent the following sixteen years trying to gain access to the profession. It was not until 1918 that women were granted the right to enter the profession under the *Women's Legal Status Act* (NSW).

It was now grudgingly accepted that women were a fact of life in the Law School, but they were still called 'gentlemen' inside the lecture halls. In class and out, women were accorded second-class status. It was a common belief that most women attended the University to achieve a 'Bachelor of Marriage', by finding a suitable husband who would ensure a socially acceptable future. To women like Gaudron the proposition was ludicrous. The strong tendency of the professional men of the day was to mate with devoted homemakers rather than clever and competitive women who were unlikely to have time to starch and iron the white shirts and collars needed for professional success. Further, the Law School was not a place where femininity was a passport to success. You had to be clever, bold and thick-skinned. As Gaudron found, it was better to find a husband outside the university walls.

There were other gates that still creaked as they were forced open. The male culture at the Law School was a reflection of attitudes Gaudron encountered when she attempted to obtain work by way of Articles of Clerkship. Before being admitted to practice, part-time law students had to complete, in conjunction with their studies, five years of articled clerkship—lowly paid labour, but compulsory work experience. Gaudron could not take up the four-year full-time course because she needed to work to support herself. She found that '[m]any distinguished lawyers took a lot of trouble and effort to explain to me that it was not their policy to take on women as articled clerks'.[19]

Gaudron obtained employment as a clerk in the Commonwealth Crown Solicitor's Office, only to find that under the determinations of the Commonwealth Public Service Arbitrator, women were paid less than men. Worse, under the *Public Service Act* (Cth), she would have to resign if she married. She reports:

> So, as a brand spanking new law student who hadn't opened a single book, I knew that the laws of this country discriminated against its women and its Aboriginal people, against more than half the population. The laws were clearly ripe for reform, as the expression now is.[20]

It did not take Gaudron long to be noticed at the Law School. She was an unconventional young woman who stood out. A law student colleague Tony (later Justice) Whealy, recalled that she could be seen engrossed in serious talk with her 'circle' at the Catalina Coffee Lounge 'enshrouded by red hair and enveloped in thick cigarette smoke':

> She liked to appear dilettante but, of course, she worked, unlike we real dilettantes, very hard indeed. She rarely missed a lecture and her prodigious academic success was won by sheer hard work.[21]

The Catalina Coffee Lounge, situated on the ground floor of the Elizabeth Street building, permitted social contact between the male and female law students that the segregated Common Rooms discouraged. The Catalina flourished when it became one of the first espresso cafés in Sydney, usurping clientele from Cahill's, previously the students' choice for coffee or morning tea. Down the road was Lorenzini's Wine Bar where men and women could drink together. Otherwise, Gaudron notes, 'more daring mixed company' could be found in the ladies' lounge of the Phillip and the Balfour hotels.[22] Another gathering place was the room of fellow student John Marsden, later a controversial NSW solicitor, where Gaudron, Frank Walker, Andrew Cunningham and others met to drink, talk and affectionately enjoy each other's company.

Gaudron was not a 'smart' dresser nor did she much care whether or not she appeared so. The smart garb of the day, as observed by Whealy, included duffel coats and desert boots 'gruesomely...known as Brothel Creepers'. Gaudron has always been simple in her tastes, and claims that she had no 'extravagances' because she could not afford them and had not been bred to them.[23] 'Extravagant', however, did apply to her personality, sense of fun and barbed sense of humour. Whealy recalls her proclamation that 'the Trots are the last bastion of the working class', a reference to the harness-racing venue known as 'the Harold Park Trots'.

Other peers remember her as a red-headed, feisty tomboy with dreadful dress sense and a fine grasp of the vernacular. She 'could swear like a trooper', confirms Whealy, as does barrister Ray Mildren, a billiard-playing law student at the time. On one occasion Mildren saw Gaudron in the men's Common Room, she having either broken the segregation convention or failed to discard her lecture room persona and walked in as a 'gentleman'. While hovering over the billiard table, he heard above the level of the general Common Room chat Gaudron raucously using the 'f' word. He recalls his shock at this, the first occasion he had heard the word used by a woman. A journalist observed that 'only Paul Keating has a broader and fruitier command of the vernacular'.[24] Another informed view is that 'only Neville Wran [former NSW Premier] had a better command of foul language'.[25]

Gaudron was well-liked for being clever, funny and different. Fellow student Greg Woods, now a NSW District Court Judge, saw her as 'a slight red-head with a temper to match'. He said at the time of their graduation,

> Mary has all the attributes of the thoroughly disconcerting, accomplished debater. She has a keen analytical mind, a magnificent command of language and sheer audacity. Opponents are demolished in a very few four-letter words.[26]

By the end of her first year at the Law School Gaudron had proved herself academically. She came fourth in her year of students enrolled in the first year of the five-year part-time law course.[27] Her first-year law subjects were accredited to her Bachelor of Arts degree, allowing her to graduate as a Bachelor of Arts in 1962.

In her second year of law Gaudron transferred to the debt collection section of the Crown Solicitor's Office. She was diligent. She tells of an agreement she reached with a particular bankrupt. As a tender of discharge he offered money and a greyhound dog, which Gaudron claims to have chained to her desk in the office while she settled with him for the discharge—a shilling in the pound.[28]

With the capacity to earn income during the day, she could afford to move into a flat with her friend, Lyn Elphick (now Williamson), who was also studying law part-time. They shared an interest in caving through which Elphick, too, met her future husband.

The Stone age

Intellectually and philosophically the Sydney Law School was a tumultuous place during Gaudron's time as a student. An understanding of the personalities engaged in conflict and the issues in contention provides an insight into influences on the students, and on the thinking they carried with them throughout their careers in the law; in Gaudron's case, influences she took to the High Court of Australia.

Gaudron's Moree childhood saw her sympathetic to viewing law as an instrument of social justice, as understood by the thinking of Professor of Jurisprudence Julius Stone. On the other hand, Gaudron's Ursuline education taught her precision and discipline, and respect for the exacting, analytical and rigorous approach to legal matters that Professors Bill Morison and Frank Hutley demanded of their students. The School had a history of conflict about its teaching approach, its educational objectives and geographic location. In the 1960s it was a place where competing approaches to the teaching role were being openly contested. Drama surrounded the debate and personality clashes were not hidden from the students. Far from being destructive, it seems that the conflicts in the Law School gave rise to a creative tension that enriched the student experience, according to a former student, Chief Justice of the NSW Supreme Court since 1998, James Spigelman.[29] They were the beneficiaries '*both* of the intellectual rigour which Morison demanded *and* of the intellectual breadth that Stone instilled', he said.

Professor Julius Stone was recognised as one of the leading legal theorists of the twentieth century. His thinking, particularly on human rights and social justice, influenced and continues to influence generations of students, including Gaudron, in their later academic, professional, political and judicial lives. He made sure that the Sydney University Law School in the 1960s did more than simply teach its students to read and learn law.

Stone's appointment in 1941 was controversial.[30] Amongst other things, his intellectual approach to legal education was regarded as a threat to the traditional practitioner-oriented teaching of law. For more than thirty years, he headed the Department of

International Law and Jurisprudence, as Challis Professor in both fields. It was part of the Law School, though located away from the Department of Law itself. But Stone's influence in the Law School was pervasive. Previously, the law course was 'legalistic and pedestrian', in Professor Tony Blackshield's view. Stone launched the *Sydney Law Review*, which later became a student publication.

Everything Stone did caused ripples. He introduced Moots as part of the standard law course. Moots, or 'mock' courts, were designed to simulate court proceedings; visiting judges and professors would role-play as judges, testing students' abilities as advocates. The innovation was short-lived, however, owing to the lack of support from the new Chair of the Law School, James Williams. This was the first clash between the two. Williams' practice of making decisions on matters concerning the Law School without consulting Stone turned into a dispute about what consultation should take place between the Professors of Law and of Jurisprudence. Stone complained of being sidelined. The showdown came when Williams insisted that one of them should resign. 'Stone remained silent, and Williams walked out.'[31]

Stone also came into conflict with law lecturer, Bill Morison, who had initially been a devout Andersonian and who had begun his academic career as a protégé of Julius Stone. Morison had studied history, philosophy and law at the University of Sydney, obtaining First-class Honours in all three disciplines, and two University Medals. He taught in the University's Faculty of Law from 1946 to 1985, becoming Challis Professor of Law in that time. His fallout with Stone in the early 1950s became personal. He was scornful of those under the spell of influential and controversial figure, and University Senate member, Alf Conlon, of which Stone was one.[32] The divisions deepened.

All students were subjected to 'Big Julie', as Stone's students called him with reference to his small stature and, no doubt, his big mind and his subject, 'Juliusprudence'.[33] High Court Justice Michael Kirby recalls that Stone wandered around the classroom 'interrogating, ruminating, challenging us all, and making theatrical use of his pipe and long scarf to offset his diminutive stature'.[34] Most students were impressed by Stone as a teacher, and Gaudron did not escape this influence, notwithstanding reservations about him as a person and the counter-influences of his antagonists. Gaudron was expressly critical of Stone on feminist grounds and, for example, thought that Stone's relationship with Zena Sachs, his research assistant, was exploitative. On the other hand, it was because of Stone's encouragement that Sachs studied law, though due to family commitments she did not pursue a professional career.

Gaudron kept an association with Stone. Twenty years after having entered the Law School, in 1981 Gaudron, as NSW Solicitor General, presented Professor Julius Stone to the NSW Attorney General on his admission to the list of Queen's Counsel, the court-recognised senior barristers.

Hutley's influence

Gaudron was also strongly influenced by Frank Hutley, another forceful personality in the Law School, and a university medallist in both philosophy and law. Gaudron has been described as a 'fiery advocate of social justice and legal reform' who was impressed with Julius Stone's concern for social justice and, at the same time, 'influenced heavily' by his intellectually rigorous foe, Frank Hutley.[35]

Hutley, a teacher at the Sydney Law School in various capacities from 1940 to 1972, could be found in the library at night ready to answer questions of students and to guide those genuinely seeking knowledge.[36] Until Stone arrived in 1942, he lectured in Jurisprudence. Hutley continued as a part-time lecturer in Probate and Succession while he practised at the Bar and as a Judge of the NSW Supreme Court. In 1973 he was appointed to the Court of Appeal from where he retired in 1984.

Hutley disliked Stone. Stone's influence arose from his now classic book, *The Province and Function of Law*.[37] It was an attempt 'to alter the way in which Jurisprudence was thought about and taught in British countries'.[38] The book examined the relationships between law and logic, law and justice, and law and society, inquiring into how the facts of social life help to develop the law, and how law affects the attitudes and behaviour of those living under it.³⁹ At the time it was generally accepted that judges merely 'declared' rather than 'made' the law. Stone challenged this. He said, first, that judges did make law and, second, that 'most judges both deny this and conceal the way in which they do it'.⁴⁰ Hutley, a 'black and white' lawyer, disagreed with Stone's view that a 'leeway of choice' was permissible for appellate judges. In 1948 Hutley gave a scathing review of Stone's work.⁴¹

Today it is recognised that changing social circumstances do shape judge-made law, though debate continues about whether or not this should be the case. The debate was not lost on Gaudron, either as a student or later as a High Court justice, when the question was actively in contention in Australia. Hutley found in Gaudron a brilliant student. She became a protégé, and he remained a great supporter for life.⁴² They both had faith that social justice could be achieved by utilising existing law. Gaudron tended to take this further, regarding law as a tool that could be adapted to social change, though not at the expense of abandoning existing law.

Hence, as a judge in later years, she was difficult to characterise in terms of whether she was 'creative' or 'declarative'. There is evidence in her decisions that she is a 'soft' judge who applied the law and logic to deliver justice that met the expectation of a developing society. Yet her reasoning was 'Hutley' in its legalism and adherence to the existing law. The complexity of her legal reasoning is not surprising, given her exposure as a student to the views of both Stone and Hutley on the proper role of judges in applying the law.

Gaudron did not see eye-to-eye, however, with everything Hutley stood for. He was conservative; she leaned to the left. While Gaudron applauded the work of Jessie Street in advancing social justice, for example, Hutley was dismissive of Street, and scathing of her association with the Communist Party, in which she held the position of Secretary for a time. Hutley was 'cantankerous'.⁴³ He regarded rudeness to be his right. He declared that 'it came naturally to be rude to people'.⁴⁴ Bill Morison suggested that when he was merely rude, people found it entertaining, but that 'merely rude' was sometimes too mild a description for Hutley's manner.

Hutley once told Morison that he 'would never amount to anything but the Methodist baker's son'. Gaudron summed him up: 'Hutley appeared to have no idea that there was a law of defamation.'[45]

The different influences on Gaudron at university were enduring and significant; enduring in that she took them with her to the High Court when she joined it in 1987; significant, because she joined the Court at a time when debate about its role was revived. Importantly, Stone's and Hutley's influences are identifiable in Gaudron's approach to the role of the courts and the way the law should be interpreted and applied. Gaudron learned from Hutley the importance of intellectual honesty, a value which restrained her manipulating the law to achieve change. As a member of the High Court, Gaudron demonstrated this by invoking a 'Hutley-like' legalistic approach. In contrast to the broad-brush approach Sir William Deane sometimes used and, more particularly, that of self-proclaimed reformer, Justice Michael Kirby, Gaudron rarely rejected the existing law in favour of making new law. Instead, a study of her High Court judgments reveals that through logic and intricate reasoning she developed a unique approach of applying the existing law, rather than overruling it, to meet changing social circumstances.

Gaudron was not alone among the brightest and best at the Sydney Law School who found their way to the High Court. The Court has been dominated by Sydney judges, most of whom were its graduates. Herbert Evatt, Sir Edward McTiernan, Sir Dudley Williams, Sir Frank Kitto, Sir Alan Taylor, Sir Garfield Barwick, Sir Cyril Walsh, Sir Anthony Mason, Sir Kenneth Jacobs, Lionel Murphy and Sir William Deane were amongst those who attended the Law School.[46] Gaudron was next to join them, and then came William Gummow, Michael Kirby, Murray Gleeson, Susan Crennan and Virginia Bell. Dyson Heydon, though not a Sydney University law graduate, was a former Dean of the Sydney Law School, and received an honorary Doctor of Laws in 2007.

To move or not to move?

A related debate within the Law School was potentially threatening to part-time students like Gaudron. It centred on the two

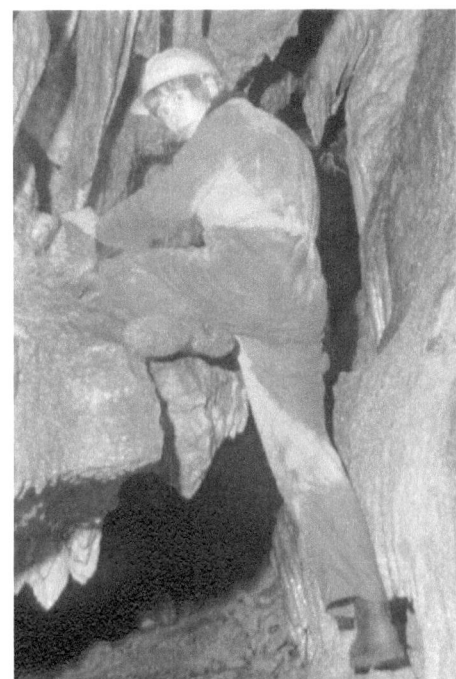

Ben Nurse, Jenolan Caves.　　　　　　　　　　Mary Gaudron, Mammoth Cave, March 1963.

(Photos Ross Ellis, reproduced courtesy of the
Sydney Speleological Society.)

Mary Gaudron's wedding day, 9 February 1963. (From left) Paul, Edward (Ted), Mary,
Robyn Wade (bridesmaid), Grace (Bonnie), Kathleen and Margaret Gaudron.

ways of thinking about legal education. Three inter-connected and controversial issues arose: the relative value of part-time lecturers drawn from the private profession as against full-time academic staff; encouragement of part-time students undertaking articles of clerkship as against full-time students; and whether the Law School should be located in the city, where connections could be maintained with the profession, or on the university campus itself.[47]

It was this last aspect of the debate that the students had fun with. They captioned the hot topic: 'To Move or Not to Move?'[48] The location question was not relevant to the universities of Melbourne or Adelaide, for example, both of which were located in the city close to the law court precinct. In Sydney, however, it 'encapsulate[d] in physical form a wider debate about the nature of legal education'.[49] When Gaudron was at the Law School, the debate was in full swing.[50] The 'old building' in the city became increasingly ramshackle and overcrowded. There was no question that there had to be a new building. Gaudron referred to the difficulties of accessing the Law School because of a 'stubbornly reluctant lift…and mean, narrow stairways.'[51] Some favoured its location on campus; others wanted to retain the city location where the part-time students and lecturers worked.

In 1963, the editors of *Blackacre*, the Law School's student magazine, gave a picture of the diversity of views within and between the full-time and part-time staff, noting that Hutley treated the matter as one of central importance.[52] In this, he and Stone were at one. Stone saw the University campus as the location for students to obtain a solid intellectual grounding. Hutley wanted the Law School to move to the campus where students would be encouraged to have a rigorous intellectual approach to their studies, undistracted by their city legal work. Though Hutley was a part-time lecturer, he nevertheless favoured full-time staff and full-time students in a modern law school.[53] Although at odds with Morison, Hutley considered that 'much of the so-called practical training to which clerks are subjected is useless and time-consuming', and that students' time should 'not be wasted in filing documents and serving writs and process'.[54] The part-time students saw this as discriminating against them. As for the suggestion that their practical training distracted them from their studies, Gaudron would provide powerful evidence to the contrary.

Morison wanted the school to stay amidst practitioners in the city, and thus to make use of part-time lecturers who were in the field more conducive to becoming fully-trained members of the profession. Were the students to be taught 'to think, or to think like a lawyer'?

Looking back, Gaudron amusingly summarised the student debate as being between the cynics and the sceptics:

> The cynics (of whom there were a few) suggested that it be an annexe to the Stock Exchange. The sceptics (female) had no reason to suppose that those responsible for their mysteriously irrelevant urinal would make good this extravagant threat.[55]

As a consequence of Hutley and Stone's thinking, course requirements were steadily tightened. By the time Gaudron arrived, students could no longer take as long as they wanted to finish their degrees. Gaudron's wry observation was that the main outcome of this was that patronage of the Phillip and the Balfour pubs suffered a decline!

The move to the campus was agreed upon, then deferred, and then abandoned as a new vote went against the move. The Phillip and the Balfour hotels were demolished to make way for the new Law School in the city at the corner of Phillip and King Streets as Gaudron and the rest of her 'class of '65' finished their degrees. The Carlton Rex stayed. It retained a 'men only' public bar, but only until the early 1970s when a new breed of bold women, including Gaudron, challenged the practice by refusing to move to the ladies' lounge upstairs.[56]

The new Law School catered for 'a new generation of students competing for entry on a quota intake which, as if by magic, caused the part-time course to disappear'.[57] Articled clerkship was abolished in the late 1960s, and the debate as to where the Law School should be located was reopened and persisted for forty years. In 2009 the School finally moved to a new building on the main campus at Camperdown.

Chapter Four

FACING CHALLENGES

> The skills of lawyering and persuasion are not found on the Y chromosome.[1]
>
> Mary Gaudron

A mum meddling in law?

Gaudron and Nurse married in February 1963 during Gaudron's third year at Law School. She became 'Mary Nurse',[2] Ben's wife, to the community of cavers and she remained Mary Gaudron, one of the boys, at Law School. They married in the Sacred Heart Catholic Church in Inverell where Gaudron's mother then lived.[3] Her father attended, too. The couple started their married life in Potts Point, moving into a unit in Lakemba, an inner western suburb of Sydney, a few years later, and later again, back to east Sydney.

The mostly happy marriage came at the cost of Gaudron's job in the public service, and was the occasion to impress on her further the reality that women did not have the same working and career opportunities as men. For women, marrying and working to complete articles to qualify to practise law were actions at odds with each other.

Forced to leave her part-time job at the Crown Solicitor's Office because of her marital status, Gaudron had some difficulty finding other work. She obtained a position as a registration clerk with a firm of solicitors, F. E. Fischer and Laws, who came to value her brilliance and enthusiasm for law. This was not before she and her friend and colleague Daphne Kok approached the Women Lawyers' Association of NSW for assistance in obtaining work as lawyers—or in 'door battering'.[4] The advice they received was that they should learn to touch-type to help them land a job. Gaudron was not impressed. In 1997, during a speech to the Association, Gaudron had her revenge by retelling the tale under the guise of applauding the fact that some improvement had taken place in women's lot.

The discrimination women law students faced was not only outside the Law School. One of Gaudron's law lecturers suggested that she should not take part in a 'moot court' exercise because, being a married woman, she was 'not going to take the practice of law seriously'.[5] Gaudron had every intention of being a wife and a mother *and* of taking the practice of law seriously. She would manage this with an understanding husband and one who was comfortable with a 'two-basket housekeeping system—one for washing and one for ironing yet to be done'. Ben Nurse was that man—and later Gaudron was able to attribute her career success to a 'tolerant husband and constant domestic chaos'.[6]

Towards the end of her studies, the force with which Gaudron demonstrated that she would do what any male could do without compromising any aspect of her life—marriage, children, study— was not one that the Law School could combat. She was nine months pregnant with her first child, when, in her fourth year, she sat her end of year Succession exam. Frank Hutley taught Succession, the study of the law of wills and the administration of deceased estates. Hutley did not suffer fools. Because of his joy in failing students, most were terrified of him. Hutley's high standards were a threat to his students. Their livelihoods were in his hands. Students were known to have failed Succession under Hutley three or four times.[7] Gaudron was not one of them.

It was a hot summer day. Gaudron had to reach over her baby

in utero to write, which, the other students believed, would slow her writing down. She finished the paper and left the examination room early and in a hurry. It is this observation of the other students from which the story probably grew that the birth was so imminent that there was an ambulance waiting outside the examination room, which rushed her to hospital in labour.[8] In fact, Danielle was born a week later.[9]

The story goes that some failed the exam, so concerned were they that Gaudron might give birth during it. The failed students were offered 'posts', the chance to sit the exam again, as passing the examination was a precondition of obtaining the degree. Gaudron, however, topped the year in the subject, having scored 'close to 100 percent', according to Tony Blackshield, teaching Jurisprudence at the time. For that effort she was awarded the Succession prize.[10] Blackshield recalls that she soon returned to the university with baby basket in tow.

More heroic is the fact that Gaudron was the only part-timer who passed the exam. The part-time articled law students were a busy bunch and were the minority of law students. Their lectures were arranged around their core hours (court hours) of work. They attended lectures before 10:00 am, rushing back to work in time for court mentions, back to lunch-time lectures, back to work, and lectures again after 4 pm. The difficulties were compounded by the attitude and behaviour of Hutley, the sole lecturer in Succession. Much to the chagrin of students, Hutley held classes at 8:30 am or earlier rather than 9:00 am. He had a reputation for locking the doors after a few concessional minutes, so a late student missed out entirely. He demanded intellectual excellence which, he believed, could not be obtained by part-timers rushing between class and work, focused only on passing in order to qualify to practise law. Frank Walker's perception is that Hutley 'fixed it' to make this virtually impossible. In this particular exam Hutley inserted a question that required a sound understanding of private international contract law principles. The full-time students had completed the private international law course and had a chance of answering the question. The part-timers, had they known it, had only one clue. A footnote to a private international law case in one of Hutley's lecture notes contained the answer. Gaudron had read her notes, followed up the references, understood the case, and correctly answered the question.

All the other part-time students failed the examination. Frank Walker was one of them and remembers the thoroughness and brilliance with which Gaudron approached the Hutley test. Walker was protective of Gaudron and suggests that other students also rallied to see that being a part-timer and mother was not used against her. Gaudron continued to attract support from Walker and others at crucial stages of her career, a factor that helps to account for her rapid rise to a permanent place in Australia's legal history. Walker, who only ever wanted to be a politician, came to law late, and was already involved in politics. It was at this time that he first identified the exceptional students, such as Gaudron and Greg Woods, whom he was able to appoint to influential legal positions when he was Attorney General of NSW from 1976 to 1983. He and others in the group talked about Gaudron's potential as the first woman to become a High Court judge.

Gaudron sometimes 'parked' baby Danielle in the women's Common Room. The baby fell into the care not only of other students but of the academic greats in the rooms next door. Tony Blackshield recalls, without any hint of annoyance, that Gaudron 'put the baby in the women's Common Room on our floor and the women students and we from the Jurisprudence Department did a lot of minding of that baby'.[11] Even 'the God of jurisprudence', Professor Julius Stone, was seen rocking her in his arms in the corridor, 'being soothed and burped by him in a cloud of pipe smoke'.[12] This was all the more notable given Stone's dependence on the two women in his life, his secretary-cum-research assistant, Zena Sachs, and his wife, Reca. Their devoted service to him, the one at work, the other at home, supported him well in all aspects of his life, and was a source of criticism of him by Gaudron.[13]

This apparently enlightened provision for a cooperative on-site child care facility arose possibly because those involved had little option but to participate in an informal baby-minding roster, if any work was to be done without the distraction of a crying baby. More probably, it came about by reason of the sheer force of

Gaudron's personality—a force to be reckoned with, according to Tony Whealy.[14] He saw her as 'fearless, even sometimes foolhardy' in her expression of her strong feelings. Her fearlessness became a feature of her professional persona. There was also the element that Gaudron, because of her determination and intellect, deserved support.

Despite the barriers, and aided by the confidence of others in her, Gaudron managed to excel and win an assortment of prizes and awards each year. For her work in each year from 1962 to 1965 she received scholarships for proficiency as well as prizes in some individual subjects. In her final year, she won six prizes, including a proficiency prize, the NSW Bar Association and Women Lawyers' Association of NSW prizes, and three others on a shared basis with other students.[15]

Gaudron's part-time and marital status, motherhood and extra-curricular activities failed to prevent her from demonstrating her excellence at University. She graduated with First-class Honours, and won the University Medal in Law, being the first part-time student to do so. Elizabeth Evatt was the only woman to have previously won the Medal. A story circulated that Gaudron had obtained the second highest pass ever, second to Herbert Evatt.

Ken Shatwell, Dean of the Law School, and in an office well away from the jurisprudence 'child-care' corner, seemed unaware of Gaudron's dual life as a law student and married woman. In the examiners' meeting that decided Gaudron was to be awarded the Medal, and in ignorance of her being married with a baby, he declared that her achievement showed the importance of students focusing on their studies 'and having no distractions'. At the same time Gaudron was a close friend of Shatwell's son, David. Ken Shatwell knew of her as 'Mary Nurse'. It amused Blackshield, present at that meeting, that Shatwell did not make the connection between Mary Gaudron, the brilliant, single-minded student, and Mary Nurse, the mum and friend of his son.[16]

Gaudron has also told of the attempt by the Vice Chancellor to award the Medal to a male student who came second to Gaudron.[17] The suggestion was that the man was more likely to obtain benefit from it, whereas Gaudron, having recently married and had a baby, had a family to look after. Famous last words they transpired to be. Such attempted interference was exceptional given that the decision of the Dean had been made. Gaudron rejected the suggestion, replying, 'The only difference between us is that I sit to pee.'[18]

Gaudron's fellow students had no doubt she would make good use of the Medal. In 1966 Greg Woods wrote:

> Mary...hopes ultimately to go to the Bar. Perhaps she will make a lot of money, but she will carry women's achievements further than the retarded New South Wales judicial system could ever expect. One can't hope to meet a nicer gal.[19]

It was fortunate that Gaudron clung tight to the Medal. The dramatic increase in the number of women studying at the Law School in recent times has been attributed to Gaudron's winning of the Medal in 1966. In her year fewer than ten percent of the Law students were women.[20] Today, more women than men enter the Law School.

Gaudron's graduating class of 1965 was notable. It included Frank Walker, in little more than a decade Attorney General in Neville Wran's NSW Labor Government, and one of the people who would help 'make' Gaudron's career. Other students at the time include three future judges, Roger Giles, John O'Laughlin and Greg Woods, and Phillip Ruddock, elected to the House of Representatives in 1973 and later a minister, John Marsden, solicitor, and barristers Paul Webb and Ernst Willheim. Gaudron's friend Daphne Kok became a NSW magistrate and headed the NSW Women's Advisory Council. Her friends Kaye Loder and Helen Gerondis also graduated that year. At Law School at the same time was financier Frank Nugan, whose business activities became the subject of Gaudron's consideration when she was NSW Solicitor General when his body was exhumed in February 1981 amid suspicions about how he died the year before, and the activities of the Nugan Hand bank, of which he was a director. After the remains were identified as being Nugan's, he was returned to his resting place in the ground. As one alumnus noted, he was the only one of them to make history by having his body exhumed.[21]

A decade of caving

Whilst studying part-time and working full-time, Gaudron had another persona as Ben Nurse's wife. As a couple she and Nurse were central figures in the caving world for more than a decade. As 'Mrs Nurse', Gaudron would don an apron and do the 'women's work' of providing suppers at Speleological Society meetings, as well as follow Ben around on excursions ready to hold the tape measure while he mapped newly discovered places in the caving underworld. It was fun, but busy. Gaudron initially took up jobs as the Society's assistant secretary, trip secretary and, when Nurse had difficulty in cajoling people to assist him with the growing job of editing the Society's monthly newsletter, *Stop Press*, she became assistant editor.

The speleologists under Nurse's leadership were a social lot. On weekends when they were not on excursions they often went to the theatre and to barbecues at each other's houses. Liking each other was important: 'In a confined mud filled tunnel in J41 [Jenolan] the only practical way of passing along shared food is from mouth to mouth. False airs and graces cannot survive under such circumstances.'[22] As for airs and graces, Gaudron put on none, 'not even after she became a judge of the Conciliation and Arbitration Commission', remarked some long-time cavers.

The Society's excursions took place almost fortnightly at weekends over a period of two to three days, to explore Bungonia, Wombeyan, Jenolan, Colong, Michelago, Abercrombie, Wee Jasper and Yarrangobilly, amongst other cave sites in NSW. They travelled by cars in convoy, perhaps two, three or more cars, and set up camp, and caved by day and ate and drank and chatted around the camp at night.

Exploration was often a muddy business, and Gaudron, clad in overalls, would crawl along the wet mud cave floors with her companions. It could be physically demanding for the keen cavers who used ladders, ropes and heavy equipment to dig and forge their way into new areas, and to map the cave surfaces and underground. Those less energetic could repair to the camp site.

The trips generally had a focus; undertaking mapping of the surfaces and underground of the caves, surveying and numbering them, testing out radio location and directional equipment, undertaking simulated search and rescue programs, and exploring and searching for new caves and uncovering new areas in existing caves. There was also the mundane work of cleaning up and removing tins and rubbish, and the more exciting work of carrying out rescues of lost or injured people.

Gaudron's friends, Lyn Elphick, and her fiancé, Dick Williamson, were the two designated hypothetically lost souls in Jenolan caves for a search and rescue trial during one very wet weekend in the middle of July 1963. Being 'lost and found' together seemed to enhance, not harm, their relationship. They married later that year and, as it transpired, made a happier couple than Ben and Mary Nurse.

Gaudron and Nurse's relationship, if initially passionate, was turbulent, partly the result of Gaudron's temperamental nature. Nurse, too, could be 'difficult' on occasions. They argued, even when on caving trips. Gaudron still 'swore like a trooper' when she was angry, according to one caver, 'though she put on an opposite face when she was in public'. On one occasion when the cavers' convoy of cars travelled to Bungonia, Gaudron and Nurse argued in the car. Gaudron threatened to jump out, and Nurse pulled the car over; the other cars pulled up behind, noting something was wrong.[23]

Despite the airing of differences in the presence of their caving friends, they were both well-liked by the caving society. Gaudron's notorious outbursts were forgiven because she was 'very bright, and as often is the case with bright people, they are temperamental'.[24] In addition, Gaudron helped with the Society's legal issues, and assisted some individual members with theirs. She mentored a daughter of one caver who studied law. In March 1963 she was a 'trip leader' in Jenolan caves. A Nurse-led group was divided into two; Nurse led one and Gaudron the other. Ross Ellis was among some first-time cavers being introduced to its intrigue by Gaudron. He was excited by the contribution they made to the mapping of the various caves of Jenolan, and soon joined the Society.

Gaudron went caving with Ben for more than a decade. In the lead up to the publication of *Bungonia Caves* by the Society in 1972, systematic mapping of the area and caves was done in a short period by a concentrated effort by a group of Society members.²⁵ In June 1972, Gaudron made her own small discovery. She observed that the fluorescein placed in the sump in Odyssey cave in Bungonia on 13 May was present at the Efflux, proving the suspected connection of the caves for the first time. By this time, Gaudron gave her all in representing cavers in their efforts to protect some caves from mining activities. She played a role in the protection of Church Creek caves in the Kanangra National Park near Warragamba Dam. More important was her role in 'saving Bungonia' from mining. She would, between 1971 and 1973, take on the conduct of legal proceedings on an *ex gratia* basis in the Mining Warden's Court in the course of a three-year battle to victory. She first had to become a lawyer.

Gender matters

Gaudron and her friend Daphne Kok both faced discrimination as women in gaining access to the professional workforce of the Law. The two friends married in the same year and produced their first babies in 1964 while still university students. In 1964, they became Student Liaison officers for the Women Lawyers' Association. On graduation, as married women, they were unable to work in the public service. They successfully found jobs as solicitors. Both faced more discriminatory attitudes against women in the workforce before overcoming them, and positioning themselves to contribute to some cultural and legal changes to the status of women in the workforce.²⁶

Gaudron later recalled that, when she commenced university, 'Ours was a society of marked inequalities, inequalities which were often entrenched or reinforced by the law itself.' She explained:

> A working woman was, by law, worth approximately two-thirds of a male worker doing the same job. In some contexts, a woman was not worth noting at all. For example, a married woman could not work in the Commonwealth Public Service. She could not sue for damages if injured by reason of

her husband's negligent driving...and she could not complain of rape within marriage.[27]

After graduating, Gaudron obtained work as part of her clerkship, initially with law firm, Maxwell Connery & Co, where she assisted with litigation, returning to F. E. Fischer and Laws to complete her articles. Graeme Laws, a partner of the firm, a great Gaudron supporter daunted by the prizes she won at University, became her master solicitor. He said, 'I had to take her up to see the Prothonotary who was supposed to read the riot act to all articled clerks. But I guess because of her University Medal, it was more of a conversation that day between him and Mary and I sat there like a schoolboy.'[28]

As a young solicitor, Gaudron found her voice. In July 1968, she addressed the National Council of Women in NSW, foreshadowing reform of family law that came about under Federal Labor's Attorney General Lionel Murphy seven years later when the *Family Law Act 1975* created a federal Family Court. She put 'the case for family courts', stating that most family disputes can be traced to one member of the family unit who has not shouldered his responsibilities, and in our present 'higgledy piggledy hotch-potch' court system, she thought, the original problem is seldom solved.[29] Her solution was to have family courts that handle the whole range of marriage, children and divorce. She believed that judges, assisted by marriage guidance counsellors and psychiatrists who could advise the court and make recommendations, might solve disputes before they reached the divorce stage.

Gaudron later headed up the litigation division in Fischer & Laws. She briefed young barrister Michael Kirby in one matter, although, when Justices of the High Court together, she did not recall the event. He did. She was offered a partnership with the firm, but turned it down to practise at the Bar.

The obstacles Gaudron saw women face by reason of their gender distressed her sufficiently to take early action to help her daughters. Gaudron insisted on her first-born daughter's name be given a masculine spelling, Daniel. She did the same for her second born, Julien. This, she argued, would give them a better chance in the workforce, at least a better chance of gaining job interviews! There were two characteristics important to compete in a male-dominated world, she asserted: 'One was a name that did not sound female and the other was to urinate standing up.'[30] Ben Nurse preferred the feminine pronunciation and spelling of his daughters' names and the girls became known as Danielle and Julienne.

Marrying Nurse was not one of Gaudron's more prudent decisions. The relationship was volatile and problems between the two became evident. Nurse was clever, but he did not have Gaudron's intellect. Not many people did. Her friends believe she 'outgrew' him. The couple remained together until the late 1970s, having produced between 1964 and 1970 two daughters, and a son who died at the age of two.

Sibling divide

There was a sad aspect to the 'plucking' of bright young Mary Gaudron out of Moree by the Catholic education system. It caused an inevitable sibling divide. None of the other children had the educational opportunities given to their oldest sister. The opening of St Ursula's gates for Gaudron gave her entry into an entirely different world from the Moree environment where she left her siblings. Margaret and Kathy went to St Philomena's High School before it closed in 1967.[31] They were intelligent children who both eventually left Moree, entered the workforce, married and had children. Paul grew up in Moree more or less as an 'only child'. He was a bright and popular young boy who participated in boys' club and football events.

Mary did not have the opportunity to develop a close relationship with Paul. He was only a baby when she was boarding at St Ursula's and she saw him only when she came home during school holidays. Once Mary moved to Sydney, she sometimes saw her father and Paul on their occasional visits. While Mary remained close to her mother and saw a reasonable amount of her two sisters and their families, a distance developed between Paul and his clever and much acclaimed eldest sister.

The overall age differences, geography and the sibling educational divide widened as Mary, the oldest, and Paul, the youngest, were propelled in opposite socio-economic directions by good and bad fortune respectively. Paul's life cruelly criss-crossed from afar with Gaudron's; she on one side or other of the Bar table as a barrister or judge, and he, for as many years, tapping on court doors to gain attention as a long-suffering litigant.

Mary entered the legal system as a student of law, and thereafter moved upward in the legal profession. Paul entered the legal system as a litigant in what became a thirty-four-year saga, with a familial twist in the tale.

While Gaudron commenced university and a new Sydney lifestyle, back home in Moree, her family was becoming increasingly dysfunctional. Ted and Bonnie's relationship had broken down. Paul was subjected to the trauma of their domestic turmoil. Bonnie left Ted, taking Paul with her when she could not stand Ted's behaviour any longer. She returned and left again. Paul was still at primary school. They went to Inverell where Bonnie obtained work in an accountant's office. Paul maintained a close relationship with his father through regular arrangements made for Paul to spend time with him in Moree where Ted still worked for the NSW Railways. But tragedy struck.

On Sunday, 26 April 1964, against departmental rules, Ted was shuttling Paul between his and Bonnie's hometowns in a goods train he was driving. According to a colleague, 'we often used to take the kids for rides on the trains'.[32] Just before midday Ted stopped the train at Mount Russell, a little railway siding between Moree and Inverell, to do some shunting operations. Ted told Paul to jump off the train and fetch some water to boil the billy. Paul jumped down, filled the billy and heard the train pulling out. Fearing he would be left behind, he ran after the train and jumped onto its steps while it was moving. Water spilled from the billy; Paul slipped and fell onto the track beneath the train. The train ran across his left foot.

In a field nearby, a wheat silo operator looked up and saw a young boy hopping alongside a moving train.[33] He saw the blood and acted quickly. Paul was rushed to Inverell Hospital and shortly after underwent the first of several partial leg amputations. He was transferred to the Far West Children's Hospital at Manly where he stayed until 16 December 1964.

There was an official inquiry into the incident. Ted was in the wrong in allowing his son on the train. However, the view was taken that he had suffered enough punishment; no disciplinary action was taken.[34] In addition, an understanding was reached that when Paul reached an employable age he would be given a job on the railways despite his physical disability. Bonnie made several informal inquiries about her son's right to compensation. Mary Gaudron was twenty-one, married and close to finishing her legal studies at Sydney University when the accident occurred. Her mother rang and asked her about Paul's legal rights. Gaudron had no practical experience in the area and knew it was beyond her competence to advise. Significantly, she raised the matter with one of her law professors and then told her mother that Paul had dim prospects of succeeding in a claim for damages against the Railways. Bonnie also made other informal inquiries and received the same negative advice. According to Paul, 'Dad was a train driver…it was a pretty poor family…We couldn't afford proper legal advice.'[35]

After the accident Bonnie returned to Moree. She and Ted later separated permanently, but never divorced. Paul was accepting of his disability as a boy. He managed well with an artificial limb. He appeared jovial and his different looking leg was a bragging point. Between 1964 and 1972, the time during which Mary graduated and started to make a name for herself at the Sydney Bar, Paul underwent four further amputations on his left leg.[36]

On leaving school Paul understood that he was guaranteed a job with the Railways and applied for an apprenticeship. However, he was denied a trade on medical grounds and instead was offered work as a junior office clerk in the Moree 'Loco' Depot. As his leg and inability to progress in the workforce plagued him, Paul started to think more about whether he had a case for damages. In 1977 Paul consulted local solicitors about it. They advised that his right to take action had expired in 1970, when he was fifteen years old.[37]

In the meantime, Ted's health was failing due to a blood

disease. As his condition deteriorated he left Moree and spent his last days in a nursing home in Sydney. This was a further blow to Paul, who had remained close to his father when he was working in Moree. Ted died at hospital at age seventy-four on 25 April 1982. He was buried at the Woronora Cemetery, in Sutherland, a southern suburb of Sydney.[38]

Paul was employed by the Railways (later the State Rail Authority) for fifteen years. He was required to move to various parts of New South Wales, which was disruptive to his family. In 1985 he resigned. In 1986 he and his wife purchased a general store, a small mixed business in the little town of Ashley, a short distance north of Moree. It was a struggle. It shut its doors within twelve months as Paul received medical advice that if he kept working on his injured left leg he would lose the whole leg. A family man with five children, Paul became an invalid pensioner. At about the same time, his eldest sister's appointment to the High Court was announced.[39]

A family litigation saga

In 1993, almost thirty years after the accident, Paul was given further legal advice. This time, he was advised that he might still pursue a claim for damages by seeking the leave of the court to proceed with the action, though the statutory time limit for lodging a claim had expired. Paul found solicitors prepared to take the case.

On 8 July 1993 the solicitors lodged a claim in the District Court in Lismore and sought an extension of the time in which he could bring the action pursuant to the *Limitation Act 1969* (NSW). The District Court dismissed the application, relying on the relevant law at the time as declared in *Dedousis v The Water Board*.[40] It ordered Paul to pay State Rail's legal costs. Then, with a twist of fate, the law took a new turn. The case of *Dedousis* went to the High Court on appeal.[41] Paul's sister, Justice Mary Gaudron, was one of the five judges comprising the full court of the High Court that unanimously overturned the lower court's interpretation of the *Limitation Act*. Gaudron and her fellow judges held that it was sufficient for the provisions of the Act to apply if the injured person was unaware of the connection between the injury suffered and the defendant's conduct that caused the injury.

A precedent was created. This decision, in which Paul's sister, albeit unwittingly, played a part, opened the way for Paul to make another bid to receive compensation that he had been denied.[42] In March 1995 Paul Gaudron's solicitors re-opened the case. They applied to the NSW District Court for an extension of time in which to proceed with the claim. This time he was successful. On 10 February 1997 Judge Dent found that Paul Gaudron did not know he had a case against NSW State Rail for his own father's negligence in moving the train without first ensuring that he was safe.

The respondent, NSW State Rail, appealed to the NSW Court of Appeal. Paul won again. The Court observed that the delay in the initiation of proceedings was a result of the inadequate and inappropriate informal advice the family had previously received, noting that his 'sister' (without mentioning her name) had a persuasive role in that process:

> In the period of twelve months during which the limitation period ran against the applicant, his sister who was a law student at the time...made enquiries into the prospects of the applicant bringing a claim for his injuries...The sister enquired of lecturing staff at the Law School of the University of Sydney and was told that any action against the Department of Railways would be unsuccessful.[43]

Paul had told the court that subsequently he never really talked about his legal rights with his sister, Mary, though he knew she might have been able to help because she was a lawyer.[44] No mention was made that 'the sister' was by this time, and had been for a decade, a Justice of the High Court; or that she had participated in the decision that helpfully changed the law; and to which court any appeal against the decision of the NSW Court of Appeal would go.

However, this was not the end of the legal saga. Fearing exposure to other similar cases, NSW State Rail applied to the

High Court for leave to appeal. Justice Gaudron, sister of the litigant, excused herself from the case.

The hearing was short and the High Court refused NSW State Rail's application. The Court seemed tired of sorting out the problems that the state's *Limitation Act 1969* caused. Chief Justice Brennan thought that if a NSW Court 'misinterpreted or chooses to misinterpret' the High Court's decision in *Dedousis* it was a matter for the NSW Court to rectify. He said '...there is a limit to which this Court can give "after sales services"...'[45] The Court, including Justice Gummow who jibed that the *Limitation Act* 'seems to obsess the New South Wales litigation profession', found that further consideration of the Act was a matter for the NSW Court of Appeal, not the High Court.

After thirty-four years and all the legal twists and turns and court proceedings, Paul Gaudron finally won his case. In 1998 the Lismore District Court, having found that the injury to Paul's leg occurred as a result of the negligence of NSW State Rail, awarded him damages of approximately $662,000 for the worsening consequences of the injury in the years following the accident and the major disturbing effect the injury had had on his life. He also recovered his legal costs.

At this point the press picked up the intertwining of the two siblings' court activities. *The Australian* reported the outcome: *Siblings' tracks cross in court.*[46] Mention was not made of the fact that Paul's litigation success, albeit delayed, arose from the law-changing decision in which his sister participated as a justice of the High Court.

The damages award was too late to provide Paul with the educational opportunities he needed to learn skills compatible with his disability. His family life and marriage had suffered from the constant pursuit of suitable work, and the family upheaval that resulted in moving around NSW. His marriage broke down irretrievably. By this time Paul's children had left home and started their own lives. Despite the support of his mother and sisters, including Mary, Paul went his own way, with less and less contact with them. Compensation in terms of the lump sum court award could not make up for the pain and loss of career, work and, indeed, life opportunities Paul had suffered. Legal victory came too late to do that. A decade later Paul remarried and moved to Warren, NSW, where he and his wife established a bus and coach service.[47]

Chapter Five

A LABOR 'GAL' AT THE BAR

The decade of the 60s was a decade of revolution, and not just the sexual revolution. The Commonwealth Scholarship scheme made it possible for more women to study law; the contraceptive pill made it possible to pursue marriage and a career in the law. But the profession was less than welcoming.

Mary Gaudron, 2002[1]

A sobering experience

Gaudron was admitted to practice as a barrister on 18 October 1968. A diminutive figure, she had red hair, a fresh open face, a direct gaze and a large smile. Although she had shed her childhood plumpness and plaits, she still 'looked about sixteen'.[2] With a First-class Honours degree in law under one arm, a University Medal under the other and some legal experience up her sleeve, Gaudron expected to slip into a career in the law with ease. She soon found that not everyone shared her egalitarian views. She had been granted scholarships and educated alongside both the poor and the rich. Now she came face-to-face with a system where much depended on social status and connections and, in particular, gender; if you were a man, you had a head start.

As the 1960s turned into the 1970s women came to assume they could be breadwinners even if men had not yet learned to be nurturers. The women's movement had taken hold as a strong force to challenge traditional views of women's role in society. Women embraced the changes; men were perplexed by them. The conservative men at the Sydney Bar did not understand how women would fit into their professional world, as women were still the child-bearers and therefore, it was believed, natural child rearers.

The big players in the Sydney legal world were housed in Wentworth and Selbourne Chambers, Phillip Street, near the law courts, and opposite the University of Sydney Law School. Gaining acceptance into those Chambers, obtaining a room and attracting briefs from male-dominated legal firms of solicitors were obstacles to be overcome by even the smartest female would-be barristers.

Wentworth Chambers had been in operation since 1957. Selbourne Chambers, located next door, opened in 1963. Barristers had to buy shares in Counsel's Chambers and these two Chambers held the majority of practising barristers in Sydney. It operated as something of a closed shop. Who you knew was also important. Mary Gaudron knew Janet Coombs. She also knew Frank Hutley, QC.

Coombs commenced practice at the Bar in March 1959. She was the only female barrister in active practice on the thirteenth floor of Wentworth Chambers. A few more women joined the Bar in the following years: Helen Knox in 1960, Kay Trevalyon and Sue Schreiner in 1962, Mary Cass in 1963, Cecily Backhouse and Anna Frenkel in 1964, and Helen Gerondis in 1965.[3] Coombs invited Gaudron to commence practice as 'a squatter' on the thirteenth floor.

Coombs, daughter of the then recently retired Governor of the Reserve Bank, Dr H. C. 'Nugget' Coombs, and sister of barrister John Coombs, was already an old hand with eight years of practice behind her, and she had her own room. She keenly encouraged women in the law and tried to protect them from the prejudice she knew they would suffer.[4] She had heard that Gaudron wished to practise at the Bar. The thirteenth floor was unusual in that sharing rooms with other barristers, and 'floating' of barristers (using rooms that were free when other barristers were away or in court), was permitted. This allowed Coombs to invite young women to share her room, or to encourage them to come to her floor and to 'float around'.

Frank Hutley had chambers on the same floor. He thought Gaudron's Succession examination paper the 'finest he had ever marked', and invited her to 'read' with him.[5] New barristers required a tutor to read with for a year as a mentoring system. 'Reading' with Hutley was good enough reason for other members of the thirteenth floor to accept Gaudron.

Gaudron, however, did not want to 'squat' in other people's rooms. She wanted her own. Janet Coombs thought it a cheeky demand of Gaudron's to seek chambers before proving her ability and staying power. She explained to Gaudron that newcomers had to share rooms initially; they had to earn their right to a place at the Bar. Custom dictated that a 'new boy on the block' had to wait to be invited. Coombs had survived for her first few years leasing chambers until her time came. She knew how to be humble. Gaudron had yet to learn that lesson. 'If you have difficulty getting chambers you can share with me,' Coombs offered. 'Oh,' said Gaudron, with what became recognised as a sharp tongue, 'I'm sure I can do better than that.'[6]

Coombs made allowance for Gaudron's brashness, reasoning that it arose from her naiveté about how the 'system' worked. But once Gaudron better understood the lie of the land, it became clear that she was brash anyway. She was confident in her ability, direct in her speech, unselfconscious about her working-class upbringing and appearance, and fearful of nothing.

Coombs was conciliatory: 'My offer remains open.' Coombs waited, knowing that soon enough Gaudron would knock on her door. It did not cross Gaudron's mind that there would be any barrier to her acceptance at the Bar, or to obtaining rooms in chambers, or to receiving briefs from solicitors. She assumed that being well qualified, ready, able and enthusiastic to start practice, offers would be made. Coombs knew otherwise. Gaudron was surprised to find that offers were not forthcoming for her to buy into chambers.

This was the beginning of an early realisation that the mere repeal of discriminatory laws was not enough to secure real equality. Gaudron reports that '[t]here was no law at that stage, not even the law of supply and demand, that said that I could not buy chambers and practise as a barrister in New South Wales'.[7]

One offer almost came her way. Michael McHugh, later a colleague on the High Court, tried to sell his room to her when he moved to another floor. He believed she was 'on her way to becoming the greatest female lawyer' that the Australian legal profession had produced. The floor refused to accept Gaudron, and selected a male barrister to buy the room.[8] Gaudron was refused chambers at the Bar a number of times because it was felt that the company of a woman on the floor would be either disruptive or, at the least, uncongenial.[9] On some of those occasions she was assured the rejection 'was neither discriminatory nor personal; it was just that I was a woman'.[10]

When the knock on the door came that Coombs was expecting, she asked: 'Would you like to sit over there?' pointing to a chair and table in the corner of her room. Gaudron then had a table at which to work. Even then, but for Hutley, it was unlikely that she would have been permitted this 'squatting' arrangement. Hutley, aware of the resistance to women at the Bar when Gaudron arrived, told her that 'our clerk has threatened to resign if we bring another woman on the floor' and, with the intention of being provocative, encouraged her to come.[11] On a later occasion he reported:

> I had to speak severely to my clerk about Mary coming to our floor. She moved in but, some time later, I overheard her giving the clerk quite a tongue-lashing. He replied, 'Look here, Mary, I don't have to take this from you. I'm not your husband!'[12]

But the clerk, Erne Stanhope, did not resign, and, according to Gaudron, they became firm friends. He secured Gaudron work that might otherwise have been difficult for her to attract, including industrial law which she had not previously practised.[13]

Paul Henke, a young solicitor and a university friend of Gaudron's, wanted to brief her on a matter, only to be told by his employers that the firm did not brief female barristers.[14] Gaudron also missed out on a high-profile brief in the Burchett defamation case by reason, it seems, only of her gender. Wilfred Burchett, controversial Australian journalist, sued Democratic Labor Party Senator Jack Kane over an accusation that Burchett served as an espionage agent for the Chinese and North Vietnamese governments and the Soviet KGB. In 1972 Clive Evatt, QC, having flown to Paris and interviewed Burchett about the matter, 'dumped' the brief he had in the case, as he was wont to do. Burchett's solicitor handed the brief to another barrister, who gallantly owned up that defamation law was not his field, and suggested that Gaudron, now a 'whip hand' in defamation, be briefed. The solicitor refused to brief Gaudron, due to the firm's policy not to brief female barristers, and insisted that the barrister handle the case himself. Burchett lost his case over the barrister's failure to raise a point of law at the trial.[15]

It did not take long for Gaudron to see and react to the anti-female culture at the Bar. The Chief Justice of the Supreme Court, Sir Leslie Herron, gave her the ideal opportunity. In the early 1970s Herron gave his usual speech of welcome to new members of the Bar. When those members included women, he thought it witty to say, 'A woman lawyer is nature's sole mistake.' Gaudron was infuriated by the remark. She, Janet Coombs and barrister Jenny Blackman approached Herron and suggested he exclude the phrase from his speech because it upset some women barristers. His retort was, 'Oh, women lawyers—I would put them all behind bras.'[16] Whether or not Herron absorbed the message, he respected Gaudron. He invited her to work with him to produce the 'Bible' on *Pleading* in the Supreme Court.[17] She edited and classified the selection of precedents of pleadings that formed the core of the work.

Gaudron shared Coombs's room for six months until she was invited to become a permanent member of the thirteenth floor. She then occupied a room on a shared basis with her university friend and industrial law barrister, Andrew Cunningham. Within two years, when Cunningham left to become an industrial court magistrate in South Australia, Gaudron had the room to herself. She shared a secretary with John McLaughlin, later Associate Justice of the Supreme Court. Despite differing political views, Gaudron proudly claiming to be left-wing and McLaughlin being 'a paid up member of the Liberal Party', they did not disagree about 'any important issue'.[18] McLaughlin respected Gaudron's intellectual honesty and rigour, which he attributed to Hutley's training.

Hutley felt responsible for his students and became a mentor to many. Well-respected, often feared, he was disliked by many for his difficult personality—'a monster'—according to one colleague.[19] He had an open door and, despite his 'rudeness' and tactlessness, he was extremely generous with his time in assisting young barristers.[20]

Hutley continued to hold Gaudron in high regard while they practised side by side at the Bar.[21] He arranged for her to succeed him as part-time lecturer in probate and succession law at the Law School. Hutley's praise of Gaudron could not be ignored. According to Kaye Loder, 'For him to recognise any sort of talent meant that student had to be very intelligent and very diligent.'[22]

In 1972 Frank Hutley was appointed to the NSW Court of Appeal and sold his chambers to Gaudron. He asked for no more than the price he paid for them, by then a ridiculously small sum.[23] 'It's our duty to assist new barristers,' he explained. Gaudron now owned her own room. Her brilliance had been her pathway to success. But more was needed: boldness.

There was a widespread view amongst male lawyers that women advocates were more suited temperamentally to working in fields associated with domestic matters and traditional women's roles, such as family law, conveyancing and probate. In NSW where the profession is divided between solicitors and barristers, most women lawyers opted to work as solicitors. Temerity was needed 'to brave that last bastion of conservatism, the Bar'.[24] A number of female lawyers elected to practise extensively in the divorce courts and in maintenance work. Others, like Gaudron, declined to do any divorce work at all, preferring to establish themselves in the mainstream, the male domain.

By this time the thirteenth floor was confident of her ability. In 1972 she was elected a member of the Bar Council of New South Wales, the first female member, evidencing the regard in which her colleagues held her. She also became a member of its Legal Education Committee.

She had come to stay, or so her Bar colleagues thought. As it turned out, she practised for only six years. Her career at the Bar was short only by reason of her success. In 1974, at age thirty-one, she was appointed a deputy president of the Commonwealth Conciliation and Arbitration Commission.

The 'defo and nello' factory

It is a barrister's duty to honour the 'taxi cab' rule. Barristers cannot pick or choose their work. They must accept the brief that comes along, subject to its being within their expertise. There are ways around this. Selecting the 'rank' helps to attract certain types of work. Gaudron's working-class background, her stated views and circles of friends led to briefs from solicitors and through senior counsel who commonly acted for the unions, the Labor Party and organisations that represented disadvantaged or vulnerable individuals.

Gaudron enjoyed industrial law. This included acting for workers in their claims for damages for injuries they sustained in the course of their employment arising from some negligence that is attributed to the employer—a faulty system of work, for example. These were the 'negligence' or 'nello' actions where unions often assisted members. The unions preferred to engage 'left wing' lawyers. It was work Gaudron was interested in, with an emphasis on acting for the individual against corporate employers and their insurers. Individuals whose reputations were impugned at the hands of the media could also take an action for damages for defamation—the 'defo' actions. Gaudron found a niche in this area as well.

Janet Coombs believes that Gaudron set out to cultivate Labor contacts and would go out of her way to meet those she regarded as heroes of the Labor Party. 'Mary always knew on which side her bread was buttered. She always knew who to look to for assistance. She was a very committed Labor person.'[25] Coombs placed Gaudron in the context of the times:

> Women were taking to the streets for equal pay and control over their bodies, when women's liberation and abortion law reform, free speech about sex, opposition to the laws of obscenity and indecency raged, when the freedom riders went to Mary's Moree where her near neighbours wanted, needed help to overcome their inequality, when Green Bans and the BLF, Mackie and the year long Mount Isa strike captured attention everywhere, when in our country Whitlam the reformer was coming into national prominence. Mary studied and entered the law across this period and its ferment. She came to know which side she was on, instinctively as it were.

While never shedding her Catholicism, Gaudron rejected the Church's teachings on some social and moral issues, like the rights of women over their bodies. This 'non-Catholic' attitude endeared her to feminists. She supported a woman's right to abortion, despite her own difficult obstetric history of miscarriages and her desire to have a large family.

Gaudron was Secretary of the Kings Cross branch of the Australian Labor Party in 1973.[26] That position would have strengthened her Labor and union connections and assisted her in attracting the kind of work in which she wanted to specialise at the Bar. Included among the Labor Party-connected lawyers who sent industrial and defamation work her way were Senator Lionel Murphy, barristers Clive Evatt and Jim Staples, and Frank Walker, who practised as a solicitor until he became Attorney General in the Wran government in 1976.

Too much involvement in party politics could, however, be detrimental to a judicial career, depending on the government in power. Being politically partisan was a two-edged sword. When Gaudron started at the Bar, the Liberal-Country Coalition Government had been in office in Canberra for twenty years. In 1969 it was returned to power with a slender majority. It was a devastating blow to left-wing lawyers, Clive Evatt, Staples and Gaudron included, who wanted to see change. In NSW, Bob Askin's first coalition Government in a quarter century had recently won a second term of office.

The era of conservatism was, however, good for the unconventional Clive Evatt's business. The newspapers revelled in attacks on militant unionists. Clive Evatt in turn revelled in running defamation cases against the papers as part of a general attack on their support of the 'establishment'. The 'defo and nello' factory flourished and, through Evatt, opportunities opened for Gaudron to prove her excellence as an advocate.

Clive Evatt, QC, the youngest brother of Doc Evatt, was a controversial and colourful figure at the Bar. Janet Coombs warned Gaudron of the dangers of associating with him. His unorthodox advocacy and ability to persuade juries and to win large awards for his clients against the newspapers unnerved the press, bringing forth complaints about the way he addressed the jury. Some members of the Bar believed he was overcharging, something never substantiated. Others regarded Evatt as the greatest common law advocate at the Sydney Bar in the 1960s. Either way—a hero to some and criticised by others—his reputation for winning was legendary. His Br'er Rabbit status was confirmed as he kept ahead of those pursuing him.[27]

Coombs's main concern, however, was Evatt's tendency to leave unsuspecting juniors to appear alone in difficult cases. Her story is that she used to hide under her desk when 'old Clive' came into her room. Jane Mathews, later a Justice of the Federal Court, also remembers Evatt brimming with charm and shuffling off, leaving her to run the case.[28]

On the other hand, he generated work, and many young barristers, Gaudron included, did not want to turn down work coming their way. She benefited from working with him and the opportunity it gave her to prove her ability as an advocate. As a newcomer to the Bar she had one of her first breaks appearing as junior counsel with him. It gave her Supreme Court civil trial experience and publicity in leading cases. As Gaudron's career 'took off', she acquired a formidable knowledge of defamation law.

She learned how to handle Evatt. Coombs noted that sometimes 'when he and his junior were in the lift together, robed and wigged, about to appear in court, he would say "Oh, I have forgotten my pen" and he would jump out of the lift to fetch it, and not come back'.[29] Gaudron was alert to this. 'She did not let him out of her sight and would accompany him back to his chambers, to ensure he reappeared.'[30]

Despite throwing herself into the 'defo' and 'nello' briar patch, Gaudron's sense of integrity kept her out of difficult and prickly situations that might have seen her tarred with the same brush as Clive Evatt. Nor did she fall into the 'factory' mentality of specialising in and taking on common law claims as they came along on a conveyor belt from law firms specialising in 'plaintiff's' claims. In pursuit of knowledge and excellence as a lawyer, she tackled all areas of law including criminal law, tax law, probate and succession.

Personality and politics

At the Bar those who knew and understood Gaudron loved her. Loyal friends were the beneficiaries of compassion and warmth. They also knew she flared up angrily when she was hurt or offended. Her flamboyant personality, unrestrained by social conventions, and her love of people and life were sufficient reasons for her friends to be forgiving of her temper, impatience and moods. Coombs was one: 'When she would go to court and lose she would be absolutely hysterical and we would have to organise rosters to take her drinking until she got over her misery.'[31]

Her success as a barrister was acknowledged by her colleagues. Her foray into the 'defo and nello' practice with Clive Evatt was seen by most as consistent with her desire to act for the 'underdog'. She drew criticism from others. More conservative members of the Bar thought that her association with Clive Evatt and the other 'soft belly lawyers' who took on work on a 'no win no fee' basis was undesirable. They viewed Evatt's conduct as a barrister, and hers by association, with suspicion. It caused some to see her as improper, greedy and unlikeable.[32]

Others objected to her coarse language and her propensity to make barbed or outright rude remarks—Gaudron's common response to offensive jokes or comments. On one occasion an insensitive male colleague asked Gaudron how many children she had. On learning that she had two daughters, he rhetorically asked: 'How is it you only have two children when you are always pregnant?' Janet Coombs heard the remark and, knowing that Gaudron had tragically lost her son from a congenital heart condition at age two, replied, 'Do you want to make her cry?' The denigration Gaudron suffered emanated mostly from the 'senior boys' on the floor.[33] Gaudron, with her sharp tongue, had insults ready to trade. Her extravagant, colourful language and her determination earned her the nickname 'Mary the Merciless' from some of her less kind colleagues.[34]

Like most barristers, Gaudron wanted to win. She seems to have been driven by a determination to establish that women were as good as men, and that she was as good as the best. Her ambition to succeed focused more on demonstrating intellectual excellence than on success for the sake of social recognition or financial reward. Demonstrating intellectual excellence had to be on her terms, within her own value system. She cared about those less fortunate than herself. She was a good listener and easily slipped into other people's shoes, enhancing her understanding of how societal values affected individuals and community groups. She learned to restrain her relatively uninhibited behaviour but did not compromise her values or principles in the process of getting what she wanted and where she wanted to be. She instinctively knew the limits of the power of her personality.

One thing she did get away with was changing from street clothes into her robes in front of the men in the 'uni-sex' change rooms. Doing what her male colleagues at the Bar did highlighted the sexist culture. There were no separate changing rooms, and the men took off their coloured shirts to don their white ones. The women, too, had to remove their top garments, and often their skirt or slacks, in order to meet the dress requirements. Walker once courteously turned his head away as Gaudron changed, and she taunted, 'Haven't you ever seen a woman in knickers before?'[35]

Gaudron inevitably found more in common with other unconventional and radical lawyers at the Bar, including Clive Evatt. Because of (or perhaps despite) this, Gaudron built up an extensive practice in equity and common law. Gaudron was unconventional in many ways, perhaps because she was, at least initially, oblivious of the expectations of her colleagues. She did not want to be addressed by her married name, Mrs Nurse, with its compassionate and feminine overtones that were, for a hard-hitting advocate, incongruous. She stuck to her birth name, Gaudron—a fairly radical decision for those times. Once asked about this decision, Gaudron replied: 'Well, marriage is so temporary,' which, as it turned out, was to be the case.

Although ignoring such social conventions, she conformed professionally and participated in professional activities. She played a modest role in the organisations to which she wanted most to contribute, sometimes taking office where she could offer some leadership. In 1972 she became the first female member of the Council of the NSW Bar Association. Holding office in the local Labor Party branch in 1973, she found herself at the wrong end of a writ for defamation following an exchange with Albie Ross Sloss, member for Kings Cross. Noted for his 'you can have the logic; I will have the numbers' attitude, he was disrupting discussion at a meeting chaired by Gaudron. Trying to adjudicate, she eventually roared at Sloss. He sued for defamation. When the claim was served, Gaudron consulted Frank Walker. He looked at the document and asked her, 'Why did you call him an [expletive deleted] Indian?' 'I didn't,' she protested, 'I called him an [expletive deleted] idiot.' When the word difference was pointed out to Sloss, he withdrew the claim: 'Ah, OK. That's all right then. My objection was to a racist remark.' Gaudron also lectured part-time at the Sydney University Law School in 1972, 1973 and 1974. She felt it kept her up-to-date and in tune with the ideas of the young students.

Socially, Gaudron was fun. Her friends loved her for the unrestrained and unselfconscious manner in which she enjoyed herself. Amongst friends, Gaudron would predictably break out into Irish revolutionary songs. Even at age sixty-five, she did so at a celebration marking Federal Court Justice Rod Madgwick's retirement, at the East Sydney Hotel at Woolloomooloo.[36] Gaudron held a class view of society and saw herself as belonging to the non-establishment end of it. She never thought it would be otherwise. She resisted acclaim for her work in the law and had a militant contempt for the 'proper' end of society.

Oz magazine hit the Sydney streets in 1963, with its irreverent satire of politicians, royalty and other public figures. In 1965 military conscription of twenty-year-olds was introduced on a selective basis. Academics joined the student agitation over Australia's entry into the Vietnam War and over other social-political issues. People had to consider their stand on current issues. Dinner party conversations turned into divisive political arguments.

Gaudron was not usually an activist when it came to the street protests and demonstrations of the late 1960s and 1970s. Her instrument for change was expertise in the law. But during the Vietnam War, she kicked off her high heels and marched barefoot in Sydney street demonstrations.[37] She supported feminist causes, particularly opposition to discrimination against women in the workforce. She was a member of the NSW Women Lawyers' Association and, for a time, on its executive. She was keen to see repeal of laws that discriminated against illegitimate children. She supported the newly-formed Women's Electoral Lobby in the early 1970s and spoke at its first national conference in January 1973 about the need for reform of laws concerning the legal status of women.[38]

When asked, she would also give her time generously for causes she believed in. The Council of Civil Liberties, of which she was a member, asked her to defend Tony Blackshield, her friend and lecturer at the Law School. She appeared for him on 20 and 21 June 1972 *pro bono* at the committal proceedings for activities associated with distributing allegedly 'offensive material'. Blackshield, then a senior lecturer in law at the University of New South Wales and a member of the Australia Party, was involved in a protest against the gaoling of Wendy Bacon on obscenity charges, over her role as an editor of *Thorunka*, an underground offshoot of the University of New South Wales' student newspaper, *Tharunka*. The principle at stake was freedom of speech.

Gaudron was unsuccessful. Blackshield was committed to trial on all counts. Legal reinforcements were required in an effort to save Blackshield from being gaoled. Trevor Martin, QC, was briefed to lead Gaudron at the trial. Gaudron went to work on keeping the case out of court. She first drafted letters to Attorney General Ken McCaw in the Askin Government, to make application for a 'No Bill' on the two 'innocent' charges relating to Blackshield's holding the broadsheets under his arm. These, she argued, should not be proceeded with as no distribution was involved. The process took about a year. Gaudron received a favourable reply, and then followed up with a second 'No Bill' submission in respect of the material that Blackshield had actually disseminated. This was also successful. In March 1974 Blackshield received written confirmation that there would be no further action on the charges.

Keep Bungonia gorgeous

More time-consuming, and of great importance to the Sydney Speleological Society, was the case Gaudron undertook in 1971 on a *pro bono* basis to preserve the Bungonia caves in the Southern Tablelands of NSW from mining activities. As the wife of Ben Nurse, the President of the Society, and a caver herself, Gaudron knew the caves well and their vulnerability to large-scale exploitation by mining interests. Limestone had been removed for many years for the making of cement, and the cavers feared that the revocation of the reserves to permit the expansion of limestone quarries would cause serious environmental degradation to an area of major natural, scenic and recreational value.

The provisions for Mining Wardens' inquiries under the *Mining Act 1906* were designed to settle conflicts between competing miners, not to provide citizens with an opportunity to play a part in environmental planning and land use. Gaudron agreed to help the cavers make innovative use of the legislation to object to further mining by seeking to restrain or limit the mining activities. Warrick Counsell, caver and student of geology, lodged an objection and the hearing opened in the Mining Wardens' Court in Goulburn in February 1972 to facilitate inspections of the caves. The Court reconvened in Sydney at the end of March 1972. The case took more than a year before it was completed.

Gaudron was nervous about her role in the case. It was an unusual action and she was aware of the implications of using the Court on behalf of what was, in reality, a public interest environmental action. The Court had discretion to award costs if, for example, it found that Gaudron's notional client, Warrick Counsell, had embarked on frivolous litigation. It was a long case in which the mining company incurred substantial legal costs, which costs Counsell, a student, could not meet.

Gaudron had no need to worry. The Society won a huge victory in its 'Keep Bungonia Gorgeous' campaign. It is for Gaudron's effective legal work that the cavers claim her as theirs. Gaudron is reluctant to take credit. She specifically requested that her role not be mentioned in the Society's book, *Bungonia Caves*, in which it describes the battle to save Bungonia.[39]

Making her mark

Gaudron made her mark at the Bar in December 1970. As a junior barrister of only two years' standing, she appeared in the High Court without a leader, in itself unusual, in a difficult defamation case, and won. In *O'Shaughnessy v Mirror Newspapers Ltd*[40] she represented the actor Peter O'Shaughnessy in a claim for defamation against the Murdoch-owned *Australian* newspaper. Clive Evatt Snr had 'dumped' the appeal case on her after she had previously appeared with him in an unsuccessful appeal to the NSW Court of Appeal.[41] Evatt saw no grounds for an appeal to the High Court. The law was against them.

The suit arose from a review of a performance of Shakespeare's *Othello*, directed by and starring O'Shaughnessy. The review essentially claimed that O'Shaughnessy had wasted the talents of the cast in a dishonest production devoted to enhancing himself at their expense.[42] In the trial itself, the judge had ruled as a matter of law that the alleged defamation was 'comment' rather than a statement of fact. He directed the jury to find so, rather than allowing the jury to decide whether or not the criticism went beyond opinion in attributing a dishonourable motive to O'Shaughnessy. The Court of Appeal held that the allegation of dishonesty was not capable of being regarded as an assertion of fact and that a new trial would serve no useful purpose. The High Court, persuaded by Gaudron, disagreed, allowed the appeal and ordered a new trial. Gaudron had succeeded in effecting a change in the High Court's approach to 'comment' as a defence in the law of defamation. The decision was authoritative and others would rely upon it in future defamation cases.

Gaudron's success is cited more often, however, as a demonstration of her courage and cleverness in dealing with the bench. There are several versions of the anecdote, with some assuming that the exchange occurred between Gaudron and the Chief Justice of the High Court, Sir Garfield Barwick (not substantiated by transcripts of the case).[43] The more likely scene of the often talked-about verbal exchange is the NSW Court of Appeal presided over by an old nemesis, Chief Justice Sir Leslie Herron. Evatt, QC, had given Gaudron the task of putting the submissions to the bench. As Tony Blackshield recalls the anecdote, Chief Justice Herron said: 'Miss Gaudron, I'm sure that if Lord Esher were with us today, he would prefer to hear his name pronounced as I have just done, rather than in the mispronunciation which you persist in using.' Gaudron responded to his pickiness by throwing the law report she was holding onto the floor and stating:

> Your Honour, I'm sure that if he were with us today under whatever appellation, *he* would have been capable of appreciating the legal argument I'm attempting to put to your Honour.

The Chief Justice considered this and conceded:

> Point, game and set to Miss Gaudron.[44]

The success Gaudron had in *O'Shaughnessy* led to briefs in other notable defamation cases. She addressed the NSW Court of Appeal, *Pearson v Australian Consolidated Press Ltd*,[45] after Evatt,

QC, again opted out, informing the bench that Gaudron, 'my learned junior', would put the submissions on the matter. Gaudron appeared with some eminent 'silks' in two other cases before the High Court in 1971, including Hutley, QC, and Harold Glass, QC (who later, like Hutley, became a Justice of the NSW Court of Appeal).[46]

Gaudron's notable professional work in 1971 was the more remarkable given the difficulties she and her family faced in the course of that year. Gaudron's marriage to Nurse was in difficulty. His high risk property developments worried her. Nor was Gaudron herself easy to live with. She was entertaining and loveable and easygoing, but she could also be histrionic, egocentric and prone to tantrums. Their busy lives took their toll. They had grave concerns about their baby boy. Gaudron was convinced there was something wrong with him. Ben was born in 1969 when she was already busy at the Bar. Perhaps she was fussing too much, Nurse hoped. But Gaudron was right. Little Ben had a fatal congenital heart condition. He required twice-daily physiotherapy treatment in the course of his very short life.

Baby Ben died on 21 June 1971. A Catholic priest buried him, attesting to Gaudron's Catholic loyalties. She was, by then, heavily pregnant with Julienne. Gaudron continued appearing in a case up to the birth of Julienne. She asked the presiding judge for an adjournment in the case knowing that it would not be finished before she gave birth. The judge agreed and asked how many weeks she would need. 'Just until after the weekend,' she replied.[47]

By 1971 Gaudron was also becoming notable for her oratory beyond the courts. She was called upon to give the traditional 'Mr Junior' speech at the Bar's annual dinner, in the basement of Wentworth Chambers.[48] She was asked to propose a toast to the guest of honour, State Attorney General Kenneth (later Sir Kenneth) McCaw, QC. Customarily, the guest of honour is 'roasted' and 'toasted' by a member of the junior bar, after 'Mr Senior', who on that occasion was Tony Larkins, QC, had buttered him up. Larkins' speech was full of praise for the work of the Attorney. There had been conflict between McCaw and the Bar, and the invitation to him to attend was, to some extent, an attempt at reconciliation.

The reply by Mr Junior is expected to be outspoken and, at the same time, demonstrate, through oratorical skills, wit and the wisdom of tact. Gaudron rose, very pregnant with Julienne, wearing a striking white maternity pants suit, and delivered a devastating critique of the conservative Askin Government's law reforms, which McCaw had introduced, on the grounds that they infringed civil liberties. A deathly silence fell over the room. Gaudron then turned to the topic of the Attorney General's judicial appointments, most of which were of conservative members of the Bar, many of whom were present. Justice Ray Reynolds of the Court of Appeal was one. He was hoping to be appointed Chief Justice.[49] While the room remained silent, Gaudron continued, stating that she had checked the biography of all of the appointees recently made in *Who's Who in Australia*:

> That check…revealed that his appointments all had a single common characteristic. It was not their religion, their politics or their schooling but it was something so apparent that one should be able to use it to predict future appointments.[50]

She paused, a breathless tension in the air. At this point a guest at the dinner, sitting opposite Justice Reynolds, observed that Reynolds 'was turning white, green, yellow and purple. He was getting more and more upset.'[51] Reynolds then rose and loudly announced, 'Mr Chairman, I do not propose to listen to any more of this rubbish,' and stormed out. Others of the guests threw bread rolls at him as he left.[52]

Gaudron assumed the Judge had taken offence at her remarks about there being so few women at the Bar, and the implied sexist attitude of the Attorney General in appointing judges only from the ranks of men.[53] Her intended punchline was more amusing and innocuous. However, in view of the stir, she did not reveal it then, saying instead, 'After that, what does one do for an encore?' She moved on to propose a toast to the Attorney General.

She told those who approached her after the event that, had

she thought it appropriate to continue, she intended to explain that with respect to each of the new judicial appointments, *Who's Who* had made mention of the appointee's father, but not the mother. It was assumed that she therefore intended to conclude something along the lines of: 'Presumably, to be eligible for appointment to judicial office under this Attorney, one needs to be motherless.'

As one member of the Bar regaled, 'No member of the Bar before or since, charged with the same duty of delivering a provocative after-dinner speech before proposing a toast to a Guest of Honour, has managed to be so spectacularly successful.' David Bennett acknowledged it as a classic moment in the life of the NSW Bar, one 'which has always been affectionately remembered by those who were not amongst the collateral damage'. He observed that, 'Whether or not Mary's speech impeded or advanced her career prospects must be left for her biographer to explain.'[54]

Mary Gaudron, barrister, and Pat Mackie leaving the Supreme Court in Sydney, 23 November 1972. (Photo by Purcell, courtesy Fairfax photos.)

Mary Gaudron, at thirty-one, with her daughter Danielle, nine, 9 April 1974. (Photo by R. Rice, courtesy Fairfax photos.)

The family home overlooking Fern Bay in Hunters Hill, built by Ben Nurse, where the family lived from 1974 to 1979. It was later condemned because of radioactivity concerns.

Chapter Six

THE PAT MACKIE CASE

In Bundaberg I saw something unequalled, in all my experience of the world's police forces, outside of Hitler's Germany, for arrogant, fascistical behaviour towards an Aborigine. He was arrested and pushed around for no reason at all and I was so incensed I followed them to the police station to make a complaint.

Pat Mackie, 2002[1]

Gaudron's luck

A last minute 'flicking' of a brief held by Clive Evatt, QC, in his frequent fashion, saw Jim Staples and Mary Gaudron become the advocates and defenders of the reputation of Mount Isa miners' strike leader, Pat Mackie. The 1972 Mackie case was significant in Gaudron's career for a number of reasons. It was in the course of this case that Gaudron began a life-long friendship with Jim Staples. It was during it that Clyde Cameron, Federal Labor frontbencher, learnt about the 'brilliant young barrister', Mary Gaudron. In December 1972, Cameron became the right politician at the right time to talk up her worth to Gough Whitlam, the incoming

Prime Minister. As a result Gaudron would win the new Labor Government's confidence that she could take on the equal pay case brief.

The Mackie case itself was notable, as it assisted in correcting the record as portrayed by the press of the reasons for the strike, and Mackie's role in it. Mary Gaudron was still at university when the Mount Isa miners' strike of 1964 attracted the nation's attention, and when, on the night of 24 October, as Mackie reports it:

> ...all over town, thousands of sheets of pink quarto paper were left lying around bearing on one side an outline drawing of my left hand showing my amputated fingers (blown off by an exploding detonator in a timber camp when I was nine years old). On the other side, there was a lurid account of my alleged criminal career consisting of a garbled list of convictions, places, and dates for a lot of 'offences'.[2]

Gaudron was finishing her final year of law in 1965 when the newspapers were looking for someone to blame for this disruption to the nation. They settled on Pat Mackie—a hero to some and a dangerous rabblerouser to others. 'Red Cap', as Mackie became known, was a charismatic and controversial unionist who worked in the mine.[3] The intrigue of Pat Mackie lies in his story of becoming unofficial popular leader of the local mine workforce in 1964, who led the local union members in a fight for better wages and conditions, in a confrontation with their own union, the Australian Workers Union (AWU), the mining company and the Queensland Government. When the press joined in the war against Pat Mackie in 1965, he commenced legal proceedings for defamation. He battled the industrial action on the one hand and litigation on the other. Mackie was fair game.

It was a lucky break when the brief came Gaudron's way. For tactical reasons Mackie's Mount Isa solicitors decided that the cases should proceed in Sydney. One case, bogged down by procedural skirmishes, took seven years to come before the Supreme Court. The stage was set for Mary Gaudron's entry. She was by then well equipped with qualifications and experience in defamation law to represent him. She was also familiar with the issues that confronted the wage-earning worker, and the need for strong union support. A strong railway union movement had resulted in good conditions for her father as a fettler and later as an engine driver. The Mackie case would enhance her understanding of the industrial environment. It also tested her emotional fortitude as an advocate when she was tasked with putting legal arguments that raised ethical issues in the case on appeal. Ultimately, it put her in good stead for running future industrial actions, and her later appointment to the Conciliation and Arbitration Commission.

Mackie's Mount Isa solicitors appointed Maurice May, a Sydney solicitor with a reputation for bold litigation in worthy cases, as their Sydney agent. May briefed the Sydney Bar's leading defamation barrister, Clive Evatt, QC. He tracked him down in Paris, taking instructions from journalist Wilfred Burchett, for his defamation case against Senator Jack Kane. On Evatt's return he picked up the Mackie brief and his enthusiasm waned. It was not a case that looked like it could be won. He wanted his fees guaranteed. No, May told him, the case had to be run 'on spec'. Mackie did not have the funds to proceed with a case of this kind against multi-millionaire Frank Packer, owner of Australian Consolidated Press. Evatt looked for another barrister to run the case.[4] There were not many members of the Bar who would appear on behalf of a litigant 'on spec'; that is, prepared to be paid from costs orders awarded in the event they won the case. But Jim Staples was one who would.

Evatt rang Jim Staples the week before with the excuse that he was 'jammed', asking him to take the case. Staples accepted the brief being 'flicked' to him at this late hour, at this stage ignorant of Evatt's view that it was unwinnable. When the brief was delivered on the Thursday morning, Staples saw what he had let himself in for. It was set down for hearing before Justice Nagle and a jury of twelve the following Monday, 30 October 1972. Packer's company was represented by Sir Jack Cassidy, QC, leader of the general Bar, and Alec Shand, son of a famous common law advocate—a formidable opposition.[5]

The next morning, Friday, as Staples recalls it, after completing his short Equity Court 'mentions' he turned his mind to the Mackie case. Entering a lift crowded with junior barristers leaving the same court, he spotted Gaudron. Staples had never spoken to her. She was a 'junior' Junior at the Bar and he thought that she possibly had free time ahead of her.[6] He knew she had been Clive Evatt's junior in several defamation cases. Somewhere between the tenth and the first floor, he asked if she was free to help with a libel case next Monday. Gaudron gladly accepted. She could not have known that this flagged a turning point in her career. According to Staples, much of her later career can be traced to the short time it takes a lift to descend nine floors.

Staples telephoned Maurice May and told him that he and Gaudron would represent Mackie. May recalls the conversation and that he challenged Staples with 'What do you know about defamation?' Staples replied, 'I'm a quick learner.' May accepted the new arrangement. He had confidence in these two junior barristers. They were closely associated with the labour movement and had strong sympathies for the 'battler' and would give the case their all.[7] May knew Gaudron. Though she was new to the Bar, he knew she was very smart and expert in defamation law. May's idea was that Gaudron would be the one to do the legal research. Staples, the more senior of the two, would lead her in the advocacy role.

Mackie received the news. He recalls being told that 'a pair of very bright young barristers, Jim Staples and Mary Gaudron', would handle the case for him.[8]

Who was Pat Mackie?

'Who was Pat Mackie?' In the middle of the turmoil surrounding the 1964 Mount Isa miners' strike this was the question people asked. On 3 February 1965 the *Daily Telegraph* thought it had the answer. Its two articles found its owners, Australian Consolidated Press (ACP), the subject of Pat Mackie's lawsuit for defamation.[9] One was headed 'Mt. Isa Strike Leader has 15 Convictions', and gave details of each of fifteen convictions Mackie had allegedly received in Australia and overseas. The other was an editorial under the heading, 'The Man Who Led Mt. Isa to Misery' which elaborated on his alleged criminal record and read, in part:

> [Mackie] entered the Mount Isa dispute in a purely disruptive role; his activities led to the AWU losing control of the dispute to a break-away group controlled by Communists and Left-wingers.
> The progress of the strike under the influence of Mackie and the men around him has been damaging to the whole Australian economy and calamitous for the miners themselves...[10]

The newspaper was confident it would not be sued. It was wrong. Mackie knew he was not a dangerous criminal. Nor was he a communist. He wanted to protect his reputation. He also wanted the true story told.

Mount Isa was a company town in north-west Queensland built in the late 1920s to support the workforce of the mines. Since the 1880s copper, and later silver, lead and zinc, have been mined there. The isolated town with its low-rent housing grew with the profitability of the mine. Since the mid-1950s discontent had been simmering among the mine's workforce. The miners found that they were working harder and harder for less and less. Some who worked a mile underground in difficult conditions tried to persuade the union to address safety concerns and the poor amenities with which they were provided.

Pat Mackie arrived in 1961 looking for regular work. His plans to sail the seven seas in his purpose-built yacht had stalled owing to a failed business venture, and working at the Mount Isa mine was his big chance to 'save a pile for my Tahiti Ketch'.[11] He presented as a tattooed man with a Canadian accent and, adding to his knock-about appearance, he wore a trademark red American baseball cap that belied his New Zealand origins.

Mackie soon found out how tough mining work was. He tried it and could not deal with the harrowing conditions, deciding instead to take up work as a contract timber man. It still required him to work in the mine, but with less of a safety risk.[12] Three years went by before he became actively and publicly involved with industrial matters at Mount Isa.[13] With mounting discontent, cold showers became the source of heated anger for the miners:

> We'd come up dirty at midnight and just got soaped up when the water cut out. We ran around to showers on the other side. No water there! Cursing, all of us just had to dress again, in our dirty working clothes, go home and, at the coldest time of night at the coldest time of year, try to wash off this grime with a cold shower, since few of the original Company built homes in Mount Isa had hot water systems. If you wanted a hot bath you had to light up a copper and fill up the bath from that, which was too much of a chore when you were tired out in the early hours of the morning…A more miserable way of getting yourself cleaned up could scarcely exist than having a cold shower at home at midnight.[14]

Mackie reports that he marched into the night supervisor's office in a bath towel complaining about the men's working conditions. His demand produced hot showers. As the news of Mackie's tantrum spread, so did the men's resolve that there was more than just the showers that needed fixing. The small success encouraged the men to believe they could achieve more. Membership of the AWU was a condition of their employment with the Mount Isa Mines Company. The men feared that the AWU was in far too cosy an arrangement with the mining company. Mackie was a tactician. He urged the men to think before calling a strike that would be unsustainable without support from outside the local workforce. By July 1964 they elected Mackie in place of an AWU official to be their local union representative.

From then on, Mackie became involved in a dispute with big league industrial and political players; he could never emerge unscathed. The men stood firmly behind Mackie as their leader as the dispute escalated.[15] Its industrial, political and economic ramifications captured the attention of the nation.[16] In the process

Mackie exposed himself to assault and ridicule by the media and emerged with his reputation ruined.

Mary Gaudron's good fortune stemmed not from the notoriety of the Mount Isa dispute alone but also from Clyde Cameron's interest in it and the later Mackie litigation. Cameron, South Australian Branch Secretary of the AWU, and State President before being elected to Federal Parliament in 1949, had had a long-running feud with Tom Dougherty, the General Secretary of the AWU, over the national body's power within the union.[17] Cameron was still at war with the AWU hierarchy over its treatment of its members. He was delighted to learn that his union enemy, Dougherty, was being linked with the bosses' struggle against the labour movement, and took pleasure in watching Pat Mackie fragment the AWU. He gave early support to the Mount Isa miners and later advised Mackie from the sidelines.[18]

The intricacies of Mackie's story had to be mastered by his legal team nearly a decade later when the hotly defended claims against Australian Consolidated Press came before a jury in the NSW Supreme Court for hearing in 1972. They had to prove he was not the troublemaker that the press had made him out to be.

The two eager barristers had little time to prepare their case. They started work on the Friday morning that Staples approached Gaudron about the case. That weekend they worked at Staples' home in Longueville. Logistically, this was difficult for Gaudron, as a young mother. She brought her two children, Julienne a baby, and Danielle about six, with her. The team worked frantically amongst a chaos of documents, the noise of children's demands, bottles and nappies. Similar scenes occurred when they met with solicitor Maurice May at his large house in Cremorne during the course of the hearing.

Their first task was to read the brief provided by the Mount Isa solicitors and Maurice May, and become thoroughly familiar with the pleadings—the claim, the defence, the particulars of each provided by the parties, the nature of the preliminary applications that the court dealt with over the years leading up to the case, and the 'proofs of evidence' or statements taken from witnesses about matters relevant to the case. They had to plan their case, making sure that all the pieces in the jigsaw needed to make out the claim would fit neatly and tightly together to establish the big picture. It also meant that they had to put themselves in the shoes of Consolidated Press's advocates—become the 'devil's advocate' in order to bring evidence that would undermine, or at least deflect, Consolidated Press's defence.

Who was Pat Mackie really? Were the things said about him true? Was he the reprobate character and criminal depicted by the press? If true, was it in the public interest to publish it? Was malice against Mackie involved on the part of those who published the damaging material? These were the questions the legal team had to answer. To do that they had the daunting task of unravelling Mackie's story and scrutinising the newspaper allegations made against him, and in particular the alleged serious criminal convictions.

In contrast to what they read about him in the newspapers, Mackie appeared to Staples and Gaudron to be a remarkable and impressive man. Staples believed in Mackie. Gaudron warmed to him. All three in their own ways were rough diamonds. All were outspoken when they saw injustices. Staples had been a 'trucker', as he described himself, before turning to law and felt a kinship with the working class.[19] Gaudron had already earned a reputation at the Bar for her tendency to rebuke in frighteningly colourful language those who espoused opinions at odds with her own values.

Mackie's description of his experience in Bundaberg is revealing of his character and illustrates his compassion for vulnerable people. He did not like the town because on his first day there he 'brushed with some rotten members of the Queensland police force' when he tried to intervene over their unfair treatment and arrest of an Aboriginal man. He tried to complain about the brutality of the two police and offered to bail the man out if he were charged, but was told to 'get right out of town as quick as you can' or he would be locked up.[20] It also provides an insight into why Mary Gaudron, similarly fearless and feisty when it comes to issues concerning human rights and discrimination, was empathetic towards him when she met him two decades later.

The material in the barristers' brief revealed the relentless campaign that had been waged against Mackie. The picture that emerged for Staples was that the mining company bosses were determined to smash Mackie's reputation as a necessary step to break the miners' will and resolve the dispute. Staples believed that the bosses used the press, radio, TV and whatever tactics could be employed to subvert Mackie's standing with the rank and file members of the union in the course of the dispute. In his view the newspaper articles were part of the propaganda war that had been waged.

Most damaging to Mackie was the vast array of material dredged up by the AWU's Edgar Williams, who had instigated an extensive investigation into Mackie's background from rumours or otherwise. It was published by S.R. Ramsden, MP, and, because it was in the course of a speech in the Queensland Legislative Assembly on 27 October 1964, it was protected by parliamentary privilege so that Mackie could not take legal action in respect of it.[21] In particular, it purported to reveal a criminal record in great detail, with such precision about the times, dates and places that they were hard to disbelieve. If true, and if believed, it seemed to the barristers to support a case that Mackie was a person of ill repute. Mackie's opponents had struck gold, according to Staples, when they discovered his police history. The case was so compelling that Consolidated Press republished it, believing that the allegations were unanswerable, and the truth of the matter and its republication were a matter of public benefit, such that it would be immune from a defamation suit.

To Staples, the press portrayed Mackie as a demagogue, a communist and a liar whose histrionics seduced the workers into the dispute. He was a drifter of no certain abode, and not a fit and proper person to lead the workers. If these were the imputations the material carried, Mackie's lawyers had to demonstrate their falsity. They would have to convey carefully to a jury of twelve the context in which the controversy about Mackie arose, in order to convince it that Mackie's name had been unfairly tarnished.

Mackie's legal team had to be ready from the very start to 'open the case' to the court; to tell the judge and the jury what the case was about. Then, to paint the 'true picture' of Mackie of which they wanted to persuade the jury, it had to be substantiated by evidence. They needed to know how Pat Mackie would answer the 'open' questions they asked him (not being permitted to ask questions that would suggest an answer). More particularly, they needed to know how Mackie would respond to the tough questions he would be asked under cross-examination. These questions would be tricky, designed to lure him into agreeing with propositions that supported Consolidated Press.

Mackie had to be interviewed at length. It is called 'proofing the punter' among barristers because litigation, like gambling, is uncertain. This process had to be undertaken with painstaking care to ensure every question asked is relevant and necessary to establish one or other element of the defamation claim. It was Gaudron's role to determine what was required to make out the case at law. Staples would have the job in court to adduce evidence from Mackie. The advocate examining his or her witness must know what the witness will say. The questions must be clear, and the assumptions on which they are based must be already established. The answers become part of the evidence that is built up piece by piece to present the totality of the case. His legal team had to hear first-hand about Mackie's life and run-ins with the law.

They ascertained that, in the course of Mackie's involvement in the union movement, he had a short-lived 'flirtation' with the philosophy of the Communist Party. The accusation, made some quarter of a century later arising out of this, that he was a communist, Mackie protested was untrue and unfair.[22] Before commencing his own mining activities, Mackie worked in Queensland in various capacities and under a number of different names. He found himself in trouble for a minor matter and pleaded 'guilty' so that he would be fined and free to go on his way or back to work. His admissions of guilt to offences he claimed he had not committed caused his lawyers further angst in court.

As to the material in the leaflet circulated at Mount Isa in 1964, Mackie explains:

In a town of forty-seven nationalities of migratory workers, a string of minor and some major convictions was not all that unusual. Most of the men there had to live by dangerous work and the use of explosives, so that scars and missing fingers were common...All of which meant that this mode of slander, pointing to a man's mutilation and convictions, was unimpressive.[23]

The barristers were satisfied that far from Mackie being a newcomer looking for a scrape, a study of his larrikin past revealed that his trouble with the authorities was the product of his industrious and adventurous attempt to survive and make good from homeless beginnings in New Zealand. They believed that his record demonstrated that Mackie was an intelligent man of initiative, with strongly held views and an innate sense of justice.

The barristers lived and breathed the case for the duration of the hearing. Forgetting to eat, Staples lost a stone in weight. According to Staples, Justice Nagle, who was hearing the case, did too. 'No one had time to eat.'[24] It was a case of high drama, and one that was hard to top for excitement.

On trial

The trial ran for a month. Clyde Cameron who, in a matter of months, would become Federal Minister for Labour, followed its progress. He hoped that evidence would unravel about the conspiratorial conduct of the mining company and the national leaders of the AWU, and that evidence of the machinations of the AWU's hierarchy would justify the stand he had taken years earlier on behalf of the rank and file union membership. Mackie's case was the first opportunity for the evidence about the workers' side of the Mount Isa strike to be put to rebut the anti-union propaganda. Evidence dealing with the conduct of the mining company and the AWU in relation to Mackie was given. Though neither was on trial, Mackie's barristers sought to establish that the unfair conduct of both was the reason for the workers rallying behind Mackie, rather than Mackie being 'a kind of pied piper leading children to their doom', as portrayed by the press.[25] With the airing of this evidence, Cameron was still hopeful that Dougherty would be dumped by the AWU rank and file. As it transpired, Cameron was cheated of that victory. Dougherty died in October 1972.[26]

Part of Mackie's case was that the newspapers had substantially overstated the nature of his previous convictions. To prove this, he had to reveal his real 'record'. That meant admitting to convictions decades earlier for such things as urinating in public, jumping ship, and crossing a State border with marijuana in the glove box of his car. Consolidated Press's legal team took advantage of Mackie's admission and were permitted by the Court to amend their pleadings to include the convictions of which they had not been aware to support the claim that the newspaper articles were true in substance. 'This was their high point,' Staples grins as he recalls the case. 'The evidence established that Mackie had indeed a criminal record. It included a conviction of riding a bike without a light down the main street of Camooweal, in the Gulf of Carpentaria!'

Consolidated Press lawyers had to concede that there were mistakes in the list of convictions, and none of note—certainly none recent. There was no evidence of the bad character the newspaper had publicly described. It revealed that Mackie was impetuous and mischievous and sometimes roguish, but not a dangerous criminal, let alone an international one.

Cassidy, counsel for Consolidated Press, mocked Mackie's trademark red cap when he cross-examined him. He was met with Mackie's quick wit:

> This red cap of yours. You wear it all the time?
> Yes.
> You're a bit of a showman?
> In that respect, I'm no different then from your Cardinal.[27]

Humorous aspects of the case were soon overtaken by a series of events whose impact Gaudron would feel later when faced with arguing the case on appeal. First, a legal skirmish arose when Mackie, under cross-examination, explained that he had pleaded 'guilty' to some offences without the benefit of legal advice, to have the matters dealt with quickly. In effect, he went back on the formal admissions made in court. Evidence to contradict the admissions made can only be brought out in court with the court's leave. Staples, in addressing the jury, compounded the difficulty by alluding to the inaccuracy of those admissions. Consolidated Press, on appeal, argued that this warranted a new trial.

Secondly, the trial had been underway for more than a fortnight when Cassidy opened the case for Consolidated Press and, according to Staples' and Gaudron's view of it, overstated matters on the evidence. More serious was Cassidy's claim that a witness would give evidence of an attempt by Mackie to run him down at Mount Isa early in February 1965, to establish that Mackie was 'a thug'. No such evidence was brought but the allegation was never retracted. Cassidy also mentioned 'threats' Mackie uttered, but failed to acknowledge that shortly after Mackie had withdrawn them and apologised. The normal courtesies and bonhomie between barristers were soon converted to coolness and hostilities. Gaudron faced an ethical dilemma when her duty to her client required her to raise these matters before the Court of Appeal.

Then tension mounted when Consolidated Press produced a 'surprise' expert witness to give evidence to support the defence of 'qualified privilege' to Mackie's claim. Gaudron provided Staples with good tactical advice to minimise the damage. The economist, Hermann Black, Chancellor of Sydney University, gave unassailable evidence that the strike was destroying the nation's exchange rate. His expertise was used to establish that it was in the public interest for the newspaper to publish matters concerning the strike. Staples commenced his cross-examination of Black just before the court went into recess on a Friday night. As they left the court Gaudron advised Staples to ask no more questions—not to risk that fatal 'one question too many', nor open the way for Black to elaborate on his evidence in re-examination. They knew that Black would 'bone up' on the weekend and have all the answers ready.

The following Monday, Staples entered the men's toilets and saw Black emerge, notes in hand. The case resumed and Black was called to the witness box. Staples stood up and announced, 'No further questions, Your Honour.' According to Staples, Cassidy was taken by surprise. As his witness had not been discharged from cross-examination the previous Friday, Cassidy had been denied the opportunity of talking to Black about what questions he should ask him in re-examination. Good tactics, and fair—but not good enough, as it transpired.

Staples painstakingly addressed the jury for six hours. It was a compelling and ultimately successful address. However, Justice Nagle took the matter out of the jury's hands by deciding as a matter of law that the publication of the article and the editorial were for the public good, a legal defence against an action for defamation.[28] Fortunately for Mackie, Nagle left to the jury the question, among others, whether the newspaper was motivated by 'malice' or ill-will when it published the articles, which, if so, would negate the defence of public good. In so doing, the judge allowed the jury to consider Cassidy's conduct at the trial in deciding the question.

The jury found for Mackie in relation to both newspaper articles. On 23 November 1972, they awarded $10,000 damages on the first count and $20,000 on the second.[29] This was a relatively large award for damages for those times. According to Mackie,

> There, after a nineteen-day marathon, a jury of 12 awarded $30,000 damages for libel to one Pat Mackie, and a vindication of the struggle itself...So little of the proceedings were reported in the Australian newspapers that it was as though it never took place.[30]

The appeal—fears and tears

It was not yet the end of the Mackie legal saga, nor Gaudron's role in it. Consolidated Press appealed on forty-seven grounds, and that the award was excessive. Significantly for Gaudron, it argued that Nagle had misdirected the jury in stating that Cassidy's conduct at the trial could in itself provide evidence of ill-will on the part of Consolidated Press at the time of publication.

An appeal is about matters of law only and is not a jury trial. As Gaudron best knew defamation law, she took the leading role in presenting arguments to the NSW Supreme Court of Appeal. It consisted of a full bench of three: Justice Reynolds, her old foe—the judge who had walked out in protest at her speech at the Bar's annual dinner the previous year; Justice Hutley, her mentor; and Justice Nigel Bowen, a former Commonwealth Attorney General. Shand, QC, was leading counsel for Consolidated Press. Neither her enemy Justice Reynolds nor the intellectual friendship she had made with Hutley would serve Gaudron well.

Hutley, while acclaiming Gaudron's brilliance, expected an exceptional performance by his protégé. While Gaudron knew the law well, this case posed a challenge. Gaudron had to justify Judge Nagle's direction to the jury. This required her to argue that Cassidy's conduct was improper, such as to provide evidence of ill-will on the part of Consolidated Press at the time of the publication. There was no transcript of what had been said. The court only transcribed the evidence taken from witnesses, not the opening statements. There was no easy way of informing an appeal court that a respected senior barrister had incorrectly or unfairly portrayed matters to a jury. It meant raising the matter of the barrister's ethical conduct. Professionally, Gaudron had to do it, or fail in her duty to her client.

The appeal case ran for six days in December 1973. The judges treated her severely at the hearing. She expected this from Reynolds, but probably not from Hutley. Unpleasantries flowed. Gaudron became visibly distressed. Her efforts to persuade the court of the injustice of what had happened in the original hearing took its toll on her. Yet the issue was crucial to the appeal. Staples was sitting beside her and felt her pain. Emotional and frustrated, she broke into tears.

The Court of Appeal at the time was known as 'a torture chamber'. According to one court-watcher, 'Grown men would faint at the withering cruelty dished out by the likes of Justices Moffitt, Hutley and Reynolds.' Gaudron did not faint. She returned to chambers after the case and broke down. Not in the form of quiet tears. In Gaudron style she flared up and amid tears shouted in colourful language words to the effect of 'I'm going to leave this fucking Bar to you bastards. You can have it all.'

The ranting continued loudly and was distressing and unsettling for everyone on the thirteenth floor. A colleague, Phil Adams, called Maurice May to come and calm her. May called a taxi and went to Wentworth Chambers. He consoled her and settled her down.

Gaudron did, as events had it, leave the Bar within months after the event, but gloriously, rather than with tears, lured by the Labor government appointment of her, at Cameron's behest, to the Conciliation and Arbitration Commission. Hutley later apologised to solicitor Maurice May when they ran into each other some years later, 'I had to test her thoroughly,' Hutley rationalised. He meant it, as he is also reported to have stated, in a submission to the NSW Law Reform Commission, that only one woman had performed competently when appearing before him.[31] He was referring to Mary Gaudron.

On 1 May 1974 Frank Packer died in hospital of cancer. On 2 May the decision on his company's appeal in the Mackie case was given. The Court found that there was insufficient evidence for the jury to have concluded that the conduct of Consolidated Press's barristers in Mackie's trial was motivated by malice. The Court as a whole did conclude, however, and fortunately for Mackie, that there was other evidence of want of good faith on the part of Consolidated Press by reason of which it was not entitled to a verdict. It referred to unjustified derogatory language used in the articles to describe Mackie.

Notably, Justice Hutley dismissed one of Consolidated Press' grounds of appeal on the authority of the High Court decision in *O'Shaughnessy v Mirror Newspapers Ltd*,[32] the case that Gaudron had successfully argued. Hutley also acknowledged that:

> The jury must have formed a very favourable view of the conduct of the plaintiff [Mackie] in the industrial disputes and seen him as the victim of what was being done by others, not as the controller of events which the defamatory material would suggest.[33]

The Court also found that the award of damages was not excessive. Accordingly, rather than allowing the appeal, it ordered that there be a new trial.

In a strange turn of events the retrial was not necessary.[34] Mackie, faced with another trial, approached Kerry Packer, now Managing Director of Consolidated Press, following Frank Packer's death. Mackie managed somehow to speak to him and demanded, 'I beat you fairly and squarely, why did you appeal?' Packer acknowledged that this was 'fair enough', and withdrew the proceedings. The matter was settled by leaving Mackie with the jury's original award, not through the efforts of the lawyers but between two men, Mackie and Packer. Gaudron's photograph nevertheless sat in Mackie's living room until he left to reside in a nursing home in 2007.

Chapter Seven

EQUAL PAY—IN PRINCIPLE

> We won equal pay for equal work in 1967. We won again in 1969, and again in 1972 and in 1974. Yet we still do not have equal pay.
>
> Mary Gaudron, 1979[1]

Cameron's 'girl' Gaudron

Within a few hours of Labor's election victory on Saturday 2 December 1972, Gough Whitlam asked Clyde Cameron to arrange for the just concluded *National Wage and Equal Pay Cases* to be re-opened.[2] It was a dramatic move. Cameron was not yet a minister, but Whitlam had confirmed that he would be the Minister for Labour.[3] Thirty years later Whitlam recalled:

> We made many decisions. First, we ordered the release of the young men who had been jailed for refusing national service for Vietnam. Next, we set in motion the recognition of the People's Republic of China as the government of One China. Then we re-opened the equal pay case.[4]

Gaudron received the brief to appear in it. The fight for gender equity in the workforce is a story of many battles in an unfinished industrial war. Gaudron's own life experiences were reason enough for her to want to see improvement in the lot of women in the workforce. Her gender, political connections and an element of fate gave her the opportunity to play an historic role. She grasped it. Representing the Commonwealth in the 1972 *Equal Pay Case* was, for Gaudron, not only a career highlight but also a turning point. It led to her appearances in subsequent national wage cases and to elevation from the Bar to the bench of judges she appeared before, to further improve working conditions for Australian men and women.

Whitlam was a keen supporter of equal pay for women. Action had to be taken quickly if his new government was to counter the submissions already put to the Conciliation and Arbitration Commission on behalf of the outgoing McMahon Coalition Government in these industrial test cases. The Commission determined awards in national wage cases as part of its dispute settling and arbitration role. The previous government had opposed the wage claims and offered no support for equal pay claims. The cases had been heard throughout October and November 1972; on 29 November, the Commission reserved its decision.

Barristers had to be briefed to put the case to the Commission on behalf of the new government. Cameron thought of Mary Gaudron.[5] He planned to brief Jack Sweeney, QC, an industrial lawyer from the NSW bar, to lead her,[6] his first choice, Dick McGarvie, QC, not being available. Cameron had reason to remember his encounters with Gaudron. On one occasion he met her and barrister Jim Staples in the public bar of a well-frequented up-market city hotel in Sydney. The bar attendant told Staples that the hotel did not 'serve women', and Gaudron replied cuttingly that her friend did not want to be 'served a woman—he'd brought his own'.[7] The bar attendant insisted that the public bar was for 'men only' and that they should leave. Cameron remembers Gaudron telling the attendant 'where to go' in explicit terms.[8] Gaudron recalls that Cameron expressed surprise that discrimination was being practised in that particular hotel and, 'already in full flight', she pointed out to him that the discrimination in that particular hotel was nothing compared to discrimination over which he would undoubtedly preside when he became Minister for Labour after the next election.[9] The three continued their drinks at the front bar.

More relevantly, Cameron remembered Gaudron for her experience in industrial law. He first met her when she was appearing as junior to Staples in the Pat Mackie case.[10] She had, by then, been acclaimed for her success in the *O'Shaughnessy* case in the High Court. Cameron recalled, 'She was just a slip of a girl in her late 20s. Her mind was so sharp and her capacity to reason was quite brilliant.'[11]

That same busy day after the 1972 election Cameron rang Staples to inquire about Gaudron's suitability for the case. According to Staples, Cameron put it this way: 'We are using Jack Sweeney. There is an issue about equal pay. How would that little girlie who was with you in Mackie's case go? Would she be of any use to Sweeney?' Staples gave an enthusiastic commendation of Gaudron for her left-wing values, her competence and her diligence. Cameron said, 'Good. I'll speak to Gough about it.'[12]

As luck would have it for Gaudron, neither Sweeney nor anyone else was briefed to lead her. Cameron consulted Jack Caine, the departmental officer handling the case in Melbourne, about reopening it. Caine raised a concern on hearing that Cameron intended to replace John Keely, QC, who had been the advocate for the outgoing government. He advised that since Keely held the brief in the case, 'even if he doesn't appear the Commonwealth will have to pay him'.[13] At that point Cameron decided he would do without senior counsel. Whether Keely, QC, was paid or not was 'something the Attorney General can settle'.[14] Gaudron, not Keely, would put the submissions. Whitlam approved the arrangement and telephoned her.

Gaudron was a few weeks short of thirty at the time, and a mother of two. She was ecstatic but circumspect. She told an interested press that she was 'aggressive' but not an 'aggressive feminist'. Nor could she say 'who chose [her] for the job, or why'.[15] Years later, however, she revealed that Whitlam had phoned her the day following his election victory and offered her the brief, saying:

> My government and I have taken three decisions. One is to bring the boys home from Vietnam, the second is to take the luxury tax off the contraceptive pill and the third is to reopen the Equal Pay case. Will you accept the brief?[16]

For Gaudron it was the chance of a lifetime. A brief to appear solo to push for equal pay in a high level government-backed case was also an opportunity to do something about discriminatory wages. She had first-hand experience of the culture of discrimination against women during her university days and her time at the Sydney Bar, as well as the Sydney city pub. On the Friday following the election, the Commission was notified of the request that the matters be re-listed to permit the barrister representing the newly-elected Federal government to put submissions.

Getting to 'Equal pay for work of equal value'

Gaudron's brief was to articulate clearly the new government's approach to equal pay in the context of the Commission's history in dealing with the issue. Women workers' call for equal pay had gathered momentum throughout the 1960s. Historically, differentials between male and female wage rates had arisen from a general acceptance that men were, and should be, the providers for their dependent families. The male basic wage was fixed as a family wage and the female basic wage was fixed for a single woman without dependants. The concept of a minimum wage for adult males emerged in 1966 to protect male income earners, and did not apply to females.

Gaudron had a difficult task, given the history of the Commission's attempts to address equal pay. Equal pay had been accepted in principle in the *National Wage Case 1967* but it was restricted to certain occupations, those traditionally occupied by men. The Commission also recognised that the concept of the man and dependent family was no longer the determining factor in fixing award wages. However, the concept of a 'family wage' nevertheless persisted in the formulation of the male minimum wage and as a bar to 'equal pay'.

Equal pay was 'won again' in the *Equal Pay Cases 1969*. The Commission accepted the basic principle that those doing the same work should be paid the same wages—'equal pay for equal work'. It noted that the concept of the family wage no longer had the significance it once had and was 'no real bar to considerations of equal pay'.[17] Once again, however, the effect of the decision was limited. The Commission decided that women should receive the same pay as men *if* they were doing the same or similar work as males employed under the same award, but it did not cover women in jobs only or predominantly done by females. Nor did the equal pay principle cover junior females. Therefore, nurses, shop assistants, typists and telephonists and junior females received no benefit from the 1969 equal pay decision.

On the occasion of the 1969 case, women workers had waged a concerted campaign for equal pay. Since the meat industry was used as a test case for the campaign, men and women workers were bussed to the city from various meat works to the Trades Hall in Melbourne. From there they marched to the courthouse where the Commission was hearing the case. They paraded up and down the street, chanting slogans and waving placards in support of equal pay. Zelda D'Aprano, an equal wage advocate and vigorous feminist meat worker, sat inside to listen to the proceedings. The noise of the demonstrators outside was in stark contrast to the quietness inside. She recorded with dismay the entrenched culture of sexual discrimination in the wage-fixing process.

> On entering the court, I immediately felt the oppressiveness of the atmosphere. People only spoke in whispers as they do at funerals…The door opened at the rear of the court and in walked the judges. All male judges. Everyone stood to attention until the judges were seated and then the proceedings began.[18]

D'Aprano's dismay did not disappear as the hearing proceeded. While Bob Hawke, the ACTU advocate in the 1960s, presented irrefutable evidence of gender wage disparity, women played no part in the proceedings:

> The women sat there day by day as if we were mute, while the men presented evidence for and against our worth. It was humiliating to have to sit there and not say anything about our own worth. I found the need to sit there silent almost beyond my control, and was incensed with the entire set up.[19]

The absence of women distressed her:

> I just couldn't believe this, and I thought, here are all the women, here we are, all sitting here as if we haven't got a brain in our bloody heads, as if we're incapable of speaking for ourselves on how much we think we're worth. And here are all these men arguing about how much we're worth and all men are going to make the decision.[20]

D'Aprano decided that something 'more than just talking was needed'.[21] On 21 October 1969 she famously chained herself to the Commonwealth Centre at the corner of Spring and Latrobe Streets, Melbourne, until she was cut free by the Commonwealth Police. She attracted publicity and roused the women's movement to further activity.[22] The next opportunity to obtain pay parity was through the *National Wage and Equal Pay Cases 1972*.

The 1972 equal pay decision

Gaudron was the first woman to appear on behalf of the Commonwealth in a national wage case. It was also her first appearance before the Commission. She had only days to become familiar with what had already occurred in the hearing, the positions put by the previous government, the employers and the unions, and to receive instructions and work with the government's legal team to prepare her submissions. It was a momentous task and she was excited by it.

So was the press. A woman appearing for the Commonwealth was news. It received very little information from Gaudron, however. According to *The Australian*, she would not discuss her personal background, political beliefs, past courtroom appearances, family connections, friends and relations. 'Talk like that' could prejudice her case, she said.[23] The paper had to make do with what it had heard. 'Merciless Mary cuts the bigwigs to size' was the headline it chose in reporting the reopening of the case: 'Mary Gaudron is said to be such a brilliant deflater of pompous argument in the courtroom that several barristers now find their wigs are too big.' The *Sydney Morning Herald* 'Back Page' feature went to the heart of the matter, commenting under the caption 'Equal Pay for Mary', that Gaudron 'will get the same fee as a male would get for the brief'. It acknowledged that the amount of the fee was not disclosed.[24] It failed to pinpoint the real issue—that Gaudron's 'fee on brief' as a junior barrister was equal to the men at the junior bar—not equal to the rate of her male predecessor, who was briefed at QC's rates. That was the rub: 'equal pay' is not achieved without 'equal opportunity', and there was, then, no female QC at the NSW Bar.

On 13 December 1972, in Melbourne, journalists confronted her on the pavement as she walked towards the court 'in her bold black and white striped suit'.[25] Having told them she had only received the brief less than a week earlier, she bravely said and no doubt believed it: 'but, I am right'.[26] She stood before the full bench of the Commission and put her application for leave to appear in simple terms. She announced:

> By reason of certain changes, of which the Commission no doubt will be aware, the Commonwealth's views and attitudes now differ significantly in respect of certain issues which were raised in these cases on a prior occasion and embodied in the previous submission placed on behalf of the Commonwealth.[27]

The unions' representative, understandably, did not object to the application. The employers' representative grudgingly conceded that they could not object in the circumstances. The Commission, presided over by Acting President, John Moore, granted the leave and Gaudron was ready to put her submissions.

There was no enthusiastic group of women in the court to cheer her on. Their interest in the work of the Commission had waned since 1969, and the re-opening of the 1972 case that offered hope for the cause occurred so rapidly that women's groups had no time to organise a large presence at the hearing. Edna Ryan, a significant figure in the fight for equal pay and who had a watching brief for the Municipal Employees' Union, was disappointed at the turnout.[28] She was, in fact, the only woman observer.[29] This would probably not have troubled Gaudron. Her adrenalin rush was not dependent upon being noticed. She had a job to do and this was her hour.

In fact, Gaudron's submission in the 1972 equal pay case took less than an hour. At the outset she forthrightly announced that the Commonwealth withdrew all recommendations it had previously made in relation to principles of equal pay. She explained that the Commonwealth now 'positively supports the concept of equal pay for work of equal value for all female workers', including those employed in work that was exclusively or usually performed by females. She highlighted the inequitable effect of work being categorised according to gender; women doing similar work to men should be eligible for the male rate of pay. Discrimination against women in the workforce covered by Commission awards was not justified and should cease.[30]

The focus of Gaudron's submission was on the need for new principles to be formulated about equal pay for females, based on a concept of 'equal pay for work of equal value' that relied on the same principles to determine wage rates for male and female employees. She was supported by the Australian Council of Trade Unions, who had called on the Commission to broaden the principle of 'equal pay for equal work' accepted in the *National Wage Cases 1969*, to 'equal pay for work of equal value' to encompass the work traditionally done by women.

Gaudron's task was to explain the shift in attitude from what had been put by the outgoing government. John Keely, QC, representing the previous government, had argued that if 'equal pay for work of equal value' was introduced, 'work value' should be measured with reference to work done by men and women within the same award. Gaudron told the Commission that this approach was too restrictive. Women doing jobs that had never been performed by men should not have to prove their worth. The new equal pay formulation should be extended to work exclusively carried out by women, where equivalent rates had not been set for males. She contended that fixing pay rates for females engaged in work exclusively performed by them could be done by making comparisons on a work value basis with the pay rates for women who have been awarded equal pay. She argued that, when it became necessary to establish new classifications to distinguish work done by women from that done by men, the pay rates should be raised to the rate males would receive if they were employed on the work.

Gaudron made another significant plea. She referred to Australia's obligations to consider its international treaty obligations.[31] Although Australia had not yet ratified the International Labour Organisation (ILO) Convention on *Equal Remuneration for Men and Women Workers for Work of Equal Value (No. 100)*, she said, with force and tact:

> The concept of equal pay for work of equal value will necessarily entail work value examinations in some awards and that is consistent with the ILO convention number 100 and recommendation number 90 concerning equal remuneration for men and women workers for work of equal value.[32]

The 1951 ILO's Recommendation 90, associated with its Convention 100 and adopted at the same time, relevantly recommended: 'Equal remuneration for men and women workers for work of equal value...with a view to providing a classification of jobs without regard to sex.' Edna Ryan praised Gaudron for the way her argument built upon the ILO Convention:

> After twenty-one years the principles of the 1951 ILO Convention on equal pay were being correctly presented for

the first time. Mary Gaudron's case rested on the inequity of determining some women's wage rates on a basis different from that of some other women workers and from male workers.[33]

Gaudron also had to address Keely's warning to the Commission about the cost of extending equal pay principles. He had urged that the 1969 equal pay decision should remain in force while any new principles were being implemented, and that any pay increases warranted on the basis of the new principles should be phased in over a period of not less than three years on the grounds that the cost 'could be very considerable'.[34] Gaudron informed the Commission that this was no longer the Government's stand. She urged that wage justice required that equal annual increments for men and women under the new concept should be implemented as quickly as possible.

On 15 December 1972, the Commission delivered its decision.[35] It noted the unusual circumstances of the election, resulting in leave having been given for Gaudron's late appearance in the proceedings.[36] It also made it clear that, despite Gaudron's request that the Commission ignore the Commonwealth's previous submission on equal pay, it took into account the Commonwealth's submissions on equal pay issues that were made both before and after the 1972 Federal election. Nevertheless, the Commission declared the new principle of equal pay in award rates for work of equal value. It meant, therefore, that women in female-dominated industries could receive pay rates comparable to the work of men in male-dominated industries.

The Commission referred to changes towards the issue of equal pay in other countries and recognised that it needed to reconsider the 1969 principles in the light of the present social and industrial climate. It decided that amending the principles would not suffice. Instead it positively stated the new principle: 'In our view the concept of "equal pay for equal work" is too narrow in today's world and we think the time has come to enlarge the concept to "equal pay for work of equal value".'

The Commission declared, as Gaudron had urged, that the

application of the principles allowed for work value comparisons to be made, where possible, between female and male classifications. The Commission explained:

> By 'equal pay for work of equal value' we mean fixation of award wage rates by a consideration of the work performed irrespective of the sex of the worker.

This time the principle would be applied to all awards and to both adults and juniors. The Commission recommended that the new rates be introduced in three stages to end on 30 June 1975, that is, in two and a half years.[37]

The 1972 decision marked a further step forward in the fight for pay equity. It enabled work that was similar to be compared for the purpose of setting equal pay rates for men and women, but it was not sufficient to bring about pay equity. It still failed to achieve work-value comparisons of dissimilar jobs. The practical effect of this was that work primarily done by women, consisting as it did of tasks that were not comparable to the work covered by current awards, was under-valued. As it transpired, the unions did not pursue work value claims for women, but rather inserted new classifications in awards by consent.[38] Where work value inquiries were conducted,

> ...jobs were not compared for relative levels of skill, effort and responsibility. Rather, attempts were made to assess where the formerly female classifications would fit into male classifications according to similarity of work content or task.[39]

It was a victory nevertheless—a victory for the unions and a victory for women. It was also a victory for Gaudron. It demonstrated that she had overcome obstacles to the pursuit of a successful legal career, and in turn it allowed her to assist women generally to get a fair go.

The interest in Gaudron's role in this case was not so much for what she did but that it was she, a woman, who did it. The application to re-open the proceedings made nine days after the decision had been reserved was a dramatic event. To have Mary Gaudron present it made it remarkable. Had Sweeney, QC, represented the Commonwealth, the outcome was likely to have been the same, but the event may have faded more quickly into the shadows of history. The unions had done much of the work in putting the case for the new principle of equal pay for work of equal value—they had an interest in ensuring that women, in doing the same jobs as men, did not displace men from jobs by undercutting their wages—and the Commission had already foreshadowed adoption of the new principle before Gaudron appeared in the case. Further, the forthcoming election had extracted a modified stand from the Coalition government on the issue, neither opposing nor supporting the extended concept of 'equal pay'.

Nevertheless, Gaudron put the case forcefully and effectively in a polished presentation. Dorothy Johnston, in a fictional account, gave Gaudron folk hero status:

> I have a clear memory of Whitlam appointing Mary Gaudron government advocate for the equal pay hearing in 1972, and the historic national wage decision that followed, with its new definition of equal pay for equal work of equal value. I remember coming across my mother sitting at the dining-room table with a fuzzy newspaper photograph of Mary Gaudron, her bobbed hair and clever, successful face.[40]

Gaudron warranted a second mention in Johnston's story:

> The smells of cooling toast and untouched tea, and my mother with that photo of Mary Gaudron at the kitchen table.[41]

Missing from the decision was women's eligibility for the same minimum wage as men. The previous government had opposed the extension of the male minimum wage to females and supported the male minimum wage being based upon the 'needs of an average or typical family unit'. Its advocate argued that '[i]t would be quite inappropriate to extend such a wage to females who, generally speaking, are not faced with the needs of a married breadwinner'.[42]

Gaudron was not briefed to address the Commission on the application of the minimum wage to females, other than to flag that the Commonwealth proposed to support the extension of the minimum wage to cover all adult employees in the next national wage case. Not much could be done until the *Conciliation and Arbitration Act*, which made provision for a minimum wage for males only, had been amended. This discrimination had to be removed before equal pay could be fully achieved. This was something Cameron, as Minister for Labour,[43] was keen to address.

The case and its outcome lifted Gaudron's profile. Importantly, Gaudron's performance pleased Cameron: 'She did a first-class job.'[44] He proclaimed,

> ...Gaudron was absolutely brilliant; for she not only gave compelling reasons why females should have the same pay as men but demonstrated that given the opportunity, a woman's performance could equal a man's.[45]

It was a significant day. It was the birthday of Edna Ryan, to whom, as a feminist and equal pay activist, the decision was particularly important. Moreover, she was born on the same day that the Conciliation and Arbitration Court was established in 1904, so it was also the Commission's anniversary. On the same day Justice Elizabeth Evatt was appointed to the Commission as a deputy president, the first woman so appointed. Gaudron, in the glow of her success, would soon follow her. Also on that day came the announcement that a Royal Commission would be established as the first move towards legal recognition of Aboriginal land rights. This was a mission to which Gaudron's subsequent career path would permit her to contribute.

The minimum wage for women

Cameron kept Gaudron in his sights. He later commented, 'It was the first time she had appeared before the Arbitration Court. It was a new field to her but she adapted herself to it almost instantaneously.'⁴⁶ Cameron arranged for Gaudron to be briefed in the *National Wage Case 1973* as junior counsel to Jack Sweeney, QC, who had missed out on the re-opened hearing in 1972. They represented the Government in the proceedings and put submissions on matters concerning the rates of pay and forms of increases in Commission awards and the adult male minimum wage.⁴⁷ These cases took four weeks to complete before the Commission issued its decision on 8 May 1973.⁴⁸ Though not significant in the chronology of equal pay decisions, Gaudron's involvement further confirmed her reputation as an effective industrial advocate.

There was more work ahead before Gaudron could play a further effective role in the push for pay equity for all working women. With the principle of 'equal pay for work of equal value' accepted, the Government was now able to ratify the 1958 ILO Convention No. 111, concerning discrimination in employment; it did so on 15 June 1973. It could not yet ratify Convention No. 100 on *Equal Remuneration for Men and Women Workers for Work of Equal Value*.

The *Conciliation and Arbitration Act* still enshrined the family wage in the form of a 'male minimum wage' that took account of the need of low-paid male workers to provide for families. A minimum wage that applied to men only was rightly seen as discriminatory. In December 1973 Cameron said,

> Australia's deplorable attitude toward the rights of women has already attracted criticism from other parts of the world…
>
> The International Labour Office has informally advised the Australian Government that the exclusively male minimum wage, and the basic wage differential on the basis of sex that operates in the States, are incompatible with the terms of the ILO's Equal Remuneration Convention No. 100. This is the agreed international standard on the question of equal pay.⁴⁹

He wanted this fixed.

Cameron introduced appropriate amendments to sections 31(1)(c) and (d) of the *Conciliation and Arbitration Act* that substituted 'adult' for 'male' in relation to the 'minimum wage'. The measure at first failed in the Senate where the Government did not have a majority. Finally, after much lobbying by women's organisations, and particularly by the Women's Electoral Lobby (WEL),[50] the legislation was passed in November 1973, ready for Gaudron, on behalf of the Commonwealth, and for Edna Ryan, as WEL's representative, to argue for payment of the full minimum wage to women in the *1974 National Wage Case*.

The main focus of this case was the wages issue, not equal pay. These were times of growing unemployment, and inflation had become a significant force in the Australian economy. The Australian Government supported the unions' call for incorporation of automatic cost-of-living adjustments in awards. It recognised that some change in the present wage fixation methods might be justified. Sweeney, having been appointed a judge of the Australian Industrial Court, was not available, and Cameron arranged for Jim Staples and Gaudron to represent the Australian Government in this case.

Staples presented the main submission on the wage matters. Recognising the importance of a woman putting the case for extension of the minimum wage to female workers, Staples allocated that aspect of the case to Gaudron. The challenge this presented was symbolised by the fact that the bench, as in the 1972 cases and those before it, consisted entirely of men.

It was a long hearing and required preparation time. Staples and Gaudron worked together for six weeks in Melbourne, allowing them only rushed trips home to Sydney at weekends. The case commenced on 19 February 1974. It consumed most days of each working week until 5 April. It was a difficult time for Gaudron. She and her family were in the process of moving from their Elizabeth Bay unit to a not yet completed waterfront home in Hunters Hill. At weekends she joined them and devoted time to such domestic tasks as selecting carpets and curtains, and arranging tree planting for the new native garden.[51]

On the first day of the hearing a small but vocal group of feminists entered the court building chanting, 'We want equal pay. We want equal pay!' John Moore, President of the Commission since July 1973, and the other five male members of the bench entered the hearing room. There was shouting from the back of the room. Moore opened with a qualified welcome to those attending: 'We cannot, however, conduct our proceedings unless we are heard in silence...I would ask that the placards be not shown in the court room.'[52] Clyde Cameron was there. He saw Gaudron turn to the hecklers to calm the commotion that broke out and heard her say, 'Pull your heads in, you bloody fools. Just shut up. You're not helping your case by shouting and carrying on with banners. For Christ's sake, shut up!'[53] Turning back to face the bench, she quickly resumed her professional composure.

The applicant unions first put their case. Rob Jolly, the ACTU's advocate, argued for protection of women's minimum pay rates in the context of their less than equal opportunities in the workforce. He highlighted the anomaly of the Commission's acceptance, on the one hand, of the principle of equal pay for work of equal value, with its simultaneous rejection of the female minimum wage on the other. The practical effect was that the male worker who received the protection of the minimum wage would receive a higher wage than the female doing the same work. However, Jolly produced no statistics, claiming that the ACTU was waiting for the outcome of the survey made for the Henderson Poverty Inquiry to obtain data. In fact, the ACTU executive was still divided about the issue, some not wanting to see a loss of the breadwinner loading.

Other organisations supported the minimum wage for women, including the National Council of Women, the Union of Australian Women and WEL.[54] Edna Ryan, representing WEL, included costings to demonstrate that approximately 226,000 families in 1968-69 had a female head, and that at least 80,000 of these families were on the poverty line. She believed that fixing this anomaly would be a small cost to the community while the benefit to affected women would be great.

Staples and Gaudron listened to the evidence for two weeks before being called upon to put submissions on behalf of the Government. Staples had a tricky task; inflation was running high and it was his brief to support the unions' case for wage indexation to offset inflationary increases in the cost of living. Staples put the case for a flat increase to the minimum wage with quarterly adjustments with reference to movement in the consumer price index.[55] On 7 March 1974, Gaudron then put the Government case for the minimum wage to adult female employees. She argued that there were compelling industrial, social and moral arguments necessitating the equal treatment of females in the workforce. By 'equal treatment', she explained, 'what is meant is the opportunity to participate equally with men in the share of economic resources distributed in the form of take home pay'.[56]

Gaudron had the benefit of WEL's submission in another aspect of the case for the minimum wage for women. Edna Ryan had explained succinctly to the Commission relevant changes that had occurred since the 1972 decision. In particular, ILO Convention No 111 had been ratified, and the *Conciliation and Arbitration Act* had been amended.[57] She told the Commission that a minimum wage for males only was a denial of wage justice to an appreciable portion of the workforce and was clearly inequitable.

The sticking point on wages parity was the 'family needs component' of the minimum male wage. Culturally, it was assumed that men were the breadwinners for their families, and needed to be guaranteed a minimum wage that took into account 'family needs'. Edna Ryan had urged that the 'family needs' concept should be abandoned. Gaudron argued that, to the extent to which the 'family needs' concept protects males on low award rates from economic and social disabilities, as a matter of logic females on low award rates ought to be afforded the same measure of protection. They toiled under peculiar employment disadvantages—physical, legal, cultural and personal handicaps—that inhibit well-rewarded employment.[58] She argued that the minimum wage was never intended to be based merely on family needs. Rather, it was the determination of ordinary hours wage rates that guarantees the minimum fair participation of a wage earner in economic distribution. She explained that if the minimum wage 'did not guarantee the bare needs of such a wage earner it would in no sense be guaranteeing to him or her, a minimum fair participation in economic benefits'.[59]

Gaudron was bolstered by the discussion of the nature of the minimum wage in the *National Wage Case 1973*. It addressed the standard of needs for the average family unit of a man, wife and two children. It considered the principle of updating the minimum wage with reference to the movement in average earnings, so that the minimum wage reflects improvements enjoyed by the community in general. Gaudron argued that, if the minimum wage was viewed in this way, it would follow that consideration of family needs would not be the sole or even substantial factor for the determination of the proper rate. She concluded that 'if that be the case there is no reason...why the minimum wage in its present conceptual framework should not be extended to females'.[60] She pointed out that unless it was extended to female workers, it could not be said to be uniformly just or useful in its application. She noted that not all male wage earners or, perhaps more relevantly, not all male minimum wage earners, could be said to have dependent families, and that '[n]ot all female wage earners, or specifically those in receipt of the minimum wage or less, can be said to be free of family responsibilities'.[61] That is, past assumptions were not reflective of social reality.

Gaudron sought to present the Commission with figures that backed up her claim that there were a number of identified areas in which women were doing less well than men, which resulted in them falling into a disadvantaged income group. In questioning the relevance of the document, one of its members suggested that the reasons why women were not doing as well as males in only one area might be irrelevant for the Commission's purposes. Gaudron feistily replied,

> Well, Your Honour, might I answer that by saying it is our submission that people are always able to explain away the reason why women are not doing so well. It is part of our case that when you add up the totality of the areas in which they are not doing so well it is just no longer good enough to make those explanations.[62]

Moore encouraged her to continue this line. He asked Gaudron whether she was attempting to paint a picture of disadvantage to women beyond the effect of the minimum wage. He summed up:

> What you are saying to us is that at least there is one part of this picture that you can rectify, namely the minimum wage. You are saying that we cannot do anything about some of these other things but that is the thing we can do something about?[63]

Gaudron confirmed that:

> ...the extension of the minimum wage to females would not eradicate all of the inequalities but it would to a significant extent for a significant sector of the workforce be an alleviating factor.

At one point, Gaudron's quick thinking put paid to a remark by Commissioner Portus. She had been referring to the example of a deserted wife with two children, whose motivation to participate in the workforce might be inhibited, given the pension to which she would be entitled compared to what she might earn in the workforce given the relatively little worth placed on that participation. Portus asked, 'Would that matter in that particular case?'[64]

Gaudron made the now legendary reply: 'Yes, Mr. Commissioner, the matters which would matter may be different depending upon who was doing the mattering about it...' Cameron, watching, enjoyed seeing Gaudron taking what she saw was pomposity out of the Commission.[65] Then Gaudron surprised everyone in the hearing room. She bluntly laid responsibility on the Commission for Australia's failure to ratify the ILO Convention concerning equal pay for work of equal value. She later marvelled at what she said. She recalled that she

> argued, with some force, about which now I think I should have perhaps had some embarrassment, that it was the fault of the Arbitration Commission that Australia could not honour

its international obligations and that the secondary consideration, of course, was that women didn't have equal pay.[66]

It was a dramatic moment in the proceedings. She put to the Commission that it had some obligation to assist the Government in its desire to eliminate discrimination based upon sex. She referred to Australia's failure to ratify ILO Convention No. 100, and said,

> In the past it has been argued that if Australia has not ratified an ILO Convention there is no legal obligation to give effect to it; the present Australian Government is not prepared to hide behind that argument. If the Commission fails to accept the responsibility to facilitate ratification the Australian Government asks it to note that it does so in full awareness that it thereby prevents the Australian Government from accepting and fulfilling its obligations as a member of the international community in this very fundamental area of human rights.[67]

The audacity of her submission captured everyone's attention. She emphasised the point with her right arm outstretched, pointing to one end of the bench, moving her arm slowly across to the other as she made the point, so that the commissioners were in no doubt about the responsibility they held. Staples cringed, worried that the judges would call upon him to 'talk to his junior', as commonly occurred when junior counsel overstepped the line, but he was awed by the strength of her words. He was not called to account and he immediately forgave 'his junior' for exceeding the parameters of her brief because of the brilliance of that submission.

The background to her proposition was that, in 1947, at the second session of the United Nations General Assembly, the Australian representative had made a statement to the effect that Australia supported the principle of equal pay, with the qualification about the Federal government's limited powers to put the principle into effect. It only had the power to legislate in respect of industrial matters concerning Federal government employees.

While the Federal government could have ratified ILO Convention 100 and then used its external affairs power, section 51(xxix) of the Constitution to enforce compliance at both the State and Commonwealth level, it was Australian policy not to ratify a Convention until it was complied with. An appropriate decision from the Commission could achieve this.

On 26 March, during the employers' submission, a group of about thirty women burst into the hearing room with placards and drowned the hearing, yelling through a loudhailer.[68] President Moore calmly welcomed them to listen, but warned that they must put down the placards and stay silent. They ignored him. He adjourned the proceedings. As the judges were leaving, the women pushed forward to the bench, and the judges' associates attempted to block them. Gaudron intervened, telling them: 'The feds will be here in a second. You'd better piss off fast.' They did, and proceedings resumed.

The Commission delivered its decision on 2 May 1974.[69] The nation was now engaged in a double dissolution election. Inflation and unemployment were major issues. Staples suffered a small blow. The Commission acknowledged 'the increased intensity of inflation'. But it took a cautious approach. It decided against Staples' submission that there should be automatic quarterly adjustments with reference to the consumer price index. A decision on that matter was deferred. The matter was not resolved and questions surrounding wage indexation were left to the Commission to determine in the 1975 *National Wage Case*, when Staples would have more success.

Gaudron had reason to be elated. The Commission extended the minimum wage to female workers. The reality that women, too, often supported families, was finally accepted. It declared that 'the family component should be discarded from the minimum wage concept'.[70] The Commission justified its changed stand, noting that since the 1972 case and the consequent phasing in of equal pay, the gap between male and female wage rates had narrowed and lowest rates applied to adult females in most awards were now close to the present minimum wage. It was therefore persuaded that the proposal to extend the minimum wage to females was economically feasible: 'We believe that this step is a logical extension of the equal pay principles which the Commission set in motion in 1972 and which will be fully applied by the middle of 1975.'[71]

Though the case was hard and tiring, and particularly taxing on Gaudron working away from home for so long, from a professional point of view it was a dream brief. She had Staples' assistance. Having the Australian Government as her client gave her an authoritative presence before the Commission. Importantly, she already had the benefit of the strong submissions put by the ACTU and WEL's Edna Ryan. In this context, Gaudron's role was small but historically significant. History remembers it because it was a woman who presented the case, and particularly because of the bold manner in which she presented it.

It was another victory in the fight for equal pay. It was another victory for Gaudron. She was again in the limelight and credited with the success. There were pats all round. Edna Ryan's submission, according to WEL's historians, was 'tightly argued' and 'was the turning point' for the Commission's decision to extend the minimum wage to some 300,000 women who had been receiving less than the male minimum wage.[72] Ryan in turn hailed Whitlam and Gaudron as the two most instrumental players in the 1972 and 1974 cases that assisted Australian women to overcome the inequitable effect of the way work was categorised and valued as women's or men's work.[73] Gaudron, for her part, credits Cameron with the success. While the women's movement campaigned in the early 1970s for an equal minimum wage, the union movement had been hesitant in pursuing the claim, possibly because it feared that it would have to trade-off award increases, or perhaps it did not want to abandon the concept of men as the breadwinners. In Gaudron's view, Cameron

> ...was determined that women should not be discriminated against in the work-place. He made a pre-emptive strike. He announced that if the ACTU were to make a claim for an equal minimum wage, it would be supported by the

Government…Clyde pursued the matter in Cabinet and eventually won the day…Clyde was well ahead of most politicians and certainly ahead of the trade union leadership.[74]

Cameron credited Gaudron for her handling of the equal pay cases, and rewarded her appropriately. On 8 April 1974, with a dissolution of the Parliament imminent and nearly a month before the 1974 decision was delivered, Cameron announced her appointment as a deputy president of the Commission.

Staples appeared in the *National Wage Case 1975*[75] led by Victorian Labor lawyer, Dick McGarvie, QC.[76] This case achieved the full wage indexation that could not be achieved a year earlier. In February 1975 Staples joined Gaudron on the bench of the Commission. The two friends-in-law became colleagues once again—this time as judges.

Gaudron was excited at seeing in her lifetime the changes that arose from the 1972 and 1974 equal pay cases, especially at being there and playing a part in effecting them. On 10 December 1974, the Government ratified the 1951 ILO *Convention No. 100 on Equal Remuneration for Men and Women Workers for Work of Equal Value*.

There was still much to be done to achieve equal opportunity in the workforce. Cameron, pleased that he had briefed Gaudron to persuade the Commission 'to jettison sixty years of sex discrimination', recognised there was more to do. He said, 'It is all very well to talk about equal pay for women, but if you don't give them equal opportunity, you have only done half the job.'[77] This reflected Gaudron's thoughts exactly, as to which she would have a great deal more to say.

Chapter Eight

A SEAT ON THE ARBITRATION COMMISSION

'Say, Bud, this here chick's a judge.'
'Sure, that's interesting. Ask her if she knows anything about Newfies.'
'She's not a goddam dog judge; she's a goddam Federal judge, a Federal aberration judge.'[1]

On the bench

Clyde Cameron needed Prime Minister Whitlam's support if Gaudron was to be appointed to the Australian Conciliation and Arbitration Commission. Cameron reasoned,

> He was a sucker for anybody who was an academic; with Gough if you had a string of degrees, that made you an ideal person for appointment. So when I told him Mary Gaudron was a gold medallist and she had first-class honours in law, he was absolutely ecstatic.[2]

Lionel Murphy, the Attorney General, supported the appointment.³ A different approach was needed to persuade the rest of Cabinet, which at that time included several former union leaders. Cameron thought it better to focus on Gaudron's working-class origins. 'Instead of talking about medals and first-class honours I talked about her father being a railway worker and coming from humble beginnings and a home with a dirt floor (at least that's what I told them) and what a solid Labor supporter she'd been and at that point Gough spoke up and said, "For Christ's sake. Next you'll be telling us she was born in a bloody manger".'⁴

It was a tempting offer. Gaudron was awed and felt the weight of the responsibility that would go with the job. It was another opportunity for her to prove she was 'equal to the best' as a lawyer, and it was work that interested her. She was enjoying the Bar and its challenges, but at times she was frustrated 'because the ground rules were wrong or the law itself was not keeping pace with changing social values'.⁵ In contrast, the Commission approached its work with less formality and more flexibility than did the courts.

Yet she initially rejected the offer. She did not lack confidence in her intellect or judgment, or her ability to apply her legal knowledge properly. It was the effect of the position on her home life, her husband and their two daughters that concerned her. Gaudron finally accepted, after being further encouraged by Cameron and Ian Sharp, then head of the Department of Labour. Gaudron's mother, Bonnie, lived in Sydney at the time, and fortunately would be there to help with the children when Gaudron was working long hours or travelling interstate. Nannies would also be needed.

Gaudron publicly acknowledged that her acceptance came only after first thinking hard about it, because it was 'a final sort of thing'.⁶ It might mean her doing the same thing for the rest of her life.⁷ At that time, only one person had resigned from the Commission. That was in 1921 when the then President of what was then the Arbitration Court, Justice Henry Bournes Higgins, clashed with Prime Minister Billy Hughes and resigned in protest. He did not, however, walk away from a judgeship; Higgins was also a Justice of the High Court.[8] As history now tells, Gaudron, for reasons she could not have foreshadowed, became only the second Arbitration justice to 'resign on principle', and the first to relinquish judicial rank in doing so.

On 1 April 1974, Gaudron's appointment as a deputy president of the Conciliation and Arbitration Commission was approved. She succeeded the late Mr Justice Aird.[9] Ms Gaudron became Justice Gaudron. She and her presidential member colleagues were entitled to be called 'Justice' although the Commission did not have a judicial function. In 1956 the Conciliation and Arbitration Court became a 'Commission'; a new Industrial Court was created to determine legal matters. This change was a consequence of the *Boilermakers' case* in which the High Court declared that as a matter of constitutional interpretation, arbitral and judicial functions could not be exercised together.[10]

On 18 April 1974 the Full Bench presided over by Sir John Moore welcomed Gaudron to the Commission. In response, she praised the Commission for 'making the law do justice', reflecting her view of the importance of the Commission's work.[11] Gaudron's mother, Bonnie, sat in court with Gaudron's husband Ben Nurse, and Danielle, aged nine, and Julienne, two. The appointment was big news. At thirty-one, Gaudron was the youngest person to be appointed to the rank of federal judge. But mostly the press was interested in the fact she was a woman and a mother, not that she was a young and competent lawyer. The reporters were assisted by Julienne making a dash for her mother, crying out 'Mummy, mummy', as Gaudron was presented with her commission.[12] Three of the city papers' headlines were:[13]

> New Justice interrupted by baby's cry,
> Judicial Genevieve; she's scored another youngest,
> The law and the laundry—Youngest judge has no time for ironing.

Had she been a man, even a man with a large family, the laundry (unless matters of dirty linen were raised) was unlikely to have surfaced in the headline.

The appointment was controversial. Gaudron's friend and colleague, Justice Frank Hutley, saw no reason to offer congratulations. He thought she was too young for judicial office; rather, he believed, she should continue at the Bar, prove her worth and gain the maturity required for a judicial appointment.

> I told her she was a silly girl. I thought it was a tragic waste of her capacity. You need patience, endurance and tolerance, things which only come with the old. I told her that the judicial office is only for the mature.[14]

The appointment drew criticism from other quarters because 'brilliant young lady barristers proud of their working-class backgrounds and with a vocabulary to match are not the sort of people you find topping legal popularity polls'.[15] The Melbourne *Herald* noted that some found it difficult to imagine this 'slip of a girl' being entitled to be called 'Your Honour', and dealing with strikes and lockouts, industry site inspections and handling the blokey culture of the mostly male workforce of the meat, wool and paper milling industries. It acknowledged, however, that she was known as a capable lawyer and it noted 'her steely determination that earned her the nickname "Mary the Merciless" when she was practising at the Bar'.[16]

Frank Walker thought it was a strange appointment for her to accept. He believed that had she stayed longer at the Bar she would have become QC (Queen's Counsel) and the top senior equity or common law lawyer. Yet, perhaps Gaudron was not being impatient, merely sensible. Realistically, a successful career at the Bar is incompatible with having the children and the family life Gaudron wanted. Could she have become as successful as the best of the men at the Bar? Would she have wanted to? It would seem not, on either count. Success means back-to-back trials, sometimes long-running ones, with case conferences, interviews of witnesses, and preparation in out-of-court hours. A fifteen-hour day could be the norm for weeks on end, with little time for anything but necessary sleep. Most mothers who miss breakfast and dinner with their children as a daily routine for the sake of their careers feel uncomfortable. Gaudron would not have forgone a family life for the sake of that kind of public success. Her goal was not to achieve fame or riches. She wanted to effect changes rather than simply win cases. As it was, she made many family sacrifices to achieve that end.

Gaudron was the second woman, following Elizabeth Evatt, to be appointed a presidential member of the Commission. Cameron was responsible for both appointments:

> The reason I appointed Elizabeth Evatt was not because she was the best potential judge available; it was because I was determined to prove that women could be good judges. The reason I appointed Mary Gaudron was because she was the best lawyer I knew.[17]

Cameron chose well. Both women proved his point.[18] The Commission was a powerful industrial force in the political and economic climate of the 1970s. Its primary functions were prevention and settlement of industrial disputes, fixation of minimum wages and conditions, and overseeing registration and management of industrial organisations.[19] Inflation was at its peak in 1974 when Gaudron joined the Commission.[20] Its decisions had to balance the need for wages to keep pace with inflation with the need to minimise the inflationary effects of wage rises. Gaudron would be one of the judges instrumental in resolving industrial disputes that threatened the nation's economy, and in securing the benefits to women of equal pay and maternity leave.

The President of the Commission, John Moore, created panels headed by deputy presidents who were responsible for specified industries or sectors of employment. From 1974 multi-industry awards were broken into industry specific awards. Gaudron's panel covered a diverse range of industries—the agricultural sector alone included dairying, flour milling, fruit growing and production, grain, hops, meat, sugar, timber and rice. Gaudron was also allocated municipal employees, non-academic staff in tertiary institutions, paper milling, cement manufacture, mineral prospecting and drilling.[21]

Gaudron moved from the thirteenth floor of Wentworth Chambers to the thirteenth floor of the Law Courts building next door, where the Commission was located at the corner of Phillip and King streets. Her first task was to choose staff. Merit selection principles were not established protocols at the time. Judges chose people they knew and trusted. Her friend Jim Staples knew and trusted Tricia Miles. Gaudron trusted Staples. Miles had been the first female barristers' clerk in Phillip Street where she worked in Frederick Jordan Chambers. She became Gaudron's 'right hand woman', her associate and long-term close friend. She came to know Gaudron well—all her faces and all her moods. Gaudron appointed an eighteen-year-old Aboriginal woman from Cowra as her secretary. Gaudron also gave some Aboriginal women from Moree the opportunity of working as her tipstaff. It did not work. In jocular fashion she conceded to a close friend, 'they were on walkabout whenever I wanted them'.

Tricia's barrister husband, Jeffrey Miles, accepted a judgeship in Port Moresby and moved there with Tricia and the family. Gaudron's then secretary Pauline Hansen asked Gaudron if she could take on the position of associate. Gaudron gruffly replied, 'You don't want this job—you will be away a lot.' Hansen did want the job and said so. Gaudron shrugged. 'Have it, if you like.' The 'interview' over and the appointment having been made, they were a good team. Hansen remained Gaudron's associate until Gaudron left the Commission in June 1980. Notably, Gaudron insisted on being Hansen's husband's 'best man' when Hansen married after they both had left the Commission. 'I'm as good as any man,' Gaudron declared, reflecting something she had perhaps been striving for all her life.

Gaudron treated her staff like family. She made time to listen to and understand them. Yet she was at times difficult to work for. She was a hard worker and a demanding boss, and could be emotional and volatile. She expected and received dedication and loyalty, and those who worked with her loved her.

Suits and singlets

Female members of the Commission were an uncomfortable fit in its entrenched male culture. Neither Gaudron's nor Elizabeth Evatt's presence apparently warranted change in how members were addressed. The women decided that their names in Commission hearing lists and decisions should not have a prefix. The male members continued to be called 'Mr Justice...' or 'Mr Commissioner...'; the female judges gave themselves no title other than 'Justice'. How difficult would it have been to remove the 'Mr' and enhance the dignity of the Commission? Very, apparently. Female judges had to wait until Gaudron joined the High Court before the conventional use of 'Mr' was dropped.

A year into her work Gaudron suffered humiliation when hearing a case that concerned 800 Victorian women meat workers' claim for wage increases following the 1974 *Equal Pay* case. On 26 February 1975 Gaudron withdrew after six days of hearing. It was understood that she stood down as a consequence of comments made by the employer representatives that as a female arbitrator, she carried a perception of bias.[22] Gaudron made no public comment about the matter. The women meat workers were incensed. 'Mad as meat axes,' was how the Meat Industry Employees Union president, Jack Sparkes, described their reaction. He, too, was livid. The suggestion that a woman was not capable of giving an unbiased decision was 'insulting'; the logic of it escaped him.[23] While Gaudron's motives for stepping down remain unknown, the act of doing so brought the sexism encountered by Australian women in the workforce to public attention.

Nor were the singleted shearers accustomed to a female in the Commission. In 1976 employers' representatives objected to Gaudron conducting an inquiry into the travelling allowance for urban shearers. They feared she would encounter resistance amongst shearers. The matter was resolved when the union representative gave an undertaking that the shearers would not call 'ducks on the pond' when Gaudron entered the sheds. The expression, author Anne Summers has explained, 'is what Australian shearers used to call out when a woman approached the shearing sheds. It was a signal to stop work, or at least to stop swearing or engaging in other behaviour the woman might find offensive, until she had left.' Summers learnt from Gaudron that it was still in use in the 1970s.[24]

There were some amusing moments during the 1975 shearers' inquiry. A shearer giving evidence solemnly swore that his name was 'Crutching Jack'. When Gaudron thanked him for his attendance, he 'volunteered with equal solemnity that he hadn't "had so much fun since Mum caught her tit in the mangle"'. Gaudron questioned why the travel claim was expressed in cents per mile, rather than per kilometre. The AWU advocate replied: 'Your Honour can do whatever your Honour likes, but I think it is only fair to warn you that my members still pay one and thruppence for their combs and cutters.'[25]

Gaudron soon demonstrated the irrelevance of gender. She was an effective arbitrator and a successful conciliator, and very much liked and respected by those who appeared before her. Her sharp tongue and quick wit kept advocates on their toes. Her interrogative voice still rings in the ears of John Blackley, often present at hearings or appearing in association with his work for the Australian National University.[26] He recalls her often asking advocates who strayed from the point: 'Where is this taking us?'; 'What turns on it?'; 'The logic of that argument completely escapes me!'; 'So, what's your point?' and 'We will not put the cart before the horse'. Gaudron's inquisitorial style did not change. According to High Court Justice, Dyson Heydon, she was not a judge who would maintain an 'enigmatic silence' when faced with a barrister's argument that she did not understand or accept. She would say so, because 'bland inscrutability was impossible for a person of her temperament, convictions and powers'.[27]

Blackley admired her ability to cut to the chase. On the bench she would sense when the time was right to intervene. She would announce the need to speak to the parties on her own and would leave the bench to talk to them in chambers. Then she would take the lead with, 'Let's sort this out and see if some agreement can be reached…' And generally she succeeded.

Gaudron did not take herself too seriously either, and entertained a little flippancy in court. In one case Gaudron waited for her associate to note the names of the people appearing and the parties they represented. There was a long list of unions and employers and the government, all having an interest in the case because it concerned the application of new Commission guidelines. The list was eventually handed to her. Gaudron considered it, looked up at those assembled expectantly before her, and said: 'Yes, I have the appearances, but who's for the money?' The atmosphere lightened, and the union representatives let her know the nature of their claim.[28]

Her unique style enhanced rather than stifled the performance of lay advocates. Lack of any preciousness about judicial rank helped to put lay advocates at ease, which in turn made it easier for her to understand and help resolve the real issues in contention behind the wide ambit of claims. Alan Anderson, representing the meat industry union, immediately warmed to Gaudron for helping him out on his first appearance before the Commission. An experienced industrial advocate, he became concerned when he could not understand the arguments put by the employer's advocate, Wally Dearlove. 'What's he talking about?' he asked himself as Dearlove went on and on. 'This woman on the bench will ask me to respond, and I don't know what to say.' He remembered his father's 'pram theory'. If someone was talking nonsense, he would say that they were 'definitely dropped out of the pram'. He rose and what came out was intended to be self-deprecatory:

> Your Honour, as a child I was dropped out of my pram on my head and I've been in a state of confusion since then. I don't know what he is talking about.[29]

Without missing a beat, Gaudron leaned forward in what looked to be an aggressive hunch, and Anderson waited for the dressing-down he thought he deserved. With feigned indignation, she said:

> I grew up in Moree, the daughter of a railway worker, and I wasn't dropped out of a pram on my head, and I don't know what he is talking about either.[30]

The earthiness of the exchange produced laughter even from Dearlove, and brought informality to the proceedings.

Off the bench, Gaudron was affable and amusing. She first visited an abattoir in Inverell in the course of an official inspection of the conditions of work. She realised that seeing an abattoir at work is not a pleasant experience, even for meat eaters. At lunchtime Gaudron declared, 'We're going off to the pub to have a meat pie. If we don't eat meat now, we'll never eat meat again.'[31] She was also disarmingly friendly towards advocates who appeared before her when chance meetings occurred at restaurants, on the way to work on a Sydney ferry, or in the bakery shop near where she lived in Canberra. She engaged them in conversation rather than make do with a nod of acknowledgment.

Fair process in the workforce

Gaudron was quick to deal with unfair or discriminatory work practices. In one 'off-the-record' conference that concerned the grievance of a female university employee, a manager was, in her view, inappropriately flippant. In response to Gaudron's question about what might be done to resolve the matter he said, 'I'd sack her.' Gaudron glared at him, and stated, 'That is not good enough Mr "T". You had better think again.' The case was quickly resolved in favour of the employee, who kept her job.[32]

Gaudron's tenacity over issues of fair process can be clearly seen in a dispute about the de-classification of an employee of the Melbourne Metropolitan Board of Works. The employer's advocate, Mr James, asserted the issue was not one for the Commission; it was a 'management prerogative' to decide whether an employee was competent to carry out his duties. Gaudron, in typical style, took him to task on procedural fairness.[33]

Gaudron J: What you are saying is: 'We are the only people competent to judge the competence of this employee'. That is what you are saying. And, 'We are not prepared to submit the reason for our decision to scrutiny'. That is what you are saying, is it not?

James: No, I am not.

Gaudron J: Are you saying the contrary?

James: I am not saying the contrary. I am saying something in between.

Gaudron J: I do not think there is somewhere in between in a decision like this, Mr James. Either the facts are disclosed and adjudged or they are not disclosed and adjudged. ...

[Discussion]

Gaudron J: He [The employee] has no choice the way you play the game, has he?

James: No, that is correct.

Gaudron J: That is not really a very satisfactory position is it, Mr James?

Gaudron adjourned the matter for further evidence.

In Gaudron's view, the success of the Commission depended very largely on the informality of its procedures and the speed with which it could act. On one occasion she said:

> Lawyers should appreciate the difference between the commission and other courts, and they should not invest it with formalism and rigidity, but promote the achievement of a solution between parties.[34]

She noted the Commission could not exercise judicial functions as did a court of law. Yet some disputes involved consideration of the legal rights of an individual, such as reinstatement of people fired for alleged misconduct, individual rights to superannuation and other employee entitlements. She encouraged unions to seek early legal advice in relation to claims of this kind, as they had to be considered in jurisdictions other than the industrial jurisdiction.

Women in the workforce

Two cases in particular were important to Gaudron. Both concerned equity for working women. One was the Queensland Local Government non-discrimination case against married women; the other, the national *Maternity Leave* case. The discrimination case arose because in Queensland it was still common for women who were working in local government to be dismissed when they married. A chief defender of the policy was the then Mayor of Rockhampton, Rex Pilbeam, who was outspoken in his views that a woman's place was in the home. Gaudron recalled that Pilbeam:

> ...a noted Royalist, decided that he was going to do something for the benefit of latch-key children, and decreed that pregnant women and women with children could no longer be employed in any agency of the Rockhampton City Council. The first beneficiary of this enlightened policy was a young library assistant who was pregnant and accordingly sacked...I remember the case quite well, and what I remember most is as we were going into Court to hear the case, the President of the Commission, Sir John Moore, said to me 'And I'll thank you not to ask the Mayor what he thinks of the Queen's child-care arrangements.'[35]

The Municipal Officers Association of Australia (the MOA) had been fighting this policy for some time and took the case of Mrs Jeanine Marshall to the Commission in 1978 for the introduction of anti-discrimination provisions in the awards. Mrs Marshall had joined the Rockhampton City Council at age fifteen, and her employment was terminated in accordance with Council policy when she married. Gaudron was only too familiar with the impact of this rule on women. Years earlier she had had to find another job when she was required to leave her government employment when she married Ben Nurse. The MOA sought a variation of the award that dictated Mrs Marshall's dismissal by the Council for being a married woman.

Gaudron was one of a bench of three hearing the case. The union claim was based substantially on provisions of International Labour Organisation Convention 111; it was supported by the Commonwealth, the United Nations Association of Australia and various women's interest groups who were granted leave to intervene. The Commission found the policy of terminating the employment of married women was discriminatory and contrary to the aims of the ILO and the Federal Government. On 24 April 1978 the Commission amended the Award by inserting a clause to prevent such terminations.[36] It was a significant decision. Following this case, the Commission began writing anti-discrimination provisions into awards, a move that delighted Gaudron. But the decision did not end the discrimination in Mayor Pilbeam's Rockhampton office. As late as 1980, Pilbeam told *New Idea*,

> People say that I hate women but I don't. The best person in the world is a woman who stays at home and brings up her children. Here in my chambers, we don't employ married women. That way, we not only keep the family together but we keep the rates down because kids will work for half the wages.[37]

The decision in the Rockhampton MOA case was tendered in evidence to the Full Bench of the Commission in the *Maternity Leave* case.[38] Pilbeam's attitude was persuasive of the need for legal intervention. If anyone needed reminding, Gaudron kept in her 'judge's notes on *Maternity Leave* case' of 19 September 1978 a press cutting dated that day from the *Age* that reported Pilbeam's views that '[w]orking mothers are behind Australia's mounting problems of drug taking, venereal disease and juvenile delinquency'.[39]

Gaudron describes participation in the *Maternity Leave* case as second only to the *Equal Pay* case of 1972 as the most exciting and important event in her career to that point.[40] The 1978 *Maternity Leave* case was heard over many months. Evidence before the

Commission was that between 1968 and 1978 in Australia the number of women in the workforce and the proportion who were married had both increased. In Australia in May 1973, 62.5% of the female workforce was married, as against 48% in 1966, and 5% in 1947.

The outcome of the lengthy hearing was that a provision for maternity leave would be inserted in the awards relevant to the proceedings. It allowed for six weeks compulsory leave after confinement, and permitted twelve to seventy-eight weeks leave which was not to affect the continuity of the mother's employment.[41] Gaudron was ecstatic at both the outcome and at having contributed to a case of such significance.

Highs and lows

The 'high' of the aftermath of the *Maternity Leave* case was evident when the commissioners relaxed in the conference room at 415 Little Bourke Street in Melbourne on 9 March 1979. As Gaudron tells it, they 'proceeded to behave in varying degrees of unladylike and ungentlemanly like behaviour accusing each other of sexism, male chauvinism, radical feminism and the like' when the telephone rang.[42] It was the associate to the Chief Justice of the High Court, Sir Garfield Barwick. He was notifying the existence of an industrial dispute. There was a picket line in place at the construction site of the new High Court building in Canberra. In the course of a strike about a disability allowance, members of the Builders Labourers Federation refused to allow Barwick himself access to the site.

The seriousness of this 'delicate matter' did not prevent Gaudron and her colleagues from deriving a measure of amusement from it. According to Gaudron, some suggested that the Chief Justice should be summonsed to a compulsory conference 'forthwith', while 'wiser counsel to the effect that the presence of the Chief Justice could only impede conciliation, prevailed'.

The compulsory conference was duly called—without the Chief Justice—and Gaudron amusingly described the BLF claim as being 'supported by two arguments, one compelling and the other cogent'. She elaborated:

The compelling argument went something like this: 'We've got the pickets in place and they're going to stay in place and we're going to keep the Chief Justice in a place which is far away from the High Court unless and until we get our disability allowance.' The cogent argument went something like, 'Well, he's always on the site. It causes an awful lot of tension and it's affecting site safety and we really don't know what the status of his instructions is.' In short they said it really was a very considerable difficulty to have to work under the supervision of the Chief Justice.

Gaudron, who enjoys the quick wit of other people, as much as her own indulging of it, reported that Justice Coldham tried to counter this with: 'But I work under the supervision of the Chief Justice, he is most critical of my work but I don't get a disability allowance for that.' Unfazed, the intelligent and quick-witted Secretary of the ACT Branch of the BLF, Peter O'Dea, replied:

> Well, if your Honour wants to make an industrial claim we would be prepared to support it with appropriate industrial action…We don't know what he's like as a Chief Justice, we just know he'd make a fine Clerk of Works on the Acropolis.

O'Dea, recalling the exchange, describes the occasion as 'a verbal duel—the sort of thing I relish'.

Gaudron, when later in a position to compare, regarded her time on the Commission as 'infinitely more fun' than on the High Court.[43] Gaudron enjoyed the work:

> Its endless variety; the industrial situations were invariably hilarious so long as you maintained sufficient distance therefrom, and one had the opportunity for inspections to quite interesting places, although in retrospect I think I could have gone without my interminable inspections of sewage works.[44]

She could, perhaps, have done without one incident. The inspections of various industries often required her to travel to remote places all over Australia. On one occasion she was involved in an incident that brought home to her the risks in the job of flying in small aircraft. It became a case of 'a wing and a prayer'—and some expletives.[45] On 5 September 1977 she and a small group of others involved in the proceedings travelled to Snuggery near Millicent in South Australia to inspect an Apcel paper mill. A seven-seater twin engine Aero Commander had been chartered to take them from Melbourne to Mount Gambier from where they travelled to Snuggery. At the end of the day they returned to Mount Gambier to fly back to Essendon Airport. About twenty minutes out from Mount Gambier a midair mishap occurred. The pilot had handed coffee to the passengers in plastic cups poured from a thermos. Gaudron, sitting at the back of the plane, lit up a thin brown cigarillo to enjoy with her coffee. There was a loud explosion followed by a hole that appeared in the roof. A man behind Pauline Hansen clutched his chest and Hansen felt a whack on the back of her neck. Gaudron was heard to gasp from the back of the plane, 'Sorry, sorry,' believing that in lighting her cigarette she had caused the explosion. The lethal weapon was not, however, the cigarillo, but a piece of metal which had broken off from the tip of a propeller. It pierced the aircraft and smashed into the cabin. The plane flew for twenty minutes on one propeller with a hole in the roof and made an emergency landing at Ballarat Airport. The shocked and injured passengers, including Gaudron who had suffered an injury to her hand and a broken finger, were taken to Ballarat Base Hospital for treatment.[46]

The proceedings at Snuggery were to be continued at Maryvale, Victoria, the following Monday. Gaudron was scheduled to carry out an inspection of another paper mill. Gaudron, in fear of another metal fatigue episode, insisted that they not fly again on an Aero Commander. Hansen booked a plane and was relieved it was a small jet. This time, she reports, in place of the plastic cups of coffee, they were served whisky in cut glass goblets from a cut glass carafe.

Gaudron enjoyed work more when her former colleague, Jim Staples, joined the Commission as a deputy president in February 1975. Staples and Gaudron's colourful collaboration in the *Mackie* and *National Wage* and *Equal Pay* cases had cemented their friendship. They had a sense of fun and political beliefs in common. Like Gaudron's, Staples' family background was working-class and, like Gaudron, he was outspoken. When he joined the Sydney Bar he befriended and mixed with the more radical lawyers and had a successful practice until he joined the Commission. As Commission colleagues, Gaudron and Staples and their staff members were gregarious, often meeting as a group for lunch and drinks after work, particularly when hearing matters interstate. Staples recalls Gaudron's tact and humour after one social lunch that included a bottle of red wine. Gaudron and Staples returned to a full bench hearing over which Gaudron presided. Staples, not unusually, engaged in an argument with counsel, and to guard against it getting out of hand, Gaudron slipped him a note. It read: 'Shut up. Your lunch is showing.'[47]

But Staples' arrival was accompanied by complexities affecting Gaudron. While Gaudron's and Staples' views coincided on how the world should be, both having a strong commitment to social justice, they had vastly different approaches about how they might use their public office to influence thinking on such issues. Staples rejected the notion that they had 'joined the establishment'; rather, he saw their role as members of the Commission as being important penetrators of political conservatism.

Staples' passion for fair play and getting things right, unlike Gaudron's, was sometimes released with the hit-and-miss consequence of an undirected missile in his effort to fire up others to support the cause. By contrast, Gaudron worked diligently within existing political and legal frameworks and took account of other people's personal or political agendas when trying to persuade them to see her way. While she had a unique personal style—frank and sometimes confrontational—she pursued a conventional approach and was smart in her use of the law and her tongue as tools for change. She embraced opportunities to make changes that people were ready to accept—changes that were sustainable and that could be built on, rather than discarded, in the future. It worked for her. She gained public positions where she could further influence development and fair application of the law.

Staples did not care what people thought about him. He cared only that they thought like him. He was unrestrained in his denunciation of absurdities and unfairness in his endeavour to persuade others not to put up with injustices. By contrast, Gaudron was sensitive to what people thought about her. She wanted to persuade people who had power to effect changes about things that mattered.

She supported Staples through his troubles, but did not 'join forces' with him as he seemed to expect of her. As Staples put it, 'she wanted to remain in the game'. He confessed that he thought Gaudron could have done better in the radical role that he assumed she would adopt on the Commission.

Staples' vision of the two being akin to conspiratorial partners in law with a mission to break down the conservative forces was guaranteed to compromise Gaudron's professional life but not their friendship. They found each other's extravagant personalities attractive. They had a high regard for each other and a strong loyalty had developed between them. This allowed their friendship to survive the crises they would suffer on the Commission.

Staples spoke out, often alienating politicians and powerful figures in the business community, and sometimes the unions, with his libertarian and individualistic approach to resolving disputes. Early in his new post Staples spoke at the University of NSW about the deplorable state of NSW prisons, with particular reference to conditions leading to the Bathurst riots of 1970 and 1974. President of the Commission, John Moore, took him to task, reminding him, 'You are a judge, not a political agitator.' Strained relations developed between them. Staples saw these as the inevitable tensions between 'the establishment and democracy', rather than merely a clash of personality.

Staples further annoyed Moore in October 1975, when he condemned the behaviour of BHP, one of Australia's largest corporations, in dealing with a dispute between it and the seamen on one of its vessels, *Iron Cavalier*. The seamen had tied the ship up in dry dock, blocking the way of other vessels. Staples found BHP had complied with the award, but he recommended that it meet some of the seamen's pay demands. The seamen, believing that

Staples' recommendation would be acted upon, freed *Iron Cavalier*, thus allowing other vessels to move. Once the ship commenced its voyage, BHP applied to Staples for the matter to be removed to the Full Bench for review. Staples saw the timing of this as 'a low act' and, from the bench, chastised BHP and commented on the powerlessness of the Commission.[48]

Moore called Staples in and told him, 'You have destroyed the confidence of the ship owners in your impartiality.' Staples retaliated. He asserted that BHP had attacked the Commission, and him and Gaudron in particular, in publicly describing their appointments as 'most regrettable'.[49] He accused Moore of standing back while they 'went after Mary and me'. Moore replied, 'They are not after Mary, they are after you!'

In the same month, Moore took an unprecedented action. He removed Staples from heading the Commission's maritime industry panel. By December 1975 Moore had reallocated most of Staples' work, reducing the industries for which he had panel responsibility. Gaudron and her staff, as well as his own, supported him, but the situation would only deteriorate for both Staples and Gaudron after the dismissal of the Whitlam Government on 11 November 1975.

The new Government wanted Staples out of the way. The Commonwealth Attorney General, Robert Ellicott, QC, arranged for Staples to undertake a twelve-month 'study tour' of international practice in the protection of human rights in Canada and the USA. Staples took the task seriously and embarrassed the Fraser Government by deluging it with voluminous reports on human rights.[50] Gaudron was upset at the Government's act of banishing Staples. Staples returned at the end of 1977 to find that he had been allocated no work and the Commission had budgeted on his absence for another year. He was being paid by the Commonwealth as a judge, but he had no work to do. He planned another work program that he could undertake while 'in exile' in Europe. Gaudron lost the companionship of her colleague for yet another year. She did, however, tolerate the new conservative political environment of the Fraser Government. She presided over some transport strikes, a concrete strike, a wool dispute, the pastoral workers' dispute, and other matters and, most importantly, the Telecom technical grades dispute.

The Telecom dispute 1978

It was Gaudron's chairing of a conference of warring parties in the long-running Telecom dispute in 1978 that put her effectiveness as a conciliator beyond doubt.[51] She offered what was later described by one commentator as the 1978 'Gaudron solution'.[52]

The dispute between Telecom and its technicians was significant in Australia's industrial history. It marked the beginning of serious concern about the job implications of technological change necessitating (as Gaudron saw it) a new approach to the management of industrial relations. The dispute arose from Telecom's announcement of a two hundred million dollar plan to computerise its exchange system. The Australian Telecommunications Employees Association (ATEA) claimed on behalf of its technician members that the new system would eliminate the need for some maintenance crew and the resulting redeployments would impair promotion opportunities.

Early in August 1978 the ATEA banned repairs and maintenance. By mid-August Telecom responded by standing down 4000 of its technicians without pay for refusing to repair the telecommunications network: 'no work as directed, no pay'. Telephone lines were falling dead across the nation as the dispute spread from state to state. Prime Minister Malcolm Fraser blamed the unions and urged Telecom management not to negotiate with them. But Fraser did not have the support of the public. Technological changes were occurring in all sectors of industry and were perceived by the community as a threat to jobs of all kinds. Further, as the STD charging systems collapsed during the dispute, the public was happy to take advantage of free or cheap long-distance calls.

The disputing parties came before Gaudron on 15 August 1978. She advised the parties to suspend retaliatory action pending further discussion, as penal bans only served to widen the dispute. ATEA agreed to lift bans on employees from doing the work of the striking maintenance workers. When the parties came before her again on 21 August, still not talking to each other, they asked that the proceedings be adjourned. Fraser was under increasing pressure to act. The business of the nation was being disrupted. On 22 August Commissioner Clarkson offered the parties a six-point 'peace plan' to be determined at a compulsory conference two days later. It envisaged a restructuring of the classification of tradesmen and technicians, taking into account other matters of concern to the employees. ATEA rejected the plan.[53]

On Saturday, 26 August, Fraser relented. 'Talking' was, after all, called for. Bob Hawke, the ACTU President and a master tactician, entered the scene to lead the union representatives in the talks with Telecom management. He said,

> The atmosphere was very taut, because Telecom believed that the introduction of new technology was a management prerogative, and rejected the idea that the workers should have any say in how it was to be introduced.[54]

He was a skilful negotiator. By Saturday afternoon Telecom had agreed to conciliation and arbitration. Gaudron was telephoned in Sydney and asked to resume the hearing in Melbourne in the morning. She telephoned her associate, Hansen. Expecting the proceedings to be drawn out, she advised her that it would be 'a toothbrush job'.

The day has been recalled as 'Bloody Sunday'.[55] By 10:30 am on Sunday morning the parties were assembled before Gaudron in the hearing room. Within minutes they adjourned for a conference which she chaired. For the rest of the day she worked with the parties and listened to their arguments. By 5 pm the parties requested a break. Gaudron kept a tight rein:

> A stylish feminine figure at the centre of a fatigued, frayed group of men, Mary Gaudron broke temporarily, lit up her long cigar, and declined to allow either the disputants to go out or food to be brought in.[56]

At 10:35 pm, after thirteen hours of verbal duelling, the parties reassembled with a settlement. This saw the end of the month-long dispute.

The negotiations took place around Commissioner Clarkson's earlier proposals on how management should deal with introduction of technology in the future, and the manner in which jobs would be protected. The parties agreed to a trial of new principles that drew substantially on those proposals, 'and indeed in many respects incorporate those proposals in their entirety', Gaudron noted, crediting him with achieving the settlement.[57]

But there was a final sticking point. The ATEA demanded back pay. The employers, for their part, could not afford, politically or economically, to destroy stand-downs as an effective management tool. Gaudron saw a way through. Some of the workers laid off had not refused to do their own jobs; they had only refused to scab on their striking mates by doing their work. She awarded them back pay, carefully ensuring that there was no back pay entitlement to those who had refused to do their own jobs:

> ...I am prepared to give special consideration to the situation of employees, members of the ATEA, who were put in a no-pay situation not as a consequence of the implementation by them of a ban, but as a consequence of a refusal to undertake work away from their normal depots and/or bases.[58]

This translated into seventy percent of those laid off receiving back pay. The ATEA was happy. Prime Minister Fraser, who had firmly and publicly stated that back pay would not be part of any settlement, was angry. Nevertheless, the disruption was over and the nation could communicate telephonically again. According to one commentator on the dispute, Gaudron's handling of the negotiations was regarded as a *tour de force*.[59]

Hawke received the media's accolade, but he credited Gaudron for the role she had played. At the conclusion of the proceedings towards 11 pm that Sunday evening, he rose to endorse Gaudron's appreciation of Commissioner Clarkson's work and thanked Gaudron herself for her 'patient assistance' without which the parties would not have been able to reach their 'happy situation'.[60] The representatives of the ATEA and the management of Telecom supported this, and thanked Gaudron for her 'patience, tolerance and wisdom'.

Hawke acknowledged that Gaudron deserved much of the credit. He told his biographer:

> We all knew she was an extraordinarily intelligent woman [and]...her sense of humour was a big help in keeping things together. In conferences of that length fatigue and frustration cause short tempers, and often the whole thing breaks down. It's a tremendous plus if the mediator can keep the atmosphere light.[61]

It was as well that Hawke had seen Gaudron working so effectively. It was his government that appointed Gaudron the first female Justice of the High Court.

Chapter Nine

A DRAMATIC DEPARTURE

> Gaudron's resignation was 'quite the most principled resignation of any public figure in a long time'.
>
> Clyde Cameron, 2003[1]

Looking to greener fields?

Gaudron had been on the Commission for a little more than a year when she accepted an appointment to head a proposed new Commonwealth statutory authority.[2] The opportunity again came from Clyde Cameron. By 1975 he was Minister for Science and Consumer Affairs. The Federal Government proposed to establish an Australian Consumer Protection Authority. Gaudron took part in some of the preparatory consultations about its role, functions and powers.[3] The new body was to be responsible for product information, safety and performance standards and would have broad powers over consumer activity and protection that would be enforced through the Australian Industrial Court. Gaudron, as its president, would retain her judicial rank. She would have been responsible for the work of five associate commissioners, to be drawn from business, the consumer movement, engineers, chemists and the law. However, the dismissal of the Whitlam Government on 11 November 1975 meant that the Consumer Protection Authority did not come to fruition.

Her willingness to leave the Commission indicates that she did not see it as the peak of her career. As it transpired, far from departing the Commission in dignified circumstances for 'something better', she became caught up in the fallout from Justice Jim Staples' confrontation with the President, Sir John Moore, and quit in spectacular and unhappy circumstances in May 1980.

The election of the Liberal-National coalition government in 1975 and its economic policy attempts to contain inflation affected the work of the Commission. It was an emotionally charged climate. Inflation had taken off. The union movement was strong. The Commission was under pressure to increase wages to keep pace with rising costs. Business now had the support of the Federal Government to try to contain wages. Gaudron had spoken out about some issues, in particular the Fraser Government's legislation in 1977 to impose penal sanctions against unionists taking industrial action, which Gaudron believed was inappropriate and futile. She also believed that the principle that the purchasing power of wages should be maintained was only questioned in times of economic downturn. Accepting the limitations of the Commission's role, she pointed out that the arbitration system cannot institute remedies to economic problems, but can only respond to situations.[4]

Gaudron was enjoying her Commission work, even in the changed political environment, but she was finding some aspects of it unsatisfactory. She had never sat on a national wage case. Further, she was travelling extensively and away from home and the children, sometimes for days on end. Significant changes were also occurring in her personal life.

Troubles at Hunters Hill

There was turmoil in Gaudron's marriage. She was unhappy. She and Nurse argued often, and pursued separate interests. She was often away, adding further strains to the marriage. A stream of nannies to look after the children came and went. By 1979 the marriage had irretrievably broken down.

Gaudron in the meantime had met and become romantically involved with John Fogarty. He was working in Sydney as a presenter of an ABC radio children's books program. Fogarty gave a picture of casual sophistication with straggly dark hair and blue rimless glasses, and he had a dry sense of humour.[5] After a career as a radio journalist, he worked for a magazine in the publicity field and then in computer accounts. Gaudron was considering a future for herself and her children with him.

Further unsettling her life was her home at Hunters Hill. It had been crumbling around her in another way—one that affected the family's relationships, their health and finances. Nurse and Gaudron had purchased a vacant block in Nelson Parade at Woolwich in Hunters Hill in 1973. Nurse, by then a developer and businessman, built the family's 'dream home', a four-level mansion extending to the waterfront overlooking Fern Bay, on the Parramatta River, and adjacent to Kelly's Bush Reserve. They moved into their nearly completed new home in 1974. During a chance conversation in the Blue Mountains in 1975, Gaudron learned from a retired professor investigating cancer clusters that there was a cluster in Nelson Parade, and that it was possibly caused by a hazardous waste dump nearby.

Inquiries revealed that the site had been used to pile contaminated tailings discarded from the refinery located on the two blocks next door. Unbeknown to Nurse and Gaudron, the NSW Department of Health had been aware of the potential health risk to the occupiers of the affected properties since late 1965. The investigations revealed that the Nurses' block had the second highest dosage rate reading.

Gaudron and other residents in Nelson Parade wanted to find out the extent of any health problem and what the NSW Government was prepared to do about it. The Government wanted to bury the issue. By 1977 a long-running battle between the residents and the State Government was under way. Gaudron put her fighting spirit to use. The department, noting the possibility of having to compensate some residents, was alarmed at the size and expense of the construction on the Nurses' block. A file note of 1977 observed that, 'Mrs Nurse is professionally Mrs Justice Gaudron, a

Deputy Commissioner in the Court [sic] of Conciliation and Arbitration,' and that No. 11 (as it was by then numbered), a previously vacant block, carried 'an extremely expensive structure, conservatively having cost in excess of $100,000'.

In March 1977 the Health Department again considered compensation. In June 1977 a full-scale investigation into the extent of contamination on several of the blocks, including that of the Nurses, and the soil on the foreshores of their block confirmed the soil contamination from radioactive material. By the end of 1977 it decided to take serious action to shift radioactive soil, and to demolish one house; the residents were not told which one. The Sydney *Sun* reported the story under the headline: '"Atom" House to Go!'[6]

Two houses were resumed. The owners of another were told to leave, but refused. The Nurses' house at No. 11 was regarded then by the department as safe. Gaudron wrote letters to the Government, which began to react to the pressure of the situation. Being a judge made her powerless in this context, as she could not be seen to use her position to put pressure on the Government. The representations were made in the name of the property owners 'Nurse'. Tom Uren, member for the nearby seat of Reid and Labor shadow minister for the environment in the Federal Parliament, came to Gaudron's aid. He obtained documents and arranged for questions to be asked about the uranium-contaminated soil and what was happening to ensure its safe disposal.[7]

More people whose relatives had died of leukemia and cancer were coming forward. Gaudron discovered that a neighbour had been diagnosed with leukemia. Panic set in. As Ben Nurse portrayed it to an inquisitive press years later, Gaudron fled with their two daughters in 1979. As a consequence, a headline in 2008 concerning a claim for compensation by current owners of the home read: 'Ex-judge fled toxic address'.[8]

Gaudron certainly feared for the health of her children—and with reason. Gaudron had told the children not to play on the split and rotting bags of soil lying at the bottom of their garden, but Julienne remembers that she did. There were no labels on the bags, and the soil was spilling out. The bags of contaminated soil would remain on the foreshore of the river for another thirty years.⁹

In 2006 the elder child, Danielle, was diagnosed with thyroid cancer and then Hashimoto's thyroiditis. Danielle's bedroom was on the eastern side of the house on the third floor. Tests later identified this bedroom as having the highest levels of radiation in the house. Danielle's health had to be closely monitored.

However, the failure of the marriage was behind Gaudron 'fleeing' without Ben Nurse. She left her home and marriage to make a new life with John Fogarty. One morning towards the end of 1979 she simply moved out, taking a small amount of furniture. Nurse might have foreseen this, but was taken by surprise. He was devastated. She and the two girls moved into a unit in east Sydney. The girls spent a good deal of their time with their father at Hunters Hill, where he chose to remain despite the radiation scare, until the home could be sold.

Gaudron and Nurse never resumed cohabitation. The public reason for Gaudron leaving the Hunters Hill home was because of the radiation contamination that her close friends said was making her ill.¹⁰ And at the time fear of ill-health and the emotional toll affected Gaudron. There was a divorce and property settlement yet to go through, and a battle with the NSW Government if the house could not be sold. The Nurses divorced soon after. The initial hostilities having been overcome, they have remained good friends as parents of the two girls. They still contend that the toxicity issue was the prime reason for Gaudron's departure from the home.

Gaudron's campaign for compensation was tenacious. The family finances depended on it. The house had declined in value. 'I'll go broke,' she told friends, 'the prices are dropping.' She had reason to be concerned, as she needed her share of the proceeds of sale to help finance her new life with John Fogarty. Nurse wanted to stay at Hunters Hill, at least until a proper price could be obtained for it. He told the press:

> The State Government has offered us $310,000 to resume the property, but it's worth $350,000, so I'm staying on. We know it's written on the file that 'if Justice Gaudron rings, fob

her off', and they have. Not even a judge can win against a government.

Under Gaudron's pressure the NSW Government purchased the home in late 1980 for the sum of around $250,000, less than originally offered, and, according to Nurse, about a third of its market value in the absence of a toxicity problem.

The 'dream house' continued to be a nightmare. It remained vacant throughout 1981. Children and dogs played and scratched about over the bags of contaminated soil.[11] Departmental staff occupied the property to assist the justification for the Government purchasing the property. Some remediation was carried out in 1987. Declared safe to occupy in 1989, the house was sold by the Government and sold again, with its last private purchasers not being informed of its history.

The matter remained quiet until 2008 when, in the course of the NSW Government revealing plans to clean up premium harbour front land and sell it for housing, it was revealed that the toxic land in Nelson Parade was never decontaminated.[12] A committee of the NSW Legislative Council was established to inquire into the level of risk to residents of Nelson Bay. Gaudron was abroad and Danielle was working in the United Kingdom when Ben and Julienne Nurse gave evidence about their knowledge of the history of the property and their concerns for their health, and that of Danielle in particular. The NSW Government bought the house back, again, in 2009.[13] In 2010 a decision was taken to demolish it.

Having moved into a home with Fogarty, Gaudron wanted to spend more time with him and start a family. Her work travel made this difficult. Her professional options were limited. She was unlikely to attract the Federal government's eye for a senior legal or judicial appointment. She was, after all, looked upon as a 'Labor lawyer'. But Labor was in government in New South Wales. Gaudron was performing well as a judicial arbitrator and was strongly identified as being part of 'left' legal circles. The NSW Attorney General at the time was Frank Walker. He was convinced that Gaudron would make a great High Court Justice and often told her so. It was not surprising, therefore, that

Gaudron was pleased to receive a telephone call from him at the end of 1979 in which he offered her a part-time position as head of the new NSW Legal Services Commission. The Legal Services Commission was to administer legal aid services and to provide better access to the justice system for the poor and disadvantaged. As its chair, Gaudron could pursue her social policy agenda, and it was compatible with her existing full-time position.

In itself, this was not something to be unduly excited about. But Gaudron was. A clerk 'temping' in the Commission's Canberra rooms where Gaudron was conducting hearings in late 1979 recalls Gaudron's reaction when she received the phone call. The clerk knew only that she was offered an exciting 'appointment'. Gaudron was ecstatic and wanted to share the news with someone, and no one else was available. The clerk never forgot the privileged occasion, given Gaudron's later elevation to the High Court, and sensed that she must have seen the appointment as one of the stepping stones to her later position. Gaudron saw the importance of accepting the part-time position to the extent that an 'in' with the NSW Government was her only way 'out' of the Arbitration Commission and its tiring travel, and into a judicial career. Predictably, by the end of 1979 her name was raised in NSW legal and political circles as the State Government's potential next appointee to its Supreme Court.

If Gaudron was to leave the Commission, now was the time. Walker had positioned her well by appointing her to the new Commission. If the NSW Government had come up with a judicial appointment Gaudron would, without doubt, have taken it. But that was not quite how events unfolded. By 1980, things at the Commission turned sour. It was Justice Jim Staples, with his unique talent for havoc, who ultimately caused Gaudron to not-so-gracefully leave the Commission.

The Staples factor

Gaudron did not anticipate the wild card that was introduced with Jim Staples' appointment to the Commission. Staples found the Fraser Government's approach to industrial relations, and the Commission's response to it, unpalatable. He stuck his neck out. It was his undoing. Gaudron stuck her neck out over some of her colleagues' actions concerning him. The entanglement of protruding necks and Gaudron's subsequent resignation became a well-publicised story. While she might have welcomed a good reason to leave the Commission, the way it occurred was not what she had in mind.

Early in 1979 Staples had returned to Australia. He was allocated a full panel of industries. Inflation was still rampant. Many argued that it was fuelled by wage increments; the Commission was under pressure to contain wage increases. When it adopted wage indexation in 1975, to deal with the wage explosion, it underpinned it with a new set of wage-indexation guidelines. Staples was outspoken about what he saw as the injustice in the Commission's application of the new guidelines to hold wages down, which he saw as wage-fixing. He believed that the law did not permit the Commission, in its arbitration role, to 'assume such a central role in wage fixation…'[14]

Gaudron accepted the guidelines, as did other deputy presidents. They worked around them, to an extent, making use of Principle 7(a) of the indexation guidelines that allowed wage increases for a change in 'work value'. It proved to be the saving 'loophole' for employees for 'catch up' movements in their wages. The Commission's award of a 'catch up' figure of $8 a week became an acceptable and expected outcome of disputes between business and the unions.

Staples regarded Gaudron as a highly effective presidential member. She had some capacity to influence Staples, demonstrated by the outcome of the 1979 Telecom linesmen hearing in which she presided on a bench of three. Staples went along with her and the third member's decision that an $8 a week increase should be awarded in compliance with the guidelines, although he wrote a separate addendum that challenged Telecom's claims about its profitability, and warned of the inflationary effect of any increase in Telecom's pricing.

Gaudron, however, was not his keeper. Staples came into conflict with the Fraser Government in October 1979 when he wrote a letter to the Government attacking proposed amendments to the *Conciliation and Arbitration Act* aimed at preventing industrial action.[15] It was leaked to the ABC and published in *The Australian*.[16] While no action was taken against him over the leaked letter, his troubles continued.

By the end of 1979 inflation had negated much of the $8 catch-up value. Staples thought it should no longer be applied automatically. He made this known in a decision in the 1979 Wool Industry (Storemen and Packers) Award subsequently overturned by a Full Bench. His handling of the dispute and the public expression of his frustrations over its outcome became the excuse needed to strip him of authority on the Commission. It was the beginning of the end of his and Gaudron's effective time at the Commission.

Arbitration of the Wool Stores dispute began in October 1979. Over-award wage increases had started to be given to factory workers who bargained directly with their employers by use of the 'work value' loophole. When the transport workers were awarded an extra $8, the 'flow-on' to other industries was inevitable. The figure of $8 was becoming an industry expectation. It was the expected outcome of the wool stores arbitration, and was in line with what the unions were likely to accept and the wool producers and brokers were prepared to give, but for political reasons were not comfortable being seen to agree to. The parties required an arbitrated award.

Staples warned the parties that he was not an 'eight dollar automaton', and that he intended to make a fair and rational decision on the wage claim on its merits. The guidelines were just that; guidelines, not mandates, and the Arbitration Commission should not become the 'national paymaster'—as 'the duty to manage is in others'.[17] Nevertheless, he faced the obstacle posed by the many constraints imposed under the guidelines. The Commission was to guard against any contrived arrangement that would circumvent the principles. The wage rate set was not to be extravagant, and its impact in economic terms must be negligible. It should help to reduce inflation and must yet stabilise industrial relations. A wage increase was not to be referenced to productivity of the workers, or adjusted to meet the burden of taxation on the wage-earner, nor to reflect the cost of living. What then, he asked, could he take into account? 'It is one thing to conclude that new minimum rates should now be prescribed. It is another to quantify the change. What shall be the measure?'[18]

At one point in the three-month long proceedings, he answered his question by suggesting that he should take heed of advice in Joseph Furphy's book *Such Is Life*. Staples provocatively reasoned:

> It may not be discovered in the profitability of the enterprise and not in the increased productivity...It may not be an adjustment to the burden of taxation on the wage earner nor reflect any movement in the cost of living...nor may it derive from a comparison with rates paid in other industries...
>
> For the quantification, then, what shall I do? I am already reeling under the advice of many prophets. There is no Polonius at hand to give me memorable precepts as he did Laertes when he fled the confusion. I shall simply select a figure as Tom Collins selected a day from his diary and we shall see what turns up. Such is life.

According to the *Sydney Morning Herald*, what turned up was what 'this style of remark might have been expected to invite—a successful appeal'.[19]

Staple handed down his decision on Christmas Eve, 1979. He raised the wool industry's storemen and packers' award by $12.50, and where the agreed $3 applied, by $15.90, which he believed reflected what the parties believed was fair. He reports that everyone in the case seemed happy when the parties' representatives had a drink with him afterwards.

But Staples had not reckoned on the ire of the Fraser Government and the recently formed National Farmers' Federation. They urged the wool brokers to appeal to a Full Bench, under the threat of the employers resorting to private treaty sales and bypassing the brokers. Staples was genuinely flabbergasted and particularly surprised that inclusions in the award that he made in response to the direct request of the parties were also appealed.

The Storemen and Packers Union called a strike. They believed that the appeal breached a promise made to them by the employers. Since an arbitrated decision was required for political purposes, it had been agreed that the parties would accept the outcome and not appeal the decision.[20] A thousand men walked off the job.

Gaudron presided over a hearing convened in late January in an effort to prevent the strike escalating into an indefinite stoppage. She directed the parties, the brokers and the union to hold a private conference, and on her own initiative she asked the media reporting the open court hearing to exercise care, urging that they not report details of the proceedings, to avoid exacerbating the already serious dispute.[21] The strike nevertheless lasted for eleven weeks. The graziers started to bypass the brokers and trade with private buyers. The brokers felt betrayed by the graziers and demanded the protection of the Federal Government by placing a ban on the export of wool. Prime Minister Fraser intervened. He froze the export of wool from Australia to save the brokers from their commercial rivals who were exporting wool during the stoppage by entering into private treaty arrangements with the graziers. The press blamed Staples.[22]

'Stapled'

Gaudron, personally supportive of Staples and loyal to the Commission's President, Sir John Moore, soon suffered at the hands of some of her fellow deputy presidents from what became torn loyalties. While the wool stores appeal and the strike were still in progress, Telecom notified a dispute with its administrative staff. The matter came before Staples on 4 March 1980.[23] The parties announced that they wanted a minimum increase of $20 a week. After what had just happened, Staples was disbelieving. He considered refusing to find the existence of a dispute, given the apparent consensus between the parties. However, the parties suggested they could have the proceedings removed to a Full Bench, as they were entitled to do under new statutory provisions. He was over a barrel. He made the finding.

Then, overnight, he changed his mind. The next morning, 5 March 1980, Staples sent Telstra a telex saying that he had cancelled the finding of a dispute. The Government was enraged. On

6 March 1980 the Prime Minister, the Attorney General, Senator Peter Durack, and other ministers met to discuss the issue and Staples' behaviour generally. They determined that Staples should be removed.

Events then moved rapidly. The Attorney General spoke to Commission President, Sir John Moore. On 10 March 1980 Moore told Staples that he should retire from the Commission and accept an offer to a non-judicial position on the Law Reform Commission under Justice Michael Kirby. Gaudron was concerned about the development and continued to support Staples. She also believed he would accept the appointment offered, but for which belief she may have avoided the dramatic way in which she resigned from the Commission. Staples considered it. However, he objected to being stripped of his judgeship. He also objected to government interference with the courts. He sought Sir John Moore's assurance by letter of 17 March 1980 that the panel of industries allocated to him would not be altered. The same day, when the assurance was not forthcoming, he wrote a longer letter of complaint, and delivered it to Moore.[24] In the meantime, he had a speech to give. He wanted to counter the unfair press publicity he had received over the Wool Stores decision.

In the controversial speech Staples gave in South Australia on 17 March 1980, he did not make any mention of the Government's attempts to remove him. Instead, he sought to justify his decisions and defend the wage rise he awarded the wool store workers. He denied any blame for the industry's unrest.[25] In doing so, he was outspoken in his criticism of the Full Bench of the Commission which had overturned his decision, and of the employers on whom he laid blame. He asserted that '[t]he employers of this country have been reduced to cowardice by the guidelines and the government, a state of ignobility which fortifies, however, their material interests'. Staples' colleagues regarded his attack on the Commission as holding it up to public ridicule. Staples would pay the price for this, and unwittingly take Gaudron down with him.

Staples returned to Sydney to continue hearing the Australian Postal Commission and Australian Postal and Telecommunications Union case (APC case) with Gaudron, presiding, and Commissioner

Clarkson. Moore did not take any action over the speech, and perhaps he did not intend to. Staples' colleagues changed that.

A letter dated 8 April 1980 signed by eight deputy presidents, Robinson, Ludeke, Williams, Gaudron, Isaac, Coldham, Alley and McKenzie, was delivered to Sir John Moore.[26] It condemned Staples' conduct of publicly criticising the Commission and expressed their confidence in Moore. It described Staples' address as 'an unprecedented breach of a fundamental convention and threatens the appeal structure in the Commission and the standing of the Full Bench decisions'. No one informed Staples beforehand. He learnt of it some three weeks later.

Gaudron later told Staples how she came to sign it. She was presiding over a matter on Monday, 7 April 1980, in Sydney when Deputy President Terry Ludeke walked into the hearing room. The advocates had their backs to the door, and Ludeke was in full view of Gaudron from the bench. He waved a piece of paper, indicating he would like to talk to her. She adjourned the proceedings and left the hearing room. Ludeke presented her with the letter. He told her that the deputy presidents were worried about Moore's health and the letter was intended to express confidence in him, given the strain he had been under owing to recent events.[27] He also pointed out that a letter in support of Moore was less damaging than a public attack on Staples by deputy presidents of the Commission.[28]

Gaudron took the time to read the letter. While she trusted Ludeke, it would be hard to imagine she would sign it without reading it carefully and considering the consequences. She agreed that Staples' speech was inappropriate and harmful to the Commission. She did not think that the letter would hurt Staples because she thought he intended to accept a position on the Law Reform Commission. She certainly intended no harm to him and she was upset and angry at the use that was made of it against him.[29]

After receiving the letter, Moore bided his time. Perhaps this was strategic and he was waiting for the completion of the long-running APC case on which Staples was sitting. He presumably did not want to put the case in jeopardy by taking the action he intended against Staples. The APC case was completed on 16 April 1980.

In late April Moore called Staples in and told him that his colleagues had lost confidence in Staples for denouncing the Full Bench which had heard the wool stores appeal from Staples' decision. Moore asserted that some of the other deputy presidents feared the prospect of sitting on appeals from decisions made by Staples. Moore informed him that he would no longer be given single judge authority over industrial disputes. He would be confined to Full Bench duties.

Gaudron—unpinned

On 1 May 1980—significantly 'May Day', a celebration for workers—as Staples and Gaudron later noted, Moore circulated a notification to Commission members of the changed arrangements which were to take effect from 7 May. The Staples story provided the headlines on Friday, 2 May 1980.[30] Gaudron was in Canberra hearing claims against the Australian National University that day.[31] She had not known that the letter she had signed was used to express concern to Moore about Staples' sitting as a single judge. She found this out during a break in her hearing. She took a telephone call in the office of the Director of the John Curtin School of Medical Research and emerged agitated and concerned. She told the advocates present that Staples had been stripped of his powers on the Commission. 'I will resign over this,' she said. 'I may not agree with what Staples did, but the fact they have done this, I will resign.'[32] She adjourned the case she was hearing to the following Monday, 5 May, and returned to Sydney for the weekend.

It was Gaudron's turn to write a 'Dear John' letter. Gaudron's Associate, Pauline Hansen, took a call on Sunday morning, 4 May. 'You'd better come in. I need you to write my letter of resignation to the Governor-General.' Hansen suffered a double shock: 'When your judge dies or resigns, your job goes with it.'[33]

Gaudron tendered her resignation to the Governor-General, Sir Zelman Cowen. She wrote a second letter the same day to President Moore.[34] It read:

Dear Sir John,

Recently I, along with other Deputy Presidents of the Commission, expressed to you disapproval of the speech made by Mr Justice Staples in Adelaide on 17 March, 1980. I do not resile from that position. However, I do not believe that the disapproval expressed either was, or should have been, a factor relevant in your decision to deprive Mr Justice Staples of his panel responsibilities.

With the benefit of hindsight, I now suspect that some of my colleagues may have foreseen the use which would be made of our expression of disapproval (a use not intended by me), and accordingly I feel no longer able to maintain an association with you, them, or the Commission.

I have therefore forwarded my resignation to the Governor-General to take effect from May 31, 1980. I have selected that date so as to permit the delivery of certain decisions which I have reserved.

Yours sincerely,
Mary Gaudron

The following morning, Monday, 5 May 1980, Gaudron flew back to Canberra. The parties in the University case were assembled. At 10:10 am, seated on the bench, she announced:

I have to inform you that I have forwarded to the Governor-General the resignation of my commission as Deputy President of the Conciliation and Arbitration Commission, with effect from 31 May 1980. This will enable me to complete matters on which I have reserved decisions, but will not permit the further hearings of these matters.

I apologise for the gross inconvenience caused to the union, the university, and in particular, the employees concerned. However, my decision was dictated by recent events, and my reasons for so deciding have been made available to the President of the Arbitration Commission, certain other Deputy Presidents, and the Minister for Industrial Relations.

I do not propose, either on or off the bench, now or at

any later stage, to say anything further on the matter. I now adjourn both matters to a date to be fixed by my successor. The Commission now adjourns *sine die*.

At 10:12 am she left the bench.[35]

Gaudron returned to Sydney. Staples went straight to her office with a copy of the Deputy Presidents' letter to Moore in his hand. He had felt flattened and confused on seeing Gaudron's signature on it. She explained that she had no idea of the use that would be made of it, and her shock at what Moore had done. Staples observed that she was shattered by it.[36] She believed that her colleagues had deliberately misled her. Feeling fooled by her colleagues, she noted the irony that she had been appointed to the Commission on April Fools' Day. The two friends talked for about an hour. Nothing was decided about what they had in mind for their futures. Gaudron did not mention her resignation.

Staples returned to his room. Hansen came in with a copy of Gaudron's letter of resignation in an envelope. For Staples it was a 'bolt out of the blue'. He raced out of his room to talk to Moore. He caught him as he was getting into a lift. He asked him to stop Gaudron's letter reaching the Governor-General. Moore replied, 'It's too late. It's already gone.' Staples then contacted the Commonwealth Solicitor General, Maurice Byers, QC, and offered to leave the Commission and accept another position, so long as it allowed him to retain his judicial rank, if the Government would refuse to accept Gaudron's resignation. Again, he was told it was too late.

Moore replied to Gaudron by letter that day, Tuesday, 6 May 1980:[37]

> Dear Mary,
>
> Thank you for sending me a copy of your letter of May 4 to the Governor-General. I sincerely regret your decision as I feel you have made a valuable contribution to the work of the Commission since you became a deputy president.
>
> I am sorry you did not discuss the matter personally with me before taking the action you have as I might have been

able to clarify matters about which you are troubled.
With best wishes for your future.
Yours sincerely
John Moore

It was Gaudron, this time, who provided the headlines: 'Judge quits over letter'.[38] At the same time, the press noted that she was 'strongly tipped to take up another judicial post in NSW'. On 7 May 1980 the Minister for Industrial Relations, Tony Street, announced that the Governor-General had accepted Gaudron's resignation. There was no turning back.

Staples laid the responsibility for Gaudron's resignation on the Federal Government 'for having promoted and condoned a most unprincipled invasion of the rules relating to the independence of the judiciary'.[39] He also blamed Ludeke for instigating the letter. He believes that Ludeke had seen Staples' speech as an opportunity to discredit him within the Commission. He later asserted that Gaudron had undoubtedly inadvertently become the sacrifice perhaps expected from him. He described her resignation as a

> logical consequence of the campaign the Government has connived at…and many other people who should have had more sense of responsibility have engaged in to drive me out of my job.

He concluded that he had been put aside because 'powerful interests in this country wanted it to be so'. And, 'They haven't got me, they've got Mary,' he lamented.[40]

Gaudron would not speak publicly about the matter.[41] The press obtained the story from her friends that she had felt 'conned' into signing the letter and that she was angry with her deputy president colleagues.[42] Amid press speculation about possible future appointments, a 'Staples' joke circulated around the Sydney legal community. The story was reported that it was suggested to Gaudron that she might find work as a magazine centrefold, to which came her quick-witted reply that, given what Staples had done to her public life, she did not want staples intruding on her private sector.⁴³ *Playboy* magazine, had, in fact, invited Gaudron to be interviewed about her work on, and resignation from, the Commission. She declined and in a written reply included the reason that she did not want to be associated with Staples (the 'S' written as an undersized capital to indicate the pun was intended).

A recent appointee to the Commission, Justice Maddern, took over Staples' previous duties. The Government made four new appointments and President Moore made some changes to the panels. He handed over some of his own panel responsibilities to Maddern, and he kept another deputy president free from specific panels, giving the appearance that Staples had not been singled out.⁴⁴ The real objective, stripping Staples of effective power, was achieved.

Public opinion was divided about the treatment of Staples. The Leader of the Opposition, Bill Hayden, called upon the other deputy presidents who signed the damning letter to clarify their positions in the light of Gaudron's resignation. 'It would be extraordinary if Justice Gaudron were the only one who felt bound to examine her conscience and principles when confronted by the result of [the letter].'⁴⁵ The legal profession was concerned about implications for the independence of the judiciary.⁴⁶ The NSW Bar specifically considered Staples' situation but did not take any particular action.⁴⁷

Later, in 1988, a new Industrial Relations Act was passed. The Conciliation and Arbitration Commission was abolished and replaced with the Industrial Relations Commission. The opportunity was taken to remove Staples from the bench. In January 1989 the appointments of judicial members of the new body were announced. Other than the omission of Staples, they were identical to those of the previous Commission. Staples was given a judicial pension of $90,000 a year.

Staples' career in the Commission overtook that of Gaudron for interest and controversy. However, in her spectacular act of resignation, it was Gaudron who was hailed as the judge who acted on principle.⁴⁸ To some, Gaudron had 'out-martyred' Staples. Staples' fearless approach to his role of arbitrator has been less readily acclaimed. Moreover, the less rebellious Gaudron remained in the mainstream where she could influence decisions, and effect change in the social justice arena. Gaudron would go on to higher things; Staples would not.

Down—but not out

When Gaudron left the Conciliation and Arbitration Commission in 1980, she became plain Mary Gaudron, with no right to 'Justice' before her name, and she had lost her $50,000-a-year job. It was a significant decision. What would she do now? Her only intimation to the press was her immediate plan to take a holiday in Europe.[49]

While her resignation was over a matter of principle, leaving the Commission, though not in the circumstances she did, might have suited her. The action of her colleagues provided her with the excuse she was perhaps looking for.[50] Just as the contamination issue at her Hunters Hill home provided Gaudron with an acceptable way of escaping from her marriage to Ben Nurse, the Staples row allowed her an 'honourable' escape from the Commission, exiting as a martyr rather than a quitter, as unwelcome as both events had been.

According to Gaudron's Associate, Pauline Hansen, it was opportune for Gaudron to leave. Though shocked at her boss's resignation, she considered that the action was not precipitant. 'It fitted,' she said. 'It was time for her to go.' Hansen noted that Gaudron had suffered some discomfort from the Fraser Government environment in which the Commission had to work; she was tired of the demands of interstate work and travel; and the prospect of a quieter life with a new husband was enticing. The Staples event may have been the decisive 'last straw' that made it easier for Gaudron to take the stand on principle that she did.

And, for Gaudron, things were not as bleak as they looked on the job front. Quitting the Commission may have looked like a backward career move, but she had good reason to believe otherwise. Gaudron may have been down, but she was not out. She had, after all, proved herself to be equal to the best and brightest at the NSW Bar. She had quickly mastered the work of the Commission.

She won the respect of the suits on the Commission bench and the singlets on the work-sites. Where law was involved, Gaudron was capable of adapting to whatever was demanded. Opportunities would be around the corner, including the expected vacancy in 1981 of the post of NSW Solicitor General. However, if she had received a whisper that something was to be offered, she did not say so. And, it was reported that an offer by the NSW Government of a judicial post was 'unlikely'.[51]

Gaudron took up the relatively peaceful life of a visiting fellow at the University of NSW Law School on 1 July, just under two months after leaving the Commission. The University was close to her Coogee home. Gaudron enjoyed university teaching, finding students to be 'intellectually provocative, demanding and stimulating',[52] and stating that it is 'always a great encouragement and challenge to be confronted with the ideas of the young'. She liked the idea of students being a conduit for her own ideas, though patience was required as 'you have to wait for your students to implement your ideas'.[53] The work, free of interstate travel, made fewer demands on her time.

She lectured in civil law, including torts and defamation, areas of law very familiar to her from her practice at the Bar, and industrial law. She designed a new and optional course for undergraduates on industrial relations. As she described it,

> The course will attempt to explain the legal limitations inherent in the Australian Constitution and the Conciliation and Arbitration Act, and the inter-relationship between state and federal jurisdiction. It will concentrate on the problems that arise in the dual state-federal system of industrial regulation and will look at specific legal responses from other countries to some of the problems that face our present system.[54]

She foresaw that discrimination, equal job opportunity, job security and new technology would become more important industrial issues for Australia in the next decade.

In her capacity as visiting fellow, Gaudron was listened to. Her new post gave her the opportunity to express her views about the arbitration system developed during her time as a deputy president. She had emerged from the Commission with strong views on the need to encourage productivity bargaining between employers and unions in the context of the current Australian industrial situation. It offered scope for smooth implementation of changes occurring in a dynamic industrial environment.

She addressed this issue at the 1980 Symposium on Industrial Relations Reform at the University of NSW, at which various speakers talked about the need for reform of the arbitration system and the difficulty of achieving change. The use of new technology continued to cause industrial problems. Gaudron drew on her experience in the Telecom cases when she talked about the need for a more cooperative approach between workers and management for greater efficiency and the avoidance of industrial disruption. She claimed that the current wage-fixing principles not only assumed a fairly static industrial environment but also provided no incentive to employees either to co-operate or to participate in changes which might result in improved productivity. She suggested a fresh approach whereby the Arbitration Commission would relax its wage-fixing principles sufficiently 'to permit, if not to encourage' productivity bargaining between employers and unions in particular industries:

> The very nature of productivity bargaining necessitates the involvement of employees in the formulation of their priorities, the assessment of achievable changes and the organisation of the changes to be effected.
>
> This in turn, necessitates the establishment of proper avenues of communication between management and employees, which in turn tends to engender mutual understanding and respect.

Her outspoken views were published in an article in the University of NSW's publication, *Occasional Papers*, in March 1981, sometime after her appointment as Solicitor General. Consequently they received headline treatment in the media: 'Gaudron backs productivity baragaining'.[55]

Gaudron continued to speak out on women's wage equity issues. She strongly supported the use of trade unions by women to press their demands for equality in the workplace. She attributed everything that women had gained in the industrial area to trade union pressure and trade union action in the arbitration process. In addressing a conference in Canberra on *Human Rights? Women's Rights?* she urged,

> In the securement and protection of industrial rights, it is important that women give attention to their rights as trade unionists, and use the trade unions appropriate to their areas of work to further their demands.[56]

For Gaudron, leaving the Commission was the beginning of a new life. She enjoyed the time now available to her with her new husband and her two girls, now aged fifteen and nine, in their new home in Coogee. She planned to have another child. But her life was not without some turmoil. She was busy battling the NSW Government over the still unresolved issue of compensation for the contamination of her former home at Hunters Hill. She had not yet secured a position beyond the short-term university appointment. She hoped that a new opportunity would present itself. The odds were in her favour, as her friend, Frank Walker, was Attorney General in the second term of Neville Wran's NSW Labor Government.

Walker's succession plan
Walker was in the University of Sydney's Law School 'Class of '65' with Gaudron. He remembered her 'steel trap' mind, beyond any other he had seen. He made no secret of his regard for her intellect and his desire to see her become a justice of the High Court of Australia; he would do anything he could to assist her up the ladder. On the Commission under a Coalition Government Gaudron was trapped in the Federal judicial system with nowhere

to go. Walker wanted to see her in the NSW arena. In recent times two High Court judges had come from the ranks of State Solicitors General.[57]

Gaudron still held the part-time statutory appointment of Chair of the NSW Legal Services Commission, giving her experience in administrative and political aspects of legal issues. She also regained visibility within the NSW legal profession and the public. It put her back amongst the NSW legal family. In June 1980 the Legal Services Commission, with Gaudron as its Chair, expanded the system of legal aid for children by establishing regional children's legal centres that offered twenty-four-hour advisory services, and set up local committees representing community interests.[58] Her high profile in this role would later help to justify her appointment as Solicitor General.

When Walker appointed her to head the Commission he already had the position of Solicitor General in mind for Gaudron. He does not believe that he specifically mentioned his succession plan to her—that is, to appoint her Solicitor General—when he offered her the Commission appointment. In considering the matter he surmised, however, that 'she knew what I thought of her. She would know that I wanted to appoint her to that position.'

Gaudron probably saw the likelihood of her being chosen for the position. The then current NSW Solicitor General, Greg Sullivan, QC, was due to retire at the end of 1980. Gaudron would see out her six-month engagement with the University of NSW in December 1980. She regarded it as a temporary position, stating that she was not 'cut out to be an academic in the long term'.[59] The practice of law was always her main interest. The evidence points to Gaudron being poised for another career leap. The Staples fiasco aside, it seems clear that Gaudron would have resigned from the Arbitration Commission, albeit six months later than she did, to accept the appointment of Solicitor General.

While her reaction in support of Staples exposed her to criticism from some traditional male thinkers who thought that such 'emotionalism' was reason enough not to appoint women to public positions, Gaudron also received credit for taking a principled stand. Speculation grew that she would take over the Solicitor Generalship. Clyde Cameron still thought highly of her, stating in July 1980 that 'she is one woman laywer who has the stature of a High Court judge',[60] and later, that

> She has one of the most brilliant legal brains in this country and will one day be lifted to the High Court. I know of no young lawyer of her age who has her ability to absorb facts and to develop an argument.[61]

Cameron's support could only serve to encourage Wran to appoint her to the post of the State's number two law officer. Walker urged it. He knew, too, that it was a step up to the High Court. It was only a matter of time.

By the end of September 1980, more than three months before the official announcement, Walker was open about his proposal to appoint Gaudron as the next NSW Solicitor General.[62] Walker wanted to use her outstanding intellect, her clear head and extensive legal knowledge. He knew her to be someone who would read the briefing material, understand the implications of an issue, weigh them up and provide timely advice. Premier Wran also had some knowledge of her from their time at the Bar together:

> Mary created interest wherever she went in legal circles. Extremely forthright in her views and quite unforgiving of people whom she thought were using the law for unworthy means or cause. She was always the centre of attention— because of her 'in your face approach' to things. She bubbled with ideas—she had a shrill voice and when excited did not leave much opportunity for anyone else to be heard, and even in the most serious argument she could inject humour and much laughter. She is a special sort of person, loved the law, and the opportunities it opened for intellectual enhancement. At the same time, no doubt she was somewhat intolerant of people who did not live up to her high standards in the

practice and understanding of the law. People not up to her intellect kept out of her way.[63]

One observer thought her appointment a tribute to the Labor Party: 'They needed a good brain, not a party hack.'[64]

Chapter Ten

NSW SOLICITOR GENERAL

The new Solicitor General is small, sandy-haired, with a vivacious grin and a ready sense of humour. She has a legendary capacity to flay with her tongue and is also noted for her mastery of the vernacular. But if anyone is to humanise the law it will be someone like her.[1]

Back on track

On 16 February 1981, Gaudron moved into her new and spacious book-lined office on the nineteenth floor of Goodsell House, Chifley Square, Sydney. Despite the lofty heights of the office, Gaudron retained her essential down-to-earth character and her cheeky sense of humour. Her youthfulness, short stature and slight build, together with her sandy hair, homely appearance and disarming smile, made it difficult to visualise her in the serious role of Solicitor General. By now, though, no one doubted her capacity in the law. Gaudron's salary of $62,351 plus an expense allowance was widely publicised.[2] It was a grand wage (for a woman) worthy of comment. And she was the first woman to hold the post in any jurisdiction in Australia. At just thirty-eight, she was also one of the youngest occupants of the office.

The Solicitor General, generally appointed from the Bar, remains a member of the Bar, but with one client, the State Government. The role requires advising the Government, including a range of departments and government agencies and, importantly, the Attorney General, on a wide range of legal issues. Premier Neville Wran was himself a highly skilled lawyer, and when Gaudron commenced in the role he and Attorney General Frank Walker were on a mission to effect social justice reforms. Their agenda suited Gaudron.

The position also involves appearances in NSW courts and the High Court of Australia to argue for outcomes that support the State Government's political agenda. In particular, the Commonwealth *Judiciary Act 1903* grants Attorneys General a right to intervene and participate in court proceedings that involve the interpretation of the Australian Constitution in ways that might affect the State's interests. The Solicitor General advises whether or not the State should intervene in a court proceeding, and then often appears to argue the case. A job for senior counsel, yet Gaudron had no 'QC' after her name. She succeeded Solicitors General Harold Snelling, QC, and Greg Sullivan, QC. So as not to fly further in the face of convention, this matter was addressed.

In February 1981 Frank Walker arranged for Gaudron to 'take silk' (a reference to the silk robes worn by Queen's Counsel). Walker also became Queen's Counsel at the same time. The rank was bestowed upon him minutes ahead of Gaudron. 'Ungentlemanly behaviour,' she quipped as they lined up to receive the honour. Gaudron became the first female Queen's Counsel in New South Wales, and the third in Australia, after Roma Mitchell in South Australia and Joan Rosanove in Victoria.[3]

Gaudron took another step to avoid controversy. By now she had become pregnant to John Fogarty. It was too early to broadcast it. While her pregnancy was apparently not a good reason to give up her long brown cigarillos with her cup of morning tea, it was a good reason to formalise her relationship with Fogarty. They married in a civil ceremony at their Coogee town house the Saturday before her ceremonial taking of silk and just days before she commenced her new job. It was an occasion for close friends and family, for solemnity and hilarity. Gaudron, true to form, over-imbibed champagne and indulged her friends with an out-of-tune duo of Irish songs performed at the bottom of the stairs with her friend, Federal Court Justice Jeffrey Spender.

The following week she informed Walker that she was travelling to Paris with Fogarty. 'Women get pregnant in Paris,' he joked. 'If you get pregnant, I'll give you one day off to have the baby.' 'You're a sexist bastard,' she responded.[4] On returning from the honeymoon, she owned up that she was pregnant. She did, in fact, have just one day off when her son Patrick was born on Monday 21 September 1981 at the Royal Women's Hospital, Paddington. Bill Bowtell, then Chief of Staff to Walker, verifies it. He went into her office the following day to deliver some material and there she was, as she said she would be, sitting at her desk with the baby in a basket behind her. Walker sent a telegram congratulating her 'on the arrival of junior counsel'.[5]

Gaudron had no idea what lay ahead in the job. She thought she did. When a judge, she had told acting Solicitor General Leslie Katz that he had the better job. He thought hers was better. She offered to swap positions with him. As Solicitor General grappling with legal issues that sometimes had far-reaching political consequences, she had reason to agree with him that it was not easy work.[6] Notwithstanding, she maintained her view that it was the best job to have in the law.[7]

In the early days she told the press of her expectations:

> [Y]ou might hope to influence the development of the law and its application, but I guess more importantly it is an area in which you advise the NSW Government in terms of its Constitutional rights, duties and the limits of its power.
>
> I suspect that there are a lot of tensions inherent in the Australian Constitutional system and I would like to see them resolved without undue conflict. It is a position from which I would hope to contribute.[8]

Asked by the *Sydney Morning Herald* what she would like to achieve, she replied:

> I should like to see a greater awareness in the community at large of legal rights, responsibilities and remedies available. Perhaps in the long term I should like to see that the law is not something apart from ordinary life…People should see that the law is there not to stand against them, but for their benefit.[9]

She also believed that her new position would give her a peaceful private life and the chance to stand back from the public limelight.[10] She expected that if she performed well, she would be unlikely to attract press publicity. If this was her first measure of success, she would in time have reason to rethink it. Her time as Solicitor General in the eventful political period of the 1980s put her in the press spotlight more than at any other time in her career. Certainly she did not foresee the unsavoury entanglements of high profile politicians and lawyers with Sydney's crime figures that set the stage for a period of political intrigue and turmoil. Some of the 'goings on' that became the subject of press headlines involved her political masters, her legal colleagues and her friends. Handling the conflict Gaudron had felt between her loyalty to her friend, Justice Staples, and her professional desire to uphold the integrity and authority of the Arbitration Commission was easy compared to the testing of her loyalties that came with being Solicitor General. Some trying times lay ahead. This was, after all, the eventful political period that became known as the 'Wran era'.[11]

The advisory role—'frank and fearless'

Gaudron's advisory role imposed enormous pressure on her. An opinion could be required at short notice on complex legal and political questions. The Premier was often under pressure from Parliament. The Attorney General was under pressure from the Premier to give advice. The material presented to Gaudron was not organised into a well-prepared brief such as a barrister might expect from a solicitor in private practice. She would be presented with large piles of files, and each file was huge. It might have many parts and bundled with it could be lengthy transcripts of proceedings. The files were often accompanied by a request that the Premier 'would like an advice by Friday with which he could brief Cabinet the following Monday'. It was not work that could be delegated. Gaudron had to read the whole of the material, identify the issues, apply her knowledge of the law and provide the advice quickly with concise reasons for her opinion that Wran could understand in order to explain it to Cabinet. And she had to get it right.

The Solicitor General is required to give 'frank and fearless' advice to the government. According to Bowtell, Gaudron gave 'the unvarnished truth'. What Wran did with it was up to him. Bowtell's observations when working for Walker were that her advices were timely, succinct and to the point, invariably correct, and always acted on. On one occasion, Wran bowed to Gaudron's legal opinion despite his intense desire to act to the contrary. He had supported a proposal to introduce legislation designed to protect national parks from logging and mining.[12] He wanted to make use of a constitutional anomaly in NSW that allowed a law to be put in place that could not be changed by future governments. All that was required was the inclusion of a 'manner and form' stipulation that the new law could only be removed or changed by the holding of a referendum or the securing of a certain majority in both houses of parliament, or by some other means that made it almost impossible to achieve. This was not constitutionally possible at the Federal level. Gaudron's advice, always visionary, warned against the proposal: 'Although...there is no legal impediment to the technique suggested, it is a technique which arouses strong passions within legal and political circles.'[13]

She was right. P.H. Lane, Professor of Constitutional Law at Sydney University at the time, said that he was strongly opposed to such a course as being 'a particularly bad practice' and a thoroughly undemocratic one.[14] 'So be it,' said Wran, adding wryly, 'but I can only say this, I think that conservation may be more important in some respects than constitutional law.'[15]

Gaudron was alert to any pressure to do another's bidding

against her will. A hint of pressure as to what course she might advise would invoke her fury. A young lad working for the Attorney General, whose office was on the floor above, when delivering papers to her, made a remark implying what was expected of her advice. It outraged her. She gripped him by the ear and pulled him out of her office, into the lift to the floor above, past a flabbergasted Bowtell who was sitting at his desk, and into Walker's office.

Despite her tendency to rage, according to Bowtell:

> She was outstanding. Honest, straightforward, and had immense integrity. She was not appointed to do the will of Wran. And on the contrary, she'd go the other way to ensure that no one could accuse her of it and that no one could assume that she could be persuaded by them.[16]

Another colourful report emerged about her organisational talents. Her method of filing papers is cited as another 'Mary Gaudron solution':

> When Mary was the NSW Solicitor General in the eighties and had a small independent office within the Attorney General's Department, she disposed of all the dross by hurling it into the bin with an appropriate expletive. This is something she could get away with because she was Mary Gaudron and she was part of a bigger department—but it is unlikely to be an available option for many of us.[17]

Gaudron had a novel way of dealing with difficult people: the 'bottom drawer' solution. When someone angered her, she would tell her friends, 'He's gone into my bottom drawer.'[18]

Undaunted by seniority, she questioned the opinions of Commonwealth Solicitors General, Sir Maurice Byers, QC, and Dr Gavan Griffith, QC. She disagreed with Byers' opinion that the media's right to report parliamentary proceedings under cover of qualified privilege could be subject to Commonwealth laws. She said so in strong terms in an advice to the NSW Attorney

General Paul Landa.[19] She also challenged the opinion of both Commonwealth lawyers that the Constitution allowed the States to hand jurisdiction to a federal court, asserting that neither Sir Maurice nor Dr Griffith addressed the issue of where, under the Constitution, the Commonwealth derived power to pass legislation for federal courts to exercise state jurisdiction.[20] She suggested instead, where joint jurisdiction was desired, that State courts be vested with Federal jurisdiction. The issue was an important one. Gaudron would later maintain her view as a Justice of the High Court that, despite the inconvenience of jurisdictional limitations on Federal and State courts, Commonwealth laws purporting to give federal courts jurisdiction to hear state matters (cross-vesting legislation) were invalid.[21]

Reform agenda

Gaudron was keen to participate in the Wran Government's reform agenda. One Sunday in May 1981 she spoke in her official capacity at the launch of the NSW *Draft Bill of Rights* by the Citizens for Democracy.[22] As well as being concerned with the environment, heritage and conservation, the Wran Government focused on women's issues, anti-discrimination and Aboriginal land rights.[23]

Gaudron contributed to NSW law reform initiatives concerning sexual assault, including domestic violence and rape, which in effect made non-consensual sex in marriage an offence. In 1979 Walker appointed their Sydney Law School friend and colleague, Greg Woods, Director of the Criminal Law Review Division of the Attorney General's Department. The work was assisted by the Women's Advisory Council, chaired for five years by Gaudron's good friend, Kaye Loder.[24] Woods also invited Gaudron's contribution because of her position and the female perspective she could offer. The extensive contribution from women was intended to assist Woods to grapple with the difficulties in balancing protection of an accused's civil rights and helping victims of sexual assault.[25] Woods produced a report that guided significant legislative reform in the area, culminating in the NSW *Crimes (Sexual Assault) Amendment Act, 1981.* It included a series of offences described as 'sexual assaults' of various levels of seriousness to replace the principal offence of common law rape. Nearly twenty years later Gaudron was disappointed to hear from critics that NSW's well-intentioned and well-informed rape-law reforms had been of little benefit to women.[26]

Gaudron contributed to other matters concerning women. She gave advice on a solution to overcome the all-male bench of magistrates. Customarily, magistrates were appointed from the Magistrates Courts administration, in which there were no suitably qualified women. Gaudron's advice to Attorney General Walker was that there was no reason in law why appointments, including appointments of women, could not be made from outside the public service.[27] An appointment of a woman followed. Another was an advice in which Gaudron agreed that the United Nations *Convention on the Elimination of all forms of Discrimination Against Women* be accepted as a benchmark at which NSW should aim in pursuit of its anti-discrimination policies.[28]

In 1986 she was critical of the Commonwealth's *Affirmative Action (Equal Employment Opportunity for Women) Bill 1986*. It is a 'constitutional smorgasbord', she wrote in her opinion, 'in that it purports to rely on every conceivable relevant constitutional head of power except perhaps those relating to lighthouses and railway construction'. She observed that 'affirmative action', which the Bill purported to support, was not necessarily the same thing as 'non-discrimination', and that nothing in the bill 'directly or indirectly favours women over men in employment'.[29]

There were other human rights issues that concerned Gaudron. At her insistence, a 'housekeeping' exercise was undertaken to abolish the death penalty, still on the statutes for treason and piracy.[30] There was one issue she did not see resolved—the Chelmsford Private Hospital scandal. Gaudron advised the NSW Government that the only avenues of investigation open were to have inquests into individual deaths, or a full inquiry into 'deep sleep' therapy, a treatment that induced patients diagnosed with a mental disorder into a coma.[31] A Police Task Force that had inquired into application of 'deep sleep' therapy to those with a supposed psychological or psychiatric disorder gave details of twenty deaths between 1964 and 1978. Four were suicides carried out with the use of prescribed barbiturates. Gaudron was familiar with the issue. As a barrister in 1970 she represented Mr Dimiter Marinoff against Chelmsford in his action for damages for injuries he allegedly sustained in Chelmsford. The case went to the High Court on appeal in which Gaudron appeared unsuccessfully.[32] Now, as Solicitor General advising on the matter in 1986, she noted that it was not until recent times that a victim received a court award for damages. The then Attorney General, Terry Sheahan, urged Cabinet to approve funding for compensation for victims, not for an inquiry. Minister for Health, Ron Mulock, disagreed, and Cabinet failed to agree on what action should be taken. It was not until 1990 that deep sleep therapy was outlawed in an overhaul of mental health legislation, subsequent to the Greiner Liberal-National Government ordering a Royal Commission.

Importantly, Gaudron also advised on the validity of indigenous land rights reform and the proposal to pay compensation to Aboriginal communities previously dispossessed by government resumption of Aboriginal reserves, introduced by Walker, who, while Attorney General, was also Minister for Aboriginal Affairs.[33] The *Aboriginal Land Rights Act* was passed in 1983. It transferred some Crown lands to the NSW Aboriginal Land Council's administrators and permitted the Council's purchase of lands for indigenous communities, funded by a percentage of land tax receipts. Part of Gaudron's role was to be watchful for any constitutional challenge to NSW legislation that advanced indigenous rights, and to similar legislation of the other States. When challenges occurred, it was also her role to don her wig and gown and appear in court to argue the case for NSW.

'Hired gun'

While objectivity was essential in her role of adviser, it was Gaudron's duty to look after the interests of the NSW Government in her role as advocate. It was her task to win cases for it, and, as required by her ministerial masters, to intervene in cases to achieve particular results. She was their 'hired gun'.

Before going to the NSW Court of Appeal, she and Walker would discuss what they wanted to achieve and what arguments and tactics could be used. Gaudron's excellence lay in her ability to see where the arguments would lead. According to Walker the conversations went like this:

> She would say, 'Frank, here's our case.' And she outlined step one, step two. 'Is that right?' She would always say 'Is that right?' I'd say 'Perfect'. Then she'd say, 'They'll think it is, but it's not. Look at step two—it's based on a false assumption. Pull it out and there's nothing left.'[34]

Walker acclaims her extraordinary legal knowledge and her intellectual creativity. They developed a close professional and personal working relationship and stood by each other in difficult times, notwithstanding one independent action she took that severely tested Walker's loyalty when the 'hired gun' almost assassinated her political master! It was over abortion. Gaudron ignored Catholic beliefs when it came to women's rights over their bodies. In the knowledge that Walker held the same strong view on the issue, she used her position to intervene in a case—but without his permission. One minister threatened to resign and a 'bitter confrontation' occurred between Walker and the Premier.[35]

Wran's Cabinet was mostly Catholic. He was not able to introduce 'abortion on demand' legislation or the legalisation of homosexuality and marijuana, which Walker and others on the left advocated. A case arose in which the then Minister for Youth and Community Services, right-wing Catholic Kevin Stewart, refused to allow an abortion for a fifteen-year-old State ward under his control. Without consulting Walker, because she knew he could not be seen to overrule another minister, Gaudron applied to the court on behalf of the Attorney General to intervene with a view to supporting the young girl's case to have an abortion. She took the risk that when the job was done, Walker would support her.

Stewart was furious and threatened to resign when he heard what Gaudron had done. Walker was annoyed, but he supported her as she knew he would. It was an example of 'the power of Gaudron'. She had gauged just how far she could go, but she had 'pushed a big boundary'.[36] Wran was angry with Walker. He told him to back out of the case. Walker agreed on the condition that Stewart, in the course of the case, did not challenge the 1971 NSW District Court 'Levine ruling' that had liberalised abortion law to the extent of placing the burden on the prosecution to prove that the abortion was unlawful.[37] Stewart agreed and was persuaded by Wran not to resign. The 'public spectacle' of two ministers opposing each other in court was avoided.[38]

Gaudron's first appearance in the High Court as Solicitor General attracted attention of a different kind. She was noticeable more because of her form than for the substance of what she had to say. On 6 August 1981 the case of *Actors and Announcers Equity Association v Fontana Films Pty Ltd* came before the Court.[39] It involved the validity of a controversial provision on secondary boycotts in the *Trade Practices Act 1974* (Cth). Gaudron intervened on behalf of NSW and Tasmania. Her black QC's robes were silk. Loose as they were, her advanced state of pregnancy was plain. The press took particular interest, reporting that there was a 'pregnant pause' in the proceedings.[40] The Full Bench of male judges kept straight faces. They had prepared for the unusual appearance, not just of a female Solicitor General but a pregnant one, although not without some concern.

The first issue they deliberated on was how to address her. By convention a Solicitor General was called 'Mr Solicitor'. What would they do? Some judges favoured 'Solicitor', others 'Miss' or 'Mrs Solicitor'. It was resolved to call her Ms Gaudron. Jack Waterford, then a young reporter, surmised that there were judges who thought the dilemma a good enough reason not to have women barristers, not to mention the problem of the shortage of women's toilets. The second concern was the possibility of Gaudron giving birth (or going into labour) before the case was completed. Gaudron's only concern was the persuasiveness of her arguments.

The case went for two days; uncompleted, it was adjourned to 1 September 1981. Gaudron, by then, was nine months pregnant with her son, Patrick. Waterford noticed that Chief Justice Gibbs was 'in a lather' about what would happen should she faint, her waters break, or start giving birth in the courtroom. Gibbs ordered that a doctor be stationed nearby, just in case. Waterford wrote a story about the court scene for his newspaper. Gaudron was not impressed.[41] It was a momentous occasion in her career and it was not her gender or motherhood that were deserving of acknowledgment, but her professional performance. 'She came up screaming at me', Waterford remembered, in what he describes as her vivid language 'which she undoubtedly had learnt to reserve for people like me'. He reported that, by contrast, she restrained herself in front of the very proper Chief Justice Gibbs.[42] Patrick was born almost three weeks later, on 21 September 1981.

Commonwealth versus State power

Gaudron displayed a high level of understanding and expertise in Australian federalism and the interaction of State and Commonwealth powers. It became one of the reasons why she was later recognised as a suitable person to be appointed to the High Court.[43] In 1982 she appeared in *Commonwealth v Hospital Contribution Fund*,[44] a case concerning the arrangements within the State courts for the exercise of federal jurisdiction. Earlier cases had held that in federal cases the judicial power of a State court could only be exercised by its judges, not by its administrative officers.[45] Gaudron put a brave and persuasive submission as to why the High Court should take the unusual step of overruling the two previous High Court decisions on the point. The Court did just that.

Gaudron appeared in the High Court in other significant constitutional cases, some arising from tensions between state and federal governments about tax matters and the distribution of revenue, including *Hematite Petroleum v Victoria* and *Stack v Coast Securities (No 9)*, in 1983 and *Gosford Meats Pty Ltd v New South Wales*, in 1985.[46] She also appeared in *Miller v TCN Channel Nine* in 1985, a case concerning the constitutional guarantee of free trade and commerce between the states (section 92).[47] She gained a reputation for what the *Australian Law Journal* described as 'outstanding and ingenious' advocacy.[48]

Gaudron was a strong advocate of matters in the states' interest. She was paid to be. Her occasional crankiness with the Commonwealth Government about Commonwealth versus State issues indicated her personal support, too, for State autonomy. In December 1983, at a dinner held in Canberra at the end of a day-long seminar conducted by the Australian National University Law School on the *Tasmanian Dam Case*,[49] another important case in which she represented NSW, Gaudron verbally attacked a Commonwealth Attorney General's departmental officer about the States not being given a fair go.[50] Officers of the department and academics, amongst others, were present at the dinner. The discussion heated up. Something was said that made her angry. She let out a loud scream and as heads turned she rose and walked out saying 'I am not going to be insulted by you and particularly not by the Commonwealth'. One of the guests advised another against following her to placate her, noting 'she often does this'.[51]

Gaudron's wariness about Commonwealth interference in the right of the states to legislate is possibly indicative of the influence of her mentor, Frank Hutley. He was a stern critic of centralised control: 'Law reform in Australia in my view should begin by dismantling much of our centralized controls so that the situation we have whereby there is apoplexy at the centre and complete apathy in the limbs is ended.'[52] Gaudron was not, however, so extreme in her view. She took a practical approach. She wanted to see NSW's social reform agenda get underway without obstruction while the people motivated to implement it were in power. On the other hand, she acknowledged that the Commonwealth was the appropriate authority to implement international conventions, such as the convention on the elimination of racial discrimination ratified by the Whitlam Labor Government in 1975. And later, as a justice of the High Court, Gaudron did not display a 'States' rights' philosophy.

In this context, Gaudron had to grapple with the philosophic dilemma that faced the NSW Government in considering whether to intervene in cases that were potential Commonwealth versus States battlefields over the limits of their respective powers. State governments sought to preserve their broad legislative power while the Commonwealth sought to expand its powers in order to achieve its particular policy agenda.

In 1982, Gaudron considered whether or not NSW should intervene to support the validity of the *Racial Discrimination Act 1975* (Cth). The Commonwealth had entered into an international treaty that called for the elimination of all forms of racial discrimination, under section 51(xxix) of the Commonwealth Constitution. To give effect to the treaty, it further relied upon its external affairs power to pass legislation that concerned racial discrimination within Australia. *Koowarta v Bjelke-Petersen*[53] was the first challenge to the Act. The case concerned Queensland Premier Bjelke-Petersen's lands legislation which John Koowarta, a member of the Winychanam Aboriginal group, challenged on the ground that the Queensland legislation was discriminatory under the Commonwealth's racial discrimination legislation.[54] The Queensland Government responded with the claim that the Commonwealth legislation went beyond its constitutional power, and that the State's legislation should prevail. The NSW Government supported the Commonwealth's racial discrimination legislation, and opposed Queensland's discriminatory laws. On the other hand, Commonwealth supremacy over State legislation in the field might put the validity of NSW's own racial discrimination and land rights legislation at risk if any aspect was claimed to be inconsistent with Commonwealth legislation. Intervention was a two-edged sword.[55]

Gaudron advised the NSW Government to take 'the elusive middle ground'. She recommended that NSW intervene to support the Commonwealth's right to legislate with respect to human rights and racial discrimination, but in restricted circumstances. She frankly admitted in her advice that '[i]t must be conceded that no ready argument achieving these objectives springs to mind—although I am not yet convinced that none exists'.[56] She did not have to find one. Western Australia and Victoria intervened to support the Queensland Government and, presumably in the interest of avoiding state divisiveness, NSW did not intervene.

The High Court found Queensland's law to be invalid as it discriminated against Aborigines. The Court held that the Commonwealth's racial discrimination legislation was validly enacted under the external affairs power in ratification of the

International Convention on the Elimination of all forms of Racial Discrimination, entered into by Australia under the external affairs power, and that it took precedence over the Queensland law.

As Gaudron feared, the decision opened the way for a direct challenge to the validity of NSW's *Anti-Discrimination Act* on the ground that the Commonwealth laws 'covered the whole field'. She appeared in the High Court to argue the legality of an investigation, authorised under the NSW legislation, of complaints by three Aborigines who alleged they were refused bar service at a Kempsey hotel in 1980. One of the complainants was Lyall Munro, known to Gaudron as he lived in Moree and had worked on the railways with Gaudron's father. Gaudron attempted to persuade the Court that the Commonwealth and State legislation were not inconsistent and were capable of 'simultaneous obedience'.[57] This was also what the Commonwealth wanted to achieve. The High Court, however, did not agree. In May 1983 it found that to the extent that the NSW provisions were inconsistent with the Commonwealth legislation, they were invalid.[58] Following this case the Commonwealth legislated to 'save' state laws in the field of racial discrimination.[59] But in the meantime, a significant battle arose over the limits of Commonwealth and State power, in the *Tasmanian Dam* case.

The Tasmanian Dam case of 1983

The *Tasmanian Dam* case, a landmark in Australia's constitutional history over the use of the Commonwealth's external affairs power, was one of the most important cases Gaudron appeared in before the High Court.[60] Representing NSW as an intervener again gave rise to a dilemma as to what support, if any, the States should give to the Commonwealth with respect to the supremacy of its legislation. The NSW Government supported the Commonwealth's power to legislate in environmental matters of national interest, yet the exercise of that power potentially infringed States' rights. In Gaudron's opinion, the Commonwealth's power to legislate in matters of national interest concerning the environment, as with human rights, should be supported so long as it could fairly be said that the legislation fell within the external affairs power. Now was the time for her to find an argument in support of that 'elusive middle ground'.

The Tasmanian Government and the Hydro-Electric Commission proposed to build a dam on the Gordon River below its junction with the Franklin River. Federal Labor had made a promise at the 1983 election that, if elected, it would stop the building of the dam in order to preserve the wilderness area of south-western Tasmania. Elected on 5 March 1983, the Hawke Labor Government acted on the issue within the month to strengthen the effect of the *National Parks and Wildlife Conservation Act 1975*,[61] by making the *World Heritage (Western Tasmanian Wilderness) Regulations 1983*, which were gazetted on 31 March. It then introduced the *World Heritage Properties Conservation Act 1983* on the first parliamentary sitting day, 21 April 1983. This Act received royal assent on 22 May 1983, barely nine days before the High Court hearing began. The intertwining issues of environmental protection and Federal-State relationships became a hot issue.

The case consisted of three separate actions. The Commonwealth first sought an injunction to stop further work on the dam on the basis of the Regulations. This pitted the Federal Government against the Gray Liberal Government in Tasmania. The Tasmanian Government responded by seeking a declaration that the Regulations were invalid as being beyond the power of the Commonwealth. After the litigation had commenced, the Commonwealth sought an injunction to stop the dam on the basis of the new Act. As it transpired the Court found the Regulations invalid, and thus the final outcome of the case depended only on the validity of the last-minute litigation over the Act.[62]

The Commonwealth pulled out all stops. It asserted that the Act was supported by the external affairs power, section 51 (xxix) of the Constitution, permitting the Commonwealth to make laws with respect to international treaties, in this case an Act to implement the United Nations Educational, Scientific and Cultural Organization (UNESCO) *Convention for the Protection of the World Cultural and National Heritage*.[63] It also relied upon the corporations power, section 51 (xx), on the basis that the Hydro-Electric

Commission was a trading corporation with respect to which the Commonwealth could make laws. Further, it relied on its power to make laws with respect to the people of any race, section 51(xxvi), arguing in this case that it was necessary to protect from flooding certain archaeological sites of cultural significance to Aborigines.

The hearing commenced in Canberra on 31 May 1983.[64] Gaudron appeared on behalf of NSW to support the Commonwealth in relation to its use of section 51 (xxix), the external affairs power, only.[65] Queensland supported Tasmania. Gaudron was concerned to limit the effect of *Koowarta* by rejecting the idea that the fact of entry into an international treaty is sufficient to trigger the Commonwealth's external affairs power. Rather, she argued that the power should be limited to cases where the treaty gives rise to a relevant international obligation to enact a law, and that the extent of that obligation is what is within the Commonwealth's constitutional power. Gaudron drew attention to Article 34 of the World Heritage convention that recognised the limits of power on a central government in a federation. It is therefore a 'question-begging' clause, she submitted. The power of the Commonwealth Government had first to be ascertained.[66] In this case, she thought that the World Heritage convention fell within this view of the power.

Given the restricted grounds on which NSW intervened, Gaudron made no reference to the Commonwealth's use of the race power or the corporations power under the Constitution. From the views she expressed later about the potential use by the Commonwealth of the corporations power to the possible detriment of the states, it is likely that she deliberately avoided that issue.

The Court, by a majority, upheld the Commonwealth legislation in a manner that broadened the scope of the external affairs power.[67] It also accepted the Commonwealth's argument as to the other heads of power. The case drew considerable criticism from supporters of States' rights and some constitutional lawyers who thought that the Court had taken an 'activist' approach to constitutional interpretation at the expense of the States. Discussion mostly centred on the use that could be made by the Commonwealth of the external affairs power. Justice Mason defended the decision, pointing out that the widening of the Commonwealth's legislative scope under the external affairs power was more a result of the widening concerns of the international community than of any activism on the part of the Court.

Gaudron, as Solicitor General, forecast adverse consequences for the legislative powers of the states. In a report on the case to the NSW Attorney General, she pointed to statements made by Mason in his judgment about the breadth of areas to which Commonwealth legislative power might extend in future.[68] She noted that the race power remained to be clarified in the course of its further use, but more particularly, she pointed out the potential for use to be made of the corporations power—greater than the external affairs power—to encroach on matters over which the States had control. She said: 'The Commonwealth power with respect to corporations poses more immediate problems for State Government than any other matter considered in the Tasmanian decision.'[69] In this regard Gaudron showed foresight as the Commonwealth subsequently made great use of the corporations power and, as it happened, in the ensuing twenty years, little use of treaties to legislate in fields generally regarded as belonging to the States.

Gaudron had already pointed out the potential reach of Commonwealth power after the High Court's decision in the case of *Fencott v Muller* a month earlier.[70] In that case the same majority as in the *Tasmania Dam* case held that 'trading corporations' include corporations which have never traded but which were incorporated for the purpose of trading. She believed that a similar view could be taken of 'financial corporations' which also come under the corporations power. She now seriously questioned whether at least some of NSW's statutory corporations should not be unincorporated to avoid such consequences. She concluded that the *Tasmanian Dam* decision emphasised and confirmed a trend towards the expansion by constitutional interpretation of central power and the practical consequence of contraction of state power 'unless co-operative arrangements are made at intergovernmental level' to ensure continued state regulation in fields considered appropriate for state governments. She warned: 'If the wider view [of the court] were to prevail and the Commonwealth were to exercise its powers, it would not be fanciful to imagine a situation in which there was one law for companies and another law for everyone else.'[71]

It was not fanciful. The High Court did just that twenty-three years later. In the 2006 *WorkChoices* case it upheld the Howard Government's 2005 WorkChoices legislation as an exercise of the corporations power.[72] It was a significant decision. Justice Kirby who dissented in the case, commented that '[o]nce a constitutional Rubicon such as this is crossed, there is rarely a going back'.[73] There was an ironic moment when the majority's reasons for decision in the *WorkChoices* case drew support from Gaudron's reasoning in a previous decision she had given as a High Court judge in 2000.[74] Kirby believes that Gaudron's reasons were 'quoted out of context and for a different purpose'. However, he added, '[t]his is the way the law sometimes develops and changes'.[75] The use, or misuse, of Gaudron's reasoning is the more notable because she was in dissent in the case and whatever she said had no binding authority. According to Professor Tony Blackshield, the joint judgment of the majority 'gives no convincing explanation of *why* the new regime is supported by corporations power'.[76]

Severing legal links to Britain

Gaudron enjoyed what might be called a gentle bullying role in contributing to Australia's movement away from the traditional constitutional links to the United Kingdom. Both privately and professionally she was committed to Australia having the final say on constitutional matters. She felt strongly about the need to sever Australia's legal ties with the British and to end the existing limited right to appeal to the Privy Council on matters heard by State supreme courts.[77] In a legal sense, the residual constitutional links meant that the States, eighty years after Federation, were still colonies of the United Kingdom. Gaudron thought this was offensive to many and was not conducive to efficient public administration. In 1982 she said: 'Perhaps one might hope that by our 200th birthday, the imperial constitutional fetters will have been recognised as inappropriate and our legislative, judicial and executive independence guaranteed.'[78]

Gaudron was thrown into the issue within weeks of commencing as Solicitor General. In reporting on a meeting of the Standing Committees of Attorneys General and Solicitors General on 10 April 1981, she noted that 'Buckingham Palace' wanted to avoid receiving conflicting advice from different Australian representatives in dealing with the severing of residual constitutional links.[79]

Gaudron recognised that the Commonwealth's support for a unified approach had, since mid-1979, been the main obstacle to progress on the issue. The States were uncomfortable with the Prime Minister of the Commonwealth providing advice to the Queen on State matters. On the other hand, they were unable to agree among themselves on what should be achieved and how it should be achieved. Not surprisingly, pronounced Gaudron when giving a speech on the matter in 1982, given the inability of the Australian States 'to agree even on the time of day'.[80] In considering ways of overcoming the problem, she suggested that the simplest approach was to press the Commonwealth to consent to legislation passed by three agreeing States, NSW, Tasmania and Victoria, so that they could proceed alone to sever the British links affecting them.[81]

In November 1979 the *Privy Council Appeals Abolition Bill* (NSW), which, if enacted would sever one aspect of legal ties to Britain, passed through both houses with bipartisan support. It had been forwarded to the Governor where, because of constitutional uncertainty, it was left 'in legislative limbo in the Governor's desk drawer'.[82] In 1982 Walker, impatient with the slow progress, wanted to proceed with the Bill. Gaudron advised against it. Respecting her advice, Walker refrained from re-presenting it to the Governor for his consent.[83]

At the Premiers' Conference of 24–25 June 1983 agreement was reached between the States on the measures to be taken, but the Commonwealth continued to be obstructive, citing the concern of 'the Palace' about receiving advice from a number of different places.[84] In October 1983 Gaudron played a remarkable role in overcoming the stalemate.[85] She travelled to London to argue a Privy Council appeal on behalf of NSW. On 25 October she took the opportunity of discussing the matter of the residual constitutional links with the British Foreign and Commonwealth Office. She left an impression. A Foreign Office official wrote to the British High Commissioner in Australia:

> Ms Gaudron came bristling with prejudice and holding a deep conviction that we were in collusion with the Commonwealth government at the expense of the States. She also thought it was the British Government which was imposing impossible restrictions on proposals for severing the residual constitutional links.[86]

The letter pointed out that it was 'abundantly clear that the Commonwealth government' had to some extent misrepresented the British position, to disguise the fact that it was Prime Minister Hawke's Department, not the British Government, which objected to some suggested proposals.

In November 1983 Gaudron provided her own report of the meeting. Although she was told that 'the Palace' was not 'overly keen' on direct access by State premiers to the Queen, she reported her understanding that there would be no objection so long as the Queen received advice from one source only in relation to any particular matter. This, however, was not the impression the British officials intended to give.[87] Nevertheless, in the light of Gaudron's report, the Commonwealth Attorney General's Department advised the British Government that the 'direct access' proposal was the 'only game in town'.[88] The British Government, in turn, accepted the importance of direct communication with the States.[89] The State Solicitors General put together a new proposal whereby advice to the Queen would be given by one Premier on behalf of all of the States to avoid future misunderstandings by the British on State positions. As a result, in November 1983, from what has been described as a 'fortuitous misunderstanding' between Gaudron and British authorities—'a clash between the direct and blunt style of the Solicitor General and the excessively subtle use of the language of diplomacy by the British officials'— the impasse was finally broken.[90]

There was still work to be done. Negotiations continued between the States and, as late as November 1984, Gaudron noted that the British authorities had not yet given agreement to direct access by State premiers to the Palace. The matter would be discussed between the Prime Minister and the Queen the following February 1985.[91] In the meantime, High Court Justice Lionel Murphy made his views known on the issue of appeals to the Privy Council. He did so in a High Court judgment he gave in November 1984 when considering the issue of leave to appeal to the Privy Council. He expressed the opinion that

> [t]he Australian parliament has ample legislative powers to abolish appeals or purported appeals to the Privy Council from State courts.
>
> This Court has been slow to accept that the States are no longer colonies of the British Empire, but are constituent parts of the Commonwealth of Australia which is an independent nation in the international community, equal in status and not subordinate to the United Kingdom.[92]

Murphy, Gaudron's friend, had been a strong campaigner for the abolition of the right of appeal to the Privy Council. According to Justice Michael Kirby, the appeal right to the Privy Council, though limited, upset and irritated Murphy throughout the course of his legal life.[93]

On 19 June 1985 the word came through that the Palace accepted the States' draft legislation incorporating the direct access proposal. Gaudron heard the news some weeks earlier through the Solicitors General grapevine.[94] She broke into song, incorporating it into her report, despite her usual atrocious lack of rhythm and rhyme. She incorporated an apology in parenthesis that signalled her awareness that her poetry was wanting:

> Ah wasn't Her Majesty so surprised
> To realise
> Premiers are well advised
> Neat and clean and civilized

Michael Emmett and the I.R.A.[95]
Whack for the diddle oh di do dé.

In 1986 the *Australia (Request and Consent) Act* was quietly passed with bipartisan support in all States as part of an exercise in which the Commonwealth Parliament, and finally the United Kingdom Parliament, legislated to end the last vestiges of colonial links.[96] This included abolition of the right to appeal from State courts to the United Kingdom's Privy Council. The right to appeal to the Privy Council was removed in time for Gaudron to take her place on the High Court of Australia as the final court of appeal in all matters, but not before the death of Lionel Murphy, who had been so strong an advocate for that outcome.

Chapter Eleven

CRIME AND CORRUPTION

The point need not be laboured, but the consequences of corruption are devastating for a police service as a whole, and for its individual members. They are similarly devastating for the community which police are expected to serve.[1]

Wran's troubles—law, but not much order

The 1980s was a decade of political and social ferment, controversy and scandal in New South Wales—a period of constant drama—demanding the Solicitor General's intense involvement. Gaudron had to advise about whatever was currently happening; and at that time everything was happening.[2] Mounting allegations of crime and corruption amongst police, politicians and the judiciary gave rise to complex legal issues. It was a role that would bring her into the public spotlight and leave her vulnerable to accusations of protecting her political bosses. Her principles, professionalism and objectivity would be tested.

The difficulty of Gaudron's role was in part the result of NSW Premier Neville Wran's reluctance to acknowledge the depth of corruption in the NSW Police.³ In 1979, he had dismissed police corruption as a problem of a few 'rotten apples in the police force barrel'.⁴ However, it was to become clear that the rotting apples rose to the top and rotted others in the process. In 1981 the Labor Party under Wran won its third successive election. Boosted by the increasing electoral popularity of his government, Wran showed little interest in dealing with corruption allegations against police and politicians.⁵ He also took little action on the growing signs of infiltration of criminal elements into the Labor Party. He was similarly slow to realise how difficult the corruption of people in powerful positions made the work of law enforcers like Gaudron.

Extraordinary demands were made of Gaudron. She commenced in her post at a time when investigations were being launched into the affairs of the Nugan Hand Bank, the 'Mr Asia' drug syndicate, the activities of crime boss 'Abe' Saffron, the 'bashing' of Member of Parliament Peter Baldwin; and the stacking of the Enmore branch of the ALP and falsification of its records, to name a few. Out of the investigations arose prosecutions and law enforcement proceedings connected with them.⁶ In the absence of a NSW Director of Public Prosecutions, a position created later, it was the Solicitor General who advised on the evidence required to support prosecutions, the investigations required, whether prosecutions should proceed, and which potential witnesses should be given indemnity against prosecution.

In 1980, Wran appointed Justice Donald Stewart to head a Royal Commission into the affairs of the Nugan Hand group. A year later he appointed Stewart to head a Royal Commission into the 'Mr Asia' drug syndicate. The political scandals unearthed by these inquiries generated speculation and disagreement about the full extent of the powerful network, police and politicians included, behind organised crime in NSW.⁷ At the same time, the closer law enforcement agencies were to bringing crime bosses to justice, the more vulnerable those who headed them were to threats. In Stewart's case, threats of physical harm required him to have round-the-clock police protection, and in Walker's case, as Attorney General, from attacks on his reputation, most notably the

Love Boat scandal. Gaudron, as Solicitor General, suffered allegations of political bias in some of her recommendations concerning prosecutions, and of 'doing deals' to protect her political bosses.

There were various reasons why prosecutions might not be pursued or, if pursued, succeed. The 'Enmore conspiracy case' that related to branch stacking activities in the branch of the Enmore Labor Party demonstrated to Gaudron the difficulty of securing convictions against powerful and well-connected people. It was a politically significant case. There was evidence that criminal elements had infiltrated inner-city branches of the ALP. The Left accused the Right of failing to act. In July 1980, left-wing Labor MP, Peter Baldwin, who, as a member of the State ALP's Credentials Committee, had been investigating complaints of branch stacking and falsification of records in the Branch, was badly beaten. No one was charged with his assault. Police did, however, lay more than 700 charges against six people, in relation to the branch-stacking allegations.

One of those charged was the Secretary of the Enmore Branch, Joe Meissner. He was also owner of the vessel, the *Kanzen*, or the *Love Boat*, as it became known. Virginia Perger, the prostitute at the centre of the *Love Boat* scandal, was his former girlfriend. The *Love Boat* scandal is thought also to have arisen from internal brawling in the Labor Party and its connections with the criminal underworld.[8] Attorney General Walker was allegedly identified with federal Labor politician Senator Graham Richardson and other public figures as having engaged in a sexual romp with prostitute Virginia Perger while partying on the *Love Boat*. Unconvincingly, Perger also named federal Liberal politician Andrew Peacock and others unlikely to be socialising with Labor politicians. Walker and Richardson, as well as Peacock, vigorously denied they were involved. Perger, lured by money to feed a drug habit, had lied. In 1986 she was charged with perjury and pleaded guilty. Frank Walker believed that the *Love Boat* scandal was a targeted attack to discredit him because of significant inquiries he had made about links between Nugan Hand's activities and the criminal underworld, and corrupt ALP members. The links were there. The problem was to unravel the network of influence.

The Enmore case might have gone some way to achieve that result. Charges laid against Meissner and others, mostly for conspiracy and forgery, were heard between February and April 1982. The prosecution case was weakened by the 'lapse of memory' of some of its witnesses. There were suggestions that some witnesses changed their mind about giving evidence. In May 1982, Deputy Chief Magistrate Bruce Brown discharged all defendants on all charges. He noted that the strength of the prosecution case appeared to have been improperly undermined.

Gaudron was asked to advise on the conduct of the case and its outcome. She concluded that Brown erred in his reasons for dismissing some of the charges relating to the Enmore records but, notwithstanding, she found that the evidence would not have supported the charges laid.[9] She was critical of the prosecution's approach. She noted the use of the 'wheelbarrow technique', whereby the prosecution puts forward everything it has, including material that is not necessarily admissible under the rules of evidence. She found that Deputy Chief Magistrate Brown was presented with a case of unmanageable proportions and that the prosecution's flawed approach made 'factual analysis well nigh impossible'.

The press snapped up the finding, according to one headline: 'Magistrate "wrong" in Enmore case'.[10] The fuss over the case caused a renewed police inquiry into it. Gaudron's assessment was confirmed, and no further action was recommended. Joe Meissner escaped culpability, although he was later gaoled for other offences.

Gaudron more controversially advised that there was insufficient evidence to prosecute Deputy Police Commissioner, Bill Allen, despite findings of criminal conduct by a police tribunal. Wran suffered from accusations that he, and by implication Gaudron, did not pursue Allen vigorously.[11] The Bill Allen affair started to unfold after the 1981 election, shaking Premier Wran out of his complacency. Public concern had been growing about police corruption when, inexplicably, Wran had appointed Allen Chief Superintendent, Metropolitan Area, against advice and ignored corruption allegations against him. Allen advanced through the ranks rapidly and became Deputy Commissioner of

Police before being brought down by his association with Abraham Saffron.

Late in 1981 Justice William Perrignon headed a police inquiry into Allen's conduct as Deputy Police Commissioner. When questioned in 1982 at the inquiry, Allen did not deny meeting Saffron at police headquarters seven times in 1981.[12] Perrignon's report in February 1982 stated that Allen had obtained free trips to Las Vegas from crime figures for himself and his family, and that he had large amounts of income for which he could not account. Perrignon found Allen's conduct brought discredit on the Police, or was likely to do so. He regarded Allen's association with Saffron 'with serious suspicion'.

Specific allegations were made against Allen that on five occasions in 1981 he had paid $500 to Sergeant Warren Molloy to induce him 'to act contrary to his duty'. Allen pleaded guilty to four departmental charges of bribery, and accepted demotion to the rank of sergeant (first class), and resigned in April 1982 on an annual pension of around $20,000, rather than being dismissed. Wran denied at the time that there had been any deal.[13] Later, Allen asserted that a deal had been done, in which he alleged Gaudron participated.

In May 1982 Gaudron studied the evidence and the findings of the 1981 Perrignon inquiry, and found that there was insufficient evidence to prosecute Allen.[14] Justice Perrignon had not made any recommendation for criminal charges to be laid against Allen, and there was no other evidence available to Gaudron. The Fraser Government was critical of the inadequacy of the penalty imposed on Allen and sought a joint Federal-State police inquiry into possible links between members of the NSW Police Force and crime syndicates in the USA. Wran, under pressure to show that he had no wrongful association with Allen, immediately made available the police inquiry report and papers concerning Allen. He requested that Gaudron re-examine whether further action should be taken against Allen for perjury, bribery, consorting, or breach of police rules.[15] In September 1982, with the benefit of the advice of the then Crown Solicitor Hugh Roberts that there was insufficient evidence to take further action, Gaudron reaffirmed her earlier advice.[16]

Criminal proceedings were eventually taken against Allen in 1987. He was committed for trial on five counts of bribery and five of obstructing the course of justice. When the proceedings eventually came to the court in 1991, Allen argued that he had done 'a deal' in April 1982 with the then Police Minister, Peter Anderson, Gaudron as Solicitor General, and the then Crown Solicitor, Hugh Roberts, that no further action would be taken if he pleaded guilty to the administrative charges.[17] Gaudron was a Justice of the High Court at the time. Hugh Roberts gave evidence denying that he or Gaudron gave any such undertaking at the meeting they had with Allen's legal counsel in 1982. Allen was eventually found guilty.

The treatment of Bill Allen by the police tribunal in contrast to the treatment of whistleblower Sergeant Philip Arantz caused a political problem for Wran, not assisted by the advice Gaudron gave in respect to Arantz's case. Gaudron inherited the Arantz claim for review of his treatment. In 1971, while working in the computer section of the NSW Police, Arantz gave various statistics to the *Sydney Morning Herald*. These showed that the crime rate in 1971 was 75 percent higher than indicated by the official figures used by the then Police Commissioner Norman Allan. For the unauthorised disclosure, Arantz was dismissed without a pension in January 1972. In a further insult, Norman Allan negotiated an early retirement in May of that year, with a pension and two years' salary. Arantz spent thirteen years seeking redress for unfair dismissal. Wran had encouraged Arantz in his fight by taking up his case when in Opposition.[18] On becoming Premier he encountered legal difficulties in meeting Arantz's claim for compensation. Gaudron, who reviewed the case, was one of the obstacles.

In 1983 Gaudron advised Wran that she agreed with the previous Solicitor General that there had been no miscarriage of justice. Arantz had breached police rules. His subsequent refusal to answer questions concerning his actions when charged with the breach gave her no confidence that he would in future abide by routine police discipline. Gaudron typically advised case by case;

she left the political consequences to others. The anomaly in the outcome was the disparity between Arantz's treatment and that of corrupt Deputy Police Commissioner, Bill Allen, who had been allowed to retire, after demotion, with a pension. Both Bill Allen and Norman Allan fared better than the whistleblower, Arantz.

Arantz pursued the matter at the political level. A compromise was negotiated in 1985. Arantz received $250,000 on his undertaking not to engage in any further public debate about the issue. It was an outcome a long time in coming. The result left Arantz with bitter feelings towards NSW Police, and Gaudron.[19]

The Barton case became another embarrassment for Wran in which Gaudron was implicated. Committal proceedings had commenced against Alexander Barton and his son Thomas for conspiring to cheat and defraud Bounty Oil Company. In the course of the mine and share boom of 1969 and 1970, speculation in mining and oil exploration companies was rife. Laurence Gruzman, QC, who had acted for the Bartons, was also charged. He reacted with allegations of a cover-up by Wran and Walker over share transactions by Sir Peter Abeles (Thomas National Transport) and his business partner Sir Arthur George. In 1982, towards the end of the long-running Barton saga, Gaudron, faced with advice that the case against the three men was not sufficiently strong to warrant the expense of continuing the proceedings, recommended that no further evidence be offered.[20] The last of the charges against the Bartons was then dropped. The Government agreed to pay Gruzman a substantial sum in legal costs and Gruzman agreed to withdraw his allegations against the Government.

The Leader of the Opposition, John Dowd, suggested that a deal had been done that involved the dropping of charges against Gruzman. Walker jumped to Gaudron's defence, stating, in the Legislative Assembly, that such a claim impugned not only the magistrates, but also Gaudron, and John Coombs, QC, who represented Gruzman:

> I knew he [Dowd] was a worm but I didn't think he would stand up in this House and reduce the reputation of a woman [Miss Gaudron] whose reputation is without peer in the legal

profession of this country and reduce the reputation of John Coombs, who is eminent in his profession.[21]

By this time, according to his biographers, 'Wran was starting to discover...that he was not immune, despite his public popularity, from strong attacks on his integrity. But his problems over corruption allegations were only just beginning.'[22]

Wran managed to quell the trouble for a time but it resurfaced in 1983. Rex Jackson, Minister for Corrective Services, resigned from the Legislative Assembly after he was exposed for corruptly receiving payments associated with development applications and the prisoners' early release scheme. This left Gaudron with the distasteful task of advising on issues surrounding the prosecution of a former minister. At the same time, a more serious crisis was unfolding.

The network of influence

Allegations surfaced against Wran himself, and later, against Gaudron's friend, High Court Justice Lionel Murphy. This put Gaudron in an awkward and unenviable position given that, as the State's second law officer, reliance was placed on her advice concerning the associated legal issues. Dubious dealings between Chief Magistrate Murray Farquhar, solicitor Morgan Ryan, George Freeman—generously described as 'a colourful racing personality'—Police Commissioner Merv Wood, and Balmain Leagues Club Secretary-Manager Kevin Humphreys, dragged Wran (a friend of the last two) and Murphy (a friend of the first two), into places from where it proved difficult to extricate themselves.

The origins of any deal were likely to be on the racecourse:

> The races, and the betting associated with them, are woven into the fabric of Sydney life. The racecourse is a meeting place for politicians, businessmen, lawyers and magistrates. It is where many illegal casino operators and other criminals spend their large earnings and make their contacts with influential members of the political and legal establishment.[23]

It has to be asked why people in public positions tend to be attracted to other powerful people without regard to whether they are of good character or repute. The racecourse, the hub of the 'network of influence', seems to provide added magnetism. Mateships are formed, alcohol flows, things are said, gambling debts become leverage for favours, favours are traded and people in public positions are compromised. The casinos that thrived on illegal gambling were patronised, too, by police, magistrates and some politicians, as well as ordinary punters.[24]

Trouble for Wran came in the form of his friend Kevin Humphreys' gambling debts. The ABC aired a *Four Corners* program in April 1983 alleging that Wran tried to influence a case in 1977 in which Humphreys was charged with misappropriation of more than $50,000 from the Balmain Leagues Club's accounts to pay gambling debts. The magistrate, Kevin Jones, had dismissed all twelve charges against Humphreys. The NSW Crown Law office sought a report from Jones. He said that Chief Magistrate Murray Farquhar told him on the morning of the hearing that Premier Wran wanted charges against Humphreys dismissed, though Jones denied that he had been influenced.

Politically the Government had no option but to launch an inquiry into the matter. Wran sued the ABC for defaming him and stood down from the premiership for three months while the Chief Justice, Sir Laurence Street, headed a Royal Commission that inquired into the committal proceedings against Humphreys, and Farquhar's role in them.

Chief Magistrate Farquhar had been involved in controversies before but had retained Wran's support. Eventually Wran pressured Farquhar to retire.[25] Before Farquhar did so, he had time to cause more havoc and more embarrassment for Wran. When Gaudron was asked to review the cases, she found that the way in which they were handled by Police Commissioner Merv Wood and solicitor Morgan Ryan had indeed been suspicious.

As Chief Stipendiary Magistrate, Farquhar presided over the cases of Roy Cessna and Timothy Milner. They had been arrested on 1 March 1979 and charged with possession of a large amount of Indian hemp. They appeared before Farquhar the next day.[26] The material available to Gaudron suggested that Police Commissioner Merv Wood had received an approach from a friend, solicitor and ALP stalwart Morgan Ryan, who was also a friend of Farquhar, raising the issue of the value placed on the drugs. Possession of illicit drugs above a certain value is an indictable offence that cannot be dealt with by a magistrate. Ryan was representing Police Commissioner Wood at the time in another matter—a conflict of interest that was ignored. The value of the drugs was reduced, permitting Farquhar to deal with the charges summarily, as less serious offences with lesser penalties. Gaudron noted the impropriety of this, given the actual quantity of drugs. Milner received a gaol sentence shorter than the minimum sentence prescribed for an indictable offence. Cessna was given a good behaviour bond and a fine. Farquhar handed out the sentences on 24 May 1979, his last day on the bench.

An internal police inquiry took place to ascertain whether there was sufficient evidence to charge the solicitor, Morgan Ryan, with conspiring with Police Commissioner Wood and Chief Magistrate Farquhar, to have Ryan's clients sentenced more leniently than the law required. Wood and Farquhar declined to be interviewed, and gave short statements. Ryan and his client Cessna refused to be interviewed. Wood resigned the next day in a letter that made no reference to this event, but to other allegations. Clarence Briese replaced Farquhar as Chief Magistrate.

Gaudron's predecessor, Greg Sullivan, QC, had investigated the matter and could not establish that Farquhar had a hand in it. Sullivan concluded that '...we can only be suspicious that the law was bent by [Wood]...to oblige a friend [Ryan], a common but tolerated source of trouble in this community'.[27] It was another case of justice being thwarted by tight connections between powerful people. Nevertheless, it was not the end of public scrutiny of the Cessna-Milner case or Farquhar's role in it. Ryan was, indeed, a central and troublesome figure with influential connections with the judiciary, the police and significant figures in the crime world. Investigations into Ryan's role in this case would lead to others.

In the meantime, the Street Royal Commission into the Kevin Humphreys matter reported in July 1983. While scathing of Chief Magistrate Farquhar, it cleared Wran of any wrongdoing. It found that Farquhar 'did influence' the outcome of committal proceedings in 1977 against Kevin Humphreys, but that he was not acting at the request or direction of Wran.[28] Wran resumed as Premier on 28 July 1983.[29]

The Street report was not released until Gaudron and the Crown Solicitor, Hugh Roberts, considered it over the weekend, though aspects of it were leaked to the press.[30] The Leader of the Opposition, Nick Greiner, accused Wran of stage-managing the release of the findings; an assertion which Attorney General Paul Landa said was unfounded. Gaudron and Roberts also advised on whether the Street Royal Commission's report should be released to the public through the media. They were in a bind. They advised that any charges to be laid against Humphreys or Farquhar should be laid before any publication of the report. However, in that event, publication of the report might be attacked as prejudicing a fair trial. They therefore concluded that if there were reasons for releasing the report, it should only be tabled in Parliament, and only after any charges were laid.[31]

In an advice of 1 August 1983, Gaudron supported the recommendation of an *ex officio* indictment against Kevin Humphreys, that is, an indictment presented directly to the court by the Attorney General, instead of after committal proceedings before a magistrate. Proceedings were also commenced in March 1984 against Farquhar for perverting the course of justice.[32]

Providing advice on the prosecution of Kevin Humphreys might have been unpalatable to Gaudron, but by 1984 she would be providing crucial advice on evidentiary matters in which her friend, High Court Justice Murphy, was implicated. She had a rough time looming ahead with political commentators suggesting that her advisory role was compromised by her political friendships and by her closeness to Justice Murphy in particular. Trouble would surface with the publication of the infamous *Age* tapes that would implicate other public officials, including Justice Murphy, in alleged criminal activities. For Gaudron, it also raised alarm bells about the extent of unauthorised and illegal police telephone tapping, which was a source of professional concern for her. The

Age tapes saga and the allegations made by then Chief Stipendiary Magistrate, Clarence Briese, that followed, put Gaudron's professional integrity and personal resources to the test.

The '*Age* tapes'

The dubbed name was a misnomer.[33] The '*Age* tapes' consisted of three cassette 'tapes' which were copies, not originals, of recordings, and some 523 pages of written material that purported either to be transcripts of intercepted telephone conversations or summaries of them, all suggestive of influential links between NSW crime figures and public officials. Extracts were published by the *Age* newspaper in a series of articles, the first of which appeared on 2 February 1984 under the heading 'Network of influence'. It did not identify the names the transcripts recorded as the speakers. However, names soon surfaced in various parliamentary proceedings, and other newspapers picked up the story.

Solicitor Morgan Ryan was central to the network. He had extensive contact with known criminal, Abe Saffron, and was one of his lawyers. He had frequent dealings with Chief Magistrate Farquhar and regular contact with High Court justice, Lionel Murphy. Ryan and Murphy had worked together as lawyers for a decade or so.[34] Wran had also worked with Ryan in the law, and Murphy and Wran were close friends.

Some of the material had come to light in July 1983 in the course of the Stewart Royal Commission into the 'Mr Asia' drug trafficking syndicate, but had not been widely publicised.[35] Further, in November 1983 the *National Times* had based an article headed 'Big shots bugged' on material sourced to Morgan Ryan's telephone.[36]

At the same time as the *Age* received the material in February 1984, the same material was delivered to Senator Gareth Evans and Paul Landa, then the Federal Attorney General and NSW Attorney General respectively. Landa referred the material to Gaudron as Solicitor General for advice on the value of the tapes and transcriptions as evidence to support prosecutions of suspected perpetrators of crime.[37] For Gaudron, there was an important preliminary issue, namely, that if the material was what it purported to be, it had been obtained illegally by the NSW Police. This was a matter needing investigation in itself. Wran, too, a decade before, had expressed concern about unlawful telephone tapping by police.[38]

It was later established that the material in the hands of the *Age* had been generated from illegal phone taps on such people as Bob Trimbole, George Freeman, Abraham Saffron and Morgan Ryan by members of the NSW Police in order to obtain evidence about drug trafficking.[39] The initial interception of Ryan's telephone conversations took place because of conversations overheard during the continuing interception of the telephone conversations of Ryan's client, Roy Cessna, after his arrest in March 1979.[40] One of the summaries of the alleged phone conversations suggested that Ryan and Farquhar were making arrangements for a 'happy' outcome for Cessna's court proceedings.

Publication of the *Age* material caught and maintained the public's attention. The focus was less on the criminal phone-tapping activity, much to Gaudron's frustration, and more on the allegations of improper conduct by 'Mr Justice Murphy of the High Court of Australia'.[41] Wran and Murphy, or names that conceivably may have referred to them, were some of the people mentioned as having been spoken to about various matters. There was nothing, though, that implicated either Wran or Murphy in any wrongdoing. In fact, the material went the other way with respect of Wran's integrity, suggesting he was an obstacle to the plans.

Gaudron advised Wran that the *Telecommunications (Interception) Act 1979* (Cth) prevented disclosure of any material obtained from telephone taps. In a twenty-two page preliminary advice of 17 February 1984, she stated that even she could be in breach of the law in the course of providing advice, as could a person quoting from them in Parliament. She set out the grounds on which she assessed that the *Age* material was unsafe and unreliable material on which to base charges, unless and until it was authenticated.[42] If the material was authentic, it appeared that the interception was not authorised under the *Telecommunications (Interception) Act*. Her advice, without the supplement that reproduced some of the material, was tabled in the NSW Parliament on 21 February 1984.

As a consequence of her advice, Gaudron was accused of facilitating delay. Wran's biographers point out that it suited Wran to 'muddy the waters' over the issue of authenticity of the 'tape' material for a considerable period, 'long enough, as it turned out, to enable the Government to be re-elected' in March 1984.[43] The Leader of the Opposition, Nick Greiner, accused the Government of 'hiding behind the skirts of the Solicitor General' to avoid holding an inquiry into the substance of the tapes and documents.[44]

However, Gaudron had studied the material carefully. The tapes were clearly not original recordings of intercepted telephone conversations, and she noted that the locations of the originals were not known. Listening to the tapes, she found that there were suggestions of editing from changes of speech patterns and speed or both, and possibly 'patching' of conversations. Only one transcript bore any relation to one of the three cassette tapes. There were no tapes corresponding to the other bundles purporting to be transcripts of or summaries of telephone conversations by which to gauge their accuracy or authenticity. She also found that the summaries were inaccurate or misleading and, in at least one, 'in a most serious respect'. She concluded: 'There is thus no measure by which their accuracy or authenticity can be assessed. Without such authentication they are wholly worthless documents from any legal perspective.'[45] Gaudron therefore recommended that a full technical assessment and evaluation be obtained from Commonwealth authorities. She recommended that the Federal and State police co-operate in any subsequent investigations, and that any member of the police found to be involved in illegal telephone interceptions be disciplined.

The dilemma was that this offered no incentive to the police involved to come forward. Yet none of the material would be admissible in a court without the evidence of those who heard the conversations to verify that the material was a true record of them. More than that, there were problems in identifying the people alleged to be conversing. Then there was the illegality of the method by which, if verified, the material was collected.

Importantly, in the supplement to her advice, not tabled in Parliament, Gaudron drew attention to the inaccurately published conversation in the *Age*, the only one with both a tape recording and a corresponding transcript. First, the speaker identified as the 'Judge' was assigned the words spoken by the 'Solicitor' according to the transcript, so that the *Age* reported that the 'Judge' talked of his drunkenness and sexual achievements, whereas the transcript revealed it was the 'Solicitor'. Secondly, the *Age* had the 'Solicitor' stating that he could arrange girls for the 'Judge', whereas there was no mention in the transcript of this having been said by anyone. Gaudron quoted from the *Age*'s purported transcript:

> Solicitor: Did you have a good time?
> Judge: If you can call getting tired and drunk and f… everything a good time, yeah…

The transcript provided to Gaudron went like this:

> Solicitor: What's happening? I only just this minute got off the plane. I just arrived home half an hour ago.
> Judge: Yeah, and how did you go?
> Solicitor: Oh, alright.
> Judge: Did you have a good time?
> Solicitor: If you can call getting tired and drunk and f…everything a good time, yeah—What's happening?
> Judge: Oh nothin'. Nothin's happening.[46]

The shabby and inaccurate reporting had already had its public effect. The *Age* acknowledged the error, but not until some two weeks later, and not by way of an apology but in the course of an article under the heading, 'Wran points out error in police tape article'.[47] The *Sydney Morning Herald* did better, reporting the error under the headline 'Newspaper gave inaccurate report of police phone taps'.[48]

Gaudron's main concern was that if NSW Police did conduct unlawful telephone taps, they should be disciplined. She said that '[t]he judge was participating in private telephone conversations. Those conversations should, in accordance with law, have remained private.' Attorney General Landa was extravagant in support of this view. On 21 February 1984, he stated that unless there had been attempts to authenticate the material, 'it would be a monstrous abuse of the legal process to subject people to some kind of inquisition as to unauthenticated documents, many of which contain hearsay, innuendo, rumour and falsity'.

Gaudron's advice that, assuming the tapes and documents were what they purported to be, disclosure of any of the material, even in Parliament, would be a breach of the *Telecommunications (Interception) Act* (Cth), further complicated an already complex matter.[49] On 22 February 1984, the Speaker, Lawrence Kelly, followed Gaudron's advice and took the unusual step of disallowing all questions in the Legislative Assembly about the crime tapes. It was a very different ruling from one he had made on 14 September 1983 when he had said, 'I do not feel that any statute—be it of this or any other State or of the Commonwealth—should, as has been stated elsewhere, take precedence over parliamentary privilege in this State.'[50] This, too, had been a direct response to Gaudron's advice at the time, triggered by a controversy caused by Attorney General Peter Duncan speaking in the House of Assembly of South Australia about Mr Justice Hope's Royal Commission into the Combe-Ivanov affair.[51] On that occasion, Gaudron declared that the law did not inhibit discussion of the Commission proceedings in Parliament, and that the press was also protected by the same privilege.[52]

Kelly, troubled by the inconsistency, revised his ruling later in the day, acknowledging that it was too restrictive, and decided to deal with matters involving the tapes as they arose. It was embarrassing for both him and Gaudron. Gaudron felt compelled to explain the apparent inconsistency. She wrote a letter the same day to the *Sydney Morning Herald* in which she explained, somewhat over-legalistically, that her advice in September 1983 concerned the operation of legislation which did not distinguish between the privilege of Parliament and the privilege of the press to report the proceedings of Parliament, unlike the *Telecommunications (Interception) Act, 1979* (Cth) which expressly bound the Crown.[53] She had not had a change of view, and she did not want to be seen as inconsistent. Landa indicated that investigations into the material would not now wait for it to be authenticated.

While concerned about the authenticity of the material, in April 1984 Gaudron nevertheless identified five lines of inquiry arising out of the material. The outcome of one in particular vindicated her cautious approach to publication of the material. It concerned an overheard conversation that implicated John Ducker, a prominent figure in the NSW Labor Party's Right faction, in accepting a bribe. Gaudron noted that Ducker was only implicated because the initials 'JD' were mentioned in the transcript and there was nothing in the material to justify the allegation.[54] In May 1984 an internal police inquiry cleared him and, on reviewing it, Gaudron and the Crown Solicitor Hugh Roberts agreed. Landa accepted their assessment. The Stewart Royal Commission also cleared Ducker of any impropriety.

Another suggested line of inquiry raised by the *Age* 'tapes' related to the possible attempt to influence the conduct or outcome of a coronial inquiry in February 1980 into a fire, deliberately lit, at the Anglers Club in Crows Nest, Sydney, in 1979. The third related to the conduct of the Cessna-Milner case—whether a lower court offence was substituted for a more serious indictable (higher court) offence. The fourth concerned George Freeman's starting price bookmaking activities and possible conspiracy to fix races. The fifth concerned speculation that NSW Police might have entered into a criminal agreement involving money in the possession of an international money courier. As to all of these, Gaudron remained pessimistic, concluding that '[u]nless and until the material is authenticated it is unlikely that inquiries would lead to any significant outcome...'

A further opinion Gaudron gave in conjunction with the Crown Solicitor in May 1984, stated:

> We have considered whether we should recommend to the Government that it appoint a Special Commission of Inquiry into the circumstances of the case. In the absence of any authentication of the transcripts, however, that seems to us to be a course that would prove completely futile.[55]

It referred to the futility of forcing witnesses into the witness box if they denied the conversations took place in the absence of reliable evidence to rebut their denials. The unverified transcript would not suffice and there was nothing of use in the tapes themselves.

Gaudron took the same view of the uselessness of the *Age* material when advising about proceedings continuing against Farquhar. He made a 'No Bill' application on the charge that he had perverted or attempted to pervert the course of justice in relation to the Humphreys case. Gaudron recommended against annulling the prosecution, noting that, while the charges would attract publicity to his public office, they 'go to the very heart of the administration of justice, and the public interest requires that they proceed to trial'.[56] Even in those proceedings, however, she doubted there was sufficient evidence on which to cross-examine Farquhar. The *Age* material would be of no help in refuting Farquhar's denials having regard to the uncertainty of its provenance.

Gaudron was criticised for this stand. One journalist, John Slee, later commented: 'she appears to have taken a quite dogmatic position that even if the tapes are authentic, the circumstances in which they were made makes them inadmissible'. The journalist continued:

> In the final analysis, it is not the NSW Solicitor General's opinion which will carry the day. It is rather that of a judge, exercising a discretion which Miss Gaudron, at least in her 1984 opinion, appears to discount or deny exists.[57]

The Briese allegations

The *Age* material did not implicate Justice Murphy in improper dealings. It did, however, trigger Chief Stipendiary Magistrate Clarrie Briese's recollection of conversations which he alleged did cast suspicion on Murphy. This set further inquiries by Gaudron in train and, inevitably, any advice she gave that was seen, no matter how indirectly, to be supportive of his interests became the subject of press comment. Gaudron's professional integrity, clear legal mind and sound judgment saw her negotiate her way through rough political terrain.

Briese's claims were suggestive of former Chief Magistrate Farquhar's and Murphy's interest in the outcome of charges of forgery and criminal conspiracy against Ryan. At first Briese made no mention of Murphy, but when he did, though some two months after Gaudron had expressed a cautious assessment of his claims, it brought with it suggestions that Gaudron's opinions were affected by bias.

In July 1984 Briese came forward first with the claim that a District Court judge, whom he then refused to name, had approached him in February 1982 and suggested that he should interfere with Magistrate Jones's handling of charges against Ryan that arose from an allegation that applications by Korean nationals for permanent resident status had been backed by false statements. Briese was fairly convincing in his detail. He said that he met the District Court judge at the Tattersall's Club. The judge, according to Briese, claimed to be acting in the interests of a senior government minister, who said that 'Neville wanted something done for Morgan Ryan'. Briese was firm in his response that no one should approach the magistrate, Kevin Jones, who was handling the Ryan matter, particularly given what Jones had suffered after his dismissal of the case against Kevin Humphreys. The judge, apparently accepting this, decided instead to arrange for senior counsel to represent Ryan.[58]

Gaudron's investigation into Briese's claim caused her to have some doubts as to the accuracy of his recollections. She gave her reasons in a twenty-five page opinion of 31 July 1984.[59] There was something unsettling about the timing of Briese's whistleblowing. Why did he wait more than two years—that is, until after publication of the '*Age* tapes'—before reporting the encounter with the District Court judge? When he did report it, why to Barrie Unsworth, then Minister for Transport and a member of the Legislative Council, and Hans Heilpern, a staff member of Frank Walker's, rather than to the Chief Judge of the District

Court and the Under-Secretary of Justice? When he did report it to the Under-Secretary on 5 July 1984, why did Briese refuse then to name the judge who approached him, and again decline on 10 July the renewed request to name the judge?

It was not until 17 July 1984 that Briese was persuaded to reveal the name of the District Court judge, John Foord. Foord denied the allegation. Wran denied that he was the 'Neville' referred to. Unsworth did not recollect any conversation with Briese about an approach by a District Court judge. Nor did Heilpern recall the conversation.

Gaudron personally questioned Briese about these discrepancies. The interview took place in the presence of the Crown Advocate and the Under-Secretary for Justice. Briese explained that his delay in reporting the matter was because the judge's approach to him had no significance until taken in the context of the '*Age* tapes'. Gaudron asked Briese why he chose to report the matter to Unsworth. He answered:

> I wanted the Labor Party to do something on a broader basis. The allegations which have been made have been very damaging—damaging to our institutions. By giving this information, maybe people at the top level may do something about them.

When asked 'Like what?' Briese replied: 'For example, change the leadership.'[60]

Gaudron knew that Unsworth and Wran were not 'mates'. Wran handed Unsworth the Ministry for Transport because he thought it better to have the politically conservative but industrially militant Unsworth 'inside the tent pissing out than outside pissing in'.[61] Unsworth was the man who had an interest in dislodging the premier. Gaudron reports: 'This was but one of the answers which caused me to conclude that Mr Briese was not entirely objective in his consideration of the matters the subject of the claim...'[62]

Nor did the story add up in other respects. By February 1982, the date that Judge Foord allegedly approached Briese, Magistrate

Jones had already found a *prima facie* case against Morgan Ryan, which indicated that the judge did not have a detailed knowledge of the case as might be expected if his motive in approaching Briese was dishonourable. Gaudron's conclusion that Briese's account was not sufficiently reliable to act on was also justified by the fact that Briese had not been concerned about the judge's remarks in the context in which they were made at the time. Briese said that the conversation only assumed significance in the context of the reported content of the taped telephone conversations by the *Age* newspaper of 2 February 1984. The *Age* material, as Gaudron had already pointed out, had already been shown to have been wrongly reported with respect to the conversation between the unnamed 'judge' and 'solicitor'.

Then, in September 1984, Briese gave evidence to the first of the two Senate Select Committees appointed to investigate the matter of High Court Justice Lionel Murphy's alleged involvement in the attempt to influence the outcome of Ryan's case. Briese claimed that he had a telephone conversation with Justice Murphy in which Murphy famously said, 'And now what about my little mate?' in relation to the same proceedings where Foord was alleged to have had attempted to influence. Murphy refused to give evidence to the committee. The Senate Committee did not find that Murphy had attempted to pervert the course of justice, but Briese's evidence did tend to support the veracity of the so-called '*Age* tapes' that made connections between Murphy and Ryan.

Briese's allegations about Murphy's conduct became the focus of a second Senate Select Committee. Again Murphy refused to give evidence. It also heard new allegations from NSW District Court Judge Paul Flannery who had presided over the 1983 Ryan conspiracy trial, which lent possible corroborative support for the Briese allegations. The committee found that on the balance of probabilities, Murphy had attempted to influence the course of justice.

In this way the snowball effect of the publication of the '*Age* tapes' culminated in the question of whether Justice Murphy had sought to interfere in criminal proceedings, a most serious allegation against a High Court justice.[63] Ryan's purported telephone conversations provided meaty stories on which the media continued to feast. Gaudron's uncomfortable situation worsened when advice she provided to the Attorney General on the authenticity of the tapes (with implications for Murphy) found its way to the press.

Chapter Twelve

TAPS, LEAKS AND BUCKETS OF MUCK

> If we are to get into the gutter or the mud, let us all get in together.
>
> Neville Wran, September 1980[1]

Plugging leaks

Amid tears and frustration, Gaudron retained her sense of humour. It was apocryphally reported that she was tempted to entitle a talk she was to give to a women's organisation in 1984: *A touch of buggery—taps, leaks, drips and buckets*.[2] She wanted to impart some light humour into some aspects of the unsavoury and malodorous muck she had to trowel through in the course of her high profile role as Solicitor General. She was reminded of *Hold the Line*, a satire on telephone tapping she had seen around 1960. She rang the author of the play, Mona Brand, for a script from which she thought she might find a suitably funny quote to include in the talk. When the time came, she thought better of it, given the sensitivity surrounding the issue as the '*Age* tapes' scandal unfolded. In fact, there was very little that was funny about the '*Age* tapes' saga and its many political ramifications.

Gaudron's advices themselves were a source of political controversy, and more so after aspects of them were 'leaked' to the press. Some on the Opposition benches and some sceptical journalists suggested that Gaudron provided guarded advice on the authenticity and value of the '*Age* tapes' material to protect the Government and her Labor friends in particular. Gaudron was, after all, known to be a committed Labor Party supporter, and a supporter of the social policies of the left. She was also a close friend of Lionel Murphy.

On the other hand, she was a stickler for fair procedural processes, and her caution on the use of the '*Age* tapes' to support prosecutions of friends of the Labor Party was consistent with her view that public officials and private citizens were alike entitled to procedural fairness before and in the course of criminal proceedings. She also wanted to hold members of the Police to account for illegally tapping telephones, if the material proved to be records of taped telephone conversations.

Further, it was her role to be an advocate for the Government when presenting legal arguments in court hearings, as well as to provide legal advice when required. It was in the Government's interest that she gave strict legal advice, and did not purport to guess what was in its political interest. Persuasively, all who worked with Gaudron in government speak with one voice about her reliability in providing legal advice that was correct. Trevor Haines, head of the Attorney General's Department, considered that 'professionally she was proper, impeccable, and perfect on matters of law'. While working with Gaudron, he knew about her left-wing politics and her friendship with Lionel Murphy, and he took these into account when considering her advice. In particular, on issues that impinged on Murphy, Haines found Gaudron to be objective; her advices followed the letter of the law and, in his opinion, were always correct.[3] But there were times when it was not certain what the outcome for Gaudron would be. In 1984 the pressures were accumulating. And more was in store.

Large extracts of Gaudron's advice of 31 July 1984 were published in a four-page edited version in the *Sydney Morning Herald* of 23 August 1984. On 28 August 1984 it was published in the

Bulletin. Gaudron's expression of doubt over the veracity of Briese's claim put her further into the press spotlight. Despite her explanation for it, she was criticised by the media for what was taken to be a strong attack on Briese's credibility and an unfavourable assessment of his evidence.

Gaudron took offence at one newspaper that quoted her as saying that Briese's allegations 'will not stand critical analysis'.[4] An apology followed the next day with an explanation that it was Wran who attributed this view to Gaudron. Wran was reported as regretting the form in which the leak occurred, but pleased that at last 'the truth has emerged'.[5] The Leader of the Opposition, Nick Greiner, sought an assurance that the leaked opinion had not come from Wran's or Landa's offices. Landa, according to press reports on 15 August 1984, had already revealed some of Gaudron's advice about the Briese matter, and of her opinion about what misconduct in office might comprise 'judicial misconduct', with reference to allegations against Judge Foord.[6] Landa was thereby forced to order an investigation into the leak.

Briese publicly stood by his claims, while Wran publicly supported Gaudron's legal stand with the remark that '[i]f we substitute the rule of Broadway [Fairfax] for the rule of law then we might as well put all our rights in our bag and pack up and go home'.[7] On any view, Gaudron's task of balancing privacy with the public's right to know, ensuring accountability of political decision-making and protecting the right of an accused to a fair trial, was a difficult one to acquit under pressure of time and press scrutiny.

With a murky picture emerging of the entanglement of Murphy with the racing clan's seedy deals and of the use of collegiate friendships to help friends in trouble, Gaudron recognised that Briese's allegations could not be disregarded, notwithstanding the discrepancies she had discovered. In an advice of 10 October 1984, taking into account evidence before the second Senate Select Committee inquiring into Murphy's conduct, she conceded that the statements of Briese and Flannery clearly indicated a strong personal interest on the part of Judge Foord in the outcome of Morgan Ryan's trial.[8] However, she found that the matters submitted by Briese did not constitute evidence of an attempt by any person to pervert the course of justice, nor of a conspiracy to do so. Nor, on their face, did Foord's actions amount to 'judicial misconduct'. In any event, she noted that misconduct was a separate matter from criminal conduct, at that time still under investigation.[9] She had already, in August, suggested that the matter be referred to the Commonwealth Director of Public Prosecutions for a full inquiry into the matter.[10]

Gaudron expressed strong views on the need for correct legal procedures to be followed. In advising that her report on the Briese allegations should not be tabled in Parliament, she said:

> I consider that such a course would be inappropriate, not only in view of the longstanding practice that Solicitor General's advices are not made public, but by reason also of the content of the report, the course of action subsequently adopted, and by reason of the need to protect the Office of Solicitor General from politicisation.[11]

She believed that the non-tabling of advices encouraged frank canvassing of the issues. She thought it 'most unfortunate' that there had been some dissemination of her views on Briese's claims because she had 'dealt frankly' with his claim and, as Briese had an important job to perform, she thought it essential that public confidence be maintained in all areas touching on the administration of the law. She asserted: 'Such confidence could not be maintained if my views on the credibility of Mr Briese were to be publicised.' She was also concerned that it might be seen as pre-emptive of the DPP's function if her report were tabled before the Senate Select Committee completed its inquiry. She concluded that she could not find 'anything exceptional which would justify the tabling of my report. On the contrary, I can only find reasons against that course.'

When Barrie Unsworth succeeded Neville Wran as Premier in 1986, Gaudron was once again accused of political bias. Unsworth reopened the matter of former Police Commissioner Wood's and Farquhar's activities and the Cessna-Milner matter. Gaudron, in advising on the sufficiency of admissible evidence to sustain a case against Wood, Farquhar or Ryan, recommended against prosecutions pending referral of the matter to the NSW Drugs Crime Commission.[12] The Government accepted her advice. This was regarded by one journalist as 'not quite independent', noting the coincidence of her advice with the political interests of the Government. She was accused of 'throttling' Unsworth's intention to act further on the matter.[13]

Gaudron was further criticised because her recommendation that the matter be referred to the Drugs Crime Commission came at the time a special police task force set up in April 1986 to investigate matters arising out of the Stewart Royal Commission was due to report. Its conclusions were understood to be that there was sufficient evidence to warrant charges being laid against at least three men in relation to the Cessna-Milner matter.[14] This led to Opposition attacks that the Government was hiding behind Gaudron's recommendation to avoid press criticism. The then Attorney General, Terry Sheahan, denied this. He said in respect of Gaudron's advice:

> The recommendation has not been to delay any prosecution. The recommendation has been to conduct further investigation because it is important that we establish whether there is sufficient evidence to institute any criminal proceedings in regard to this matter.[15]

Whether Gaudron was able to maintain impartiality was a matter of controversy, with the press continuing to criticise what it saw as Gaudron's loyal support of Murphy. Accusations that she was biased drew support from subsequent inquiries that found there was sufficient evidence for charges to be laid against Murphy and to have him committed for trial. One commentator suggested that in making an adverse assessment of the credibility of Briese's allegations against Judge Foord, Gaudron was in effect putting in doubt the credibility of the chief witness against her friend Justice Murphy.[16]

The criticism surfaced again when Gaudron became a Justice

of the High Court in 1987. Her assessment of the veracity of Briese's claim continued to be regarded by some with suspicion:

> Ms Gaudron did nothing to promote the statutory standing and impartiality of her office by ostentatiously joining Murphy and his coterie while the jury weighing the question of his guilt...was still out.[17]

It did not seem to matter that Gaudron's assessment of Briese's claims was made in February 1984, before Briese gave evidence before the Senate Select Committee in September 1984 of Murphy's alleged involvement in the attempt to influence the outcome of Ryan's case. What the press found important was that Murphy was not merely her friend but her known supporter. One journalist asserted that her expressed doubts about the authenticity of the 'telephone tap' material made her seem unduly protective of Murphy's interests. The journalist cynically suggested that Murphy engineered, with calculative intent, Wran's appointment of Gaudron. He wrote:

> It is a plausible enough contention that Ms Gaudron was compromised in her role as NSW Solicitor General by her loyalty to the Premier responsible for her appointment and to her patron, Mr Justice Murphy, and there has been no dissimulation in her admiration for him.[18]

The 'indemnity' dilemma

Gaudron was also subject to criticism for her handling of the vexed issues of 'No Bill' submissions (whether a prosecution should proceed), and applications for 'indemnity' which would guarantee a person immunity from prosecution in exchange for evidence that would assist in the prosecution of others. The Attorney General decided these matters on advice from the Solicitor General. Gaudron faced criticism mostly because of her recommendations that proceedings be dropped or not proceeded with for lack of evidence. But she was also criticised for her stand in wanting prosecutions to proceed against those police associated with illegal telephone taps, when others argued they should be given immunity from prosecution if they agreed to provide information about the phone tapping operations. There must have been times when she felt she could not win.

By 1985 controversy had grown surrounding prosecutions that were dropped on Gaudron's advice. The NSW Ombudsman, George Masterman, criticised the 'No Bill' system (and Gaudron by implication) in his 1985 annual report. Anti-corruption campaigner, South Coast MP John Hatton, in a typical comment, said:

> There have been some very suspicious no-bills in recent years, and it has always been defended by the Attorney General, every time the issue has been raised, on the grounds that he was acting on the best Crown Law advice.[19]

The NSW Bar and the Law Society, having some understanding of the complexities that arose in the prosecution process, supported Gaudron, expressing confidence in her work as Solicitor General.[20] Legal processes behind the scenes were sometimes difficult for the general public to comprehend.

Despite the difficulties in securing convictions, Gaudron was firm that police should be prosecuted for illegally tapping telephones. In September 1984 Justice Stewart's 'Mr Asia' inquiry into drug trafficking was extended to examine the unauthorised telephone tapping by NSW Police that had led to the so-called '*Age* tapes'. The Commission wanted to hear from the police who conducted the interceptions between January 1980 and June 1981 to determine the source and extent of the activity. Stewart's inquiry revealed that several hundred police were involved in unlawful interception of telephone conversations. All of the police officers interviewed denied any knowledge of the telephone taps. Individual police involved were not going to admit they had broken the law, even though it was known that it had become commonplace since 1968.[21]

Stewart's solution was to arrange for police who were prepared to give evidence about illegal phone tapping activities to be given a guarantee that they would not be charged with those offences. He requested the NSW Government to grant immunity to some thirty-one police involved in unlawful interceptions. Gaudron advised against this course. Stewart and Gaudron knew each other from Law School. They had been colleagues on the same floor in Selbourne Chambers. Stewart had previously been a policeman and had left because of the extent of corruption. Stewart and Gaudron shared the same law-enforcement objectives but they did not always see eye to eye on how these could best be achieved.

Attorney General Walker had taken the view that indemnity should not be granted to a principal perpetrator of a crime but only to lesser offenders, and only then where their evidence was likely to secure the conviction of more serious offenders. Gaudron shared these sentiments. She caused more controversy in saying as much to Justice Stewart in 1984.

She first wanted to know whether the evidence of the police witnesses would produce the original tapes—unlikely, as Stewart discovered that the tapes and a mass of transcripts had been destroyed as soon as the '*Age* tapes' story broke—and also what offences they were being indemnified for, and what prosecutions would result from their evidence. To Gaudron, it seemed that the indemnities sought were not to secure prosecutions against other police but to assist Stewart in his inquiries into drug trafficking. It did not fit with her guiding principle, namely, that if a person was to avoid prosecution for a criminal offence, the trade-off should be successful prosecution of others for more serious crimes.[22]

The stand-off lasted a year. Gaudron argued that those guilty of criminal conduct, particularly corrupt police officers, should be prosecuted. Stewart, on the other hand, knew that without the evidence of the police, there could be no prosecutions beyond a few members of the police force, for the extensive illegal activity or for possible crimes and public corruption revealed from the tapped and taped conversations. Gaudron stood firm.[23] The press criticised her for this, too.[24]

Little wonder that when Gaudron was asked to provide advice on draft legislation to establish a NSW Director of Public Prosecutions who would take over the functions of the Attorney

General in relation to 'No Bill' and 'Indemnity' applications, and found flaws in the proposals, she concluded: 'I consider that the only advantage of the present proposal is that it will save me a lot of trouble, anxiety and bad press.'[25]

Disillusionment and distractions

Gaudron suffered more angst on discovering that lurking behind some indemnity applications was further unacceptable police conduct relating to serious drug trafficking rackets. In 1985 Gaudron was asked to review a request for indemnity against prosecution of cannabis grower Giuseppe Verduci, a police informant, for conspiracy to cultivate Indian hemp. In October 1980, NSW Police, in conjunction with an Australian Federal Police (AFP) initiative, took part in an illegal drug trafficking 'entrapment plan', code named *Operation Seville*.[26]

In August 1981 the AFP 'authorised' Verduci to engage in the 'controlled' cultivation of Indian hemp on his own land at Bungendore, a half-hour drive from Canberra.[27] The 'authority' extended to harvesting and selling the marijuana crop. The stated aim of the operation was to arrest people engaged in transportation and sale of the harvest. Verduci had been recruited as an informant in the early 1980s by the AFP. One of the AFP officers involved was Superintendent Colin Winchester.[28] Winchester later became Assistant Commissioner who headed the ACT police force and was gunned down and killed in Canberra in 1989.

It was a cosy arrangement. Verduci cultivated, harvested and arranged for the distribution and sale of the produce under the watchful eye of the two police forces, on two separate occasions, the second being carried out on Crown land. The Bungendore project came to an end in 1982. But in 1984 Verduci repeated the exercise on a property he purchased in the name of his wife at Guyra, NSW. There he grew another crop of Indian hemp, this time without police approval.[29] Verduci, along with five others, was arrested and was due to stand trial in May 1985. Verduci claimed he had been acting as an agent for the AFP at Guyra as well as Bungendore, and sought immunity from prosecution in return for providing information.

In the course of providing advice, Gaudron recommended that material on Verduci and the information supplied by him be referred to the National Crime Authority (NCA), set up to target crime and drug trafficking, for evaluation.[30] During 1986 Gaudron held discussions with Justice Donald Stewart, Chairman of the NCA, on the value of Verduci's information.[31] The NCA found Verduci tricky to deal with, and Stewart, like Gaudron, held concerns about the role of the AFP in the Bungendore project and the use of information obtained through unlawful conduct.[32]

In 1987, after Gaudron had relinquished office, Verduci was granted indemnities in return for becoming a Crown witness in respect of other offenders in relation to the Bungendore and Guyra plantations.[33] However, as key Crown witness, Verduci provided no significant information, either refusing to answer questions on the ground that his answers might incriminate him or that he could not 'remember' what happened.[34] Verduci's immunity was subsequently withdrawn in relation to the Bungendore matters. Nevertheless, the NCA was ultimately unable to obtain sufficient information to secure a conviction against him. In 1989, charges against eleven other alleged offenders associated with the plantations were dismissed or 'no billed'.[35]

Gaudron consistently held the view that illegally obtained evidence should not be used to secure criminal convictions. She had taken the approach in relation to the unlawful police telephone taps that no one was above the law, and held the same view about the legitimacy of 'entrapment' operations. Nearly ten years later, as a justice of the High Court, she had the opportunity to express her objections to drug-trafficking entrapment exercises. They were twofold. She believed that a fair trial required that proceedings be conducted strictly in accordance with the law, and that unlawful conduct on the part of law enforcement officers was an abuse of fair process. Secondly, abuse of process could only bring the administration of justice into disrepute and diminish public confidence in the courts.[36]

In January 1989, when Colin Winchester was killed outside his home in Canberra, Verduci was spoken to at length by investigators.[37] In the early days of the investigation, it was suspected that

Winchester might have been killed to stop him giving evidence against those charged with drug offences from the Verduci arrangements. Inquiries into this were not fruitful. A Canberra public servant, a troubled and troublesome person David Eastman, was charged and convicted of Winchester's murder as a self-motivated lone action. In a twist, more than a decade later, Eastman would limp through unsuccessful appeals to the High Court against his conviction. Gaudron was a Justice on two of these in which issues arose as to whether Eastman had received a fair trial.[38]

By October 1984, faced with an increasing volume of work, Gaudron found she was frequently deferring routine tasks to attend to the unexpected. On the same day as her July 1984 assessment of Briese's claims, Gaudron had to consider recommendations arising out of a special inquiry conducted by Justice John Slattery that Rex Jackson, former Minister for Corrective Services who had resigned in 1983 in disgrace, should be prosecuted for corruption.[39] The pressure of these matters delayed her from providing timely advice in respect of whether or not the State of NSW should intervene in proceedings listed for hearing for 2 August, relating to the Hilton Hotel bombing.[40]

Her time was being spent less and less on social justice issues and increasingly on police corruption. She became disappointed, disillusioned and frustrated as the fight against crime revealed the extent to which members of the NSW Police—the law enforcers—were associated with, and in some cases formed part of, the criminal underworld.

A ministerial reshuffle in 1983 saw Paul Landa take over from Gaudron's friend, Frank Walker, as Attorney General. She did not like Landa.[41] She threatened to resign on several occasions in the short period in which she worked with him. She found him inconsiderate and abrasive, even though he took her advice and supported her. He yelled when he wanted something done, and demanded action from whomever he could first get hold of by telephone. Most people found him difficult to work with. He died after nine months in the portfolio. Gaudron thereafter referred to him as 'the deceased'.[42]

Wran then stepped briefly into the Attorney General portfolio.

He was particularly demanding, and tensions arose in his relationship with Gaudron. With reference to police corruption, she warned him:

> Evidentiary problems associated with intended prosecutions cannot be overstated, nor the degree of adverse comment which will attend these Chambers and the administration of this Department, if the problems are not addressed in a thorough and professional manner.[43]

She outlined the increase in and mounting pressures of work and the giving away of routine tasks to attend to the unexpected. She became overwrought, at least for a time. She confided to a close friend that she wanted to quit, jesting that she would go abroad and join the Irish Bar. Nevertheless, as a woman with remarkable recuperative capacities and resilience, she found the necessary emotional resources to push on.

Some of the tension was relieved when Attorney General Terry Sheahan took over from Wran at the end of 1984. Sheahan and Gaudron worked effectively together. Sheahan regarded her well and did not interfere with her work. He inherited a mass of files from Landa's days, all awaiting decisions. Gaudron was the recipient. No one would ignore her advice, Sheahan declared, because it was always correct. He also knew how to manage Gaudron's tantrums. When it was reported that, 'Mary's gone off again,' Sheahan would ring his departmental head, Trevor Haines, and send him to see Mary with a bottle of champagne.

Throughout her time as Solicitor General, Gaudron's law was a powerful force behind the scene. Despite adverse publicity in the press about her findings, neither her opinions nor her professionalism was questioned by those who relied on her, irrespective of the inconvenience her advice might cause the Government. Her opinions on the law were always taken as correct, and she was forceful in ensuring fair process was followed, particularly where individuals' rights required protection. Her worth was confirmed by Cabinet's reaction to her leaving the post for appointment to the High Court. When Jack Hallam, the Minister for Agriculture, responded to suggestions for Gaudron's successor, he simply said: 'We need another Mary.'[44]

Gaudron also had other interests that added to her busy life and also served to distract her from office tensions. In 1984 she found the time to present a joint paper to the first Equal Opportunity in Employment conference in Sydney. That the battle for equal opportunity in the workforce had yet to be won was illustrated by the remark of a permanent head who was heard to say that 'equal opportunity is a health hazard'.[45] Gaudron and her co-author, Ann Fieldhouse, a lawyer in the Crown Solicitor's Office, urged that the task of implementing equal opportunity in the public sector should not be left to the employer. They argued that it was one for a properly trained external authority, such as an Equal Opportunity in Public Employment Director.

Gaudron had a full life in Sydney outside her office. She was an unpaid board member of the Nimrod Theatre in Darlinghurst. It was founded in 1970 by a group of young writers and directors, including Gaudron's friends and legal colleagues Lillian and Ken Horler, who converted an old stable into a small and atmospheric theatre. The Nimrod staged new Australian plays and new and radical versions of Shakespeare. Its success allowed it to move into bigger premises in 1974. Gaudron, then a young lawyer, had worked behind the scenes, as she often did for what she saw as good causes, assisting with the legal paperwork of its establishment.

Gaudron became a government-appointed member of the Council of Macquarie University from 1981 to 1986, and chaired the Advisory Council of the Centre for Technology and Social Change at the University of Wollongong from 1984 to 1986. Her time on the Macquarie University Council overlapped with her friend, Joan Bielski, as well as with Elizabeth Evatt and Jocelynne Scutt.[46]

Even these external interests were not without dramas. The Nimrod Theatre's survival was threatened in 1983 when it became cash-strapped.[47] Then, arguments between academics at Macquarie University broke out. The dispute over composition of the fifteen-person selection committee to choose a law professor was noisy enough to gain the attention of the press.[48] The Council rejected most of the names proposed by the academics and substituted their own, including Gaudron and Justice Elizabeth Evatt.

Despite the constant dramas associated with her work, Gaudron regarded her time as Solicitor General as her best days. She had around her a loyal and supportive staff, including lawyer Tim Robertson, brother of celebrity barrister Geoffrey Robertson. Tim Robertson and his partner, Fran Davis, became close friends of Gaudron and her family. The job allowed Gaudron much more time with her family and friends in Sydney. She had a young son to raise and teenage daughters to look after.

Midway into her term as Solicitor General, Gaudron was one of five lawyers rumoured as being considered for President of the NSW Court of Appeal. She was 'amused and bemused' by this and indicated that she was not interested in a judicial appointment.[49] Well, not this one, and not at this time. Better was to come. And when it did, as a Justice of the High Court, it was a challenge that she was able to grasp fully.

Testing Lionel Murphy

On 21 November 1984 the Commonwealth Director of Public Prosecutions, Ian Temby, QC, recommended that Lionel Murphy, a Justice of the High Court of Australia, be prosecuted on two counts of attempting to pervert the course of justice. One concerned the allegations of Chief Magistrate Clarence Briese about the approach he alleged Murphy had made to him late in 1981 or early 1982. The other concerned the allegations regarding conversations with District Court Judge Paul Flannery on 9 July 1983. Both involved criminal proceedings against the solicitor, Morgan Ryan. Murphy proclaimed his innocence and stood down from the bench of the High Court, but he refused to resign.

He was committed for trial at the Castlereagh Street local court. At the close of committal proceedings in April 1985, Murphy declared: 'I am angry at these false charges. I did not attempt to pervert the course of justice. To do so would have been a betrayal of what I have fought for all my life.' He fought the charges all the way. He had already sought a review of the committal proceedings in the Federal Court and was unsuccessful.[50] In August 1985 he appealed to the High Court on some twenty-one technical legal and constitutional grounds.

It was well known that Gaudron wanted to see her friend, Lionel Murphy, acquitted. She might have anticipated press criticism, therefore, when she provided professional advice that NSW should intervene in the proceedings before the High Court to challenge the application of section 43 of the *Commonwealth Crimes Act* under which Murphy was prosecuted to the committal proceedings involving Morgan Ryan that took place before a NSW magistrate. The section dealt with the obstruction of justice 'in relation to the judicial power of the Commonwealth'. Ryan's committal proceedings were before a NSW magistrate's court, though they related to an indictable offence against Commonwealth law. The imperative for NSW to put the argument was to preserve the independence of the NSW court system. But, had Gaudron's argument been successful, Murphy too, would have won his appeal. She was unsuccessful.[51]

Criticism from the press came.[52] It upset her. Wendy Bacon, in the *National Times*, questioned how NSW's intervention in the proceedings could be to the advantage of the citizens of NSW. She also commented on Gaudron's association with Murphy, and on Gaudron's advice to the Attorney General concerning Briese's allegations against Judge Foord. In the course of these comments Bacon stated that Gaudron, as a junior barrister, was 'a protégé' of Murphy's.[53]

Gaudron had upset Bacon on a previous occasion. In 1984 Bacon had written an article for the *National Times* entitled 'Roger Rogerson and the barbecue set', in which she wrote about allegations of police cover-ups that implicated Detective Sergeant Rogerson. As a result, inquiries were made and Rogerson was charged with bribery. He was, however, acquitted; it was another case where the evidence of police corruption was insufficient to secure a conviction. Rogerson then audaciously requested that the NSW Government launch contempt proceedings against Bacon and the *National Times*. Gaudron, in considering the request and Rogerson's legal rights, recommended that proceedings be instituted against the newspaper and Bacon for contempt of court.[54]

Gaudron was nevertheless angry that Bacon had attacked her impartiality and impugned her professionalism. She had provided a character reference for Bacon in 1981 when Bacon had appealed against the NSW Barristers' Admission Board's rejection of her application to practice.[55] Now Bacon was questioning her integrity. Gaudron complained to the Australian Press Council about Bacon's article.[56] The Council found that Bacon had made some errors, but it took into account the pressure of space within which the journalist had to work and found the comments were made in good faith, or were legitimate. It concluded:

> While acknowledging that some of the points made by Ms Gaudron have force, the Council thinks it is unfortunate that she did not air them at the time in a letter to the editor. The Council considers that, having discussed the complaints, it does not need to take any further action.

Murphy's trial started on 5 June 1985. Alec Shand, QC, one of the barristers for Consolidated Press and against Gaudron in the *Mackie* case, represented Murphy. Ian Callinan, QC, later a High Court Justice on the bench with Gaudron, was the Crown Prosecutor. Callinan urged that Murphy's position as a High Court Justice relative to the standing of the judicial officers he allegedly sought to influence was 'right at the heart of the case'. He highlighted the close personal and professional relationship Murphy had developed with Ryan over thirty years. On 5 July 1985 the jury found Murphy guilty on the charge relating to Briese's allegations and acquitted him on the charge arising out of Flannery's allegations. He was sentenced to eighteen months' imprisonment.

John Slee, a *Sydney Morning Herald* columnist, took the opportunity to attack Gaudron.[57] He stated that her advice to the NSW Government about Briese's evidence in relation to Justice Murphy would not stand up in court and that this 'assessment took a battering from the Murphy jury'. Gaudron again complained to the Press Council. Her advice had referred to Briese's suggestion that there may have been a conspiracy involving Murphy and Foord, but she had not advised on Briese's allegations against Murphy—

only those made against Foord. The Press Council upheld her complaint. However, it accepted Slee's explanation that his intention was simply to convey that Gaudron's general assessment of Briese's evidence was not shared by the jury in Murphy's trial. The Council found that Slee's error was an honest mistake and it took no action.[58]

Murphy's supporters, including Wran, criticised the prosecution. Temby QC's opinion supporting the decision to prosecute in November 1984 was released to the press in August 1986. It revealed that he had been of the opinion that a conviction was 'not probable' in that there was insufficient evidence to make a conviction 'more likely than not'.[59] Specifically, Temby concluded that on the available evidence Murphy was not likely to have intended to interfere in Ryan's committal proceedings. Therefore, a jury was not likely to find 'beyond reasonable doubt' that Murphy had broken the law. However, he took the view that as Murphy was a high standing public official, his prosecution should proceed to 'clear the air' and avoid any public perception of a 'cover up'.[60] On the other hand, there were many lawyers who believed that, while public officials should be brought to account according to the law, they must be given the same protection that the law gives to others, and therefore the charges should not have been proceeded with.[61]

Murphy appealed to the NSW Court of Criminal Appeal. On 28 November 1985, it quashed the conviction on the Briese allegations and ordered a new trial on the grounds that the trial judge's summing up to the jury had been wrong.[62] It ruled against him on other technical legal arguments. Joy over Murphy's success was dampened by the trouble Murphy's plight caused for his friend, Neville Wran. In the course of a media frenzy concerning Murphy's court proceedings, Wran remarked that 'I have a very deep conviction that Mr Justice Murphy is innocent of any wrongdoing.' Wran was charged and found guilty of contempt of court.[63] Professor of Law, Tony Blackshield also stated publicly that the jury verdict was wrong. He was not charged.[64] Wran's conviction put an end to the 'Wran for Canberra' political campaign. Wran resigned as Premier on 4 July 1986, but not before he put forward Mary

Gaudron's name to the Commonwealth as a potential appointee to the High Court.

Murphy's retrial commenced in mid-April 1986. In his first trial Murphy had gone into the witness box and subjected himself to cross-examination. He declined to give sworn evidence before the jury at the second trial. Journalist and Murphy watcher, Roderick Campbell, thought the explanation Murphy gave for this was not convincing.[65] Nor did it convince Murphy's High Court colleagues who thought that if Murphy wanted to return to the High Court he ought to explain his behaviour. Nevertheless, it was the correct tactical decision. On 28 April the jury acquitted Murphy.

Gaudron was by Murphy's side with his family and other friends while the jury considered their verdict. When they acquitted him, she could not contain her excitement. Her exuberant cheering was audible from the back of the court.[66] Murphy stood on the steps of the Court and told the nation's media that he had been dragged through a political trial, but that the first thing he planned to do was take his young sons to see *Crocodile Dundee*. He also declared his intention to return to the High Court bench.

But more trouble awaited Murphy. A few days later, the second report of Justice Donald Stewart's inquiry into the authenticity of the '*Age* tapes' was released. It found the tapes to be authentic, in the limited sense that they emanated from the NSW Police. The Commission was also satisfied that the voices were real and not simulated but no further authentication tests were carried out on the material. It accepted that the accuracy of the transcription by police of conversations varied widely and, even with apparently verbatim transcripts, there was, in all but a few cases, no way of knowing whether the transcripts came from an unedited tape. No tapes survived from the police tap on Ryan's phone. Usually the tapes were erased as soon as they were transcribed and any surviving tapes were destroyed in 1984 when their existence became public knowledge.[67]

The material contained in the tapes about organised crime seemed to be forgotten in the press frenzy over rumours that circulated about Murphy. He was again under great pressure to resign. His supporters urged him not to lest it be perceived as an admission of guilt. Eminent Australians grouped together to call for an end to the pursuit of the judge. Murphy did not resume his seat on the Court, nor did he resign. The publicity embarrassed the Hawke Government. Acting Attorney General Senator Gareth Evans felt particularly uncomfortable, as he had worked closely with Attorney General Murphy in 1974. In May 1986 the Hawke Cabinet established a Special Parliamentary Commission of former judges, Sir George Lush, Sir Richard Blackburn and Andrew Wells, to inquire into whether Murphy's conduct amounted to 'misbehaviour', sufficient grounds to remove him from the High Court under section 72 of the Constitution. In June 1986 Murphy took injunctive proceedings in the High Court to prevent this, and failed.[68] Callinan, QC, was appointed counsel assisting the inquiry.

On 31 July 1986 Murphy announced that he had cancer of the colon and a short time to live. He stated his intention to return to the High Court and sit for as long as possible. The announcement caused terrible angst. Chief Justice Gibbs wrote urging him not to sit again. Murphy rejected that suggestion. Gibbs had to accept his return.[69] Roderick Campbell concluded that '[as] history shows, anything less final than death would not have diminished his determination to press on'.[70] Murphy returned to the High Court on 1 August 1986. The following day, visitors to the public gallery of the High Court, in a stand of support for his assertion of innocence, included Professor Manning Clark, Professor Harry Messel, Clyde Cameron, Senator George Georges and Commonwealth Solicitor General Dr Gavan Griffith, QC. A rally outside was addressed by historian Humphrey McQueen, union leader Peter O'Dea and prominent Canberra barrister and subsequently Chief Justice of the ACT Supreme Court, Terry Higgins, QC.

Murphy sat as a Justice of the Court for a week before becoming too ill to continue. He heard a criminal case, *King v The Queen* (1 August) and a civil case, *Miller v TCN Channel Nine Pty Ltd* (5 and 6 August). At around lunchtime on 21 October 1986 the Court received a call from Murphy's wife, Ingrid, to say that her husband was failing. He would not see the day out. Murphy had prepared judgments in both cases. The Court had scheduled the delivery of the judgments for the following day. If Murphy died before then, his judgments would have 'died with him'. While it would not have made any difference to the outcome of the cases (he had dissented in both), in a chivalrous gesture to ensure that Murphy's last two judgments were delivered, Chief Justice Gibbs and Justice Gerard Brennan rushed into court in Canberra and delivered the two judgments at 3:30 pm the same day. Murphy died an hour later, aged sixty-four, at his home in Forrest.

Before Murphy's death the Irish Ambassador arranged 'a wake' to celebrate his life, something that Murphy could enjoy. It was on a Sunday at the Embassy of Ireland. Gaudron was there for her friend. Tony Blackshield recalls the sweet sadness of the occasion. Gaudron sang a song. She made up the words and put them to a recognisable Irish melody, the Australian version known as *Moreton Bay*, although ironically, another version of the same tune is called *Father Murphy*.[71] 'It was terrible,' laughed Blackshield. 'It didn't scan; it didn't rhyme; and Gaudron could not sing.' It went like this:

> O Lionel Murphy, O Lionel Murphy
> A fearless champion of right and law
> They tore you from your rightful status
> But to the court you are now restored

There was more. Once started, Gaudron did not want to stop.

The Irish Ambassador spoke (partly in Gaelic), and Murphy gave a spirited response. He said, 'I didn't understand everything the Ambassador said. What did he mean "*If* Lionel was still involved in politics"?' It was an emotional and happy evening with people occasionally breaking into tears. One of those weeping was Neville Wran.[72]

A public memorial service was held for Lionel Murphy at Sydney Town Hall on 27 October 1986. Gaudron spoke. She referred to his contribution to human rights, civil liberties, the advancement of the rights of minorities and the disadvantaged. She alluded to Murphy's scientific curiosity (he was a Bachelor of

Science) and told of a conversation that she had had with him that illustrates the connection she felt to him:

> 'Look,' he said. 'Did you ever think about the electric light?' I didn't, so rather than answer his question I offered some vague self-evident statement about its having improved the quality of life. 'You know', he said, 'they resisted it. Oh yes, the gas light companies, they resisted it. They took it to court—the cases are in the law reports.' The conversation was turning to the law, and I was on safer ground. Before I could inject another platitude, he had tacked clear away. 'See,' he said, 'the electric light must have changed human metabolism. It stands to reason. Longer exposure to light must speed up the maturing process. Look at all those hot house flowers—they bloom out of season because the light speeds up the maturing process.' Perhaps we were again on easy conversational ground, but no. 'See,' he said. 'If it affects the maturing process, it has to affect the emotions.' Emotions are dangerous topics of conversation—particularly for lawyers who are presumed not to have any, unless of course they are women. 'See,' he said, picking up a scientific journal. 'There is a theory here that everybody needs a precise amount of light. Too much or too little, and some individuals will become emotionally ill. If you can ascertain the precise amount of light for the individual, you can solve the problem. Have a look at it,' he said. 'There could be something in it.'[73]

Lionel Murphy, Gaudron concluded, was and is 'the electric lighting of the law'. She explained: 'He would take an ordinary old abstraction—like equal justice—he would expose it, he would illumine the abstraction, he would make its form stark.' She referred to Murphy's espousal of equal justice in *McInnis'* case, where he said: 'Where the kind of trial a person receives depends on the amount of money he or she has, there is no equal justice.'[74] Equal justice was a concept Gaudron had a special interest in developing over the next decade or so. She talked then of Murphy's way of getting beyond abstractions, seeing individual people with particular problems who looked to the law to help them. She finished her talk with: '"Look!" he'd say. "See!" he'd say. Look! See! It is the least we should do.'

It was a good speech. The Town Hall was packed. Amongst his many friends and supporters were Murphy's federal Labor friends. They liked it. They were about to choose a replacement for Murphy's seat on the High Court.

Chapter Thirteen

HIGH GROUND

I pulled up behind an old yellow station-wagon and saw this woman in the driver's seat with the *Sydney Morning Herald* spread out over the steering wheel and a fag in her mouth...It was Mary Gaudron, High Court Justice, just being a parent.[1]

From left field

Even before Lionel Murphy's demise, Gaudron's name was canvassed in legal and political circles as a possible successor because the Chief Justice, Sir Harry Gibbs, himself about to retire, predicted that a woman would soon be appointed to the Court.[2] Several factors were in Gaudron's favour. It was time for a woman to join the bench. There was no other obvious female lawyer. And there was precedent for appointing a state Solicitor General.[3] Gaudron was well-known and well-respected for her sharp legal mind. She had the formal support of the NSW Attorney General, Terry Sheahan, and former Premier, Neville Wran.[4] Each State now submitted recommendations to the Federal Attorney General. In anticipation of Chief Justice Gibbs' retirement, Wran and Sheahan had nominated

NSW Chief Justice Laurence Street and, in the event of the Chief Justice being replaced by an existing member of the Court, they nominated Mary Gaudron to fill the subsequent vacancy.[5]

Her chances were enhanced by Murphy's death. It left the Hawke Government with two vacancies to fill. The timing was right: the 'when you are in favour', is as important as the 'who you know' adage. But her mooted appointment invited public controversy.[6] In some circles, appointing Gaudron had broad appeal. She was Murphy's friend. Her appointment would make up for the injustice his supporters thought Murphy suffered and which, they believed, hastened his death. On the other hand, her support of Murphy and her work as Solicitor General for Premier Wran caused others to doubt her political impartiality. Her emotional disposition was raised as making her unsuitable for appointment. Some Labor Party members called Gaudron's resignation from the Arbitration Commission a display of emotionalism not befitting a High Court judge.[7]

At the political level, Attorney General Lionel Bowen had Michael McHugh on top of his list to replace Murphy. McHugh was highly regarded within the legal profession. But Murphy had a last wish. He and his wife Ingrid were at dinner at the Prime Minister's Lodge in Canberra just before he died. Murphy was very unwell. Prime Minister Bob Hawke took him into the study where they had 'a good yarn' in which Murphy opened up to Hawke.[8] Hawke did not always see eye-to-eye with Murphy, but he respected him. It can be imagined that both men shed tears. In the course of the conversation Murphy made his wish known that he would like to see a woman appointed to the High Court.[9] As others heard the story later, Hawke, emotionally, if rhetorically, asked: 'Mate, mate…what can we do?' Murphy replied: 'Appoint a woman to the High Court.'

Hawke understood that Murphy had Gaudron in mind. He was receptive to this. He saw in her two very important attributes: a keen mind and a good heart.[10] Further, as ACTU President, he had observed her capacity to absorb arguments and make sound decisions when she was a deputy president of the Conciliation and Arbitration Commission.[11]

Judge Mary Gaudron at home with Peggy, 10 June 1980.
(John O'Gready, courtesy Fairfax photos.)

Mary Gaudron, QC, on the announcement of her appointment
as Justice of the High Court of Australia, 8 December 1986.
(©Newspix/Alan Pryke)

Full Court in session, December 1998. (Left to right) Justices Kenneth Hayne, William Gummow, Mary Gaudron, Chief Justice Murray Gleeson, Justices Michael McHugh, Michael Kirby and Ian Callinan. (©Newspix/Michael Jones)

A decision on the appointments was deferred. Cabinet did not meet to consider the vacancies until after Murphy's funeral. This, too, proved fortunate for Gaudron. The outstanding eulogy she gave at Murphy's memorial service was noticed. It also put paid to the suggestion that 'emotionalism' was a disqualification for judicial appointment. She cleverly wove in a snipe at her critics by demonstrating that Murphy was all the better a lawyer for his belief in the importance of feeling and emotions. According to Senator Susan Ryan, her polished performance melted the hearts of the doubters.[12] She became a frontrunner.[13] McHugh would have to wait. He did, and was appointed when the next vacancy occurred. This was the moment for the Hawke Cabinet to approve the appointment of a woman, Gaudron, to the High Court.

Appointments to the High Court are a major matter. The Court plays an important and powerful role in the lives of Australians. Gaudron described the Court as being the chief dispute mechanism of society—'the glue that keeps society together' and enables society to work harmoniously.[14] It is the final court of appeal on what the law means in Australia.[15] It interprets and applies the laws made by the parliaments of Australia and can declare laws invalid if the Commonwealth or States overstep their legislative competence under the Constitution. This can affect a government's legislative program. Professor R. S. Parker noted, 'When we face future questions in Australian politics we cannot reckon without the Constitution.'[16] Legal historian Professor John Williams says that Australian history 'can be told through the High Court'.[17]

In the 1980s and 1990s, when Gaudron was sitting on the Court, most Australians became aware of its power with the publicity attracted by its decisions on *Mabo* and *Wik* concerning indigenous title to land.[18] Its decision in the *Patrick Stevedores* case ended the waterfront dispute of 1998.[19] The divisiveness of the political, legal and industrial issues raised by this dispute, and its resolution, was dramatised in a television docu-drama, *Bastard Boys*. There was further public attention on the Court's role in 2007, when it upheld the validity of the Howard Government's *WorkChoices* legislation.[20]

On 6 February 1987, Justice Anthony Mason, the then longest

serving member of the Court, was appointed Chief Justice on the retirement of Sir Harry Gibbs. Justice John Toohey and Mary Gaudron were appointed to fill the vacancies. Toohey was deliberately made the more senior of the two to make it clear that it was he, not Gaudron, who was being appointed to the vacancy created by Murphy's death.[21] The *Australian Financial Review* wrote, 'The Federal Government has produced the unlikely result of an ecstatic Labor Party…The Gaudron-Toohey team also delivers the type of liberalisation of the court which will appeal to Labor supporters.'[22] American political scientist Jason Pierce, in a study of the High Court under Chief Justice Mason, wrote in 2002, that '[b]y the late 1980s a coterie of like-minded, reform-oriented judges was assembled, skeptical about the orthodoxy and intent on advancing a new institutional vision.'[23]

Gaudron's appointment was of particular interest to the public. It was also the more controversial of the two.[24] When Gaudron's appointment was announced on 8 December 1986, the Opposition called for her to sever all links with the Labor Party.[25] There were cries of cronyism and 'jobs-for-the-mates'.[26] *The Australian* summed up her appointment as 'essentially political', under the caption: 'Gaudron: controversy is certain.'[27] The article gathered the views of those who regarded her appointment as tokenism, and who thought there were State court judges with more experience than Gaudron could offer. It also referred to those who credited the Government for making the appointment on the grounds that it furthered the affirmative action program. Gaudron was offended by the suggestion that she was a 'token woman'.[28]

While recognising she was a 'brilliant advocate' with vast experience in the High Court arguing for NSW, the *Sydney Morning Herald* explained the Opposition's 'barely disguised criticism' of her appointment:

> Miss Gaudron's appointment will be controversial only in part because of her closeness to the Labor Party. Past political affiliation is not a bar to the High Court. The concern about Miss Gaudron's appointment arises from her political connections and questions about her judgment. Those questions stem

very largely from her handling of three controversies: the demotion of the Arbitration Commissioner, Justice Staples; the Age Tapes; and the allegations by the Chief Stipendiary Magistrate against Judge Foord.[29]

Controversy about some of her last actions as Solicitor General followed the announcement of her appointment to the High Court. One *Sydney Morning Herald* headline read 'New judge in row over drug appeal'.[30] It dealt with Gaudron's opinion that a light sentence imposed on a drug trafficker should not be appealed. The Shadow Attorney General John Dowd claimed that there had been too many decisions made in the past two years which defied common sense.[31] The article referred to the suggestion of independent NSW MP John Hatton that her 'slip-shod' decision was made without reading the trial judge's remarks on sentence. Gaudron did not like it. She sought and received an apology in the newspaper early in January 1987.[32]

The criticism was painful to Gaudron.[33] She was powerless to refute it.[34] What she could do would be to prove herself on the Court, converting criticism to high praise. She intended to be seen as equal to the best, and up to the task. She wanted not only to prove the critics wrong but to make a significant contribution to Australia's legal justice system.

One voice in support of Gaudron's appointment was that of Geoff Kitney, a political journalist, who had an idea of what that contribution might be: 'The appointment of two new judges, Mary Gaudron and John Toohey, at the same time as Sir Anthony [Mason] became Chief Justice, is seen as being likely to strengthen the "contemporary values" credentials of the court.' He referred to the reported comments of Chief Justice Mason that it was appropriate for the Court to take into account the changing values of the community. Kitney concluded that rather than Gaudron being regarded as a 'token woman' appointed by a Labor Government, 'a much fairer view of her appointment would be that it represents a major step in the sophistication of the court'.[35]

The NSW Bar responded to her appointment with restraint.

Early in May 1987, the NSW Bar Association held a dinner for her, attended by about 200 barristers and judges in the Association's banqueting rooms in Phillip Street. A good number of female barristers attended, and a disappointing number of males.[36] Tony Whealy, QC, as he then was, enjoyed the task of honouring Gaudron without acclaiming her:

> This vivacious, forceful, often troublesome but always exuberant personality has taken upon herself that which (in a different context—I think he was speaking of Death!) Dickens described as 'The grim solemnity of the Sages and Patriarchs.' It is a long and awesome task that confronts Mary Gaudron. It is also an important one, not only for her but for Australians and Australia too. It is my hope that in meeting the challenge of that task, she will retain her vivacity, her force and exuberance.[37]

Seconding the toast was a junior barrister, who had not previously met Gaudron. While Gaudron received good wishes from all, not much was said of the way in which the Court, and Australians generally, might benefit from her intellect, as is normally the case, nor a word of confidence in her ability to complement the excellence of the High Court bench.[38] The press attributed this muted enthusiasm to the Bar's view that Gaudron did not have the legal standing, experience and depth in law of, for example, Justice McHugh of the NSW Court of Appeal, whom the NSW profession generally would have preferred.[39]

Gaudron's home town of Moree reported her appointment with a front page story in the *Moree Champion* on 9 December 1986, in which it listed her career achievements.[40] Two days later a small article appeared on page sixteen, headed 'The Gaudron decision was made years ago'. It included a blurred class photograph produced by one of Gaudron's childhood friends in which Mary Gaudron's face as a six-year-old was circled. It attributed the appointment to the family kitchen table around which Mary sat with her father and where her passion for law and politics was kindled, mentioning the influence of Evatt's visit to her home town during the 1951 referendum to ban the Communist Party. Thereafter, Moree seemed to forget its clever daughter.

Richard Ackland's periodical, *Justinian*, noticed her. On her joining the High Court, under the caption, 'The High Court's junior', it said:

> There was no hint at the welcoming ceremony that she had been the present government's most controversial appointment to that jurisdiction, or that almost every criterion the Australian Bar Association had urged should not count in High Court appointments had in her case proved decisive, or that the sole criterion the Association had commended would have placed the claims of a host of other possible candidates well ahead of hers.[41]

While it acknowledged that Gaudron was a University Medallist, it was dismissive of her achievement by claiming that 'academic distinction alone cannot make a practitioner strong in professional merit'. On the contrary, the columnist thought that 'this melancholy catalogue of sins of omission and commission as well as the better claims of other candidates' should have counted against her appointment.[42]

Against this background of reservations and outright criticisms, Gaudron's appointment was also a 'good news story' for women. In her inaugural speech Gaudron lamented that her situation was unique, and she applauded the women who helped the struggle for equality:

> Because I believe that too often, we emphasise differences at the expense of common cause, I would wish that the day had arrived when the appointment of a woman to this Court was unremarkable. Whilst I am the first woman appointed to this Court, my appointment is the result of the courage, determination and professionalism of women who made their mark in the profession in days when the value of women's contribution had to be established.

She made particular reference to Dame Roma Mitchell, who was present at the ceremonial sitting,[43] continuing:

> Of the many women lawyers who were instrumental in advancing the status of women within the legal profession, Dame Roma Mitchell's contribution merits particular acknowledgement…My constitutional duty is to all Australians but I hope that consistent with and by reason of the discharge of that responsibility, I shall be able to contribute as effectively to the status of women lawyers as has Dame Roma.[44]

Gaudron was less restrained in her language about the role of the Court. She acknowledged the changing times and the need to adapt jurisprudential thinking within the limits allowed by the law in the attempt to achieve equal justice. Mentioning that Jeremy Bentham dismissed the idea of a natural right, even to liberty, as 'terrorist talk' and 'nonsense on stilts', she continued with a passage that clearly reflected the formative influences of her education as a lawyer:

> Of course, the law has changed since the time of Jeremy Bentham, and so too have people's expectations of it. Social, political, technological and economic changes have placed added demands on the law, and have also given impetus to new patterns of jurisprudential thought and a requirement for the critical evaluation of conventional judicial method.
>
> Whatever be the long term implications of that evaluation, three things will, I believe, remain inevitably unchanged: the need for rigorous and dispassionate intellectual analysis; the obligation to ensure equality before and under the law; and the obligation to ensure that justice is done in accordance with the law.[45]

The first paragraph reflected Julius Stone's teachings; the second, the teachings of Frank Hutley. The speech provided an early indication of her intention to apply a combination of two judicial methods to her judging role on the Court.

Given Gaudron's association with the Labor Party and the social reform issues she had supported, High Court watchers expected her to move beyond this to attempt, through the law, to achieve active social reform. To an extent, with others on the Court, she did. Interestingly, as Professor Tony Blackshield observed, if social justice was the goal, Gaudron developed 'more intricate' legal reasoning to achieve it compared to her fellow judges, while remaining faithful to the existing law.[46] Throughout her time on the High Court she was portrayed as 'progressive', and yet her interpretation of many aspects of the law appeared to some legal commentators to be 'conservative'.[47]

The Court Gaudron joined coincided with the opening of a new chapter in its history. As a consequence of the 1977 amendment to the Constitution, judges now retired no later than seventy. This meant a speedier turnover of judges. A second change in 1984 was the abolition of the automatic right of appeal from other courts to the High Court; instead, such appeals could only be heard if the High Court granted special leave. This change allowed the High Court to confine appeals to cases in which an issue of special or public importance was raised. Third, the Privy Council in London no longer had a role in Australia's judicial system. The remaining right of appeal from State Supreme Courts had ended with the *Australia Act 1986* (UK) and the *Australia Act 1986* (Cth), an achievement Gaudron actively supported as NSW Solicitor General. The High Court had no competing authority. Finally, Gaudron and Justice Toohey were fresh blood for the bench newly headed by Chief Justice Anthony Mason. And Gaudron, of course, was the Court's first female appointee. Change was in the air.

Out with the old

Each newly appointed High Court Justice is expected to sit for a large portrait-style photograph to be hung in the gallery of judges in the foyer of the High Court building. Perhaps wanting to avoid a staid image, Gaudron's photograph is not of the forty-four-year-old who joined the Court in 1987. She chose the photograph taken on the occasion of her becoming Solicitor General in 1981, at age thirty-eight. It is an attractive photo of her youthful and smiling face, brightened by her white blouse with black and tan spotted motifs. It stands out as a bright reminder in the Court's photographic history of the moment in time when a woman first joined its bench.

One change was made in direct response to the novelty of a female Justice. The judges decided that the title 'Mr Justice' would no longer be used. The term 'Justice' was adopted. Eventually, other courts made the same change to overcome the 'Mrs or Madam Justice' dilemma. Another oddity was the convention of judges referring to each other as 'brother judges'. The notion of judges referring to their 'sister judge' did not take hold. When, in 2009, three of the seven judges were women, the judges accepted that they would refer to each other as 'colleagues'.

Gaudron made a few changes of her own. The first concerned the roles her three staff would play and, as other judges followed her lead, a tradition disappeared. She wanted to be surrounded by less pomp and more brains. In addition to an associate, Gaudron was entitled to a tipstaff (or 'Justice's assistant') as well as a secretary or personal assistant. A tipstaff is a minder of sorts who attends to the personal needs of the judge, runs errands, assists the judge to robe, and even pulls out their chair to ease their judge into position behind the bench. While the tipstaff sat in court and followed the proceedings only to the extent necessary to anticipate their judge's in-court needs, the associates, whose job it was to research and assist the drafting of judgments, were not necessarily in court. The Chief Justice's associate, for example, may be the only associate listening to the case. Gaudron saw no sense in this division of labour. She preferred two legally trained people with research capacity. Judgment writing is hard: 'daunting', according to Justice Hayne; 'unremitting', requiring intellectual intensity and long hours, according to Justice Gummow; and, according to Gaudron a decade into the work, 'the writing never gets easier', requiring research and 'articulation of issues with precision'.[48]

On commencing, Gaudron asked candidates for the associate position if they would be prepared to share the two allocated salaries for an associate and tipstaff, and the duties that went with them. This meant that one or other of the associates could be in the courtroom performing the 'tippy's' role and hear the case on which Gaudron was sitting. It made it easier for the associates to assist with the case research and decision-writing. Other judges, envious of Gaudron's new arrangement, adopted it. Some of the more traditional judges clung to their tipstaves for a time, if only because they had provided long and loyal service.

Gaudron did not have protégés in mind for the associate positions. She contacted Macquarie University. It was a lucky day for Margot Stubbs, a country girl who had just returned home after completing her law degree. She had a good relationship with the receptionist at the law school who knew Stubbs would jump at the opportunity. The first 'job share' appointees were Stubbs and Kevin Connor.

Stubbs' interview was memorable. She saw Gaudron, the professional and very much a mother, in action. It took place in Gaudron's book-lined room in the Goodsell Building in Sydney where the Solicitor General's office was then housed. Gaudron's son, Patrick, then about five-and-a-half years old, was there too. He was causing his own special havoc with a stick that he was poking into the back of his mother's chair. The effect was to push his mother forward into her desk. Gaudron interviewed Stubbs while her body moved involuntarily backwards and forwards in a jerking fashion as Patrick poked away. The telephone rang and Gaudron excused herself to take the call. Patrick returned to his toys and Stubbs was left on the leather settee, whiling away her time. She asked Patrick why he was not at school. He came and sat on the lounge beside her and deliberately rubbed his body against hers. Then he answered, 'chicken pox', and added as he rubbed, 'and now you are going to have it'.

She got the job but not the chicken pox. Gaudron was amused when Stubbs told her the story many years later. Gaudron's recall of the interview was Stubbs' self-description that she was a 'neo-Marxist feminist with a sense of humour'. That, according to Gaudron, is what gave her the job. Her sound intellect and ability to make good coffee also played their part.

Gaudron, keen on supporting gender equity, selected one male and one female for her associates when she could. Associates' terms were generally for a period of one to two years before they moved on to practise at the Bar, or take up some other aspect of their career. In the event, up to the year before her retirement, twenty-four (two-thirds) of Gaudron's thirty-five associates were women. Justice McHugh favoured women. One of his explanations for why most of his associates were women was that the majority of the best law graduates were women. Another, he admitted, was that 'I very much like women.'[49] Justice Gummow generally appointed men. Justice Kirby's chambers, when he later joined the Court, became known as the 'Ken and Barbie' chambers, as he seemed always to appoint not only highly intelligent associates, but beautiful ones, one male and one female.

One of Gaudron's associates secured an interview at age ten. Janine Lapworth was interested in law as a child, and she wrote a letter to Gaudron when she first took her place on the bench in 1987. Gaudron, no doubt remembering Doc Evatt's response to her own curiosity about the law at a similarly impressionable age, invited the girl to the High Court. Stubbs was charged with the task of showing young Janine around. Lapworth pursued her interest in law and, at the turn of the century, became one of Gaudron's associates.

Gaudron was behind a change in the dress of the Court's justices. The issue of whether barristers and judges should continue to wear wigs and gowns sparked a lively debate in Australia's legal circles. It was raised at the High Court's planning meeting in Gaudron's first year at the Court. She argued strongly to be rid of both wigs and gowns for the Court's justices (other than on ceremonial occasions). She failed to persuade them then, but succeeded in having the matter included as a standing agenda item for future meetings. In 1988 the justices agreed that wigs would no longer be worn, although they would still wear their black robes. It was not until 1997 that the Federal Court adopted a similar practice.

Gaudron bucked another tradition. In 1988 she declined appointment as Companion of the Order of Australia in the Bicentennial Australia Day honours list.[50] Gaudron has refused to say why she turned it down. 'It's one of those things protocol says you do not talk about,' she said.[51] It has been suggested that her stand was a show of solidarity with Lionel Murphy, who refused to accept the then customary knighting of High Court Justices.[52] It is also consistent with her stand on equality. She did not want to encourage social distinctions, particularly in a circumstance where the honour was bestowed because of the office held, not because of the exceptional work of the person holding it. 'I am only doing my job,' she would say.[53]

There was one aspect of new thinking that she did not embrace. In the year of her appointment in 1987, smoking was banned in the Australian public service. On being informed of the ban, Gaudron made a request of the young person responsible for the delivery rounds. She said:

> Well, they may have banned smoking in the High Court building, but my chambers are not part of the building, and I would like a circular to go out to everyone telling them that if they want to smoke, they can come to my chambers.[54]

Fortunately for Gaudron, all the judges' chambers have access to a balcony where those who wanted to smoke could do so.

Gaudron was ready for the task ahead. She had large reserves of emotional energy, was a sound judge of character and had great confidence in her own intellectual ability.[55] She did not lose her capacity to be ferocious when angry, nor her essential kindness and acute awareness of other people's feelings. Despite the seriousness of the job, she retained her sense of humour. She continued, as far as she could, her life as an 'ordinary person', including the obligation of an ordinary mother to drive her child to his sporting activities.[56]

Incarcerated in Canberra

The High Court moved to its own building in Canberra in 1980. Its new building was designed to accommodate three impressive courtrooms lined with sound-absorbing Australian timbers and comfortable chambers befitting the highest judges in the land. With the public in mind, it is light and spacious, with a large entrance hall, a cafeteria and, as well as stairs, ramps to give access to the elderly, those with disabilities, and people with children in strollers. Outside it is surrounded by nearly a hectare of quarry tiles featuring a long and gently sloping waterfall.[57] Its large size and height reflect its importance, yet its heavy asymmetrical architecture projects an air of uncertainty, no doubt reflecting the feeling of litigants who come before it. The large concrete structure is daunting against the backdrop of placid Lake Burley Griffin. The High Court became known as 'Gar's Mahal' in legal circles, the new building having been former Chief Justice Garfield Barwick's idea.[58]

As comfortable as the daytime environment was, the judges had to contend with the difficulties of isolation and loneliness. Chief Justice Mason described it thus:

> I found working in the Court in Canberra artificial and insular. The Court is a Canberra monument, virtually on the lakeside, surrounded by green parkland. It is a world away from shops or restaurants except for those in the National Gallery and the National Library. The entire working day was spent in the building. If you went out to lunch, which one did rarely, it was necessary to make a car trip. In Canberra, a High Court Justice is more removed from the community than is a judge on a court in one of the State capitals.[59]

The Court usually sits in Canberra for the first two weeks of each month except for January and July, and for most of those months most of the judges work in the Court researching and preparing judgments, as they might in the second two weeks of the sitting month. In addition to more regular trips to Sydney and Melbourne to hear special leave applications, the Court sometimes travels to Hobart, Brisbane, Adelaide and Perth. It hears special leave applications in the more distant capital cities by video link from Canberra. Sir Anthony Mason remembers when the new technology to do this was still to be perfected. There was an occasion when the video link was interrupted and the image of the justices on the screen was replaced by characters from *Sesame*

Street. The Registrar reported that counsel did not think that there was much difference between the Justices and Big Bird and his companions.[60]

Life at the top can be lonely at night, too, after the day's work is over. Some stay or eat at the Commonwealth Club; on one occasion three Justices were observed to be sitting and eating at separate tables. Understandably, people do not necessarily seek the company after work of those with whom they work each day. Most judges whose families are interstate find an apartment or town house suitable for a single person. They soon discover that they are in a city that turns in early on weeknights, and most crave the company of their own family and the comfort of their own bed. Aspiring lawyers, in their eagerness to climb the judicial summit, might underestimate the loneliness of a long-distance judge. One lower court judge remarked that 'life on the High Court bench would be like serving twenty years hard labour'. Another, considering this, concluded: 'and I think that after all the ceremony has ended, and the congratulations have faded away that his assessment was and is a chillingly accurate one'.[61]

Sir Ronald Wilson experienced the cold fact that with the prestige of a judicial appointment comes some loneliness.[62] Sir Daryl Dawson described why:

> Canberra in the middle of winter at night is not exactly...a glamorous life...You get back to your little flat, freezing cold. You stand there watching the television while eating your solitary sandwich night after night. It is not glamorous, I can tell you.[63]

It was no different for Gaudron. Her husband and children were in Sydney. Not that going home brought her much peace. As she acknowledged, 'Problems with teenage children do not evaporate when their mother becomes a High Court Judge.' She went home to be a mother where she was used 'as a taxi service'.[64]

Gaudron found ways to combat loneliness in Canberra. She would often dine with Jeffrey and Tricia Miles at their Canberra home, and sometimes dine with friends who were Federal Court judges when they were hearing cases in Canberra. She also accepted invitations from the local Bar and Women Lawyers' Associations to speak at their dinners. She was always entertaining at these events and offered enthusiastic encouragement to women lawyers to pursue their careers with vigour.

Gaudron initially leased a flat close to the Court. She later moved to the prestigious suburb of Yarralumla, a more convivial place to live, with a local shopping centre where people gather to shop and eat. It is a leafy suburb nestled between a golf course and the shores of Lake Burley Griffin. Gaudron enjoyed visiting the local bakery in the mornings, where the coffee was good—always important to her. She was not too proud to say 'hello' and have a chat to people she had met during her forays into Canberra as a judge of the Arbitration Commission, and mingle with the patrons, without any pomp.[65]

Learning curve

It was fitting that Gaudron's first Full Bench case as a Justice of the High Court should concern procedural fairness. *Fadel Zecevic v DPP*[66] is cited as an early example of how she:

> ...combined technical mastery with a general tendency to insist on strict compliance by trial judges with their obligations in directing juries—a tendency that seems motivated by an interest in ensuring both procedural fairness for the accused and due respect for the function of the jury in the administration of criminal justice.[67]

Fresh from her role as NSW Solicitor General, she had a preoccupation with fairness in the justice system, sensitive to what she believed were unfair processes employed in the course of the Wran and Murphy prosecutions.

On Gaudron's second day the Full Court heard *Jackson v Sterling Industries*.[68] This time she agreed with the minority decision of Chief Justice Mason and Justice Deane, the beginning of a common alignment in the three's views. Nevertheless, she wrote a separate decision. The case concerned the scope of the judicial powers under the Constitution, an area in which Gaudron had gained some specific insight and expertise as NSW Solicitor General.

On her third sitting day she heard a case concerning the application of the Captain of HMAS *Penguin* for the issue of a Writ of Prohibition directed to Kim Beazley, Minister for Defence.[69] It was now that she found her voice on the bench, asking questions of counsel in the course of their submissions.

Voicing her opinion sparked a new controversy. In September 1987, still affected by the pursuit of Premier Wran and Justice Murphy by enforcement agencies and the media, she spoke at the 24th Australian Legal Convention in Perth about the criminal justice system—the dangers of the current trends in the criminal investigative process—and the competing aims of using electronic eavesdropping to fight crime and the maintenance of people's rights. She talked of the need for review mechanisms to improve the accountability of agencies like the Director of Public Prosecutions and the National Crime Authority that had wide investigatory powers.[70] Her colleague, Sir Ronald Wilson, a former Crown prosecutor, speaking at the same conference, openly disagreed with her view that decisions to prosecute should be the subject of review. He said that in balancing the need for checks and accountability against speedy trials, he favoured speedy trials.[71]

The press had a good time with it. Gaudron was voicing her views in a public debate over a sensitive question of government policy. John Slee of the *Sydney Morning Herald*, and a frequent Gaudron critic, portrayed her as carrying emotional baggage from her time as NSW Solicitor General: 'Old wounds from the Justice Murphy prosecution have clearly been opened at the 24th Australian Legal Convention...'[72] The editorial in the *Sydney Morning Herald* asked, 'Was it the High Court judge or the former NSW Solicitor General' talking?[73] More followed, linking Gaudron's friendship and support for Justice Murphy to her speech, and implicitly criticising her use of her judicial status to bat for a cause.[74] Her remarks, it was suggested, were a veiled attack on Ian Temby's decision to prosecute Murphy in November 1984 after the second Senate inquiry. Temby was also at the conference and defended the role of the Director of Public Prosecutions.

Gaudron did not like the publicity. She declined to be interviewed about it.[75] Thereafter she kept a low public profile. She agreed to speak at Women Lawyers' Association functions (mostly on the basis that it was not recorded), and at some ceremonial or special occasions.[76]

The boys on the bench

Gaudron was the smiling new girl on the block. She took her seat on the bench alongside her six male colleagues: Chief Justice Sir Anthony Mason, and Justices Ronald Wilson, Gerard Brennan, William Deane, Daryl Dawson and John Toohey. Since Toohey was appointed on 2 February 1987 and Gaudron on 6 February, he established seniority over her. This meant that during sittings of the Full Court, Gaudron, the smallest in stature, trailed in at the end of the line of male judges, headed by the Chief Justice. The judges enter the Court from the side of the bench, which is raised on a platform at the front of the Court. The Chief Justice sits in the middle, the most senior puisne judge on his right, the next on his left, and so on in alternating positions down to Toohey and Gaudron, the 'bookends' at each end of the bench.

Being the only woman on the High Court, Gaudron said, 'I do not want to be the first and last. People might say "we tried a woman once and it did not work".' Asked what it was like to be the only woman, Gaudron answers with the word, 'improbable'. She described one of her more improbable experiences that concerned a colleague who showed an interest in feminism. He asked her what sort of feminist she thought he was.[77] She told a group of women lawyers that until then she had not thought he was any sort of feminist, but she knew what sort he would admire—educated, intelligent, witty and individual—so she said, 'I think you might be a Mary Wollstonecraft feminist.' She reported:

> He thereafter read much of her writings and delved into the life of that great philosopher and would-be revolutionary who advocated radical political reform and, who, as a single woman in London in the last part of the 18th Century, wrote

and published works of fiction and philosophy, as well as political tracts, openly engaged in sexual liaisons, gave birth to and reared an illegitimate child, twice attempted suicide and then died giving birth to the child who later wrote Frankenstein. It was a mistake to introduce him to Mary Wollstonecraft for he thereafter categorised me, rather churlishly, I thought, as 'wimp feminist'.[78]

Gaudron's presence awakened some of the other Justices to issues of discrimination against women. In October 1989 she was flying with her colleagues to Perth in an Air Force Hercules, because of a pilots' strike that made commercial flights irregular at the time. There was 'a certain camaraderie in the plane' until, by way of general conversation, Gaudron informed her colleagues that she would be speaking to a gathering of women lawyers in Perth. She did not expect the reaction she received. 'It might have been better if I had started dancing the Can-Can. It was clearly inappropriate for me to attend, much less speak at, such a gathering.'[79] One suggested that she was being discriminatory by attending and questioned the need for women to have separate professional organisations, because 'there is no discrimination in the law'. Another, according to Gaudron, 'by way of final judgment on the ignominy of what I was about to do, said, "Not even Lionel [Murphy] would have done such a thing".' Their attitude, she said, was short-lived, because that evening the judges were to dine at Perth's exclusive 'men only' Weld Club. Gaudron was accepted as an 'honorary male' but she refused to eat anywhere that barred women.[80]

Gaudron established sound relationships with her male colleagues. Chief Justice Mason was a little reserved in his new position to start with. But soon enough, and to the surprise of many High Court watchers, Mason, Deane and Gaudron formed a regular core of the Court's majority, often delivering joint judgments.[81] 'Surprised', because it was not expected that Gaudron would be embraced by two senior, well-respected jurists, both appointed by a Liberal-National Coalition Government. Both men regarded her highly, intellectually and personally, and she remained firm friends with each of them. Gaudron enjoyed a particularly relaxed relationship with Mason.[82] He, in turn, enjoyed her refreshing style and provocative nature. He recalled a case where, with another judge, they were sitting on a special leave application in Perth relating to Rugby League salary caps. During the course of the argument, Gaudron said sarcastically in a voice that he thought could be heard by others, rather than a whisper that would not, 'It's nothing more than a slave market.'[83]

Deane, so well-liked when he later became Australia's Governor-General, had little time for pomp and circumstance, and was more outspoken than Gaudron. Gaudron, so very informal when she was out of the public eye and always free of professional self-importance, was mindful that her performance was being closely scrutinised because, as a woman, she was an oddity on the bench. She did not want to jeopardise the prospect of other women being appointed to the bench, and so was most careful to present publicly as appropriate and professional.

Wilson was the most senior puisne judge when Gaudron joined the Court. He had previously been Solicitor General in Western Australia. He felt an outsider in the course of his successful legal career, humbled by his ordinary education. He also felt that Sydney-based High Court judges, who then dominated the Court, were inclined to be centralists, supporting Federal Government moves to extend its powers over the States. Wilson expressed delight at Gaudron's appointment, happy to see a female on the bench. He was pleased about Toohey's appointment, too, because he was a fellow Western Australian.[84] Both, he believed, were appointed because of their ability to do the job.[85] Nevertheless, Wilson and Gaudron did not have much to do with each other. While there was no sign of animosity between them arising from their early public clash of views, they were not likely buddies.[86] She was fiery. He was at all times a model of courtesy.[87] He was a devout Christian and had an abhorrence of swearing. Further, while Wilson related well to all the justices, he thought that socialising with them should be limited 'to avoid interest groups and power blocs forming on the bench'.[88]

Gaudron also had a good working relationship with Dawson,

a Victorian, who also came to the bench from the position of state Solicitor General. He was, though, more conservative in his approach to decision-making, and was regarded as a traditionalist. Gaudron also developed a long-standing friendship with Justice Gerard Brennan, who became Chief Justice in 1995 on Mason's retirement. Gaudron's chambers were next door to Toohey's and they became good friends, and she enjoyed his company when she was in need of a balcony-cigarette. She had given up smoking for a brief time during Chief Justice Mason's reign but she took up again at the end of 1997. Despite doctors' advice to the contrary, she told her friends that smoking made her 'feel better'.

Michael McHugh joined the bench when Wilson retired. He and Gaudron were friends, McHugh being the barrister who attempted to sell his chambers to Gaudron when she first came to the NSW Bar and was thwarted by the opposition of male barristers on the floor. Bill Gummow, who joined the bench in 1995, became a special friend of Gaudron's. He and Gaudron had attended the University of Sydney Law School together, competing for prizes in equity law. She topped the year, winning the John Geddes Equity prize, while Gummow won the E. D. Roper Memorial prize in equity and commercial law. She regarded his intellect highly and he was impressed with Gaudron's reasoning in her decisions, though he can be regarded as generally jurisprudentially more conservative. The more radical Justice Michael Kirby, already a friend of Gaudron's, joined the bench in 1996, filling the vacancy created by Deane's departure to become the Governor-General in 1995.

Official 'informal' photograph of the justices during Sir Anthony Mason's Court leadership, 1987. (Sitting, left to right) Chief Justice Anthony Mason, Daryl Dawson, John Toohey; (standing) Ronald Wilson, Gerard Brennan, Mary Gaudron and William Deane. (Courtesy the High Court of Australia.)

Official 'informal' photograph of the justices on the induction of Chief Justice Murray Gleeson, 1998. (Sitting, left to right) Chief Justice Murray Gleeson, William Gummow; (standing) Michael Kirby, Ian Callinan, Kenneth Hayne, Michael McHugh and Mary Gaudron. (Photo David Coward, courtesy the High Court of Australia.)

Justice Mary Gaudron 'holding court'. Official 'informal' photograph on induction of Justice Michael Kirby, February 1996. (Sitting) Justice John Toohey, Chief Justice Gerard Brennan, Justice Mary Gaudron; (standing), Justices Michael Kirby, Daryl Dawson, Michael McHugh and William Gummow. (Photo David Coward, courtesy the High Court of Australia.)

Chapter Fourteen

GETTING TO MABO: THE MASON COURT AT WORK

There was a point when Australia led the world in the quality of its judges. Three stand out: Mason, Deane and Gaudron.
Geoffrey Robertson, 1998[1]

Judicial activism v black-letter law

Gaudron joined the High Court at an exciting time. A new era was about to begin. Sir Anthony Mason, sworn in as Chief Justice on 6 February 1987, declared that '[o]ur courts have an obligation to shape principles of law that are suited to the conditions and circumstances of Australian society and lead to decisions that are just and fair'.[2] Some commentators claimed that the age of 'black letter' law or 'legalism' had ended, replaced by an age of 'judicial activism'.

One international observer saw the period from the mid-1980s to the mid-1990s as no less than 'a revolution'.[3] Mason, Chief Justice from 1987 to 1995, portrayed the Court's shift in approach 'more as a reaction to a series of changed circumstances' of which there were many and which 'would be very difficult to catalogue'.[4]

It was undoubtedly a significant decade in the Court's history.[5] Gaudron was in the thick of it.

The Court's approach to its tasks became the subject of extensive debate. Controversy about Gaudron's appointment was subsumed in controversy about the 'Mason Court'. Two issues in particular branded the Mason Court as activist. One was its handling of indigenous land rights in the *Mabo* case. The other was its expansive approach to implied constitutional rights and freedoms.

Judges have some latitude in how they approach their role. In part, it derives from the knowledge and experience they bring to the bench. It is also necessary because the British system of law practised in Australia consists not only of parliament-made laws, but also of 'judge-made' law, the common law. High Court judges, for example, look to the Court's previous decisions concerning cases with similar-fact situations (precedents) to guide their decision-making. The dynamic process of 'distinguishing' one set of circumstances from another permits the law to grow incrementally. As new precedents are established, the common law develops. The Court's decisions can move with or veer away from previous decisions as new situations and new circumstances confront it. Which way it has swayed and how far has depended on the jurisprudential thinking of the judges composing the Court at any particular time.

At the heart of the debate about the Mason years is whether the Court went beyond legitimate incremental law-making, 'long recognised as their proper role', and actively intruded into matters properly the preserve of parliament.[6] Crucial questions included the extent to which the Court should develop the law to meet changing circumstances in society, or leave it to the parliaments to legislate when new laws are required? Should judges assert their own values, or avoid doing so?

Two schools of thought have developed on the proper role of the Court. The traditionalists—'black letter lawyers'—favour an approach that relies on the text and structure of legislation when interpreting it, adhering to legal principles derived from existing law and previous authoritative cases (legal precedents), strict analytical and conceptual techniques of formal legal reasoning, notwithstanding that outcomes might not meet contemporary societal expectations.[7] They are often associated with legal positivism.[8] According to Sir Owen Dixon, in 1952:

> close adherence to legal reasoning is the only way to maintain the confidence of all parties in Federal conflicts…It may be that the court is thought to be excessively legalistic. I should be sorry to think that it is anything else. There is no other safe guide to judicial decisions in great conflicts than a strict and complete legalism.[9]

The High Court is generally said to have approached its role this way, though the Court's leading student, Professor Leslie Zines, has shown that even Dixon did not invariably adhere to the strict legalism he advocated, and periodically took account of social and policy considerations.[10]

By contrast, others interpret the law liberally, permitting adjustment where existing law does not sufficiently cover new circumstances or meet contemporary values. This has been called 'realism', and those who practise it, 'judicial activists'.[11] Justice William Deane is said to fall into this category; Justice Michael Kirby, who joined the Court after Mason's retirement, is another recent judge regarded as adopting this approach.

Gaudron does not fall comfortably into either of these categories. Her judicial reasoning is noted for its legalism and the rigorous application of principle and logic. Nonetheless, because during the Mason years she joined the majority in some notable cases that interpreted the law to reflect contemporary values, she has frequently been cast as an activist. In fact, she combined the two different approaches to the judge's role, using the existing law in an original way as a tool for social justice, displaying the influences on her thinking of both Frank Hutley and Julius Stone. Professor Julius Stone's progressive social values and his jurisprudential teachings underpin Gaudron's decisions. At the same time, her regard for the existing law is reminiscent of Frank Hutley.

Politics behind the Court

A central question is how the Constitution, a document drawn up at the end of the nineteenth century to fit the political circumstances at the time, should be interpreted in conditions more than a century later. Should the Court interpret it as it was intended to be read when it was adopted and confine itself to declaring what the law is in relation to the case before it, or should it consider the contemporary consequences of its decisions? Even before his appointment as Chief Justice, Mason expressed a more liberal approach to constitutional interpretation than Dixon. Mason regarded constitutions as documents framed in general terms to accommodate the changing course of events so that courts interpreting them must take account of community values. In 1986 he observed that '[t]he ever present danger is that "strict and complete legalism" will be a cloak for undisclosed and unidentified policy values'.[12] Dixon's protégé Sir Robert Menzies perhaps came close to the truth in the statement attributed to him that 'constitutional law is only half law and half philosophy, political philosophy'.[13]

A study of the Court's decisions during its first century illustrates that the Constitution is a document that can be read literally, liberally, flexibly, in conjunction with the social thinking of the times, consistently or inconsistently with prevailing attitudes, approached as a dynamic or fixed document, depending on the boldness or otherwise of the Court. When the Constitution was drafted in the late nineteenth century, the imperative was for nationally uniform laws relating to, for example, national defence, immigration, customs and currency. It was designed to provide the national parliament with the necessary powers to present a unified nation to the international community, and a domestic uniformity that would facilitate interstate commerce and freedom of movement. At the same time its mission was to preserve the authority of various States to make laws with respect to their own domestic affairs and, in particular, education and health. Its present form represents a compromise—the maximum agreement that could be reached between States of varying sizes, population, resources and interests.[14]

A century later, advances in information technology, communications and transport, the impact of a global economy on national affairs, and changing societal expectations, mean that the Constitution has to be worked with and worked around. It has proven difficult to amend. Formal alteration essentially requires a Bill to be passed by both houses of the Commonwealth Parliament, and approved in a referendum by a majority of Australian voters nationwide as well as by a majority in a majority of the States.[15] This has happened only on eight occasions out of forty-two referenda to date.[16] Thus, as Professor Geoffrey Sawer noted in 1949, judicial interpretation has often been the means of effective change.[17]

The High Court's interpretation of the Constitution and its application to today's society has often been difficult and sometimes controversial. Its rulings on the validity of Commonwealth and State legislation and other decisions inevitably have implications for Australian society and citizens.[18] It was commonly believed that judges drawn from the law, a politically conservative profession, would construe the Commonwealth's legislative powers narrowly, even emphasising the meaning of the Constitution given to it in 1900. Conversely, the Labor Party was seen to favour greater central powers to accommodate its social welfare programs or its environmental agenda, as in the *Tasmanian Dam* case of 1983, and therefore looked to appoint judges likely to favour a broader interpretation of the Commonwealth's specific powers to make laws under section 51 of the Constitution.

Cases featuring Commonwealth versus State powers as a significant issue did not arise during Mason's chief justiceship (with two and, after 1989, three Justices appointed by Labor governments). Mason later noted it was significant that 'the two most sensationalised decisions of the High Court in the last half-century' were not constitutional decisions but decisions on indigenous land rights.[19] In later years the Mason Court gave expansive interpretation to a number of Commonwealth powers, but this approach was not confined to Labor-appointed judges. Further, the decision in one important case that did reach the Court on the question of the Commonwealth's use of its legislative power surprised those who assumed the Court would support the expansion of the corporations power. The Commonwealth Parliament had passed the *Corporations Act 1989* to provide for a uniform national corporations law. The Court (including Gaudron), in an almost-unanimous joint judgment in the *Incorporations Case* found the law invalid; only Deane dissented.[20] Ironically, the next landmark case after the *Tasmanian Dam* case of 1983 that would extend the Commonwealth's powers at the expense of the States occurred under the more conservative Court in 2007—the *WorkChoices Case*. Justice Callinan, who (along with Kirby) dissented in *WorkChoices,* highlighted the irony in suggesting that, as a result, the majority decision in the *Incorporations Case* 'may well now be effectively overruled'.[21]

By Mason's time, the political focus had changed, and the 'centralist' and 'States' rights' boxes ceased to be appropriate for the placement of judges. The boxes had been re-labelled 'judicial activism' and 'black-letter law'. The popular view was that Labor governments would look for judicial activists who would pursue social justice in their decisions, while Coalition appointees might be expected to take a more restricted approach, applying the law as they found it to the case before them. This simplistic typecasting ignored the fact that Chief Justice Mason and Justice Deane of the so-called 'activist era' were Coalition appointees (Mason in 1972 and Deane in 1982). And they formed part of the six to one majority in *Mabo*, the case most responsible for the Court being seen as 'activist'; Deane with Gaudron delivering the most radical of the Court's judgments.

Mabo: 'the darkest secret of our history'

As a child brought up in Moree's divided community of 'black' and 'white' peoples, Gaudron had witnessed, first-hand, discrimination against Aborigines. The *Mabo* decision,[22] which pronounced the law on indigenous land rights, was of crucial importance to her. While she had spoken of her appearance in the 1972 *Equal Pay Case* and her participation in the *Maternity Leave Case* as important and exciting points in her career, *Mabo* was the high point of her work on the High Court. It was as if her whole life experience and legal career had been a preparation for her participation in *Mabo* when it came to the Court in 1992. When a ten-year-old girl wrote to Gaudron and asked her, 'What is the most important case to you?', Gaudron's lengthy reply, in essence, was '*Mabo*'.[23]

In June 1987, during her first year on the Court, Gaudron considered the place of indigenous customary law in Australian law in *Walden v Hensler*.[24] Walden, an elder of the Gungalida tribe in North Queensland, was prosecuted for a breach of Queensland's fauna conservation law. He had been hunting on a property with the permission of the station manager, and had killed a bustard (bush turkey) for food. He had, all his life, hunted for traditional food in accordance with his people's custom. He also took a turkey chick for his child as a pet, intending to release it into the bush when it grew up, as was required by custom. He was charged with having the two birds in his possession without a permit. His defence was based partly on an honest claim of right derived from Aboriginal custom. The Court accepted that Walden honestly believed that he was doing nothing wrong but the majority held that customary rights alone were not sufficient to form the basis of a defence under the legislation.

Toohey dissented. He had been Aboriginal Land Commissioner from 1977 to 1982. In that role he heard claims under the *Aboriginal Land Rights (Northern Territory) Act 1976* (Cth), and perhaps, among the judges, had the best understanding of Aboriginal and Torres Strait Islander customary law.[25] Gaudron, also in dissent, considered that customary law could form part of the law in Australia and provide a defence in a case such as this where the legislation *permitted* its recognition. It was also an early expression of Gaudron's concept of equal justice. Her decision, legalistic and intricate, incorporated the paradoxical notion that discriminatory treatment that accommodated different legal systems and different peoples was required for the delivery of equal justice.

In 1999, post-*Mabo*, in *Yanner v Eaton*, Walden's defence was raised again, this time successfully.[26] Yanner was a member of the Gungaletta tribe. Like Walden, he was charged under the same Act with taking two young estuarine crocodiles without a permit. In this case, with Gaudron in the majority, it was held (consistently with *Mabo*'s recognition of title rights) that the customary law applied because it was not *excluded* by the legislation.

The history-making decision in *Mabo* gave legal recognition of the relationship of indigenous Australians to their lands. It provided a new lens through which all Australians could view their past. In May 1992 five people from the Murray Islands in the Torres Strait took proceedings against the State of Queensland to the High Court. Led by Eddie (known as 'Koiki') Mabo, they claimed that since time immemorial the Meriam people had continuously occupied and enjoyed the islands and had established settled communities with a social and political organisation of their own. In 1912 the islands, except for two acres leased to a mission, were 'permanently reserved and set apart for use by the Aboriginal inhabitants of the State' pursuant to the *Land Act 1910* (Qld). The claimants sought a declaration that, while acknowledging that the islands came under the sovereignty of the Crown as part of the Colony of Queensland in 1879, they were subject to the Meriam people's rights to the lands according to their local custom, their original native ownership and their actual possession, use and enjoyment of the islands. They also sought payment of compensation for any impairment of those rights by the State.

The *Coast Islands Declaratory Act 1985* (Qld) was the State Government's response. The object of this law was to extinguish any native title that might otherwise exist upon annexation of the Murray Islands, and in so doing it provided that no compensation was payable in respect of any rights that existed prior to annexation. The High Court did not dismiss the claim out of hand. It remitted the case to the Supreme Court of Queensland so that it could take evidence and make findings of fact, on the basis of which the High Court could then determine the legal issues.[27] The proceedings in the Supreme Court were assigned to Justice Martin Moynihan, who began taking evidence on 13 October 1986. But legal objections (known as demurrers) continued before the High Court and, on 13 February 1987, the hearings before Moynihan were adjourned until the issues on demurrer were decided.

Gaudron joined the High Court in time for the hearing of *Mabo v Queensland (No. 1)* in 1988, generally known as *Mabo No. 1*.[28] The matter concerned Queensland's reliance on the *Coast*

Islands Declaratory Act 1985 (Qld). Six of the seven judges agreed that, if valid, the statute was sufficiently 'clear and plain' to extinguish native title. A majority of four to three, however, held it was invalid because it was inconsistent with the *Racial Discrimination Act 1975* (Cth).

Gaudron joined Brennan and Toohey in holding that 'the attempt to extinguish the traditional legal rights...is undone by s10(1) of the *Racial Discrimination Act*.'[29] Deane formed the same view in a separate judgment. Whether the claimants had a valid claim was not decided at this stage.[30] The case returned to the Queensland Supreme Court for determination of the facts as to whether native title could be established. Justice Moynihan resumed his hearings. On 5 June 1989, he found that the claims relating to offshore waters could not be sustained. He therefore made an order dismissing the Commonwealth from the action. He handed down his findings as to the remaining claims relating to the Murray Islands on 16 November 1990.

In the meantime two of the claimants died. In addition, Eddie Mabo's claim was undermined by arguments about his heritage rights. He had been adopted under customary law. The litigation was at risk of being sidetracked by arguments about whether his adoption was recognised at law. He reluctantly withdrew from the proceedings. He maintained his interest, and the proceedings retained his name. It was pursued by the surviving claimants, David Passi and James Rice. The case came before the High Court again in 1992 in *Mabo v Queensland (No. 2)*, generally referred to as *Mabo*. The High Court now had to decide the substantive issue of whether native title could exist in Australian law, and whether the Meriam people had established their title right. It heard argument from 28 to 31 May 1991, delivering its decision on 3 June 1992, ten years after the litigation had commenced. Eddie Mabo had died on 21 January 1992.

In *Mabo No. 2*, the High Court found that native title did exist in Australia. It was the first common law determination of native title in Australia. The majority held, amongst other things, '[t]hat the Meriam People are entitled as against the whole world to possession, occupation, use and enjoyment of the Murray Islands'.

Although the Court's declaration was expressed to apply in principle to 'the Murray Islands', it in fact only related to the Island of Mer, where the remaining two claimants had an interest. No final decision was made about the other Murray Islands of Dauar and Waier. This was significant because it had implications for indigenous land right claims elsewhere in Australia. The traditional rights of the holders of native title could no longer be ignored.

The Court dispelled the notion that Australia was *terra nullius* (a term in the judgments borrowed from international law) when the British established sovereignty over Australia and denied that the Crown obtained full legal and beneficial ownership of all lands. This aspect of the Court's findings does not reflect the intricacies of the decision. The Court did not undo existing law. It has long been accepted that indigenous peoples occupied Australia before the British claimed sovereignty. The Court accepted the legitimacy of the occupation and settlement of Australia by the British and the establishment of British laws, despite their finding that New South Wales was not 'unoccupied' when it was settled by the British.

The crux of the decision of the majority, Mason, Brennan, Deane, Toohey, Gaudron and McHugh, with only Dawson dissenting, was that the British common law as it applied to Australia recognised native title to the land; but only to the extent that it had not been extinguished by the law under British and later Australian rule. It held that native title could be extinguished by the grant of an interest in the land by the executive government or the legislature, as had legitimately been done since British settlement.

Deane, Toohey and Gaudron, though in the minority in this aspect of the decision, found that native title could not be lawfully extinguished without a clear and unambiguous legislative intention. In their view it followed that there might be situations where native title had been unlawfully extinguished and, where that had occurred, the title-holders had a right to compensation. The federal Labor Government seemed to think this was a reasonable proposition. Following the decision in *Mabo*, the *Native Title Act 1993* (Cth) was passed, validating land titles given to non-indigenous interests from 1975 (following the racial discrimination legislation) to 1994 when the *Native Title Act* took effect. In return, compensation had to be paid to the dispossessed indigenous groups. It also gave indigenous people the right to negotiate native land titles.

Once the notion of *terra nullius* was rejected, the High Court looked to the common law concerning land rights of indigenous people. The largely unanticipated and unique aspect of the decision was that the Court used international law to inform it about the common law that applied to the Meriam people's claim. It held that Australian common law, like the common law of other places colonised by the British, recognised the pre-existing land rights of indigenous people. The decision was consistent with court decisions in the United States, Canada and New Zealand, as well as with later decisions of the Privy Council dealing with indigenous rights in British colonies in Africa.[31]

In raising and rejecting the notion of *terra nullius*, the Court, without overturning previous case law, did depart from a view taken by the Privy Council in 1889 in *Cooper v Stuart*[32] on the status of the early occupation of NSW. The High Court was free to do so. The Privy Council's acceptance of the proposition that NSW was 'unoccupied' at the time of white settlement in the late 1800s (although without using the term *terra nullius*) had already been questioned by Justice Blackburn in relation to Gove Peninsula in the Northern Territory, in the *Gove Land Rights* case. Blackburn acknowledged Aboriginal occupation of their traditional lands and the injustice they had suffered.[33] However, he regarded himself as bound by the Privy Council decision.[34] The High Court, in 1992, had no such constraint.[35]

A significant aspect of the majority decision in *Mabo* is that future action to remove native title will be difficult because State legislation is subject to the *Racial Discrimination Act*. Further, the Commonwealth has to comply with the constitutional requirement that acquisition of property must be effected on 'just terms'—that is, that it must be accompanied by the payment of compensation.

The *Mabo* decision has been the subject of much criticism, in particular, that the Court had engaged in law-making. It did, as every case that declares new law does. More serious is the criticism that, in going beyond what was necessary to decide the case before it, the Court was adopting an inappropriately political role.

Critics argued that the decision to allow the existence of native title throughout Australia was wrong because the issue before the Court was not mainland Australia but the Murray Islands in the Torres Strait.[36] Those who take this view point out that the island of Mer had a long history of settlement, agriculture and land tenure that did not necessarily exist on the mainland.

Mabo is also the case that is most cited by critics of the High Court as evidence of its 'activism'—in giving a decision that was thought to go beyond a declaration of what the law is, to making the law into what the Court thought it ought to be. Criticism also centred on the language of the decision and not simply the decision itself.[37]

The emotions expressed by Deane and Gaudron came under particular criticism. One judge said with reference to Deane and Gaudron's joint judgment, that '[i]t was one thing for the court to overturn *terra nullius* but quite another to do so with such moralising tones'.[38] Judges customarily do not reveal who is the lead writer of a joint decision. The fact that Deane and Gaudron gave their decision jointly indicated that they both saw a place for expressing emotions in their reasons for decision in *Mabo*. In contrast to Brennan, who reasoned that a 'factual error' set the common law on a mistaken path in relation to native title, Deane and Gaudron were of the view that the facts concerning indigenous occupation were known but ignored.[39]

The decision formed part of the development of a notion of justice that raised the complex issues of what amounts to equal treatment and what amounts to discriminatory behaviour.[40] Deane and Gaudron regarded acknowledgment of past injustices as necessary if the integrity of the law was not to be undermined, because long acceptance of legal propositions, particularly those relating to real property, 'can of itself impart legitimacy and preclude challenge'.[41]

Supported by scholarly research, they told the story of dispossession of the original inhabitants. They were unrestrained in describing the past treatment and dispossession of indigenous Australians. They declared:

An early flash point with one clan of Aborigines illustrates the first stages of the conflagration of oppression and conflict which was, over the following century, to spread across the continent to dispossess, degrade and devastate the Aboriginal peoples and leave a national legacy of unutterable shame.[42]

They went on to describe the shame of the dispossession of the Aboriginal peoples of most of their traditional lands:

The acts and events by which that dispossession in legal theory was carried into practical effect constitute the darkest aspect of the history of this nation. The nation as a whole must remain diminished unless and until there is an acknowledgment of, and retreat from, those past injustices.[43]

Later in their judgment they explained their use of emotive language. (Pierce suggests that they explained their use of language because they were '[c]ognizant that [their] supercilious tone may offend the orthodox norms').[44] They said:

[W]e are conscious of the fact that, in those parts of this judgment which deal with the dispossession of Australian Aborigines, we have used language and expressed conclusions which some may think to be unusually emotive for a judgment in this Court. We have not done that in order to trespass into the area of assessment or attribution of moral guilt. As we have endeavoured to make clear, the reason which has led us to describe, and express conclusions about, the dispossession of Australian Aborigines in unrestrained language is that the full facts of that dispossession are of critical importance to the assessment of the legitimacy of the propositions that the continent was unoccupied for legal purposes and that the unqualified legal and beneficial ownership of all lands of the continent vested in the Crown.[45]

These few sentences angered some jurists because Australian judges had historically 'avoided writing in moralising tones'.[46] According to Pierce, one judge said Deane and Gaudron's opening paragraph shocked the profession: 'It was over the top—way over. That wasn't logical thinking. It was anger, emotion. Judges don't write that way.'[47] Another judge considered that the legal community was particularly taken aback by the 'moralising' tone the majority judgments employed, and that of Deane and Gaudron 'caught the most ire'.[48]

Other judges applauded it.[49] And, outside the legal profession, Deane and Gaudron's judgment is often quoted for its incorporation of understanding of the indigenous relationship to land. The academic philosopher Raimond Gaita explores issues of justice and the place of acknowledgment of collective responsibility for wrongs done by our 'political ancestors'.[50] He questions the morality of the 'practical' stand that only looks forward; that refuses to look backward to acknowledge the deep shame of the past. This, he says:

> ...treats as morally and politically irrelevant the fact that the Aborigines are landless because they were dispossessed rather than because of a natural catastrophe. More generally, it treats as irrelevant that their suffering is saturated by a justified sense that they have been terribly wronged. To ignore that, to insist high-mindedly that real moral concern focuses on the present and the future rather than the past, is to compound their humiliation and our shame.

Gaita names Deane and Gaudron as the judges who saw this matter quite clearly. In his view their use of uncharacteristically emotive language did not detract from, but made more powerful, the logic of their reasoning. It was essential, for 'they were applying a concept of justice that went beyond the simplicity of the formula that "equal treatment *equals* equal justice".' According to Gaita, 'justice' demands more than a declaration of indigenous land rights, because that declaration alone could not return the original occupiers of the land to their land.

Gaudron, as a judge in *Mabo*, played a part in what has been described by historian Henry Reynolds as 'the correction of

Australia's documented history'. According to Reynolds, a mentor to Eddie Mabo, the case was about both law and history. *Mabo* re-directed past thinking about the place of indigenous land rights in the British legal system that Australia acquired on colonisation. He said of the six majority judges:

> Their main business was jurisprudence. But the passion, which drove the judgment, came from a deep sense of the need to remedy historical injustice with Justices Deane and Gaudron referring to a legacy of unutterable shame.[51]

Gaudron knew before studying the research presented to the Court that as a people, Aborigines and Torres Strait Islanders belonged to their land and lived by established customs, and were not nomads who lived without rules. She had lived amongst Aborigines in Moree, later employed them, befriended them, and heard their stories. However, while Moree left an impression on Gaudron, her decision in *Mabo* made none, sadly, on Moree. Gaudron's role in it, as a girl from Moree, was not brought to the community's attention. Noeline Briggs-Smith, Aboriginal Researcher for the Moree Library, was unaware that Gaudron participated in the case. She believes that *Mabo* was of little significance to the local indigenous community.[52] This is in contrast to their awareness of the land surrender at Wave Hill in 1975, resulting from the wide publicity given to a photograph of Prime Minister Gough Whitlam pouring sand into Vincent Lingiari's hand. The photograph was taken by an indigenous photographer, Mervyn Bishop, who came from Brewarrina, near Moree.

The *Mabo* outcome and Gaudron's role in it were not even mentioned in Moree's local newspaper. The day after the decision, the *Moree Champion* carried a story about a 'bitter row' between 'ousted Moree Aboriginal Land Council Chairman, Mr Lyall Munro Snr, and the State and Regional Land Councils' over the appointment of an administrator to the Council. It also reported that the Moree Plains Shire Council would unanimously oppose the Aboriginal Amaroo land claim in favour of a development proposal.[53] This was perhaps indicative of the slight significance

Mabo played in the day-to-day lives of most Aborigines affecting, in principle, large tracts of relatively unusable land in Australia.

The Constitution: rights and freedoms

Mabo was not the only reason that the Mason Court was labelled 'activist'. Another significant feature which invited criticism of the High Court during Mason's chief justiceship was that it led exploration and development of implied rights contained in the Constitution. The Court found that the Constitution offered a range of human rights protections to individuals despite the absence of a Bill of Rights.

In 1988, in *Davis v The Commonwealth*, the Court applied the common law principle in support of freedom of expression in its consideration of the scope of the Commonwealth's legislative power to make laws for the planning of the 1988 Bicentenary celebrations.[54] Indigenous protestors sued the Australian Bicentennial Authority for its refusal to permit the sale of T-shirts bearing slogans such as '200 years of suppression and depression'. The High Court held that the statutory regime under the *Australian Bicentennial Authority Act 1980* (Cth) went beyond what was reasonably necessary to achieve its legitimate objects and impinged on freedom of expression. Mason, Deane and Gaudron wrote in their majority joint judgment:

> Although the statutory regime may be related to a constitutionally legitimate end, the provisions in question reach too far. This extraordinary intrusion into freedom of expression is not reasonably and appropriately adapted to achieve the ends that lie within the limits of constitutional power.[55]

In the 1989 case of *Street*,[56] the Court declared that section 117 gave a constitutional guarantee of equality by protecting individuals from discrimination by reason of the State in which they lived.[57] Section 117 states that a resident of one State shall not be subject in any other State 'to any disability or discrimination which would not be equally applicable to him' if the person were resident in such other State. Three years later there were controversial decisions in *Nationwide News* and *Australian Capital Television* cases,[58] in which the Court recognised that the Constitution implied a freedom of communication about government and political matters, including election advertising. It did so with reference to the Constitution having provided for a system of government that entails representative democracy. If democracy was the object, then, according to the Court, there was an implied right that people were free to communicate. It was not an 'absolute freedom', Gaudron acknowledged, because a law which curtails the freedom of communication is valid if its purpose is not to impair freedom but to secure some other end within the Commonwealth's power. However, it must do so in a manner that 'is reasonably and appropriately adapted to that end'.[59]

In *Cunliffe*, one of a trilogy of cases delivered on the same day on the implied freedom, Gaudron said:

> If a law which operates to curtail political discussion is not reasonably and appropriately adapted to its stated purpose, it may be inferred that its purpose is other than as stated... Similarly, if a law imposes a direct prohibition on political discussion in an area where none previously existed, it will ordinarily be concluded that it has the impermissible purpose of curtailing that discussion unless it can clearly be seen to be serving some overriding and important public interest.[60]

In *Stephens*, one of the other cases, Mason, Toohey and Gaudron held that the implication of freedom to communicate as to political matters related to government at state level.[61] The third case, *Theophanous*, controversially extended this right in offering protection against defamation laws.[62] While aspects of this decision, as outlined in the joint judgment of Mason, Toohey and Gaudron, were ultimately rejected by the Court, *Lange v Australian Broadcasting Corporation* affirmed the essential idea that actions for defamation in political cases are subject to the implied freedom.[63]

In a later case, *Kruger* (the *Stolen Generation Case*), Gaudron found that the implied right of freedom of political communication extended to freedom of association and movement. The case concerned the validity of a Northern Territory law that authorised the removal of children from their Aboriginal families between the years 1925 to 1960. The issues raised in it were complicated by the fact that the Commonwealth legislation was based on its 'Territories power' (section 122 of the Constitution), and the members of the Court differed as to whether the freedoms implied in the Constitution applied to the Commonwealth's exercise of this power. Gaudron thought they did. She also found that the law infringed the express constitutional prohibition on 'the free exercise of any religion' contained in section 116. She was alone in this view, although Toohey and Gummow were sympathetic to the idea.[64]

Also important was a series of cases in which the Court implied the right to a measure of procedural fairness in the exercise of the judicial power dealt with in Chapter III of the Constitution. This arose from recognition in the Constitution of the need for an independent federal judiciary. Separation of the three branches of government—executive, legislative and judiciary—and their powers, is a constitutional safeguard against arbitrary power and a protection of liberty. This is reflected in Chapters I, II and III of the Commonwealth Constitution which deal with the Commonwealth Parliament, the Executive Government, and the Judicature respectively. In 1956 the High Court reinforced this in the *Boilermakers' Case*, when it held that it was unconstitutional for the Commonwealth Court of Conciliation and Arbitration to exercise both arbitral and judicial powers because of the acceptance in the Constitution of the separation of administrative and judicial powers.[65] As a result, two separate bodies were established, one of which was the 'non-judicial' Conciliation and Arbitration Commission of which Gaudron became a deputy president, the other, the Commonwealth Industrial Court. According to Gaudron, *Boilermakers'* was about the 'protection of individual rights and freedoms'.[66]

The High Court had recognised that the separation of powers doctrine operated to promote the independent and impartial exercise of judicial power and the rule of law.[67] But until the Mason Court, the Chapter III provisions were regarded merely as delineating the Commonwealth's jurisdiction to exercise judicial power. The Mason Court, however, inferred from the Constitution the requirement that the judicial power had to be exercised with a level of judicial due process. 'Due process' is the essence of procedural fairness. It implies the like treatment of like persons in like circumstances. The results might differ, but the processes should always be fair. 'Procedural fairness' is often termed 'natural justice' and includes the right to be given a fair hearing and the opportunity to present one's case.

Deane and Gaudron were the strongest promoters of the implied constitutional requirement that due process had to be followed in the exercise of judicial power. Deane took a broad view, believing that this was implicit from the democratic system of government recognised by the Constitution as a whole. He said in Dietrich v The Queen, a case concerning fair trials:

> The fundamental prescript of the criminal law of this country is that no person shall be convicted of a crime except after a fair trial according to law. In so far as the exercise of the judicial power of the Commonwealth is concerned, that principle is entrenched by the Constitution's requirement of the observance of judicial process and fairness that is implicit in the vesting of the judicial power of the Commonwealth exclusively in the courts which Ch. III of the Constitution designates.[68]

Gaudron, in the same case, was not so sweeping in approach, but as strong in result. She believed that the exercise of judicial power by definition incorporated the requirement of due process:

> The fundamental requirement that a trial be fair is entrenched in the Commonwealth Constitution by Ch. III's implicit requirement that judicial power be exercised in accordance with the judicial process.[69]

She argued that the judicial function had to be exercised in accordance with the judicial process or it was not an exercise of judicial power under section 71, and cannot be exercised by a federal court.[70] Gaudron had regard to the text of Chapter III, and in keeping with 'the law matters' principle, she developed her view of the meaning of federal judicial review by drawing on principles extracted from previous cases. She reasoned that a law that required a court to exercise its power in an arbitrary or discretionary way, or in any way other than in accordance with the judicial process, was invalid, because it would be contrary to the proper exercise of 'judicial power'.

The common thread of the Court's decisions concerning the exercise of judicial power by federal courts is the putting of 'justice' into 'judicial power' in Chapter III of the Constitution. Mason explained:

> There was a time when it was thought that the courts administered the law as distinct from justice. This is not the position today. And judicial concern with the idea of justice is at bottom one of the reasons why the courts have refined some of the principles of substantive as well as procedural law.[71]

The development by the High Court of an implied right in the Constitution to a fair trial exposed it (and Gaudron) to more criticism.

The High Court criticised

The head-turning case of *Mabo*, cases concerning implied rights, and some other important but less controversial cases led Jason Pierce to claim that the High Court became politicised under Chief Justice Mason. Gaudron does not escape. He states:

> Justice Gaudron frequently lined up as a Mason reformer and promoted the politicized role. Sometimes she provided just her vote. Other times she pushed reforms even further than her reform-minded colleagues.[72]

Pierce asserts that 'from the mid-1980s to the mid-1990s, a group of High Court judges embarked on a concerted effort to redefine substantively their institution's role within the political system'.⁷³ He calls the work of the Court during the Mason years a transformation from 'an orthodox judicial role to a new politicized judicial role', stating that the Court's politicisation of the judicial role represented one of the most, if not the most, significant developments in Australia's history. He wrote:

> ...the role transformation depended heavily upon the right collection of judges assembling at the Court. Chief Justice Mason was central to the transformation, but he needed willing collaborators—judges who shared in a larger, more politicized vision of the Court. He got just that with the appointment of Deane, Toohey, and Gaudron.⁷⁴

These judges, he concluded, in showing their willingness to recognise that matters of public policy cannot be divorced from difficult and ambiguous questions of law, advanced the 'politicised' role of the Court.

One High Court Justice interviewed by Pierce 'circumspectly confessed the Court's preference for fairness over certainty'; another 'confessed' to the possibility that the judges were more mindful of social justice issues than their predecessors. This judge explained that they provided a forum for those who do not have voices elsewhere in the political system, partly because there is no bill of rights in the Constitution.⁷⁵ Pierce describes this as 'the Mason Court's penchant for fairness'.⁷⁶

To some it might seem strange that a court could be criticised for pursuing 'fairness'. Yet the Mason Court was seen by many as guilty of straying from its 'proper' role in its pursuit of fairness and social justice. Pierce included Gaudron in his list of those whom he believed used the Court to achieve 'social justice', stating that 'both Mason and Gaudron would bring leadership to the role of transformation'.⁷⁷ Gaudron, he noted, consistently supported the most controversial Mason-era decisions such as *Mabo*, the Court's landmark case on indigenous land rights; *Wik*, which extended the land rights concept; *Cole v Whitfield*,⁷⁸ which clarified the meaning of section 92 of the Constitution dealing with the freedom of interstate trade and commerce; *Australian Capital Television* and *Nationwide News*, on freedom of the press; and *Dietrich*, on fair trials.[79]

Pierce's case examples, however, do not always illustrate his point. *Wik* was not a decision of the Mason-led Court. And the decision of *Cole v Whitfield* was welcomed, rather than being the subject of controversy, because, as Professor Ronald Sackville explained, 'the Court abandoned an economically and historically indefensible construction on s92 of the Constitution...'[80] Mason's view is that Pierce overstates the extent of the change made by the Court's decisions and its realist methodology.[81]

Most Australian legal commentators would agree that the shift in the High Court's jurisprudence was substantial. Some applauded it while others welcomed what they saw was an equally significant shift back to a narrower and more legalistic approach from the mid-1990s. Whether or not it is accurate to describe it as a politicisation of the Court is also a matter of debate. Sir Gerard Brennan, who succeeded Mason as Chief Justice, for example, does not regard the Mason Court as having been politicised, except in the sense that the members of that Court displayed the policy and value considerations which underlie legal principles and were prepared to articulate legal rules in accordance with the principles as properly understood.[82]

One writer's analysis is that Mason led the Court with a 'realist' methodology, while Deane and Toohey were notable for their 'natural law' perspective, one that saw the role of the law to protect the interests of individuals, an aspect which drew Gaudron's support.[83] Possibly relevant to this is the unusual factor that six out of the seven Justices in the Mason Court were raised as Catholics, though not all were practising Catholics when members of the Court.[84] Whether or not they adhered to the faith, their Catholic background might well have instilled a strong sense of social justice. Further, the dependence of Catholic doctrine on a theory of natural law might have reinforced the social justice approach which some regard as distinctive of the High Court during this period.

Gaudron was a bold but nevertheless legalistic lawyer. She

did not like to strain the language of legislators. Her decisions supported social justice outcomes where logical reasoning and correct application of legal principle allowed. Her judicial method supported protection of individuals, particularly those vulnerable by reason of their history or particular circumstances. If she set herself the challenge of achieving just outcomes consistent with current values while adhering to the existing law, she would face a difficult task. She might have taken an easier track and embraced a broader policy-driven approach to the application of legal principles, as Deane and Toohey did on occasions. Justice Kirby, for example, openly concedes that where the law permitted, he took public policy considerations into account in forming judgments.[85] Gaudron, by working through existing law, often arrived at similar outcomes supported by different reasoning. In this respect she was neither a 'Kirby' nor a 'legal positivist' at the other end of the spectrum, like Justice Wilson.[86]

The comments Pierce recorded in his interviews of past and present Australian judges were, necessarily, unattributed. But they do not provide evidence that the supposed 'ring-leaders' of the group in fact collaborated or intended to do so. The Justices have always discussed cases during or after the hearings, at least in the course of the inevitable chatter in the lift taking them to their chambers at the completion of a case. They need to identify which judges will draft the majority, or a joint minority, decision. They rarely act alone in developing their reasons for judgment. The circulation of proposed decisions and the supporting reasons can assist others, as can discussion or conferences.[87] The High Court building has a spacious book-lined room containing a large round table designed for this very purpose. The judges also meet on a one-to-one basis. Gaudron and Deane did so because they worked well together.[88] Some judges are less willing to engage in discussion than others.

While Mason hoped that there would be more joint judgments to clarify the reasons for decisions, it did not happen as much as he would have liked. He had no control over the matter.[89] Mason recalled:

> We met regularly to discuss the judgments, something which had not occurred before in my experience, though there had been meetings to discuss particular cases. Moreover, we made a conscious effort to produce joint judgments rather than a series of individual judgments and, if possible, to bring about judgments which, if not unanimous, were supported by a clear majority, say 5 to 2, rather than by a bare majority of 4 to 3, particularly in important cases. Our efforts were not as successful as I had hoped but, given the extent of our underlying differences of opinion, the outcome was probably as much as could be expected.[90]

A study of the High Court's decisions under Mason does not indicate that there was any 'collaborative plot'. A catalogue of decisions and dissenting judgments demonstrates how the views of the judges diverged. They often wrote separate judgments to express their different thinking about a case. Gaudron did this neither more nor less than others.[91] She addressed issues in separate majority judgments in several significant cases, notably in the case of *Mabo* (jointly with Deane) and in the high profile *Patrick Stevedores* case. She did this when she wanted to explore any issue that was important, or where her views went further on development of the law than the rest of the Court on some aspect of a case.

Intellectually Gaudron was comfortable in the company of Mason and Deane. Both demonstrated a humanitarian approach to the administration of justice. She quickly gained their respect and that of the other judges because of her own intellectual discipline. All liked her for her outspokenness and sense of humour. The High Court under Mason provided a liberal judicial environment in which Gaudron dared to develop some aspects of her notion of justice, under her own constraint of legalism. This was a court on which she felt at home.

Chapter Fifteen

EQUAL JUSTICE: GAUDRON AT WORK

The modern application of the doctrine of equality, particularly in relation to Aborigines, demands that we confront ourselves, confront our preconceptions and our prejudices; it demands that we know ourselves.

Mary Gaudron, 1993[1]

The elusive concept of 'equality'
Nothing in Gaudron's upbringing, at home or at school, taught her that different people should be treated differently, or with varying degrees of fairness. But she witnessed that they were. Aborigines were savagely discriminated against, and treated unfairly; hardworking railway workers lived in poverty and makeshift housing, unlike the families living on the other side of the river. Gaudron had no reason to reconstruct the core values she had grown up with. Her understanding developed in her childhood of what was unfair, unjust or discriminatory, and deepened when she and other women met prejudice in pursuing a career. Her experiences awakened her not only to the racism indigenous Australians suffered but to the injustice of all forms of discrimination.[2] She recognised

that discrimination, often disguised or indirect, had to be exposed and eliminated if a fair system of justice were to be achieved. She looked at discrimination against all minority groups—and how the law could be used to redress it. While perfection would never be achieved, she was watchful for flaws in the justice system and ready to grapple with their underlying causes.

Gaudron's exploration of the notion of justice, and the concept of 'equal justice' and its interrelationship with discrimination, is a strong feature of her decisions during her time on the High Court. She started with the meaning of 'equality' itself. Gaudron acknowledged that it was a difficult concept to define, observing that '[o]utside the field of mathematics, "equality" is an infuriatingly elusive concept'.[3]

She admits to once falling into the trap of assuming the fairness behind the concept of 'equality before the law', when she failed to recognise a difference in a case in which she was involved as a barrister. She recalled what she described as her 'arrogance' when acting for a young mother, Aboriginal, who was gaoled for a minor offence. The mother's young daughter was made a ward of the State and placed in the care of a white Australian couple. On release from prison, the mother sought to regain custody. But she failed to appear at the hearing. When she was located, Gaudron asked why she had not come to court. 'I didn't want to go to gaol.' The answer, Gaudron noted,

> [t]old eloquently of her only experience of the law, namely, of going to court through one door and coming out several months later via prison. And it need hardly be said that she did not get her daughter back, partly because her failure to appear at the earlier hearing was taken to indicate a want of genuine concern for the welfare of the child.[4]

Gaudron conceded, 'It never occurred to me. I didn't know.' She drew on this experience to illustrate that as a general rule, lawyers are not always sensitive to the thinking or feelings of those who, because of their circumstances or history, require additional or special differential treatment.[5]

Gaudron demonstrated a deeper understanding of the need for differential treatment for people when she was Solicitor General. A non-custodial sentence had been imposed on an Aboriginal man for robbery. Gaudron had to consider whether the Crown should appeal against the leniency of the sentence. She acknowledged that, on its face, the sentence was 'manifestly inadequate'. On reviewing the facts and circumstances she advised against an appeal. The man, twenty-seven, was a heroin user. He had been in and out of institutions since he was fourteen. She thought that the non-custodial sentence offered the only hope that he might adjust to life as an ordinary citizen. What swayed her was the insight he had shown in giving evidence. With 'telling poignancy' he had said, 'My grandfather didn't know my father and I didn't know my father, now I am not going to get to know my sons.'[6]

Gaudron's experiences were important to her view that understanding equality has much to do with understanding differences. She emphasised that equality is not uniformity; it is not sameness:

> How could it be when we are all different with different talents, different intellectual abilities, different needs, different interests, different priorities and different personalities. Equality is the recognition of relevant difference and, where there is relevant difference, adaption appropriate to that difference.[7]

Put simply, a requirement that all people, including those who are wheelchair-bound, use stairs to access a public building is one that treats people equally, but is unfair because it indirectly discriminates against those who cannot climb stairs. This can be addressed by a law requiring installation of ramps and lifts in public buildings.

Gaudron's succinct definition of equality's opposite, 'inequality', as 'the different treatment of persons who are equal and the equal treatment of persons who are different',[8] reveals the twist that makes the concept of equality difficult to grasp. She stressed that equality requires not only the rejection of 'irrelevant distinctions', but must, at the same time, take 'genuine differences' into account.[9]

In *Street* she found that discrimination consists in treatment that is not 'appropriate' to a real or 'relevant difference'.[10] Her judgment in that case is said to have provided what has since become a leading statement of the meaning of discrimination within Australian law.[11] As she put it on another occasion, important to her notion of equal justice was that it must be free of discrimination—'blind to differences that don't matter but...appropriately adapted to those that do'.[12]

She recognised that such differences as race, religion or sex are generally not relevant differences, but they may be where they give rise to different needs.[13] She noted that Sir Richard Blackburn, when a justice of the Northern Territory Supreme Court, articulated the complexity of delivering equal justice as early as 1968.[14] In hearing an appeal by a noted Aboriginal leader, Dexter Daniel, against a conviction of having insufficient visible lawful means of support, Justice Blackburn pointed out that although the law applied to whites and to Aborigines, it was 'an error to assume that there is one standard of living which is regarded as the norm for all persons in the community'. He ruled that the court must have regard to Mr Daniel's 'actual standard of existence and address itself to the means that he has for support at that standard'.[15]

The simple notion that 'equality' requires not only that similar cases must receive similar treatment but that different cases must get different treatment permeates Gaudron's understanding of justice. That is, injustice occurs when *equal* treatment ignores a relevant difference; it requires *different* treatment which must be 'appropriate and adapted to a relevant difference'. Once the concept of recognition of relevant differences is encompassed in the notion of equal justice, unfair discrimination can be identified, and the law adjusted to remove it. In *Leeth*, Gaudron said:

> Leaving aside the special problems associated with the equal treatment of persons or things that are different, in a constitutional context discrimination is constituted by the different treatment of persons or things that are not relevantly different. And even if there is a difference of that kind, different treatment will constitute discrimination if it is not

reasonably capable of being seen as appropriate and adapted to that difference.[16]

And, of the judicial process, she said:

> All are equal before the law. And the concept of equal justice—a concept which requires the like treatment of like persons in like circumstances, but also requires that genuine differences be treated as such—is fundamental to the judicial process.[17]

In *Kruger*, members of the Stolen Generation argued that there was an implied guarantee of legal equality. Gaudron emphasised that equality before the courts permits discriminatory laws, because the legal concept of discrimination is one that differentiates discrimination *between* people from discrimination *against* people. She explained that there is a limited constitutional guarantee of equality before the courts, not an immunity from discriminatory law.[18]

Gaudron applied her notion of equal justice to identify discriminatory actions or laws in many cases that came before the Court concerning the different treatment of things, such as application of taxes, as well as of people.[19] She promoted the recognition of discrimination in operation as essential to achievement of 'equal justice'. But unfair discrimination is sometimes indirect and not always easy to identify.

Nailing discrimination

In 1989 Deane and Gaudron delivered a joint majority judgment in *Banovic*, the leading case on indirect discrimination in the workplace.[20] Direct discrimination, where there is different treatment, is more readily addressed under the law. Indirect discrimination is where, notwithstanding the same treatment, there is a different outcome. Deane and Gaudron formed a majority with Dawson (Brennan and McHugh dissenting), to unmask the apparently equal treatment of a company's workforce to reveal indirect discrimination against female workers.

The case concerned the employer's practice of 'last on, first off' for retrenching workers. On its face it was not discriminatory, as more men than women were retrenched. A group of eight retrenched female workers claimed they were discriminated against because of the employer's preference for recruiting men. They argued that because women waited longer to be employed, they lacked employment seniority and were therefore more vulnerable to retrenchment. The majority agreed that the 'last on, first off' formula was flawed in a workforce that was predominately male. Deane and Gaudron found that the retrenchment policy was 'indirect' discrimination as a consequence of past discriminatory recruitment practices of a preference for men, and held that it offended the anti-discrimination legislation.

Gaudron was also attuned to discrimination against women in a domestic situation. In a civil action concerning the amount of an award of damages to an injured man, Gaudron identified what she saw as erroneous assumptions made about the role of women in the home. In 1992 the High Court, in *Van Gervan v Fenton*, considered the method of assessing the notional value of the time spent by a wife who provided attendant care services to her injured husband.[21] The Court held that compensation should be measured by reference to the market value of the services provided rather than to the family member's forgone earnings. Gaudron agreed. But, for good measure, she wrote a separate judgment addressing arguments put to the Court with which she strongly disagreed. She explained why no deduction from market value should be made for the domestic services previously provided by the injured man's wife. She said, first, that the assumption that the services given by his wife before the accident were 'needed' by her husband, rather than part of a normal domestic relationship, is an assumption that implies 'incompetence and selfishness of a very high order'.[22] She also refuted the argument that the injured man already had the services of a wife and, therefore, to the extent that the accident gave rise to a need for those services, no requirement for compensation for those services arose. She said, 'At best, that equates a wife to an indentured domestic servant—which she is certainly not.'

The relationship of discrimination to Gaudron's special notion of equality is an essential starting point for Gaudron's evolving concept of judicial due process. This is demonstrated in *Leeth*.[23] Richard Leeth had been convicted under Commonwealth law by a State court of conspiring to import into Australia a commercial quantity of cannabis resin. The *Commonwealth Prisoners Act* 1967 provided for a non-parole period which differed depending on the law in the State where the prisoner was convicted. Leeth claimed that the provisions in the Act that authorised the unequal treatment of Commonwealth offenders were discriminatory and invalid. Mason, Dawson and McHugh said they were not. They denied that the Constitution contained an implied right to substantive legal equality, only recognising the right to procedural equality. Brennan did not agree that the right had been violated, and thus the majority found the sentencing process in accordance with the Act was a valid exercise of federal judicial power.

Deane, Toohey and Gaudron dissented. Deane and Toohey took a broad approach in holding that there was an implied right to substantive legal equality in the exercise of the judicial power. In part, they drew support from fundamental concepts of equality at common law, though the common law, as Gaudron well knew, often relegated women to a status very much unequal to men. Deane and Toohey took a holistic approach to the Constitution, even referring to the words in the preamble (*Whereas the people...have agreed*) to suggest 'the inherent equality of the people'. Importantly, they regarded Chapter III of the Constitution as extending its protection to require a need for 'equal justice', together with express constitutional provisions in particular contexts that required equal treatment or prohibited discrimination.

Gaudron did not support Deane's and Toohey's broad approach. Through more circumscribed and complex reasoning, she found the same implication to be supported by the text of Chapter III of the Constitution; that is, that it was an essential feature of the judicial function that its exercise had to be fair and impartial in accordance with the judicial process. She relied on previous cases in which other members of the Court, including herself, had said as much.[24]

Gaudron's evolving view of equal justice can be seen in a wide range of cases, both criminal and civil. The analysis she undertook of 'citizenship', a concept not referred to in the Constitution but which emerged with the *Australian Citizenship Act 1948* (Cth), reveals her concern about the legal development that treated non-citizens as synonymous with 'aliens' over whom the Commonwealth had constitutional power to legislate. Her special notion of justice is also seen in her thinking about requirements of procedural fairness in administrative decision-making, and where the line is drawn between the judicial and executive functions, particularly in relation to detention of people who have not been found guilty of an offence, and the restriction of rights of specific groups of people.

Right to a fair trial

Gaudron has been portrayed as the 'High Court's chief supporter of due process'.[25] Although the requirement of due process extends beyond the criminal process, the right to a fair trial, an aspect of due process, is most clearly understood in the criminal context. It was described by the majority of the Court in *McKinney v The Queen* (1991) as 'the central thesis of the administration of criminal justice'.[26] But issues arose for the Court as to what requirements were essential to a fair trial.

In *Dietrich v The Queen* (1992)[27] the Court considered whether a fair trial meant that a person charged with a serious offence punishable by a term of imprisonment was entitled to be represented. Dietrich could not afford representation and he had exhausted avenues for legal aid save what was available to him if he pleaded guilty. He had unsuccessfully sought an adjournment of the trial. The High Court considered whether there had been a miscarriage of justice by reason of his not being represented by counsel. The Court held that while there is no common law right to legal counsel at public expense, an indigent accused has a right to a fair trial. If having no legal representation resulted in an 'unfair trial', there must be a stay of proceedings until counsel is provided.

Deane and Gaudron went further. They suggested that the right to representation in this case was founded in the Constitution which, in vesting judicial power exclusively in the courts, requires that judicial process and fairness be observed. Gaudron, in a separate majority judgment, set out the principle, as propounded unsuccessfully by Justice Lionel Murphy in *McInnis*, that every accused person has the right to a fair trial and that this included the right to counsel in all serious cases. Gaudron formulated her ideas more precisely than Murphy, and justified them.[28] On this issue, neither she nor Murphy believed that the Court should take into account government budgetary concerns when considering matters of criminal justice. Murphy, in *McInnis*, had said in dissent:

> If a person on a serious charge, who desires legal assistance but is unable to afford it, is refused legal aid, a judge should not force him to undergo trial without counsel. If necessary, the trial should be postponed until legal assistance is provided.[29]

Gaudron, in *Dietrich*, explained the import of 'fairness':

> In most cases a trial is fair if conducted according to law, and unfair if not. If our legal processes were perfect that would be so in every case. But the law recognizes that sometimes, despite the best efforts of all concerned, a trial may be unfair even though conducted strictly in accordance with law. Thus, the overriding qualification and universal criterion of fairness.

Mason had been in the majority in *McInnis*, where the Court had considered that there had not been a miscarriage of justice by reason of the accused being unrepresented by counsel. On this occasion, he joined with McHugh in finding that, in all the circumstances, Dietrich was deprived of his right to a fair trial and a real chance of acquittal. Brennan and Dawson dissented, agreeing with the decision in *McInnis*, noting that entitlement to representation by counsel is not the same as entitlement to have counsel provided at public expense.

The decision was criticised. Pierce treats it as an illustration of the High Court adopting a 'politicised judicial role'. He considered that the Court was entering into the realm of political and economic policy, since legal aid offices with their scarce resources would need to concentrate on funding criminal trials to the detriment of civil litigants as a consequence of the decision.³⁰ The contrary can equally be cogently argued, namely that Deane and Gaudron, in upholding the right to a fair trial under the Constitution, applied the law as they saw it without regard to the political and financial policies of the governments concerned. In any event, Mason in his judgment in *Dietrich* pointed out that the Commonwealth and States had been given notice of the issues to be canvassed before the Court so that they might exercise the right to intervene. Only the Commonwealth and South Australia intervened. And no argument was put to the Court that recognition of such a right for the provision of counsel at public expense would impose an unsustainable financial burden on government.

In *Ridgeway v The Queen* (1995) Gaudron took a stronger line than the rest of the Court on an aspect of an accused's right to a fair trial.³¹ Members of the Australian Federal Police assisted the Royal Malaysian Police Force in illegal importation of heroin sold to John Ridgeway as part of an entrapment plan to catch Ridgeway 'red-handed'. The Court for the first time considered the common law defence of 'entrapment' to the commission of a crime.

The majority found that evidence of an offence which is obtained by unlawful conduct on the part of law enforcement officers could be admissible, although a court has discretion to exclude it on public policy grounds where, for example, admission of the evidence made it impossible for the accused to receive a fair trial. The Court nevertheless held that, because of the illegal police conduct, Ridgeway's conviction must be quashed, and a new trial was ordered.

Gaudron had a broader concern. As Solicitor General of New South Wales, she had previously confronted the issue of law enforcement agencies 'turning a blind eye' to illegal police activities in pursuit of convictions, namely, use of illegal telephone taps (the '*Age* tapes' saga) by the NSW Police and the unlawful Federal and ACT Police authorisation of the growing, harvesting and distributing for sale of marijuana crops as part of a supposed entrapment plan ('Operation Seville'). In *Ridgeway* she stated her view that public confidence in the courts is diminished when the illegal actions of law enforcement agents lead to a prosecution of an offence, and particularly where the law enforcement agents are not brought to account for their own criminal acts.[32]

The Commonwealth Government did not share her concern. It reacted to *Ridgeway* by amending the *Crimes Act 1914* (Cth) to provide for 'controlled operations' in which law enforcement officers might engage in otherwise illegal conduct to obtain evidence for prosecution concerning narcotic goods. It removed court discretion to exclude evidence by reason of its being obtained illegally, where certain conditions were met. The validity of the new provision was challenged in *Nicholas v The Queen*, a case with similar facts, on the ground that it was directing the Court to act in a manner inconsistent with the nature of judicial power.[33] Gaudron agreed with the majority in holding the provision valid, despite her own view on the direction the law should take. In what has been described as Gaudron's 'ungrudging adoption of views that have prevailed over hers', she accepted the decision in *Ridgeway* as law.[34]

Fortunately for Gaudron, the majority emphasised that the new provision only required the Court to disregard the official's unlawful behaviour, and did not require the Court to disregard any resultant unfairness of the unlawful behaviour in its exercise of discretion of whether the unlawfully obtained evidence should be excluded. She said:

> And so construed, it is also clear that it neither authorises nor requires a court to proceed in circumstances which bring or tend to bring the administration of justice into disrepute. And although it is perhaps not quite so clear, it does not offend against the requirements of equal justice.[35]

Gaudron's decision in *Nicholas* was a retreat from her position in *Ridgeway*, where she had argued that any prosecution based on illegal conduct by law enforcement officers must always be an abuse of process, since its inevitable consequence is to weaken public confidence in the administration of justice.[36] She therefore took the opportunity to restate her broad view of the implied right to equal justice, and the principles involved in a fair trial, in the constitutional exercise of the judicial power. She said in *Nicholas*:

> It means, moreover, that a court cannot be required or authorised to proceed in any manner which involves an abuse of process, which would render its proceedings inefficacious, or which brings or tends to bring the administration of justice into disrepute.[37]

She set out her formulation of what, as a minimum, the judicial power entails:

> ...equality before the law, impartiality and the appearance of impartiality, the right of a party to meet the case made against him or her, the independent determination of the matter in controversy by application of the law to facts determined in accordance with rules and procedures which truly permit the facts to be ascertained and, in the case of criminal proceedings, the determination of guilt or innocence by means of a fair trial according to law.[38]

It was worth stating. In the following year, six judges on the High Court endorsed the due process principle, citing Gaudron's passage written the previous year in *Nicholas* and specifying what it entailed.[39]

Justice for citizens and others

Gaudron's analysis of the meaning of citizenship and the difference between non-citizens and non-enemy aliens provided the High Court with a different perspective on how to deal with the impact on individuals of legislation relating to deportation of 'aliens'. Again, her notions of equality and discrimination informed her approach.

The Constitution grants the Commonwealth power to legislate with respect to 'naturalization and aliens' (section 51 (xix)) but makes no reference to Australian citizenship. The notion of citizenship was first introduced in 1948 by the *Australian Citizenship Act* (Cth). In *Nolan* (1988), the Court (except for Gaudron) held that after 1948 anyone was an alien unless they became an Australian citizen.

British subjects, some of whom had been in Australia all their lives and who had not considered themselves 'aliens', became liable to deportation when the *Migration Act 1958* (Cth) was amended in 1984. Therrance Nolan was one of them. He had resided in Australia since 1967, when he was ten. In 1984, under section 12 of the amended Act and as a 'non-citizen', he became liable for deportation because of serious criminal convictions committed before he had lived continuously in Australia for ten years. His British citizenship had protected him against deportation prior to the 1984 amendments to the Act. After that, it did not and a deportation order was made against him.

Nolan challenged the new law and its application to him on the grounds that the Constitution only gives the Commonwealth power to legislate with respect to 'aliens', not 'non-citizens', and that British subjects are not 'aliens'.[40] Gaudron agreed, but she was alone on the Court in that view. She conceded that section 12 of the Act applied to non-citizens and, in that context, Australian citizenship became the criterion for admission to membership of the Australian community. In *Nolan*, however, the legislation was being applied retrospectively. In her view the Act was invalid in so far as it purported to operate with respect to non-alien British subjects who had already been absorbed into the Australian community prior to the section coming into operation in 1984. The majority held that a person who did not meet citizenship criteria and who had not become a citizen of Australia was constitutionally an 'alien'; being a British subject could no longer exclude such a person from being classified as such. Gaudron spoke forcefully against the majority view that 'non-citizens' had become equivalent to 'aliens' under the Constitution.[41]

In *Lim* (1992) Gaudron spoke further on the implications of Australian citizenship being an 'entirely statutory' concept. She said that Parliament could not authorise the transformation of a 'non-alien' to an 'alien' by statutory redefinition of citizenship. But, leaving room for a change of the Court's view in the future, she held the Act valid 'only insofar as "non-citizen" is synonymous with the constitutional meaning of "alien".' In *Lim*, Gaudron acknowledged but questioned the conclusion in *Nolan* that 'alien' was synonymous with 'non-citizen':

> But that conceals a number of questions: when did it become synonymous? with what effect in relation to persons, if any, who were not aliens but did not become citizens? and must it remain so?[42]

The raising of questions, to which her answers might run counter to the declared law, was a technique Gaudron employed to keep issues, if not alive, at least on ice, ready to be thawed when new circumstances permitted. She continued:

> It may be that the occasion to answer the questions that I have formulated will never arise. However, membership of the community constituting the Australian body politic, for which the criterion is now, but was not always, citizenship, is a matter of such fundamental importance that, in my view, it is necessary that the questions be acknowledged even if they are not answered.[43]

She further challenged the Commonwealth's assumption that it could detain 'aliens', not because it was wrong in *Lim* (which concerned a group of Cambodian nationals who had arrived in Australian territorial waters by boat), but because it was sometimes wrong, and she hoped she could limit the direction initiated in *Nolan*.

Nearly a decade later, a Gaudron-led majority managed to steer further away from *Nolan* in the case of *In Re Patterson; Ex parte Taylor*.[44] Graham Taylor was born in the United Kingdom and came as a child in 1966, with his parents, to Australia, where he lived for the next thirty years. Acting Immigration Minister Kay Patterson cancelled Taylor's 'notional' visa in 1999 pursuant to the *Migration Act 1958* (Cth) after he had been released from a term of imprisonment for a serious offence. The Court found that the decision to deport Taylor had failed to take into account a relevant factor under the Act, namely, whether the deportation was in the national interest. This failure to follow 'due process' was a jurisdictional error in the exercise of administrative power, one which rendered invalid the Department's decision in relation to Taylor. The Court held that as no 'decision' had been made, there was no 'decision in law'.

The Court also found that Taylor, a statutory 'non-citizen', was not an 'alien', thereby rejecting the *Nolan* view that 'non-citizen' was synonymous with 'alien'. Gaudron based her finding on the fact that Taylor, having been a member of the Australian community and having been in Australia before 1987 (when Australia by reason of the *Australia Acts 1986* (UK and Cth) attained sovereignty), was not an alien within the meaning of the Constitution. Kirby held that Taylor was not an alien when he arrived in Australia and having been absorbed into the people of the Commonwealth, Parliament could not retrospectively declare him to be an alien. This aspect of the majority decision was persuasive, but arguably not essential, to the decision in *Patterson*. This permitted a later Court to regard *Patterson* as not authoritative on that issue, and to reaffirm *Nolan* instead.

Ex parte Te (2002) presented a different aspect of the issue. The majority of judges, with whom Gaudron agreed, declared that Meng Tok Te, a Cambodian, was an 'alien' because, unlike Taylor, he had arrived as an alien. However, Gaudron emphasised that the constitutional issue was whether someone was an 'alien' or a 'non-alien', and that the fact that a person was not an Australian citizen 'is irrelevant if he is not an alien'.[45] Te was born in Cambodia in 1967. He entered Australia as a refugee in 1983 and was granted a permanent resident visa. He had never become an Australian citizen. He was convicted of criminal offences concerned with drug trafficking and sentenced to a term of imprisonment; an order of deportation was made against him. Gaudron reiterated her view, explaining that *Patterson*

> clearly held that provisions of the Act permitting the detention and removal of non-citizens were invalid in their application to a person who had been born in the United Kingdom, had entered Australia before the coming into effect, in 1987, of the *Australian Citizenship Amendment Act 1984* (Cth)...and had

been absorbed into the Australian community but had not taken out Australian citizenship.[46]

It was claimed that '[a]lmost single-handedly, Justice Gaudron added the problem of citizenship to the Australian Constitutional agenda, despite its absence from the written text, by questioning and probing the concept of alien as a foundation for Commonwealth constitutional power'.[47]

Gaudron, however, did not win out with her view. In 2003, after Gaudron had retired, the Court, in *Shaw v MIMA*, halted the direction the Court was taking in respect of 'non-citizens'.[48] Jason Shaw, a British citizen, had lived permanently in Australia since 1974 when he was two, but had never become an Australian citizen. The Court upheld the provision in the *Migration Act 1958* (Cth) that authorised the minister to deport him. Shaw had, by this time, two children who were Australian citizens. The majority, Gleeson, Gummow and Hayne, reaffirmed the earlier decision of *Nolan*, a judgment of six members of the Court, from which Gaudron had dissented. Had she not retired earlier that year, the decision was likely to have been four to three in Shaw's favour, rejecting the decision in *Nolan* that non-citizens were constitutionally 'aliens'. It was an example of the importance of who is sitting on the Court at any particular time.

Gaudron's influence was still present in *Shaw*, but not, as might be expected, from what she had said in *Patterson*. The majority drew support from Gaudron's decision in the quite different citizenship case of *Sue v Hill*.[49] They cited what she had said there with respect to the phrase, 'foreign power'. Gaudron had made the point that '[t]o acknowledge that, in some constitutional provisions, some words and phrases are capable of applying to different persons or things at different times is not to change the meaning of those provisions. It is simply to give them their proper meaning.'

In *Sue v Hill*, Gaudron formed part of the majority which found that British citizens who resided in Australia became 'aliens' for the purpose of eligibility for election to Commonwealth Parliament. Hill was an Australian citizen and a British citizen by reason of her birth. She had not taken any steps to renounce her

British citizenship prior to her election on the One Nation ticket in Queensland to the Senate in 1998. The Court had to decide whether Hill was a citizen of a 'foreign power' for the purposes of deciding her eligibility, under section 44 of the Constitution, for election to the Parliament. Britain was not a 'foreign power' at the time of Federation. Under the *Australian Citizenship Act 1948* (Cth) an Australian citizen was also a British subject. The 1984 amendments removed all reference to the status of British subject in favour of the status of Australian citizen. According to Gaudron, the enactment of the *Australia Acts 1986* (UK and Cth) transformed the Commonwealth of Australia into a sovereign independent nation, making Britain thereafter a 'foreign power' for the purpose of section 44 of the Constitution.

Gaudron's approach to citizenship, according to Professor Kim Rubenstein, is founded on a fundamental concern for human rights. She has concluded that Gaudron's linking of various aspects of citizenship 'elaborated a vision that enhanced her country's capacity to be inclusive and humane in its treatment of its members. In this she left judicial markers, perhaps dormant for the present, but certainly lying in wait for the spark of future jurisprudence.'[50] Rubenstein points to *Teoh* as an example of Gaudron's use of citizenship as a source of protection for the most vulnerable in society.[51] In *Teoh* Gaudron gave a separate decision in which she focused on the consequence to the young child and six young step-children of the deportee, Teoh, of a decision refusing his application for resident status. She noted that Teoh's deportation would mean that 'the children would be placed in a position where they grew up either fatherless or in another country, denied an upbringing in the country of which they are citizens.'[52] This was a factor that an administrative decision-maker should reasonably take into account. Gaudron regarded citizenship as involving 'obligations on the part of the body politic to the individual, especially if the individual is in a position of vulnerability. And there are particular obligations to the child citizen in need of protection...No less is required of the government and the courts of a civilised democratic society.'[53] From this stand point Gaudron concluded that it was arguable that:

> citizenship carries with it a common law right on the part of children and their parents to have a child's best interests taken into account, at least as a primary consideration, in all discretionary decisions by governments and government agencies which directly affect that child's individual welfare, particularly decisions which affect children as dramatically and as fundamentally as those involved in this case.[54]

The case is a further example of Gaudron promoting the view that procedural fairness was a requirement of administrative decision-making processes. Later, in *Kruger* (the 'Stolen Generation' case), the Court, while rejecting other aspects of her views in that case, accepted her notion that the judicial power under the Constitution implicitly carries with it the requirement for due process in the exercise of administrative discretion.[55]

In *Teoh*, due process required that relevant matters be taken into account. It was reasonable that the best interests of Teoh's child and step-children were taken into account as a matter of course because of 'the special vulnerability of children, particularly where the break-up of the family unit is, or may be, involved, and because of their expectation that a civilised society would be alert to its responsibilities to children who are, or may be, in need of protection'.[56]

The power to detain

The Commonwealth's power over 'aliens' raised the question: in what circumstances could the executive power be used to involuntarily detain people who have not been found guilty of an offence? As Professor Zines has pointed out, 'Lurking beneath the disagreement in the immigration detention cases is the basic issue of the weight to be given to the protection of Chapter III.'[57] *Lim* and *Kruger* established that the power to authorise detention in custody is not exclusively judicial in character.

Lim was one of a group of people who arrived by boat from Cambodia who, while not enemy aliens, were detained in custody. The High Court held that the 'aliens' power in section 51(xix) of the Constitution provided the basis for administrative detention of immigrants in some circumstances.[58] The Court made it clear that express authority is required to detain an 'alien', and the constitutional limits of the executive power are to be determined by what is 'reasonably necessary' to achieve the object of the legislative power. It was therefore relevant to ask whether detention can reasonably be regarded as necessary in achieving the non-punitive end.

Gaudron accepted that detention of an alien in custody without a determination of guilt did not contravene the judicial power of the Commonwealth. She denied, however, that the power to legislate with respect to aliens meant that laws could be made for detention of aliens 'because they were aliens'. Her starting point was that aliens are 'people' and a special law with respect to them, to be valid, must have some connection with their status as aliens and which was 'appropriate and adapted to regulating entry or facilitating departure as and when required'. This meant that aliens might lawfully be detained in custody for the purposes of expulsion and deportation and, also, for the purposes of the receipt, investigation and determination of applications for admission to Australia.

Gaudron took a broader and more flexible view than the majority in *Lim* of the categories of people whose detention in custody might be authorised by the exercise of executive power in respect of other people. Brennan, Deane and Dawson recognised that arrest and custody under a warrant pending trial, detention by reason of mental illness or infectious disease, and punishment for contempt of Parliament and for breach of military discipline were well-accepted categories where detention can be authorised other than by a court order in exercise of the judicial function. Gaudron said:

> Detention in custody in circumstances not involving some breach of the criminal law and not coming within well-accepted categories of the kind to which Brennan, Deane and Dawson JJ. refer is offensive to ordinary notions of what is involved in a just society. But I am not presently persuaded that legislation authorizing detention in circumstances involving

no breach of the criminal law and travelling beyond presently accepted categories is necessarily and inevitably offensive to Ch. III.[59]

This proved insightful. In *Kruger*, where the *Lim* principle to establish the limits of the executive power was applied, the removal of children from their Aboriginal families and their detention in reserves or institutions was found not to be in breach of the exercise of Chapter III judicial powers.[60] Gaudron agreed with Toohey and Gummow, forming part of the majority, that the law was not in breach of Chapter III because its object was the welfare of the children. In *Kruger* she affirmed her view that the well-accepted categories referred to in *Lim* could not be regarded as precise and confined; they include for example, in the case of mental illness and infectious disease, people being detained in custody for their own welfare and for the safety of the broader community. She said:

> it cannot be said that the power to authorise detention in custody is exclusively judicial except for clear exceptions. I say clear exceptions because it is difficult to assert exclusivity except within a defined area and, if the area is to be defined by reference to exceptions, the exceptions should be clear or should fall within precise and confined categories.[61]

Her disagreement with the joint judgment in that respect was later accepted by Hayne and Heydon in *Al-Kateb v Godwin*,[62] and by McHugh in *Re Woolleys*[63] and Gummow in *Fardon v Attorney General (Qld)*.[64]

Gaudron preferred not to rely on the question of whether the purpose of the law was 'non-punitive' as a test of its validity. She applied the stricter view she expressed in *Lim* that, subject to exceptions, a law authorising detention of a person not found guilty of a crime could not be a valid law on a topic with respect to which section 51 confers legislative power on the Commonwealth.[65]

An aspect in *Kruger* that complicated the thinking on the various issues considered, was whether the exercise of the Commonwealth's power to legislate with respect to Territories was subject to Chapter III concerning the exercise of judicial power. The same question arose with respect to whether section 116, forbidding laws that prohibited the free exercise of any religion, applied to the Commonwealth in its exercise of the Territories power. Gaudron held that it did, and Toohey and Gummow were strongly inclined to agree; but Dawson and McHugh thought otherwise.

The judgments on this issue became part of a significant movement within the High Court towards putting the Northern Territory and the Australian Capital Territory on the same constitutional basis as the rest of Australia, in contrast to an older view that when the Commonwealth legislated for the Territories it could do so without regard to constitutional limitations. Blackshield observed that Gaudron's judgments, including that in *Kruger*, have given repeated impetus to that movement. This position, again, is guided by her views on equality.[66]

Gaudron's view of the role of equality and due process in the administration of justice shaped her approach to her role on the Court. Her unique approach is seen in her application, logically and legalistically, of principles of law extracted from her notion of equal justice, without resort to more general notions concerning personal liberty. Her intricate thinking, often original, showed a consistent regard for the law as it stands.[67] The Court in the Mason years provided an encouraging environment for Gaudron's exploration of the concepts of equal justice, discrimination and due process.

However, after Mason's retirement, some changes in the thinking and approach of the Court became inevitable. There were changes in the membership and dynamics of the Court, a change of government and a number of policy initiatives which brought new issues to the Court for determination. Gaudron proved adept at adapting to change.

Chapter Sixteen

ADAPTING TO CHANGE: THE COURT UNDER CHIEF JUSTICES BRENNAN AND GLEESON

> It might have crossed your mind that you could be the Associate to the Chief Justice of the High Court...Well uncross it.[1]
>
> Mary Gaudron, 1995

'No' to the top job

On the eve of Sir Anthony Mason's retirement press speculation was rife that the Keating Government would appoint Gaudron to succeed him as Chief Justice of the High Court.[2] Gaudron offered no encouragement. In 1995 she firmly told a newly appointed associate that if it had crossed her mind that she could become associate to the Chief Justice, she should 'uncross it'.

Gaudron was in the right place and in sufficient political favour to make history as the first female to be appointed Chief Justice of a western country's highest court. But the timing was not right. She was then the second most junior member of the Court. Sir Gerard Brennan was the most senior judge; Sir William Deane and Sir Daryl Dawson were ahead of her in seniority. That would not have been sufficient to deter Prime Minister Keating from elevating her, but it did deter Gaudron. She would not consider upsetting the order of seniority within the Court.³

Gaudron 'screamed down the phone' to Keating when he sounded her out about the proposition.⁴ It was unacceptable, Gaudron thought, since Brennan was next in line. Her friends, politicians Clyde Holding, Peter Duncan and Frank Walker, tried to persuade her to accept Keating's choice. She would be regarded as a 'government judge', she insisted, and lose the authority she had on the Court. 'You would be leading it,' they responded. 'You don't understand,' she countered.⁵

Gaudron knew the dynamics of the bench and the consequences of breaking with tradition if she were to 'leap frog' those senior to her. It had not been done before in the High Court. Appointments had been made from outside the Court, but from within the Court only the most senior judge—Isaac Isaacs in 1930, Gavan Duffy in 1931, Owen Dixon in 1952, Harry Gibbs in 1981 and Anthony Mason in 1987—had ever been elevated to Chief Justice.

Her respectful stand was not without precedent. When Sir Garfield Barwick retired, there was speculation that the post was offered to Sir Ninian Stephen, who resisted the possibility on the ground that Harry Gibbs was his senior. Gaudron's rejection of the idea was in all likelihood not only a matter of tradition and courtesy. She knew her power: she had an influence within the Court, her reasoning processes were persuasive and she was listened to. Frank Walker believes that acting alone, Mason could not have led the Court in the direction it took, and that Gaudron's intellectual influence was significant. Tony Blackshield is another observer who believes Gaudron was more influential behind the scenes than is widely understood. Sir Anthony Mason, preferring not to use the word 'influence', confirms that Gaudron's views were always listened to. An unorthodox elevation to the chief justiceship could well diminish a stature she had won in nearly a decade on the Court.

She knew her chance might not come again. Politics might make her unacceptable to the government in power, even when it was 'her turn', as, it would transpire, was the case. It was the right decision for another although unanticipated reason. In 1995, shortly before Brennan took his place as Chief Justice and Bill Gummow was appointed to fill the vacancy, Gaudron was diagnosed with having a brain aneurism; and it had to be removed, or she would die. She was warned that she might not survive the operation. It was a frightening time. She feared, not so much death but, waking up to find she had suffered 'cognitive function impairment'.[6] She went into the anaesthetic knowing that this, or death, were real possibilities. She recovered. Gummow was surprised and delighted when she attended his inauguration, despite her frailty from the surgery. But it was a while before her energy levels returned, and she continued to face troubling health issues.

In a collegiate sense Brennan headed a particularly happy court. Everyone was fond of Gerard Brennan. Although reserved by nature, he was always friendly, kind and considerate. His quiet style was a contrast to Gaudron's. She is a raconteur and would capture the attention of her colleagues with her voluble story-telling. The relaxed mood under Brennan's leadership was reflected in the Court's photographs. David Coward, the Court's official photographer from 1996, noticed the light atmosphere when he came to record their images for history: 'they were like a bunch of high school kids, having a ball'. Brennan continued Mason's practice of an informal photograph being taken of all the judges in the ante-room near the main court, following the formal photograph of the full bench routinely taken on ceremonial occasions. One depicts the justices surrounding Brennan, all of whom, including Brennan, have their heads turned to Gaudron, obviously 'holding court'. On retirement, Brennan arranged for a photograph to be taken of all the Court's staff. The familial atmosphere of the group, assembled on the staircase, was apparent.

Brennan, Gaudron, Dawson and Toohey walked around the Parliamentary Triangle each sitting day at lunchtime, chatting in a relaxed manner and, being relatively unknown, happy to be free to walk outdoors without security officers in tow. Justice Ken Hayne joined the walks when he succeeded Sir Daryl Dawson on the Court. In addition, all the Justices met in Brennan's Chambers at the close of each sitting for refreshments. Brennan recalls that over a glass of scotch or wine 'these informal gatherings would last as long as the conversation went on—a conversation dealing with shoes and ships and sealing wax'.[7]

The Court in this period appeared to be less adventurous, jurisprudentially speaking, with the loss of two of its major influences, Mason and Deane. Deane left the Court in 1995 shortly after Mason to become Governor-General. Dawson and Toohey also retired during Brennan's term. Brennan and Gaudron missed them all greatly.[8] However, Brennan was not Chief Justice for a sufficiently long period to conclude that there was some retreat by him, or other members of the Court under his leadership, from the progressive posture of the Mason era.[9] From the time he first joined the Court he had sometimes dissented where he thought a majority was applying a legal principle 'too generously'.[10] On the other hand, as with many judges, to some extent he may have been affected by the thinking of new members on the Court.[11] What can be said is that predicting the thinking of new members of the Court and how they will decide a particular case was as difficult during Brennan's term as Chief Justice as at any other time. The Court's handling of the important cases of *Wik* and *Kartinyeri v Commonwealth* (the *Hindmarsh Island Bridge* case), each of which was decided shortly after changes in the Court membership, illustrates this.

The Wik case

On 23 December 1996 the decision in *Wik* was delivered, further developing the *Mabo* principle concerning indigenous land rights.[12] What was at issue was the nature of pastoral leases. In the words of Henry Reynolds, 'If anything, history was even more important in the *Wik* case [than *Mabo*].'[13] He observed:

> The Commonwealth and the State governments argued that they had to be considered in terms of common-law doctrine. The Wik people asserted that pastoral leases had to be considered historically as a unique product of Australian colonial development, created specifically to allow for the mutual use of land by pastoralists and traditional owners.

Though it had less impact than *Mabo* in terms of symbolism, the decision in *Wik* had more practical effect because it dealt with productive lands under cultivation.

Toohey, Gaudron and newcomers Bill Gummow, and Michael Kirby, who was appointed 6 February 1996, formed the majority on the main issue concerning the rights of the Wik and Thayorre peoples in respect of pastoral lands. The majority held that the grant of certain pastoral leases by the Crown under the *Land Act 1910* (Qld) and the *Land Act 1962–1974* (Qld) did not confer exclusive possession of the leased areas on the lease holders, and therefore did not necessarily extinguish native title rights and interests in the relevant areas. The decision was supported by reasons drawing on long-established principles of real property law. Although called leases, the majority found that relevant interests in the lands were no more than licences; as such they did not terminate whatever indigenous title subsisted in the land.

Gaudron and Gummow had special knowledge of equity principles in their application to real property rights and entitlements. They applied property law principles to find that a pastoral lease might restrict the rights of the native titleholders, but that native title could survive and coexist.[14] They held that application of the common law principle of coexistence placed native title on an equal footing with other interests. The question of whether native title was extinguished by the grant of a pastoral lease, according to the majority, had to be determined by a consideration of the specific terms of the laws that created these leases and the particular rights and interests that were thereby asserted and established. In the event of inconsistencies, however, the rights of a pastoral leaseholder would take precedence.

Each judge in the majority gave a separate judgment. Gaudron's judgment provides a clear demonstration of her analytic textual approach and application of logic to reach what might be described as a social justice-oriented outcome. She noted that the features of pastoral leases differed significantly from leases under the common law. They granted the pastoralist a bundle of statutory rights over land but not ownership of the land.[15] By contrast, a feature of a common law lease is the right to exclusive possession for the period of the lease, and the right to exclusive possession is sufficient to extinguish the former title. The Queensland statute did not grant that right.[16]

For support, Gaudron relied on the provisions of the statute that denied the pastoral lessee the right to ringbark, cut or destroy trees, and that denied the pastoralists power to stop authorised people from cutting or removing timber or material within the holding. She drew on the 'rule of construction', that generally legislation with respect to waste lands or Crown land 'is not to be construed, in the absence of clear and unambiguous words, as intended to apply in a way which will extinguish or diminish rights under common law native title'. She explained that this rule was not a special rule with respect to native title; it was simply a well-settled rule of properly reading a statute.[17]

Brennan dissented. He held that a pastoral lease was to be treated as a lease as generally understood at common law, and that it granted a right of exclusive possession that was inconsistent with the survival of any native title rights.[18] He had alluded to this in his influential decision in *Mabo* and, consistent with that thinking, pronounced it in *Wik*. Dawson and McHugh joined Brennan in dissent.

The *Wik* decision had major implications for the development of the common law relating to native title, the operation of the *Native Title Act 1993* (Cth), and land management generally. It became the subject of widespread public debate about its implications and about the proper role of the Court. At the same time, the decision defies attempts to associate it with the 'activism' for which the Court became known during the Mason years. The supposedly jurisprudentially more conservative new member, Gummow, formed part of the majority of four with Toohey, Gaudron and Kirby. Gummow explained the decision in *Wik* not as being an exercise in 'activism but the result of the correct application of existing law on property rights'.[19] Further, Brennan and Dawson dissented along with Labor appointee, McHugh, all members of the Court during the Mason period. This did not deter National

Party leader, Tim Fischer, as acting Prime Minister, from accusing the four majority judges in *Wik* of unacceptable activism, and from wanting to do something about it.[20]

A capital 'C' conservative

On 2 March 1996, the Howard Liberal-National Coalition Government was victorious in the general election. The Labor Government's appointment in early 1996 of radical jurist Justice Michael Kirby to the bench, and the Court's decisions of *Mabo* and *Wik*, prompted National Party leader and Deputy Prime Minister Tim Fischer to call for a capital 'C' conservative to be appointed to the High Court. Fischer wanted the High Court's advance into areas of social justice to cease.[21]

Fischer attacked the Labor Government's appointment of Kirby in particular, saying his decision in *Wik* was 'awful'. He accused all four majority judges, Toohey, Gaudron, Gummow and Kirby, of making law rather than applying it.[22] Brennan defended the Court in a letter to Fischer, and correspondence between them over political criticism of the Court was released to newspapers.[23] This generated a public brawl stepped up by an attack on Brennan by Queensland Premier Rob Borbidge. Federal Attorney General Daryl Williams urged coalition members of parliament to cease their attack on the judiciary, at the same time as Prime Minister Howard appeared to support the critics of the Court.[24]

On 4 March 1997, Fischer reportedly stated that Brennan's retirement would open the door for the appointment of 'someone who's somewhat conservative on the matter of judicial activism', and that he was 'attracted to the thought that it would be a capital C Conservative' lawyer appointed Chief Justice of the Court.[25] Williams responded quickly with an assurance that the next Chief Justice would be 'the best person for the job'.[26] That did not stop Fischer repeating his view.[27] As new appointments were made to the Court, journalists recalled Fischer's words.

When Dawson retired in August 1997, Victorian Supreme Court Justice Kenneth Hayne was appointed to the Court. His appointment was regarded as the replacement of a conservative by a conservative, and drew comment to that effect.[28] Hayne was expected to be an intellectually rigorous and disciplined lawyer, attributes which would not displease Gaudron. He was assessed as unlikely to be 'activist or extremist in his legal interpretation'.²⁹ One barrister reportedly commented: 'Ken Hayne will be a capital-C Conservative on the bench. He's the sort of person Tim Fischer would like to have there. He's clever. He won't be a supporter of Mabo and Wik and all those things. He won't be a believer in implied rights.'³⁰

Two more vacancies would arise the following year with Toohey's and Brennan's retirements. Press speculation continued about the Government's agenda:

> For the first time since Federation, the Government has explicitly stated—through the Deputy Prime Minister, Tim Fischer—an intention to stack the High Court with 'Capital C conservatives' on the pending retirement of three judges…'³¹

Ian Callinan, QC, of the Queensland Bar was appointed to fill the vacancy created by Toohey's retirement in April 1998. It was seen as an 'attempt to redress the balance'.³² An early assessment was that Callinan was a political conservative and favoured 'States' rights' rather than an expansion of 'citizens' rights'.³³ There was little doubt about where he stood jurisprudentially. He said on the announcement of his appointment: 'I think it's important that the High Court decide cases in an orthodox way and I hope I do that.'³⁴

Callinan's appointment to the Court was the Coalition Government's response to pressure to appoint not only a conservative but also a Queenslander. The appointment seemed to be influenced not only by Fischer but also by National Party State Premier Rob Borbidge. The Queensland Government wanted native title to be 'expunged'. Prime Minister John Howard wanted the support of Queensland for the *Wik* legislation. Callinan was not otherwise a leading contender for the appointment. A practising barrister with extensive experience in all jurisdictions, he had not previously been a judge. His involvement in the prosecution of Justice Lionel Murphy had lifted his profile as an advocate to national status.³⁵ The mood of the time is captured in comments attributed to one jurist:

> I don't think anyone who knew the work of the High Court would have considered Callinan as an acceptable appointee to the High Court, in terms of experience or ability. He was a very good trial advocate. That's what he was—the beginning and end of it I think. He wouldn't have appeared in the High Court more than a half-dozen times in his life. He was a surprise appointment and he was appointed for that reason.³⁶

Though his political philosophy was so different from Gaudron's, Callinan had, in common with her, a colourful and witty personality. With interests in art, literature, Australian history and politics, cricket, rugby union and rugby league, he also wrote plays, short stories and novels—one, *The Lawyer and the Libertine*,³⁷ with its love and sexual overtones, was a racy novel for a High Court judge to have written.

The appointment of Justice Ian Callinan to the High Court caused tensions on the bench. Gaudron was not happy about it, at least initially. There were many reasons for her apprehension. At the outset, Callinan was appointed in circumstances of an apparent search for a conservative to counter the Court's 'activist' tendencies. Callinan was the barrister who had successfully led the prosecution team against her friend, Lionel Murphy, at both the committal proceedings and the two trials. Further, Callinan had cross-examined Kirby when he gave evidence for Murphy.

Gaudron was also aware of a story circulating in the press gallery in Parliament House that a deal had been struck between the Liberal and National parties that Callinan would be appointed Chief Justice when Brennan retired towards the end of the year.³⁸ Callinan, the story implied, was chief justice-in-waiting. The argument of the Nationals was that Callinan might lead the Court to dismiss any challenge to the Howard Government's '10 point plan' embodied in the 1997 *Native Title Amendment Bill*, legislation designed to wind back the effect of the High Court's earlier decisions. Aboriginal interests flagged the possibility of a challenge to the legislation on the ground, amongst others, that the Commonwealth's power to pass legislation in respect to people of any race—the 'race power' (applicable to the Aboriginal race since the 1967 referendum on the Constitution)—could not be validly used to disadvantage Aborigines.

The aim was for Callinan to take his place in time for *Kartinyeri v Commonwealth* (the *Hindmarsh Island Bridge* case), scheduled for hearing in April 1998. The then Attorney General, Daryl Williams, recommended appointment of Justice John von Doussa from the Federal Court to fill the vacancy created by Toohey's retirement. A compromise strategy evolved, as legal circles understood it. Callinan would be appointed first as a Justice, and then elevated to Chief Justice when Brennan retired; the vacancy thus created would go to von Doussa.[39] The plan required Howard to do what Keating had wanted to do in respect of Gaudron, and appoint a Chief Justice from the bench who was not the next 'in line of seniority'. Whether Howard, given his reported intention to appoint his Sydney University contemporary, Murray Gleeson, then Chief Justice of the NSW Supreme Court, initially accepted the plan is unclear. In any event, it went awry when controversies about Callinan erupted.[40]

The day after Callinan was sworn in, questions immediately arose over his involvement in the very case in which the Government wanted him to participate—*Kartinyeri*. On Wednesday, 4 February 1998 Callinan was faced with an application by Doreen Kartinyeri seeking that he disqualify himself from participating in the hearing because he had previously acted for one of the other parties.[41] As a barrister Callinan had advised on aspects of the *Hindmarsh Island Bridge Bill* (Cth) at the request of Coalition Government ministers, the constitutional validity of which was being challenged in the proceedings. It was argued that his association with people and political events underlying the case might give rise to a reasonable apprehension of bias. Callinan considered the matter overnight. He sought consultation with his judicial colleagues, but they took the view that the decision was one, at least initially, that he must make.[42]

Callinan gave his decision not to withdraw on Thursday 5

February 1998.⁴³ Up to this point there had been nothing untoward; it became so when Callinan refused to disqualify himself. He reasoned that there was no more need for him to disqualify himself than other of his judicial colleagues who had also previously expressed views on the issue. He referred to previous statements of Brennan and Gaudron, which might indicate a predisposition in *Kartinyeri*. He referred to a view Brennan had expressed in the *Tasmanian Dam* case that approval by the people of Australia of the amendment to the Constitution to permit the Government to legislate in respect to the Aboriginal race was 'an affirmation of the will of the Australian people that the odious policies of oppression and neglect of Aboriginal citizens were to be at an end, and that the primary object of the power is beneficial'. This, Callinan suggested, could be taken as indicating a predisposition to a favourable result for *Kartinyeri*. Gaudron, he said, also expressed a view on the matter in *Lim* where she suggested that the race power only authorises laws for the *benefit* of the race concerned, and in *Kruger* where she expressed a similar view. Callinan likened his comments to those of lawyers who may have expressed views as advocates when at the Bar, or advising governments. Thus, he reasoned, his own expression of views as an advocate was not a ground on which to disqualify himself.

He commenced sitting with the other six judges on the main hearing of the case the same day and continued the next. By 18 February his colleagues persuaded him to change his mind. It was an embarrassment for the Court. Some of the other Justices feared that the litigants might claim that the Court was responsible for their extra legal costs.

Gaudron expressed relief. 'Thank goodness he was put on training wheels,' she said, with reference to the rumour that Howard had considered appointing him direct to the Court as Chief Justice.⁴⁴ *Kartinyeri* was not the only matter to disturb Callinan's arrival on the Court. In mid-1998 the ABC *Four Corners* program raised questions about Callinan's professional conduct as a barrister in the *White Industries* litigation.⁴⁵ He had allegedly advised the commencement of litigation in the case as a 'delay tactic', advising at the same time that the case was weak and would not succeed if put to the test, but that taking proceedings would enhance his client's bargaining position. It was a serious allegation; if true, it would constitute conduct by a barrister that could warrant disciplinary action. Callinan, now a judge, was called to give evidence in the case in April 1998. He did not recall giving any advice to the solicitors, Flower and Hart, to try and obstruct the progress of the proceedings. On the contrary, his evidence was that the steps he recommended were those that he thought should and could be properly taken in the litigation.

The Federal Court found that the conduct of the firm of solicitors, acting on Callinan's advice, was an abuse of process and an attempt to obstruct or defeat the administration of justice. The solicitors appealed.[46] In July 1998, the Law Council of Australia, and later the ALP, called for an inquiry into Callinan's conduct.[47]

There was an irony. Callinan had been Counsel Assisting the Senate inquiry into whether the allegations against Justice Lionel Murphy would support Murphy's removal from the High Court. Now, the rare issue of impeachment of a High Court justice arose over Callinan's own conduct.[48] Attorney General Daryl Williams was uncomfortable, but on 26 August 1998 he declared that an inquiry was not warranted.[49]

In June 1999, the Federal Court dismissed the solicitors' appeal in the *White Industries* case, and the Opposition renewed calls for an inquiry into Callinan's conduct. The Government refused to act. The view was taken that a judge's conduct as a barrister, rather than conduct as a judge, could not amount to 'proved misbehaviour or incapacity' under section 72 of the Constitution which covers removal of judges from office.[50]

Notwithstanding Gaudron's initial horror at a conservative such as Callinan being appointed, and the controversy that accompanied and followed his appointment, she enjoyed his company. Both had a particular interest in criminal law. She found she could work well with him, and she acknowledged that he had acquitted himself well on the Court.[51] Callinan, in turn, found Gaudron to be good company as well as a good lawyer.[52]

The Hindmarsh Island Bridge case

Callinan's absence from *Kartinyeri* made no difference to its outcome. Legalism, not activism, prevailed. The decision showed the limit to which the Court, including Gaudron, as a matter of law could go to progress indigenous rights.[53] The case is significant in the context of the development of Gaudron's thinking, as she reviewed her previous analysis of the race power that Callinan had referred to. Not indecisive by nature, her change of mind demonstrated strength—a determination to get the law right—even if that required reviewing her own thinking.[54]

The case concerned the validity of the Coalition's *Hindmarsh Island Bridge Act 1997* (Cth) that exempted the Hindmarsh Island Bridge in South Australia from the *Aboriginal and Torres Strait Islander Heritage Protection Act 1984* (Cth). The area included land and waters around Hindmarsh Island and between the island and the coast of South Australia. A proposal to build a bridge linking the island with the mainland was opposed by several groups of indigenous women on Aboriginal heritage grounds. In 1988 archaeological and anthropological surveys had identified a number of sites, including burial and camp sites in the development area. It was the beginning of a long-running battle. In 1994, the claim was framed in terms that the development would intrude on a site for 'secret women's business'. The original application, as cited by Gaudron in an earlier related hearing, contended that the bridge would 'undermine cosmological and human reproduction and cause Ngarrindjeri society and its traditions to ultimately disappear'.[55]

By the time the case reached the High Court in 1998, it was thought that it would be an indicator of whether the Howard Government's proposed amendments to the Labor Government's *Native Title Act* were constitutionally valid. In particular, it was thought that the case would provide the Court with an opportunity to consider whether the 'race power' under the Constitution authorised laws detrimental to Aboriginal people. While the 1967 amendment to include Aboriginal people was intended to benefit Aboriginal people, there had been no judicial determination of whether it permitted the Parliament to pass laws to the detriment of Aborigines. Could it, for example, take away long held but newly declared land rights?

Kartinyeri was not however, a good test case on the point of concern, as the decision of the majority of the Court did not turn on the issue of how the race power should be interpreted and applied. The majority, including Gaudron, found the Hindmarsh Island Bridge legislation valid on the ground that it did no more than amend the 1984 Aboriginal heritage protection legislation. The Court held that Parliament could validly amend or revoke what it had validly enacted. Gaudron agreed, even though the withdrawal of a benefit previously granted to Aboriginal people imposed a disadvantage on those whom the law had previously benefited. There were, as well, opposing Aboriginal views on the issue.[56] Gaudron's heart might not have been in the decision she gave, but the law was the law, and had to be honestly applied.

Gaudron's decision in this case applied her concept of discrimination 'appropriate and adapted to relevant difference' in giving meaning to the words of the provision that granted power to single out a race as the subject of legislation. While a decision on the limits of the race power in the Constitution was not necessary for the majority's decision, Gaudron took the opportunity to reconsider what she had said in *Lim* about the race power. In that case she had stated that there was 'much to commend' the view that the race power could only be used for the *benefit* of a race. She had considered that the words 'for whom it is deemed necessary' implied 'for the benefit of' a race.

She abandoned that view in *Kartinyeri*. She considered the effect of the 1967 amendment to the provision that included the Aboriginal race, and decided that even if the inclusion was intended to advantage the Aboriginal race, it did not change the meaning of the rest of the provision. And, on a close study of its words, she reasoned that the qualifying phrase in the provision that granted the power to make special laws with respect to a particular race—'for whom it is deemed necessary'—was significant. She reasoned that the test of the validity of the law in question was whether it was reasonably capable of addressing a real and relevant difference that exists. On its face, that test, she thought, led to the conclusion that the race power could not in present circumstances support legislation that was to the detriment of Aboriginal Australians. From this stance, she recognised that the scope of the power can change, depending on what is 'deemed necessary' in the circumstances and the times. She said:

> Although the power concerned…is, in terms, wide enough to authorise laws which operate either to the advantage or disadvantage of the people of a particular race, it is difficult to conceive of circumstances in which a law presently operating to the disadvantage of a racial minority would be valid.[57]

This, she noted, was especially so for Aboriginal people, who were presently seriously disadvantaged in their material circumstances and in terms of the vulnerability of their culture. Thus, through this complex process of reasoning, Gaudron came to a view not so very different in outcome from that she had expressed in *Lim*.

The application of the race power was central to Kirby's dissenting decision. He was alone in finding the legislation unconstitutional. He placed importance on the reasons for the 1967 amendment in holding that the race power did not extend to the enactment of laws detrimental to, or discriminatory against, people of the Aboriginal race, or of any race. Gaudron did not support this view. The other Justices in the majority either disagreed, stating that the race power did not confine Parliament to make laws of benefit to a racial group, or they avoided giving an opinion.

While Gaudron joined Kirby in placing much stronger limits on the use of the race power than the rest of the Court and reached much the same practical result, though by 'more circumscribed and elaborately-constructed chain of reasoning',[58] her reasoning will possibly have more appeal to future courts than Kirby's more policy-driven approach because it is open to accommodating future circumstances.

The glass ceiling intact

When Toohey left the Court in 1998, Gaudron was the most senior member after Chief Justice Brennan. If there had been any truth in the rumour that Callinan was being groomed for the position of Chief Justice, by July 1998 he was no longer a contender. Gaudron had acted as Chief Justice during Brennan's absence before his retirement. She was capable. Her lively personality guaranteed the engagement of the other judges. She pulled them together.[59]

But the Coalition was in power and again the timing was not in her favour. It is unlikely that Prime Minister Howard approached Gaudron about the appointment. She did not want it anyway, deciding about this time on an early retirement from the Court.[60] According to friends, she was not interested in getting old waiting for a further change of government. Rather, she planned to spend a long retirement enjoying her French cottage in the Loire with her second husband, John Fogarty. She was fifty-five years old. Her health, if a factor, was not given as a reason. She had faced and survived a serious operation to remove a brain aneurism. Stress was not good for her (and that, she reasoned, was why she did not give up smoking her cigarillos!). She announced her intention to retire in 2003. In that year, she told her friends, she would be sixty and the High Court would be 100, and that would be a good year to leave. On turning sixty she would also qualify for her retiring superannuation—ten years earlier than the statutory age of 'senility'.

The Howard Government appointed Murray Gleeson, Chief Justice of the NSW Supreme Court, to head the High Court. Overlooking Gaudron was newsworthy. Given that politics play a part in the selection of High Court judges, Gaudron was not expected to be appointed. But she was next in line; and a woman. One paper's headlines read: 'Gleeson's outside run pips Gaudron to top job.'[61] Gleeson took up his appointment on 22 May 1998.

Gleeson's personal style was very different from Brennan's convivial manner. Jack Waterford reported in May 2003:

> The High Court is not necessarily a bunch of happy chappies. Three stay at the Commonwealth Club whenever they are in

> town...A disloyal club member remarks he never sees any of the three, Chief Justice Murray 'Smiler' Gleeson, Ian 'Tub' Callinan or new boy 'Dirty' Dyson Heydon, share a table at breakfast, lunch or dinner, or, indeed, speaking to one another. And each day three sleek Commonwealth cars arrive, often together, to take them singly to the High Court.[62]

The difference in atmosphere, which photographer David Coward claimed was palpable, can be seen in the contrasting photographs of a relaxed 'Brennan' group of judges depicting a natural camaraderie, and of a 'Gleeson' arranged group of judges in the same ante-room, lined up like a football team. Coward's photo history is evocative of a new era of formality that many believed would characterise the Gleeson Court.

Gaudron had her own issues about being photographed after her brain surgery. It had left her with some facial nerve irritation which, she perceived, distorted her image. On one occasion, Gaudron complained about the photographs taken of her. The photo-shoot produced only one reasonable picture of her, but it was not the best of the group as a whole. With a lot of fiddling, Coward managed to make a composite photograph by cutting out the acceptable image of Gaudron from one image and superimposing it over her less flattering image in what was otherwise the best photograph of the group.

Less activism—more restraint: the Gleeson Court

Gleeson favoured legalism as the proper basis for judicial interpretation—an indication to some that the Court would be less activist than the previous decade.[63] Only Gaudron, McHugh, Gummow and Kirby remained of the Labor appointees, following the Howard Government appointments of Hayne, Callinan and Gleeson.

Professor Zines did not agree that the Gleeson Court demonstrated a general pattern or direction in constitutional interpretation.[64] The 1999 case of *Yanner v Eaton* was a case in point. The Court upheld the native title right to hunt as a defence to a charge of hunting native fauna contrary to a state enactment that declared certain fauna to belong to the Crown.[65] Chief Justice

Gleeson was in the majority in the case with Justices Gaudron, Kirby, Gummow and Hayne. McHugh and Callinan dissented. The case illustrates the difficulty of predicting judges' approaches to their role with reference to the political philosophy of the Government that appointed them.

On the other hand, the important 1999 case of *Re Wakim* demonstrated the Court's reluctance to base an argument on social 'convenience and efficiency', and favour legal analysis and the strict application of the law. *Re Wakim* thwarted State and Commonwealth plans for a statutory scheme devised to rectify significant jurisdictional procedural differences across Australia.[66] This outcome cannot be attributed to Gleeson's influence. Gaudron was, for example, one of the majority judges. While the decision was not the outcome she wanted, it was the outcome dictated by the proper application of the law as she saw it. Her decision was consistent with the view she expressed as NSW Solicitor General in 1984, namely, that States could not vest jurisdiction in federal courts, and federal courts could not exercise it. Gaudron had believed in the correctness of the stand she had taken as Solicitor General on the limits of federal and State court jurisdiction, even though, on arriving at the High Court, she stated publicly her view that there was a need for greater uniformity of legal procedures within the nation, and at least within a State, regardless of whether a court proceeding was under a State or Commonwealth law.[67] Indeed, she would like to see one identifiable judicial system in Australia, rather than simply an aggregation of State and federal courts. But the law as Gaudron saw it did not permit it, and inconvenience and social consequence were no reason for Gaudron to ignore the law.

Kirby was disappointed that the Court missed the opportunity given by *Re Wakim* to obtain procedural unity throughout Australia.[68] He was the sole dissenter on the main point in the case. He argued that the Constitution must be read liberally to accommodate the changing needs of society; in this case, the nation's need for uniformity in its legal processes. There was precedent to support this view. In *Gould v Brown* the Court upheld the power of the States to confer jurisdiction on federal courts, and of the

Commonwealth Parliament to permit it.[69] Its value as a precedent, however, was weak. It was a three-three decision, Chief Justice Brennan being the decider with Toohey and Kirby; Gaudron, significantly, and McHugh and Gummow disagreeing.[70] The need for judges to be and to be seen to be consistent is an acknowledged one.[71] Their background and experience, particularly those who have held Commonwealth or State posts as solicitors general, inevitably influence their legal thinking. Gaudron's stand in *Re Wakim* could be anticipated.

Brennan and Toohey had left the Court by the time *Re Wakim* was considered. It is, in Kirby's view, a good example of the importance of who sits on the Court in the making and unmaking of the law.[72] If ever Kirby had a case for his pragmatic interpretive approach, *Re Wakim* demonstrated it. All of the State and Commonwealth governments of all persuasions supported the legislation.[73] They had worked towards it for more than a decade. This case demonstrates Gaudron's legalism, certainly in contrast to the approach of Kirby.

If any two judges shared similar humanitarian values, it was Gaudron and Kirby. However, she and Kirby had quite different approaches to their role as judges, and to giving expression to their views in their decisions. Kirby took opportunities to effect social reform if he thought the law was outdated. It is apparent that Gaudron distanced herself from Kirby's liberal interpretative style, being a 'lawyer's lawyer' first and foremost, and a social reformer only where the law allowed. Kirby was critical of his colleagues, including Gaudron, for being excessively technical in one case in which the Court decided that it could not provide guidance to a South Australian Director of Public Prosecutions on a criminal procedural matter. Kirby disagreed. He said: 'An unconstructive and unhelpful response ill becomes the courts, as a branch of government, in contemporary Australia. The law should not "draw up its skirts" and refuse all assistance.'[74]

Kirby had another outburst in 1999. He accused the Court majority of three—Gaudron, Gummow and Callinan—of allowing a man who had deliberately flouted a court order to walk away, unpunished, 'laughing at justice'. He and McHugh dissented in the decision to overturn a contempt conviction of Sydney real estate agent Karl Pelechowski, and the six-month gaol term that had been imposed upon him in 1998. According to Kirby, this was 'not a shining moment for the authority and effectiveness of judicial orders in Australia'.[75] The NSW District Court had ordered that Pelechowski not dispose of or deal with a property that he had mortgaged to obtain a credit facility. A creditor to whom Pelechowski owed a large sum of money had sought the order. Eleven days later Pelechowski breached the order and was subsequently gaoled for being in contempt of court. The High Court found that the District Court did not have the power to grant the type of order it had. Pelechowski walked free.[76]

Perhaps because of these experiences, Kirby tended to work on his own rather than as part of a team. 'He never did any alliance building,' McHugh observed. 'His work methods excluded it.'[77] Gaudron and her colleagues felt reluctant to ask Kirby to write the lead reasons for decision. It is rumoured that on one occasion, as the judges were leaving the court, Gaudron said loudly, 'Michael, can't you bloody well agree with us just once?' She screamed at him another time, with affection and exasperation, and in response he called her 'emotional'.[78]

Kirby upset Gaudron on occasions when she was standing in for Chief Justice Brennan, by contradicting remarks she made in exchanges with counsel. Kirby, like Gaudron, could be outspoken on the bench. In *Garcia v National Australia Bank Pty Ltd* the issue before the Court was whether a woman had been subjected to undue influence when she was persuaded to enter into an unfair financial transaction for the benefit of her partner. Gaudron observed that cases of this kind, coined as 'sexually transmitted debts', not infrequently involve women who are described as educated and articulate. Counsel agreed, adding that such women are often 'the object of cads'. 'Naturally,' Gaudron acknowledged. Kirby would have none of it, and said as much: 'I must not allow that. That sounds a rather sexist statement. Some articulate and educated men are the objects of cads…it makes me feel uncomfortable that we are slipping into stereotypes.'[79]

The views of the judges at this time were the subject of little discussion between them before or after hearings. At the conclusion of the hearing in *Garcia*, one of the judges suggested that they meet over a cup of tea before drafting their judgments. Gaudron embraced the idea and consensus was reached, with Gaudron, McHugh, Gummow and Hayne delivering a joint majority decision; Kirby and Callinan agreed with the majority but delivered separate judgments.[80] The practice of meeting after a hearing to discuss the issues over a cup of tea continued.[81]

Gaudron and Kirby: a complex relationship

Gaudron and Kirby were firm friends despite their rifts and tiffs and different judicial methods. Along with McHugh, Gaudron attended Kirby's farewell ceremonial sitting on the High Court. The Court has no formal ceremonial practice to farewell retiring judges. Gaudron and McHugh sat in the body of the court amongst the family members and distinguished guests specially invited by Kirby. Kirby sat on the bench alone.[82] No other current or former High Court Justice was present.[83]

Gaudron also gave Kirby her unequivocal support and was at the forefront of moves to defend him when Liberal Senator Bill Heffernan, the then Parliamentary Secretary to Prime Minister Howard, attacked. Heffernan wrongly accused Kirby of improper use of a Commonwealth car and 'trawling' for under-age male prostitutes in Sydney's Kings Cross. Heffernan had previously targeted Kirby after Kirby had given a talk in 2000 to the 'Hot Potato Club', a lunchtime group of schoolboys at St Ignatius' College, Riverview, a Jesuit school in Sydney. In the course of the talk he spoke of the importance of people feeling comfortable with themselves being homosexual.[84] In response to Heffernan's accusations, the High Court and the Department of Finance and Administration investigated and found that there had been no misuse of official cars, that the accusations were without foundation and that documents suggesting otherwise had been falsified.[85]

In March 2002 Heffernan renewed the allegations under protection of parliamentary privilege (presumably not having been informed by the government of the previous investigation), but in breach of conventions and Senate practice designed to protect judicial independence and impartiality. A standing order states that a senator 'shall not use offensive words…against a judicial officer, and all imputations of improper motives and all personal reflections on those…officers shall be considered highly disorderly'.[86] In support of his claim, Heffernan produced what purported to be a Comcar document recording Kirby's movements at Easter 1994. The *Sun Herald* published a photocopy of it on which, fortuitously, there were also references to car travel by Laurie Brereton, then a minister in the Labor Government, and Frederick Peterson, former Industrial Relations Commissioner.[87] Neither had travelled by Comcar that Easter.

In 2002, armed with a copy of the Registrar's earlier report on the matter, Gaudron participated in drafting a press statement about Heffernan's attempt to discredit a judge of the High Court. She showed it to Chief Justice Gleeson and informed him that the accusations were wrong, and that Heffernan knew them to be wrong. Gleeson, as a matter of principle, was opposed to judges making press statements. In this case, an expression of a view might compromise the Court if it had to determine an objection taken to Kirby sitting on a particular case. He urged her not to release it. Gaudron insisted on something being done. Others of her colleagues came to her chambers to urge her not to release the statement. This fired her up more. She ordered them out of her chambers Gaudron-style. Laurie Brereton came to the rescue. Fortunately, he had diary records of his movements as a minister that did not tally with the document Heffernan produced. Brereton was holidaying with his family in Queensland at the time. He called a press conference to expose the fake document. Further, he revealed that the Government had already examined the Comcar record on which Heffernan relied and had found it to be a forgery.[88] Heffernan was forced to apologise in the Senate on 19 March 2002 and he resigned from his position as Parliamentary Secretary.[89]

The Attorney General Daryl Williams did nothing to protect or defend Justice Kirby or the dignity of the Court. It was his view that it was not his role to do so.[90] Gaudron's view was simple. If neither the Chief Justice nor the Attorney General would intervene to counter Heffernan's attack on Kirby, individual judges could and should. Those who know her see the story as 'pure' Gaudron—at work behind the scenes when she saw the need to right a perceived injustice.[91]

An example of Gaudron's and Kirby's shared humanitarian values, and one which illustrates well the emphatic way in which Gaudron expresses a point of view, relates to the High Court judges' discussion of pension entitlements to same-sex partners of judges under the *Judges' Pensions Act 1968* (Cth). Gaudron was a supporter of a pension entitlement for Kirby's partner. Not long before Gaudron retired, the judges, other than Kirby, were equally divided on the issue. Gaudron said to Kirby: 'You've gotta vote. I'm not fuckin' doing this for you Kirby. I'm doing this for everyone in this fucking situation. You've gotta vote!'[92] Vote he did, and Kirby reports that the Justices, by majority, voted that the Chief Justice should write to the Howard Government seeking a change in the law.[93] According to Kirby, '[o]n such issues Mary was "the sea green incorruptible"; strong, principled, voluble'. The anecdote is revealing of Gaudron's concern about people's rights generally, not just the rights of women or the rights of people she knows, but of all people, and that she will express this in the strongest terms.

While Kirby did not escape Gaudron's sharp tongue, she liked and respected him. She told a journalist that although she did not always agree with him, and though he was sometimes naively optimistic, she particularly admired what she thought was his greatest asset—his courage.[94] Kirby says that he learned a great deal from her:

> Justice Gaudron is a real teacher, and she's taught me many things, particularly about indigenous matters and fairness matters. I think I'm a sort of honorary feminist, and that may be explained by the fact that I have felt discrimination and maybe if you never feel it, you don't quite understand what all the fuss is about.[95]

Their relationship was bound to be complex, given their similarities and differences. Kirby is religious. He was brought up an

Full Court bench 2002, (from left to right) Justices Kenneth Hayne, William Gummow, Mary Gaudron, Chief Justice Murray Gleeson, Justices Michael McHugh, Michael Kirby and Ian Callinan. (Courtesy the High Court of Australia).

Anglican and supports the values of his faith. He is a monarchist, and respects traditional institutions, like the church, family and Parliament. Gaudron denies being influenced by her religious background. She is a republican. Both Gaudron and Kirby admired Lionel Murphy and shared his liberal and humanitarian values. They are both hard workers who have devoted their lives to the law and its use to improve justice in society.

There is little doubt that Gaudron blended in better than Kirby with the Court's more conservative leadership, as she had on the Arbitration Commission in comparison with the radical Justice Jim Staples. She was gregarious, well-liked, and a cooperative team player. Her approach was more traditional than Kirby's, who incorporated common sense values into his reasoning when he felt 'either constrained by a pre-existing rule, precedent and legislation, or is particularly troubled by an identified injustice'.[96]

The question arises whether Gaudron effected a shift in her approach in the absence of the influence of her colleagues from the Mason years and in the presence of Gummow and, later, Hayne. Or did she, in Gaudron-style, continue to differentiate her views from those of the newer members of the Court, as she did when she took a different perspective of an issue from the members of the Court she first joined? What is clear is that Gaudron, in her judicial role, displayed an individual approach and style.

Chapter Seventeen

LAW, GAUDRON-STYLE

Now if life as a judge teaches you anything at all, and I readily confess it doesn't teach you much...it does teach you that even in Australia, there will always be those who, by virtue of their superior social, economic or political power, can and will deny or trample on the rights of others.

Mary Gaudron, 2005[1]

A certain style

Despite her apparent blending in with the changing membership and judicial thinking of the High Court, Gaudron was not one to desert a view she held.[2] Nor did her feisty attitude fade with longevity in years on the Court. As her retirement approached, she became less restrained on the bench and expressed more passion (and sometimes anger) about the rights of vulnerable members of society.

She had a unique style. Gaudron often saw a case from an angle no other judge had taken, sometimes giving it a new direction. Gummow regards this as a very great skill of Gaudron's.[3] She was a sharp thinker, and formulated her ideas comprehensively so that, when the time came to draft a decision, she did so—with fountain pen full of purple ink—in hand-written form. Her reasons unfolded logically as her thoughts transferred to paper. Some considered it was her habit of writing decisions by hand which gave them their distinctively flowing quality.[4] Her photographic memory must have assisted in this process. She could read a page of notes and have near-perfect recall, according to her former husband, Ben Nurse.

Gaudron was also an able administrator. She was efficient, undertook large workloads and completed tasks in a timely manner.[5] She showed strength and leadership, even when—especially when—she was fired up over issues she felt strongly about. This did not alienate her from other members of the Court. She sometimes took the initiative and talked with judges in an effort to forge consensus.[6] She was a team leader, as well as a team player. Gaudron was also the judge who was 'mother' in her collegiate role. She remembered people's birthdays, reminded others of them, and, when appropriate, organised parties.[7]

At the same time she was a mother who missed her family when she was away, frequently for lengthy periods during many of the years when her children were growing up and establishing their careers. Gaudron is a family woman. She loved children and, despite her busy career, would have had more if she could.[8] Both her daughters followed their mother's footsteps in taking up law. Her oldest, Danielle Nurse, graduated in Arts (Asian studies) and Economics at the Australian National University in 1988, and later made use of her acquired languages when she worked as a Qantas international air steward. She then studied law at the University of Technology, Sydney, graduating in 1998 with First-class Honours.[9] She practised in a large Sydney legal firm for a time before taking up work with Warner Bros in the United Kingdom. Julienne Nurse graduated in Arts in 1993 and Law in 1995 at the Australian National University. She decided at first not to practise law. Instead, with the help of her father, she established a health store in Hunters Hill shopping village. She ran the shop successfully for many years before returning to law, where she works as in-house counsel in the industrial sector for a large union in Sydney. Gaudron's youngest child, Patrick Fogarty, like his mother, won a University of Sydney Medal, in his case awarded by the Faculty of Science in 2003. In the same year, Patrick won an Australian Young Statisticians' book prize for a conference talk he gave, later the subject of a jointly published work.[10] As Gaudron's planned retirement from the Court approached, Patrick's promising career in statistics took him further away from her, to London, where he works as a statistician in medical research.

By 2001 Gaudron was enjoying her work less and looking forward to life after the bench more. She wanted to see more of her family, and spend more time at her cottage in the Loire from where she could more readily visit Danielle and Patrick in London. Her health was also a factor. Not that Gaudron allowed ill health to affect her capacity to work, nor did she raise it later as a matter relevant to her decision to retire early. Even during periods of extreme fatigue she worked at a high level, always ready to volunteer to take on work required in the Court. Nevertheless the state of her health and her diminished feeling of wellbeing after 1998 took its toll. This might account for her impatience in the 'Nigger Brown' case.

Gaudron had a particular way of giving a message that can be seen from comments she made in the course of some hearings. She was particularly testy in *Hagan v Trustees of the Toowoomba Sports Ground Trust*, known as the '*Nigger Brown*' case, in which she thought that a complaint of racism went too far. She made her feelings about it obvious in the course of Hagan's application before the Court. Aboriginal activist Stephen Hagan from Toowoomba, Queensland, sought unsuccessfully to have the word 'nigger' removed from a football ground grandstand. Hagan had also campaigned unsuccessfully for a ban on the name *Coon cheese*. The Toowoomba athletics' oval had a stand named after Edward Stanley 'Nigger' Brown, an old rugby league player. Blond-haired and blue-eyed Brown was nicknamed 'Nigger' by his teammates because he used to polish his shoes with 'Nigger Brown' polish.[11] Hagan applied to the High Court for special leave to appeal against the Federal Court's decision in the case.[12]

Gaudron and Hayne sat as a bench of two; Gaudron presiding.

Kirby, also in Brisbane with his High Court colleagues at the time, was scheduled to sit on the case but was absent, listening to and responding to Senator Heffernan's apology in the Senate for the false allegations he had made against the judge.[13] Upstairs, Gaudron was unimpressed with Hagan's case from the start. Unusually for Gaudron, she appeared to be underprepared. Counsel for Hagan, Ernst Willheim, referred to a section of the *Racial Discrimination Act 1975* (Cth). This exchange took place:

> Gaudron J: Well, I will tell you how important it seems to have been to your case, Mr Willheim. Section 18B is not reproduced in the bundle of materials before the Court. ...
> Willheim: It is the very first page of our bundle, your Honour.
> Gaudron J: Yes, thank you.[14]

She later remarked that the issue of whether a person might be likely in the circumstances to be offended had already been decided in the court below. Willheim corrected her, and pointed out that since the trial judge had in fact found against Hagan on that point, the court below did not find it necessary to address the issue, which was one reason for the appeal.

A transcript does not indicate body language or voice intonation. Those present, however, heard Gaudron over-emphasise the German pronunciation of 'Willheim', and her stinging delivery was indicative of more to come. Willheim put the submission that the nickname 'Nigger' was applied to Brown because of his colour. Gaudron asked whether this was because of the colour of Brown's boots or because of the colour of Hagan's skin. She remarked that it was no more offensive than the word 'pinky' on a cement mixer: 'Let us assume for a moment that I'm "pink"—and it's not an unreasonable assumption—and I'm offended by a sign that says "Pinky's Porkies". Now is that made out?'

Gaudron and Hayne rejected the application for leave with, as it has been described, 'what seems to have been unseemly judicial impatience and insensitivity.'[15] Gaudron's attitude was uncharacteristic in *'Nigger Brown'*, given it was a case concerning discrimination. Gaudron did not see it that way. Gaudron and Willheim were contemporaries at the University of Sydney Law School, and the irritation she directed to him might be attributable to a pre-existing rivalry reminiscent of that of Oscar Wilde and Sir Edward Carson. Another explanation, though not relevant to their decision, is that she and Hayne possibly assumed that the case was funded by the Aboriginal Legal Service and, given their view that the case was without merit, they may have thought the funding inappropriate and wasteful. The case was, in fact, undertaken *pro bono* by Willheim.

Discrimination—a woman's perspective

As a mother, a wife, a child of a working-class father, a woman, and as a thoughtful individual with a forceful personality, Gaudron brought a different perspective to the High Court, as judges from different walks of life are expected to do. She brought her perspective to some domestic cases concerning the role of women. Kirby cites the 2002 case of *U v U* as an example.[16] As with *Van Gervan*[17], it was another case that built on unjust assumptions about women's domestic roles. In *U v U* Gaudron saw its indirect effect in custody and family disputes and said so. The majority of the Court dismissed an action in which a mother, the prime carer of a child, asked to be allowed to return with her daughter to live in Mumbai where her wealthy family resided. Her estranged husband, also from India, was an Australian citizen who did not want to return, and wanted their child to stay with him if the mother returned to India. Gaudron and Kirby dissented. They thought it an unreasonable imposition on the mother to have to abandon her life and the career she had in India after the marriage had broken down.

Gaudron was crotchety. She said the case highlighted the 'inherently sexist' nature of custody rights in which women with children were considered 'selfish' if they did not fit in with the plans of their former male partners:

> [I]t is noteworthy that in this case there was no consideration of the possibility that the father could return to India

permanently to avail himself of frequent and regular contact with his daughter. The failure to explore that possibility... seems to me to be explicable only on the basis of an assumption, inherently sexist, that a father's choice as to where he lives is beyond challenge in a way that a mother's is not.[18]

Later, when talking about the case, Kirby told a journalist that 'it was important, I think, symbolically and substantively, to have the point of view of a woman...'[19]

Gaudron let slip her own uncertainty about her role as a mother in an exchange with a barrister in the case when she said, 'Well, no mother is ever going to say...if asked, "My life is more important than the child's",' and she added, 'except perhaps me'. Justice Hayne agreed: 'Just so', he said (presumably not intending to agree with Gaudron's self-denigration!)[20]

Gaudron worked to weed out insidiously discriminatory and unjust assumptions that society made about the domestic role of women. She thought that women's lives were diminished by 'motherhood' statements about contact with and shared responsibility for children incorporated in the *Family Law Reform Act 1995*. During the hearing of *U v U* she explained:

> Because if [the mother] does not say 'I will subordinate my interests', the values of this society will immediately judge her to be a bad mother. We are dealing with notions, male notions, that are going to be imposed on any woman in this situation which are essentially, in my view, unfair and it puts the mother in an absolutely impossible position...[21]

The special perspective Gaudron brought to the Court by reason of her experience and gender was highlighted by Ruth (later Justice) McColl. McColl recalls a case in which a father argued that his children should carry his name for what he called 'genetic reasons'. He was separated from his partner who had given the children her surname. Gaudron, not impressed, asked, 'Well, on which gene is the surname carried?' She thought that the father's argument was irrelevant to the best interests of the child, only relevant to the paramount interest of the father, and she questioned why female children had ever needed to bear their father's name.[22]

In the *Superclinics* case Gaudron had already made her views on gender discrimination very clear. The issue was abortion. It involved a controversial 'wrongful birth' claim for damages for the cost of raising a child. A woman took legal action against a medical clinic for negligent failure to diagnose her pregnancy at a time when she could have had an abortion. It came before the High Court in 1996 as an application for special leave to appeal from the NSW Court of Appeal in which, in a dissenting judgment, Justice Roderick Meagher said that, should a court sanction an action for damages, it would seem to him to be 'improper to the point of obscenity'.[23] These sentiments outraged Gaudron.

So did some of the submissions put to the High Court by counsel for the medical clinic, Steven Rares, QC. He mentioned the option of having the child adopted as a means of mitigating the damages claimed by the mother. Gaudron reacted forcefully:

> That would be about the cruellest and most inhuman submission I have heard put in this Court since I have been here. I must say, it took my breath away when I read the judgments below suggesting that that was a proper form of mitigation.[24]

One issue in the case was whether the mother had suffered compensable economic loss. When it was put by counsel that the loss was mitigated by the enhanced enjoyment of life in having the child, Gaudron countered, 'There may be joy in motherhood, but I would hardly have thought it was enhanced enjoyment of life. There be it.' Apparently Brennan—a father of seven—wanted to distance himself from the remark. He said, 'Justice Gaudron is one member of the Court; others may see it differently.'

Gaudron also slipped in a quip when Rares submitted that it was impossible to value the benefit that a healthy child brings to a parent. She remarked: 'Yet, for obvious reasons, sometimes they do not bring any.' Gaudron continued her cynical wit. Rares mentioned people who suffer post-natal depression, and whilst Justice Dawson jumped in first to point out that only women suffer from it, Gaudron added, 'You can take gender neutral language too far.' When Rares suggested the totality of a child's financial circumstances should not be ignored and raised, by way of example, the possibility of a child inheriting a large sum of money from a grandparent who 'was able to commodiously provide the child's mother', Gaudron was ready with: 'You must know different children from the ones I know.'[25]

Justice Kirby observed in 2003 that the High Court became a more 'blokey' place after Gaudron had retired:

> She brought a different value-added. She brought her perspective of the law and her great experience. She also brought a woman's perspective. That, after all, is half the population. I think her capacity to see things in a slightly different way was a great benefit to the High Court and you can see it in many cases.[26]

He concluded: 'a woman's life experience is not that of a man. It's a different life experience, a different perspective. So I miss Mary Gaudron.'

Protecting the vulnerable

Gaudron's humanitarianism was strongly demonstrated in cases involving the rights and dignity of refugees. Cases concerning rights of migrants to judicial review of decisions made by immigration officers reveal Gaudron's continuing pursuit of procedural fairness as part of her concept of equal justice. In 1994 the Keating Labor Government introduced significant reforms to the *Migration Act 1958* (Cth). It was the first step towards restricting judicial review of migration decisions.[27] Time limits were introduced in which applications for judicial review could be made to the Federal Court.[28] The Government's intention was to deprive people who had arrived by boat as prospective migrants from Indo-China from seeking judicial review of decisions taken by officers of the

Department of Immigration and Ethnic Affairs about their status as migrants or refugees. Other restrictions on the right to judicial review were imposed.

In particular, section 476 in Part 8 of the amended Act excluded a breach of the rules of natural justice and the unreasonable exercise of power from grounds of review of a decision by the Federal Court. In 1999 the High Court, in *Abebe*, considered the effect of section 476.[29] The majority held the provision valid, finding that the Commonwealth could limit the grounds on which an administrative decision could be reviewed by the Federal Court, even though full review was available in the High Court under section 75(v) of the Constitution.[30] Gaudron, Gummow and Hayne disagreed. Gaudron, noting that an applicant could seek review by the High Court under section 75(v) on wider grounds than was permitted by the Federal Court, held the provisions invalid because there was no final determination of the matter and it was not, therefore, an exercise of judicial power.[31] In the event, however, the whole Court found that there was no error that attracted the High Court's jurisdiction under section 75(v). The significance of the case was that the whole Court considered that the jurisdiction which section 75(v) confers on the High Court to review executive decision in the case of serious error could not be limited by a law of the Parliament.

In May 2001 the High Court held, in *Yusuf*,[32] that the *Migration Act* did not exclude judicial review where the relevant migration tribunal had made a jurisdictional error. Importantly, it defined jurisdictional error broadly and suggested that it included a breach of the rules of procedural fairness. If the tribunal went beyond its jurisdiction in the way it arrived at its decision, it was not 'a decision' under the Act as to which a review was prohibited. The Court's stand was akin to the line of cases in which it accepted that the judicial power in the Constitution had to be exercised with due process. This decision posed a problem for the Howard Government. This led to a large increase in people approaching the High Court under section 75(v) of the Constitution for a review of a decision made about their migration or refugee status.

In August 2001 the Howard Government's refusal to permit the *Tampa* to dock in Australia to disembark some rescued refugees received some public support. In October 2001, tenuous claims were made, later proved to be false, that refugees on a small intercepted boat had deliberately thrown their children overboard, in a bid to be rescued and taken to Australia. In the lead-up to a federal election the Howard Government, stung by the *Yusuf* case, used these claims to build up public support to further restrict the appeal rights of similar 'undesirable' arrivals.

On 2 October 2001 the *Migration Legislation (Judicial Review) Act 2001* (Cth) came into effect with the intention of negating the effect of *Yusuf*. It introduced a new Part 8 of the *Migration Act*. It included section 474 which declared that administrative decisions by an immigration official or one of the tribunals that reviewed the decisions would be 'final and conclusive and must not be challenged, appealed against, reviewed, quashed or called in question in any court'. It was known as a 'privative clause'.[33] Immigration Minister, Philip Ruddock, explained that the amendment 'will restrict access to judicial review in all but exceptional circumstances'.[34]

On its face the new provision seemed to clash with section 75(v) of the Constitution that permits review of executive decisions by the High Court.[35] Deane and Gaudron, in an earlier case concerning a challenge to a taxation assessment by a Deputy Commission of Taxation, acknowledged that the 'distinction between what laws are and what laws are not consistent with section 75(v) is admittedly an elusive one'.[36] The section reads, in part:

> 75. In all matters
>
> ...
>
> (v) In which a writ of Mandamus or prohibition or an injunction is sought against an officer of the Commonwealth: the High Court shall have original jurisdiction.

It thus gives the High Court jurisdiction in all matters in which an applicant is seeking a writ of mandamus (where the Commonwealth is asked to carry out a function it is obliged to perform) or a writ of prohibition or an injunction against an officer of the Commonwealth (to prevent the Commonwealth from doing something). As technical and dry as section 75(v) reads, it is a powerful tool cherished by Gaudron as one that can be used by any individual, including non-citizens, who consider they have been wronged by an executive decision of the Government.

At least some High Court judges perceived section 474 as an attack on the Court's role. Justice Kirby thought the Government's plans were Orwellian in their scope. He said:

> We are here to do justice, that is the oath we take, and you want to take it away from us. Well, I would need to be convinced that it is not part of the essence of the constitutional writ, for you to have the power to take it away, because it is in the Constitution.[37]

For her part Gaudron used her 'question' technique:

> It brings us back to the question of what power does the Parliament have to direct this Court, as to what it shall and shall not do. That is the first question, and the second really is by what right can the Parliament take away inherent power from a constitutional court. Now I would have thought that they were big questions.[38]

It had earlier been claimed that the Government's pre-2001 legislative scheme already was an 'attempt to nullify section 75(v)'.[39] Another lawyer argued that the 2001 amendments contravened the Constitution by circumventing section 75(v) by drafting devices, while not directly ousting the jurisdiction conferred by the section.[40]

In March 2002 the High Court threw a spanner in the works in its decision in *Bhardwaj*.[41] Gaudron and Gummow, in the majority, acknowledged that the privative clause, section 474, in the *Migration Act* in restricting judicial review of decisions of Commonwealth officers made under the Act was valid, not inconsistent with section 75(v). But they found that the clause was subject to section 75(v) in the case of a Commonwealth officer making a jurisdictional error. On the facts of *Bhardwaj*, they held that the Minister's decision was made in circumstances that denied Bhardwaj a reasonable opportunity to answer the case against him. It was in breach of the rules of natural justice, and could be set aside under section 75(v). In this way, the amendment to the *Migration Act* did not change the Court's view of the power of section 75(v).

By then there had been a sharp fall in the number of asylum seekers arriving by boat or plane. The problem remained, however, of the hundreds of men, women and children in detention centres whose refugee applications had been rejected but who had nowhere to go. They looked to the High Court.

In February 2003, in *Plaintiff S157*, the Court confirmed that section 474 did not conflict with section 75(v) of the Constitution.[42] But again the Court found that the plaintiff was denied procedural fairness and that this amounted to a jurisdictional error. It held that the flawed decision was therefore not a 'decision' from which section 474 in the *Migration Act* prohibited a review. Gaudron delivered the joint judgment of five judges; Gleeson and Callinan agreed in separate judgments. Immigration Minister Ruddock was faced with a seven-judge ruling that allowed federal courts to continue to review cases where the applicant asserted that a decision under the *Migration Act* was defective by failing to observe procedural fairness.

The volume of migration cases continued to rise. With the Howard Government's clamp down on 'boat people', the use of section 75(v) increased. There was an increasing flow of writs as people challenged migration decisions and a growing incidence of cases in which a litigant personally presented his or her argument found worthy by the Court.

Gaudron did not like the Government's approach to dealing with asylum seekers. In Gaudron-style she put her point of view. *Plaintiff S157* was so named because another amendment to the *Migration Act* imposed a prohibition on identifying the litigant by name. Gaudron had plenty to say about this de-identification. In the 2002 case of *275-02 v MIMA and anor* the applicant was referred to only as 'S200'. She vented her anger on counsel representing Minister Ruddock in the proceedings who had omitted to announce his own name, as is the convention when appearing in a court. Referring to the prohibition on her from referring to the litigant by name, she asked at the outset:

> Now, would somebody kindly tell me what happens now? I am aware of section 91X. I presume I cannot say to this person, 'Mr So-and-So, do you represent yourself?' which is what I would normally say. I presume I cannot extend to him the normal courtesies that I would extend to any person at the Bar table. Mr X, I am addressing you.

'Yes', acknowledged the barrister, Geoffrey Johnson. 'Shall I call you Mr X?' she asked the barrister. 'Well, it is a matter for your Honour,' he replied. 'Well, it is not a matter for me. It is a serious question. I take it that you appear for the Minister,' she responded. Mr Johnson realised that he had not announced his name, and apologised to the Court. Gaudron did not let the matter go:

> Gaudron J: No. You see, you are very lucky. You have a name.
> Johnson: Well, your Honour, if it is of assistance, the practice in the Federal Court...has been to call the applicant by the assigned name.
> Gaudron J: The assigned name?
> Johnson: Well, there is an assigned, I think probably randomly allocated, set of letters in the Federal Court.
> Gaudron J: That is ridiculous. That is ridiculous.

Gaudron then questioned Johnson about the constitutional validity of the amendment in issue:

> Gaudron J: You repeat that it is valid and that I am to treat this person as if he had no name. Do you assert that? I am to sufficiently ignore the man's humanity as to deny him a name in these court proceedings and to deny him the ordinary courtesies that I would extend to anyone at the Bar table?

> Johnson: Your Honour, my suggestion to the Court is that he be referred to as S200.
> Gaudron J: Well, let me call you Mr J41, shall I?
> Johnson: That is a matter for your Honour, but, your Honour...

And round it went:

> Gaudron J: Well, it is not. I would not do it. I would not do it because it is discourteous.
> Johnson: Well, your Honour, could I respectfully suggest to your Honour that if it is explained to the applicant that...
> Gaudron J: No, no, explain it to me. It is my problem; not the applicant. It is my problem. I was brought up understanding that there were certain courtesies and considerations to be extended to all fellow creatures. I was brought up at the Bar to believe that you treated people at the Bar table with respect. My time on the Bench has reinforced that learning; that one is to treat them with respect.

Gaudron underlined that it was the Act and not the Minister's representative that she was criticising. 'The Act is denying me my right to treat this gentleman with the respect I would normally afford to anybody I met in society, in the street, or with whom I had to have any professional dealings, including in terms of listening to his submissions.' She apologised to Mr 'S200' in Court for being unable to address him by his name.[43] She called him 'Sir', and told him she would prefer to call him by his given name but that an amendment to the Act in 2001 forbade it. 'I realise it is a gross discourtesy. It is not of my making,' she declared. At this point, 'S200', who had been listening to this exchange through the interpreter, rose to his feet to express his appreciation for the respect Gaudron paid to him.

At the time of this case, Gaudron's retirement was only a few months away. She had nothing to lose in airing her view on government policy in the case. She had formally notified the Attorney General Daryl Williams in June 2002 that she would retire in January 2003, shortly after her sixtieth birthday.

Type-casting Gaudron

Gaudron's jurisprudential style has proved difficult to place in any of the conventionally labelled boxes. Most commentators on the High Court tend to assess jurists' philosophical approaches with reference to the 'black and white' and 'activist' labels. Gaudron defies these. It is the combination of her ability to mould the law to meet the needs of contemporary society, without abandoning existing law, that defeats attempts to place her in one or other of the conveniently described legal camps. This is well illustrated by Justice Heydon finding no place for Gaudron in his classification of the various approaches of High Court justices to constitutional interpretation. In 2007, in the Sir Maurice Byers Lecture on the High Court and the Constitution, Heydon included Gaudron's colleagues in his taxonomy but ignored her, other than including her name with others in some footnotes.[44]

It is clear that Gaudron felt intellectually comfortable with Mason, Deane and Toohey in her first eight years on the Court. It is also apparent that she found intellectual compatibility with the jurisprudentially more conservative justices Gummow and Hayne on the Gleeson Court. They were more legalistic in their judicial approach than Kirby on the same Court, and Deane from the Mason Court. But then, so had Gaudron been from the time she joined the Court.

After Chief Justice Gleeson's arrival at the Court, there was no noticeable change in Gaudron's propensity to agree or disagree with the majority decision. She was not a conspicuous dissenter. On the contrary, she was part of the majority of the Court in a significant number of cases. This would be partially explained if it is accepted that there was no dramatic 'shift back' in the Court's jurisprudential thinking following the Mason Court's approach of realism. Most legal commentators believe there was. The perception might arise therefore, that Gaudron adapted her approach in different circumstances. Like a chameleon, did she change her colours to blend in with the changing legal environment on the Court as she found it?

There is another explanation as to why Gaudron managed to stay more or less in tune with the majority of judges under all three Chief Justices—Mason, Brennan and Gleeson. Heydon, though apparently unable to classify Gaudron under one of the conventional jurisprudential headings, did recognise the influence on her at the University of Sydney Law School of the rigorous and legalistic law lecturer, Frank Hutley. When Heydon paid tribute to Gaudron on succeeding her on the Court, he said: '[s]he stood high among those best equipped for the task by capacity, by training, particularly at the hands of the late Mr Justice Hutley, by experience and by achievement'.[45] If it is accepted that Gaudron was equally influenced by the Law School's progressive jurist, Julius Stone, a clue is provided about Gaudron's capacity to use the law as a precision tool for advancing social justice. First, it must be remembered that support Gaudron gave to some of Deane's and Toohey's decisions was limited by the more legalistic approach she adopted. This was the case too in respect of the limited support she gave Kirby's reasons for his decisions, even though they often arrived at similar conclusions.

In *Leeth*, in which Gaudron joined Deane and Toohey in dissent, she formulated narrower and more legalistic reasons than those of Deane and Toohey in finding a Commonwealth law invalid that permitted different sentencing provisions depending on where the individual being sentenced lived.[46] Deane and Toohey concluded that the Constitution contained a general principle of legal equality. Gaudron's decision focused on the narrower ground that the judicial power itself incorporated the concept of equal justice. She held that a law requiring the courts to exercise a judicial power, such as the non-parole period of an offender, on geographical grounds rather than grounds particular to the offender, was discriminatory and 'inconsistent with the judicial process'.[47] Her method led to the same outcome, but avoided the broad-brush application of legal principles.

Further, when the implied freedom of political communication developed in the Mason years continued, with a more legalistic approach to constitutional interpretation, Gaudron felt comfortable. Her moderation at times is likely to have more to do with her analysis of text and application of the declared law than shifts to accommodate the mainstream thinking of members of a particular Court. This is illustrated by the separate reasons for decisions she often delivered in which she distanced herself from an approach with which she did not agree, though agreeing with the decision of the majority or minority of which her decision formed a part.

To suggest Justices of the High Court are capable of 'influencing' each other, in the sense of 'prevailing' upon them to change their views, would be wrong. The Court's Justices have proved to be independent thinkers, as evidenced by the many separate judgments delivered by majority and dissenting judges. Gaudron's personality, in particular, was too strong to be swayed by others to abandon her world view, her notion of equal justice and the way in which it should be applied as a principle of law. This is not to say that the dynamics of a changing Court did not have some influence over the thinking of individual members of the Court. Judges are likely to be open to the particular thinking of some judges more than others.

Gaudron had high regard for the well-regarded equity lawyers Gummow and Hayne. Mason had lectured both Gummow and Gaudron in equity at the University of Sydney. Gaudron had bettered Gummow in class, but by the time Gummow joined the Court, he was one of the acknowledged authorities on the subject, having co-authored *Equity, Doctrines and Remedies*, an authoritative text on equity in Australia.[48] Gaudron's ability to dissect a statute and analyse the meaning of a provision from the text is another of her skills that Gummow admired. But they did not always agree with each other's views.

Brennan suggests that while Gaudron would have responded in some way to changes of Court membership (notably her regard for Gummow and Hayne, in some measure compensating for the departure of Deane and Toohey), it is unlikely that this led to any substantial change in her judicial method.[49] Presumably he considers the same applied to him.

The nature of the role of the judges requires they have an open mind; that they exchange views, and listen to what each other has to say. Gaudron was at her best when what Blackshield describes as her 'original thinking' was supported by those whose intellects she admired. And the intellectual energy she devoted to developing arguments and supporting them with concise and logical reasoning is likely to have had as much persuasive effect on other justices as their views did on her.

The placement of judges on the bench, in itself, can be important to decision outcomes. Gummow recalls the importance to the physical dynamics of the bench in *Plaintiff 157*, for example. Chief Justice Gleeson, presiding, sat in the centre with Gaudron to his right; on her right was Gummow, and to his right, Hayne. The latter three talked amongst themselves in the course of counsel addressing the Court. It is common to see one or two of the judges exchanging whispered comments during a hearing. By the time the judges rose, Gaudron, Gummow and Hayne had reached a consensus.

Gaudron has demonstrated that as difficult as it sometimes is for a lawyer intent on being true to the law and to effect social change, this is what she achieved on the whole, by her individualistic style.[50] This is illustrated in her decision in the controversial and highly political *Patrick Stevedores* case in 1998.[51] It concerned the dismissal of some 1400 waterfront workers, most of whom belonged to the Maritime Union of Australia. It occurred on the evening of Tuesday 7 April 1998, when the Patrick group of stevedoring companies claimed that the work practices of the waterfront workforce had placed the company in a position of insolvency. The Patrick companies were put into voluntary administration. Controversially, an entirely new non-union workforce was recruited through the use of employer companies that provided labour on an agency basis. The dismissed workers, angry, set up a picket line on the docks of Melbourne.

The waterfront stoppage caused havoc on the docks. The hostilities between employer and workers matched those of the Mount Isa dispute with which Gaudron was familiar when representing Pat Mackie, the leader of the mining workforce.[52] The workers applied to the Federal Court to be reinstated. They were successful. The Patrick group appealed. The issue for the High Court was whether a court could order the resumption of trading by one of the employer companies, or whether that was a matter only for its administrator to decide.

Those who knew of Gaudron's working-class background and sympathy for the rights of workers would expect her to find for the waterfront unionists, and she did. The majority of the Court also upheld the Federal Court's orders that the dismissed workers should be reinstated. However, the majority judges, other than Gaudron, found that the Federal Court orders went too far, and interfered with the administrator's discretion to determine whether or not to resume trading by the employer companies. The error, the majority held (with Callinan dissenting) was not fatal. They held that the orders could be rectified and they were amended accordingly. Gaudron disagreed with that aspect of the decision, and with her usual legalistic and analytical approach, upheld the Federal Court orders on the ground that their clear effect was to permit the possibility that the employer companies might trade their way back to solvency, without interfering with the administrator's discretion. She delivered a separate judgment setting out her reasons for dismissing the Patrick group's appeal in its entirety.

Another significant instance of her aptitude for applying the law to meet contemporary expectations was her contribution to the groundbreaking medical negligence case, *Rogers v Whitaker*.[53] Gaudron's decision is again revealing of her notion of equality. She approached the doctor-patient relationship as one of inequality, in that the medical practitioner holds the specialist information that the patient requires in order to make decisions about his or her own medical treatment. Whitaker was advised that the patient might benefit from surgery to her near-blind right eye. She specifically talked to her surgeon about her concerns that she retained good sight in her left eye. As a result of the surgery to her right eye, she developed inflammation in the left eye that led to loss of sight in that eye from a condition known as sympathetic ophthalmia. She took legal action against the doctor for his failure to warn her of that risk of the procedure.

The High Court had to consider the scope of the duty the surgeon owed to a patient to exercise reasonable care and skill, and whether failure to warn the patient of the possibility of this adverse outcome constituted a breach of this duty. The English *Bolam* test had previously applied, to the effect that whether a doctor is guilty of negligence is a matter of medical judgment.[54] The majority in *Rogers v Whitaker* found that a doctor has a duty to provide information about the material risks of any planned procedure and, importantly, that medical opinion was not the only, or prime, determinate of what the duty of care involved—certainly not with respect to the duty to warn.

Gaudron agreed with the majority. In a separate decision she enlarged on what she thought was required to satisfy the duty of care owed by the doctor to the patient. Implicit in her reasoning is recognition that the power imbalance that exists in the doctor-patient relationship should be addressed. She described later, in another case, the Court's rejection in *Rogers* of the doctor-patient relationship 'as basically paternalistic'.[55] In *Rogers* she emphasised that the obligation for a doctor to provide information that was 'reasonably required' by a patient was a minimum requirement, and that what was reasonable was a matter 'of commonsense'.[56] It included warning the patient of a risk that is 'real and foreseeable', not 'far-fetched or fanciful'. She also suggested that other types of information, such as the need for or desirability of alternative treatment that promised greater benefit, was within the duty of disclosure.[57]

Chappel v Hart affirmed the view that medical opinion is not the sole test in determining whether a medical practitioner has acted negligently in diagnosing or treating a patient and in giving advice about the risks associated with treatment.[58] By this time, Gaudron had first-hand experience of being in the position of a vulnerable patient who on medical advice agreed to undergo a serious procedure. Hart underwent surgery on her oesophagus without being warned about the possible consequences should the oesophagus be perforated and infection set in. That course of events occurred, although not through any negligence on the part of the surgeon. Hart's claim for damages for negligence was based on the failure of the surgeon to warn her of the risks of the surgery. She argued that as a consequence of that failure she lost the opportunity of choosing to defer the procedure and arrange for a more experienced surgeon to undertake it. The Court, Gaudron presiding, agreed that compensation could be awarded for a 'lost opportunity' even though the outcome may have been the same at the hands of a more experienced surgeon. Again Gaudron went further than the rest of the Court. She thought a medical practitioner, in fulfilling the duty to advise a patient about options available, also had a duty to inform Hart 'that there were more experienced surgeons practicing in the field'.[59]

Her lead was followed in *Naxakis*.[60] A bench of five unanimously confirmed that the test for medical negligence was no longer what the medical profession considered was accepted as proper medical practice at the time. The case concerned a twelve-year-old boy who had been admitted to hospital with a head injury after having been involved in an altercation with a schoolmate. It transpired that he had a pre-existing brain aneurism that burst after he had been discharged from hospital and left him severely disabled for life. The possibility of an aneurism, rare in a child, was not checked before he was discharged. The Court found it was for the jury to conclude on the evidence whether other medical steps should reasonably have been taken to exclude other causes of the boy's symptoms. Gaudron emphasised that it was not for expert medical witnesses to give their opinion on whether the steps taken were reasonable, or whether the hospital or surgeon was negligent in failing to take them. Gaudron's strong statements in these cases have been referred to in subsequent cases and legal journals indicating the direction in which medical negligence law homegrown in Australia might head.[61]

An enduring legacy

Sir Anthony Mason describes Gaudron's outlook on life and the law as essentially that people should be treated fairly, with respect and dignity.[62] This is evident in her notion of equal justice and its relationship to discrimination, and her promotion of due process in providing a fair system of justice. Gaudron's influence on the meaning of equality and the application of due process, particularly in decisions she gave concerning criminal law, forms part of the legacy Gaudron leaves to Australian law.[63]

Professor Fiona Wheeler, in examining Gaudron's decisions concerning the requirements of due process, paid particular attention to *Ebner v Official Trustee in Bankruptcy*.[64] In that case Gaudron found that impartiality was a constitutional requirement of the exercise of Federal judicial power. The case concerned a contention that a judge who heard and determined proceedings at first instance should be disqualified by reason of a shareholding he or she had in a listed public company. Gaudron, again in the majority but delivering a separate decision from the joint majority judgment, emphasised that impartiality, and the appearance of it, is a significant principle of natural justice, and one required by Chapter III of the Constitution.[65] Kirby states that it is in this case that the constitutional implication of 'judicial impartiality' began its 'journey to acceptance'.[66] According to Wheeler, who noted that the High Court continued to recognise the due process principle after the departures of Mason and Deane, the legitimacy of the principle, whether based on Deane's or Gaudron's view, must now be regarded as settled. She stated that the legacy of Deane and Gaudron 'seems assured, even if not all elements of their due process vision come to pass'.[67]

Blackshield views the way Gaudron articulated her notion of 'equality' in *Leeth* as providing a more 'circumscribed and elaborately constructed chain of reasoning' than the broad-brush approach in the joint dissenting judgment of Deane and Toohey in that case.[68] For that reason, Blackshield believes, it is likely to have increasing appeal. He suggests that it is probably this aspect of Gaudron's reasoning that has been most influential on Gummow, who has carried the notion forward in a variety of contexts. While the broader approach of Deane and Toohey has been rejected, Gaudron's approach has continued to have influence.[69] Wheeler likewise claims that Gaudron's notion of justice may have long-lasting influence on the Court beyond that of other judges.

If this is correct, the full extent of Gaudron's legacy may not yet be apparent. Her influence might be long-lasting. Her combination of original thinking with logical reasoning may have broad appeal to judges who take an 'activist' approach in their decision-making role, as well as to jurists more inclined to 'declare' rather than 'make' law. This view is supported by constitutional lawyer, Professor Adrienne Stone, in the context of Gaudron's interpretive approach to the Constitution. She concludes that Gaudron's decisions are likely 'to be very attractive to a rights-sensitive but moderate court, which would like to reinvigorate constitutional rights without overturning established precedent'.[70] Professor Cheryl Saunders also describes Gaudron as having a different and original approach. It is one that is entirely within the Australian text-based tradition of constitutional interpretation, highly logical, and also 'novel by comparison to other members of the same Court'.[71] Professor George Williams likewise suggests that Gaudron's legalism did not restrain her progressive approach to developing the law better to reflect the society in which we live.[72]

Others would undoubtedly argue otherwise. One 'legal academic' (a male), who asked not to be named, told the *Age* that Gaudron had failed to live up to the reputation for brilliance advanced by her supporters; that she had written some good judgments, but was 'erratic' and certainly not among the court's greats.[73] Gaudron did, on occasions, revise a view she previously held, and openly stated her reasons for doing so. Heydon made a virtue of Gaudron's preparedness to admit a change of view when he said:

> ...if she realised that she had been misapprehending the problem or if she worked out for herself some possible solution to it, she would reveal her changed thinking at once. She never left the pursuit of truth for the pursuit of victory.[74]

This was not indicative of weakness. Heydon spoke of the force of Gaudron's intellect and personality, noting the effect of these on the barristers who appeared before her: 'They often had to summon up all their reserves of fortitude and calmness...'

Heydon also hinted at a legacy likely to unfold when he said of Gaudron's judgments:

If they are read slowly, line by line, repeatedly, carefully and sympathetically, they create a much fresher and clearer vision of the issue. One might not agree with either her reasoning or her conclusion, though very often one would, but the question of agreement is not to the point. The value of her judgments lies not so much in compelling acceptance of a conclusion as in aiding readers to their own conclusions. For that reason they will be read as long as any parts of the Commonwealth Law Reports continue to be read.[75]

Sir Anthony Mason considers Gaudron made a very significant and genuine contribution to the development of Australian law. In acclaiming her as an outstanding lawyer, he notes in particular her 'very fine' command of and insight into constitutional law and her 'outstanding' criminal law judgments.[76] Ruth McColl, SC, considered that Gaudron had an 'extraordinarily humanising effect on the law', making special reference to her insights in cases concerning women and families, the law of discrimination and the development of principles of equality.[77] As early as 1994, Professor Michael Detmold of Adelaide University said of Gaudron, 'I think she has turned into one of the sharpest constitutional lawyers on the Court. She is at the forefront of working out new constitutional law concerned with citizenship, individual liberties, rights and so forth.'[78] Justice Jane Mathews was open about her view: 'When history has its say [Mary Gaudron] will go down as an outstanding High Court Judge.'[79]

Chapter Eighteen

MOVING ON: A TIME TO SPEAK OUT

> The trouble with the women of my generation is that we thought if we knocked the doors down, success would be inevitable: the trouble with the men of your generation is that so many still think that, if they hold the doors open, we will be forever grateful.
>
> Mary Gaudron, 1995[1]

Equal opportunity

Up to the time of her retirement Gaudron regretted that so little progress had been made in the equal participation of women in the law. In one of her last cases she was rewarded with the appearance before the High Court of one of her Associates, Naomi Sharpe, with a 'speaking role'.[2] Gaudron had often commented about how few women had appeared in the Court,[3] an indication that equal opportunity was proving to be as elusive as equal pay. Once she asked Hartog Berkeley, Victoria's Solicitor General, 'Why don't you bring a woman with you to Canberra?' And he did. He persuaded the Victorian Government to brief a woman to appear with him: Susan Crennan, who, with the help of that professional break, became the next woman appointed to the High Court.[4]

Achieving silk was a breakthrough for women. In the years up to 2003 Gaudron invited the women silks and their families, including their children, to drinks in her chambers at the High Court, to celebrate the rarity of the occasion.[5] Before she retired she spoke out about issues concerning equal opportunity of employment, of women lawyers in particular, and the issue of merit in appointments to the Court.

While married women were an integral part of the paid labour force, cultural and structural obstacles to equality of opportunity continued, and not only for professional lawyers. The assumption was made that paid work can be performed without heed to childcare needs at the end of the school day and during school holidays.[6] Gaudron saw a connection between the failure of governments to address the problem, the declining birth rate and the growing number of women in the workforce: 'As one who has been the mother of a teenager for 24 years straight, and is still not out of the woods in that regard, I find it very difficult to make an argument in favour of motherhood.'[7] She was quick to point out that there was perhaps one, if you subscribed to the theory of geneticist, Gillian Turner—that male children inherit their intelligence from their mothers. Gaudron facetiously concluded that intelligent women 'just need to wait a few generations until men are completely dumbed down and then we take over completely'.[8] In the same sarcastic vein she once said: 'It is often said that, for a woman to succeed in a traditional male area, she has to be better than her male counterparts. We know this is true. We also know that it is not very hard to be better than the average male.'[9]

Gaudron regarded failure to address the issue of equal pay as a disgrace. She made the observation in 1979 that equal pay had been 'won' in 1968, again in 1972 and 1974, and, over twenty years later, lamented that 'it may have to be won again'.[10] Her words were quoted as still true at the turn of the century.[11] In 1992, Gaudron noted sadly that in 1972 average male and female earnings were far from equal, with women earning only 84 percent of the average ordinary time weekly wages for Australian men.[12] In 2008 it had not changed. Women's salaries were still 16 percent behind men's.[13]

Anti-discrimination legislation had not had much bearing on the position of women in the workforce either:

> It is generally accepted that, notwithstanding their greater participation and notwithstanding some individual achievements in male dominated areas, the general pattern of women's employment has not changed greatly since 1970, with women still clustered in the lower paid jobs and, increasingly, in part-time or casual employment.[14]

The notion of 'the glass ceiling', she noted, is a euphemism suggesting that women are held back, not by reason of discriminatory practices or unequal treatment, but on account of some mysterious indefinable *je ne sais quoi*. She considered that the modern anti-discrimination legislation had influenced, or perhaps shaped, current attitudes, but not entirely for the good: 'In particular it may have entrenched some inexact, if not inaccurate, notions of equality; and it may be blinding some of us to what justice or equality demands in the particular case.'[15]

Gaudron saw a role for lawyers to help address this:

> One fundamental question that emerges is how to maintain equality of opportunity—in the vernacular, a fair go for all—in the face of changes that appear to have wrought significant inequality in wealth and in bargaining power. From the perspective of a mere lawyer, that translates as a challenge to ensure equal justice.[16]

Gaudron's own experiences confirmed the barriers that professional women encountered. They all added up—her mother's expectation that she should work for a radio station; the local solicitor ridiculing her for considering a career in law; the loss of her job in the public service because she married.[17] Earlier in her career she stated that equal pay for women would not be achieved until women had equal opportunity to access the same employment opportunities as men, and the higher paid jobs 'that men had so successfully guarded for themselves for so long'.[18]

By 1998 she had noted small signs of progress. When addressing a Bench and Bar dinner in Sydney, she observed that all the speeches were delivered by women at a gathering of some six hundred people. But there was still a dearth of female 'silks'. In 1989 there were no women among the newly appointed QCs throughout Australia. Dame Roma Mitchell told a tale about Gaudron's solution to this.[19] At a Canberra dinner gathering of men newly appointed to that rank, Gaudron said to Dame Roma in the hearing of fellow judges, 'Perhaps it would be a good idea if there were a rule that no liquor be served at the dinner unless there is at least one woman among the new silks.' According to Dame Roma, this 'suggested' threat was effective. In the next year two female barristers were appointed in NSW and two in Victoria—incremental but noteworthy progress.[20]

By 2000, Gaudron had abandoned her view that equality of opportunity would give women lawyers 'a fair go'. Opportunity was *not* everything.[21] It would not secure equality of participation:

> I believe there are [men in] positions of power and influence who simply pay lip-service to the notions of equality and equity but in truth do not believe in them...There are, I think, people who do not accept that men and women are equal; who do not think equality is a good thing and, indeed, who actually fear the equal participation of women in the professions and in the workplace.[22]

Gaudron tirelessly encouraged women lawyers in their battle for equality and to discourage and shame those men who harped that women were not appointed to the bench on merit. Never one to miss an opportunity, in 2002 she singled out Justice Roderick (Roddy) Meagher for perpetuating problems for female lawyers. She commented:

> With the growing influence of feminism in the 1970s and the enactment of anti-discrimination legislation, blatant

rudeness and discrimination went underground in the profession, save in the case of the wilfully unreconstructed who, I should think, included Roderick Pitt Meagher. I mention him because, only recently, he was reported as saying: 'The Bar desperately needs more women barristers [because] there are so many bad ones that people may say that women...are hopeless by nature.'[23]

Gaudron pointed out that Meagher, one of the most senior judges of the NSW Court of Appeal, knew the probable consequence of his remark, namely that few, if any, women barristers would be briefed to appear in that Court. Gaudron was kind to him in the circumstances. Meagher also referred to 'hairy-legged lesbians' and court corridors 'thronged with unmarried mothers and abused children, people who are stoned, or were hatched in bottles, or have been raped or cloned'.[24]

Federal Attorney General Daryl Williams claimed that there were few senior women in the profession to choose from for judgeships. He was correct in that there were relatively few women of 'QC' or 'SC' rank. However, there were many women in the profession worthy of, but who had not achieved, that rank.[25] The distinguishing initials are bestowed without any transparent 'merit' process. The 'secret committee' process of granting or rejecting applications of barristers to become silk has remained an obstacle to the appointment of more women judges.

Gaudron had something to say about the depressingly low numbers of senior women at the Bar, and the standard explanation that women of merit will eventually obtain silk: it is only a matter of time. This explanation, she said, is one 'that is as insidious and counter-productive as Justice Roddy Meagher's ingenious argument in support of more women going to the Bar'. The explanation is dishonest, she told a group of women lawyers,

> ...and it is calculated to ensure that the number of women taking silk remains pathetically low. It is dishonest because it slyly conveys the message that men of silk are men of

merit—a proposition which, if true, would mean that there were many, many fewer than 300 men with silk in New South Wales, and many, many fewer than 700 Australia-wide. It is doubly dishonest because it is predominantly those men who have benefited from not having to compete with women on equal terms who decide what constitutes merit, a task at which they have often enough demonstrated something short of complete competence. And the explanation is calculated to ensure that the number of women who take silk remains low because it conveys the message that those who have sufficient years of practice do not have the necessary ability, thereby ensuring that they are not given the briefs which would indicate their ability to carry silk. So catch-22—back where we started.[26]

Issues of 'merit'

Gaudron suggested that 'merit' was a relevant criterion for the appointment of judges only when it came to women. When it came to men, there was no evidence that merit is 'the sole—or even—a criterion which is regularly applied.' She said: 'The way in which debate turns to merit when, and only when, a woman is considered for a particular position or office is not only insulting in my view, it is clear evidence of a belief that women are inferior and ought to be treated as such.'[27]

Gaudron's point was made following a vacancy that occurred on the ACT Supreme Court bench in mid-2000. The local press reported the Government's expressed preference for a woman to be appointed: 'Suggestions that the Government is extremely keen to appoint the ACT's first resident female judge have sparked public debate over the judicial appointment processes in general, and issues of merit versus gender balance in particular.'[28] One ACT Supreme Court judge had even thought it necessary to warn the Government against a token appointment of a woman to the bench.[29] He thought it 'appalling nonsense' that the judiciary should be 'representative' of the broader community in terms of gender and ethnic background. Gaudron joined the debate, 'noting with disdain' the fact that the merit issue only seemed to arise when a woman was being considered for a senior post.[30] She said in 2002:

> The merit fiction is by no means the sole deterrent to women's success at the Bar. Perhaps the most significant barrier is patronage. Patronage still governs who gets the chambers and where; it still governs the passing of briefs, the selection of juniors and, to the extent briefing patterns result from recommendations, briefing itself.[31]

She also criticised the existing system of patronage at the Bar as incompatible with originality of thought and promotion to the bench based on merit:

> Patronage is about creating people in one's own image, about perpetuating the status quo, securing conformity, protecting the prevailing ethos and stifling originality of thought. Patronage means that merit is not the sole criterion for success; it explains why, for some, mere incompetence is no handicap and, for others, outstanding ability is no guarantee against failure. Patronage is, thus, inequality. Patronage is discrimination and, ultimately, patronage is contrary to the interests of justice.[32]

She pointed out that the first Australian women lawyers to succeed did so at enormous cost. They adopted masculine career models and practised law no differently from their male colleagues, selling short both themselves and the proper development of the law.[33] They had to if they were to become, as sociologist Clare Burton pointed out, 'the odd woman' who rose to a position of influence and power, 'the peculiar exception to the rule'.[34] Gaudron tried to change the culture that let so few women reach positions of power, but succeeded only in becoming more noteworthy for her oddness, not part of a group of women walking through to the top with her. On her retirement she was a 'peculiar exception to the rule' who wanted to be an unexceptional one of many.

A bench of men again

Gaudron thought that the best chance of getting a second woman on the High Court was for her to go. She had other good reasons to resign, but this, she said, was a motivating force. It did not work. 'We muffed it!' she acknowledged.[35] When she resigned on 10 February 2003, the Court again became a bench of men.

The nation's papers had been awash with speculation about which woman would replace Gaudron. He, not she, arrived in the person of Dyson Heydon. The Howard Government did not regard Gaudron's seat as reserved for a female. October 2003 came and went, marking a century since the High Court first sat in 1903, and a century in which time Gaudron was the sole female on its bench.

The last cases Gaudron heard were in Sydney on Friday 13 December 2002. Tom Hughes, QC, appearing before her, made a sincere and heartfelt farewell on behalf of the Bar:

> We shall miss your Honour. We shall miss the pungency and the directness of your clearly-expressed contributions to argument...your Honour has demonstrated a great capacity to go straight to the heart of any problem...We shall also miss your strict adherence to legal principle in the formulation of judgments...In your Honour's distinguished career as a justice of this Court, you have justified in the fullest possible measure sanguine expectations that people of sound judgment entertained about you when you were appointed. For us it is a pity that your Honour is leaving early.[36]

Gaudron did not expect this, but was pleased. Her last judgment was handed down on Friday 7 February 2003. It was not marked by any formal farewell ceremony. A farewell was held for her, however, which she had not expected or requested, at the Buena Vista Café on the nineteenth floor of the NSW Supreme

The brooch was designed and produced by John Tarasin on behalf of AWL. It depicts a Picasso-type face, which incorporates the scales of justice. A fire above and a sword below signify feminine wisdom and power. (Photos Jennifer Batrouney, courtesy AWL).

AWL presenting the brooch, 25 January 2003. (Left to right) Justice Mary Gaudron, Dominique Hogan-Doran (President), Jennifer Batrouney, SC, and Noor Blumer.

Mary Gaudron, QC, handing the AWL brooch to High Court Justice Susan Crennan at the AWL conference, 29 September 2006.

Court building, a common meeting place of the legal profession with views of the city and the harbour.

Gaudron made her last appearance on the bench on the day of her retirement, in Canberra on Monday afternoon, 10 February 2003, when the Full Bench sat for the ceremonial announcement of the new Queen's and Senior Counsel. Chief Justice Gleeson referred to the fact that it was the last occasion on which Gaudron would sit as a member of the Court. He paid tribute to her wealth of learning and practical experience, and to the 'profound understanding of and commitment to legal principle' that she brought to the Court. He spoke of her outstanding career achievements and concluded that '[s]he will be missed by her colleagues, not only for her personal companionship, but also for the experience, insight and learning she brought to the Court's decision-making process.'[37]

The then Attorney General Daryl Williams addressed the House of Representatives briefly on the same day, referring to the positions she had held before appointment to the High Court, and the many times she was a pioneer in being the 'youngest' or 'first woman' to hold those positions, as well as to her sixteen years on the Court. 'I would like to put on record my appreciation of her dedication and commitment over a long period to her duties within the Court and to the law,' he said.[38] And that was that. She was again just Mary Gaudron, QC.

Justice Dyson Heydon was sworn in the next day. The ceremony conjured a picture of a men's club. Attorney General Williams, with whom Heydon was at Oxford University, spoke and in joshing style, reminded the new judge of how, cross-examining a famous football player Heydon asked for his autograph. Welcome speeches were given by the Presidents of the Law Council of Australia, the Australian Bar Association and the NSW Bar Association. Not one woman was amongst the speakers. Former Chief Justice Sir Harry Gibbs and Gaudron were seated on the bench, as recognised 'dignitaries'. Outside, a very young girl stood beside the entrance to the High Court building holding a piece of cardboard upon which was written, 'Mum, can women be High Court judges?'

The main controversy surrounding Justice Heydon's appointment was that he was not a woman. Once again, 'merit' became a debated concept.[39] It was another example of Gaudron's view that merit is given a public airing only when there is a possibility that a woman might be appointed to the bench. In April 2003 former Chief Justice of the Family Court, Elizabeth Evatt, criticised the Howard Government's record on gender equity in the nation's courts and tribunals.[40] As to the appointment of Heydon she said: 'What sort of message does that bring to the community and to women in Australia when they see their highest court solely made up of men?'[41]

Gaudron thought women should and would be here again, not just as a matter of equity but through merit, and because they make a difference.[42] Pondering the issue of gender inequity in 1999, Gaudron considered that if judges are to exercise the discretion required of them when formulating their judgments, they should be drawn from all sectors of society. Laws are often expressed in broad terms, leaving it to courts and tribunals to decide what is 'fair and reasonable', 'just and equitable', or 'appropriate in all the circumstances'. Gaudron observed:

> I have always held it to be self-evident that, because judges exercise wide discretionary powers, it is essential that our lawyers should be drawn from the entire social spectrum. No matter what our field of endeavour, it is important to remember that equality is not uniformity.[43]

It was ironic that the first case before the new bench of men concerned a woman's reproductive rights—another controversial 'wrongful birth' claim by the mother for the cost of raising an unplanned child. Gaudron and Kirby had granted special leave the previous year for the case to proceed.[44] The case, *Melchior*, was scheduled for hearing by the Full Court on the day Heydon was sworn in, and a day after Gaudron retired.[45]

Gaudron's decision to retire from the High Court a decade ahead of the compulsory retirement age surprised those who did not know her. She had made her choice in the knowledge that had she stayed until Labor came to power federally in 2007, the chances were strong that she would have been shuffled to the middle of the bench to become the Court's first female Chief Justice. She was the most senior member of the Court and had proved herself capable of the task. She ended her judicial career early. She knew that it was time to leave. Gleeson retired in 2009 and Federal Court Justice Robert French succeeded him as Chief Justice.

After she retired, there was a moment of speculation about 'Gaudron for Governor-General' when Dr Peter Hollingworth resigned and talk began about his successor.[46] It is not likely that even this prestigious position would have appealed to Gaudron. This, too, would have been a further step away from the ordinary and happier and healthier life she longed for. Her cottage in the Loire in France had been for too long too far away. A better life beckoned.

Just prior to retirement, Gaudron was presented by the Australian Women Lawyers' Association with a specially commissioned diamond and gold brooch. She declared she would retain it only until another woman was appointed to the High Court. It would become a perpetual, if unofficial, badge of office for Australia's highest-ranking female lawyer. The brooch depicts the scales of justice and a diamond-encrusted sword of Themis, the ancient Greek goddess of justice. Gaudron optimistically suggested that a second brooch be made 'just in case two women were ever appointed simultaneously'.[47]

On retiring, and with Justice Heydon appointed to take her place, she had to review her plan for the brooch. She held on to it until 2005. In 2005 the Howard Government appointed Justice Susan Crennan to the High Court. While it was certainly an occasion for celebration among women lawyers, Gaudron remained aware of all the work still to be done to achieve genuine gender equity. In a private conversation she humorously put the achievement into perspective: 'When there is a full court of seven females for close on a century—then we will have achieved equality!'

Gaudron duly handed the brooch to Justice Crennan. However, in the hope that other women would follow Justice Crennan to the bench, Crennan handed the brooch back to Gaudron to facilitate a change in plan. The symbolic brooch became the Australian Women Lawyers' patron's brooch, and Gaudron remained its custodian until 2009 when, as outgoing patron of the Association, she handed the exquisite brooch to the new patron, Diana Bryant, Chief Justice of the Family Court.[48]

Then the remarkable occurred. The same Government appointed another woman, Justice Susan Kiefel, to the next vacancy in 2007. The two Susans took their place as the junior 'bookends' at each end of the High Court bench. Two years later, the Rudd Labor Government appointed Virginia Bell to the bench. On 3 February 2009, Gaudron looked on as Justice Bell was welcomed as Australia's forty-eighth High Court judge, sitting with two other women and four men on the Court.[49]

The lure of the Loire—and the ILO

Unassuming, unrenovated and much-loved for its unpretentiousness, 'La Marge' sits looking across to a small castle, the Chateau Rouge. Off the beaten tourist track, it is still close to regional centres in a beautiful and unspoiled rural area of France. Access is by narrow sealed roads that wind through fields golden with sunflowers that raise their bowed heads to the morning light. Tractors pulling loaded wide carts take priority over oncoming tourists' hire cars that pull over in time or face being forced to reverse up a hill and around corners to a passable point in the road.

On retirement the first plan Gaudron intended to put into action was to relax with her family and friends in the French countryside. Gaudron had purchased the cottage for a modest sum in the 1980s from her very good friend and former caving comrade Sybil Davis, who had settled in France many years earlier. As luck would have it, the cottage next door became available for sale and Gaudron and her husband, Fogarty, acquired two small cottages with adjoining stone walls in the centre of the tiny village to which they belong. It was in the course of a stay with Sybil Davis that Gaudron was introduced to the Domaine Sylvain Gaudron vineyard that produces the regional Vins de Vouvray at Vernou in the Loire. Soon after, she discovered the resting place of a family of Gaudrons in the little cemetery behind Davis's cottage.

Never a loner, Gaudron encourages her friends and family to stream in and out, and judicial colleagues make European detours to visit Gaudron and Fogarty after attending legal conferences. To Gaudron, the Loire was a lure to the peace and simple life it offers, but also because it is an exotic environment where she can entertain friends 'on her patch'. Being on her own turf is important to Gaudron. She is comfortable when she is the centre of attention. A private person by nature, she becomes an extrovert when she is with her intensely loyal and trusted friends. She spends time there with her friends travelling by river barge on the smaller rivers and canals of the Loire valley while watching the French countryside slide by. She guides them around the Loire's grand chateaux, and introduces them to the pleasures of the region's wines. One guest observed that all she had to do was to learn to love the backpackers that her children kept sending to her door.

But Gaudron did not retire from the Court only to rest. Nor did she leave the law. On her retirement, her health and spirits picked up, and so did her momentum. And with it came a willingness to accept appointments and speak out on social justice issues in a way that she felt unable to do as a judge. Desiring more time with her husband and family but not wanting to be intellectually idle, Gaudron first accepted a three-year appointment as Visiting Professor in the Faculty of Law at the University of New South Wales, reminiscent of her retreat to the university in 1980 when she resigned from the Arbitration Commission. Her assignment was a series of lectures on a range of topics including the rule of law, inequality and minority rights, judicial discretion and criminal trial processes.

In addition and most importantly, in June 2003 she commenced a part-time appointment to the International Labour Organisation's Administrative Tribunal in Geneva, under the auspices of the United Nations. This work commitment was for a period of four months a year in two sessions. The Australian Government was not responsible for putting her name forward. She had, during her time on the High Court, participated in international criminal law initiatives, and the international reputation she enjoyed was responsible for the recommendation.[50] Geneva was a stone's throw from her second home, her cottage in the Loire, and it fitted neatly with the couple's plan to spend more recreation time in France. As the children established careers and lives of their own, this allowed the couple to see Danielle and Patrick in London, and Julienne and other relatives at home in Sydney. Sharing time between Australia and Europe became their lifestyle.

The International Labour Organisation (ILO) had been established to define and protect the rights of workers. The Administrative Tribunal hears complaints from serving and former staff members of the ILO, the World Health Organization, the United Nations Educational, Scientific and Cultural Organization and other organisations associated with the United Nations. The work on the Tribunal suited Gaudron. She had an interest and experience in labour relations. She worked with six other members from different countries, and she became Vice-President when her appointment was renewed in 2006, and President late in 2009.[51] She had participated in more than 300 cases by then, taking the work of drafting decisions home to Australia after the sittings in Geneva concluded.

Gaudron's association with the United Nations brought other interesting work. Towards the end of 2003 the ILO appointed her to a commission of three to examine trade union rights in Belarus. She accompanied a Finn and a Croat to Minsk, Belarus, in April 2004 and interviewed trade union and government officials. One of the complaints of the trade unionists was that presidential decrees and laws violated international standards for dealing with human rights issues. Gaudron found that the Constitution of Belarus guaranteed all kinds of basic human rights, including those of trade unionists, and that '[t]he terms of that Constitution would make ours look like a very meagre document indeed'.[52] She also learned that the Constitution of the newly-independent republic provided for immediate ratification of international treaties and incorporation into law, something not done in Australia. Even so, some independent trade unionists were arrested and incarcerated for exercising what she thought appeared to be a constitutionally guaranteed freedom of association. Worse, the main right of appeal by those serving periods of 'administrative detention' could only be exercised once the sentence had been served.[53] Gaudron observed: 'The constitutional guarantee was of no account in the absence of a right on their part to initiate action in the courts to enforce their constitutional freedom, the right to initiate action being vested solely in government bodies.'[54]

The experience was important to her. She noted that, regrettably, there was no equivalent in the Belarus Constitution to section 75(v) of the Australian Constitution to overcome the 'black hole situation' for someone wanting judicial review of an administrator's decision.[55] She said:

> There are aspects of the Australian Constitution which might appear outdated, unwieldy or fraught with ambiguity, but my fleeting contact with the legal system in Belarus reminded me of the particular genius of the Australian Constitution—a genius which, so far as I am aware, is not replicated in any other country's constitution—namely s 75(v) which gives to everyone in Australia the right to approach the High Court to compel Commonwealth authorities to perform their constitutional and statutory duties and to prevent them from acting in excess of their powers.[56]

In January 2006 Gaudron was also appointed to the high-level 'Redesign Panel' established by then United Nations Secretary-General Kofi Annan. This panel had been established to review the ethics, accountability, compliance and dispute resolution systems as a key component of the organisation's management reform. Gaudron chaired the panel, consisting of six independent international experts, and which consulted widely, taking members to Geneva, Vienna, Nairobi, Santiago, the International Criminal Tribunal for Rwanda at Arusha and the United Nations Stabilisation Mission in Haiti. The Panel presented its major recommendations in New York on 20 July 2006, recommending a 'redesigned' system that met the basic human rights standards to which staff members are entitled, and that ensured accountability of managers and staff.[57]

At home, Gaudron chaired an advisory board to Queensland's

Secretary-General of the United Nations, Kofi Annan (seated opposite Mary Gaudron) meets with the 'Redesign Panel', including Louise Otis of Canada, Ahmed El-Kosheri of Egypt, Diego Garcia-Sayan of Peru, Kingsley Moghalu of Nigeria and Sinha Basnayake of Sri Lanka. UN Headquarters, New York, 8 June 2008. (United Nations photo/Eskinder Debebe.)

Griffith University's Innocence Project, founded in 2001 under the Directorship of Lynne Weathered of Griffith Law School. A group of lawyers, academics and students work together, *pro bono*, on special cases where injustices may have occurred to pursue proof of innocence by use of DNA testing.[58] In 2009, in conjunction with this work, Gaudron launched an exhibition of art works that captured the emotions of the wrongfully convicted and of prisoners' families who felt the justice system had made a mistake.[59] Typically, Gaudron refused to be interviewed, but spoke to the guests about the importance of Australia following the United Kingdom and the United States in their preparedness to use DNA innocence testing.

The 'genius' of the Constitution's section 75(v)

On leaving the Court, there were matters Gaudron wanted to speak about, particularly matters concerning human rights, and the potential of section 75(v) of the Australian Constitution to protect them. As she put it, 'If abuses can occur, they will occur.'[60] She stated that she was not prepared for the shocking stories that came before the High Court in the 1990s from the mouths of asylum seekers. She reflected:

> Now, I've never been accused of lacking imagination, but my theoretical knowledge and my conviction that, without the protection of the law, human rights abuses will occur did absolutely nothing to prepare me for the horror stories given by those asylum seekers whose despair led them to this country and, ultimately, to the High Court in a quest to obtain status as refugees...[61]

She spoke about the refugee crisis in her Chairperson's address to the 15th Conference of the International Society for the Reform of Criminal Law, in Canberra on 27 August 2001.[62] Her starting point was that asylum seekers were refugees because the laws of their own countries did not protect their basic human rights, or where there were such laws, the courts and tribunals of their countries either could not or would not protect their rights.[63] That led her to explain the importance in Australia of the Constitution's section 75(v).

Gaudron enshrined section 75(v) as the most important human rights provision in the Australian Constitution, and as 'undoubtedly the genius of our Constitution in this country'.[64] Understanding its intricacies is not easy, as, according to Gaudron, the 'small subsection…has been known to reduce grown men to tears'.[65] It 'guarantees the rule of law' in Australia, Gaudron explains, because it operates to ensure that the right to a hearing is not thwarted by arbitrary decisions. She said:

> The section, like lamingtons and Australian Rules football, is all our own; our own peculiar genius. Not surprisingly, governments of both sides have sought from time to time to cut down the operation of that little subsection; and equally not surprisingly, the High Court has resisted their attempts every time. That little subsection is quite unique. It has no equivalent, as far as I know, in any other Constitution. Certainly it has no equivalent in the United States of America. And it is only because America hasn't got that equivalent provision that we have that legal black hole known as Guantanamo Bay.[66]

Gaudron spoke often about her experience in Belarus as an example of how abuse of human rights can occur, even in the presence of, at least on paper, legal protection against it. In Belarus detention of the trade unionists was called 'administrative detention'—and, Gaudron considered, this was 'not a bad euphemism' for the detention in Australia of asylum seekers who commit no crime but who merely seek to claim their rights under international law. She said: 'It's also a useful euphemism for the detention of "enemy combatants" in Guantanamo Bay, who, by virtue of being called "enemy combatants", are denied the protection of international law embodied in the Geneva Convention'.[67] She expressed her faith in the role of international law in the protection of human rights, explaining that:

> [W]hen governments themselves fail to respect the basic human rights of their people, it is only international bodies that can then protect those people whose rights are abused, even if the protection is limited only to offering them the benefit of the Refugee Convention. It is, thus, very disconcerting when countries which claim to be governed by the rule of law fail to respect international laws and norms or to any extent and for whatever reason, themselves fail to observe the Rule of Law.[68]

Gaudron believed that respect for the rule of law and human rights was dependent upon universal access to courts or tribunals vested with jurisdiction and empowered to protect them. To this end, she advocated an international rule of law involving universal jurisdiction to protect human rights and punish those who ignore those rights.[69] She also saw the importance of an independent judiciary and an independent and fearless legal profession. She observed:

> It takes very little imagination to appreciate what abuses can and do occur in those countries where there is no rule of law or where, to any extent, the rule of law is abrogated in the name of some supposedly greater good, for example, the war on terrorism.[70]

In 2006 Gaudron lamented that the United Nations' sixtieth anniversary in 2005 had passed unnoticed in Australia.[71] The San Francisco Conference in 1945 established the United Nations, wrote the United Nations Charter and drafted the Universal Declaration of Human Rights adopted in 1948. Gaudron noted,

> It is truly bizarre that, although Australians, notably Dr Evatt and Jessie Street, should play such a significant role in the drafting of the Universal Declaration, it took so long for Australia to put into effect any of the obligations by which it was at least normatively bound from 1948 and earlier.

Gaudron decried Australia's action of being willing to permit Australians David Hicks and Mamdouh Habib to be held at Guantanamo Bay for more than two years without charge.[72] It has proved convenient for the US Government to hold prisoners at Guantanamo Bay Detention Centre inside the United States naval base in Cuba, where prisoners do not have access to the American legal system. Gaudron pointed out that the United States made no attempt to hide the fact that it held, without charge, 200 people there with the intention of denying prisoners a fair trial and the benefit of being classified as prisoners of war. She noted that '[d]etention centres are set apart and isolated from the mainstream of society and deliberately so, so that you won't know what's going on'. A 'legal no-man's land' was created in which there would be 'no rule of law, only the rule of military victory'—a serious breach of the human rights of the detainees. The United States military commission process that was set up to try, among others, David Hicks put human rights and the truth at risk, Gaudron said, noting its procedures are not consistent with the rule of law or the notion of a fair trial. She again criticised the Australian Government's failure to intervene.[73]

She reasoned that if Hicks had committed a crime against the United States, he should have been dealt with there in that country's justice system with all the judicial safeguards. If Hicks had committed a crime against Afghanistan, he should be tried there. Alternatively, Hicks could have been brought back to Australia and charged with conspiracy at common law if there had been some relevant connection with the country that brought the charges. If he had committed a crime against international law or international norms, then, Gaudron argued, there was a need for an international solution.

The then Attorney General Philip Ruddock claimed that Gaudron's outcry was about Government policy dressed up as a rule of law issue. He dismissed Gaudron as 'an armchair critic' and asserted the right of the United States to determine the lawfulness of its actions.[74] Gaudron accepted her relegation to 'armchair critic' but was nevertheless highly critical of what she saw as the unethical behaviour of the Australian Government:

> Let me not argue the point; but I can still read and I can tell you that the indefinite detention without trial before a properly constituted and independent tribunal is a breach of several of the provisions of the Declaration of Human Rights.

She cited them chapter and verse.[75] She also said that:

> In dismissing my criticisms of Guantanamo Bay, the Attorney General quite correctly said that it was the courts of the United States that would decide if David Hicks' detention was lawful and it is true. At this stage they are four years too late in doing so. There is no point in my doing anything more because I'm sure you all know the United Nations and the European Union have both called for the closure, the immediate closure, of Guantanamo Bay.

A cute legal fiction

In 2004 Gaudron spoke out about the Howard Government's method of limiting asylum seeker applications by creating a 'migration zone'.[76] She spoke about the laws passed by the Coalition Government in September 2001 to excise a group of islands and other offshore places from the 'migration zone'. She called Australia's asylum law 'a cute legal fiction'—the declaration of land as Australian for one purpose, and not for another, was a contrived concept—with the law declaring it to be something that it was not.

As fate would have it, on 4 March 2004, the day Gaudron was giving the Dame Roma Mitchell International Women's Day Memorial Lecture to Victorian Women Lawyers, a boatload of fifteen suspected asylum seekers that had entered Australian waters was intercepted by customs vessel, *Dame Roma Mitchell*. The asylum seekers were taken to Ashmore Reef, 400 kilometres off the northwest coast of Australia, an area excised from the 'migration zone', in order to prevent them from gaining access to Australia's legal system. As the news came in that Dame Roma's naval persona was being employed in such an unfortunate way, Gaudron condemned the Government's asylum policies. She claimed that creation of a 'migration zone' demonstrated the Government's unwillingness or inability to respect the rule of law:

> By means of the legal fiction that Australia is less than the sum of its parts, Australia denies to persons who would assert a right to asylum under international law, access to tribunals and courts which might otherwise rule upon their claims—claims based upon an international convention which Australia has ratified and, at least indirectly, incorporated into its domestic law.[77]

Like Guantanamo Bay, Australia's islands were excised from an artificially created 'migration zone' to physically isolate asylum seekers in a 'legal no-man's-land'.

In 2006 Gaudron made a positive call for action. She drew attention to Article 14 of the United Nations Declaration of Human Rights that supported everyone's right to seek asylum in other countries. 'Not a word about detention centres there,' she said, 'and because of that I think today is an appropriate occasion to call for the immediate closure of immigration detention centres.' She referred to the reported Commonwealth Government settlement of a claim by a child who had been severely traumatised as a result of the two years he spent in immigration detention. The Supreme Court hearing was said to have taken sixty-three days. Aware of the huge costs likely to be involved—'there will not be any change out of a million dollars, I promise you'—and the likelihood of damages being awarded in a similar amount, Gaudron appealed to people to support the call for closure of detention centres on practical grounds.[78] She stated that if people could not call for such closure on humanitarian grounds, or because of the terms of Article 14, '[a]t least there is a better than respectable argument that we should do it on economic grounds'.[79]

Gaudron felt ashamed to have to name Australia as an offender when it came to listing human rights abuses occurring throughout the world. In this context she referred to the treatment of Cornelia Rau and Vivian Solon, detained in the one case and detained and deported in the other, after being mistakenly taken to be 'aliens'.[80]

In talking about human rights abuses, Gaudron spoke about them often being driven by political, ethnic or religious differences. She said,

> In the case of white Australia, human rights abuses also occur, and they occur at individual levels. The victims of those abuses are usually the most vulnerable. As a general rule the authorities don't interfere with nice middle class men and women like us. They pick on the difficult people. They pick on the non-conformists, the troublemakers, the dissidents, and as often as not they pick on the mentally ill and the mentally disabled.[81]

Harking back to the policy of depriving a person of the right to use his or her name, she spoke of newspaper reports that two men, nameless and unidentified, had been in Australian immigration detention for three and five years respectively. She asked rhetorically: 'How much more vulnerable can you be than to lack a name and an identity?'[82]

The many faces of Gaudron

Sally Robinson had not met Mary Gaudron when she rang the doorbell of her Lilyfield home in Sydney. Gaudron opened the door and thrust a glass of French champagne into Robinson's hand, and asked, 'Are you nervous?' Robinson had not been—not until then. So the first word on her list of character traits for Mary was 'formidable'!

Robinson was commissioned by the NSW Bar Association to produce a portrait to hang in the Association's rooms after Gaudron retired from the High Court. Gaudron chose Robinson from the three or four artists offered because she was the least likely to produce a staid picture of a serious and aloof High Court Justice.

The artist observed there was much more to Gaudron:

> ...as we talked about her life and work, I added many other words. It seemed to me that Mary had two sides to her life

and personality: the unnerving, fiercely intelligent, forthright and sharp legal mind and the good-humoured, compassionate, worldly lover of life.[83]

Robinson perhaps understood that Gaudron's formidable presence was to mask her own nervousness—a 'Gaudron technique' used to overcome her feelings of vulnerability—about exposing herself by being splashed all over a canvas.

Gaudron has many faces. When provoked, she will flare up. Fluctuation between warmth and wrath can occur rapidly. Her quick wit is used, more often than not, as a barbed weapon of war against those whose conduct offends her. When beyond wit, she can be ferocious. As one barrister put it, 'The redhead temper is reserved for injustice and for spurious arguments.'[84] And she enjoys provoking others. Sir Anthony Mason noted, 'Everything she says is designed to provoke.'[85]

Robinson saw only Gaudron's warmth, not her wrath, and was saved from hearing expletives. She was fascinated by Gaudron's love of words—'whether it is words she reads or writes or uses to talk about the law; the French language; or words in her beloved crossword puzzles'.[86] It did not take Robinson long in her mission to understand the personality behind the face she was portraying, to conclude that one portrait could not say it all.

Robinson produced two portraits, both of which were far from staid. She colourfully captured what she saw as Gaudron's two main and contrasting faces. One depicts Gaudron the professional, making a serious point. Unexpectedly, the colourful image is infused with Gaudron's own words about section 75(v) of the Constitution, the provision she so applauds. Robinson extracted Gaudron's sentiment for section 75(v) when she asked Gaudron whether she had a favourite saying or phrase that could be stencilled into the commissioned work. There was no stopping Gaudron. She told Robinson all about the value of section 75(v), and while Robinson did not understand its legal ramifications, she saw how passionate Gaudron was about matters concerning the protection of human rights. Gaudron took her time crafting the words. With her trademark purple ink, she penned more than a phrase. Robinson incorporated the full text provided by Gaudron in the portrait.

Robinson's second portrait, by way of contrast, portrays the gregarious, fun-loving, carefree side of Gaudron, smoking the notorious cigarillo, clearly careless about her own health. It was created for the Archibald exhibition, but perhaps, mused Robinson, it was not 'politically correct' to hang a picture of a judge smoking. It shows a relaxed and happy Gaudron; one with which her friends are familiar from socialising with her, whether at her cottage in the Loire, or at the Fogarty-Gaudron Great Mackerel Beach weekender, north of Sydney, near Pittwater, the East Sydney hotel where she and her friends often meet up, or at home in Lilyfield. The image typifies the uninhibited personality of the woman who can discard her professional persona and enjoy a glass of champagne while entertaining those around her by bursting into raucous singing of Irish revolutionary songs.

Gaudron is a complex person who displays apparently contradictory traits. Noted for refusing invitations to speak at professional functions, including dinners at which she is invited to participate as guest speaker, Gaudron generally makes exceptions for women lawyers, and has given her time generously to attend their associations' conferences and dinners.[87] Women had been exposed to discrimination in the workforce. Gaudron supported them and espoused her views when she was with them. She was reluctant, however, to attend a one-day conference held by the Centre for Comparative Constitutional Studies at the University of Melbourne on 5 March 2004 to honour her contribution to the law.[88] Notwithstanding, the organisers proceeded with the conference. Gaudron turned up, apparently cranky, and sat quietly in the back of the room for most of the day. Towards the close of the proceedings, she rose to give a warm and inspirational 'off the cuff' speech. She concluded her remarks with typical humour that on this occasion combined her sarcasm about conventional attitudes to women with a dash of self-deprecation. She stated that she hoped Catherine Branson would not be appointed as the next woman to the High Court because how she and Gaudron looked would be compared and Branson's stunning beauty would show Gaudron up!⁸⁹

At a dinner in 2007, feigning protest, Gaudron said to the person introducing the speakers, 'Don't ask me to get up', whilst pulling out a mirror from her handbag and applying lipstick and combing her hair. Those around her understood she wanted to speak, and she did—about the way in which women lawyers should and could influence development of the law.⁹⁰ Gaudron made a passionate appeal to women lawyers to use the law as an adaptive tool to 'create justice', not just for women or any other section of the community, but for all people.⁹¹ The catch cry, 'Get out and create justice', has been repeated in Gaudron's name on many occasions since.⁹²

Gaudron has expressed a dislike of the press and refused to provide comments and interviews throughout the course of her career. On Michael Kirby's retirement, in commenting about how he will amuse himself, Gaudron suggested that much of his time will be taken up by 'journalists ringing up and asking damn ridiculous questions'.⁹³ Nor did she want her biography written. 'I have a horror of biographies' and 'I don't really want to delve into things that are past and best left there,' she said.⁹⁴ She told friends that she preferred they did not cooperate with her biographer. Yet she gave an interview to the author of Michael Kirby's biography, presumably agreeing that some judicial biographies are stories worth telling.⁹⁵

Contradictions of personality aside, with courage, intelligence and drive, Gaudron has made the law and her family her life. Her oldest child, Danielle, and her youngest, Patrick, both live and work in London, the two half-siblings sharing a flat. Julienne works and lives in Sydney. As yet, there are no grandchildren, just a willing grandmother-in-waiting. But Gaudron gave her mother, Bonnie, that joy who, living in Sydney, has been a cohesive family force into her nineties. Gaudron does not pretend she has had good relations with her children all of the time. Does any parent, let alone a Justice of the High Court? Mary Gaudron was ambitious to make a real contribution to improving social justice in Australia. She was driven to prove that, despite being a woman, she was

Three-year-old Vivien Clarke outside the High Court in Canberra, during a reception of the swearing-in of Justice Dyson Heydon to replace Justice Mary Gaudron, 11 February 2003. (Photo Alan Porritt/ AAP Image)

Trish Muller and Justice Mary Gaudron celebrating with members of Australian Women Lawyers, 25 January 2003. (Photo Jennifer Batrouney, courtesy AWL).

The Hon. Mary Gaudron, QC, opening Gaudron Chambers, Melbourne, 5 March 2004, with barristers Richard Maidment, Stephen Whybrow and James Glisson. (Photo courtesy Jeanette Morrish.)

intellectually equal to the best. She was determined to be a wife and mother too, and a good one. She did it all.

Gaudron remembered

Gaudron has had a lasting influence in the development of Australia's law. Her important contribution to Australian law is acknowledged by the legal community. The Law Council of Australia awarded her honorary membership, only the fourth person so honoured for her 'distinguished service to the law and legal profession'.[96] She was made a life member of the Australian Bar Association.[97] David Curtain, QC, President of the Australian Bar Association at the time of Gaudron's retirement, referred to her work in the development 'of every important area of Australian law—the common law, criminal law, equity, conflicts of laws, constitutional and administrative law, native title, free speech and natural justice'. And he added:

> Justice Gaudron has spoken powerfully on the issues of women in the profession: on discrimination and differences; on the viciousness of the system of patronage in the legal profession; on the importance of equality of opportunity, both in education, and in the profession; and on the contributions women have made, and have yet to make, to the law.[98]

On 5 March 2004, she opened Gaudron Chambers, established at the initiative of Jeanette Morrish, QC, named in her honour, in Republic Tower, Queen Street, Melbourne.[99] On the same day the conference honouring Gaudron's crucial work in law took place. The papers, published as a collection in the *Public Law Review* in 2004, attest to the fact that Gaudron played a substantial role in developing the law in Australia and to jurisprudential thinking about relationships between law, morals and theories of justice.[100] They provide a thorough analysis and appraisal of Gaudron's thinking on the judicial role and responsibilities of judges; her approach to interpretation of the Constitution, to citizenship, and to protection of indigenous rights; her theory of discrimination and understanding of equality; and her views on criminal law procedures and the fundamental importance of a fair trial.

Gaudron never lost faith in the law. Humble about the role she has played, she described herself as privileged 'to be a bit player in the maintenance of the rule of law in Australia'.[101] As a 'bit player' she had a far-sighted vision. She thought of social problems and their solutions in legal terms. She believed that the role of the law was to improve people's lives, rather than regulate them. She searched for systemic sources of injustice, sometimes by questioning the meaning of high-sounding concepts, such as 'equality before the law', to unmask inequalities that arise from people being different or vulnerable. She left a High Court that now accepted that 'equality' no longer meant 'sameness':

> So much is now established constitutional principle. Surely, it is not too much to hope that it will soon be the reality, if for no other reason than the failure to acknowledge and tolerate difference is, in truth, cruel oppression.[102]

Having left the High Court, Gaudron's horizons expanded. She holds the rule of law as important to international peace and understanding; and speaks of the need for the establishment of an international rule of law that involves universal jurisdiction over basic human rights.[103] At sixty-seven Mary Gaudron continues to 'get out and create justice'. She is an ordinary and extraordinary Australian who has worked to embed humanity in the Australian legal system.

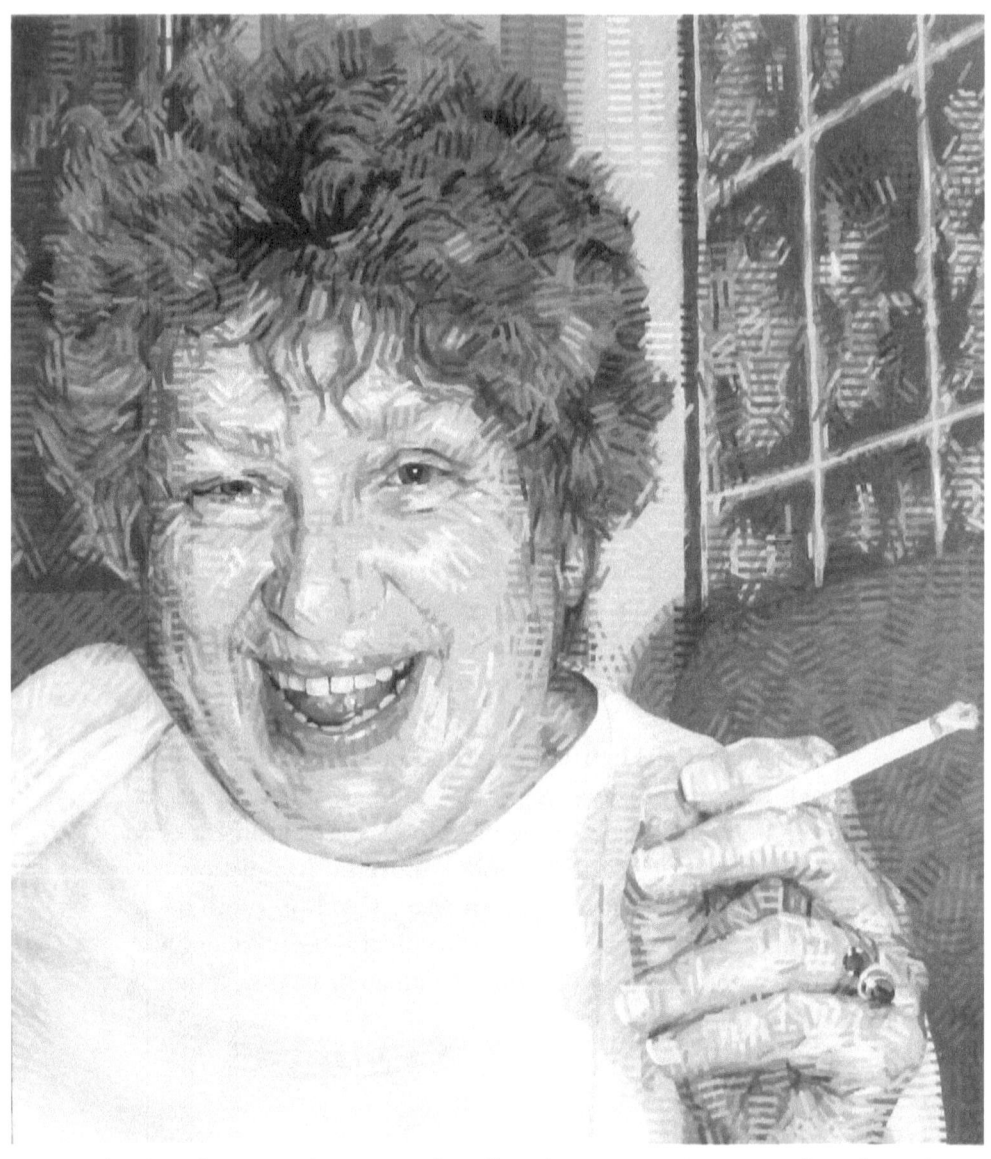

Another face of Mary Gaudron. Portrait by Sally Robinson, 2006. (Courtesy Sally Robinson.)

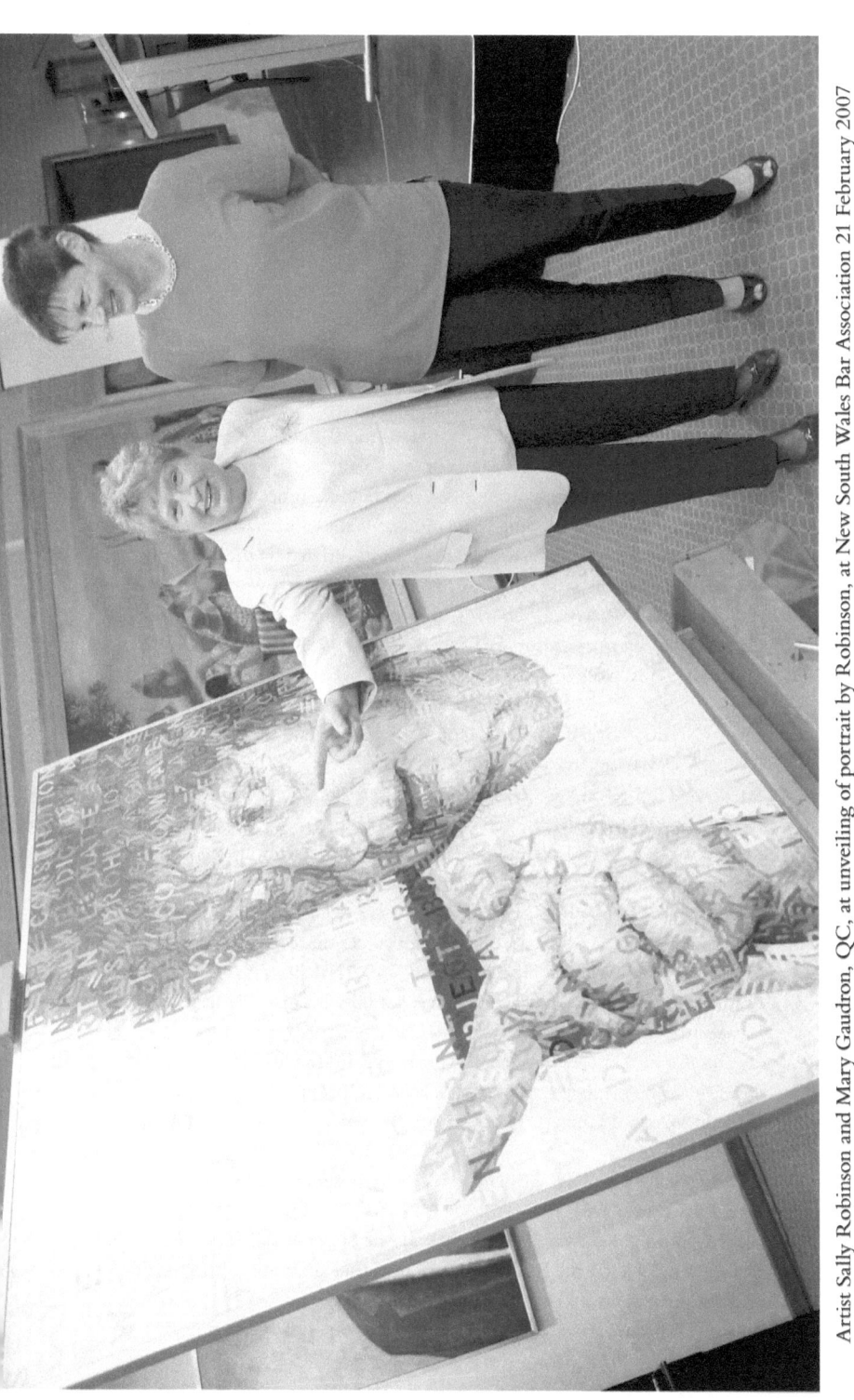

Artist Sally Robinson and Mary Gaudron, QC, at unveiling of portrait by Robinson, at New South Wales Bar Association 21 February 2007 (Courtesy Bar News and NSW Bar Association, with permission of Sally Robinson.)

NOTES

PROLOGUE: THE EVATT CONNECTION

1. In 1950 Prime Minister Menzies introduced the *Communist Party Dissolution Bill* that gave power to the government to publicly declare any citizen a Communist and to bar Communists from holding office in a range of public organisations, including trade unions. With Labor Party support the bill became law on 20 October 1950. Evatt, briefed by the Waterside Workers' Federation, led the successful panel of barristers who represented the Communist Party and ten trade unions. In March 1951 the High Court declared the Act unconstitutional, leading to the 1951 referendum.
2. 'Evatt says "Yes" vote too risky', *Sydney Morning Herald*, 7 September 1951, p. 4.
3. Mary Gaudron, QC, 8 March 2005 (speech, UNIFEM International Women's Day Breakfast, Adelaide).
4. 'Mary Gaudron: Tomboy, idealist—High Court Judge', *Woman's Day*, 22 December 1986; Gaudron, 2005 (speech, UNIFEM).
5. Lenore Nicklin, 'The Law and the laundry: Australia's youngest judge has no time for the ironing', *Sydney Morning Herald*, 9 April 1974, p. 7.
6. Gaudron, 2005 (speech, UNIFEM).
7. Yvonne Preston, 'Mary Gaudron: brilliant career dotted with firsts', *Sydney Morning Herald*, 10 March 1981, p. 7; *Herald*, 10 April 1974, p. 18.
8. Preston, 'Mary Gaudron: brilliant career dotted with firsts', *Sydney Morning Herald*, 10 March 1981, p. 7.
9. Henrik Kalowski, 'Gaudron, Mary Genevieve' in *The Oxford Companion to the High Court of Australia*, eds. Tony Blackshield, Michael Coper, George Williams, Oxford University Press, 2001, p. 293; and Gaudron, 2005 (speech, UNIFEM).
10. Preston, 'Mary Gaudron: brilliant career dotted with firsts', *Sydney Morning Herald*, 10 March 1981, p. 7.
11. Mary Gaudron, 3 March 2006 (Address, Jessie Street Trust, Parliament House Sydney) available on the Evatt Foundation website at: www.evatt.org.au/publications/papers/163.html, viewed 25 June 2010.
12. Nicklin, 'The law and the laundry', *Sydney Morning Herald*, 9 April 1974, p. 7.

13 H.V. Evatt won the University of Sydney Medal in Law in 1918; Elizabeth Evatt in 1955; and Mary Gaudron in 1966.
14 17 September 1980 (University of Adelaide ALP Club), reported on by Angela Biven, 'Rights of workers her forte', *The Advertiser*, Adelaide, 18 September 1980, p. 14.
15 *Mabo v Queensland (No 2)*, (1992) 175 CLR 1 at 76; Justices Deane and Gaudron delivered a joint judgment.

CHAPTER 1: HOME GROUND
1 Northern Regional Library, Indigenous Unit, Moree, NSW: http://www.indigenousunit.com.au, viewed 16 March 2010.
2 Also, State Records of NSW Naturalisation Index 1834-1903, in 1877 Jacob declared his 'native place' to be Germany.
3 Information provided by Cathie Allan, cousin of Mary Gaudron and Gaudron family historian, and various other Gaudron descendants (telephone interview with author 21 February 2005). Allan's research suggests that the Australian authorities permitted self-determination of nationality. See also reference to Australian authorities' recognition of the Rhine River border region's turbulent history of various French and German rule and the difficulty of identifying the inhabitant's country of origin in *Alsace-Lorraine Past, Present and Future*, Coleman Phillipson, T. Fisher Unwin Ltd, 1918.
4 *Blackacre*, Journal of the Sydney University Law Society, March 1966, p. 15.
5 Justice Robert French, then of the Federal Court, on the occasion of the 1987 Australian Legal Convention in Perth, 22 September 1987.
6 Janet Coombs, barrister, telephone interview with author 29 May 1998.
7 Roland Parsons, *Migrant Sailing Ships*, Gould Books, 1993, p. 14; and see http://mariners.records.nsw.gov.au/1855/03/035cat.htm, viewed 6 July 2008.
8 *Emigrants from Hamburg to Australia*, 1854, Pt 2, November 1854, indexes compiled by Eric Kopittke, Rosemary Kopittke and Valerie Dieckmann, Queensland Family History Society Inc.
9 At: http://www.records.nsw.gov.au/indexes/searchform.aspx, viewed 6 July 2008.
10 This seems to be its arrival date according to the story as told by others from families who arrived on the same vessel, though shipping records indicate its arrival date of 12 March.
11 *Mabo v Queensland (No 2)* (1992) 175 CLR 1.
12 Information from Lyall Munro, Sam Sabine, interviews with author 2–3 May 2006; Jeanette Jackson, telephone interview 17 July 2009.
13 Thompson Row, now Maude Street. A soap factory operated there until 1937.
14 Noeline Briggs-Smith, interview with author 3 May 2006.
15 Jennifer Byrne, 'Di Yerbury', *Bulletin with Newsweek*, 28 June 2005, p. 32.
16 Briggs-Smith, interview with author 3 May 2006.

17 Lalie Schmidt (now Fletcher) and Allan Ross, classmates, interviews with author 10 March 2010.
18 Preston, 'Mary Gaudron: brilliant career dotted with firsts', *Sydney Morning Herald*, 10 March 1981, p. 7.
19 Ibid.
20 Justice Mary Gaudron, 29 October 1999, on conferral of an honorary Doctorate of Laws (Occasional Address, University of Sydney), *Sydney Law Review*, 2000, Vol. 22, p. 151, at p. 152.
21 Gaudron, 2005 (speech, UNIFEM).
22 *Mabo v Queensland (No 2)* (1992) 175 CLR 1, at 109.
23 *The Rising Sun—A history of Moree and District, 1862–1962*, R. J. Webb, Moree, North West Champion for the Moree Centenary Celebrations Committee, 1962. More about the lives and times of the original inhabitants of the region can be found in *Moree Mob*, Volumes 1-3, researched by Noeline Briggs-Smith with the support of the Indigenous community, published by the Northern Regional Library and Information Service, Moree NSW, 1999-2003.
24 *Moree Mob*, Vol. 2: 'Burrul Wallaay (Big Camp)', researched by Noeline Briggs-Smith, Northern Regional Library and Information Service, Moree, NSW, 2003, p. 1.
25 The Royal Australian Historical Society Journal, Aborigine Place Names in Northern NSW, Vol. XVI, Part 11, gives 'spring' and 'long waterhole' as possible meanings.
26 The name 'Moree' was thought to have meant 'rising sun' in the Kamilaroi (Gamilaraay) language, and consequently appears on Moree's crest. Webb, *The Rising Sun*, regarded this as correct. However, the Kamilaroi word for 'sun' is 'Yaraay', and it now seems clear that the Kamilaroi people referred to Moree, pronounced by the Aboriginal people as 'Moee', as the 'place of water holes and springs'. Further, one of the pastoral runs established in 1844 was named *Moree*, and it is thought to have been adapted from the Kamilaroi 'Moee'.
27 *The Rising Sun*, Webb, p. 82.
28 *Moree*, Moree Shire Council Visitor Information Centre, 2006, p. 7, which page, devoted to Kamilaroi culture, was included in the publicity brochure for the first time.
29 *Outcasts in White Australia*, C.D. Rowley, Penguin, 1972, p. 211.
30 'We all have lives', film clip 3, *The Highest Court*, 1998, ABC documentary broadcast 26 May 1998, Film Art Doco, National Film and Sound Archive.
31 The council passed a resolution to this effect in 1950, which it reaffirmed in 1955 and actively enforced.
32 Gaudron, 2005 (speech, UNIFEM).
33 *Moree Mob*, Vol. 2, p. 12.
34 See *Moree Mob*, Vol. 2; *Outcasts in White Australia*, Rowley, p. 211.
35 Terry Hie Hie was the site of an Aboriginal initiation and ceremonial ground. It is derived from the word Terrihihi, meaning 'a place of small birds in

abundance' (*Moree Mob*, Vol. 2, pp. 8, 9).
36 *Moree Mob*, Vol. 1, 'Winanga Li', Family research by Noeline Briggs-Smith, Northern Regional Library and Information Service Moree, NSW, 1999, p. 4.
37 Before 1909, removal of Aboriginal children from their families was authorised under general child welfare laws. In 1943, the Aborigines Welfare Board took over from the Aborigines Protection Board, and continued to regulate the residence, movement, employment and child-rearing practices of Aborigines' lives; see *Moree Mob*, Vol. 1, p. 5.
38 Munro and Betty Carter, interviews with author 2 May 2006.
39 See also *Freedom Ride: A freedom rider remembers*, Ann Curthoys, Allen & Unwin, 2002.
40 *Moree Mob*, Vol. 2, Preface, p. 15.
41 *Moree Mob*, Vol. 2, Preface, p. vii.
42 Janet Coombs, telephone interview with author 29 May 1998.
43 Noel Houlahan, telephone interview with author 12 July 2008.
44 Sabine, interview with author 3 May 2006.
45 Houlahan, telephone interview with author 12 July 2008.
46 Sabine, interview with author 3 May 2006.
47 *Ibid*.
48 Sabine, interview with author 3 May 2006.
49 Information collected from various neighbours and work colleagues of Ted at the time.
50 Carter, interview with author, 2 May 2006.
51 *Moree Mob*, Vol. 2, p. 13.
52 Catherine Branson, 24 August 1990 (introducing Mary Gaudron, The Mitchell Oration, Adelaide, p. 4).
53 Shipping migrant records at: http://members.iinet.net.au/~perthdps/shipping/mig-nsw.htm, viewed 14 July 2008, *Migrant ships arriving in NSW 1837-99*: SIROCCO (2) 03 10 1864, Sydney Plymouth (Film AL reel 2139: People on Bounty Ships).
54 Church of England records, Local history room, Northern Regional Library, Moree, NSW.
55 Dux Board, Moree public primary school.
56 Munro, interview with author 2 May 2006.
57 Sabine, interview with author 3 May 2006.
58 Sabine, Munro, interviews with author 2-3 May 2006.
59 Impression of friends and colleagues.
60 Jeanette Jackson, telephone interview with author 17 July 2009.

CHAPTER 2: THE GETTING OF KNOWLEDGE—AND RELIGION
1 Attributed to Francis Xavier, the co-founder of the Jesuit Order.
2 *The Making of a Diocese: Maitland, its bishop, priests and people 1866–1909*, Beverley Zimmerman, Melbourne University Press, 2000, p. 165: this system 'catered for and reinforced class differences'.

3   Fr Paul McCabe, interview with author 30 June 2008.
4   Monica Horan, letter to author dated 3 August 2008.
5   Allan Ross, interview with author 10 March 2010.
6   Mavis Dick, telephone interview with author 6 August 2009, received letter in reply to letter of congratulations when Gaudron became Justice of the High Court in 1987.
7   Moree community members.
8   *WEL-Informed*, 163, Monthly newsletter of the NSW Women's Electoral Lobby, January 1987.
9   Mary Gaudron spoke of her father's words to a school friend.
10 Kate Legge, 'Gaudron's Law', *Weekend Australian Review*, 19-20 November 1994, p. 2.
11 Milton Cockburn, 'Mary Gaudron ponders another first', *Sydney Morning Herald*, 19 November 1994, p. 3.
12 *This Land of Promise: The Ursuline Order in Australia 1882–1982*, Pauline Kneipp, Armidale, University of New England Press, 1982, pp 113-118.
13 *Ibid*, p. 91.
14 Sean Flood, student of De La Salle College, Armidale, telephone interview with author 15 February 2005.
15 Gaudron has talked of this to various friends and colleagues, although according to some of the Sisters who were teaching at St Ursula's at the time, punishments were meted out only for misbehaviour, and were usually 'white cards', blue cards being reserved for good behaviour.
16 Sister Pat Kennedy, telephone conversation with author 21 August 2000.
17 *This Land of Promise*, Kneipp, photo caption opposite p. 109.
18 Various friends and colleagues.
19 Preston, 'Mary Gaudron: brilliant career dotted with firsts', *Sydney Morning Herald*, 10 March 1981, p. 7.
20 Anon. Citation on presentation of Justice Mary Gaudron to the Chancellor of the University of Sydney, on the Occasion of the ceremony of the conferral of the degree of Doctor of Laws on 29 October 1999, http://www.usyd.edu.au/senate/committees/advisoryGaudron.shtml, viewed 24 April 2010.
21 Mary Gaudron, 7 September 2007 (speech, 10th Annual Dinner of Australian Women Lawyers, Melbourne); Sister Pat Kennedy, telephone conversation 21 August 2000.
22 Legge, 'Gaudron's Law', *Weekend Australian Review*, 19-20 November 1994, p. 2.
23 'Bursaries in Secondary Schools', *Sydney Morning Herald*, 25 January 1957, p. 10.
24 Conversation reported to and information provided by solicitor, Mark Houlahan, Webb and Boland solicitors, Moree, interview with author 2 July 2007.

25 Margaret McCabe, telephone interview with author 3 June 2008.
26 Published results *Sydney Morning Herald*, 7 January 1959, p. 10.
27 *Sydney Morning Herald*, 14 January 1959, p. 14.

CHAPTER 3: SYDNEY UNIVERSITY LAW SCHOOL
1   Preston, 'Mary Gaudron: brilliant career dotted with firsts', *Sydney Morning Herald*, 10 March 1981, p. 7.
2   Justice Mary Gaudron, 'Part Time and Partisan' in *A Century Down Town: Sydney University Law School's first hundred years*, eds. John and Judy Mackinolty, Sydney University Law School, 1991, p. 141.
3   University of Sydney Senate by-laws require a candidate for LLB to be 17 years of age; Gaudron, *A Century Down Town*, p. 141.
4   Gaudron, 29 October 1999, *Sydney Law Review*, 2000, Vol. 22, p. 151.
5   Calendar of the University of Sydney for the years of 1961 and 1962 for results of end of year examinations in 1959 and 1960.
6   Sydney Speleological Society website, http://www.sss.org.au/html/The_society.htm viewed 24 April 2010.
7   Gaudron had been inspired by Sister Pat Kennedy's enthusiasm and the detail she provided in Gaudron's Ancient History class at St Ursula's College. Sister Pat Kennedy, telephone interview with author 21 August 2000.
8   Bob Ellis, 19 October 2001, 'Bare Ruin'd Choirs Where Late the Sweet Birds Sang' (Evatt Foundation paper, *What are we here for?*), at: http://evatt.labor.net.au/publications/papers/69.html, viewed 28 June 2010.
9   See 'The Push' http://www.cultureandrecreation.gov.au/articles/push/, viewed 29 December 2008.
10 Annabel Stafford, 'Going Boldly into the minefield that is health', *The Age*, 29 December 2007, http://www.theage.com.au/articles/2007, viewed 18 June 2010.
11 Eugene Kamenka, 'The Andersonians' philosophy and criticism in Australia'. *Quadrant*, July 1987, p. 6, quoted and commented on in *Julius Stone: An intellectual life*, Leonie Star, Melbourne, Oxford University Press in association with Sydney University Press, 1992, p. 167.
12 *Mediator: A biography of Sir Richard Kirby*, Blanche d'Alpuget, Melbourne University Press, 1977, p. 237.
13 Whealy QC, NSW *Bar News*, Winter Edition 1987.
14 Gaudron, 2005 (speech, UNIFEM).
15 In 1961, 7.6% of the University's law students were women, *A Century Down Town*, p. 209.
16 Gaudron, *A Century Down Town*, p. 142.
17 In full: 'which gave Mr Leopold Bloom's palate a fine tang of faintly scented urine'.
18 A full account is contained in *The First Women Lawyers: A comparative study of gender, law and the legal professions*, Mary Jane Mossman, Hart Publishing, 2006,

p. 156; see also Bec McPaul, *A Woman Pioneer*, (1948) 22 ALJ 1 at p. 2; and Anabel Dean, *The University of Sydney Alumni*, November 2005.
19　Gaudron, 2005 (speech, UNIFEM).
20　*Ibid*.
21　When, as a leading QC at the NSW Bar, Whealy spoke on the occasion of Gaudron's appointment to the High Court, recorded in NSW *Bar News*, Winter Edition 1987.
22　Gaudron, *A Century Down Town*, p. 142.
23　David McKnight, 'A career of firsts and controversy', *Sydney Morning Herald*, 9 December 1986, p. 19.
24　Jack Waterford, Canberra journalist, personal communication with author April 2002 and 26 May 2003.
25　Frank Walker, interview with author 2 August 2008.
26　*Blackacre*, 1966, p. 15.
27　Calendar of the University of Sydney for the year 1963.
28　Jim Staples, interview with author 15-16 May 1999.
29　Chief Justice James Spigelman, 5 November 2005 (Address, Sesquicentenary of the University of Sydney Law Faculty, Sydney).
30　His appointment in 1941 was strenuously opposed by some lawyers on the University Senate who argued that vacancies should not be filled during wartime while men were on active service. Their opposition was perceived by some as anti-Semitism. Sir Laurence Street acknowledged this 'quite extraordinary anti-Semitic activism' (Anabel Dean, *The University of Sydney Alumni*, November 2005). The appointment was confirmed by the Senate, and then rescinded, and then reinstated following protests by the Students' Representative Council, and public controversy.
31　Julius Stone, *Star*, p. 106 provides a full account of the event.
32　Stone's appointment received the strong support of Conlon, a student representative on the Senate. *Australian Dictionary of Biography*, on line: http://www.adb.online.anu.edu.au/biogs/A130529b.htm viewed 22 January 2009. See also, *Julius Stone*, Star, p. 68.
33　Blackshield, interview with author 28 February 2008.
34　Michael Kirby, personal communication, 1 August 2010.
35　Legge, 'Gaudron's Law', *Weekend Australian Review*, 19-20 November 1994, p. 2. Blackshield's view is that Gaudron's personality and background drove her passion for social justice. See *Australian Constitutional Law and Theory: Commentary and materials*, Tony Blackshield and George Williams, 5th ed, The Federation Press, 2006, p. 285, where Mason, Jacobs, Murphy, Deane and Kirby are listed as High Court judges who were influenced by Stone, and in which list Gaudron is not included.
36　John M. Ward, 'The Law School in World War II', *A Century Down Town*, p. 97.
37　Julius Stone, *The Province and Function of Law: Law as logic, justice and social*

control; a study in jurisprudence, Sydney, Associated General Publications Pty. Ltd., 1946.
38 Julius Stone, *Star*, p. 81.
39 *Ibid*, pp. 86-88.
40 *Ibid*, p. 88.
41 F. C. Hutley, 'Logic and the legal process', *University of Western Australia Annual Law Review*, 1948-9, Vol. 1. No 2, p. 172.
42 Liz Hickson, 'Mary Gaudron's brilliant career', *Woman's Day*, 17 July 1980, pp. 34-35.
43 *Encounters with the Australian Constitution*, Michael Coper, CCH Australia Ltd, 1987, p. 200. The caption under a photograph of Hutley when he was Justice of the NSW Court of Appeal reads: 'In his characteristically cantankerous way, Justice Hutley was a constant critic of those who would glibly equate reform with centralism.'
44 W. L. Morison, 'Law School People 1941-1973', *A Century Down Town*, p. 109.
45 *Ibid*, p. 110.
46 Samuel Griffith, Edmund Barton, Richard O'Connor and Adrian Knox were also graduates of Sydney University, but not of the Law School.
47 The debate was not unique. It arose at the University of Melbourne Law School, but was resolved earlier in favour of professional academic teaching, and with less conflict, see *Memoirs of Zelman Cowen: A public life*, Zelman Cowen, Miegunyah Press, 2006, pp. 227-8.
48 *Blackacre*, 1963, 'To move or not to move', p. 7.
49 Spigelman, 5 November 2005 (address, University of Sydney Law Faculty).
50 Plans for a new Law School on the main university campus at Camperdown had commenced some three or four years before.
51 Gaudron, 'Part Time and Partisan', *Sydney Law School Reports*, 1, No. 12, 1989, University of Sydney, p. 14.
52 *Blackacre*, 1963, 'To move or not to move?' pp. 7–12.
53 *Ibid*, p. 12.
54 *Blackacre*, 1966, 'Legal education', p. 12.
55 Gaudron, *A Century Down Town*, p. 142.
56 Blackshield, interview 28 February 2008.
57 Gaudron, *A Century Down Town*, p. 142.

CHAPTER 4: FACING CHALLENGES
1 Justice Michael Kirby, quoting Mary Gaudron, 22 October 2003 (speech, *Women in the Law—Doldrums or Progress,* Women Lawyers of Western Australia, Perth), at: http://www.hcourt.gov.au/speeches/kirbyj/kirbyj_22oct.html, viewed 24 February 2009.
2 So named in the membership list in the Society's Annual 1962-63 report.
3 Sacred Heart Parish records.

4   Mary Gaudron, 19 September 1997 (speech, Australian Women Lawyers' Association, Melbourne).
5   'Women at the top: Mary Gaudron', *Law Society Journal* (NSW), Vol. 22, No. 7, August 1984, p. 431; see also Justice Margaret McMurdo, 22 February 2003 (speech proposing a toast to Mary Gaudron on her retirement from the High Court, Australian Women Judges Dinner, Sydney), http://archive.sclqld.org.au/judgepub/2003/mcmurdo050303.pdf, viewed 26 June 2010; and *Queensland Bar News*, April 2003, p. 37.
6   Legge, 'Gaudron's Law', *Weekend Australian Review*, 19-20 November 1994, p. 2.
7   Gaudron, *A Century Down Town*, p. 141; Associate Justice John McLaughlin, Supreme Court of New South Wales, interview 7 April 2005.
8   NSW WEL newsletter, January 1987.
9   *Blackacre*, 1966, 'Woman student wins medal', p. 15.
10 The Permanent Trustees Company of NSW Ltd prize, announced *Sydney Morning Herald*, 8 January 1965, p. 8.
11 Legge, 'Gaudron's Law', *Weekend Australian Review*, 19-20 November 1994, p. 2.
12 Blackshield, interview with author 28 February 2008; and *Julius Stone*, Star, p. 102.
13 Blackshield, interview with author 28 February 2008.
14 Whealy, speaking on the occasion of Gaudron's appointment to the High Court; NSW *Bar News*, Winter Edition 1987.
15 Calendar of the University of Sydney for the years 1964–1967.
16 Blackshield, interview with author 28 February 2008.
17 Emeritus Professor Sir Stephen Henry Roberts CMG, historian, was Vice-Chancellor 1947–1967.
18 Gaudron, when Deputy President of the Conciliation and Arbitration Commission, told the story to Stephan (Steve) Lukass, Australian National University Industrial Officer. He recounted the story to John Blackley, then the Australian National University's Staff Classifications Officer, during an adjournment in a hearing over which Gaudron presided, in the context of expressing high regard for Gaudron's legal ability. Gaudron's then husband, Ben Nurse, recalls that the attempt by the University of Sydney Law School to award the medal to the man who came second included a proposal to award the medal jointly. Hutley opposed that proposal.
19 *Blackacre*, 1966, p. 15.
20 Law Graduates 1966, *A Century Down Town*, p. 226. Of 140 graduates, 11 were women.
21 Whealy QC, reported in 'Meal gives the law something to chew over', *Daily Telegraph*, 11 May 1987, p. 11, talking of the 'class of '65'. In fact Nugan finished his law degree in 1963 (University of Sydney records).
22 *1963 to 1964 Yearbook*, Sydney Speleological Society, p. 34.
23 Harry Pemble, telephone interview with author 19 April 2008.

24 *Ibid.*
25 *Bungonia Caves, Sydney Speleological Society Occasional Paper No. 4*, eds. Ross Ellis, Lyndsey Hawkins, Robert Hawkins, Julia James, Gregory Middleton, Benjamin Nurse, Gleniss Wellings, Sydney Speleological Society, 1972.
26 Daphne Kok was President of the Women Lawyers' Association and President of the International Federation of Women Lawyers, in the course of her legal career.
27 Gaudron, 1999 (Occasional Address, University of Sydney).
28 Cockburn, 'Mary Gaudron ponders another first', *Sydney Morning Herald*, 19 November 1994, p. 3.
29 'The case for family courts', *Sydney Morning Herald*, 26 July 1968, p. 11.
30 Legge, 'Gaudron's Law', *Weekend Australian Review*, 19–20 November 1994, p. 2.
31 It re-opened as a central school, years 1–10, in 1999.
32 Sabine, interview with author 3 May 2006.
33 'Boy's foot cut off by father's train', *Sydney Morning Herald*, 30 April 1964, p. 1.
34 Finding of Judge Peter Dent, NSW District Court, as set out by Justice Priestly in *State Rail Authority v Gaudron* [1997] NSWSC 302 (12 August 1997).
35 Bernard Lane, 'Siblings' tracks cross in court', *The Australian*, 2-3 May 1998, p. 3.
36 Findings of Judge Dent, as set out by Justice Priestly in *State Rail Authority v Gaudron* [1997] NSWSC 302.
37 *Ibid.*
38 Memorial plaque Woronora Cemetery, Sutherland, NSW; death notice, *Sydney Morning Herald*, 27 April 1982.
39 *Moree Champion*, 11 December 1986, p. 16.
40 *Dedousis v The Water Board* (1992) 9 NSW CCR 417.
41 *Dedousis v Water Board* (1994) 181 CLR 171.
42 The NSW Court of Appeal accepted that Gaudron was unlikely to have her brother's situation in mind, it having been dealt with so many years earlier.
43 Judge Dent, NSW District Court, quoted by Justice Priestley in *State Rail Authority v Gaudron* [1997] NSWSC 302.
44 Lane, 'Siblings' tracks cross in court', *The Australian*, 2-3 May 1998, p. 3.
45 *State Rail Authority of NSW v Gaudron*, 1 May 1998, S101/1997 (1998) HCA Transcript 144.
46 Lane, 'Siblings' tracks cross in court', *The Australian*, 2-3 May 1998, p. 3.
47 Cathie Allan (cousin of Mary Gaudron and Gaudron family historian), telephone conversation with author 13 April 2010.

CHAPTER 5: A LABOR 'GAL' AT THE BAR

1 Justice Mary Gaudron, 13 June 2002 (speech, Women Lawyers' Association of NSW); see High Court website: http://www.hcourt.gov.au/publications_05_2.html#MaryGaudron, viewed 1 January 2009.

2 John McLaughlin, interview with author 7 April 2005.
3 Eva Curran, 'Women in the Law NSW 1970–1984', unpublished research paper, 1984.
4 Janet Coombs was appointed Honorary Life Member of the Bar Association in 1998, 'in recognition of her exceptional service to the Association and the philanthropic support and interest shown to new barristers, particularly to women members', *Stop Press*, NSW Bar Association monthly newsletter, No. 52, June 1998, p. 2.
5 Cockburn, 'Mary Gaudron ponders another first', *Sydney Morning Herald*, 19 November 1994, p. 3.
6 Coombs, telephone interview with author 29 May 1998.
7 Gaudron, 2005 (speech, UNIFEM).
8 Justice Michael McHugh, 27 October 2004, 'Women Justices for the High Court' (Speech, Western Australian Law Society), at: http://www.hcourt.gov.au/speeches/mchughj/mchughj_27oct04.html, viewed 14 June 2020.
9 'Women at the top: Mary Gaudron', *Law Society Journal* (NSW), Vol. 22, No. 7, August 1984, p. 431.
10 Gaudron, 2005 (speech, UNIFEM).
11 *Ibid*.
12 Hickson, 'Mary Gaudron's brilliant career', *Woman's Day*, 17 July 1980, p. 35.
13 Gaudron, 2005 (speech, UNIFEM).
14 Cockburn, 'Mary Gaudron ponders another first', *Sydney Morning Herald*, 19 November 1994, p. 3.
15 Maurice May, telephone interview with author 14 August 2007; and see *Burchett v Kane* [1980] 2 NSWLR 266, where the consequences of the barrister's omission were raised on appeal.
16 *The Bulletin*, 31 March 1992, p. 42.
17 *Pleading under the Supreme Court (Amendment) Act 1970*, by the Hon. Sir Leslie Herron, Chief Justice of NSW, with Appendix of Precedents edited by M.G. Gaudron, Barrister-at-Law, Government Printer, New South Wales, 1971.
18 McLaughlin, interview with author 7 April 2005.
19 Ken Horler, QC, telephone interview with author 18 November 2008.
20 McLaughlin, Blackshield. See entry by John McLaughlin, 'Hutley, Francis Charles (Frank) (1914–1985), *Australian Dictionary of Biography,* on line edition, http://adbonline.anu.edu.au/biogs/A170571b.htm, viewed 25 Aril 2010.
21 McLaughlin, interview with author 7 April 2005.
22 Cockburn, 'Mary Gaudron ponders another first', *Sydney Morning Herald*, 19 November 1994, p. 3.
23 Coombs, telephone interview with author 29 May 1998.
24 Justice Jane Mathews, 1982, 'The changing profile of women in the law' (paper, ANZAAS Congress, Sydney).
25 Coombs, reported in Legge, 'Gaudron's law', *Weekend Australian Review*, 19-20 November 1994, p. 3.

26 ALP 1974 NSW Kings Cross Branch Returns, ML MSS 5095/624, item 2306.
27 Jim Staples, interview with author 15-16 May 1999.
28 Justice Jane Mathews interviewed by John Farquharson, 23 October 2001, ORAL TRC 4647, National Library of Australia (Tape 2, 'Women in the law and at the Bar').
29 Paul Donohoe, QC, interviews with author September 1999.
30 Coombs, telephone interview with author 29 May 1998.
31 Coombs, reported in Legge, 'Gaudron's law', *Weekend Australian Review*, 19-20 November 1994, p. 4.
32 Donohoe, QC, interviews with author September 1999.
33 Coombs, telephone interview with author 29 May 1998.
34 *Queensland Bar News*, April 2003; Barrie Watts, 'Merciless Mary cuts bigwigs to size', *The Australian*, 12 December 1972, p. 3.
35 Frank Walker, interview with author 2 August 2008.
36 Horler, QC, telephone interview with author, 18 November 2008.
37 John Blackley, interview with author 25 September 2007. Lyn Williamson recalls Gaudron joining demonstration marches against the war.
38 Text of paper, 'Women and the law', in *The WEL Papers* (The National Journal of the Women's Electoral Lobby 1973/4), pp. 29–33; and see *Making Women Count: A history of the Women's Electoral Lobby in Australia*, Marian Sawer with Gail Radford, UNSW Press, 2008, p. 9; Suzanne Baker, 'WEL: A hard row still to hoe', *Sydney Morning Herald*, 22 January 1973, p. 8.
39 Ross Ellis, co-editor of *Bungonia Caves*, 1972.
40 *O'Shaughnessy v Mirror Newspapers Ltd* (1970) 125 CLR 166.
41 *O'Shaughnessy v Mirror Newspapers Ltd* (1968–70) 72 SRNSW, 347.
42 Judgment of Barwick CJ, McTiernan, Menzies and Owen JJ.
43 A version involving Chief Justice of the High Court Sir Garfield Barwick is reported by Hickson, 'Mary Gaudron's brilliant career', *Woman's Day*, 17 July 1980, p. 35.
44 This version also accords with the memory of the instructing solicitor in the case, and a carefully detailed account told by the Chancellor of the University of Sydney in 1999 in the presence of Gaudron on the occasion of the conferral on her of an honorary degree of Doctor of Laws.
45 *Pearson v Australian Consolidated Press Ltd* [1971] 1 NSWLR, 189.
46 *R v Flight Crew Officers' Industrial Tribunal, ex parte Australian Federation of Air Pilots* [1971] 45 ALJR 659, raising industrial issues; *Leslie v Mirror Newspapers* (1971) 125 CLR 332, a defamation case. Gaudron made 37 appearances in the High Court whilst at the Bar, including the period during which she was NSW Solicitor General, see *The Oxford Companion to the High Court*, Table of Reported High Court Appearances by Counsel later appointed as Justices of the High Court, p. 165.
47 McKnight, 'A career of firsts and controversy', *Sydney Morning Herald*,

9 December 1986, p. 19; Roderick Campbell, 'Gaudron's extraordinary career comes to an end', *Canberra Times,* 12 February, 2003, p. 15.
48 David Bennett, QC, 'Mary Gaudron's "Mr Junior" speech and High Court debut', *No Mere Mouthpiece: Servants of All, Yet of None,* eds. Geoff Lindsay and Carol Webster, Butterworths, 2002, pp. 262-3.
49 Former NSW Premier Neville Wran, telephone interview 16 December 2005.
50 This account is based partly on Bennett, QC, *No Mere Mouthpiece,* 2002, pp. 262-3, and reports of others present. Pamela Tate, SC, Solicitor General for Victoria, Australia, also told the story on 22 September 2006, 'Extending the boundary of right—Flos Greig, Joan Rosanove and Mary Gaudron—Three Australian women lawyers,' (*10th Ethel Benjamin Commemorative Address,* Dunedin, New Zealand).
51 Legge, 'Gaudron's Law', *Weekend Australian Review,* 19-20 November 1994, p. 1.
52 Neville Wran, telephone conversation with author 16 December 2005.
53 1998 speech by Gaudron following the Mr Junior speech of that year at the Bench and Bar dinner.
54 Bennett, QC, *No Mere Mouthpiece* (2002), pp. 262-3.

CHAPTER 6: THE PAT MACKIE CASE
1 Pat Mackie, *Many Ships to Mount Isa: Autobiography,* Pat Mackie, ed. Elizabeth Vassilieff, Seaview Press, 2002, p. 268.
2 *Mount Isa: The Story of a Dispute,* Pat Mackie with Elizabeth Vassilieff, Hudson Publishing, 1989, p. 49.
3 *Red Cap* became the title of a musical production about Pat Mackie and the Mount Isa dispute, performed in Mount Isa in July 2007.
4 Maurice May, solicitor, telephone interview with author 14 August 2007.
5 Staples, interview with author 15-16 May 1999; See also Cockburn, 'Mary Gaudron ponders another first', *Sydney Morning Herald,* 19 November 1994, p. 3.
6 'Junior' being the term used for those barristers appearing with Queen's Counsel (Senior Counsel) or on their own without a 'silk' to lead them.
7 May, telephone interview with author 14 August 2007.
8 *Mount Isa,* Mackie with Vassilieff, p. 241.
9 *Mackie v Australian Consolidated Press Ltd* (unreported) came before Nagle J. in a jury trial in the Supreme Court of NSW in 1972. Staples and Gaudron represented Mackie.
10 As set out in the judgment of Hutley J. A. in the case on appeal, *Mackie v Australian Consolidated Press Ltd* [1974] 1 NSWLR, 561 at 567.
11 *Many Ships to Mount Isa,* Mackie, p. 263.
12 *Mount Isa,* Mackie with Vassilieff, pp. 2-3.
13 *Mackie v Australian Consolidated Press Ltd* [1974] 1 NSWLR, 561 at 569, per Hutley J.A.

14 *Mount Isa*, Mackie with Vassilieff, pp. 6-7.
15 *Ibid*, p. 88.
16 Mackie was expelled from the union and sacked by the Company, but he continued to lead the men. On 10 December 1964, the Country-Liberal Party Government of Queensland under Premier Frank Nicklin declared a state of emergency. The stalemate continued for many months. It had a severe impact on the economy, not only in north Queensland but in the nation as a whole. The miners rejected direction from Tom Dougherty, throwing the labour movement into disarray. The Queensland Trades and Labour Council supported the miners' industrial action. The AWU was seen as conspiring with the bosses and condemning their own members, and the AWU's control of its own members slipped through its hands. The mine re-opened on 17 February 1965 after a 32-week dispute and a work stoppage of some two months. By April 1965 the Company agreed to re-engage most of the previous work force. Mackie was not re-employed. See *Mackie v Australian Consolidated Press Ltd* [1974] 1 NSWLR 561 at 567-573.
17 In 1950 Dougherty expelled Cameron, together with the whole leadership of the Committee of Management of the South Australian Branch, for breaches of new rules. Cameron and his supporters successfully challenged the validity of the rules in the Industrial Court. In 1959 Cameron and the other Committee members were reinstated and Cameron set up the CMC. See: *Papers of Clyde Robert Cameron*, National Library of Australia, MS 4614.
18 *Mount Isa*, Mackie with Vassilieff, pp. 117-118.
19 Jim Staples and Australia Party founder and businessman, Gordon Barton, studied law together at the University of Sydney Law School (both graduating in 1953). Barton established an interstate road transport business and his fellow law students served as his drivers, Staples being one of them.
20 *Many Ships to Mount Isa*, Mackie, p. 268.
21 Queensland Parliamentary Debates, 1964-5, Vol. 239, p. 1032.
22 Hansard Queensland Legislative Assembly, 4 March 1965, speech of Minister for Labour, J. D. Herbert, referred to by Mackie in *Many Ships to Mount Isa*, p. 276.
23 *Mount Isa*, Mackie with Vassilieff, pp. 49-50.
24 Staples, interview with author 15-16 May 1999.
25 Justice Hutley's description of what a jury might have found in *Mackie v Australian Consolidated Press Ltd.* [1974] 1 NSWLR, 561 at 573.
26 Alan Ramsey, 'Camerons come and Camerons go on', *Sydney Morning Herald*, 12 February 2003, p. 15.
27 Staples, interview with author 15-16 May 1999.
28 The proceedings are not reported but described in the decision on appeal of Justice Hutley, p. 574.
29 'Mackie awarded $30,000', *Sydney Morning Herald*, 24 November 1972, p. 3.
30 *Mount Isa*, Mackie with Vassilieff, p. 242.

31 *Politics of Law Reform*, Stan Ross, Penguin, 1982, p. 182.
32 *O'Shaughnessy v Mirror Newspapers Ltd* (1970) 125 CLR 166, referred to by Hutley in Mackie on appeal at 579.
33 *Mackie v Australian Consolidated Press Ltd* [1974] 1 NSWLR. 561 at p. 572.
34 McLaughlin, interview with author 7 April 2005. McLaughlin took over the brief from Gaudron when she left the Bar.

CHAPTER 7: EQUAL PAY—IN PRINCIPLE
1 Mary Gaudron and Michal Bosworth, 'Equal Pay?' *In Pursuit of Justice: Australian women and the law 1788–1979*, eds., Judy Mackinolty and Heather Radi, Hale & Iremonger, Sydney, 1979, p. 171.
2 *Unions in Crisis*, Clyde Cameron, Hill of Content, 1982, p. 93-4.
3 *The Confessions of Clyde Cameron 1913–1990*, as told to Daniel Connell, ABC, 1990, p. 201.
4 E. G. Whitlam AC, QC, 2 December 2002, *Thirty Years Later: The Whitlam government as modernist politics*, (Keynote Address, Old Parliament House, Canberra).
5 *Confessions*, Cameron, p. 201.
6 Staples, interview with author 15–16 May 1999.
7 Gaudron, 2005 (speech, UNIFEM).
8 *A Life on the Left: A biography of Clyde Cameron*, Bill Guy, Wakefield Press, 1999, p. 255.
9 Gaudron, 2005 (speech, UNIFEM).
10 *A Life on the Left*, Guy, p. 255; Cockburn, 'Mary Gaudron ponders another first', *Sydney Morning Herald*, 19 November 1994, p. 3.
11 Michael Grealy, 'First lady at court?' *Adelaide Advertiser*, 8 April 1981, p. 4.
12 Jim Staples, interview with author 15-16 May 1999.
13 *Unions in Crisis*, Cameron, p. 95.
14 *Ibid*.
15 Barrie Watts, 'Merciless Mary cuts the bigwigs to size', *The Australian*, 12 December 1972, p. 3.
16 Gaudron, 2005 (speech, UNIFEM); see also report, 'It's law, but there's still no equal pay', *Adelaide Advertiser*, 9 March 2005, p. 13.
17 *The Australasian Meat Industry Employees Union & Others v Meat and Allied Trades Federation of Australia & Others (Equal Pay Cases)* (1969) 127 CAR 1142, at p. 1156, decision 19 June 1969, available at Australian Industrial Relations Commission, Sir Richard Kirby Archives, http://ww3.e-airc.gov.au/archives/1969equalpay, viewed 20 June 2009.
18 State Library of Victoria http://www.slv.vic.gov.au/ergo/equal_pay_for_women:_zelda_daprano viewed 16 November 2008; *Women's Web: Women's stories—Women's Actions*, http://home.vicnet.net.au/~womenweb/actions/EqualPay.htm, viewed 26 June 2010.
19 *Women's Web: Women's stories—Women's Actions*, http://home.vicnet.net.au/~womenweb/actions/EqualPay.htm, viewed 26 June 2010.

20 *Equal pay for women: Zelda D'Aprano*, http://www2.slv.vic.gov.au/ergo/equal_pay_for_women:_zelda_daprano, viewed 26 June 2010.
21 *A Wealth of Women*, Alison Alexander, Duffy and Snellgrove, 2002, p. 261-2, and see http://www.slv.vic.au/ergo/equal_pay_for_women:_zelda_daprano viewed 16 November 2008; http://www.australianbiography.gov.au/subjects/daprano/intertext4.html viewed 20 June 2009.
22 Other women joined D'Aprano when she repeated the stunt some three weeks later. It led to her establishing the Women's Action Committee which campaigned on equal pay for women, and other forms of sexual discrimination.
23 Watts, 'Merciless Mary cuts the bigwigs to size', *The Australian*, 12 December 1972, p. 3.
24 *Sydney Morning Herald*, 17 December 1972, p. 129.
25 Janet Hawley, 'Legal tipsters say decision in week', *The Australian*, 14 December 1972, p. 4.
26 Ibid.
27 *1972 National Wage and Equal Pay Cases*, transcript of proceedings, 13 December 1972, p. 828 at 829.
28 Daily with Deiley, 'Mary makes a womanly plea', *Daily Telegraph*, 14 December 1972, p. 9.
29 *Making Women Count*, Sawer with Radford, p. 195.
30 Transcript of proceedings, 13 December 1972, p. 837.
31 The provisions of the Convention had already been raised in the proceedings through Exhibit K2, p. 47.
32 Transcript of proceedings, 13 December 1972, p. 838.
33 *Gentle Invaders: Australian women at work 1788–1974*, Edna Ryan and Anne Conlon, Nelson, 1975.
34 *Gentle Invaders*, Ryan and Conlon, p. 160.
35 *1972 National Wage and Equal Pay cases* (1972–73) 147 CAR 172.
36 *Gentle Invaders*, Ryan and Conlon, p. 173.
37 Whitlam decided to disregard this recommendation in respect of the Australian public service and have it introduced immediately, *Confessions*, Cameron, p. 202.
38 Kathy MacDermott (former head of the Equal Pay Unit) email, 9 January 2009.
39 *The Promise and the Price*, Clare Burton, Allen & Unwin, 1991, p. 132.
40 *The Trojan Dog*, Dorothy Johnston, Wakefield Press, 2000, p. 14.
41 Ibid, p. 17.
42 *Unions in Crisis*, Cameron, p. 94.
43 From 1974 to 11 November 1975, the Department was retitled 'the Department of Labor and Immigration' without the 'u' in Labor.
44 *The Confessions of Clyde Cameron 1913–1990*, as told to Daniel Connell, p. 202.
45 *Unions in Crisis*, Cameron, p. 95.
46 Grealy, 'First lady at court?' *The Advertiser*, Adelaide, 8 April 1981, p. 4.

47 See also, Fred Wells, 'ACTU seeks $12.10 rise in total wage', *Sydney Morning Herald*, 10 March 1973, p. 10.
48 *1972–3 Equal Pay and National Wage Cases* (1973) 149 CAR 75.
49 Clyde Cameron, 14 December 1973 (speech, Women's Electoral Lobby of Victoria, Melbourne).
50 *Making Women Count*, Sawer with Radford, p. 196.
51 Nicklin, 'The law and the laundry', *Sydney Morning Herald*, 9 April 1974, p. 7.
52 *National Wage Case 1974*, transcript, 19 February 1974, p. 1.
53 *A Life on the Left*, Guy, p. 255.
54 Transcript of proceedings 27 February 1974, p. 328, at 332-342; and see *Gentle Invaders*, Ryan and Conlon, p. 170.
55 Transcript of proceedings, 5 March 1974, pp. 344-5.
56 Transcript of proceedings, 7 March 1974, p. 499.
57 Transcript of proceedings, 27 February 1974, p. 341.
58 Transcript of proceedings, 7 March 1974, p. 510.
59 *Ibid*, p. 505.
60 *Ibid*.
61 *Ibid*, p. 506.
62 *Ibid*, p. 517.
63 *Ibid*, p. 518.
64 *Ibid*, p. 523.
65 As reported to the *Woman's Day*, 17 July 1980.
66 Gaudron, 2006 (Address, Jessie Street Trust). She incorrectly attributed this submission to the 1972 *Equal Pay Case*.
67 Transcript of proceedings, 7 March 1974, p. 534.
68 According to a report of an anonymous witness, *The New Province for Law and Order: 100 years of Australian industrial conciliation and arbitration*, eds. Joe Isaac and Stuart MacIntyre, Cambridge University Press, 2004, 'Justice and Equity: Women and Indigenous Workers', Gillian Whitehouse, p. 234.
69 *National Wage Case 1974* (1974) 157 CAR 293.
70 *Ibid*, p. 299.
71 *Ibid*, p. 300.
72 *Making Women Count*, Sawer with Radford, p. 197; and see Australian Women Biographical Entry, http://www.womenaustralia.info/biogs/AWE0004b.htm, viewed 16 November 2008.
73 According to Susan Carcary, ACT CPSU, *Obituary of Edna Ryan*.
74 *A Life on the Left*, Guy, p. 256, letter from Cameron to Bill Guy, January 1997.
75 *The National Wage Case 1975* (1975) 167 CAR 18.
76 Later Governor of Victoria.
77 *The Confessions of Clyde Cameron*, as told to Daniel Connell, ABC, 1990, p, 209.

CHAPTER 8: A SEAT ON THE ARBITRATION COMMISSION
1 The exchange occurred when Gaudron was introduced by one USA sewage engineer to another in the course of a 72 hour layover in the Middle East due

to mechanical difficulties with the aircraft on which she was travelling, story told by Gaudron, *Bar News*, Winter 1987, p. 14; repeated by Justice Margaret McMurdo, President of the Queensland Court of Appeal, 22 February 2003 (proposing a toast to retiring Justice Gaudron, Australian Women Judges Dinner, Sydney).
2   *A Life on the Left*, Guy, p. 257.
3   Jocelynne A. Scutt, 'Murphy the Attorney General', in *Lionel Murphy: A radical judge*, ed. Jocelynne A. Scutt, McCulloch Publishing, 1987, p. 55.
4   Legge, 'Gaudron's Law', *Weekend Australian Review*, 19–20 November 1994, p. 3.
5   Nicklin, 'The law and the laundry', *Sydney Morning Herald*, 9 April 1974, p. 7.
6   Ibid.
7   'Hectic time for judge', *The Herald*, Melbourne, 9 April 1974, p. 9.
8   Pamela Coward, *Henry Bournes Higgins and the Australian Constitution*, unpublished thesis presented for the degree of Master of Laws, School of General Studies, Australian National University, 1975, p. 225; *H. B. Higgins: The rebel as judge* John Rickard, Allen & Unwin, 1984, pp. 253-62. See also Anne Summers, 'Justice Mary Gaudron's resignation', *Australian Financial Review*, 6 May 1980, p. 8.
9   Cabinet Minute, Decision No. 2161, National Archives of Australia A 5925.
10 *The Queen v Kirby: Ex Party Boilermakers' Society of Australia* (1956) 94 CLR 254.
11 'New Justice interrupted by baby's cry', *Sydney Morning Herald*, 19 April 1974, p. 10. See also, 48 *Australian Law Journal* (April 1974) p. 220.
12 '"Mummy, mummy" as judge welcomed', *The Age*, 19 April 1974, p. 12.
13 *Sydney Morning Herald*, 19 April 1974, p. 10; *The Herald*, 10 April 1974, p. 18; *The Advertiser*, 10 April 1974, p. 4, respectively.
14 Hickson, 'Mary Gaudron's brilliant career', *Woman's Day*, 17 July 1980, p. 35.
15 Maximilian Walsh, 'Candid comment: Ms Solomon', *Sydney Morning Herald*, 18 May 1980, p. 42; Hickson, 'Mary Gaudron's brilliant career', *Woman's Day*, 17 July 1980, p. 34.
16 John Yeomans, 'Mary set unions buzzing' *The Herald*, 13 August 1974, p. 19.
17 *Unions in Crisis*, Cameron, p. 97. The appointment of Evatt was on the recommendation of ACTU leader, Bob Hawke. However, Hawke was not consulted about the appointment of Gaudron (Hawke, telephone interview 7 June 2010). See also *Confessions of Clyde Cameron 1913–1990* as told by Daniel Connell, p. 210.
18 Elizabeth Evatt became Chief Justice of the Federal Family Court in 1976.
19 In 1973 changes to the structure and operation of the Commission were made. It became known as the Australian Conciliation and Arbitration Commission, then changing in 1988 to the Australian Industrial Relations Commission. Further changes to the nature and role of the Commission occurred subsequently.

20 See Australian Money Forum table *Inflation in Australia, 1970–2008*, http://www.moneyforum.com.au/node/1 viewed 14 January 2010.
21 Anne Summers, 'Mary Gaudron resignation', *Australian Financial Review*, 6 May 1980, p. 8.
22 McKnight, 'A career of firsts and controversy', *Sydney Morning Herald*, 9 December 1986, p. 19.
23 'Woman out of pay case', *Daily Telegraph*, 27 February 1975, p. 14.
24 *Ducks on the Pond*, Anne Summers, Penguin/Viking, 1999, p. 176-7.
25 Michael Kirby and Breen Reighton, 'The Law of Conciliation and Arbitration', in *The New Province for Law and Order:100 years of Australian industrial conciliation and arbitration,* eds. Joe Isaac and Stuart Macintyre, Cambridge University Press, 2004, pp. 100–101.
26 Blackley, the University's Staff Classifications Officer responsible for position evaluation at the time.
27 *Ceremonial—Heydon J—Swearing in C0/2003,* 11 February 2003, High Court of Australia transcript of proceedings, p. 562.
28 Staples, interview with author 13 June 2009.
29 Anderson, telephone interview with author 18 April 2008.
30 A version of this story is recorded in *What About the Workers?* Barry Cohen, Allen & Unwin, 2000, p. 118 with the dropping of 'e's in the voice of an uneducated working class 'fella'. The gist of the exchange is correct, but the working-class language attributed to Anderson is not.
31 Pauline Hansen, interview with author 22 March 2005.
32 Blackley was present at the conference (Blackley, interview with author 25 September 2007).
33 *The Association of Professional Engineers Australia – and – Melbourne and Metropolitan Board of Works,* transcript of proceedings 9 March 1979, pp. 5A—8.
34 Mary Gaudron, 30 June 1979 (speech, first National Conference of Labor Lawyers, Adelaide) reported by Trish Evans, 'Huge task to change industrial law—judge', *Australian*, 2 July 1979, p. 7.
35 Gaudron, 2005 (speech UNIFEM).
36 The decision was delivered by President Moore; Gaudron and Commission Brack *in absentia* (1978) 203 CAR 584.
37 S. Hogan, 'The cavalier mayor likes women—as stay-at-homes', *New Idea*, 5 January 1980, p. 23, cited and commented on by Grace Johansen in her study, *Women in Central Queensland: A study of three coastal centres 1948 to 1965*, January 2002, p. 295, at: http://library-resources.cqu.edu.au/thesis/adt-QCQU/uploads/approved/adt-QCQU20060921.120038/public/07chapter6.pdf, viewed 27 April 2010.
38 Exhibit M 4, tendered 20 September 1978 in support of the ACTU's case, 'Mary Gaudron' papers, MS 7628 Boxes 1, 2 and 3, Australian National Library Archive, contain material including some exhibits and transcript of proceedings, *National Maternity Leave Case.*

39 Bruce Best, 'Working mothers hit: Rockhampton mayor's blast', *The Age*, 19 September 1978, p. 15; news clipping and note book in 'Mary Gaudron' papers, MS 7628, Box 2, Australian National Library Archive.
40 Preston, 'Mary Gaudron: brilliant career dotted with firsts', *Sydney Morning Herald*, 10 March 1981, p. 7.
41 *The FMWU v ACT Employers Federation (Maternity Leave Case)* (1979) 218 CAR 120, decision 9 March 1979.
42 Gaudron, 8 May 1987, NSW *Bar News*, Winter 1987, p. 13.
43 Justice Michael Kirby, 22 October 2004, 'Industrial Conciliation and Arbitration in Australia—a centenary reflection' (speech, The Centenary Convention Conciliation and Arbitration in Australia), quoting Justice Mary Gaudron in *The New Province for Law and Order*, eds. Isaac and Macintyre, p. 100, n 5.
44 Gaudron, 8 May 1987, NSW *Bar News*, Winter 1987, p. 14.
45 In the matter of *Australian Paper Manufacturers Limited – and – the AMW&SU and ors,* inspection 5 September 1977.
46 Hansen, interview with author 22 March 2005; and see 'Judge in mishap', *Sydney Sun*, 6 September 1977, p. 3.
47 Staples, interview with author 13 June 2009.
48 *The Broken Hill Proprietary Company Limited and The Seamen's Union of Australia* (1975) 171 CAR p. 711, decision 15 October 1975.
49 In the course of an address by a BHP executive to the annual conference of the NSW Industrial Relations Society in Bathurst.
50 Blackshield, interview with author 28 February 2008; Staples, interview with author 15-16 May 1999.
51 *Australian Telecommunications Technical and Trade Staff (Salaries and Specific conditions of employment Award 1976).*
52 Maximilian Walsh, 'Candid comment', *Sydney Morning Herald*, 22 February 1981, p. 50.
53 *Clear Across Australia: A history of telecommunications,* Ann Moyal, Thomas Nelson, 1984, p. 327.
54 *Robert J. Hawke: A biography,* Blanche d'Alpuget, Schwartz/Penguin, 1984, p. 351.
55 *Clear Across Australia,* Moyal, 1984, p. 328.
56 *Ibid,* p. 329.
57 Transcript, p. 121.
58 Transcript, p. 120.
59 *Clear Across Australia,* Moyal, 1984, p. 328.
60 Transcript, p. 121.
61 *Robert J. Hawke,* Blanche d'Alpuget, p. 352.

CHAPTER 9: A DRAMATIC DEPARTURE
1 Roderick Campbell, 'Gaudron's extraordinary career comes to an end', *Canberra Times*, 12 February 2003, p. 15.

2   Richard Ackland, 'Cameron's new consumer czar', *Australian Financial Review*, 2 September 1975, p. 1; 'Protect buyers, warns Cameron', *Sydney Morning Herald*, 9 October 1975, p. 12.
3   Staples, interview with author 15-16 May 1999.
4   Mary Gaudron, February 1977 (speech, Victorian Chamber of Commerce luncheon), reported in the *Australian Financial Review*, 16 February 1977, pp. 1, 8.
5   Jacqueline Kent, author, then colleague of Fogarty (personal communication with author 10 November 2009).
6   Murray Trembath, 'Atom house to go!' *Sydney Sun*, 2 December 1977, p. 3.
7   *Uren papers*, Box 123 MS 6055, National Library of Australia.
8   Alexandra Smith, *Sydney Morning Herald*, 5 July 2008, Fairfax digital http://www.smh.com.au/news/national/exjudge-fled-toxic-addr ess/2008/07/04/1214951042657.html, viewed 5 July 2008.
9   Submission of Julienne Nurse, 25 June 2008, at http://www.parliament.nsw. gov.au/prod/parlment/committee.nsf/0/f8f6bd650d862975ca25747a0082276 6/$FILE/Submission%202.pdf, viewed 25 April 2010.
10 Janet Hawley, 'Mary Gaudron's brilliant career', *The Age*, 10 May 1980, p. 17, in which Nurse talked about Gaudron leaving the home six months earlier with the children because of the radioactive toxicity discovered five years earlier.
11 Peter Diegutis and Paul Ellercamp, 'Hunters Hill radioactive soil lies in rotting bags', *Sydney Morning Herald*, 3 July 1981, p. 2.
12 Simon Benson, 'Nuclear waste disgrace', *Daily Telegraph*, 29 January 2008, p. 5; Editorial, 'Waste plan a mess', 29 January 2008, p. 16; Simon Benson, 'Nuclear waste may stay', *Daily Telegraph*, 30 January 2008, p. 7.
13 Ben Cubby, 'Luxury home is too radioactive to live in', *Sydney Morning Herald*, 25 June 2008, p 1 and 7; Ben Cubby, 'Government buys back radioactive home', 5 March 2009, *Sydney Morning Herald*; and *The North West Star*, Fairfax Digital, 5 March 2009, http://www.northweststar.com.au/news/ national/general/for-the-second-time-government-buys-back-radioactive- home/1450753.aspv?storypage=2, viewed 5 March 2009.
14 J. F. Staples, 17 March 1980 (Address, 'Uniformity and Diversity in Industrial Relations', South Australian Industrial Relations Society, Adelaide), *Journal of Industrial Relations*, September 1980, Vol. 22, No 3, p. 356.
15 *Politics of Law Reform*, Ross, p. 187. Despite the opposition of all 25 Arbitration Commissioners the legislation was passed.
16 Malcolm Colless, 'Judge's blast at law change rocks Street', *The Australian*, 13-14 October 1979, p. 1: Errol Simper, 'Eloquent rebel with no shortage of causes', *The Australian*, 13–14 October 1979, p. 15.
17 From the decision, as reported by Staples, Address to the South Australian Industrial Relations Society, 17 March 1980, *Journal of Industrial Relations*, Vol. 22, No. 3, September 1980, pp. 353, 356–7.

18 *Ibid*, p. 354.
19 Editorial, 'Tangled skein', *Sydney Morning Herald*, 14 March 1980, p. 6.
20 Staples, interview with author 15–16 May 1999.
21 Keith Martin, 'Wool stoppage likely to go on', *Sydney Morning Herald*; Larry Kornhauser, 'Judge seeks suppression of wool row story', *Australian Financial Review*, 16 January 1980.
22 *Sydney Morning Herald*, 14 March 1980; *Adelaide Advertiser*, 17 March 1980; *Canberra Times*, 11 March 1980.
23 Transcript of proceedings, 4 March 1980 *Australian Telecommunications Commission and the Administrative and Clerical Officers Association*, Sydney.
24 The texts of the letters are reproduced in full in article P. P. McGuinness, 'Staples, Moore—High Noon', *Australian Financial Review*, 8 May 1980, p. 6.
25 *Journal of Industrial Relations*, September 1980, Vol. 22, No. 3, p. 354.
26 Geoff Walsh, 'Hayden presses judges on Staples issue', *Australian Financial Review*, 12 May 1980, p. 3; and see John Slee, 'Judge quits over letter', *Sydney Morning Herald*, 6 May 1980, p. 1.
27 Staples, interview with author 15-16 May 1999.
28 Anne Summers, 'Wage judge resigns', *Australian Financial Review*, 6 May 1980, pp. 1, 8.
29 *Ibid*; and Slee, 'Judge quits over letter', *Sydney Morning Herald*, 6 May 1980, p. 1.
30 Keith Martin, 'Staples stripped of power', *Sydney Morning Herald*, 2 May 1980, p. 1; Anne Summers, 'Moore moves against Staples', *Australian Financial Review*, 2 May 1980, pp. 1-2.
31 *The Association of Architects, Engineers, Surveyors and Draughtsmen of Australia – and – The Australian National University*, Australian Commonwealth Conciliation and Arbitration Commission transcripts 2 May 1980, p. 103.
32 John Blackley was present when Gaudron was called to the phone. The Director of the School, Professor Fenner, was away at the time (Blackley, interview 25 September 2007).
33 Hansen, interview with author 7 April 2005.
34 Text reproduced in article, Anne Summers, 'Wage judge resigns', *Australian Financial Review*, 6 May 1980, p. 8.
35 Transcript of proceedings, 5 May 1980, p. 104.
36 Staples, interview with author 15-16 May 1999.
37 Text reproduced in article, Malcolm Colless, 'Sir Zelman may be asked to stall over resignation of Judge Gaudron', *The Australian*, 7 May 1980, p. 1.
38 Slee, 'Judge quits over letter', *Sydney Morning Herald*, 6 May 1980, p. 1; 'Justice Mary Gaudron resigns, ABC reports', *Canberra Times*, 6 May 1980, p. 1; Summers, 'Wage judge resigns', *Australian Financial Review*, 6 May 1980, p. 1.
39 'Staples tells of Gaudron move', *Sydney Morning Herald*, 7 May 1980, p. 2.
40 *Ibid*; and Grealy, 'First lady at court?' *The Advertiser*, 8 April 1981, p. 4.
41 Janet Hawley, 'Mary Gaudron's brilliant career', *The Age*, Melbourne, 10 May

1980, p. 17, tells of Gaudron's daughter answering the phone politely saying, 'Mummy says "no comment".' Some months later, in response to being asked if she had any regrets about her resignation, Gaudron said, 'I don't answer questions about that. I'm sorry', Angela Biven, 'Rights of workers her forte', *The Advertiser*, Adelaide, 18 September 1980, p. 14.

42 Summers, 'Wage judge resigns', *Australian Financial Review*, 6 May 1980, pp. 1, 8.
43 Staples interview; *Sydney Sun*, 25 September 1981, p. 4.
44 Anne Summers, 'Moore moves against Staples', *Australian Financial Review*, 2 May 1980, p. 2.
45 Geoff Walsh, 'Hayden presses judges on Staples issue', *Australian Financial Review*, 12 May 1980, p. 3.
46 *Sydney Morning Herald*, 3 April 1980, p. 2; *Sydney Morning Herald*, 8 May 1980, p. 6.
47 *Justinian*, 'Bar grapples with Staples', June 1980, p. 4; *Australian Financial Review*, 6 May 1980.
48 Clyde Cameron described her action as 'quite the most principled resignation of any public figure in a long time', (Roderick Campbell, 'Gaudron's extraordinary career comes to an end', *Canberra Times*, 12 February 2003, p. 15).
49 *Australian Financial Review*, 6 May 1980, pp. 1, 8.
50 Cockburn, 'Mary Gaudron ponders another first', *Sydney Morning Herald*, 19 November 1994, p. 3.
51 'Offer of NSW post "unlikely"', *Canberra Times*, 7 May 1980, p. 2.
52 'Women at the top: Mary Gaudron', *Law Society Journal* (NSW), Vol. 22, No. 7, August 1984, p. 432.
53 Preston, 'Mary Gaudron: brilliant career dotted with firsts', *Sydney Morning Herald*, 10 March 1981, p. 7.
54 'Ms Gaudron silent on the inside story,' *The Australian,* 21-22 June 1980, p. 3.
55 'Gaudron backs productivity bargaining', *Sydney Morning Herald*, 27 March 1981, p. 12.
56 At the then Canberra College of Advanced Education, reported in, 'Use unions, Gaudron urges women', *Canberra Times*, 28 September 1980, p. 3.
57 Justices Ronald Wilson and Daryl Dawson.
58 John Slee, 'More legal aid urged for children', *Sydney Morning Herald*, 19 June 1980, p. 12.
59 Michael 'First lady at court?' *The Advertiser*, 8 April 1981, p. 4.
60 Hickson, 'Mary Gaudron's brilliant career', *Woman's Day*, 17 July 1980, pp. 34-5. Cameron retired from Federal Parliament in 1980.
61 Grealy, 'First lady at court?' *The Advertiser*, 8 April 1981, p. 4.
62 Anne Summers, 'Gaudron to NSW post', *Australian Financial Review*, 30 September 1980; John Slee, 'NSW post to Miss Gaudron', *Sydney Morning Herald*, 1 October 1980, p. 13.
63 Neville Wran, telephone interview with author 16 December 2005.

64 Bill Bowtell, former Chief of Staff to NSW Attorney General Frank Walker, telephone interview with author 17 March 2008.

CHAPTER 10: NSW SOLICITOR GENERAL
1 Preston, 'Mary Gaudron: brilliant career dotted with firsts', *Sydney Morning Herald*, 10 March 1981, p. 7.
2 Malcolm Brown, 'Justice Gaudron gains $62,351 post', *Sydney Morning Herald*, 7 January 1981, p. 3; *Daily Telegraph*, 8 January 1981, p. 6, 'New Solicitor General', *Sydney Morning Herald*, 17 February 1981, p. 11.
3 Justice Jane Mathews, 1982, 'The changing profile of women in the law' (paper, ANZAAS Congress, Sydney).
4 Frank Walker, interview with author 2 August 2008.
5 'Column 8', *Sydney Morning Herald*, 23 September 1981, p. 1.
6 Jackie Elliot, High Court Librarian, short contact with author 27 January 2000.
7 As she told Michael Sexton, barrister, before he became NSW Solicitor General (Sexton, short contact with author 28 February 2008).
8 Grealy, 'First lady at court?' *Adelaide Advertiser*, 8 April 1981, p. 4.
9 Preston, 'Mary Gaudron: brilliant career dotted with firsts', *Sydney Morning Herald*, 10 March 1981, p. 7.
10 Debbie Byrne, 'Lady of the law faces a new test', *The Herald*, Melbourne, 5 March 1981, p. 9.
11 See *The Wran Era*, ed. Troy Bramston, The Federation Press, 2006.
12 Proposed by Bob Carr, the Minister for the State Planning and Environment.
13 Ross Dunn, 'The Greening of the NSW Constitution by Robert Carr', *Sydney Morning Herald*, 13 January 1986, p. 1, pointing out that the Wran Government had exercised this power already in the past. In 1979 the NSW Government had inserted in the State Constitution five provisions on compulsory voting at Legislative Assembly elections.
14 Dunn, 'The Greening of the NSW Constitution by Robert Carr', *Sydney Morning Herald*, 13 January 1986, p. 1.
15 Pilita Clark, 'Wran sorry, but greenery plan not politically sound', *Sydney Morning Herald*, 14 January 1986, p. 3.
16 Bowtell, telephone interview with author 17 March 2008.
17 Don Colagiuri SC, Parliamentary Counsel, September 2005 (paper on the organisation of a drafting office, conference, London), www.opc.gov.au/calc/docs/calc_loophole_july_2007.pdf, viewed 1 April 2009.
18 Robyn Henderson, conversation with author 7 February 2010, recalled Gaudron informed her and Jim Coombes of this.
19 Ross Dunn, 'NSW tilts at Canberra legal view', *Sydney Morning Herald*, 5 January 1984, p. 3.
20 SG 461/84, 21 August 1984, concerning provisions in the Commonwealth's *National Crime Authority Model States Bill*.

21 *Gould v Brown* (1998) 193 CLR 346. Cross-vesting legislation was upheld by reason of Chief Justice Brennan's decisive vote, while Gaudron was one of the three justices holding it invalid. In *Re Wakim; Ex parte McNally* (1999) 198 CLR 511, cross-vesting legislation was held invalid, with Justice Kirby the single dissentient on the point.
22 *Sydney Morning Herald*, 16 May 1981, p. 56, public notice for the launch the following day.
23 Frank Walker, 'Social Policy and the Reform Agenda', in *The Wran Era*, ed. Bramston, p. 169. For more about the Wran Government reforms of the 1970s and 1980s, see also Chapter 10, 'Health', Laurie Brereton; Chapter 16, 'Social Policy and the Reform Agenda', Frank Walker; Chapter 18, 'Women's Policy', Carmel Niland.
24 Wran had established the advisory body because there were so few women in Cabinet, parliament and administrative decision-making positions. Carmel Niland claimed that 'In the 1980s, NSW created the best machinery for government for women in the world,' 'Women's Policy', *The Wran Era*, ed. Bramston, p. 189.
25 *Politics of Law Reform*, Ross, p. 16.
26 Mary Gaudron, launch of a text on rape-law reform, 'Balancing the Scales', ed. Dr Patricia Easteal, speech reported in *Canberra Times*, 4 September 1998.
27 SG 27 May 1981, p. 1–3.
28 SG 24 July 1981, p. 181.
29 SG 67/86 24 February 1986, and see SG 93/86, 12 March 1986.
30 *The Crimes (Death Penalty Abolition) Amendment Act 1985* (NSW) was assented to on 15 May 1985.
31 SG 262/86 4 June 1986.
32 *Bailey v Marinoff* (1970) 125 CLR 52.
33 In 1981 Gaudron advised on the validity of revocations of certain reservations for the use of Aborigines, and in 1982 she provided advice with regard to land taken from Aborigines.
34 Walker, interview with author 2 August 2008.
35 Mike Steketee, 'Ministers avert clash in court on abortion law', *Sydney Morning Herald*, 15 April 1982, p. 2.
36 Walker, interview with author 2 August 2008.
37 The ruling of Judge Aaron Levine in *R v Wald* (1971) 3 DCR (NSW) 25. When Judge Levine died in 1972, Gaudron, then at the Bar, cosigned a letter, published in the *Sydney Morning Herald*, 21 July 1972, p. 6, expressing regret over his death and acknowledging his 'truly liberal approach to present problems, which made him a bridge between the community and the normally entrenched conservatism of the law'.
38 Steketee, 'Ministers avert clash in court on abortion law', *Sydney Morning Herald*, 15 April 1982, p. 2.
39 *Actors and Announcers Equity Association v Fontana Films Pty Ltd* (1982) 150 CLR 169.

40 'Pregnant pause', *The Australian*, 7 August 1981, p. 23.
41 Jack Waterford, *Canberra Times* journalist, personal communication with author 26 May 2003.
42 *Ibid*.
43 According to Pamela Tate SC, Victorian Solicitor General, Gaudron's arguments 'invariably illustrated a depth of understanding of Australian federalism and the integrated system of federal and State courts', 22 September 2006 (speech, 10th Ethel Benjamin Commemorative Address, Dunedin, New Zealand).
44 *Commonwealth v Hospital Contribution Fund* (1982) 150 CLR, 49, 50.
45 *Kotsis v Kotsis* (1970) 122 CLR 69 and *Knight v Knight* (1971) 122 CLR 114.
46 *Hematite Petroleum v Victoria* (1983) 151 CLR 599 and *Stack v Coast Securities (No 9)* (1983) 154 CLR 261, over the validity of state fees and the Commonwealth's exclusive power to impose excise duties; *Gosford Meats Pty Ltd v New South Wales*, (1985) 155 CLR 368, also concerned excise duties, in which Gaudron argued that a state licence fee for abattoir operators was not a tax on goods and therefore not an excise duty. She also defended the State fee as not being discriminatory as it applied even-handedly to all abattoirs in the State, directing this argument to Justice Murphy, who in earlier cases had argued that an 'excise duty' should be confined to a discriminatory tax. She failed to convince Murphy, or the rest of the Court.
47 *Miller v TCN Channel Nine* (1985) 161 CLR 556.
48 Kalowski, entry on Gaudron in *The Oxford Companion to the High Court*, p. 294.
49 *Commonwealth v Tasmania* (1983) 158 CLR 1, discussed further below.
50 The seminar papers delivered on 3 December 1983 about the case, *Commonwealth v Tasmania* (1983) 158 CLR 1, are contained in 14 *Federal Law Review*.
51 This account was drawn from conversations with several of the people present at the dinner.
52 *Encounters with the Australian Constitution*, Michael Coper, CCH Australia Limited, p. 199.
53 *Koowarta v Bjelke-Petersen* (1982) 153 CLR 168.
54 The Aboriginal Land Fund Commission sought to purchase a lease of Crown land in Northern Queensland for the Winychanam Aboriginal group. Under the *Land Act 1962* (Qld), the consent of the Minister for Lands was required. He refused to dispose of a large tract of land to Aborigines; see *Sir Ronald Wilson: A matter of conscience,* Antonio Buti, University of Western Australia Press, 2007, p. 205.
55 Gaudron was supportive of a suggestion made by Commonwealth Solicitor General, Maurice Byers, that Federal legislation should contain express provision to preserve State legislation which conferred rights of no less advantage than those created by Federal legislation. She provided advice to the NSW Attorney General to this effect on 26 October 1981.

56 SG Advice, 9 November 1981, p. 302.
57 'Aborigines' complaints spark test of race law', *Sydney Morning Herald*, 16 March 1983, p. 3. The complaints were investigated by the NSW Counsellor for Equal Opportunities, as a result of which the hotel owner sought a declaration in the NSW Supreme Court that NSW had no jurisdiction to investigate a matter that was being investigated by the Commonwealth Commissioner for Community Relations. The proceedings were transferred to the High Court to consider whether the Federal and State laws were in conflict.
58 *Viskauskas v Niland* (1983) 153 CLR 280.
59 The *Racial Discrimination Amendment Act 1983*(Cth), purporting to remove the inconsistency retrospectively as well as prospectively. The relevant provision (s. 3) was then challenged successfully in the High Court in *Metwally v University of Wollongong* (1985) 60 ALR 68, the Court holding that the Commonwealth by its own Act could not revive a state law already invalid as inconsistent with a Commonwealth law under s. 109 of the Constitution.
60 *Commonwealth v Tasmania* (1983) 158 CLR 1.
61 Section 69 of the *National Parks and Wildlife Conservation Act 1975* and sections 6(2)(b), 6(3) and 9 of the *World Heritage Property Conservation Act* 1983.
62 Justice Deane, one of the majority judges in the case, joined the dissenting judges, Chief Justice Gibbs, and Justices Wilson and Dawson, to form a majority in holding that the Regulations were invalid. Deane's reason was that they involved an acquisition of property without sufficient provision for it being on 'just terms'.
63 The dam site fell within national parklands that in December 1982 had been entered on the World Heritage List of UNESCO. The new Government passed the *World Heritage Properties Conservation Act 1983* to strengthen its power to stop the damming of the Gordon River.
64 Patrick Walters, 'First shots fired in High Court dam war', *Sydney Morning Herald*, 7 April 1983, p. 3.
65 With James Spigelman and Tim Robertson, assisting. Gaudron put submissions on 9 June 1983; transcript of proceedings, p. 713. See summary of Gaudron's argument (1983) 158 CLR 1, at pp. 47-8.
66 Blackshield believes that none of the judgments gave sufficient weight to this point. For elaboration see *Australian Constitutional Law and Theory Commentary and Materials,* Blackshield and Williams, 5th ed., The Federation Press, 2010, pp. 898-9.
67 *Commonwealth v Tasmania* (1983) 158 CLR 1, decision 1 July 1983; Mason, Murphy, Brennan and Deane, with Chief Justice Gibbs, and Wilson and Dawson in dissent.
68 Justice Mason (as he then was) at pp. 84-5.
69 SG Report 14 June 1983.
70 *Fencott v Muller (O'Connors Winebar case)* (1983) 152 CLR 570, a decision given 28 April 1983.

71 SG Report 14 June 1983. The potential use of the corporations power had been considered by others well before the *Tasmanian Dam* case. Justice Mason, as Commonwealth Solicitor General in the 1960s, had seen the importance of the development of the corporations power as a source of power for the Commonwealth but, in those days, he doubted whether the Court, despite Chief Justice Barwick's progressive attitude on that aspect of the Constitution, would entertain its use to expand Commonwealth powers (Sir Anthony Mason, interview 7 October 2009).
72 *New South Wales v Commonwealth* (2006) 229 CLR 1; see joint judgment pp. 114–15, 14 November 2006.
73 Tim Dick, 'High noon for the states', Fairfax digital, *Sydney Morning Herald*, 15 November 2006, http://www.smh.com.au/news/national/high-noon-for-the-states/2006/11/14/1163266550361.html, viewed 1 May 2010.
74 *Re Pacific Coal* (2000) 203 CLR 346, a development of her views in an earlier case, *Re Dingjan; Ex parte Wagner* (1995) 183 CLR, 323, in which cases she was in dissent.
75 Tim Dick, 'High noon for the states', Fairfax digital, *Sydney Morning Herald*, 15 November 2006, http://www.smh.com.au/news/national/high-noon-for-the-states/2006/11/14/1163266550361.html, viewed 1 May 2010.
76 Tony Blackshield, 'Case note *New South Wales v Commonwealth* Corporations and connections', (2007) 31 *Melbourne University Law Review*, No 3, p. 1135 at 1136, and for discussion of *Pacific Coal*, pp. 1141–4. The 'ironies' of the decision in the *WorkChoices* case are further discussed below.
77 Staples, interview with author 15-16 May 1999.
78 Address to graduates at Macquarie University in Sydney, reported by the *The Australian*, 29 July 1982, and see the *Australian Financial Review* 31 May 1982.
79 Gaudron, 10 April 1981, 'Residual Constitutional Links', report to the NSW Attorney General.
80 Mary Gaudron, 'How Britain is still ruling Aust States', *Australian Financial Review*, 31 May 1982, p. 10.
81 SG Advice 17 June 1981.
82 *The Chameleon Crown: The Queen and her Australian governors,* Anne Twomey, The Federation Press, 2006, p. 186.
83 Walker, interview with author 2 August 2008.
84 SG Report, 28 June 1983.
85 For a full account of the story, see *The Chameleon Crown*, Anne Twomey, The Federation Press, 2006.
86 *The Chameleon Crown*, Twomey, p. 241, and for a full account see pp. 204–31.
87 *The Chameleon Crown*, Twomey, p. 241.
88 *Ibid*, p. 242.
89 *Ibid*, pp. 243, 246.
90 *Ibid*, p. 240–2.
91 SG 607/84.

92 *Caltex Oil (Australia) Pty. Ltd. v X. L. Petroleum (NSW) Pty. Ltd.* (1984) 155 CLR 72, at p. 86.
93 A tribute by Justice Michael Kirby, Canberra, 21 October 1996 on the tenth anniversary of Lionel Murphy's death.
94 SG 214/85, 3 June 1985.
95 Her apology was 'to Michael Emmett and the IRA', perhaps intending to refer to Michael ('Mick') Collins, Irish revolutionary leader (16 October 1890–22 August 1922), or Robert Emmet (4 March 1778–20 September 1803), Irish nationalist rebel leader. She also explained that the acute was an attempt for the last line to rhyme with 'ized'!
96 *Australia Act 1986* (UK) and *Australia Act 1986* (Cth).

CHAPTER 11: CRIME AND CORRUPTION
1 The Hon. Justice J. R. T. Wood, *Royal Commission into the New South Wales Police Service Final Report*, Vol. 1: Corruption, May 1997, NSW Government, 1997, p. 36.
2 Bill Bowtell, telephone interview with author 17 March 2008.
3 Graham Freudenberg, 'Neville Wran: The voice of Sydney', in *The Wran Era*, ed. Bramston, p. 103.
4 23 April 1979; *Wran: An unatuthorised biography*, Mike Steketee and Milton Cockburn, Allen&Unwin, 1986, p. 285.
5 *Wran*, Steketee and Cockburn, p. 253.
6 SG Advices 11 December 1981 and 16 June 1983; February 1982. Gaudron represented Police Minister Anderson to oppose Saffron's court application to have his name removed from Justice Perrignon's terms of reference for his police inquiry into corruption. See 'Court dismisses Saffron summons', *Sydney Morning Herald*, 9 February 1982, p. 3.
7 *Wran*, Steketee and Cockburn; *Killing Juanita*, Peter Rees, Allen & Unwin, 2004; *Recollections of an Unreasonable Man*, Don Stewart, ABC Books, 2007.
8 *Wran*, Steketee and Cockburn, provides an account of the 'Love Boat' story, p. 252.
9 SG 272/85, 23 July 1985.
10 Andrew Keenan, *Sydney Morning Herald*, 14 November 1986, p. 7.
11 *Wran*, Steketee and Cockburn, p. 280–3; Police Commissioner Anderson was also criticised.
12 May 1982, Mr Justice Perrignon, sitting as the Police Tribunal inquiring into the misconduct of Deputy Police Commissioner Bill Allen.
13 Greg Turnbull and Mike Steketee, 'After Allen, Canberra seeks US link inquiry', *Sydney Morning Herald*, 28 April 1982, p. 1.
14 SG Opinion, 19 May 1982.
15 Turnbull and Steketee, 'After Allen, Canberra seeks US link inquiry', *Sydney Morning Herald*, 28 April 1982, p. 1.
16 SG Opinion, 23 September 1982.

17 'Former policeman claims he did a deal', *Sydney Morning Herald*, 14 February 1991, p. 4; 'Judge looks at delay in Allen case', 15 February 1991, p. 5.
18 *A Collusion of Powers*, Philip Arantz, self-published, 1993, p. 276.
19 Friend of Arantz (email to author 15 August 2007); Rod Frail, 'The high price of speaking out', *The Age*, 8 August 1988, p. 11.
20 SG Opinion, 16 August 1982.
21 Mike Steketee, 'Walker and Dowd clash over Bartons', *Sydney Morning Herald*, 5 November 1982, p. 10.
22 *Wran*, Steketee and Cockburn, p. 291.
23 *Ibid*, p. 294.
24 See also Andrew Clarke, 'Policing, law and order', in *The Wran Era*, ed. Bramston, p. 154.
25 *Wran*, Steketee and Cockburn, pp. 267-8, 271-2.
26 Summary of facts in SG 453/84.
27 Report tabled in the NSW Parliament on 28 February 1980, Rodney Frail, 'Suspicion that law was "bent"', *Sydney Morning Herald*, 29 February 1980, p. 3.
28 Paul Byrnes, 'Wran: "completely exonerated" but Farquhar "did influence"', *Sydney Morning Herald*, 29 July 1983, p. 1.
29 Laurie Ferguson having been Acting Premier from 16 May 1983.
30 Paul Byrnes, 'The Street findings—a Government leak?' *Sydney Morning Herald*, 30 July 1983, p. 1.
31 SG/83 29 July 1983.
32 'A February hearing for Farquhar', *Sydney Morning Herald*, 23 December 1983, p. 1. Farquhar had tried to delay the hearing until after Magistrates were selected for the Local Court that would replace the Magistrates Court under the new *Local Court Act*. Gaudron was a member of the panel that would select the magistrates, and Farquhar's counsel argued that her interest in the prosecution might influence the Magistrate allocated to hear the case. The application was rejected.
33 Garry Sturgess, 'Murphy and the Media', in *Lionel Murphy: A radical judge*, ed. Jocelynne A. Scutt, McCulloch Publishing, 1987, pp. 211, 215.
34 *Wran*, Steketee and Cockburn, p. 38.
35 Journalist, John Silvester, produced notes he had made from documents given to him by the investigative journalist Bob Bottom.
36 Marian Wilkinson, 'Big shots bugged', *National Times*, 25 November-1 December 1983, p. 3.
37 On 21 February 1984, Senator Evans appointed the new Commonwealth Director of Public Prosecutions, Ian Temby, QC, as Special Prosecutor under the provisions of the *Special Prosecutors Act 1982* (Cth).
38 *Wran*, Steketee and Cockburn, pp. 314–15.
39 Others included Ronald Diaz, Fredrick Anderson, Karl Bonnette and Stanly Smith. See the Stewart Royal Commission report, May 1986, SG 636/84, 19 December 1984.

40 Stewart Royal Commission into drug trafficking.
41 *Ibid.*
42 SG 161/84 17 February 1974 on the authenticity of the material and its usefulness in evidence.
43 *Wran*, Steketee and Cockburn, p. 318.
44 Mike Steketee, 'Tapes: the 5 vital questions', *Sydney Morning Herald*, 22 February 1984, p. 1.
45 SG 161/84, 17 February 1984.
46 SG 161A/84, 17 February 1984.
47 See Sturgess, 'Murphy and the Media', *Lionel Murphy: A radical judge,* ed. Scutt, p. 219, about this and other errors.
48 Stephen Rice, 'Newspaper gave inaccurate report of police phone taps', *Sydney Morning Herald*, 16 February 1984, p. 3.
49 Steketee, 'Tapes: the 5 vital questions', *Sydney Morning Herald*, 22 February 1984, p. 1; see 'The Gaudron Report', p. 4, 'Tapes, documents "legally worthless"', for edited version of Gaudron's report.
50 Editorial, *Sydney Morning Herald*, 24 February 1984, p. 8.
51 ASIO had concerns when David Combe, who had close associations with the Hawke Labor Government, together with his wife developed a relationship with Valery Ivanov, the First Secretary for the USSR, in the course of the Combes preparing for a trip to the USSR in 1982. Ivanov, who was thought to have KGB links, was expelled from Australia in 1983 by Prime Minister Bob Hawke.
52 Gaudron openly disagreed with the Commonwealth Attorney General, Gareth Evans, and Solicitor General, Sir Maurice Byers, in her view that the privilege extended to press reports of the proceedings. See Mike Steketee, 'Speaker switches tapes ruling', *Sydney Morning Herald*, 23 February 1984, p. 2; 'Gagged and ungagged', Editorial, *Sydney Morning Herald*, 24 February 1984, p. 8.
53 Mary Gaudron, 'Courts must rule on phone taps', Letters to the Editor, *Sydney Morning Herald*, 28 February 1984, p. 8.
54 John Campbell, 'Ducker totally exonerated over tapes', *The Australian*, 24 May 1984; Ross Dunn, 'Landa's advice clears Ducker', *Sydney Morning Herald*, 24 May 1984, p. 2, and see *Wran*, Steketee and Cockburn, p. 321.
55 SG 454/84 3 May 1984, and 454A/84 9 May 1984.
56 SG 328/84 19 June 1984.
57 John Slee, 'Use of police tapes for judge to decide', *Sydney Morning Herald*, 11 November 1986, p. 12.
58 7 August 1981, Ryan was charged with forgery (preparing false documents); on 5 November 1981, a charge of conspiracy was added to the forgery charge. It was alleged that the application was supported by false statements by the Koreans' employers as to their special skills and employment qualifications. On 29 January 1982, Kevin Jones, SM, committed Ryan for trial on both

charges. Later the forgery charge was dropped. In July 1983 Ryan was convicted on the conspiracy charge, but on 26 July 1984, the conviction was quashed by the NSW Court of Criminal Appeal (*R v Ryan* (1984) 55 ALR 408). A new trial was ordered but never proceeded with because the flood of prejudicial publicity arising from the *Age* tapes had made a fair trial impossible.

59 SG 448/84, 31 July 1984.
60 SG 448/84, 31 July 1984. See report by Dennis Shanahan, 'Briese thought Labor might change leader, Gaudron says', *Sydney Morning Herald*, 22 August 1984, p. 1; Briese gave evidence on 18 April 1985 of the interview he had with Mary Gaudron; reported by Lindsay Simpson, *Sydney Morning Herald*, 19 April 1985, p. 2.
61 *Wran*, Steketee and Cockburn, p. 218.
62 SG 448/84 31 July 1984.
63 *Odgers' Australian Senate Practice*, eleventh edition, Ch. 20, 'Relations with the judiciary'. Report of the first committee, pp. 168/1984.

CHAPTER 12: TAPS, LEAKS AND BUCKETS OF MUCK

1 Graham Freudenberg, 'Neville Wran: The voice of Sydney', in *The Wran Era*, ed. Bramston, p. 103.
2 *Sydney Morning Herald*, 27 August 1984, 'Stay in Touch' reported a rumour that this was the title of the address. The following day, 28 August 1984, the *Sydney Morning Herald*'s 'Stay in Touch', under the heading 'Legal mischief', p. 12, (and see 'Column 8', p. 1), reported that Gaudron had contacted them and told them there was no formal title for her speech. She had been asked to present a lighthearted talk on topical issues like bio-ethics, family law, and technology and the law. She thought she might be able to include some reference to illegal recording of telecommunications under the last heading.
3 Trevor Haines, telephone interview with author, 18 May 2010.
4 Paul Lynch, 'Crime tapes linked with NSW court row', *The Australian*, 4-5 August 1984, p. 1.
5 Paul Lynch, 'Landa orders probe into Gaudron leak', *The Australian*, 13 August 1984, p. 3.
6 Dennis Shanahan, 'Judge is sidelined until inquiry ends', *Sydney Morning Herald*, 15 August 1984, p. 1; see also, Ross Dunn, 'No inquiry into drug case', *Sydney Morning Herald*, 15 August 1984, p. 3.
7 Dennis Shanahan, 'I stand by my claims, says Briese', *Sydney Morning Herald*, 4 August 1984, p. 1.
8 SG 530/84.
9 SG 530/84, 10 October 1984.
10 SG 449/84, 2 August 1984; 450/84, 13 August 1984.
11 SG 451/1984, 13 August 1984.
12 SG 561/86, 6 November 1986.

13 John Slee, *Sydney Morning Herald*, 17 November 1986, p. 28.
14 Inquiry established 30 April 1986, Parliamentary Paper No. 155/1986 (Cth), and near completion by mid-November 1986.
15 Dennis Shanahan, 'Sheahan denies delaying Cessna-Milner prosecutions', *Sydney Morning Herald*, 12 November 1986, p. 2. See also Andrew and Mark Coultan, 'Police angry at Government move on Cessna-Milner inquiry', *Sydney Morning Herald*, 10 November 1986, p. 4; Evan Whitton, 'The case that just refused to go away and the Cessna file: ready to explode', *Sydney Morning Herald*, 13 November 1986, p. 2.
16 Editorial, 'Cessna–Milner: getting it right', *Sydney Morning Herald*, 12 November 1986, p. 12.
17 *Justinian*, 'The High Court's junior', No. 50, March 1987, p. 11.
18 *Ibid*.
19 Independent MP Mr John Hatton, *Sydney Morning Herald*, 29 December 1986.
20 John Slee, 'Legal profession backs Gaudron in no-bill row', *Sydney Morning Herald*, 4 December 1985, p. 4.
21 *Recollections of an Unreasonable Man*, Don Stewart, ABC Books, 2007, p. 173; See also *Wran*, Steketee and Cockburn, pp. 314–15; Wran had expressed concern over telephone tapping in early 1973.
22 SG 636/84, 19 December 1984.
23 SG 128/85, 11 February 1985 and see SG 69/86 24 February 1986.
24 *Telegraph*, 5 November 1986 pp. 1 and 2.
25 SG 571/86, 20 November 1986, p. 5.
26 NCA 1988-89 Annual Report, p. 26.
27 The project was apparently endorsed by Detective Sergeant Blissett of the NSW Bureau of Crime Intelligence. Under the supervision of Detective Sergeant Bill Cullen of Goulburn, they monitored the progress of the crop, and two officers from the Bureau undertook observations. In January 1982 Detective Sergeant Slade of the Bureau became involved in the project.
28 NCA 1988-89 Annual Report, p. 26.
29 *Ibid*, p. 28.
30 *Ibid*.
31 NCA 1988-89 Annual Report, p. 28.
32 Donald Stewart, personal communication with author 19 November 2008; and see NCA 1988-89 Annual Report, p. 29, referring to the rationale for the involvement of members of the AFP and the NSW Police in the two Bungendore plantation exercises being the subject of criticism. In 1987 Stewart forwarded to the Commissioner of the AFP a summary of the NCA's investigation in so far as it concerned the conduct of members of the AFP in their dealings with Verduci.
33 NCA 1988-89 Annual Report, p. 28.
34 *Ibid*, p. 29.
35 *Ibid*, and see *Parliamentary Joint Committee on the National Crimes Authority*, Third Report, Appendix 1, Australian Government Publications Service,

Canberra, 1989, at: http://www.aph.gov.au/SENATE/COMMITTEE/acc_ctte/completed_inquiries/pre1996/third_report/report/report.pdf., viewed 10 July 2010.

36 *Dietrich v The Queen* (1992) 177 CLR 292; *Ridgeway v The Queen* (1995) 184 CLR 19; *Nicholas v The Queen* (1998) 193 CLR 173, discussed further below.
37 See NCA 1988-89 Annual Report, p. 25.
38 *Re Governor, Goulburn Correctional Centre; Ex parte Eastman* (1999) 200 CLR 322, in which she suggested that the doctrine that there was a constitutional requirement for judicial impartiality and independence might apply to courts in the Territories, at p. 340; *Eastman v The Queen* (2000) 203 CLR 1, concerning fitness to plead.
39 31 July 1984, SG 433/84, concerning recommendations made by Justice Slattery in his 1984 report arising out of the Special Commission for Inquiry.
40 SG 421/84.
41 Work colleagues; confirmed by Ben Nurse, interview 24 May 2010.
42 Justice Terry Sheahan, former NSW Attorney General, interview with author 12 August 2009.
43 SG 559/84, 25 October 1984.
44 Justice Terry Sheahan, interview with author 12 August 2009.
45 Rosanne Robertson, 'Call for experts on equal opportunity', *Sydney Morning Herald*, 7 June 1984, p. 2.
46 Scutt 1981-1984; Evatt 1979-1985.
47 *Sydney Morning Herald*, 5 February 1983, p. 14. It folded in 1988.
48 Luis M. Garcia, 'The case of Macquarie's law chair v the academics', *Sydney Morning Herald*, 1 June 1984, p. 1.
49 Robert Thomson, 'After President Moffit steps down, it's Kirby or McHugh', *Sydney Morning Herald*, 22 June 1984, p. 1. The post went to Justice Michael Kirby.
50 *Murphy v Director of Public Prosecutions* (1985) 60 ALR 299.
51 *R v Murphy* (1985) 158 CLR 596, 14 August 1985. Murphy also challenged the proceedings before the Parliamentary Commission of Inquiry, which the High Court rejected.
52 *Justinian*, No 50, March 1986, p.11.
53 *National Times*, 16-22 August 1985.
54 8 January 1985, SG 17/85. Rogerson was later convicted and gaoled in 1990 for conspiring to defeat the course of justice.
55 'Bacon questioned over protests', *Sydney Morning Herald*, 22 September 1981, p. 2.
56 Adjudication No. 265 (January 1986) [1986] APC 1.
57 John Slee, 'The luck of Judge Foord', *Sydney Morning Herald*, 8 October 1985, p. 14.
58 Adjudication No. 266 (January 1986) [1986] APC 2.
59 *Sydney Morning Herald*, 4 August 1986, p. 4.

60 Tony Blackshield, 'The "Murphy Affair"' in *Lionel Murphy: A radical judge*, ed. Scutt, p. 248.
61 *Ibid*, p. 250.
62 *R v Murphy* [1985] 4 NSWLR 42; 63 ALR 53.
63 *DPP v Wran* [1986] 7 NSWLR 616. The newspaper which published Wran's remarks was fined $200,000. Wran was fined $25,000; *DPP v Wran* (1987) 86 FLR 92.
64 As a result of which public statement a juror wrote a private letter to Blackshield complaining that the trial judge's directions had made the jury believe that they must convict even though they were convinced that Murphy had not done anything wrong (Tony Blackshield, personal communication 20 April 2010).
65 Roderick Campbell, 'The maelstrom that was the Murphy affair', *Canberra Times*, 'Binding Authority; 100 years of the High Court of Australia', High Court Centenary magazine, 3 October 2003, p. 12.
66 Roderick Campbell was present in Court (Campbell telephone conversation with a friend 21 March 2008).
67 Blackshield, 'The "Murphy Affair"', *Lionel Murphy: A radical judge*, ed. Scutt, p. 233.
68 *Murphy v Lush* (1986) 65 ALR 651.
69 The texts of the letters exchanged between Gibbs and Murphy, 31 July and 1 August 1986 respectively, are set out in *Sir Harry Gibbs: Without fear or favour*, Joan Priest, Scribblers Publishing, 1995, pp. 111-12.
70 Campbell, 'The maelstrom that was the Murphy affair', *Canberra Times*, 'Binding Authority; 100 years of the High Court of Australia', High Court Centenary magazine, 3 October 2003, p. 12.
71 The original tune of the Irish ballad by Patrick McCall, 'Boolavogue' and the very similar 'Father Murphy' (who hailed from Boolavogue, County Wexford, Ireland) was later used in Australia's 'Moreton Bay' about an Irish convict in Australia.
72 Blackshield, interview with author 28 February 2008.
73 Gaudron's full speech is contained in the Epilogue to *Lionel Murphy: A radical judge*, ed. Scutt.
74 *McInnis v R* (1979) 143 CLR 575 at p. 583.

CHAPTER 13: HIGH GROUND
1 Tim Barrett, barrister and occupant of Gaudron's room, thirteenth floor, Wentworth Chambers (interview with author 7 April 2005).
2 Verge Blunden, 'With one down and two in doubt, the guard at the High Court is changing', *Sydney Morning Herald*, 29 July 1986, p. 15.
3 On the Court at the time were Chief Justice Mason, a former Commonwealth Solicitor General, and Justices Dawson and Wilson, previous State Solicitors General.

4   Since Sir Garfield Barwick's days as Chief Justice, when the High Court became responsible for its own administration, the *High Court of Australia Act 1979* made provision for the States to be consulted by the Federal Attorney General.
5   Sheahan, interview with author 12 August 2009.
6   Verge Blunden, 'Woman mooted for High Court', *Sydney Morning Herald*, 6 November 1986, p. 3; *Sydney Morning Herald*, 9 December 1986, John Slee 'Politics and the High Court', p. 16, where Slee also said that Gaudron had a 'formidable grasp of legal principle' and he acknowledged her technical competency as a lawyer.
7   John Slee 'Politics and the High Court', *Sydney Morning Herald*, 9 December 1986, p. 16. Senator Susan Ryan, and member of the Hawke Cabinet, witnessed some of her colleagues' coolness, according to Legge, 'Gaudron's Law', *Weekend Australian Review*, 19–20 November 1994, p. 2.
8   Robert Hawke, telephone conversation with author 8 June 2010.
9   *Ibid*; and Clyde Cameron reportedly talked about the meeting to Kate Legge, as reported in 'Gaudron's Law', *Weekend Australian Review*, 19-20 November 1994, p. 3.
10 Hawke, telephone conversation with author 8 June 2010.
11 Mike Steketee, 'Gaudron not a token, Hawke says', *Sydney Morning Herald*, 10 December 1986, p. 3.
12 Legge, 'Gaudron's Law', *Weekend Australian Review*, 19–20 November 1994, p. 2.
13 Mike Steketee, 'Mary Gaudron in field for High Court vacancy', *Sydney Morning Herald*, 6 December 1986, p.13.
14 'We all have lives', film clip 3, *The Highest Court*, 1998, ABC TV documentary broadcast 26 May 1998, Film Art Doco, National Film and Sound Archive; William West, 'Judge warns on need for equality', *The Australian*, 1 April 1987, p. 11.
15 *Australia Act 1986* (Cth).
16 Meredith memorial lectures, 'The future of the Constitution' p. 1, in *Future Questions in Australian Politics*, Bundoora, Victoria, La Trobe University, 1979.
17 In speaking of the High Court history exhibition at the National Archives of Australia, July 2009.
18 *Mabo v Queensland (No 2) (Mabo case)* (1992) 175 CLR 1; *Wik Peoples v Queensland (Pastoral Leases case)* (1996) 187 CLR 1.
19 *Patrick Stevedores Operations No. 2 Pty Ltd v Maritime Union of Australia* (1998) 195 CLR 1.
20 *New South Wales v Commonwealth (WorkChoices)* (2006) 229 CLR 1.
21 Blackshield, personal communication 20 April 2010.
22 David Solomon and Greg Earl, 9 December 1986, 'Gaudron, Toohey get nod as new High Court Judges', p. 1.

23 *Inside the Mason Court Revolution: The High Court of Australia transformed,* Jason L. Pierce, Carolina Academic Press, 2006, p. 208.
24 Slee, 'Politics and the High Court', *Sydney Morning Herald*, 9 December 1986, p. 16.
25 Paul Willoughby, '"Awed" High Court judge sets her first precedent', *The Advertiser*, Adelaide, 7 February 1987, p. 5.
26 Rod Frail, 'Keep mates off High Court, Labor advised', *Sydney Morning Herald*, 8 December 1986, p. 3, reporting on National Party Leader, Ian Sinclair's criticism.
27 William West, 'Controversy is certain', *The Australian*, 9 December 1986, p. 13.
28 Prime Minister, Bob Hawke, denied Gaudron's appointment was 'tokenism', Steketee, 'Gaudron not a token, Hawke says', *Sydney Morning Herald*, 10 December 1986, p. 3.
29 McKnight, 'A career of firsts and controversy', *Sydney Morning Herald*, 9 December 1986, p. 19.
30 Ross Coulthart, 'New judge in row over drug appeal', *Sydney Morning Herald*, 29 December 1986, p. 1.
31 *Ibid.*
32 'Miss Mary Gaudron, QC', *Sydney Morning Herald*, 3 January 1987, p. 1.
33 Margot Stubbs, interview with author 27 February 2008.
34 'We all have lives', film clip 3, *The Highest Court*, 1998, ABC TV documentary broadcast 26 May 1998, Film Art Doco, National Film and Sound Archive.
35 Geoff Kitney, 'Top judge lends weight to constitutional reform', *Times on Sunday*, 9 August 1987, p. 5.
36 'Meal gives the law something to chew over', *Daily Telegraph*, 11 May 1987, p. 11.
37 8 May 1987 (speech, NSW Bar paying tribute to Gaudron on her appointment), *Bar News*, Winter 1987, p. 11.
38 Heather J. Roberts, 'Women Judges, "Maiden Speeches" and the High Court of Australia', observed the same trends in the welcome speeches at Gaudron's swearing-in ceremony, in Beverley Baines, Daphne Barak Erez, and Tsvi Kahana (eds), *Feminist Constitutionalism*, Cambridge University Press, 2010 (forth-coming).
39 Slee, 'Politics and the High Court', *Sydney Morning Herald*, 9 December 1986, p. 16; West, 'Controversy is certain', *The Australian*, 9 December 1986, p. 13.
40 'Former Moree student makes High Court history', *The Champion*, 9 December 1986, p. 1.
41 'The High Court's junior', *Justinian*, No 50, March 1987, p. 11.
42 *Ibid*, and the remarks were republished in 'A different kind of Justice', Fergus Shiel, 9 December 2000, *The Age,* Fairfax Digital, http://www.theage.com.au/articles/2002/12/08/103895027061.html, viewed 16 February 2009.

43 Dame Roma Mitchell was Australia's first female justice, appointed to the South Australian Supreme Court in 1962, Australia's first female QC (1965), and later Governor of South Australia (1991-96).
44 Transcript of Proceedings, *Swearing-in Ceremony, Gaudron J* (High Court of Australia, 6 February 1987) pp. 2–7; (1987) ALR xxxvii. See also 'Women Judges', Roberts, commenting on Gaudron's 'downplaying the difference that [gender] identity would make in her performance of the judicial role', p. 6 in *Feminist Constitutionalism*, CUP 2010 (forth coming).
45 Transcript of Proceedings (High Court of Australia, 6 February 1987); (1987) ALR, p. xxxviii.
46 Blackshield, personal communication with author 20 April 2010.
47 Richard Yallop, 'A battle still to be won', *The Australian*, 10 February 2003, p. 10.
48 'We all have lives', film clip 3, *The Highest Court*, 1998, ABC TV documentary broadcast, 26 May 1998, Film Art Doco, National Film and Sound Archive.
49 Justice Michael McHugh, 27 October 2004, 'Women justices for the High Court' (dinner speech, hosted by the Law Society of Western Australia), at: http://www.hcourt.gov.au/speeches/mchughj/mchughj_27oct04.html, viewed 27 June 2010.
50 There had been a long-standing tradition that High Court judges were given a knighthood shortly after their appointment. Murphy, however, refused to accept one. The last appointees to be knighted were Deane and Dawson (appointed in 1982). Thereafter, the Australian honours system replaced British knighthoods. The Order of Australia Council, chaired by Sir Anthony Mason, decided to give a Companion of the Order of Australia (AC) to all High Court Justices. Since 1987, Gaudron has been the only appointee to refuse an AC.
51 Jennie Curtin, '13 take honours but one says no', *Sydney Morning Herald*, 26 January 1988, p. 1.
52 Anne Davies and Peter Smark, 'The faces of justice', *Sydney Morning Herald*, 10 July 1993.
53 Frank Walker reports that Gaudron approved of the Order of Australia for people who had done work in or for the community beyond their job (interview with author 2 August 2008).
54 Kylie Hawkins had then just commenced in her first employment with the public service at the High Court.
55 Margot Stubbs, one of her two first Associates, interview with author 27 February 2008.
56 Tim Barrett, barrister, interview with author 7 April 2005.
57 Crispin Hull, 'A design for the people' in *Binding Authority: 100 years of the High Court of Australia*, described the aspects of the Court and made some of these observations in the *Canberra Times*, special lift out, 3 October 2003.

The Oxford Companion to the High Court has several entries about the Court's architect, Colin Madigan (pp. 452-3), the architecture of the building (pp. 27-30), the courtrooms (pp. 171-3), symbolism of the building (pp. 654-6), and artworks within it (pp. 32-4).

58   Liz Jackson, ABCTV *Four Corners*, 3 April 1995, edited transcript in *The Mason Papers*, ed. Geoffrey Lindell, The Federation Press, 2007, p. 399.
59   Sir Anthony Mason, November 2008, *23 Years on the High Court*, (speech, Probus Club, Sydney), http://www.sydneyprobus.org/Previous%20talks/23%20years%20on%20the%20High%20Court%20Mason.pdf viewed 27 April 2009.
60   *Ibid.*
61   Whealy QC, 8 May 1985 (Congratulatory speech) *Bar News*, Winter 1987, p. 11.
62   *Sir Ronald Wilson: A matter of conscience*, Buti, p. 213.
63   *Ibid.*
64   Justice Mary Gaudron, 19 September 1997 (speech, Australian Women Lawyers' Association, Melbourne).
65   Blackley, interview with author 25 September 2007.
66   *Zecevic v Director of Public Prosecutions (Vic)* (1987) 162 CLR 645.
67   Kalowski, in *The Oxford Companion to the High Court*, p. 294. Other examples cited to illustrate this are her joint judgments in *Doney v The Queen* (1990); *Edwards v The Queen* (1993); *Farrell v The Queen* (1998); *H.G. v The Queen* (1999).
68   *Jackson v Sterling Industries Ltd* (1987) 162 CLR 612.
69   *Re Bolton; Ex Parte Douglas Beane* (1987) 162 CLR 514.
70   24th Australian Legal Convention, 22 September 1987.
71   Tony Robertson, 'Judge calls for end to committal proceedings', *The Australian*, 26–27 September 1987, p. 8; Slee, 'Call for constraints on crime bodies', *Sydney Morning Herald*, 23 September 1987, p. 7; Robert Thomson, 'When two titans of the judiciary clash', *Sydney Morning Herald*, 29 September 1987, p. 15.
72   John Slee, 'Gaudron stirs old memories of Murphy', *Sydney Morning Herald*, 25 September 1987, p. 8.
73   Editorial, 'How reasonable a judge's doubts?' *Sydney Morning Herald*, 28 September 1987, p. 12.
74   Slee, 'Call for constraints on crime bodies', *Sydney Morning Herald*, 23 September 1987, p. 7; 'Judge warns of phone-tap danger', *The Sun* (Melbourne), 23 September 1987, p. 23; 'Judge sees danger in crime authorities', *Age*, 23 September 1987, p. 6; David Solomon, 'Judge calls for review of prosecuting agencies', *The Australian*, 23 September 1987, p. 2; John Slee, 'The ghost of Lionel Murphy', *Sydney Morning Herald*, 29 September 1987, p. 14.
75   *The Australian*, 10 February 2002.

NOTES 441

76 For example, 19 September 1997, 'Speech to Launch Australian Women Lawyers' published under that title in (1997) 72 *Australian Law Journal*, p. 119; 29 October 1999 (Occasional Address, University of Sydney); 13 June 2002 (Speech, Women Lawyers Association of New South Wales, 50th Anniversary Gala Dinner, NSW Parliament House, Sydney) at: http://www.hcourt.gov.au/publications_05_2.html#MaryGaudron, viewed 14 June 2010; Gaudron, *The Sir Richard Blackburn Lecture 1992*.
77 *Australian Feminist Law Journal*, Vol. 12, March 1999, 'A happy coincidence of self-interest and the public interest: Equality of opportunity for women at the Victorian Bar', p. 117 at p. 119.
78 *Ibid*.
79 Mary Gaudron, 19 September 1997 (speech, launch of Australian Women Lawyers' Association in Melbourne) 72 *Australian Law Journal*, p. 119 at p. 121.
80 Yallop, 'A battle still to be won', *The Australian*, 10 February 2003, p. 10.
81 See '"Some are more equal than others"—an empirical investigation into the voting behaviour of the Mason Court', Russell Smyth, *The Canberra Law Review*, Vol. 6, Nos. 1 & 2, 1999, 193 at 202 and Table 2 at p. 212.
82 Jeffrey Miles, personal communication with author 29 September 2009.
83 Sir Anthony Mason, interview with author 7 October 2009.
84 South Australia and Tasmania remained unrepresented on the Court.
85 *Sir Ronald Wilson*, Buti, p. 227.
86 Margot Stubbs, interview with author 27 February 2008.
87 *Sir Ronald Wilson*, Buti, p. 191.
88 *Ibid*, p. 197.

CHAPTER 14: GETTING TO MABO: THE MASON COURT AT WORK

1 Geoffrey Robertson, reported by Michele Field in 'Advocate for the good fight', Panorama, *Canberra Times*, 28 March 1998, p. 3, at p. 4.
2 Swearing in speech (1987) 162 CLR ix-xi.
3 *Inside the Mason Court Revolution*, Pierce.
4 Sir Anthony Mason, interview with author 7 October 2009.
5 Fiona Wheeler and John Williams, '"Restrained activism" in the High Court of Australia' in *Judicial Activism in Common Law Supreme Courts*, Brice Dickson (ed.), Oxford University Press, 2007, p. 20; George Williams, *Canberra Times*, 1 July 2002. See also Andrew Lynch, 'The once and future Court?' *Federal Law Review*, Vol. 28, p. 145.
6 Justice Robert French, *Ethos*, August 1998, ACT Law Society, p. 7 at p. 10; and see Jason L. Pierce, 'Speaker's Notes', *Reactions to the Mason Court: What are Australia's Judges thinking?* at: http://www.gtcentre.unsw.edu.au/publications/papers/docs/2008/351_JasonPierce.pdf, viewed 27 June 2010.
7 See Haig Patapan, 'High Court Review 2001: Politics, Legalism and the Gleeson Court', *Australian Journal of Political Science*, (2002), Vol. 37, No. 2, pp. 241-253.

8   The term 'black letter lawyers' originates from the United States Law Institute's annual restatement of the law, produced since 1921, in which in black print, the succinct and narrow proposition of the law heads the more detailed statement that follows. Over time the term has, however, been coined to describe legalistic lawyers who apply principle and logic.
9   *Swearing in of Sir Owen Dixon as Chief Justice* (1952) 85 CLR xi, xiv.
10 *The High Court and the Constitution*, Zines 5th edn, 2008, p. 603; 4th edn, 1997, pp. 429-30 quoted and commented on by George Williams, 'The High Court and the Media', *University of Technology Sydney Law Review*, 1999, Vol. 10.
11 Patapan, 'High Court Review 2001', *Australian Journal of Political Science*, (2002), p. 241-2, defines the terms.
12 Sir Anthony Mason, 'The Role of a Constitutional Court in a Federation: A Comparison of the Australian and the United States Experience' *Federal Law Review*, 1986, Vol. 16, p. 5, quoted and commented on by Andrew Lynch, 'The Once and Future Court?' *Federal Law Review*, Vol. 28, p. 156.
13 Noted by Creighton Burns, in 'Constitutional Pandora's box opens', *The Age*, 24 November 1975, p. 9.
14 *Federalism in Australia*, Geoffrey Sawer et al., Cheshire, 1949; Papers read at the fifteenth Summer School of the Australian Institute of Political Science.
15 The Australian Constitution, section 128.
16 Parliamentary Library Research Paper 2, 1999-2000, *Constitutional Referenda in Australia*, Scott Bennett and Sean Brennan, 24 August 1999 at, http://www.aph.gov.au/library/pubs/rp/1999-2000/2000rp02.htm#FACTS, viewed 28 June 2010.
17 Sawer, *Federalism in Australia*, p. 16.
18 See also Professor Leslie Zines' observations in extract from ABC's *Four Corners*, 3 April 1995, quoted in *The Mason Papers*, ed. Lindell, p. 401.
19 Sir Anthony Mason, 2008, *23 Years on the High Court*.
20 *New South Wales v Commonwealth* (1990) 169 CLR 482.
21 *New South Wales v Commonwealth (WorkChoices Case)* (2006) 229 CLR 1 at 376.
22 *Mabo v State of Queensland (Mabo No 2)* (1992) 175 CLR 1.
23 Recollection of an associate to Justice Gaudron.
24 (1987) 163 CLR 561.
25 See also Maureen Tehan, 'Difference, equality, recognition and justice: Indigenous issues in the High Court judgments of Justice Mary Gaudron' in *Public Law Review*, 2004, Vol. 15, No. 4, Law Book Co, p. 261 at pp. 320-27. On the broader issue of recognition, there had been previous criminal cases prior to 1987 in which sentencing judges had taken Aboriginal customary law into account in mitigation of sentence; see also Blackshield & Williams, 5th edn., p. 191.
26 *Yanner v Eaton* (1999) 201 CLR 351.

NOTES

27 Chief Justice Gibbs on 26 February 1986, *Mabo v Queensland* (1986) 64 ALR, 1.
28 (1988) 166 CLR 186.
29 *Mabo No. 1*, at 219.
30 See for history of action *The Mabo Decision*, commentary by Richard H Bartlett, Butterworths, 1993, pp. vi-viii.
31 Sir Anthony Mason, 2008, *23 Years on the High Court*, p. 15.
32 *Cooper v Stuart* (1889) 14 Appeal Cases 286. The Privy Council referred to NSW as 'a tract of territory practically unoccupied, without settled inhabitants or settled law' and several decisions in the NSW Supreme Court had used similar language. But none of them used the term *terra nullius*.
33 *Milirrpum v Nabalco Pty. Ltd* (The *Gove Land Rights Case*) (1971) 17 FLR 141.
34 *Politics of Law Reform*, Ross, p. 195.
35 Technically, Justice Blackburn had not been bound by *Cooper v Stuart* either. The position is set out in Blackshield & Williams, 5th ed., 2010, p. 155, where it is explained that relevant case law, 'arose within the context of the transplanted British system of Crown grants, reservations and dedications of land. The relationship of that transplanted system to any Indigenous system or scheme of interests was never in issue.'
36 For comment based on views of senior appellate judges in Australia and some barristers and officials, see *Inside the Mason Court Revolution*, Pierce.
37 *Inside the Mason Court Revolution*, Pierce, Appendix A, pp. 293-5.
38 *Ibid*, p. 211.
39 Sandra S. Berns, 'Constituting a Nation: Adjudication as Constitutive Rhetoric', *Interpreting Constitutions, Theories, Principles and Institutions*, eds. Charles Sampford and Kim Preston, Federation Press, 1996, p. 109. Berns points out that Deane and Gaudron, in expressing this view, 'fatally undermine' Brennan's 'attempted rescue' of the common law by his assertion that had the 'facts' been properly understood, the law would have recognised common law native title from the outset. See pp. 105-109 for an analysis of the use of language by Deane and Gaudron.
40 See Tehan, 'Difference, equality, recognition, justice: Indigenous issues in the High Court judgments of Justice Mary Gaudron', in *Public Law Review*, 2004, Vol. 15, No. 4, p. 261 at p. 320.
41 *Mabo* (1992) 175 CLR 1, at 91, and the story of dispossession, pp. 104–109.
42 *Mabo* (1992) 175 CLR 1, at 104.
43 *Ibid*, at 109.
44 *Inside the Mason Court Revolution*, Pierce, p. 68.
45 *Mabo* (1992) 175 CLR 1, at 120.
46 Pierce, *Inside the Mason Court Revolution*, p. 69.
47 *Ibid*.
48 *Ibid*, p. 68.

49 Pierce acknowledges that judges were divided in their views, p. 109; pp. 152-3.
50 *A Common Humanity*, Raimond Gaita, Text Publishing, Melbourne, 1999, p. 88.
51 Henry Reynolds, 'The public role of history', paper presented at the National Library of Australia conference 14–15 April 2000, by permission of NLA.
52 Researcher for *Moree Mob*, Vols. 1-3, Moree Northern Regional Library and Information Service.
53 4 June 1992, pages 2 and 3 respectively.
54 *Davis v Commonwealth* (1988) 166 CLR 79.
55 *Ibid*, at 100.
56 *Street v Queensland Bar Association* (1989) 168 CLR 461.
57 The principle established, the practical effect of the case was limited. It meant that NSW barristers could now cross State borders and practise in other States!
58 *Australian Capital Television v Commonwealth* (1992) 177 CLR 106, and in *Nationwide News Pty Ltd v Wills* (1992) 177 CLR 1.
59 *Nationwide News* (1992) 177 CLR 106 at 95. See also, *Australian Capital Television* (1992) 177 CLR 106 at 217-18.
60 *Cunliffe v Commonwealth (Migration Agents Case)* (1994) 182 CLR 272, delivered 12 October 1994. *Cunliffe* concerned the validity and operation of Pt 2A of the Migration Act, and Gaudron considered the implied constitutional freedom of political communication in the context of the Commonwealth's exercise of the aliens power (Constitution, s.51(xix)), and the validity of a law where its operation can curtail political discussion.
61 *Stephens v West Australian Newspapers Ltd* (1994) 182 CLR 211.
62 *Theophanous v Herald and Weekly Times Ltd* (1994) 182 CLR 104, Mason, Toohey and Gaudron again delivering a joint majority judgment.
63 *Lange v Australian Broadcasting Corporation* (1997) 189 CLR 520.
64 The Court held that section 116 meant 'for the purpose' of prohibiting the free exercise of religion, and that even if a law interferes with that freedom, it is valid so long as it was not enacted for that purpose. They found that the law authorising the forcible removal of Aboriginal children from their families was not a law made for the purpose of prohibiting the free exercise of religion simply because one of the objects of the law was to prevent Aboriginal parents from bringing up their children in their tribal culture. Toohey agreed with Gaudron that the section 116 implied that right, but because the case was on demurrer, he felt that without any detailed exploration of factual evidence, there was insufficient evidence to allow such a finding. Gummow, while holding that the Ordinance was not made for the purpose of prohibiting the free exercise of religion, also acknowledged the possibility that a different conclusion might be drawn if there was appropriate evidence from which it could be drawn.

65   *R v Kirby; Ex parte Boilermakers' Society of Australia* (1956) 94 CLR 254.
66   Mary Gaudron, 'Some reflections on the *Boilermakers' case*', (1995) *Journal of Industrial Relations*, Vol. 37 (2) p. 309.
67   Fiona Wheeler, 'Due process, judicial power and Chapter III in the new High Court', 2004 *Federal Law Review*, Vol. 32, No. 2 pp. 208–94.
68   *Dietrich v The Queen* (1992) 177 CLR 292 at 326.
69   Ibid.
70   Fiona Wheeler, 'Due process', pp. 209-10.
71   'The role of the courts at the turn of the century', (1993) 3 *Journal of Judicial Administration*, p. 156, at 165.
72   *Inside the Mason Court Revolution*, Pierce, p. 213; and see p. 210 where Pierce cites *Leeth* as an example of wanting to push the Court further.
73   *Inside the Mason Court Revolution*, Pierce, Introduction, p. 3.
74   *Inside the Mason Court Revolution*, Pierce, p. 211.
75   Ibid, p. 88.
76   Ibid, p. 83.
77   Pierce, Speaker's Notes, 'Reactions to the Mason Court: What are Australian Judges thinking?' p. 8, UNSW 2008 Constitutional Law Conference, at: http://www.gtcentre.unsw.edu.au/publications/papers/docs/2008/351_JasonPierce.pdf, viewed 28 May 2010.
78   (1988) 165 CLR 360.
79   *Inside the Mason Court Revolution*, Pierce, p. 210.
80   Ronald Sackville, 'Why do Judges make law? Some aspects of judicial law making', 2001, *University of Western Sydney Law Review*, p. 5.
81   Sir Anthony Mason, interview with author 7 October 2009.
82   Sir Gerard Brennan, personal communication with author 6 May 2010.
83   *The Constitutional Jurisprudence and Judicial Method of the High Court of Australia*, Dr Rachael Gray, Presidian, 2008, p. 57.
84   Mason, for example, had a Catholic mother, as Gaudron had a Catholic father, and in both cases the children were brought up as Catholics. Dawson was the exception.
85   Kirby's view is that the Constitution is a document intended to be long-lasting and that latitude in its interpretation and application has to be given to accommodate the changing times. See also Heather Roberts and John Williams, 'Constitutional Law', in *Appealing to the Future: Michael Kirby and his legacy*, eds. Ian Freckelton, SC, and Hugh Selby, Law Book Company, 2009, p. 30.
86   Wilson's biographer refers to Wilson's 'legal positivism', *Sir Ronald Wilson*, Buti, p. 189.
87   Rebecca Craske and Richard Haigh, 'Judgment production', in *The Oxford Companion to the High Court*, pp. 369-70.
88   Margot Stubbs, interview with author 27 February 2008.
89   Sir Anthony Mason, interview with author 7 October 2009.

90 Sir Anthony Mason, 2008, *23 Years on the High Court*.
91 Matthew Groves and Russell Smyth, A century of judicial style: changing patterns in judgment writing on the High Court 1903–2001, [2004] *Federal Law Review* 11, Table 1: Judgment Writing of Individual Justices, at: http://www.austlii.edu.au/au/journals/FedLRev/2004/11.html#Heading198, viewed 27 June 2010. For voting behaviour generally under Chief Justice Mason, '"Some are more equal than others"—an empirical investigation into the voting behaviour of the Mason Court', Russell Smyth, *The Canberra Law Review* (1999) Vol. 6, Nos 1 & 2.

CHAPTER 15: EQUAL JUSTICE: GAUDRON AT WORK

1 'Equality before the law with particular reference to Aborigines', (1993) *The Judicial Review*, Vol. 1, No. 2, p. 81 at p. 88.
2 'We all have lives', film clip 3, *The Highest Court*, 1998, ABC TV documentary broadcast 26 May 1998, Film Art Doco, National Film and Sound Archive.
3 Justice Mary Gaudron, 24 August 1990 (The Mitchell Oration 1990, 'In the Eye of the Law: The Jurisprudence of Equality', Adelaide); see also Mary Gaudron, address to the Bar Readers' Course, Brisbane 20 July 1994, p. 1; and Gaudron's speech, 9 October 1998, at the launch by the Victorian Bar Council of its plans for responding to *Equality of Opportunity for Women at the Victorian Bar: A Report* commissioned and published by the Victorian Bar Council, Melbourne.
4 Article based on 'Speech to launch Australian Women Lawyers', Melbourne, 19 September 1997, *The Australian Law Journal*, Vol. 72, 119, p. 123. The launch of AWL attracted the highest attendance of all events at the 30th Australian Legal Convention.
5 Justice Mary Gaudron, 19 September 1997 (Speech, launch of Australian Women Lawyers, Melbourne), published, *The Australian Law Journal*, Vol. 72, 119, p. 123.
6 SG 403/86, 25 July 1986.
7 *Equality: The Guarantee of Excellence*, Australian Women Lawyers, Sydney, 29 September 2006. And see *Speech to Launch Australian Women Lawyers*, 1998 *Australian Law Journal* Vol. 72, 119, p. 123. Gaudron expresses this in a range of cases, *Leeth v Commonwealth* (1992) 174 CLR 455, being an example.
8 Gaudron, 24 August 1990, 'In the Eye of the Law'; and see *Street v Queensland Bar Association* (1989), 168 CLR 461 at 571 and 573-4. See also, Tehan, 'Difference, equality, recognition, justice', *Public Law Review*, 2004, Vol. 15, No. 4, Law Book Co, p. 261 at p. 320.
9 Gaudron, 19 September 1997, *Australian Law Journal*, Vol. 72, 119, p. 123. See *Castlemaine Tooheys v South Australia* (1990) 169 CLR 436, 480, in which Gaudron and McHugh delivered a joint judgment; *Street v Queensland Bar Association* (1989) 168 CLR 461.

NOTES 447

10 *Street v Queensland Bar Association* (1989) 168 CLR 461 at 571–3.
11 'The High Court's Conception of Discrimination: Origins, Applications, and Implications', Amelia Simpson, [2007] *Sydney Law Review* 10, p. 267
12 Foreword, p. vii, *The Hidden Gender of Law*, 2nd edn., Regina Graycar, Jenny Morgan, The Federation Press, 2002.
13 1997, speaking at the launch of Australian Women Lawyers.
14 Gaudron, *Sir Richard Blackburn Lecture 1992*, pp. 1–2.
15 *Daniel v Belton* (1968) 12 FLR 101, at p. 104.
16 *Leeth v Commonwealth* (1992) 174 CLR 455.
17 *Ibid*; and see Chief Justice Marilyn Warren, 'Justice Gaudron's contribution to the jurisprudence of the criminal law', in *Public Law Review*, 2004, Vol. 15, No. 4, Law Book Co, p. 261 at p. 328.
18 *Kruger* (1997) 190 CLR 1. In other cases Gaudron developed and adjusted her notion of equality and the concept of discrimination, for example, *Kartinyeri v Commonwealth* (the *Hindmarsh Island Bridge Case*) (1998) 195 CLR 337; *Austin v Commonwealth* (2003) 215 CLR 185 (joint judgment of Gaudron, Gummow and Hayne); *Wong v The Queen* (2001) 207 CLR 584 (joint judgment of Gaudron, Gummow and Hayne, especially at p. 608: 'Equal justice requires identity of outcome in cases that are relevantly identical. It requires different outcomes in cases that are different in some relevant respect').
19 *Street v Queensland Bar Association* (1989) 63 ALJR 715 at pp. 759-60; *Castlemaine Tooheys Ltd v South Australia* (1990) 169 CLR 436, joint judgment with McHugh, at p. 478.
20 *Australian Iron and Steel Pty. Ltd. v Banovic* (1989) 168 CLR 165.
21 *Van Gervan v Fenton* (1992) 175 CLR 327.
22 *Ibid*, at 350.
23 *Leeth v Commonwealth* (1992) 174 CLR, 455 (Gaudron, at 502).
24 *Street v Queensland Bar Association* (1989) 168 CLR 461; Gaudron 564 at 570–4, and see Mason CJ at 487–9; Brennan at 508–11; Deane at 528-9; Toohey at 555; *Castlemaine Tooheys Ltd. v South Australia*, (1990) 169 CLR 436, at 478.
25 Wheeler, 'Due process' p. 207. See Wheeler's introduction, p. 205, where she provides case examples of the Court's recognition that litigants are entitled to a minimum level of procedural due process, and of Deane and Gaudron going further in arguing that the due process principle guaranteed a fair trial for a federal offence, prohibited the application of retroactive federal criminal laws (*Polyukovich v Commonwealth (the War Crimes case)* (1991) 172 CLR 501 (Gaudron at 704-8)), and required 'equal justice' in the exercise of federal judicial power.
26 *McKinney v The Queen* (1991) 171 CLR 468 at 478.
27 *Dietrich v The Queen* (1992) 177 CLR 292.
28 Sir Anthony Mason, interview with author 7 October 2009.
29 *McInnis v The Queen* (1979) 143 CLR 575, at p. 592.

30 *Inside the Mason Court Revolution*, Pierce, pp. 52-53.
31 *Ridgeway v The Queen* (1995) 184 CLR 19.
32 *Ibid*, p. 78.
33 *Nicholas v The Queen* (1998) 193 CLR 173.
34 Kalowski in *The Oxford Companion to the High Court*, p. 295.
35 *Nicholas v The Queen* (1998) 193 CLR 173, at 211.
36 *Ridgeway v The Queen* (1995) 184 CLR 19, at 78.
37 See discussion of *Nicholas* by Wheeler, 'Due process', p. 8.
38 (1998) 193 CLR 173, at 208–9.
39 *Bass v Permanent Trustee Co Ltd* (1999) 198 CLR 334, at 359.
40 Gaudron, at pp. 183–4.
41 *Nolan v Minister for Immigration and Ethnic Affairs* (1988) 165 CLR 178. For a detailed examination of the issue see Kim Rubenstein, 'Citizenship and the Centenary—Inclusion and Exclusion in 20th Century Australia', *Melbourne University Law Review*, 2000, p. 24. See also Kim Rubenstein, 'Citizenship', in *The Oxford Companion to the High Court*, p. 99.
42 *Chu Kheng Lim v Minister for Immigration, Local Government and Ethnic Affairs* ('*Lim*') (1992) 176 CLR 1 at 53.
43 *Ibid*, (note omitted).
44 *Re Patterson; Ex parte Taylor* (2001) 207 CLR 391, Gaudron, McHugh, Kirby and Callinan making up the majority.
45 *Re Minister for Immigration and Multicultural Affairs; Ex parte Te* (2002) 212 CLR 162 at 179.
46 *Ibid*, at 178.
47 Cheryl Saunders, 'Interpreting the Constitution' in *Public Law Review*, 2004, Vol. 15, No. 4, Law Book Co, p. 261 at p. 294.
48 *Shaw v Minister for Immigration and Multicultural Affairs* (2003) 218 CLR 28.
49 (1999) 199 CLR 462.
50 Kim Rubenstein, 'Meanings of membership: Mary Gaudron's contributions to Australian citizenship' in *Public Law Review*, 2004, Vol. 15, No. 4, Law Book Co, p. 261 at p. 313.
51 *Minister of State for Immigration & Ethnic Affairs v Ah Hin Teoh* ('*Teoh*') (1995) 183 CLR 273.
52 *Ibid*, at 303.
53 *Ibid*, p. 304.
54 *Ibid*.
55 *Kruger v Commonwealth* (the *Stolen Generation* case) (1997) 190 CLR 1.
56 *Teoh*, p. 304.
57 *The High Court and the Constitution*, Zines, 5th ed., p. 288.
58 *Chu Kheng Lim v Minister for Immigration Local Government & Ethnic Affairs* (1992) 176 CLR 1.
59 *Ibid*, at 55.
60 Some judges came to this conclusion because of their view that Ch. 111 provisions did not apply to the Commonwealth's exercise of its power to

legislate with respect to the Territories. Toohey, Gummow and Gaudron found so because of the evident welfare purpose of the legislation, although Gaudron preferred not to rely on the test of whether the detention was 'non-punitive'.
61 *Kruger* (1997) 190 CLR 1, at 110.
62 *The High Court and the Constitution*, Zines, 5th ed., p. 288; *Al-Kateb v Godwin* (2004) 219 CLR 562.
63 *Re Woolleys* (2004) 225 CLR 1 at 13-14.
64 *Fardon v Attorney General* (Qld) (2004) 223 CLR 575 at 653.
65 *The High Court and the Constitution*, Zines, 5th ed. p. 290, cites Gummow, for example, in *Al Kateb v Godwin* (2004) 219 CLR 562, at 610–11.
66 Blackshield points to her judgments in *Newcrest Mining (WA) Ltd v Commonwealth* (1997) 190 CLR 513 and *Northern Territory v GPAO* (1999) 196 CLR 553, by way of examples (personal communication with author 20 April 2010).
67 Blackshield, personal communication with author 20 April 2010.

CHAPTER 16: ADAPTING TO CHANGE
1 Gaudron, in the course of an interview with a new Associate in 1995.
2 Margo Kingston, 'Gaudron tipped to be Chief Justice', *Sydney Morning Herald*, 22 October 1994, pp. 1 and 13; Michelle Coffey, 'Mary, Mary riding High', *Herald Sun*, 27 October, 1994, p. 13; Milton Cockburn, 'Mary Gaudron ponders another first', *Sydney Morning Herald*, 19 November 1994, p. 3; Kate Legge, 'Gaudron's law', *Weekend Australian Review*, 19–20 November 1994, p. 1.
3 Cockburn, 'Mary Gaudron ponders another first', *Sydney Morning Herald*, 19 November 1994, p. 3; Bernard Lane, 'Gaudron baulks at High Court's top job', *The Australian*, 14 February 1995, gathered from legal sources that Gaudron's view was that her promotion, not being the most senior justice on the bench, would call judicial independence into question.
4 Gaudron later told a friend.
5 Frank Walker, interview with author 2 August 2008.
6 *Ibid.*
7 Sir Gerard Brennan, personal communication to author 6 May 2010.
8 *Ibid.*
9 See *The Brennan Legacy: Blowing the winds of legal orthodoxy*, eds Robin Creyke, Patrick Keyzer, The Federation Press, 2002.
10 Brennan implied no criticism in making this observation. He stated that he was not conscious of any judgment of the Mason Court that was not logically defensible (personal communication 6 May 2010).
11 George Williams, *Canberra Times*, 14 November 2005, Opinion p. 11, suggests that when Deane left in 1995 to take up the appointment of Governor-General, McHugh moved towards a more legalistic approach, and that Brennan was influenced by his shift.
12 *Wik Peoples v State of Queensland* (1996) 187 CLR 1.

13 Henry Reynolds, *The Public Role of History*, 2000, by permission of the National Library of Australia.
14 *The Great Land Grab*, Michael Bachelard, Hyland House, 1997, p. 59.
15 *Wik Peoples*, at 209.
16 See 'An overview of the Wik decision', Daniel Gal (1997) *University of New South Wales Law Journal*, 488, http://www.austlii.edu.au/au/journals/UNSWLJ/1997/5.html viewed 15 March 2010.
17 *Wik Peoples* at 204.
18 Garth Nettheim, '*Wik*', in *The Oxford Companion to the High Court*, p. 712.
19 Justice Bill Gummow, interview with author 12 April 2010.
20 James Woodford, 'Fischer lashes High Court on Wik', *Sydney Morning Herald*, 11 January 1997, p. 1.
21 Niki Savva, 'Fischer seeks a more conservative court', *The Age*, 5 March 1997, p. 1; Kathryn Bice, 'Pledge on next Chief Justice', *Australian Financial Review*, 6 March 1997, p. 8; Ross Peake, 'Judges make targets of themselves with a capital T: Howard', *Canberra Times*, 6 March 1997.
22 Woodford, 'Fischer lashes High Court on Wik', *Sydney Morning Herald*, 11 January 1997, p. 1.
23 Alan Ramsey, 'High Court gets short shrift', *Sydney Morning Herald*, 8 March 1997, p. 43.
24 Gervase Greene, 'Attorney pleads for peace in court row', *The Age*, 1 March 1997, p. 5; and see 'Fischer won't be muzzled', *Daily Telegraph*, 1 March 1997, p. 2; Adrian Rollins, 'Attacks "undermine" role of High Court', *Sunday Age*, 9 March 1997, p. 9.
25 Savva, 'Fischer seeks a more conservative court', *The Age*, 5 March 1997, p. 1.
26 Bice, 'Pledge on next Chief Justice', *Australian Financial Review*, 6 March 1997, p. 8.
27 Innes Willox, 'Deputy PM maintains court attack', *The Age*, 28 April 1997, p. 4.
28 Bernard Lane, John Kerin and Dennis Shanahan, 'Conservative to fill High Court vacancy', *The Australian*, 13 August 1997, p. 1.
29 Karen Middleton, Laura Tingle and Tim Colebatch, 'Victorian appointed a High Court judge', *The Age*, 13 August 1997, p. 3.
30 *Ibid.*
31 Margo Kingston, 'The assault on dissent', *Sydney Morning Herald*, 11 October 1997, p. 1.
32 Helen McCabe, 'Balancing the scales', *Daily Telegraph*, 19 December 1997, p. 4.
33 Lane, 'Conservative tilts bench', *The Australian*, 19 December 1997, p. 1; David Marr, '"Civilised Bloke" is just the right man for the job', *Sydney Morning Herald*, 19 December 1997, p. 2.
34 Ian Callinan, QC, 18 December 1997, reported by Lane, 'Conservative tilts bench', *The Australian*, 19 December 1997, p. 1.

35 See Nicholas Hasluck, 'Callinan, Ian David Francis' in *The Oxford Companion to the High Court*, p. 78.
36 *Inside the Mason Court Revolution: The High Court of Australia transformed*, Pierce, p. 280.
37 Published by Central Queensland University Press, 1997.
38 Comment in presence of author 5 March 1998; Canberra Press Gallery journalist (conversation with author 1998); and other legal sources.
39 Tony Blackshield, personal communication to author 20 April 2010.
40 When controversies about Callinan erupted, Murray Gleeson was appointed Chief Justice, and von Doussa missed out on an appointment to the Court. Von Doussa was later appointed President of the Human Rights Commission in 2003.
41 *Kartinyeri v The Commonwealth* (1998) 156 ALR 300.
42 Transcript of proceedings, Brennan, *Kartinyeri and Anor v The Commonwealth of Australia* A29/1997 (18 February 1998).
43 *Kartinyeri v The Commonwealth* (1998) 156 ALR 300.
44 Conversation in presence of author 5 March 1998.
45 Roderick Campbell, 'Court links Callinan to process abuse', *Canberra Times*, 16 July 1998, p. 1.
46 *White Industries (Qld) Pty Ltd v Flower & Hart (a firm)*, (1998), ALR 169; *Flower & Hart (a firm) v White Industries (Qld) Pty Ltd*, [1999] FCA 773 (11 June 1999).
47 Roderick Campbell, 'Law council urges Government to act over Callinan', *Canberra Times*, 22 July 1998, p. 1; Roderick Campbell, 'Opposition backs Law Council's call for Callinan inquiry', *Canberra Times*, 23 July 1998, p. 3; Roderick Campbell, 'Attorney General says no to Callinan problem', *Canberra Times*, 27 August 1998, p. 3; Margo Kingston, 'Government refuses to act over Callinan', *Sydney Morning Herald*, 27 August 1998, p. 2; Roderick Campbell, 'ALP calls for inquiry into judge's conduct', *Canberra Times*, 13 June 1999, p. 3.
48 In 1980 Senator Gareth Evans unsuccessfully formally moved for a committee to examine various financial interests of Chief Justice Barwick.
49 Kingston, 'Government refuses to act over Callinan', *Sydney Morning Herald*, 27 August 1998, p. 2; *Canberra Times*, 27 August 1998, p. 3.
50 For a full account of the controversy see A. R. Blackshield, 'The Appointment and Removal of Federal Judges', in *The Australian Federal Judicial System*, eds. Brian Opeskin and Fiona Wheeler, Melbourne University Press, 2000, p. 400 and pp. 422-6.
51 Friends and colleagues.
52 Ian Callinan, telephone conversation with author 4 May 2010.
53 *Kartinyeri v Commonwealth* (1998) 195 CLR 337.
54 See Kalowski, *The Oxford Companion to the High Court*, p. 295; and Cheryl Saunders 'Interpreting the Constitution' in *Public Law Review*, 2004, Vol. 15, No. 4, Law Book Co, p. 261 at p. 294.

55 *Wilson v The Minister for Aboriginal and Torres Islander Affairs* (1996) 189 CLR 1.
56 Refer Justice Jane Mathews interviewed by John Farquharson, 23 October 2001, ORAL TRC 4647, National Library of Australia (Tape 2, 'Women in the law and at the Bar') for a detailed account of the litigation, and Mathews' suggestion that but for the cultural vulnerability of the women, their claim might have been resolved satisfactorily before reaching the High Court.
57 *Kartinyeri v Commonwealth* (1998) 195 CLR 337; Gaudron, 359 at 367.
58 Blackshield, personal communication to author 20 April 2010.
59 Observation of Gaudron's capacity by an associate of the High Court.
60 Fia Cumming, 'Gaudron to quit High Court?' *Sun Herald*, 5 April 1998, p. 21; personal communication to author, 3 May 1998.
61 Jack Waterford, *Canberra Times*, 1 April 1998, pp. 1 and 2.
62 'Lone rangers through the legal thickets', *Canberra Times*, Public Sector Informant, May 2003.
63 In an address to the Australian Bar Association, 2000, commented upon by Leslie Zines, 'Gleeson Court', in *The Oxford Companion to the High Court*, p. 307.
64 Leslie Zines, 'The Present State of Constitutional Interpretation', in *The High Court at the Crossroads*, eds. Adrienne Stone and George Williams, Federation Press, 2000, pp. 224 and 238. See Patapan, 'High Court Review 2001', *Australian Journal of Political Science* (2002), pp. 241 and 22-3, where his discussion of the meaning of 'legalism' reveals a more complex picture.
65 *Yanner v Eaton* (1999) 201 CLR 351.
66 (1999) 198 CLR 511. The case concerned the constitutional validity of cross-vesting of jurisdiction, in particular, the vesting of state companies law jurisdiction in the Federal Court.
67 Gaudron, July 1987 (*Sir Samuel Griffith Memorial Lecture*).
68 *Australian Law News*, Vol. 22 No. 6, July 1987, p. 6, 'Justice Gaudron calls for an "Australian" judicial system', reporting on her expressed view in the 1987 Sir Samuel Griffith Memorial Lecture.
69 193 CLR 346, 511.
70 See Michael Coper, 'Tied vote', in *The Oxford Companion to the High Court*, p. 672.
71 Sir Anthony Mason, interview with author 7 October 2009.
72 Michael Kirby, interview with author 14 August 2009.
73 *Re Wakim* (1999) 198 CLR 511, Kirby at 598-9.
74 *Director of Public Prosecutions v B* (1998) 194 CLR 566 at 609. Roderick Campbell, 'Kirby criticizes judges for "unhelpful" answers', *Canberra Times*, 24 July 1998, p. 4.
75 Michael Kirby, 'Judgment in black and white', Fairfax digital *Canberra Times*, 1 August 2002, at http://www.canberratimes.com.au/news/local/news/columns/judgment-in-black-and-white/660629.aspx?storypage=0, viewed 28 June 2010.
76 *Pelechowski v Registrar, (Court of Appeal)* 198 CLR 435 at 492.

77 *Sydney Morning Herald*, Fairfax Digital, 'Now history will be the judge', David Marr, 31 January 2009, at: http://www.smh.com.au/articles/2009/01/30/1232818725589.html?page=3, viewed 4 September 2009.
78 Gaudron, remark in presence of author 5 March 1998.
79 *Garcia v National Australia Bank Ltd*, application for leave, 4 March 1998. Gaudron expressed her feelings about the exchange privately the next day. Transcript at http://www.austlii.edu.au/au/other/HCATrans/1998/50.html, viewed 14 June 2010.
80 *Garcia v National Australia Bank Ltd* (1998) 194 CLR 395.
81 Justice Bill Gummow, interview with author 12 April 2010.
82 His speech in which he mentioned many of the guests present is accessible at http://www.michaelkirby.com.au/index.php?option=com_content&view=article&id=79:judicial-farewell&catid=13:2009&Itemid=93, viewed 27 May 2010.
83 Observations of one of the guests.
84 See Frank Brennan, 'My friend Justice Kirby', *Eureka Street*, Vol. 19, Issue 2, 2 February 2009, at: http://www.eurekastreet.com.au/uploads/File/pdf/090202.pdf, viewed 2 April 2009.
85 ABC *7.30 Report*, 'Justice Kirby accepts Heffernan's apology', Fran Kelly, 19 March 2002, transcript at http://www.abc.net.au/7.30/content/2002/s508367.htm, viewed 23 May 2009.
86 Standing Order 193(3). See *Australasian Parliamentary Review*, ed. J. R. Nethercote, Spring, 2002, Vol. 17, No 2, News and Notes p. 3.
87 *Sunday Telegraph*, 17 March 2002, p. 1; see also Michelle Grattan and Mike Seccombe, 'Heffernan sunk by false claims', *Sydney Morning Herald*, 19 March 2002, p. 1, showing the name of Ian Sinclair, former National Party MP, as a traveller who also thought it unlikely he was in Sydney that Easter.
88 ABC radio transcript, *7.30 Report*, Fran Kelly, 'Justice Kirby accepts Heffernan's apology', 19 March 2002, at http://www.abc.net.au/7.30/content/2002/s508367.htm, viewed 28 June 2010.
89 The story is reported in the *Canberra Times*, 27 June 2009, 'Forum', p. 5; *The Australian*, 15 December 2008; also *Melbourne Star*, 'Asking for trouble: Michael Kirby and the homophobes', March 2002, at: http://www.adam-carr.net/bnews/2002/bnm2.txt, viewed 5 August 2008; Staples, interview 22 September 2002; Stubbs, interview 27 February 2008.
90 Jack Waterford, 'Courting trouble: the judiciary's woes', *Canberra Times*, The Public Sector Informant, April 2002, p. 7. See also, Patapan, 'High Court Review 2001' *Australian Journal of Political Science*, (2002), p. 245 on Williams' attitude to protecting the dignity of the Court.
91 Staples, interview with author 22 September 2002; Stubbs, interview with author 27 February 2008.
92 Michael Kirby, personal communication to author 13 February 2010.
93 The Chief Justice wrote to the Government but the request was all but ignored. See Mark Metherell, *Sydney Morning Herald*, 'Ruddock

refuses Kirby on same-sex pensions', July 13, 2007, http://www.smh.com.au/news/national/ruddock-refuses-kirby-on-samesex-pensions/2007/07/12/1183833688051.html, viewed 14 February 2010. After the election of the Rudd Government the changes were passed, and just before Justice Kirby's retirement.
94 Leonie Wood, 'Exit the great dissenter', *The Australian*, 15 December 2008; Fairfax digital: *WA Today National*, 30 January 2009, http://www.watoday.com.au/national/exit-the-great-dissenter-20090130-7u19.html; Doug Conway, 'Time's up for the great dissenter', *Independent Weekly*, 29 January 2009, http://www.independentweekly.com.au/news/local/news/general/times-up-for-the-great-dissenter/1419582.aspx, on line reports viewed 21 February 2009.
95 Jade Tyrell and Bonita Silva, 'Justice Kirby interview', *Vertigo*, 16 February 2009, http://www.utsvertigo.com/2009/02/justice-kirby-interview/ viewed 7 July 2009.
96 Ian Freckelton, SC, *Appealing to the Future: Michael Kirby and his legacy*, Ian Freckelton, SC, and Hugh Selby (eds.), Law Book Company, 2009, p. 30.

CHAPTER 17: LAW, GAUDRON-STYLE
1 Gaudron, 2005 (speech, UNIFEM).
2 Sir Anthony Mason, interview with author 7 October 2009.
3 Justice Bill Gummow, interview with author 12 April 2010.
4 *Ibid*.
5 Sir Anthony Mason, interview with author 7 October 2009; Justice Bill Gummow, interview 12 April 2010.
6 Ian Callinan, telephone conversation with author 4 May 2010.
7 *Ibid*.
8 Frank Walker, interview with author 2 August 2008.
9 http://www.law.uts.edu.au/careers/graduates/1998/ug5may1998.html, viewed 15 August 2009.
10 P. Fogarty and N.C. Weber, 'The smoothness criterion as a trend diagnostic', *Journal of Applied Mathematics and Decision Sciences*, School of Mathematics and Statistics, University of Sydney, 2006.
11 *The Age*, 'Judge rejects bid on "nigger" sign', 20 March 2002, at: http://www.theage.com.au/articles/2002/03/19/1016519809826.html, viewed 14 July 2009.
12 *Hagan v Trustees of the Toowoomba Sports Ground Trust* B17/2001, 19 March 2002, HCA Transcript 132.
13 Michael Kirby, interview with author 14 August 2009; 'Justice Kirby accepts senator's apology', *Daily Telegraph*, 20 March 2002, p. 4.
14 Transcript, p. 2. See also, Ernst Willheim, 'Australia's Racial Vilification Law Found Wanting? "Nigger Brown" Saga: HREOC, the Federal Court, the High Court and the Committee on the Elimination of Racial

Discrimination', (2004) 4, *Asia-Pacific Journal on Human Rights and the Law*, No 1.
15 'The Golden Thread at the Heart of Tort Law: Protection of the Vulnerable', Jane Stapleton, *Centenary Essays for the High Court of Australia*, ed. Peter Cane, Butterworths, 2004, p. 254; Willheim, 'Australia's Racial Vilification Law Found Wanting?' (2004) 4, *Asia-Pacific Journal on Human Rights and the Law*, No 1. A petition on Hagan's behalf to the United Nations Committee on the Elimination of Racial Discrimination eventually resulted in a recommendation that the sign be removed.
16 *U v U* (2002) 211 CLR 238.
17 *Van Gervan v Fenton* (1992) 175 CLR 327.
18 *U v U* (2002) 211 CLR 238 at 248.
19 Interview by Monica Attard, ABC radio, 16 November 2003, *Sunday Profile*.
20 *U v U* S256/2001 [2002] HCATrans 155 (11 April 2002), at http://www.austlii.edu.au/au/other/HCATrans/2002/155.html, viewed 17 July 2010.
21 *Ibid*. See also the views Gaudron expressed in *AMS v AIF* (1999) 199 CLR 16, at 180, a similar case, in which she wrote a separate majority decision.
22 Ruth McColl, President of the NSW Bar Association, later Justice of the NSW Court of Appeal, interview with Damien Carrick, Radio National, *The Law Report*, 'Changing of the Guard at the High Court', 4 February 2003, referring to a special leave application before the High Court; and see 'Sit Down Girlie', (2003) *Alternative Law Journal*, Vol. 28, No. 1, p. 41.
23 *CES v Superclinics (Australia) Pty Ltd* (1995) 38 NSWLR 47.
24 *Superclinics Australia Pty Ltd v CES & Ors* S88 (1996) HCA Transcript 357 (11 September 1996).
25 *Superclinics Australia Pty Ltd v CES & Ors* S88 (1996) HCA Transcript 359 (12 September 1996).
26 Interview by Monica Attard, ABC radio, 16 November 2003, *Sunday Profile*.
27 The *Migration Reform Act 1992* (the *Reform Act*) commenced 1 September 1994; See Linda J. Kirk, 'Chapter III and Legislative Interference with the Judicial Process: *Abebe v Commonwealth* and *Nicholas v The Queen*', in *The High Court at the Crossroads*, eds. Stone and Williams, p. 119 and 127, for a history of the legislation.
28 Sections 475 and 478 of the *Migration Act 1958* (Cth).
29 *Abebe v Commonwealth* (1999) 197 CLR 510.
30 See *The High Court and the Constitution*, Zines, 5th ed. p. 607.
31 *Abebe v Commonwealth* (1999) 197 CLR 510; Gaudron: at 552-3, 550; Gummow and Hayne at 561.
32 *Minister for Immigration and Multicultural Affairs v Yusuf* (2001) 206 CLR 323.
33 *Migration Legislation Amendment (Judicial Review) Act 2001* which included a new Part 8 of the *Migration Act* in which section 474 was inserted. Section 474 declared that administrative decisions by an immigration official or one of the tribunals that reviewed the decisions would be 'final and conclusive and must

not be challenged, appealed against, reviewed, quashed or called in question in any court'.
34 Ruddock, second reading: *Migration Legislation Amendment (Judicial Review) Bill 2001*, House of Representatives, *Debates*, 26 September 2001, p. 31559.
35 Section 474 provoked controversy among lawyers. A statutory provision which seeks to remove from the courts their power to review an administrative action is referred to as a *privative clause*.
36 *Deputy Commissioner of Taxation of the Commonwealth of Australia v Richard Walter Pty Ltd* (1995) 183 CLR 168.
37 *Plaintiff S157/2002 v Commonwealth*, transcript 4 September 2002, [2002] HCA Trans 423.
38 Ibid. Decision: *Plaintiff S157/2002 v Commonwealth* (2003) 211 CLR 476.
39 Evidence of Professor Kim Rubenstein cited in Senate Legal and Constitutional Legislation Committee, Parliament of Australia, Canberra, Inquiry into *Migration Legislation Amendment Bill (No 4) 1997*; *Migration Legislation Amendment Bill (No 5) 1997* (1997) 31.
40 Sarah Ford, 'Judicial Review of Migration Decisions: Ousting the *Hickman* Privative Clause?' [2002] MULR 28, at: http://www.austlii.edu.au/au/journals/MULR/2002/28.html, viewed 2 April 2009.
41 *Minister for Immigration & Multicultural Affairs v Bhardwaj* (2002), 209 CLR 597.
42 *Plaintiff S157/2002 v Commonwealth* (2002) 211 CLR 476.
43 *275-02 v MIMIA and Anor, S200/2002*, 23 September 2002, Chambers in Sydney; *Applicant S275-02 v MIMIA & Anor S200/2002* [2002] HCATrans 465 (23 September 2002).
44 'Theories of Constitutional interpretation: a taxonomy', delivered 3 May 2007, published in *Bar News*, Winter 2007, p. 12.
45 Swearing in of Justice John Dyson Heydon, High Court of Australia, transcript C0/2003 [2003] HCATrans 562 (11 February 2003) at http://www.austlii.edu.au/au/other/HCATrans/2003/562.html, viewed 16 July 2010.
46 Fiona Wheeler and John Williams, '"Restrained Activism" in the High Court of Australia', in *Judicial Activism in Common Law Supreme Courts*, ed. Brice Dickson, Oxford University Press, 2007, p. 51.
47 *Leeth v Commonwealth* (1992), 174 CLR 455, at 503.
48 Originally co-authored with Justices Roderick Meagher and John Lehane. In the book's fourth edition, 2002, Justice Dyson Heydon replaced Gummow as a co-editor.
49 Sir Gerard Brennan, personal communication with author 6 May 2010.
50 Legge described Gaudron as 'a curious mix of ideological passion and intellectual discipline', 'Gaudron's law', *Weekend Australian Review*, 19–20 November 1994, p. 1.
51 *Patrick Stevedores Operations No. 2 Pty Ltd v Maritime Union of Australia* (1998) 195 CLR 1, at 49.

52 It became the subject of an ABC docudrama in 2007.
53 *Rogers v Whitaker* (1992) 175 CLR 479.
54 *Bolam v Friern Hospital Management Committee* (1957) 1 WLR, at p. 587, which held that a medical practitioner is not guilty of negligence if he or she acts in accordance with a practice accepted as proper by a responsible body of doctors skilled in the relevant field of practice.
55 Gaudron, in *Breen v Williams ('Medical Records Access case')* (1996) 186 CLR 71, summarising the effect of *Rogers v Whitaker*.
56 *Rogers v Whitaker* (1992) 175 CLR 479 at 493.
57 *Rogers v Whitaker* (1992) 175 CLR 479, at 494. And see, 'Does a doctor have a duty to provide information and advice about complementary and alternative medicine?', Elizabeth Brophy, *Journal of Law and Medicine*, Vol. 10, No. 3, February 2003, p. 271, at pp. 275, 279.
58 *Chappel v Hart* (1998) 195 CLR 232.
59 *Ibid*, at 520.
60 *Naxakis v Western General Hospital* (1999) 197 CLR 269.
61 In *Rosenberg v Percival* (2001) 205 CLR 434 at 456; Gummow referred to Gaudron's statement in *Rogers v Whitaker*, about the need for a risk to be real and foreseeable. See also Ian Freckelton, 'The new duty to warn', in *Alternative Law Journal* [1999] Vol. 4, at: http://www.austlii.edu.au/au/journals/AltLJ/1999/4.html, viewed 7 June 2010.
62 Sir Anthony Mason, interview with author 7 October 2009.
63 *Cameron v The Queen* (2002) 209 CLR 339, see McHugh J at pp. 352–3. Some members of the Court indicated support for the idea that Federal judicial power must be exercised in accordance with 'equal justice'.
64 *Ebner v Official Trustee in Bankruptcy* (2000) 205 CLR, 337; see Wheeler, 'Due process', Vol. 32, No. 2 (2004) *Federal Law Review*, p. 205 at p. 215.
65 *Ebner* at p. 368.
66 *Roberts v Bass* (2002) 212 CLR 1 at 55, discussed by Wheeler, 'Due process', (2004) *Federal Law Review*, p. 224.
67 *Ibid*.
68 Blackshield, personal communication to author 20 April 2010.
69 The difference between the two approaches is explained by Christine Parker, 'Protection of judicial process as an implied constitutional principle', (1994) 16 *Adelaide Law Review* 341 at 350-5.
70 Adrienne Stone, 'Justice Gaudron and constitutional rights' in *Public Law Review*, 2004, Vol. 15, No. 4, Law Book Co, p. 261 at p. 304. Stone also stated that Gaudron's concept of discrimination 'became a pervasive feature of her interpretation of the Constitution'.
71 Cheryl Saunders, 'Interpreting the Constitution' in *Public Law Review*, 2004, Vol. 15, No. 4, Law Book Co, p. 261 at p. 294.
72 University of NSW constitutional law professor, George Williams, reported by Yallop, in 'A battle still to be won', *The Australian*, 10 February 2003, p. 10.

73 Fergus Shiel, 'A different kind of Justice', *The Age*, 9 December 2000, Fairfax Digital, http://www.theage.com.au/articles/2002/12/08/103895027061.html, viewed 16 February 2009.
74 Swearing in of Justice John Dyson Heydon, High Court of Australia, transcript C0/2003 [2003] HCATrans 562 (11 February 2003) at http://www.austlii.edu.au/au/other/HCATrans/2003/562.html, viewed 16 July 2010.
75 Ibid.
76 Interview with author 7 October 2009; and see Fergus Shiel, 'A different kind of Justice', *The Age*, 9 December 2000, the *Age*, Fairfax Digital, http://www.theage.com.au/articles/2002/12/08/103895027061.html, viewed 16 February 2009.
77 McColl, 4 February 2003, *The Law Report*, 'Changing of the guard at the High Court' , Radio National, interview with Damien Carrick, http://www.abc.net.au/rn/talks/8.30/lawrpt/stories/s774889.htm, viewed 24 June 2010.
78 Legge, 'Gaudron's law', *Weekend Australian Review*, 19-20 November 1994, p. 4.
79 Justice Jane Mathews interviewed by John Farquharson, 23 October 2001, ORAL TRC 4647, National Library of Australia (Tape 2, 'Women in the law and at the Bar').

CHAPTER 18: MOVING ON: A TIME TO SPEAK OUT
1 Gaudron wrote this in a note to a High Court colleague in 1995, telling the tale in a speech 19 September 1997 (Australian Women Lawyers' Association, Melbourne).
2 *New South Wales v Lepore* (2003) 212 CLR 511.
3 Benjamin Haslem, 'Women lawyers must dare to be themselves', *Weekend Australian*, 20-21 September 1997, p. 5, reporting Gaudron's words the previous day at a speech to Australian Women Lawyers in Melbourne. During the year 1996-97 Gaudron noted that women appeared to put argument only twice before the Full Bench of the High Court.
4 Justice Goldberg, Victorian Bar dinner address, 'Living legends at the Bar', 29 August 2003, *Victorian Bar News*, No. 126, Spring 2003.
5 David Curtain, QC, President of the Australian Bar Association, 10 February 2003, speech at a dinner at the High Court of Australia to welcome new silks, and to honour Justice Mary Gaudron, reported on the Victorian Bar website, http://www.vicbar.com.au/webdata/VicBarNewsFiles/124%20Career.pdf as at 5 June 2009.
6 *Subordination: Feminism and social theory*, Clare Burton, George Allen & Unwin, Sydney, 1985, p. 132.
7 Bernard Lane, 'Men fear equality of sexes', *Weekend Australian*, 15-16 July 2000, p. 1.
8 Ibid.
9 The view that women have to be better than men but that, fortunately, this is not very difficult, was first articulated by Charlotte Whillon, a former mayor

of Ottawa. Gaudron repeated it in a speech to launch the Australian Women Lawyers' Association, 19 September 1997.
10 Gaudron, *The Sir Richard Blackburn Lecture 1992*, p. 10.
11 Gaudron's words were quoted by Professor Rosemary Hunter on 27 October 1999 and by Jocelynne Scutt on 5 October 2000, delivering separate addresses at the Clare Burton Memorial Lecture, in Canberra. See also Rosemary Hunter, *Indirect Discrimination in the Workplace*, Federation Press, 1992, p. 187.
12 Gaudron, *The Sir Richard Blackburn Lecture* 1992, p. 11.
13 Australian Bureau of Statistics, Average Weekly Ordinary Time Earnings, May 2008; see ACTU 'Equal Pay Day 2008: Australian women still treated as cheap labour', 27 August 2008, at http://www.actu.org.au/Media/Mediareleases/EqualPayDay2008Australianwomenstilltreatedascheaplabour.aspx viewed 11 July 2010.
14 Gaudron, *The Sir Richard Blackburn Lecture* 1992, p. 12.
15 *Ibid*, pp. 14–15.
16 Gaudron, 29 October 1999, 'Occasional Address', *Sydney Law Review*, 2000, Vol. 22, p. 151.
17 This barrier was removed in NSW in 1969, following the Commonwealth's lead in 1966.
18 Clare Burton, *Subordination: Feminism and social theory*, George Allen & Unwin, Sydney, 1985, p. 132.
19 Dame Roma Mitchell, by note sent to the Roma Mitchell Oration held in Adelaide on 24 August 1990 on the occasion of Gaudron's speech, 'In the Eye of the Law: The Jurisprudence of Equality'.
20 The issue of how applications for silk are treated is ongoing. See *Australian Financial Review*, 'Secret society decides who gets silk', Legal Affairs, 'Hearsay', 20 March 2009, p. 46.
21 *10th Ethel Benjamin Commemorative Address*, 22 September 2006, Dunedin, New Zealand, Pamela Tate, SC, Solicitor General for Victoria, Australia, 'Extending the boundary of right—Flos Greig, Joan Rosanove and Mary Gaudron—Three Australian Women lawyers'.
22 14 July 2000, at the launch of Juliet Bourke's report *Corporate Women, Children, Careers and Workplace Culture*, reported by Bernard Lane, 'Men fear equality of sexes', *Weekend Australian*, 15–16 July 2000, p. 1; and see *The Sydney Institute Quarterly*, Vol. 4, No. 2, August 2000, 'Judges and the Media'.
23 Justice Mary Gaudron, 13 June 2002 (Speech, Women Lawyers Association of NSW 50th Anniversary Gala Dinner, Sydney), at: http://www.hcourt.gov.au/speeches/gaudronj/gaudronj_wlansw.html, viewed 7 June 2010. Meagher in fact qualified his words, adding, 'that is not so. It's a pity the able people don't come.'
24 *Sydney Morning Herald Good Weekend Magazine*, 4 May 2002, p. 46; *Sydney Morning Herald*, 15 June 2002, p. 3.
25 In February 2003, for example, 13.5 per cent of all barristers holding New South Wales practising certificates were women, of which only approximately

three per cent of the senior Bar were female: Rachel Davis and George Williams, critique and comment, 'Reform of the Judicial Appointment Process: Gender and the Bench of the High Court of Australia', (2003) 27 *Melbourne University Law Review*, No. 3. See also Davis and Williams, 'A century of appointments but only one woman' (2003) 28 *Alternative Law Journal* 54.

26 Gaudron, 13 June 2002 (Speech, Women Lawyers Association of NSW).
27 Geesche Jacobsen, 'Women still seen as inferior: judge', *Sydney Morning Herald*, 15 July 2000, p. 3.
28 Roderick Campbell, 'ACT Government stressing our judges, say top lawyers', *Canberra Times*, 20 July 2000, p. 1.
29 Justice John Gallop, 'The Attorney General: A Hybrid Character who Needs to be Versatile', 16 May 2000 (the fifteenth *Sir Richard Blackburn Lecture*).
30 Roderick Campbell, 'ACT Government stressing our judges, say top lawyers', *Canberra Times*, 20 July 2000, p. 1.
31 Gaudron, 13 June 2002 (Speech, Women Lawyers' Association of NSW).
32 *Ibid.*
33 'Treating Unequals Equally', Launch of Australian Women Lawyers' Association, Melbourne, 19 September 1997.
34 Clare Burton, 'Women's Accommodative Strategies in the Labour Market', in *Gender, Politics & Citizenship in the 1990s*, eds. Barbara Sullivan and Gillian Whitehouse, UNSWP, 1996, pp. 148-60, 153.
35 Gaudron, 25 January 2003 (speech, AWL Summer Twilight Retirement Reception for Justice Mary Gaudron, Centennial Parklands Restaurant, Sydney).
36 High Court of Australia transcript, 636, 13 December 2002, *Ceremonial— Remarks of Final Sitting of Gaudron J—Sydney S00/2002* (2002).
37 High Court of Australia transcript (2003) 555, 10 February 2003, *Ceremonial Sitting—Announcement of Appointments of Queen's Counsel and Senior Counsel C00/2003*.
38 10 February 2003, http://parlinfo.aph.gov.au/parlInfo/download/media/pressrel/71I86/upload_binary/71i864.pdf;fileType=application/pdf#search=%22retirement%20of%20justice%20gaudron%22, viewed 24 June 2010.
39 Editorial, 'Woman may be best one for the job', *Canberra Times*, 22 June 2002, p. C6; Ross Peake, 'Justice Gaudron to leave High Court', *Canberra Times*, 22 June 2002, p. 4.
40 15 April 2003 on the occasion of the launch of a *Women and the Commission* exhibition at the Commission's Melbourne headquarters.
41 'Judge slates lack of female justices', *Canberra Times*, 16 April 2003, p. 13.
42 Gaudron's retirement reception, over the 2003 Australian Day Long weekend in Centennial Parklands Restaurant in Sydney hosted by Australian Women Lawyers.

43 Gaudron, 29 October 1999 (Occasional Address, University of Sydney), *Sydney Law Review*, 2000, Vol. 22, p. 152.
44 Brisbane, 9 March 2002.
45 The case came before the full Court, including Justice Heydon on 11 February 2003, *Cattanach v Melchior* (2003) 215 CLR 1. The prospect was reported on in *The Australian*, 7 February 2003, p. 11.
46 'New Governor-General in weeks', *Canberra Times*, 27 May 2003, pp. 1, 2, 3 and 10.
47 *Australian Financial Review*, 31 January 2003, p. 57.
48 On 20 February 2009.
49 *The Australian*, 4 February 2009, http://www.theaustralian.news.com.au/story/0,25197,25005594-2702,00.html, viewed 4 February 2009.
50 According to Justice Bill Gummow, the recommendation was made by a member of the British Parliament (interview with author 12 April 2010).
51 Its members rotate the Presidency.
52 Gaudron, 2005 (speech, UNIFEM).
53 See July 2004 *Report of the Commission of Inquiry appointed under Article 26 of the Constitution of the ILO, to examine trade union rights in Belarus*, (paras. 326, 508-516, 619), at: http://www.ilo.org/wcmsp5/groups/public/---dgreports/---dcomm/documents/meetingdocument/kd00067.pdf viewed 14 June 2010.
54 Mary Gaudron, QC, 17 September 2004, 'The Rule of Law—its role in international governance' (*2004 Annual World Understanding and Peace public lecture,* Australian Centre for Peace and Conflict Studies, University of Queensland, Brisbane).
55 See *Victorian Bar News*, 'Celebratory Dinner: The Honourable Mary Gaudron QC', 15 September 2005, p. 38.
56 *Ibid.*
57 The Panel found that the United Nations did not have an efficient, effective, independent and well-resourced justice system. It concluded that a fundamental overhaul of the internal justice system was required. It made recommendations that offered redress to staff with grievances and for dealing with staff or managerial misconduct quickly and effectively. It even recommended changes in the Administrative Tribunal of which Gaudron was a member, as well as in other aspects of the informal and formal system of justice. United Nations Press Release Org/1470, 20 July 2006.
58 http://www.griffith.edu.au/law/innocence-project, viewed 9 August 2009.
59 Gold Coast exhibition, *Innocence? Capturing the Wrongfully Convicted*, 31 July 2009.
60 Mary Gaudron, 3 March 2006 (Address, Jessie Street Trust, Parliament House Sydney) available on the Evatt Foundation website at: www.evatt.org.au/publications/papers/163.html, viewed 25 June 2010.
61 Gaudron, 2005 (speech, UNIFEM).

62 The conference commenced 27 August 2001; reported in *Canberra Times*, 27 August 2001, p. 3.
63 Gaudron, 2005 (speech, UNIFEM).
64 *Ibid.*
65 *Ibid.*
66 Gaudron, 2006 (Address, Jessie Street Trust). She expressed the same sentiments in 2005 (speech, UNIFEM).
67 Gaudron, 2004 (*Understanding and Peace public lecture*).
68 Gaudron, 2005 (speech, UNIFEM).
69 Address delivered at the Dame Roma Mitchell International Women's Day Luncheon, hosted by the Law Institute of Victoria, 4 March 2004.
70 Gaudron, 2005 (speech, UNIFEM).
71 Gaudron, 2006 (Address, Jessie Street Trust).
72 Mary Gaudron, 4 March 2004 (speech, Victorian Women Lawyers, Melbourne).
73 Interview with Narda Gilmore reported on ABC's *Lateline*, 4 August 2005.
74 *ABC News Online*, Govt rejects 'armchair criticism' over Hicks, 4 August 2005, at, http://www.abc.net.au/news/newsitems/200508/s1430481.htm, viewed 16 July 2010.
75 Gaudron, 2006 (Address, Jessie Street Trust).
76 'Asylum law is a fiction: ex-judge', *The Age*, 5 March 2004, p. 3; Gaudron, 2004 (*Understanding and Peace public lecture*).
77 'Liberty, Justice and Sorority', the Victorian Women Lawyers Dame Roma Mitchell Memorial Lecture, Law Institute of Victoria, Melbourne, 4 March 2004.
78 Gaudron, 2006 (Address, Jessie Street Trust).
79 Gaudron was no longer on the High Court when the case of *Al-Kateb v Godwin* (2004) 219 CLR 562 was decided. Had she been, she is likely to have found that the indefinite detention of a person awaiting deportation was in breach of the Australian Constitution. If so, the case would have gone the other way, since it was a 4:3 decision.
80 Victorian Women Lawyers' Association, 4 March 2004.
81 Gaudron, 2006 (Address, Jessie Street Trust).
82 *Ibid.*
83 Sally Robinson, interview with author 1 May 2008.
84 David Curtain, QC, 10 February 2003, speech at a dinner at the High Court of Australia to welcome new silks, and to honour Justice Mary Gaudron.
85 Sir Anthony Mason, interview with author 7 October 2009.
86 Sally Robinson, interview with author 1 May 2008.
87 For example, 19 September 1997, Launch of Australian Women Lawyers' Association, Melbourne; 1998 Australian Women Lawyers, published (1998) 72 ALJ, 123; 29 October 1999 (Occasional Address, University of Sydney),

Sydney Law Review, 2000, Vol. 22, p. 152; 13 June 2002, 50th Anniversary, Women Lawyers' Association of New South Wales; 8 March 2005, UNIFEM International Women's Day Breakfast, Adelaide.
88 From which emanated 'A collection honouring Justice Mary Gaudron', *Public Law Review*, 2004, Vol. 15, No. 4, eds. Cheryl Saunders, Fiona Wheeler, Michael Taggart, Janet McLean, Law Book Co, p. 280.
89 Professor Kim Rubenstein, conversation with author 29 May 2010.
90 Janean Richards, observation of Gaudron, 7 September 2007 (10th Australian Women Lawyers' Dinner, Melbourne).
91 Mary Gaudron, 7 September 2007 (Impromptu speech, Australian Women Lawyers' 10th Anniversary dinner). Gaudron also agitated for women to take 'direct action', January 1973 (speech, WEL National Conference), 'Women and the law', *WEL Papers*, p. 29.
92 Theme of Australian Women Lawyers 2nd National Conference, 'Creating Justice', 12-14 June 2008.
93 *The Australian* on line, 'Justice Michael Kirby bows out still jousting', Michael Pelly, 30 January, 2009, at: http://www.theaustralian.news.com.au/business/story/0,,24981424-17044,00.html, viewed 2 April 2009.
94 Gaudron, personal communication to author, 3 May 1998.
95 A. J. Brown, forthcoming biography of Michael Kirby, The Federation Press, 2010.
96 Ron Heinrich, the then President of the Council, reported by the *Canberra Times*, 4 February 2003, p. 9.
97 David Curtain, QC, 10 February 2003 (speech, dinner at the High Court of Australia to welcome new silks, and to honour Justice Mary Gaudron).
98 *Ibid.*
99 The Chambers were short-lived due to Morrish becoming a judge of the District Court of Victoria a year later.
100 'A Collection honouring Justice Mary Gaudron', *Public Law Review*, 2004, Vol. 15, No. 4, p. 261.
101 Gaudron, 2005 (speech, UNIFEM).
102 Speech to Launch Australian Women Lawyers, 1998 *Australian Law Journal*, Vol. 72, 119, p. 123. In support she noted the line of cases dealing with tax impositions and discrimination against interstate trade and commerce: *Cole v Whitfield* (1988) 165 CLR 360; *Bath v Alston Holdings Pty Ltd* (1988) 165 CLR 411, and *Castlemaine Tooheys Ltd v South Australia* (1990) 169 CLR 436.
103 Gaudron, 2004 (*Understanding and Peace public lecture*).

SELECT BIBLIOGRAPHY

WORKS BY MARY GAUDRON

PAPERS

'Mary Gaudron' papers 1959–79, National Library of Australia (NLA) MS 7628, Boxes 1, 2 and 3.

ORAL HISTORY

Justice Mary Gaudron, Deputy President of the Australian Conciliation and Arbitration Commission, 1974–79 (interviewer: Amy McGrath, 12 March 1979), ORAL TRC 665, NLA. Access now closed for both research and public use until 5 January 2043.

ABC TV documentary broadcast, 'We all have lives', film clip 3, *The Highest Court,* 1998, 26 May 1998, Film Art Doco, National Film and Sound Archive.

BOOKS, FOREWORDS AND ARTICLES

Herron, the Hon. Sir Leslie, Chief Justice of NSW, *Pleading under the Supreme Court (Amendment) Act 1970*, with Appendix of Precedents edited by M. G. Gaudron, Barrister-at-Law, Government Printer, New South Wales, 1971.

Gaudron, Mary and Michal Bosworth, 'Equal pay?' in *Pursuit of Justice: Australian Women and the Law 1788–1979*, Judy Mackinolty and Heather Radi (eds), Hale & Iremonger, 1979, ch. 15.

Gaudron, Mary, in 'Women at the top: Mary Gaudron', *Law Society Journal* (NSW), Vol. 22 (7), August 1984.

Gaudron, Justice Mary, foreword to G. L. Certoma, *The Law of Succession in New South Wales*, Law Book Company, 1st edn 1987; 2nd edn 1992; 3rd edn 1997.

Gaudron, Justice Mary, 'Part time and partisan', *A Century Down Town: Sydney University Law School's first hundred years*, John and Judy Mackinolty (eds), Sydney University Law School, 1991.

Gaudron, Justice Mary, 'Equality before the Law with particular reference to Aborigines', *The Judicial Review, 1993,* Vol. 1 (2).

Gaudron, Justice Mary, 'Some reflections on the *Boilermakers' case*', (1995) *Journal of Industrial Relations*, Vol. 37 (2), p. 306.

Gaudron, Mary, 'A happy coincidence of self-interest and the public interest: Equality of opportunity for women at the Victorian Bar', *Australian Feminist Law Journal*, March 1999, Vol. 12.

Gaudron, Justice Mary, foreword to Regina Graycar and Jenny Morgan, *The Hidden Gender of Law*, 2nd edn, Federation Press, 2002.

Gaudron, Mary, foreword to Susan Purdon and Aladin Rahemtula (eds), *A Woman's Place: 100 years of Queensland's women lawyers*, Supreme Court of Queensland Library, 2005.

SPEECHES

January 1973, 'Women and the law', *The WEL Papers,* The National Journal of the Women's Electoral Lobby 1973/4.

30 June 1979, first National Conference of Labor Lawyers, Adelaide.

1980 Herbert Vere Evatt Memorial Lecture, University of Adelaide ALP Club.

23 November 1981, 'Women in the workforce and the elimination of discrimination—whose responsibility?' Anne Conlon memorial lecture, Sydney, NSW Women's Advisory Council, 1982.

17 June 1986, 'The Australia Acts', Lecture given at Macquarie University.

27 October 1986, Memorial Service for Lionel Murphy, Sydney Town Hall.

1987, 'Control of delegated government functions in relation to the maintenance and enforcement of the criminal law', 24th Australian Legal Convention, Perth.

1988, 'Human rights, changing contexts', Commemorative address on the occasion of the 40th anniversary of the Universal Declaration of Human Rights.

24 August 1990, 'In the eye of the law: The jurisprudence of equality', The Mitchell Oration, Adelaide.

20 July 1994, address to the Bar Readers Course, Brisbane.

19 September 1997, launch of Australian Women Lawyers' Association, Melbourne, *The Australian Law Journal*, 1998, Vol. 72 (2), p. 119.

9 October 1998, launch by the Victorian Bar Council of its plans for responding to *Equality of Opportunity for Women at the Victorian Bar: a Report*, commissioned and published by the Victorian Bar Council, Melbourne.

29 October 1999, 'Occasional address, University of Sydney, conferral of degrees', *Sydney Law Review,* 2000, Vol. 22, p. 151.

13 June 2002, Women Lawyers' Association of NSW 50th Anniversary Gala Dinner, Sydney.

25 January 2003, Australian Women Lawyers Summer Twilight Retirement Reception for Justice Mary Gaudron, Centennial Parklands Restaurant, Sydney.

4 March 2004, 'Liberty, justice and sorority' the Victorian Women Lawyers', Dame Roma Mitchell Memorial Lecture, Law Institute of Victoria, Melbourne.

17 September 2004, 'The rule of Law—its role in international governance', 2004 Annual World Understanding and Peace public lecture, Australian Centre for Peace and Conflict Studies, University Queensland, Brisbane.

8 March 2005, UNIFEM International Women's Day Breakfast, Adelaide.

3 March 2006, Jessie Street Trust, Parliament House, Sydney, found at the Evatt Foundation website: www.evatt.org.au/publications/papers/163.html, viewed 25 June 2010.

29 September 2006, 'Equality: The guarantee of excellence', Australian Women Lawyers, Sydney.

7 September 2007, 10th Annual Dinner of Australian Women Lawyers, Melbourne.

ORAL HISTORY

Justice Jane Mathews (interviewer: John Farquharson, 23 October 2001), ORAL TRC 4647, NLA, (Tape 2, 'Women in the law and at the Bar').

SELECTED BOOKS and ARTICLES

Arantz, Philip, *A Collusion of Powers*, self-published, 1993.

Attard, Monica, 'Record of interview of Justice Michael Kirby', *Sunday Profile*, Australian Broadcasting Corporation, 16 November 2003.

Bachelard, Michael, *The Great Land Grab*, Hyland House, 1997.

Bartlett, Richard H., *The Mabo Decision*, Butterworths, 1993.

Berns, Sandra S., 'Constituting a nation: Adjudication as constitutive rhetoric', *Interpreting Constitutions, Theories, Principles and Institutions*, Charles Sampford and Kim Preston (eds), Federation Press, 1996.

Blackshield, A. R., 'The appointment and removal of Federal judges', in *The Australian Federal Judicial System*, Brian Opeskin and Fiona Wheeler (eds), Melbourne University Press, 2000.

Blackshield, Tony, Michael Coper and George Williams (eds), *The Oxford Companion to the High Court of Australia*, Oxford University Press, 2001.

Blackshield, A. R. and George Williams, *Australian Constitutional Law and Theory Commentary and Materials*, 5th edn, Federation Press, 2010.

Blackshield, Tony, 'Case note *New South Wales v Commonwealth*: Corporations and connections', (2007) 31 *Melbourne University Law Review*, No. 3, p. 1135.

Bramston, Troy (ed.), *The Wran Era*, Federation Press, 2006.

Brennan, Frank, 'The 1998 Revisiting of Wik and the Ten Point Plan', *The Australian Journal of Forensic Sciences*, Vol. 31 (2), July–December 1999.

Briggs-Smith, Noeline, *Moree Mob*, vols 1–3, with the support of the Indigenous community, published by the Northern Regional Library and Information Service, Moree NSW, 1999–2003.

Burton, Clare, *The Promise and the Price*, Allen & Unwin, 1991.

Burton, Clare, *Subordination: Feminism and social theory*, George Allen & Unwin, Sydney, 1985.

Burton, Clare, 'Women's accommodative strategies in the labour market', in *Gender, Politics & Citizenship in the 1990s*, (eds) Barbara Sullivan and Gillian Whitehouse, UNSW Press, 1996.

Buti, Antonio, *Sir Ronald Wilson: A matter of conscience*, UWAP, 2007.

Cameron, Clyde (as told to Daniel Connell), *The Confessions of Clyde Cameron 1913–1990*, ABC, 1990.

Cameron, Clyde, *Unions in Crisis*, Hill of Content, 1982.

Campbell, Enid, 'Intervention in constitutional cases', *Public Law Review*, 1998, Vol. 9, p. 255.

Campbell, T. W., 'Nuns in the Diocese of Armidale 1890–1940', a paper read before the Australian Catholic Historical Society, 8 April 2001, Sydney, NSW.

Cane, Peter, (ed.), *Centenary Essays for the High Court of Australia*, Butterworths, 2004.

Creyke, Robin and Patrick Keyze (eds), *The Brennan Legacy: Blowing the winds of legal orthodoxy*, Federation Press, 2002.

Coper, Michael, *Encounters with the Australian Constitution*, CCH Australia Ltd, 1987.

Curthoys, Ann, *Freedom Ride: A freedom rider remembers*, Allen & Unwin, 2002 .

d'Alpuget, Blanche, *Mediator: A biography of Sir Richard Kirby*, Melbourne University Press, 1977.

d'Alpuget, Blanche, *Robert J. Hawke: A biography*, Schwartz/Penguin, 1984.

Davis, Rachel and George Williams, critique and comment, 'Reform of the judicial appointment process: Gender and the Bench of the High Court of Australia', *Melbourne University Law Review*, 2003, Vol. 27 (3).

Davis, Rachel and George Williams, 'A Century of Appointments But Only One Woman', *Alternative Law Journal*, 2003, Vol. 28, p. 54.

Ellis, Ross, Lyndsey Hawkins, Robert Hawkins, Julia James, Gregory Middleton, Benjamin Nurse, and Gleniss Wellings, (eds), *Bungonia Caves*, Sydney Speleological Society Occasional Paper No. 4, Sydney Speleological Society, 1972.

Freckelton, Ian and Hugh Selby (eds), *Appealing to the Future: Michael Kirby and his legacy*, Law Book Company, 2009.

Gaita, Raimond, *A Common Humanity*, Text Publishing, Melbourne, 1999.

Gal, Daniel, 'An overview of the Wik decision', *University of New South Wales Law Journal*, 1997, p. 488.

Gray, Rachael, *The Constitutional Jurisprudence and Judicial Method of the High Court of Australia*, Presidian Legal Publications, 2008.

Groves, Matthew and Russell Smyth, 'A Century of judicial style: Changing patterns in judgment writing on the High Court 1903–2001', *Federal Law Review*, 2004, Vol. 11.

Guy, Bill, *A Life on the Left: A biography of Clyde Cameron*, Wakefield Press, 1999.

Heydon, Justice John Dyson, 'Theories of Constitutional interpretation: a taxonomy', the 2007 Sir Maurice Byers Lecture on the High Court and the Constitution, *Bar News*, Winter, 2007.

Hunter, Rosemary, *Indirect Discrimination in the Workplace*, Federation Press, 1992.

Hussey, Marie, *In simplicity of heart: Guyra, the Ursuline years, 1919–1969*, Ursuline Convent, Lyneham, ACT, 1983.

Hutley, F. C., 'Logic and the legal process', *University of Western Australia Annual Law Review*, 1948–9, Vol. 1 (2).

Isaac, Joe and Stuart Macintyre (eds), *The New Province for Law and Order—100 years of Australian Industrial Conciliation and Arbitration*, Cambridge University Press, 2004.

Kamenka, Eugene, 'The Andersonians: Philosophy and Criticism in Australia', *Quadrant,* July 1987, Vol. 31, p. vii.

Kirby, Justice Michael, 'A. F. Mason—from *Trigwell* to *Teoh*', 1996, Sir Anthony Mason Lecture, *Melbourne University Law Review*, 1996, Vol. 20 (4).

Kirby, Justice Michael, 'H. L. A. Hart, Julius Stone and the struggle for the soul of law', *Sydney Law Review*, 2005, Vol. 14.

Kneipp, Pauline, *This Land of Promise: The Ursuline Order in Australia 1882–1982*, Armidale, University of New England Press, 1982.

Lindell, Geoffrey (ed.), *The Mason Papers*, Federation Press, 2007.

Lindsay, Geoff and Carol Webster (eds.), *No Mere Mouthpiece: Servants of all, yet of none*, Butterworths, 2002.

Lynch, Andrew, 'The once and future court?' *Federal Law Review*, Vol. 28, p. 145.

Mackie, Pat, with Elisabeth Vassilieff, *Mount Isa: The story of a dispute*, Hudson Publishing, 1989.

Mackinolty, John and Judy (eds), *A Century Down Town: Sydney University Law School's first hundred years*, Sydney University Law School, 1991.

Mackinolty, Judy and Heather Radi (eds), *In Pursuit of Justice: Australian women and the law 1788–1979*, Hale & Iremonger, Sydney, 1979.

Mason, Sir Anthony, 'The role of a constitutional court in a federation: a comparison of the Australian and the United States experience', *Federal Law Review*, 1986, Vol. 16.

Mason, Sir Anthony, 'The role of the courts at the turn of the century', *Journal of Judicial Administration*, 1993, Vol. 3, p. 156.

Mossman, Mary Jane, *The First Women Lawyers: A comparative study of gender, law and the legal professions*, Hart Publishing, 2006.

Parker, Christine, 'Protection of judicial process as an implied constitutional principle', *Adelaide Law Review*, 1994, Vol. 16, p. 341.

Patapan, Haig, 'High Court Review 2001: Politics, legalism and the Gleeson Court', *Australian Journal of Political Science*, 2002, Vol. 37 (2), p. 241.

Pierce, Jason L., *Inside the Mason Court Revolution: the High Court of Australia transformed*, Carolina Academic Press, 2006.

Priest, Joan, *Sir Harry Gibbs—without fear or favour*, Scribblers Publishing, 1995.

Rickard, John, *H. B. Higgins, the rebel as judge*, Allen & Unwin, 1984.

Ross, Stan, *Politics of Law Reform*, Penguin, 1982.

Rowley, C. D., *Outcasts in White Australia*, Penguin, 1972.

Rubenstein, Kim, 'Citizenship and the Centenary—inclusion and exclusion in 20th century Australia', *Melbourne University Law Review*, 2000, Vol. 24.

Ryan, Edna and Anne Conlon, *Gentle Invaders: Australian women at work 1788–1974*, Nelson, 1975.

Sackville, Ronald, 'Why do Judges make law? Some aspects of judicial law making', *University of Western Sydney Law Review*, 2001, Vol. 5.

Sampford, Charles, and Kim Preston (eds), *Interpreting Constitutions: Theories, principles and institutions*, Federation Press, 1996.

Saunders, Cheryl, Fiona Wheeler, Michael Taggart, and Janet McLean, (eds), 'A collection honouring Justice Mary Gaudron', *Public Law Review*, 2004, Vol. 15 (4), Law Book Co.

Sawer, Geoffrey, and others, *Federalism in Australia*, F. W. Cheshire, 1949.

Sawer, Marian, with Gail Radford, *Making Women Count: A history of the Women's Electoral Lobby in Australia*, UNSW Press, 2008.

Scutt, Jocelynne A. (ed.), *Lionel Murphy: A radical judge*, McCulloch Publishing, 1987.

Simpson, Amelia, 'The High Court's conception of discrimination: Origins, applications, and implications', *Sydney Law Review*, 2007, Vol. 10, p. 267.

Smyth, Russell, '"Some are more equal than others": An empirical investigation into the voting behaviour of the Mason Court', *Canberra Law Review*, 1999, Vol. 6 (1) & (2), p. 193.

Star, Leonie, *Julius Stone: An intellectual life*, Melbourne, Oxford University Press, 1992.

Steketee, Mike and Milton Cockburn, *Wran: An unauthorised biography*, Allen & Unwin, 1986.

Stephens, Tony, *Sir William Deane: The things that matter*, Hodder, 2002.

Stewart, Don, *Recollections of an Unreasonable Man*, ABC Books, 2007.

Stone, Adrienne and George Williams (eds), *The High Court at the Crossroads*, Federation Press, 2000.

Stone, Julius, *The Province and Function of Law: Law as logic, justice and social control; a study in jurisprudence*, Sydney, Associated General Publications, 1946.

Sydney Speleological Society, *1963 to 1964 Yearbook*.

Twomey, Anne, *The Chameleon Crown: The Queen and Her Australian governors*, Federation Press, 2006.

Vassilieff, Elizabeth, (ed.), *Many Ships to Mount Isa: Autobiography, Pat Mackie*, Seaview Press, 2002.

Webb, R. J., *The Rising Sun—A history of Moree and District, 1862–1962*, Moree, North West Champion for the Moree Centenary Celebrations Committee, 1962.

Women's Executive Development, *The Promise and the Price: Ten years of the Clare Burton Memorial Lectures*, Australian Technology Network of Universities, 2009.

Wheeler, Fiona, 'Due Process, judicial power and Chapter III in the new High Court', *Federal Law Review*, 2004, Vol. 32 (2), p. 208.

Wheeler, Fiona, and John Williams, '"Restrained activism" in the High Court of Australia', Brice Dickson (ed.), *Judicial Activism in Common Law Supreme Courts*, Oxford University Press, 2007.

Willheim, Ernst, 'Australia's racial vilification law found wanting? "Nigger Brown" Saga: HREOC, the Federal Court, the High Court and the Committee on the Elimination of Racial Discrimination', *Asia-Pacific Journal on Human Rights and the Law*, 2004, Vol. 4 (1).

Williams, George, 'The High Court and the media', *University of Technology Sydney Law Review*, 1999, Vol. 10.

Zimmerman, Beverley, *The Making of a Diocese: Maitland, its bishop, priests and people 1866–1909*, Melbourne University Press, 2000.

Zines, Leslie, *The High Court and the Constitution*, 5th edn, Federation Press, 2008.

NEWSPAPERS AND MAGAZINES

Adelaide Advertiser, 1974, 1981; *Age*, 1974, 1980; *Australian*, 1972, 1986, 1994, 1998; *Australian Financial Review*, 1972, 1980; *Blackacre*, Journal of the Sydney University Law Society, 1963, 1966; *Bulletin* with Newsweek, 2005; *Canberra Times*, 1980; *Daily Mirror*, 1981; *Daily Telegraph*, 1981, 1987; *Herald* (Melbourne), 1974, 1981; *Moree Champion*, 1959–2000; *NSW Bar News*, 1987–2009; *Queensland Bar News*, 2003; *Sun* (Sydney) 1981; *Sydney Morning Herald*, 1951, 1957, 1959, 1964, 1965, 1968, 1972, 1974, 1980, 1981, 1983, 1986, 1994, 2003; *Victorian Bar News*, 1987–2009; *WEL-Informed*, monthly newsletter of the NSW Women's Electoral Lobby, 1987; *Woman's Day*, 1980, 1986.

NEWSPAPER COLLECTIONS

Collection of Janet Coombs (Bar Association of New South Wales Library) of news clippings relating to early female barristers in NSW.

COURT DECISIONS AND TRANSCRIPTS

Commonwealth Conciliation and Arbitration Reports 1972–1980

Commonwealth Law Reports 1981–2009

High Court of Australia, transcripts of proceedings, 1987–1993

High Court of Australia transcript of proceedings 1994–2004, available http://www.austlii.edu.au/au/other/HCATrans/.

Commonwealth Conciliation and Arbitration Commission transcripts of proceedings, 1972–1981.

SPEECHES

French, Justice Robert, on the occasion of the 1987 Australian Legal Convention, 22 September 1987, Perth.

Kirby, Justice Michael, 'Women in the Law: doldrums or progress?', 22 October 2003, Women Lawyers of Western Australia, Perth.

Kirby, Justice Michael, A tribute on the 10th Anniversary of Lionel Murphy's death, 21 October 1996.

Mason, Sir Anthony, 'Twenty-three years on the High Court', Probus

Club, Sydney, November 2008.

Mathews, Justice Jane, 'The changing profile of women in the Law', ANZAAS Congress, 1982, Sydney.

McHugh, Justice Michael, 'Women Justices for the High Court', Western Australian Law Society, 27 October 2004, Perth.

McMurdo, Justice Margaret, proposing a toast to Mary Gaudron on her retirement from the High Court, Australian Women Judges Dinner, 22 February 2003, Sydney.

Spigelman, Chief Justice James, NSW Supreme Court, Sesquicentenary of the University of Sydney Law Faculty, 5 November 2005, Sydney.

Staples, Justice J. F., 'Uniformity and diversity in industrial relations', South Australian Industrial Relations Society, Adelaide, 17 March 1980, *Journal of Industrial Relations,* September 1980, Vol. 22 (3).

Tate, SC, Pamela, Solicitor General for Victoria, *10th Ethel Benjamin Commemorative Address*, 'Extending the boundary of right—Flos Greig, Joan Rosanove and Mary Gaudron—three Australian women lawyers', 22 September 2006, Dunedin, New Zealand.

Whitlam, E. G., 'Thirty years later: the Whitlam Government as modernist politics', 2 December 2002, Keynote Address, Old Parliament House, Canberra.

INTERVIEWS

Cathie Allan (phone) 21 Feb & 24 Mar 2005, 29 & 30 Jan 2008, 13 Apr 2010; John Blackley (Canberra) 25 Sep 2007; Professor Tony Blackshield (Sydney) 28 Feb 2008; Noeline Briggs-Smith (More) 3 May 2006, 10 Mar 2010; Tom Campbell (Canberra) 21 Jan 2009; Betty Carter (Moree) 2 May 2006, 9 Mar 2010; Warwick Counsell (phone) 29 Apr 2008; Ross Ellis (phone) 29 Apr 2008; Lalie Fletcher (Moree) 10 Mar 2010; Peter Gaudron (Canberra) 17 Mar 2009; Justice William Gummow (Canberra) 12 Apr 2010; Pauline Hansen (Sydney) 7 Apr 2005; Noel Houlahan (phone) 12 Jul 2008; The Hon. Michael Kirby (Sydney) 14 Aug 2009; Sir Anthony Mason (Sydney) 7 Oct 2009; Margaret McCabe (phone) 3 June 2008; Associate Justice John McLaughlin (Sydney) 5 Apr 2005; Lyall Munro (Moree) 2 May 2006, 10 Mar 2010; Ben Nurse 24 May 2010; Sam Sabine (Moree) 3 May 2006, 10 Mar 2010; Justice Terry Sheahan (Sydney) 12 Aug 2009; Former Justice Jim Staples (Canberra) 15–16 May 1999, 22 Sep 2002, 13 June 2009; The Hon. Don Stewart QC (phone) 31 Oct 2008, 1 November 2008; Margot Stubbs (Sydney) 27 Feb 2008; Sally Robinson (Sydney) 1 May 2008; Allan Ross (Moree) 10 Mar 2010;

The Hon. Frank Walker QC (Sydney) 2 Aug 2008; Judge Greg Woods (Sydney) 1 Aug 2008.

BRIEF CONTACTS

Alan Anderson (phone) 19 Apr 2008; Tim Barrett (Sydney) 7 Apr 2005; Bill Bowtell (phone) 17 Mar 2008; Sir Gerard Brennan (phone, email) 4 May 2010, 6 May 2010; Bruce Bromhead (phone) 20 Jul 2008; The Hon. Ian Callinan QC (phone) 4 May 2010; Janet Coombs (phone) 29 May 1998; David Coward (phone) 17 Mar 2008; Stella Cusack (phone) 14 Jul 2008; Mavis Dick (phone) 16 Aug 2009; John Dunkley (Canberra 22 Jan 2009; The Hon. Elizabeth Evatt (Sydney) 3 May 2003; Sean Flood (phone) 15 Feb 2005; Fr Bernie Frize (phone) 14 Jul 2009; Phil Hardman (Moree) 29 Apr 2005; The Hon. Robert Hawke (phone) 8 June 2010; Rhonda Henderson (Sydney) 7 Apr 2005; Molly Hethrington (Moree) 9 Mar 2010; Ken Horler QC (phone) 18 Nov 2008; Sister Monica Horan (letter) 3 Aug 2008; Mark Houlahan (Moree) 2 Jul 2007; Kevin Humphries (phone) 18 Aug 2000; Janette Jackson (phone) 17 Jul 2009; Phillip Jenkyn (phone) 10 May 2008; Sister Mary Kneipp (phone) 12 Sept 2007; Pat Madden (Moree) 8 Mar 2010; Maurice May (phone) 14 Aug 2007; Fr Paul McCabe (Moree) 30 June 2008; Sister Gerard McGlynn (phone) 29 Nov 2007; The Hon. Jeffrey Miles (Canberra) 29 Sep 2009; Leslie Moore (phone) 12 June 2008; Harry Pemble (phone) 19 Apr 2008; Jack Waterford (email) 26 May 2003; Ernst Willheim (Canberra) 3 Sept 2009; The Hon. Neville Wran QC (phone) 16 Dec 2005; Pat Young (phone) 20 Mar 2008.

INDEX

Abebe v Commonwealth (1999), 353
Abeles, Sir Peter, 212
Abercrombie Caves (NSW), 64
Aboriginal and Torres Strait Heritage Protection Act 1984 (Cth), 332, 333, 334
Aboriginal community (Moree), 10, 11, 12, 289
　discrimination against, 4, 16–21, 23–24, 29, 110, 280, 299
　dispossession from land, 17, 286–87
　employment, 14–15
　Top Camp, 12, 14, 19, 20
Aboriginal Land Rights Act 1983 (NSW), 191
Aboriginal Land Rights (Northern Territory) Act 1976 (Cth), 281
Aboriginal Legal Service, 25, 349
Aboriginal people
　children, removal of, 20, 318
　　see also Stolen Generation case
　culture and heritage *see* Hindmarsh Island Bridge case (1998)
　customary law, 281–82
　discrimination against, 10, 14, 16–21, 23–24, 29, 95, 102, 280
　land rights *see* indigenous land rights
　Moree community *see* Aboriginal community (Moree)
　see also Torres Strait Islander people
Aborigines Protection Act 1909 (NSW), 20
Aborigines Protection Board, 20
abortion, 34, 82, 192–93, 193, 351
　Superclinics case (1996), 351–52
Ackland, Richard, 258
ACT Bar Association, 267
ACT Police Force, 236
ACT Supreme Court, 246, 374

activism *see* judicial activism
Actors and Announcers Equity Association v Fontana Films Pty Ltd (1981), 193
ACTU *see* Australian Council of Trade Unions (ACTU)
Adams, Phil, 110
Advisory Council of the Centre for Technology and Social Change (University of Wollongong), 240
affirmative action *see* equal employment opportunity (EEO)
Affirmative Action (Equal Employment Opportunity for Women) Bill 1986 (Cth), 190
Afghanistan, war in, 389–90
Age, 147, 367
Age tapes, 216–23, 224, 225, 226, 228, 233, 234, 235, 256, 308
Aird, Justice, 137
Al-Kateb v Godwin (2004), 318
Alcoholics Anonymous (Moree), 25
'aliens,' Commonwealth power over *see* refugees
Allan, Norman, 211, 212
Allen, Bill *see* Bill Allen affair
Allen, Peter, 21
Alley, Deputy President, 170
Aloysius, Mother Mary, 28
Amaroo land claim, 289
Anderson, Alan, 143
Anderson, Peter, 211
Anderson, Professor John, 44, 51
Anglers Club (Sydney), 222
Annan, Secretary-General Kofi, 384, *385*
Anti-Discrimination Act 1977 (NSW), 197
ANZAC Day, 19
Arantz, Philip, 211–12
Archibald exhibition (Sydney), 394
Armidale High School, 39
Armidale (NSW), 14, 22, 29, 42
Ashley (NSW), 71
Askin, Bob, 83

Askin Government (NSW), 88, 92
asylum seekers *see* refugees
Attorney General's Department (Cth), 203
'Auntie Noeline' *see* Briggs-Smith, Noeline
Australia Act 1986 (Cth), 260, 313, 315
Australia Act 1986 (UK), 260, 313, 315
Australia Party, 87
Australia (Request and Consent) Act 1985 (Cth), 205
Australian Bar Association, 378
Australian Bicentennial Authority, 290
Australian Bicentennial Authority Act 1980 (Cth), 290
Australian Broadcasting Commission (ABC), 160
　annual concert, 37
　Four Corners (tv program), 214, 330
Australian Capital Television v Commonwealth (1992), 291, 296
Australian Citizenship Act 1948 (Cth), 306, 310, 315
Australian Citizenship Amendment Act 1984 (Cth), 313
Australian Consolidated Press
　Pat Mackie case *see Mackie v Australian Consolidated Press Ltd* [1974]
　Pearson v Australian Consolidated Press Ltd [1971], 90–91
Australian Constitution, 1, 2, 3, 4, 19, 30–31, 177, 184, 185, 189, 260, 295, 337
　association and movement, freedom of, 294–95
　press, freedom of, 291, 296
　referenda on, 279, 329
　rights and freedoms, interpretation of, 276, 278–80, 290–94, 359, 398
　Chapter I – Parliament, 292
　Chapter II – Executive, 292
　Chapter III – Judicature, 292,

INDEX

293, 294, 305, 316, 318, 319, 366
s 44 – election to Parliament, 315
s 51(xix) – 'aliens' power, 310, 313, 314, 316
s 51(xx) – corporations power, 132, 196, 197, 198, 199, 200, 201, 280
s 51(xxix) – external affairs power, 132, 196, 197, 198, 199, 200
s 51(xxvi) – race power, 199, 200, 329, 332, 333, 334
s 72 – judge's appointments etc., 246, 331
s 75(v) – judicial review, 353, 354–56, 384, 386–87, 393
s 92 – interstate trade, 295–96
s 116 – religion, free exercise of, 292, 319
s 117 – residents of states, discrimination between, 290
s 122 – Territories power, 292, 318–19
Australian Consumer Protection Authority, 158–59
Australian Council of Trade Unions (ACTU), 116, 119, 127, 133, 155, 251
Australian Federal Police (AFP), 308
  Operation Seville, 236–37, 308
Australian Financial Review, 255
Australian Industrial Court (formerly Commonwealth), 126, 137, 158, 292
Australian Iron and Steel Pty. Ltd. v Banovic (1989), 303–4
Australian Labor Party (ALP), 1, 2, 14, 15, 22, 67, 81, 182, 225, 229, 251, 255, 279, 331
  criminal infiltration of, 207, 208
  DLP, 'Split' with, 35
  Enmore branch stacking, 207, 208, 209
  MG's association with, 260
  see also Cameron, Clyde; Murphy, Lionel; Walker, Frank; Wran, Neville
  NSW Branch *see* NSW Branch (ALP)

Australian Law Journal, 194
Australian National University (ANU), 39, 142, 346
  dispute, 171, 172–73
  Law School, 195
Australian Postal and Telecommunications Union, 169, 170–71
Australian Postal Commission case (APC case), 169, 170–71
Australian Press Council, 243, 244
Australian Telecommunications Employees Association (ATEA), 154–57
  Telecom dispute (1978), 154–57, 178
Australian Women Lawyers' Association, 380–81
  AWL brooch, *377,* 380–81
Australian Workers Union (AWU), 96, 142
  Mount Isa miners' strike *see Mackie v Australian Consolidated Press Ltd* [1974]

baby boomers, 43
Backhouse, Cecily, 76
Bacon, Wendy, 87, 242–43
Baldwin, Peter, 207, 208
Balfour Hotel (Sydney), 48, 57
Balmain Leagues Club (Sydney), 213, 214
Bar Association of Queensland, 327
Barton, Alexander, 212
Barton, Thomas, 212
Barton case, 212–13
Barwick, Chief Justice Sir Garfield, 54, 90, 148, 265, 321
Bastard Boys (docu-drama), 254
Bathurst riots (prison), 152
Beazley, Kim, 268
Belarus
  Constitution, 383–84, 387
  ILO Commission, 383–84, 387
beliefs and values (MG), 87–88
  anti-discrimination *see* discrimination
  Britain, severing legal ties to, 201
  equal justice *see* equal justice
  human rights *see* human rights

procedural fairness, 292–94, 305, 306, 316
  social justice *see* social justice
  women's rights *see* women's rights
Bell, John, 43
Bell, Virginia (later Justice), 54, 381
Bennett, David, 93
Bentham, Jeremy, 259
Beresford, Bruce, 43
Berkeley, Hartog, 369
Bernardine, Sister Mary *see* Horan, Monica
Bhardwaj case (2002), 355–56
BHP dispute (1975), 152
Bielski, Joan, 240
Bill Allen affair, 209–12
  Perrignon inquiry, 210
bill of rights, 290, 295
  NSW, 189
Bishop, Mervyn, 289
Bjelke-Petersen, (Joh), 196
Black, Hermann, 107–8
black-letter law, 275, 332
  judicial activism, *versus,* 275–77, 280, 286, 367
Blackacre (magazine), 56
Blackburn, Justice Richard (later Sir), 246, 285, 302
Blackley, John, 142
Blackman, Jenny, 79
Blackshield, Professor Tony, 51, 60, 61, 62, 90, 201, 244, 247, 260, 319, 321, 362, 366
  MG's defence of, 87–88
boat people *see* refugees
Boilermakers' case (1956), 137, 292
Bolam test (UK), 364
Borbidge, Rob, 326, 327
Borgia, Sister Mary, 30
Bounty Oil Company, 212
Bowen, Justice Nigel, 109
Bowen, Lionel, 251
Bowtell, Bill, 185, 187, 188
Bradshaw, Richard, 43
Brand, Mona, 228
Branson, Catherine, 394–95
Brennan, Justice Gerard (later Chief Justice, Sir), 73, 247, 269, 296, 305, 317, 330, 338, 361
  Chief Justice, appointment as, 320, 321, 322

dissenting judgments, 303, 307, 323, 325
Mabo (No. 2), 284, 286
MG, relationship with, 272
retirement, 326, 327, 328, 329, 335
Wik judgment, 325, 326
Brennan, Richard, 43
Brennan Court, 274, 322–35
cases *see* Brennan court cases
Brennan court cases
Hindmarsh Island Bridge case (1998), 329–30, 332–34
Wik case (1996), 254, 295, 296, 323–26, 327
Brereton, Laurie, 341
Briese, Chief Magistrate Clarence, 215
corruption allegations by, 217, 223– 227, 229–31, 232–33, 238, 241, 242, 243–44, 256
Briggs-Smith, Noeline, 12, 17, 19, 21, 24, 289
Britain, severing legal ties with, 201
British Foreign and Commonwealth Office, 203
Brown, Deputy Chief Magistrate Bruce, 209
Brown, Edward Stanley ('Nigger'), 347
Bryant, Diana, 381
Builders Labourers Federation (BLF), 82
High Court picket, 148–49
Bulletin (magazine), 230
Bundaberg (Qld), 95, 102
Bungendore (NSW), 236, 237
Bungonia Caves (book), 65–66, 88
Bungonia Caves (NSW), 64, 65
Odyssey Cave, 66
protection from mining, MG's role in, 66, 88–89
Burchett, Wilfred, 79, 97
Burchett v Kane [1980], 79, 97
Burton, Clare, 375
Butler, Richard, 43
Byers, Sir Maurice, 173, 188, 189

Callinan, Ian (later Justice), 243, 246, 327–31, 335, 336, 338
dissenting judgments, 280, 337, 363

High Court, appointment to, 327, 329, 336
Hindmarsh Island Bridge case (1998), 329–30
The Lawyer and the Libertine (novel), 328
MG, relationship with, 328, 331
White Industries cases (1998), (1999), 330–31
Cameron, Clyde, 95–96, 101, 105, 106, 110, 112, 124, 125–26, 127, 133–34, 158, 181, 246
Conciliation and Arbitration Commission, recommends MG for, 134, 135–36, 139
national wage cases, recommends MG for, 113–14, 134
Camooweal (Qld), 106
Campbell, Roderick, 245, 246
career (MG), 38
Advisory Council of the Centre for Technology and Social Change, chair of, 240
Articles of Clerkship, 47, 58, 67
Australian Bar Association, life member of, 398
Commonwealth Crown Solicitor's Office, clerk with, 47, 49, 59
Conciliation and Arbitration Commission *see* Deputy President of Conciliation and Arbitration Commission (MG)
Council of Civil Liberties, member of, 87
Council of NSW Bar Association, member of, 81, 86
F. E. Fischer and Laws, clerk with, 59, 67
High Court of Australia *see* Justice of High Court of Australia (MG)
ILO Administrative Tribunal, appointment to, 382–84
Innocence Project (Griffith University), appointment to, 384–85
legacy of law career, 365–68
Legal Education Committee

(NSW), member of, 81
Macquarie University Council, member of, 240–41
Maxwell Connery & Co, clerk with, 67
Nimrod Theatre, board member of, 240
NSW Bar *see* NSW Bar, MG at
NSW Legal Services Commission, chair of, 164, 180
obstacles for women, 38, 40, 47, 48, 58, 59, 62, 66–68, 76–79, 80–81
Queen's Counsel, 184, 185
Solicitor General (NSW) *see* Solicitor General of NSW (MG)
Supreme Court of NSW, work in, 5
UN 'Redesign Panel,' appointment to, 384, 385
UNSW Law School, Fellow at, 177–79, 180, 382
Women Lawyers' Association of NSW, member of, 87
Carlton Rex Hotel (Sydney), 57
Carve Her Name in Pride (book), 33
Casino (NSW), 9
Cass, Mary, 76
Cassidy, Sir Jack, 97, 106–9
Cateaux Wattel (ship), 9
Cattanach v Melchior (2003), 379
Cessna, Roy, 214–15, 218
Cessna - Milner case, 213, 214–215, 218, 222, 231–32
Chappel v Hart (1998), 364–65
character and personality (MG), 8, 26, 31, 32, 33, 48–49, 62, 77, 91, 144, 151, 152, 181, 183, 188, 239, 257, 263, 349, 361, 367, 393
bench, on the, 140, 142, 143, 157, 239, 345
drive and ambition, 38, 41, 48, 62, 85, 395–98
'Mary the Merciless' epithet, 85, 118, 138
politics, and, 84–88
Chelmsford Private Hospital scandal, 190–91
Chifley, Ben, 1

INDEX

childhood in Moree (MG), 10–17, 21–26, 39, 50, 68, 280
  birth, 12
  Catholic upbringing, 8, 10, 21, 27
  'Doc' Evatt, meeting with, 1–2, 3, 4, 30, 258, 263
  education *see* education (MG)
  home life, 6, 21–26
  railway community, 10, 11, 12–16, 22, 25, 28
'children overboard affair,' 354
Chu Kheng Lim v Minister for Immigration, Local Government and Ethnic Affairs (1992) *see* Lim case (1992)
Church Creek cave site (NSW), 66
citizenship, 306, 310–16, 398
  Ex parte Te (2002), 313–14
  Lim case (1992), 311–12, 316, 317, 318, 330, 333, 334
  Nolan v Minister for Immigration and Ethnic Affairs (1988), 310–11, 312, 313, 314
  Re Patterson; Ex parte Taylor (2001), 312–13, 314
  Shaw v MIMA (2003), 314
  Sue v Hill (1999), 314–15
  Teoh case (1995), 315–16
civil liberty, 92, 247
  Blackshield, MG's defence of, 87–88
Clark, Professor Manning, 246
Clarkson, Commissioner, 155, 156, 157
Coast Islands Declaratory Act 1985 (Qld), 282, 283
Cobbett, Professor Pitt, 46
Coffs Harbour (NSW), 9
Cold War, 3
Coldham, Deputy President, 149, 170
Cole v Whitfield (1988), 295, 296
Colong Caves (NSW), 64
Combe-Ivanov affair, 221
Comcar, 341
common law, 46, 83, 84, 86, 97, 190, 305, 325, 389, 398
  equal justice, and, 305, 306, 316
  Mabo (No. 2), and, 283, 284, 285, 286

Commonwealth Club (Canberra), 266
Commonwealth Constitution *see* Australian Constitution
Commonwealth Court of Conciliation and Arbitration, 292
Commonwealth Prisoners Act 1967 (Cth), 305
Commonwealth Public Service, 47, 58, 66
Commonwealth Public Service Arbitrator, 47
Commonwealth v Hospital Contribution Fund (1982), 194
Commonwealth v State power (MG), 194–201, 279
  Anti-Discrimination Act 1977 (NSW), 197
  Commonwealth v Hospital Contribution Fund (1982), 194
  Fencott v Muller (1983), 200
  Gosford Meats Pty Ltd v New South Wales (1985), 194
  Hematite Petroleum v Victoria (1983), 194
  Miller v TCN Channel Nine (1985), 194
  Racial Discrimination Act 1975 (Cth), 196–97
  Stack v Coast Securities (No 9) (1983), 194
  Tasmanian Dam case (1983), 195, 197–201, 280, 330
Commonwealth v Tasmania (1983) *see* Tasmanian Dam case (1983)
communism, 1, 35
Communist Party of Australia (CPA), 1, 53, 104
  referendum to ban (1951), 1–3, 258
Companion of the Order of Australia (AC), 263
Conciliation and Arbitration Act 1904 (Cth), 166, 177
  amendments to, 124–25, 128
Conciliation and Arbitration Commission, 113, 137, 139, 140, 175, 292
  ANU dispute, 171, 172–73
  APC case, 169, 170–71
  BHP dispute (1975), 152
  Maternity Leave case (1979), 139, 146, 147–48, 280

  meatworkers dispute, 141
  MG as Deputy President *see* Deputy President of Conciliation and Arbitration Commission (MG)
  national wage and equal pay cases *see* national wage and equal pay cases
  shearers dispute, 141–42
  Telecom dispute (1978), 154–57, 178
  Telecom linesmen dispute (1979), 165, 178
  wool stores dispute, 166–68, 169, 171
Conciliation and Arbitration Court, 124, 136, 137
Conlon, Alf, 51
Connor, Kevin, 262
conscription (Vietnam War), 87, 112
conservation *see* environment and conservation
Constitution *see* Australian Constitution
Convention for the Protection of the World Cultural and National Heritage (UNESCO), 198
Coombs, Dr H. C. ('Nugget'), 76
Coombs, Janet, 76–78, 79, 80, 82, 83, 84, 85
Coombs, John, 76, 212, 213
Cooper v Stuart (1889), 285
Coraki (NSW), 9
Corporations Act 1989 (Cth), 280
Council of Civil Liberties, MG as member of, 87
Council of NSW Bar Association, 81, 86
Counsell, Warrick, 88, 89
Coward, David, 322, 336
Cowen, Sir Zelman, 171, 172, 173, 174
Cox, Eva, 44
Crennan, Justice Susan, 54, 370, 377
  High Court, appointment to, 380
crime and corruption (NSW), 238, 239
  Age tapes, 216–23, 224, 225, 226, 228, 233, 234, 235, 256, 308

Barton case, 212–13
Bill Allen affair *see* Bill Allen affair
Briese allegations, 217, 223–227, 229–31, 232–33, 238, 241, 242, 243–44, 256
Enmore branch stacking, 207, 208, 209
Jackson, resignation of, 213, 238
Nugan Hand Bank, 63, 207, 208
Operation Seville, 236–37, 308
Stewart Royal Commissions *see* Stewart Royal Commissions
Street Royal Commission, 213–14, 215–16, 224
Crimes Act 1914 (Cth), 242, 309
Crimes (Sexual Assault) Amendment Act 1981 (NSW), 189–90
Criminal Law Review Division (NSW AG's Department), 189
Crocodile Dundee (film), 245
cross-vesting laws, 189, 337–38
Crown Solicitor (NSW), 210, 211, 214, 216, 222, 234, 240
Crown Solicitor's Office (Cth), 47, 49
Cunliffe v Commonwealth (1994) *see* Migration Agents case (1994)
Cunningham, Andrew, 48, 80
Curtain, David, 398
Cusack, Dymphna, 33
Cutmore, Betty (later Carter), 18, 23–24, 29
Cutmore, Daisy ('Nan'), 23
Cutmore, Dorothy, 23

Daily Telegraph, 98–99
d'Alpuget, Blanche, 45
Dame Roma Mitchell (ship), 390
Daniel, Dexter, 302
D'Aprano, Zelda, 116–17
Davis, Fran, 241
Davis, Sybil, 381
Davis v The Commonwealth (1988), 290
Dawson, Justice Daryl, 269, 303, 305, 317, 320, 322, 352
dissenting judgments, 307, 325

Mabo (No. 2), 284
MG, relationship with, 271–72
retirement, 323, 326
Wik judgment, 325
De La Salle College (Armidale), 36, 37
Deane, Justice William (later Sir), 17, 54, 267, 269, 283, 290, 295, 303, 304, 308, 317, 320, 354
dissenting judgments, 280, 305, 360, 366
Governor-General, appointed as, 271, 272, 323
judicial activist, 277, 280
Mabo (No. 2), 284, 286–88, 289
MG, relationship with, 270–71, 297, 359
'natural law' perspective, 296
procedural fairness, 293
Dearlove, Wally, 143–44
death penalty, abolition of, 190
Dedousis v The Water Board (1992) and (1994), 71–72, 73
deep sleep therapy *see* Chelmsford Private Hospital scandal
defamation, 54, 81, 82, 83, 84, 86
Burchett case, 79, 97
Lange v Australian Broadcasting Corporation (1997), 291
O'Shaughnessy v Mirror Newspapers Ltd, 89–90, 110
Pat Mackie case *see* Mackie v Australian Consolidated Press Ltd [1974]
Pearson v Australian Consolidated Press Ltd [1971], 90–91
Theophanous v Herald and Weekly Times Ltd (1994), 291
Democratic Labor Party (DLP), 79
ALP, 'Split' with, 35
Dent, Judge, 72
Department of Finance and Administration (Cth), 340
Department of Health (NSW), 160–61
Department of Immigration and Ethnic Affairs (Cth), 353
Deputy President of

Conciliation and Arbitration Commission (MG), 5, 64, 81, 97, 110, 176–77, 178, 251, 344
anti-female culture, 141–46
ANU dispute, 171, 172–73
appointment, 134, 135–39, 180
BLF High Court picket, 148–49
fair work practices, 144–46
Maternity Leave case (1979), 139, 146, 147–48, 280
meatworkers dispute, 141
office and staff, 139–40
resignation, 159, 164, 165–76, 180, 251
shearers dispute, 141–42
Telecom dispute (1978), 154–57, 178
Telecom linesmen dispute (1979), 165, 178
torn loyalties, 168–71, 180, 186
travel duties, 149–50, 163, 164, 176
detention *see* refugees
Detmold, Professor Michael, 368
Dick, Mavis, 30
Dietrich v The Queen (1992), 293, 296, 306–7, 308
Dignam, Arthur, 43
Director of Public Prosecutions (Cth), 231, 241, 268, 269
Director of Public Prosecutions (NSW), 207, 235
Director of Public Prosecutions (SA), 338
discrimination, 5, 19, 177, 189, 190, 299–300, 319, 398
equality, and, 302–4
racial *see* racial discrimination
Street v Queensland Bar Association (1989), 290, 302
women, against *see* women's rights
see also equal justice
Discrimination (Employment and Occupation) Convention (ILO), 125, 128, 147
Dixon, Chief Justice Owen (later Sir), 277, 278, 321
domestic violence, 189

INDEX

Doody (Bishop of Armidale), 29, 37
Dougherty, Tom, 101, 106
Dowd, John, 212, 256
DPP *see* Director of Public Prosecutions (Cth)
drug trafficking, 256
  Operation Seville, 236–37, 308
  Ridgeway v The Queen (1995), 308–9
  see also 'Mr Asia' drug syndicate; National Crime Authority (NCA); NSW Drugs Crime Commission
Ducker, John, 222
due process *see* procedural fairness
Duffy, Chief Justice Gavan, 321
Duke, William, 15
Duncan, Peter, 221, 321
Durack, Peter, 169

E. D. Roper Memorial prize, 272
Eastman, David, 238
Ebner v Official Trustee in Bankruptcy (2000), 366
education (MG), 21, 27–39
  St Francis Xavier Primary School (Moree), 23, 28–31, 32
  St Ursula's College (Armidale), 14, 31, 32–39, 44, 50, 68
    bursary, 31, 37–38
    music and song, 36–37
  University of Sydney 1959-1960, 40–45
    changing social mores, 43–45
    Commonwealth Scholarship, 39, 41
    feminism, 44, 45
    Law School *see* Sydney University Law School, MG at
    Moree and Bullaroo Council prize, 41
    Ngunngan Club, 42
    part-time work, 40, 41
    'The Push,' 43–44, 45
Ellicott, Robert, 153
Ellis, Bob, 43
Ellis, Ross, 65
Elphick, Lyn (later Williamson), 49, 65

Embassy of Ireland (Canberra), 247
Enmore branch stacking, 207, 208, 209
entrapment, 236, 237, 308
environment and conservation, 187, 279
  Tasmanian Dam case (1983), 195, 197–201, 280, 330
equal employment opportunity (EEO), 134, 177, 190, 240, 255, 369–74
  legal profession *see* legal profession, EEO in the
equal justice, 299–319, 365
  citizenship *see* citizenship
  common law, and, 305, 306, 316
  discrimination, and, 302–4, 365
  'equality,' concept of, 299–303, 363, 366, 398
  fair trial *see* fair trial, right to
  Leeth v Commonwealth (1992), 302–3, 305, 360, 366
  procedural fairness, 305, 306, 316, 319, 352, 353, 356, 365
equal pay cases *see* national wage and equal pay cases
Equal Remuneration for Men and Women Workers for Work of Equal Value (ILO Convention), 120–21, 125, 130–31, 132, 134
Equity, Doctrines and Remedies (book), 361
Esher, Lord, 90
Evans, Ada, 46
Evans, Gareth, 217, 246
Evatt, Clive, 5, 79, 82, 83–84, 86, 89, 90, 98
  'defo' and 'nello' practice, 81–84, 95, 97
Evatt, Elizabeth, 4–5, 62, 240, 241, 379
  Chief Justice (Family Court of Australia), 4
  Deputy President (Conciliation and Arbitration Commission), 5, 124, 139, 141
Evatt, Herbert Vere ('Doc' or 'Bert'), 5, 30, 62, 83
  Chief Justice (Supreme Court of NSW), 4

CPA, 1951 campaign against referendum to ban, 1–3
  Justice (High Court of Australia), 5, 54
  MG, meeting with, 1–2, 3, 4, 30, 258, 263
  UN, role in formation of, 4, 388
Ex parte Te (2002), 313–14

F. E. Fischer and Laws, 59, 67
fair trial, right to, 294, 306–10, 399
  Dietrich v The Queen (1992), 293, 296, 306–7, 308
  McKinney v The Queen (1991), 306
  Nicholas v The Queen (1998), 309–10
  Ridgeway v The Queen (1995), 308–9
family background (MG), 7–10
  'French connection,' 7–8, 381
  'Irish connection,' 8
Family Court of Australia, 4, 67, 379
Family Law Act 1975 (Cth), 67
Family Law Reform Act 1995 (Cth), 350
Fardon v Attorney General (Qld) (2004), 318
Farquhar, Chief Magistrate Murray
  Age tapes, 217, 218, 223
  Cessna-Milner case, 213, 214–215, 231–32
  Street Royal Commission, 213–14, 215–16, 224
Federal Court, 241, 263, 329, 331, 347, 353, 363
federal elections
  1972, in, 112, 121
  1974, in, 132
  1975, in, 159
  1983, in, 198
  1996, in, 326
Federation (Australia), 201, 327
Fellow at UNSW Law School (MG), 177–79, 180, 382
feminism and feminists, 44, 45, 52, 57, 82, 87, 124, 126–27, 148, 262, 269–70, 342
  see also women's movement
Fencott v Muller (1983), 200
Fieldhouse, Ann, 240
Fischer, Tim, 326, 327

Fisher Library (University of Sydney), 41
Fitzgerald, Father Tom, 34
Flannery, Judge Paul, 226, 230, 241, 243
Flower & Hart cases *see White Industries* cases (1998), (1999)
Fogarty, John
  marriage to MG *see* marriage to John Fogarty (MG)
  relationship with MG, 160, 162, 163
Fogarty, Patrick (MG's son), 193, 262, 347, 383, 395
  birth, 185, 193
Foord, Judge John
  Briese allegations, 225, 226, 230, 231, 232, 242, 243, 244, 256
Four Corners (tv program), 214, 330
Franklin River (Tas), 198
Fraser, Malcolm, 154, 155, 156, 168, 169
Fraser Government (federal), 153, 159, 176, 179, 210
  Staples, conflict with, 164–66, 167, 168–69
Frederick Jordan Chambers (Sydney), 8, 140
freedom of speech, 1, 82, 88, 398
  Davis v The Commonwealth (1988), 290
freedom of the press
  Australian Capital Television v Commonwealth (1992), 291, 296
  Nationwide News Pty Ltd v Wills (1992), 291
  Stephens v West Australian Newspapers Ltd (1994), 291
  Theophanous v Herald and Weekly Times Ltd (1994), 291
Freeman, George, 213, 218, 222
French, Chief Justice Robert, 380
Frenkel, Anna, 76
Frize, Bernie, 29–30
Furphy, Joseph, 167

Gaden, John, 43
Gaita, Raimond, 288
Garcia v National Australia Bank Pty Ltd (1998), 339–40

Gaudron, Alfred (MG's uncle), 10
Gaudron, Appoloniae (MG's great-great grandmother), 8, 9
Gaudron, Bernie (MG's uncle), 10
Gaudron, Edward John Michael ('Ted') (MG's father), 2, 10, 11–12, 14, 15, 16, 25–26, 31, 55, 68, 97, 136
  death, 71
  Paul's railway accident, 69–70
  political views and social values, 21–22, 23, 25–26, 35, 257
  separation from Bonnie, 69, 70
  violence and aggression, 22, 23, 25
Gaudron, Elizabeth (MG's great grandmother), 6, 9
Gaudron, Grace ('Bonnie') (MG's mother), 11–12, 14, 21, 22, 24, 25, 27, 55, 68, 70, 73, 136, 137, 395
  personality, 24, 25
  separation from Ted, 69, 70
Gaudron, Jacob (MG's great-great grandfather), 8, 9
Gaudron, Jacob (MG's great-great uncle), 9
Gaudron, James (MG's uncle), 10
Gaudron, Johann ('John') (MG's great grandfather), 6, 9
Gaudron, John ('Jack') (MG's grandfather), 6, 9
Gaudron, John (MG's uncle), 10
Gaudron, Joseph (MG's uncle), 10
Gaudron, Kathy (MG's sister), 55, 68–69, 73
Gaudron, Margaret (MG's sister), 55, 68–69, 73
Gaudron, Mary Ann (MG's grandmother), 8, 9, 10
Gaudron, Mary Genevieve
  beliefs and values *see* beliefs and values (MG)
  career *see* career (MG)
  caving, interest in, 35, 37, 42, 49, 64–66, 381
    Bungonia Caves case, 66, 88–89

  childhood *see* childhood in Moree (MG)
  education *see* education (MG)
  health issues, 322, 335, 347, 382, 394
  Hunters Hill home *see* Hunters Hill home (MG)
  influences on *see* influences on MG
  intellectual ability, 31, 35, 36, 38, 62, 80, 85, 157, 179, 181, 264, 270, 367
  Loire Valley home, 7, 347, 380, 381–82, 382, 383, 392
  marriages *see* marriage to Ben Nurse (MG); marriage to John Fogarty (MG)
  personality *see* character and personality (MG)
  photos and portraits, *18, 55, 94, 252,* 322, *336, 377,* 392–94, *397, 400, 401*
  political views *see* political views (MG)
  prizes and awards *see* prizes and awards (MG)
  public speaking and debating skills, 35–36, 38, 91
    see also speeches and addresses (MG)
  religious beliefs, 35, 44–45, 82, 91, 192, 344
  roots *see* family background (MG)
  smoking, 8, 44, 48, 264, 272, 335, 394
  speeches *see* speeches and addresses (MG)
Gaudron, Paul (MG's brother), 55, 68–69
  litigation and damages, 69, 70, 71–74
  railway accident, 69–70
Gaudron, Peter (MG's uncle), 10
Gaudron, Robert James ('Bobbie') (MG's brother), 22–23
Gaudron, Susannah (MG's great-great aunt), 9
Gaudron Chambers (Melbourne), 398
Geneva Convention, 387
George, Sir Arthur, 212
Georges, George, 246

INDEX

Gerondis, Helen, 63, 76
Gibbs, Chief Justice Harry (later Sir), 193, 194, 246, 247, 250, 255, 321, 378
Giles, Roger (later Judge), 63
Glass, Harold (later Justice), 91
Gleeson, Chief Justice Murray, 29, 54, 314, 337, 341, 378
   High Court, appointment to, 329, 335–36
   retirement, 380
Gleeson Court, *253, 273, 336–40, 343,* 345–65
   judicial activism v black-letter law, 336–40
   Justices on, 336
Gleeson Court cases
   Abebe v Commonwealth (1999), 353
   Al-Kateb v Godwin (2004), 318
   Bhardwaj case (2002), 355–56
   Cattanach v Melchior (2003), 379
   Chappel v Hart (1998), 364–65
   Ebner v Official Trustee in Bankruptcy (2000), 366
   Fardon v Attorney General (Qld) (2004), 318
   Garcia case (1998), 339–40
   Gould v Brown (1998), 337–38
   Naxakis case (1999), 365
   'Nigger Brown' case (2000), 347–49
   Patrick Stevedores case (1998), 254, 298, 362–63
   Pelechowski v Registrar, Court of Appeal NSW (1999), 338–39
   Plaintiff S157 case (2003), 356, 362
   Re Wakim (1999), 337–38
   Re Woolleys (2004), 318
   Rogers v Whitaker (1992), 363–64
   Shaw v MIMA (2003), 314
   Superclinics case (1996), 351–52
   275-02 v MIMA and anor (2002), 356–58
   U v U (2002), 349, 350
   Yanner v Eaton (1999), 281–82, 336–37
   Yusuf case (2001), 353–54

Goodsell House (Sydney), 183
Gordon River (Tas), 198
Gorton Government (federal), 83
Gosford Meats Pty Ltd v New South Wales (1985), 194
Goulburn (NSW), 89
Gould v Brown (1998), 337–38
Gove land rights case (1971), 285
Governor-General of Australia, 271, 272, 323, 380
Gray Government (Tas), 198
Great Depression, 22
Green Bans, 82
Greenland, Hall, 43
Greer, Germaine, 43–44, 230
Greiner, Nick, 216, 219
Greiner Government (NSW), 191
Griffith, Dr Gavan, 188, 189, 246
Gruzman, Laurence, 212
Guantanamo Bay (Cuba), 387, 389, 390, 391
Gummow, Justice William, 54, 73, 261, 263, 292, 314, 318, 322, 336, 337, 338, 344, 345, 366
   dissenting judgments, 338
   Equity, Doctrines and Remedies (book), 361
   GM, relationship with, 272, 359, 361
   Wik judgment, 324, 325, 326
Gungaletta (Aboriginal tribe), 281
Gungalida (Aboriginal tribe), 281
Guyra (NSW), 236, 237
Gwydir River (NSW), 20

Habib, Mamdouh, 389
Hagan, Stephen, 347, 348
Hagan v Trustees of the Toowoomba Sports Ground Trust (2000) *see* 'Nigger Brown' case (2000)
Haines, Trevor, 229, 239
Hallam, Jack, 239–40
Hand, Burt, 16
Hansen, Pauline, 140, 150, 155, 171, 173, 176
'Harold Park Trots' (Sydney), 48
Hatton, John, 234, 256
Hawke, Bob, 116, 155, 156–57, 251

Hawke Government (federal), 198, 203, 246, 251, 379
Hayden, Bill, 175
Hayne, Justice Ken, 261, 314, 318, 322, 337, 344, 347, 348, 350
   High Court, appointment to, 326–27, 336
   MG, relationship with, 359, 361
Heffernan, Bill, 340–42, 348
Heilpern, Hans, 224, 225
Hematite Petroleum v Victoria (1983), 194
Henke, Paul, 79
Herald, 138
Herron, Chief Justice Sir Leslie, 79, 90
Heydon, Justice Dyson, 54, 142, 318, 336, 367–68
   High Court, appointment to, 376, 378, 379
   Sir Maurice Byers Lecture, 359
Hicks, David, 389, 390
Higgins, Chief Justice Terry, 246
Higgins, Justice Henry Bournes, 136–37
High Court cases
   Abebe v Commonwealth (1999), 353
   Actors and Announcers Equity Association v Fontana Films Pty Ltd (1981), 193
   Al-Kateb v Godwin (2004), 318
   Australian Capital Television v Commonwealth (1992), 291, 296
   Australian Iron and Steel Pty Ltd v Banovic (1989), 303–4
   Bhardwaj case (2002), 355–56
   Cattanach v Melchior (2003), 379
   Chappel v Hart (1998), 364–65
   Cole v Whitfield (1988), 295, 296
   Commonwealth v Hospital Contribution Fund (1982), 194
   Davis v The Commonwealth (1988), 290
   Dedousis v The Water Board (1994), 71–72, 73

481

Dietrich v The Queen (1992), 293, 296, 306–7, 308
Ebner v Official Trustee in Bankruptcy (2000), 366
Ex parte Te (2002), 313–14
Fardon v Attorney General (Qld) (2004), 318
Fencott v Muller (1983), 200
Garcia case (1998), 339–40
Gould v Brown (1998), 337–38
Hindmarsh Island Bridge case (1998), 329–30, 332–34
King v The Queen (1986), 246
Leeth v Commonwealth (1992), 302–3, 305, 360, 366
Lim case (1992), 311–12, 316, 317, 318, 330, 333, 334
Mabo case see Mabo v Queensland (No. 2) (1992)
Mabo v Queensland (No. 1) (1988), 282–83
McInnis v The Queen (1979), 248, 307
McKinney v The Queen (1991), 306
Migration Agents case (1994), 291
Miller v TCN Channel Nine (1985), 194, 246–47
Nationwide News Pty Ltd v Wills (1992), 291
Naxakis case (1999), 365
Nicholas v The Queen (1998), 309–10
'Nigger Brown' case (2000), 347–49
Nolan v Minister for Immigration and Ethnic Affairs (1988), 310–11, 312, 313, 314
O'Shaughnessy v Mirror Newspapers Ltd, 89–90, 110
Patrick Stevedores case (1998), 254, 298, 362–63
Pelechowski v Registrar, Court of Appeal NSW (1999), 338–39
Plaintiff S157 case (2003), 356, 362
Re Patterson; Ex parte Taylor (2001), 312–13, 314
Re Wakim (1999), 337–38
Re Woolleys (2004), 318
Ridgeway v The Queen (1995), 308–9

Rogers v Whitaker (1992), 363–64
Shaw v MIMA (2003), 314
Stephens v West Australian Newspapers Ltd (1994), 291
Street v Queensland Bar Association (1989), 290, 302
Sue v Hill (1999), 314–15
Superclinics case (1996), 351–52
Tasmanian Dam case (1983), 195, 197–201, 280, 330
Teoh case (1995), 315–16
Theophanous v Herald and Weekly Times Ltd (1994), 291
275-02 v MIMA and anor (2002), 356–58
U v U (2002), 349
Van Gervan v Fenton (1992), 304, 349
Walden v Hensler (1987), 281
Wik case (1996), 254, 295, 296, 323–26, 327
WorkChoices case (2006), 201, 254, 280
Yanner v Eaton (1999), 281–82, 336–37
Yusuf case (2001), 353–54
High Court of Australia
Anti-Discrimination Act 1977 (NSW), 197
Canberra, life in, 264–67
cases see High Court cases
Constitution, interpretation of, 276, 278–80, 290–94, 359, 398
Limitation Act 1969 (NSW), 71–72, 73
MG as Justice on see Justice of High Court of Australia (MG)
Racial Discrimination Act 1975 (Cth), 196–97
seniority, 320, 329, 335
Hillë, Elizabeth see Gaudron, Elizabeth (MG's great grandmother)
Hilton Hotel bombing, 238
Hindmarsh Island Bridge Act 1997 (Cth), 332
Hindmarsh Island Bridge Bill 1996 (Cth), 329
Hindmarsh Island Bridge case (1998), 329–30, 332–34
Callinan involvement, 329–30

Hindmarsh Island (SA), 332
Hitler (Adolf), 102
HMAS Penguin, 268
Hogan, Margaret, 34, 35, 39
Hold the Line (play), 228
Holding, Clyde, 321
Hollingworth, Dr Peter, 380
Hope, Justice, 221
Horan, Monica, 30
Horler, Ken, 240
Horler, Lillian, 240
House of Assembly (SA), 221
House of Representatives (federal), 378
Howard, John, 326, 327, 329, 330, 335
Howard Government (federal), 201, 254, 256, 326, 328, 332, 335, 336, 342, 353–54, 376, 380, 389
Afghanistan, war in, 389–90
'children overboard affair,' 354
'migration zone,' 390–91
Hughes, Billy, 136
Hughes, Robert, 43
Hughes, Tom, 376
human rights, 4, 5, 50, 102, 131, 153, 179, 190, 196, 197, 247, 315, 383
Constitution, interpretation of, 276, 278–80, 290–94, 398
s 75(v) Constitution, and, 384, 386–87, 393
see also indigenous land rights; refugees; women's rights
Humphreys, Kevin
Street Royal Commission, 213–14, 215–16, 223, 224
Hunters Hill home (MG), 94, 126, 160–63, 176, 179
compensation claim, 160, 161, 162–63, 179
NSW Government, battle with, 160–61
radiation contamination, 160, 161–62
Hutley, Professor Frank, 91, 195, 259, 277, 360
Judge (NSW Supreme Court and Court of Appeal), 34, 50, 52–54, 80, 109, 110, 138
Julius Stone, conflict with, 52–53

INDEX

MG 's 'reading' with, 77, 78
Hydro-Electric Commission, 198, 199

ILO *see* International Labour Organization (ILO)
Incorporations case, 280
indemnity from prosecution, 207, 233–36
  Operation Seville, 236–37, 308
indigenous land rights, 189, 191, 398
  Amaroo land claim, 289
  Gove land rights case, 285
  Mabo case *see Mabo v Queensland (No. 2)* (1992)
  Mabo v Queensland (No. 1) (1988), 282–83
  Royal Commission, 124
  Wik case *see Wik Peoples v Queensland (Pastoral Leases case)* (1996)
  see also Native Title Act 1993 (Cth)
industrial disputes, 159
  Mount Isa *see Mackie v Australian Consolidated Press Ltd* [1974]
  Patrick Stevedores case (1998), 254
  Storemen and Packers Union, 167–68
  see also Conciliation and Arbitration Commission
Industrial Relations Commission, 175
inflation, 126–27, 128, 132, 139, 159, 165, 166
  see also national wage and equal pay cases
influences on MG
  Catholic upbringing, 8, 10, 21, 27, 344
    see also St Ursula's College (Armidale)
  'Doc' Evatt, 1–2, 3, 4, 30, 258, 263
  father's political views and social values, 21–22, 23, 25–26
  Hutley, 34, 50, 52–54, 195, 259, 277, 360
  Stone, 50–52, 54, 259, 277, 360
Innocence Project (Griffith University), MG appointed

to, 384–85
International Convention on the Elimination of all forms of Discrimination Against Women (UN), 190
International Convention on the Elimination of All Forms of Racial Discrimination (UN), 195, 196, 197
International Criminal Tribunal for Rwanda, 384
International Labour Organization (ILO), 120, 125
  Administrative Tribunal, MG's appointment to, 382–84
  Discrimination (Employment and Occupation) Convention, 125, 128, 147
  Equal Remuneration Convention, 120–21, 125, 130–31, 132, 134
Inverell Hospital, 69
Inverell (NSW), 22, 69, 144
Iron Cavalier (ship), 152–53
Isaac, Deputy President, 170
Isaacs, Chief Justice Isaac, 321

Jackson, Rex, 213, 238
Jackson v Sterling Industries Ltd, (1987), 267–68
Jacobs, Sir Kenneth, 54
James, Clive, 43
Jenolan Caves (NSW), 64, 65
Jock Strap and his Elastic Band, 36–37
John Geddes Equity prize, 272
Johnson, Geoffrey, 357–58
Johnston, Dorothy, 123
Jolly, Rob, 127
Jones, Magistrate Kevin, 214, 224, 226
Jordan, Mary Ann *see* Gaudron, Mary Ann (MG's grandmother)
Jordan, Sir Frederick, 8
Joye, Col, 21
Judges' Pensions Act 1968 (Cth), 342
judicial activism, 199, 286, 325–26, 326, 327, 328, 332, 367
  black-letter law, *versus*, 275–77, 280, 286, 367
Judiciary Act 1903 (Cth), 184
Justice of High Court of

Australia (MG), 29, 38, 53, 54, 61, 141, 149, 163, 164, 179, 181, 211, 241, 330, 336, 337, 338, 345–46
  AC, declines, 263–64
  appointment as, 4, 5, 8, 71, 157, 239, 245, 250–60, 276, 336
  Callinan, relationship with, 328, 331
  Canberra life, 266–67
  cases *see* Brennan Court cases; Gleeson Court cases; Mason Court cases
  Chief Justice speculation, 320–23, 329
  citizenship *see* citizenship
  criticism of, 294, 295
  cross-vesting laws, 189, 337–38
  Dawson, relationship with, 271–72
  Deane, relationship with, 270–71, 297, 359
  discrimination against women *see* women's rights
  dissenting judgments, 281, 305, 314, 338, 359, 360
  fair trial *see* fair trial, right to
  Gummow, relationship with, 272, 359, 361
  Hayne, relationship with, 359, 361
  Heffernan allegations, 341–42
  Hindmarsh Island Bridge case (1998), 332–34
  Judges' Pensions Act 1968 (Cth), 342
  judicial activism v black-letter law, 53, 195, 259, 277, 296–97, 338, 359–61, 367
  Kirby, relationship with, 272, 339, 340–44, 352
  legacy of career, 365–68
  Limitation Act 1969 (NSW), 71–72, 73
  Mabo (No. 2) judgment *see Mabo v Queensland (No. 2)* (1992)
  Mason, relationship with, 270–71, 298, 359
  McHugh, relationship with, 272
  'Nigger Brown' case (2000), 347–49

procedural fairness *see* procedural fairness
refugees *see* refugees
retirement and farewell, 335, 358–59, 359, 376–78, 379–80
social justice, 295, 296–97
staff, 261–63
titles, wigs and robes, 261, 263
Toohey, relationship with, 272, 359
Wik judgment, 324, 325, 326
Wilson, relationship with, 271
woman's perspective, 349–52
Justinian (journal), 258

Kamenka, Eugene, 44
Kamilaroi people, 19
Kanangra National Park (NSW), 66
Kane, Jack, 79, 97
Kanzen (ship) *see Love Boat* scandal
Kartinyeri, Doreen, 329
Kartinyeri v Commonwealth (1998) *see* Hindmarsh Island Bridge case (1998)
Katz, Leslie, 185
Keating, Paul, 49, 321, 329
Keating Government (federal), 320, 326, 332, 352–53
Keely, John, 119–20, 121
Kelly, Lawrence, 221
Kennedy, Sister Pat ('Mother Campion'), 32, 33–34, 35, 39
KGB (Soviet Union), 79
Kiefel, Justice Susan, 381
King v The Queen (1986), 246
Kirby, Michael (later Justice), 43, 51, 54, 67, 169, 201, 204, 263, 297, 313, 328, 337, 350, 355
dissenting judgments, 334, 338
Heffernan allegations, 340–42, 348
High Court, appointment to, 324, 326, 336
Judges' Pensions Act 1968 (Cth), 342
judicial activist, 277, 338
MG, relationship with, 272, 339, 340–44, 352
Re Wakim (1999), 337–38
retirement, 340, 395

Wik judgment, 324, 325, 326
Kitney, Geoff, 256
Kitto, Sir Frank, 54
Kneipp, Sister Pauline, 34
Knox, Helen, 76
Kok, Daphne, 59, 63, 66
Koowarta, John, 196
Koowarta v Bjelke-Petersen (1982), 196, 199
Kruger v Commonwealth (Stolen Generation case) (1997) *see* Stolen Generation case

Labor Party *see* Australian Labor Party (ALP)
Land Act 1962–1974 (Qld), 324
Land Act 1910 (Qld), 282, 324
Landa, Paul, 189, 216, 217, 220, 222, 230, 238, 239
Lane, P.H., 187
Lange v Australian Broadcasting Corporation (1997), 291
Lapworth, Janine, 263
Larkins, Tony, 91
Law Council of Australia, 331, 378, 398
Law Society of NSW, 234
Laws, Graeme, 67
Leeth v Commonwealth (1992), 302–3, 305, 360, 366
legal aid, 164, 180, 306, 307
Legal Education Committee (NSW), 81
legal positivism *see* black-letter law
legal profession, EEO in the, 369–70, 371–74
High Court, on the, 376–81, 380–81
judges, appointment of, 374–76
magistrates, appointment of, 190
merit, 370, 372, 373, 374–75, 379
legalism *see* black-letter law
Legislative Assembly (NSW), 212, 213, 221
Legislative Assembly (Qld), 103
Legislative Council (NSW), 224
Leuralla (Evatt family home), 5
Liberal–Country Coalition, 83
Liberal–National Coalition, 159, 270

Liberal Party, 328
Lim case (1992), 311–12, 316, 317, 318, 330, 333, 334
Limitation Act 1969 (NSW), 71–72, 73
Lindsay Range (NSW), 22
Lingiari, Vincent, 289
Lismore District Court, 71, 73
Lismore (NSW), 9
Loder, Kaye, 63, 80, 189
Lorenzini's Wine Bar (Sydney), 48
Love Boat scandal, 207–8
Ludeke, Deputy President Terry, 170, 174
Lush, Sir George, 246

Mabo, Eddie ('Koiki'), 282, 283, 289
Mabo v Queensland (No. 1) (1988), 282–83
Mabo v Queensland (No. 2) (1992), 5, 10, 17, 254, 276, 280–90, 294, 323, 326, 327
common law, and, 283, 284, 285, 286
criticism of decision, 285–86
MG and Deane joint judgment, 286–88, 289, 295, 298
terra nullius, 284, 285, 286
MacCallum, Mungo, 43
Mackie, Pat ('Red Cap'), 94, 95, 96, 99, 101, 102, 362
Mackie v Australian Consolidated Press Ltd [1974], 82, 95–111, 150, 243, 362
appeal, 108–11
Daily Telegraph articles, 98–99
mining dispute, background to, 98–101
'proofing the punter,' 104–5
trial, 105–8
Macquarie University, 262
Council, 240–41
Maddern, Justice, 175
Madgwick, Justice Rod, 87
Magistrates Courts Administration, 190
Marinoff, Dimiter, 191
Maritime Union of Australia, 362
marriage to Ben Nurse (MG)
caving life, 64–66, 88
children *see* Nurse, Ben;

INDEX

Nurse, Danielle; Nurse, Julienne
family life, 58, 59, 65, 68, 91, 136, 138–39, 346
Hunters Hill home *see* Hunters Hill home (MG)
marriage breakdown, 159–60, 162, 176
meeting, courtship and marriage, 42–43, 55, 58, 146
marriage to John Fogarty (MG), 176, 179, 184–85, 241, 266, 335, 346, 381, 382
Marsden, John, 48, 63
Marshall, Jeanine, 146–47
Martin, Trevor, 88
Maryvale (Vic), 150
Mason, Chief Justice Anthony (later Sir), 54, 199, 254–55, 256, 267, 269, 275, 284, 290, 291, 305, 307, 308, 322, 365, 368
   Chief Justice, appointment as, 224–25, 321
   Mabo (No. 2), 284
   MG, relationship with, 270–71, 298, 359, 393
   retirement, 272, 277, 320, 323
Mason Court, 255, 260, 273, 275–98, 319, 323, 344, 359, 360
   cases *see* Mason Court cases
   Catholic background, 296
   Constitutional rights and freedoms, interpretation of, 276, 278–80, 290–94, 398
   criticism of, 294–98
   judicial activism v black-letter law, 275–77, 280, 286, 290, 297, 325
   Justices on, 269–72
   social justice, 295, 296–97
Mason Court cases
   Australian Capital Television v Commonwealth (1992), 291, 296
   Australian Iron and Steel Pty Ltd v Banovic (1989), 303–4
   Cole v Whitfield (1988), 295, 296
   Davis v The Commonwealth (1988), 290
   Dedousis v The Water Board (1992) and (1994), 71–72, 73

Dietrich v The Queen (1992), 293, 296, 306–7, 308
Ex parte Te (2002), 313–14
Jackson v Sterling Industries Ltd, (1987), 267–68
Leeth v Commonwealth (1992), 302–3, 305, 360, 366
Lim case (1992), 311–12, 316, 317, 318, 330, 333, 334
Mabo case *see Mabo v Queensland (No. 2)* (1992)
Mabo v Queensland (No. 1) (1988), 282–83
McKinney v The Queen (1991), 306
Migration Agents case (1994), 291
Nationwide News Pty Ltd v Wills (1992), 291
Nicholas v The Queen (1998), 309–10
Nolan v Minister for Immigration and Ethnic Affairs (1988), 310–11, 312, 313, 314
Re Patterson; Ex parte Taylor (2001), 312–13, 314
Ridgeway v The Queen (1995), 308–9
Stephens v West Australian Newspapers Ltd (1994), 291
Street v Queensland Bar Association (1989), 290, 302
Sue v Hill (1999), 314–15
Teoh case (1995), 315–16
Theophanous v Herald and Weekly Times Ltd (1994), 291
Van Gervan v Fenton (1992), 304, 349
Walden v Hensler (1987), 281
Zecevic v DPP (Vic) (1987), 267
Masterman, George, 234
maternity leave, 139, 146, 147–48, 280
Maternity Leave case (1979), 139, 146, 147–48, 280
Mathews, Jane (later Justice), 83, 368
Mawkes, Albert (MG's great-grandfather), 24
Mawkes, Grace ('Bonnie') *see* Gaudron, Grace ('Bonnie') (MG's mother)
Mawkes, Violet Grace ('Nan')

(MG's grandmother), 24
Maxwell Connery & Co, 67
May, Maurice, 97, 98, 101, 110
McAuley, Catherine, 28
McCabe, Paul, 36
McCanna, Marie, 36, 38
McCaw, Kenneth (later Sir), 88, 91–92
McColl, Ruth (later Justice), 350, 368
McElphone Hotel (Moree), 22
McGarvie, Dick, 113, 134
McHugh, Michael (later Justice), 78, 251, 254, 257, 263, 305, 307, 318, 336, 339, 340
   dissenting judgments, 303, 325, 337, 338
   Mabo (No. 2), 284
   MG, relationship with, 272
   Wik judgment, 325
McInnis v The Queen (1979), 248, 307
McKenzie, Deputy President, 170
McKinney v The Queen (1991), 306
McLaughlin, John, 80
McMahon Government (federal), 113, 123
McMaster Ward (Moree District Hospital), 20
McQueen, Humphrey, 246
McTiernan, Sir Edward, 54
Meagher, Justice Roderick, 351, 372–73
Meat Industry Employees Union, 141, 143
meatworkers dispute, 141
medical negligence, 363, 365
   Chappel v Hart (1998), 364–65
   Naxakis case (1999), 365
   Rogers v Whitaker (1992), 363–64
Meehan, Father Edward, 30
Mehi River (NSW), 11, 12
Meissner, Joe, 208, 209
Melbourne Metropolitan Board of Works, 144
Meng Tok Te, 313–14
Menzies, Sir Robert, 278
Menzies Government (federal), 1
Meriam people, 282, 283, 285
Messel, Professor Harry, 246

485

Michelago Caves (NSW), 64
Migration Act 1958 (Cth), 311, 312, 314, 352–53, 354, 355–56
Migration Agents case (1994), 291
Migration Legislation (Judicial Review) Act 2001 (Cth), 354
Mildren, Ray, 48–49
Miles, Jeffrey, 140, 266
Miles, Tricia, 140, 266
Milirrpum v Nabalco Pty Ltd (1971) see Gove Land Rights case (1971)
Miller v TCN Channel Nine (1985), 194, 246–47
Milner, Timothy, 214–15
Mining Act 1906 (NSW), 88
Mining Warden's Court (NSW), 66, 88–89
Minister for Immigration & Multicultural Affairs v Bhardwaj (2002) see Bhardwaj case (2002)
Minister for Immigration and Multicultural Affairs v Yusuf (2001) see Yusuf case (2001)
Minister of State for Immigration & Ethnic Affairs v Ah Hin Teoh ('Teoh') (1995), 315–16
Mitchell, Dame Roma, 184, 259, 372, 390
MOA see Municipal Officers Association of Australia (MOA)
Moffitt, Justice (Athol), 109
Molloy, Warren, 210
Moore, John (later Sir), 119, 126–27, 130, 132, 137, 139, 146, 152, 153, 168
  MG's resignation, 171–76
  Staples, fallout with, 159, 168–71
Moore, Lesley, 39
Moree Cemetery, 23
Moree Champion (newspaper), 257, 289
Moree Council, 20
Moree Library, 289
Moree (NSW), 37, 82
  Aboriginal community see Aboriginal community (Moree)
  Aboriginal Land Council, 289
  Mabo (No. 2), reaction to, 289–90

MG's childhood in see childhood in Moree (MG)
  railway community, 10, 11, 12–16, 22, 25, 28
  settlement of, 11, 17
Moree Plains Shire Council, 289
Moree Public School, 24
Moree Swimming Pool, 21–22
Morison, Professor Bill, 50, 51, 53, 54, 56, 57
Mount Isa Mines Company, 100
  miners' strike (1964) see Mackie v Australian Consolidated Press Ltd [1974]
Mount Russell (NSW), 69
Moynihan, Justice Martin, 282, 283
'Mr Asia' drug syndicate, 207
  Stewart Royal Commission, 207, 217, 222, 232, 234–35, 245
Mulhall, Mother Mary Vincent, 28
Mulock, Ron, 191
Municipal Employees' Union, 119
Municipal Officers Association of Australia (MOA), 146–47
Munro, Lyall (Snr), 15, 25, 197, 289
Murdoch (Rupert), 89
Murphy, Ingrid, 251
Murphy, Lionel (later Justice), 54, 67, 82, 136, 229, 264, 268, 270, 307, 344
  Age tapes, 213, 216, 217, 218, 233
  Briese allegations, 223, 224, 226–27, 230, 232–33, 241, 242, 243–44
  illness and death, 246–47, 250, 251, 255
  Senate Select Committee inquiries, 226, 230, 231, 233
  trial, retrial and aquittal, 241–45, 267, 268, 327, 328, 331
  'wake' and memorial service, 247–49, 254
Murray, Les, 43
Murray Islands (Torres Strait), 282, 283, 284, 286
  Dauar, 284

Mer, 284, 286
Waier, 284

Nagle, Justice (John Flood), 97, 105, 108
national census (1967), 19
National Council of Women, 67, 127
National Crime Authority (NCA), 237, 268
National Farmers' Federation, 167
National Parks and Wildlife Conservation Act 1975 (Cth), 198
National Party, 326, 327, 328
National Times, 217, 242
national wage and equal pay cases, 96, 112–34
  1967, 115, 126
  1969, 116, 119, 121, 126
  background, 113, 115–17
  MG's role
    appointment, 112–15, 123, 134
  1972 – equal pay for work of equal value, 117–24, 125, 126, 127, 128, 133, 134, 147, 151, 280, 370
  1973, 125, 129
  1974 – minimum wage for women/indexation, 123, 124–34, 141, 374
  1975 – indexation, 128, 132, 134, 151, 165
  see also inflation
Nationwide News Pty Ltd v Wills (1992), 291
native title see indigenous land rights
Native Title Act 1993 (Cth), 284–85, 325, 332
Native Title Amendment Bill 1997 (Cth), 328–29
natural justice see procedural fairness
Naxakis v Western General Hospital (1999), 365
New Idea (magazine), 147
New South Wales v Commonwealth (1990) see Incorporations case
New South Wales v Commonwealth (Workchoices) (2006) see Workchoices case (2006)

Ngarrindjeri people, 332
Ngunngan Club (University of Sydney), 42
Nicholas v The Queen (1998), 309–10
'Nigger Brown' case (2000), 347–49
Nimrod Theatre (Sydney), 240
'No Bill' submissions, 88, 223, 233–34, 236, 237
Nolan, Therrance, 311
Nolan v Minister for Immigration and Ethnic Affairs (1988), 310–11, 312, 313, 314
Northern Territory Supreme Court, 302
Notaris, Peter, 16
NSW Bar, MG at, 67, 70, 75–93, 136, 138, 176, 177
  anti-female culture, 76–79, 80–81, 85, 272
  Bungonia Caves case, 66, 88–89
  commencing practice, 76–81
  'defo' and 'nello' practice, 81–84
  'Mr Junior' speech (Sydney Bar), 91–93, 109
  national wage cases *see* national wage and equal pay cases
  O'Shaughnessy v Mirror Newspapers Ltd, 89–90, 110
  Pat Mackie case *see Mackie v Australian Consolidated Press Ltd* [1974]
  'reading' with Hutley, 77, 78, 80
  securing chambers, 76–78, 80, 272
  Tony Blackshield, defence of, 87–88
  women barristers, 76–77, 79
NSW Bar Association, 151, 175, 184, 234, 378, 392
  High Court, MG's appointment to, 256–57
  member, MG as *see* NSW Bar, MG at
  prize, 62
  see also Council of NSW Bar Association
NSW Barristers' Admission Board, 243
NSW Branch (ALP), 222
  Credentials Committee, 208

NSW Court of Appeal, 72, 73, 80, 89, 92, 191, 241, 257, 351, 373
  Mackie v Australian Consolidated Press Ltd [1974], 107
  O'Shaughnessy v Mirror Newspapers Ltd, 89–90, 110
  Pearson v Australian Consolidated Press Ltd [1971], 90–91
NSW District Court, 72, 226, 339
  'Levine ruling,' 193
NSW Drugs Crime Commission, 232
NSW Law Reform Commission, 110, 169, 170
NSW Legal Services Commission, MG chair of, 164, 180
NSW Ombudsman, 234
NSW Police Force, 222, 238, 239
  Bill Allen affair *see* Bill Allen affair
  Cessna – Milner case, 213, 214– 215, 231–32
  Operation Seville, 236–37, 308
  Roger Rogerson case, 242
  Street Royal Commission, 213–14, 215–16, 224
  unlawful telephone tapping *see Age* tapes
NSW prisons, riots at, 152
NSW Railways (later State Rail Authority), 10, 12
Paul Gaudron litigation, 69, 70, 71, 72–73
NSW Solicitors' Admission Board, 38
NSW Supreme Court, 4, 5, 8, 79, 84, 96, 329, 335, 376
  Pat Mackie case *see Mackie v Australian Consolidated Press Ltd* [1974]
NSW Women's Advisory Council, 63
Nugan, Frank, 63
Nugan Hand Bank, 63, 207, 208
  Stewart Royal Commission, 207
Nurse, Ben (MG's husband), 55, 137, 161, 163, 346
  caving life, 64–66, 88

marriage to MG *see* marriage to Ben Nurse (MG)
Nurse, Ben (MG's son), 68, 85
  birth, 91
  death, 91
Nurse, Danielle (MG's daughter), 59–60, 61, 67–68, 94, 101, 136, 137, 161–62, 163, 179, 346, 347, 383, 395
  birth, 60
Nurse, Julienne (MG's daughter), 68, 91, 92, 101, 136, 137, 161–62, 163, 179, 346, 383
  birth, 91
Nurse, Mary *see* Gaudron, Mary Genevieve

Oakes, Laurie, 43
obscenity and indecency laws, 82, 87
Occasional Papers (UNSW publication), 178
O'Dea, Peter, 149, 246
O'Laughlin, John (later Judge), 63
One Nation (party), 315
Operation Seville, 236–37, 308
O'Reilly, Father Lynami ('Bulldog'), 21, 22, 25, 30
Orwell, George, 16
O'Shaughnessy, Peter, 89–90
O'Shaughnessy v Mirror Newspapers Ltd, 89–90, 110
Othello (play), 89
Oz (magazine), 87

Packer, Frank, 97, 110
Packer, Kerry, 111
Parker, Professor R. S., 254
Passi, David, 283
Pat Mackie case *see Mackie v Australian Consolidated Press Ltd* [1974]
Patrick Plains (NSW), 9
Patrick Stevedores Operations No. 2 Pty Ltd v Maritime Union of Australia (1998), 254, 298, 362–63
Peacock, Andrew, 208
Pearson v Australian Consolidated Press Ltd [1971], 90–91
Pelechowski, Karl, 339
Pelechowski v Registrar, Court of Appeal NSW (1999), 338–39

People's Republic of China, 112
Perger, Virginia, 208
Perkins, Charles, 21
Perrignon, Justice William, 210
Peterson, Frederick, 341
Phillip Hotel (Sydney), 48, 57
Pierce, Jason, 255, 287, 288, 294–96, 297, 307
Pilbeam, Rex, 146, 147
Plaintiff S157/2002 v Commonwealth (2003), 356, 362
Playboy (magazine), 175
Pleading under the Supreme Court (amendment) Act 1970 (book), 79
political views (MG), 35, 53, 80, 82–83, 229, 344
  Kings Cross Branch (ALP), secretary of, 82, 86
  personality, and, 84–88
Portus, Commissioner (J.H.), 130
Postmaster-General's Department, 37
Poulis, George, 16, 25
Premiers' Conference (1983), 202
Privy Council Appeals Abolition Bill 1979 (NSW), 202
Privy Council (UK), 202, 285
  right to appeal to, abolition of, 201–5, 260
prizes and awards (MG), 62, 67
  Bachelor of Arts (1962), 49
  bursary to St Ursula's College, 31, 37–38
  Commonwealth Scholarship, 39, 41
  honorary Doctorate of Laws (University of Sydney), 41
  John Geddes Equity prize, 272
  Moree and Bullaroo Council prize, 41
  NSW Bar Association prize, 62
  Succession prize (University of Sydney), 60
  Sydney University Medal in Law, 4, 62–63, 67, 75, 258
  Women Lawyers' Association of NSW prize, 62
procedural fairness, 292–94, 365

equal justice, and, 305, 306, 316, 319
fair trial *see* fair trial, right to
refugees, 352, 353, 356
productivity bargaining, 178–79
Public Law Review, 398
Public Service Act (Cth), 47

Queen (Elizabeth II), 202, 203, 204

racial discrimination, 10, 14, 16–21, 23–24, 29, 95, 102, 280, 299
  Anti-Discrimination Act 1977 (NSW), 197
  Koowarta v Bjelke-Petersen (1982), 196, 199
  'Nigger Brown' case (2000), 347–49
  Racial Discrimination Act 1975 (Cth), 196–97, 283
  see also Aboriginal people
Racial Discrimination Act 1975 (Cth), 196–97, 283, 285, 348
Railway Institute Library (Moree), 25
Railway Workers' Union, 2, 10, 14, 15, 97
Ramsden, S.R., 103
rape, 189, 190, 373
  marriage, within, 67, 189
Rares, Steven, 351, 352
Rau, Cornelia, 391
Re Patterson; Ex parte Taylor (2001), 312–13, 314
Re Wakim; Ex parte McNally (1999), 337–38
Re Woolleys (2004), 318
refugees, 352–59, 386–88, 390–92
  Abebe v Commonwealth (1999), 353
  Australian 'migration zone,' 390–91
  Bhardwaj case (2002), 355–56
  detention, 316–19
  Plaintiff S157 case (2003), 356, 362
  procedural fairness, 352, 353, 356
  Refugee Convention, 388
  275-02 v MIMA and anor (2002), 356–58
  Yusuf case (2001), 353–54

Reid, Lyndall, 36
Reynolds, Henry, 288–89, 323
Reynolds, Justice Ray, 92, 109
Rice, James, 283
Richardson, Graham, 208
Richmond River (NSW), 9
Roberts, Hugh, 210, 211, 216, 222
Robertson, Geoffrey, 43, 241, 275
Robertson, Tim, 241
Robinson, Deputy president, 170
Robinson, Sally, 392–94, *401*
Rockhampton City Council, 146
Rogers v Whitaker (1992), 363–64
Rogerson, Roger, 242
Rosanove, Joan, 184
Roxon, Lillian, 44
Royal Commissions
  Hope Royal Commission, 221
  Stewart *see* Stewart Royal Commissions
  Street Royal Commission, 213–14, 215–16, 224
Royal Malaysian Police Force, 308
Royal Women's Hospital (Sydney), 185
Rubenstein, Professor Kim, 315
Rudd Government (federal), 381
Ruddock, Phillip, 63, 354, 356, 389
rule of law, 230, 292, 382, 387, 388, 389, 391, 399
Ryan, Edna, 119, 124, 126, 127, 128, 133
Ryan, Morgan, 213, 214, 215
  Age tapes, 217, 218, 245
  Briese allegations, 224, 226, 227, 230, 233, 241, 242, 243, 244
  Cessna–Milner case, 213, 215, 232
  Street Royal Commission, 213, 214
Ryan, Susan, 254

Sabine, Sam, 15
Sachs, Zena, 52, 61
Sacred Heart Catholic Church (Inverell), 58

INDEX 489

Saffron, Abraham ('Abe'), 207
  Age tapes, 217, 218
  Bill Allen affair, 210
San Francisco Conference (1945), 4, 388
Saunders, Professor Cheryl, 367
Schmidt, Lalie, 15–16
Schreiner, Sue, 76
Scutt, Jocelynne, 240
Second World War *see* World War II
Selbourne Chambers (Sydney), 76, 235
Senate Select Committee inquiries, 226, 230, 231, 233
separation of powers doctrine, 292–93
Sesame Street (tv program), 265–66
sexual assault, 189–90
Shakespeare, (William), 89, 240
Shand, Alec, 97, 109, 243
Sharp, Ian, 136
Sharpe, Naomi, 369
Shatwell, David, 62
Shatwell, Ken, 62
Shaw, Jason, 314
Shaw v Minister for Immigration and Multicultural Affairs (2003), 314
Sheahan, Terry, 191, 232, 239, 250
shearers dispute, 141–42
Simms, Vic, 20
Sir Maurice Byers Lecture, 359
Sirocco (ship), 24
Sisters of Mercy (Moree), 28
Slattery, Justice John, 238
Slee, John, 223, 243–44, 268
Sloss, Albie Ross, 86
Snelling, Harold, 184
Snuggery (SA), 150
social justice, 5, 10, 22, 28, 35, 50, 52, 53, 128, 151, 238, 248, 260, 277, 280, 326, 395
  Mason Court, 295, 296–97
  reforms, 184, 189–91, 195, 338, 362
  see also equal justice
Solicitor General (Cth), 173, 188, 246
Solicitor General of NSW (MG), 177, 178, 183–205, 206–27, 228–49, 251, 267, 268, 301
  advisory role, 184, 186–89

advocate for NSW Government, 184, 191–94, 229
Age tapes, 216–23, 224, 225, 226, 228, 233, 234, 235, 256, 308
appointment, 179–82, 233, 260
Barton case, 212–13
Bill Allen affair *see* Bill Allen affair
Briese allegations, 217, 223–227, 229–31, 232–33, 238, 241, 242, 243–44, 256
Britain, severing legal ties to, 201–5, 260
Commonwealth v State power *see* Commonwealth v State power (MG)
Enmore branch stacking, 207, 208, 209
High Court, appearance before, 193–94
  see also Commonwealth v State power (MG)
Hilton Hotel bombing, 238
indemnity from prosecution issues, 207, 233–36
Jackson, resignation of, 213, 238
logging and mining, 187
'Mr Asia' drug syndicate *see* 'Mr Asia' drug syndicate
'No Bill' submissions, 223, 233–34, 236
Nugan Hand Bank *see* Nugan Hand Bank
Operation Seville, 236–37, 308
press, criticism by, 242–43, 244, 256
Roger Rogerson case, 242–43
social reform agenda, 184, 189–91, 195
Street Royal Commission, 213–14, 215–16, 224
trial and aquittal, 241–45
Solon, Vivian, 391
Sparkes, Jack, 141
speeches and addresses (MG), 202, 228, 267, 270, 394
  Centre for Comparative Constitutional Studies (University of Melbourne), 394–95
  Dame Roma Mitchell

International Women's Day Memorial Lecture, 390–91
Equal Opportunity in Employment conference, 240
15th Conference of the International Society for the Reform of Criminal Law, 386–87
Herbert Vere Evatt Memorial Lecture (1980), 5
High Court, appointment to, 258–59
'Human Rights? Women's Rights?', 179
Lionel Murphy eulogy, 247–49, 254
'Mr Junior' speech (Sydney Bar), 91–93, 109
National Council of Women in NSW, 67
'Remembering the Universal Declaration and Australia's human rights record' (2006), 4
Symposium on Industrial Relations Reform (1980), 178–79
24th Australian Legal Convention, 268
Women Lawyers' Association of the ACT, 267, 269
Women's Electoral Lobby (1973), 87
Spender, Justice Jeffrey, 185
Spigelman, Chief Justice James, 50
St Francis Xavier Primary School (Moree), *13*, 23, 28–31
St Ignatius' College (Sydney), 340
St John and St Henry Catholic Church (Moree), 12, 29
St Joseph's (College, Sydney), 29
St Philomena's (Convent School, Moree), 28, 29, 31, 68
St Ursula's College (Armidale), 14, 31, 32–39, 44, 50, 68
St Vincent de Paul (Moree), 25
Stabilisation Mission in Haiti (UN), 384
Stack v Coast Securities (No 9) (1983), 194

Standing Committees of
  Attorneys General and
  Solicitors General (1981
  meeting), 202
Stanhope, Erne, 79
Staples, Jim, 82, 83, 113, 140
  Conciliation and Arbitration
    Commission, Deputy
    President of, 134, 150–53,
    164–76, 344
  APC case, 169, 170–71
  BHP dispute (1975),
    152–53
  fallout with Moore and
    demotion, 159, 168–71,
    175–76, 256
  Fraser Government,
    conflict with, 164–66,
    167, 168–69
  MG's resignation, 159, 164,
    165–76
  removal from Panel, 153
  wool stores dispute, 166–68,
    169, 171
  National Wage Case 1974, 126,
    127–28, 131, 133
  National Wage Case 1975,
    132, 134
  Pat Mackie case *see* Mackie v
    Australian Consolidated Press
    Ltd [1974]
Stephen, Sir Ninian, 321
*Stephens v West Australian
  Newspapers Ltd* (1994), 291
Stewart, Justice Donald, 207,
  217, 234–35, 237
Stewart, Kevin, 192–93
Stewart Royal Commissions
  'Mr Asia' drug syndicate, 207,
    217, 222, 232, 234–35, 245
  Nugan Hand Bank, 207
Stock Exchange (Sydney), 57
Stolen Generation case, 291–92,
  303, 316, 318, 319, 330
Stone, Judy, 21
Stone, Professor Adrienne, 367
Stone, Professor Julius, 50–52,
  54, 56, 57, 61, 259, 277, 360
  Hutley, conflict with, 52–53
  Moot courts, introduction
    of, 51
  Morison, conflict with, 51
  *The Province and Function of
    Law* (book), 52–53
  Williams, conflict with, 51
Stone, Reca, 61

Stop Press (newsletter), 64
Storemen and Packers Union,
  strike by, 167–68
Street, Chief Justice Laurence
  (later Sir), 214, 251
Street, Jessie, 53, 388
Street, Tony, 174
Street Royal Commission,
  213–14, 215–16, 224
*Street v Queensland Bar
  Association* (1989), 290, 302
Stubbs, Margot, 38, 262
Such Is Life (book), 167
Sue v Hill (1999), 314–15
Sullivan, Greg, 180, 184, 215
Summers, Anne, 141–42
Sun Herald, 341
Sun (Sydney), 161
*Superclinics Australia Pty Ltd
  v CES & Ors* S88 (1996),
  351–52
Supreme Court of Queensland,
  282, 283
Sweeney, Jack (later Justice),
  113, 123, 125, 126
Sydney Bar *see* NSW Bar
  Association
Sydney Law Review, 51
Sydney Morning Herald, 118,
  167, 186, 211, 220, 221, 229,
  243, 250, 255–56, 268–69
Sydney Speleological Society,
  42, 64, 65–66
  Bungonia Caves case, 88–89
  Stop Press (newsletter), 64
Sydney Town Hall, 247, 249
Sydney University Law School,
  MG at, 39, 45–57, 59–63,
  70, 72, 179, 235, 272, 349,
  360
  babysitting duties, 61–62
  Catalina Coffee Lounge, 48
  Crown Solicitor's Office
    (Cth), work at, 47, 49, 59
  full-time v part-time, 54–57,
    60–61
  Hutley's Succession course,
    59–61, 77
  John Geddes Equity prize,
    272
  part-time lecturer, 86
  segregation, sexism and
    discrimination, 45–47, 49,
    59–60, 62–63
  University Medal in Law, 4,
    62–63, 67, 75, 258

Sylvain Gaudron (vinyard),
  7, 381
Szabo, Tania, 33
Szabo, Violette, 33
Szeps, Henri, 43

Tampa (ship), 354
Tasmanian Dam case (1983),
  195, 197–201, 279, 280, 330
Tattersall's Club (Sydney), 224
taxation and revenue, 84, 115,
  166, 167, 191, 194, 303, 354
Taylor, Graham, 312–13
Taylor, Sir Alan, 54
Telecom dispute (1978),
  154–57, 178
Telecom linesmen dispute
  (1979), 165, 178
*Telecommunications (Interception)
  Act 1979* (Cth), 218, 221
telephone tapping (unlawful)
  see Age tapes
Temby, Ian, 241, 244, 268–69
Terry Hie Hie (Aboriginal
  reserve), 20
Tharunka (newspaper), 87
Thayorre people, 324
The Australian, 73, 89, 118,
  166, 255
The Economist (journal), 34
*The FMWU v ACT Employers
  Federation* (1979) *see Maternity
  Leave* case (1979)
The Lawyer and the Libertine
  (novel), 328
The Province and Function of Law
  (book), 52–53
'The Push' (University of
  Sydney), 43–44, 45
*The Queen v Kirby: Ex
  Party Boilermakers' Society
  of Australia* (1956) *see
  Boilermakers'* case (1956)
*Theophanous v Herald and
  Weekly Times Ltd* (1994), 291
Thomas National Transport,
  212
Thorunka (newspaper), 87–88
Toohey, Justice John, 255, 269,
  283, 291, 292, 295, 318, 322,
  338
  dissenting judgments, 281,
    305, 360, 366
  High Court, appointment to,
    255, 256, 260, 271
  Mabo (No. 2), 284

MG, relationship with, 272, 359
'natural law' perspective, 296
retirement, 323, 327, 329, 335
Wik judgment, 325, 326
Top Camp (Aboriginal camp in Moree), 12, *13,* 14, 19, 20
Torres Strait Islander people, 19
land rights *see* indigenous land rights
see also Aboriginal people
Trade Practices Act 1974 (Cth), 193
trade unions, 2, 81, 82, 83, 136, 143, 145, 152, 159, 166, 179, 383
ATEA *see* Australian Telecommunications Employees Association (ATEA)
Australian Postal and Telecommunications Union, 169, 170–71
Australian Workers Union *see* Australian Workers Union (AWU)
BLF *see* Builders Labourers Federation (BLF)
Maritime Union of Australia, 362
Meat Industry Employees Union, 141
Mt Isa miners' strike (1964) *see Mackie v Australian Consolidated Press Ltd* [1974]
Municipal Employees' Union, 119
national wage cases, 118, 122, 123, 126, 127
Railway Workers' Union, 2, 10, 14, 15, 97
Storemen and Packers Union, 167–68
women, and, 179
see also Australian Council of Trade Unions (ACTU)
Trades Hall (Melbourne), 116
Trevalyon, Kay, 76
Trimbole, Bob, 218
Turner, Gillian, 370
275-02 v MIMA and anor (2002), 356–58

U v U (2002), 349, 350
UNESCO, 383
Convention for the Protection of the World Cultural and National Heritage, 198
Union of Australian Women, 127
unions *see* trade unions
United Nations, 383–84
'Doc' Evatt's role in formation, 4
establishment, 388
Geneva Convention, 387
International Convention on the Elimination of all forms of Discrimination Against Women, 190
International Convention on the Elimination of All Forms of Racial Discrimination, 195, 196, 197
'Redesign Panel,' MG appointed to, 384, *385*
Refugee Convention, 388
United Nations Association of Australia, 147
United Nations Charter, 4, 388
United Nations General Assembly, 131
Universal Declaration of Human Rights, 4, 388, 390
Article 14, 391
University of New England, 34
University of New South Wales (UNSW), 87, 88
MG as Fellow at Law School, 177–79, 382
Occasional Papers (publication), 178
University of Sydney, 21, 34, 329
Fisher Library, 41
MG at *see* education (MG)
University Libertarian Society, 44
University Medal, 21, 34, 329347
University Speleological Society, 42
University of Technology, Sydney, 346
UNSW *see* University of New South Wales (UNSW)
Unsworth, Barrie, 224, 225, 231, 232
Uren, Tom, 161
Ursuline Order *see* St Ursula's College (Armidale)

Van Gervan v Fenton (1992), 304, 349
Verduci, Giuseppe, 236–37, 238
Vianney, Siser Mary *see* Dick, Mavis
Victorian Women Lawyers, 390
Vietnam War, 87, 112
von Doussa, Justice John, 329

Walden v Hensler (1987), 281
Walker, Frank, 48, 60, 61, 63, 82, 85–86, 138, 163, 164, 224, 235, 238, 321
Love Boat scandal, 207–8
Solicitor General, MG as, 179–82, 184, 185, 187, 188, 189, 191–93, 202, 212
Walsh, Richard, 43
Walsh, Sir Cyril, 54
Warragamba Dam (NSW), 66
Warren (NSW), 74
Warrener, Roy, 15
Waterford, Jack, 193, 194, 335–36
Wave Hill (NT), 289
Weathered, Lynne, 386
Webb, Dick, 38
Webb, Paul, 63
Wee Jasper cave site (NSW), 64
WEL *see* Women's Electoral Lobby (WEL)
Weld Club (Perth), 270
Wells, Andrew, 246
Wentworth Chambers (Sydney), 76, 91, 110, 140
Werris Creek (NSW), 32
Whealy, Tony (later Justice), 48, 62, 257
Wheeler, Professor Fiona, 366
Wherrett, Richard, 43
White Industries cases (1998), (1999), 330–31
Whitlam, Gough, 82, 95, 112, 113, 114, 115, 123, 133, 135, 136, 289
Whitlam Government (federal), 96, 195
dismissal of, 153, 159
national wage cases *see* MG's role *under* national wage and equal pay cases
Who's Who in Australia (book), 92, 93
Wik Peoples v Queensland (Pastoral Leases case) (1996), 254, 295, 296, 323–26, 327

criticism of decision, 326
Willheim, Ernst, 63, 348–49
Williams, Daryl, 326, 329, 331, 341, 359, 373, 378
Williams, Deputy President, 170
Williams, Edgar, 103
Williams, James, 51
Williams, Professor George, 367
Williams, Professor John, 254
Williams, Sir Dudley, 54
Williamson, Dick, 65
Wilson, Justice Ronald (later Sir), 268, 269, 272, 297
  MG, relationship with, 271
Winchester, Colin, 236, 237–38
  murder of, 236
Winychanam Aboriginal group, 196
Wollstonecraft, Mary, 269–70
Wombeyan Caves (NSW), 64
Women Lawyers' Association of NSW, 59
  member, MG as, 87
  prize, 62
  Student Liaison Officer, MG as, 66
Women Lawyers' Association of the ACT, 267, 269
Women's Advisory Council, 189
women's domestic roles, 304, 349–51
  U v U (2002), 349, 350
  Van Gervan case (1992), 304, 349
Women's Electoral Lobby (WEL), 87, 126, 127, 128, 133
Women's Legal Status Act (NSW), 46

women's movement, 76
  see also feminism and feminists
women's rights, 16, 40, 46, 58–59, 66–67, 76, 78, 115, 130, 270, 349–52
  abortion *see* abortion
  domestic roles *see* women's domestic roles
  domestic violence, 189
  rape *see* rape
  reproductive rights, 379
  sexual assault, 189–90
  trade unions, and, 179
  workforce, in *see* workforce, women in
  see also Women's Electoral Lobby
Wood, Merv (Police Commissioner)
  Cessna-Milner case, 213, 214– 215, 231–32
Woods, Greg (later Judge), 49, 61, 63, 189
Wool Industry (Storemen and Packers) Award (1979), 166–68, 169, 171
WorkChoices case (2006), 201, 254, 280
workforce, women in
  equal employment opportunity *see* equal employment opportunity (EEO)
  equal pay, 47, 66, 113, 139, 370–71
    see also national wage and equal pay cases
  indirect discrimination, 303–4
  married women, 47, 59, 66, 146–47, 370

maternity leave, 139, 146, 147–48, 280
minimum wage *see* national wage and equal pay cases
World Health Organization, 383
World Heritage Properties Conservation Act 1983 (Cth), 198
World Heritage (Western Tasmanian Wilderness) Regulations 1983 (Cth), 198
World War II, 10, 33
Woronora Cemetery (Sydney), 71
Wran, Neville, 49, 63, 181–82, 184, 186, 187, 188, 192–93, 228, 231, 244, 247, 250, 251
  Age tapes, 217, 218, 219, 220
  Attorney General, as, 238–39
  Briese allegations, 225, 230
  prosecution then resignation, 244–45, 267, 268
  Street Royal Commission, 213–14, 215–16
Wran Government (NSW), 63, 82, 179, 186, 189
  crime and corruption *see* crime and corruption (NSW); Royal Commissions

Xavier, Francis, 27

Yanner v Eaton (1999), 281–82, 336–37
Yarrangobilly Caves (NSW), 64
Yusuf case (2001), 353–54

Zecevic v DPP (Vic) (1987), 267
Zines, Professor Leslie, 277, 316, 336

www.ingramcontent.com/pod-product-compliance
Lightning Source LLC
Chambersburg PA
CBHW020752020526
44116CB00028B/73